AF623878

PROTOHISTORY

Archaeology of the Harappan Civilization

INDIAN ARCHAEOLOGY IN RETROSPECT

VOLUME II

PROTOHISTORY

Archaeology of the Harappan Civilization

Edited by

S. SETTAR
RAVI KORISETTAR

Indian Council of Historical Research

MANOHAR

2002

First published 2002

© Indian Council of Historical Research, 2002

All rights reserved. No part of this publication may be
reproduced or transmitted, in any form or by any means,
without prior permission of the editors and the publisher

ISBN 81-7304-318-3 (Set)
ISBN 81-7304-320-5 (Vol. II)

Published by
Ajay Kumar Jain for
Manohar Publishers & Distributors
4753/23 Ansari Road, Daryaganj
New Delhi 110002

Typeset by
A J Software Publishing Co. Pvt. Ltd.
305 Durga Chambers
1333 D.B. Gupta Road
Karol Bagh, New Delhi 110005

Printed at
Lordson Publishers Pvt. Ltd.
C 5/19 Rana Pratap Bagh
Delhi 110007

Contents

Foreword

As one of the editors of this series and also as one associated with the Indian Council of Historical Research, I am delighted to present the *Indian Archaeology in Retrospect* in four volumes. This series has taken the present form, undergoing several transformations during the last four years. When it was originally planned in 1995 at Dharwad, we had only a limited aim of attempting a historiographical account, covering the Pre and Early history of India in two volumes (from Palaeolithic to the Early Historical Period); we had also somewhat vaguely nourished one-volume retrospect on Indian Art History to complement it. During the early years of the preparation, we kept our options open, sought and considered suggestions from others, tried to involve as many established scholars as possible—all these experiments taught us how much easier it is to write for oneself than get others write for one. Of about a hundred odd scholars with whom we corresponded at the early stages, only about eighty could stand by us till the end. Some could not respond to our invitation and they proved to be the most helpful ones, because their silence remained golden; some others reacted enthusiastically in the beginning, pleaded for more time subsequently, but faded away at the concluding stages. No doubt, the latter should have had justifiable reasons for their withdrawal, but this upset our planning badly, and denied us about a dozen important papers. Critics who notice obvious gaps should not overlook the inherent hazards involved in such collective efforts while assessing the academic content of these volumes.

The four volumes of *Indian Archaeology in Retrospect* are shaped by a combination of factors: our original plan apart, the suggestions and modifications made by colleagues and friends, the range of available scholarship, generous offers and voluntary participations, drop outs and withdrawals, and also accidents of various other kinds, are the most obvious ones among them. All these led to alter the original plan on the one hand and to accommodate new ideas on the other. The latter resulted in the expansion of the series from the original two to four volumes; it also made possible one full volume on the Indus Studies and another on the Interactive Sciences. The most useful addition came from scholars who have more or less devoted their entire lifetime to their respective fields of specialization: this explains the most useful, informative and meticulously prepared Appendices and Bibliographies.

While working on this series with Ravi at Dharwad, I had also initiated several bibliographical projects in the Indian Council of Historical Research at New Delhi. Besides liberally funding such projects (both for their preparation and publication), the ICHR had also made efforts to create opportunities to bring out bibliographical accounts in *The Indian Historical Review*, and in publications brought out under the new monograph series as well as several other publications of the Council. When these volumes were finalised, I thought that a comprehensive bibliography of Indian archaeology, covering the entire nineteenth and twentieth centuries, would be an appropriate complement to this series. I hope Professor V.N. Misra of the Deccan College, who is siezed with this task since 1997, would present it one day. The original plan of making this Bibliography an integral part of this series, as Volume V, had to be, abandoned, however to avoid further delay in the publication of these volumes. I am happy that the Indian Council of Historical Research is able to complement the excellent work done by a community of Dutch, South Asian and South-East Asian scholars under the *ABIA South and Southeast Asian Art and Archaeology Index* project, sponsored by the International Institute of Asian Studies at Leiden, Netherlands. The ABIA offers annotated bibliography of the publications of the year; our volume comprises only bibliographical entries of important publications brought out during the past century and half.

Dr. Ravi Korisettar, Professor and Chairman of the Department of History and Archaeology, Karnatak University, Dharwad, had to bear the major brunt of the responsibility, especially after I took over the Chair of the ICHR and became increasingly involved with the responsibilities of the Council. In fact, his share of contribution is far more than mine. My contribution to it is almost nil. I deem it a privilege to associate myself with these works and to present them on behalf of the ICHR. Both these projects were completed within a reasonable period of time, thanks to the initiative and cooperation of scholars and editors: in fact, the ICHR grant given to it is only nominal and symbolic.

S. SETTAR

Chairman
Indian Council of Historical Research
New Delhi
30 June 1999

Acknowledgements

Edited works are always built on the labour and cooperation of contributing scholars and the *Indian Archaeology in Retrospect* series is no exception to this. Ever since 1995, when this idea was first seriously and systematically formulated, nearly every scholar approached by us responded favourably, contributed his paper well in time and cooperated with us whenever we reached him on editorial details. Some of them helped with the names and addresses of scholars who may be interested to contribute to this series. As valuable as this was the share of experts who carefully went through the papers refereed and helped us ensure the standard.

All the contributors whose names are easily accessible in these volumes, the reviewers of papers who remain invisible, and those who gave us advice to extend the field of enquiry and also suggested names of scholars, deserve to be remembered here.

The project sprouted on the campus of Karnatak University, Dharwad, an old town located on the eastern edge of Western Ghats. Sylvan, quiet, cool though it is, in the mid-nineties, it was hardly suitable for establishing a global communication. This initial handicap was overcome by the electronic mailing facility established in the University. Soon this bug caught us both and invaded into our homes too. From this locale at Dharwad, we maintained contact with more than hundred scholars across the world, and more intensely with about eighty who stood by us till the end. We should recall the facilities generously provided by the authorities of Karnatak University, and in particular, the help given by Dr. S.C. Kendadmath, Librarian, and Mr R.M. Vatnal of the Information Centre. To fill the blanks in the Bibliography and to cross-check references, we had to reach centres within and outside India. The help given by Dorian Fuller, Nicky Boivin, Gregory Possehl, Rabi Mohanty and V. Selvakumar is gratefully remembered here. The Geological Society of India (Bangalore), Indian Society for Prehistoric and Quaternary Studies (Pune), and the Ethnographic and Folk Culture Society (Lucknow), permitted us to reproduce the papers of R.S. Pappu, M.D. Petraliglia, M.K. Dhavalikar and K.A.R. Kennedy published in their respective journals. Professor C. Venugopal of Karnatak University spared his valuable time to read the text and made suggestions to improve the diction. We are obliged to all these individuals and institutions.

The series needed a sponsor and a publisher and there was none in sight at the early stages of its implementation. Even when the volumes were nearing completion in 1998, its institutional base remained uncertain. When we approached the Indian Council of Historical Research, the authorities of the Council accepted to publish these volumes and also met the contingent expenses. The Manohar Publishers & Distributors, especially Mr. Ramesh Jain and Ajay Jain, have done nothing less than a miracle by producing these volumes in a record time. The authorities of the ICHR and the proprietors of Manohar deserve our whole-hearted thanks.

S. Settar
Ravi Korisettar

Introduction

S. SETTAR and RAVI KORISETTAR

Research on the Harappan archaeology goes back to the year 1922, when Mohenjo Daro, the 'mound of the dead' in Sindh, was found. This discovery raised immense interest world-over because of its extraordinary urban character. Since then the archaeology of the Harappan Civilization has been growing, both in terms of geographic frontiers and cultural dynamics. In the post-Independence period, this study has been occupying a paramount place in the archaeology of South Asia and the last twenty-five years, in particular, have witnessed excavation of scores of Harappan sites, bringing to light the most exciting results. Intensive explorations and excavations of several sites both in India and Pakistan have caused a tremendous knowledge explosion, facilitating a far better understanding of the fundamentals of its origin, its efflorescence and of its ultimate 'end'. Archaeologists in these two countries, either independently or in collaboration with Western scholars, have launched multidisciplinary investigations to reconstruct the spatio-temporal framework of this civilization. The radiocarbon determinations and the evidence of the early food-producing cultures within the Greater Indus Valley have put the civilization in the perspective of indigenous origins. A vast body of cultural data, brought out from recent excavations, have accompanied paradigms shifts in the study, necessitating concomitant changes in the projection of this civilization.

Recent investigations of early sites like Mehrgarh, Kili Ghul Mohammad (Baluchistan) and Gar-I Mar and Gar-I Asp (Afghanisthan) have proved crucial to the understanding of the precursors of this civilization. The spurt of calibrated radiocarbon dates and increasing number of multi-pronged investigations on the excavated sites (especially the bio- and geo-archeological studies), have compelled the Bronze Age archaeologists to re-evaluate their earlier theories and interpretations. The purposefulness of this multi-pronged investigations may be made out from the publications brought out by the European Association of South Asian Archaeologists, the Archaeological Surveys of India and of Pakistan and several such others. Publication on various aspects of the civilization have kept pace with the progress of research made in the field. For instance, a stimulating paper of G.L. Possehl (1998; *The Journal of World Prehistory* 11 [4]: 425-72), which offers an admirable summary of our understanding of the decline of the Harappan Civilization as well as the processual perspectives on this civilization, provokes a thorough scrutiny of the old problems in light of new evidence. Serving as a critique of arguments hypothesizing the 'eclipse' of the civilization, he proposes, in the light of the evidence from north-western India and Gujarat, to look at this phase of civilization as a process of de-urbanization and a shift to eastwards in the general distribution of the settlements and population. This means that the ongoing debate on the rise, development and collapse of the civilization revolves round the relative roles played by climate and tectonics in controlling the drainage patterns, landscape evolution as well as the stability and agricultural suitability of alluvial tracts in the Indus Basin. There is now compelling evidence pointing to the net effects of tectonics and climate, both from the continental and marine stratigraphic records (see Schuldenrein, this volume).

Studies made so far on the palaeoclimate of the Harappan Civilization are yet to reach an agreement. While some favour prevalence of a relatively wetter monsoon during 2500-1900 BC others feel that conditions were comparable to those of the present times. The most convincing reconstruction of monsoon conditions of the Mid-Late Holocene period has been made by Enzel and her collaborators (1999; *Science* 284: 125-7). Based on the limnology of the dry Lunkaransar lake in Rajasthan, they argue that this region experienced wet climate between the (radiocarbon) years 6300 and 4800 BC; they also point out that the Harappan Civilization (as well as the present climate) emerged a thousand years after this lake dried up and that it 'was not synchronous with the lacustral phase'.

The major achievements of the post-Independence archaeology of the Harappan Civilization may be summed up as follows:

- The distribution, settlement patterns and site densities in some of the crucial regions of the Harappan province provide a clear picture of the history of the civilization supported by a firm radiocarbon chronology.
- The beginnings of food-production go back to *c.* 7000-5000 BC (Kili Ghul Mohammad phase).
- The cultural development between the Early Harappan and Kili Ghul Mohammad is distinguished by the character of the ceramics: (a) Burj Basket Marked phase (*c.* 5000-4300 BC); (b) Togau phase (*c.* 4300-3800 BC): and (c) Kechi Beg/Hakra Wares phase (*c.* 3800-3200 BC).
- The Early Harappan is located at 3200-2600 BC; the Early to Mature Harappan transition at 2600-2500 BC; the Mature or Urban Harappan at 2500-1900 BC; and Post-Urban Harappan at 1900-1400 BC.
- The Post-Urban Harappan sites have multiplied in number but they reveal a decrease in the 'net settled area and average site size'.
- The French Archaeological Mission to Pakistan, the excavations at Mehrgarh and Nausharo in particular, has provided vital information on the food-producing way of life in the north-western parts of South Asia. In a decade long excavations conducted at Harappa, the French archaeologists have brought to light evidence of a continuous sequence of cultural growth from the Early Harappan to the Post-Urban Harappan (Cemetery H Culture) phases, besides throwing fresh insight into the technique of craft production and the complexity of the urban civic architecture.
- Excavations at Ghazi Shah have provided vital clues for understanding the transition from Early Harappan to Mature Harappan in the time range of *c.* 2600-2500 BC.

- Evidence of the expansion of settlements towards the Indus heartland is scanty prior to 3000 BC.
- While the major urban settlements witnessed a dramatic collapse by 2000 BC, the satellite settlements continued to thrive nearly undisturbed.

This background probably serves as a base for understanding the studies made in this volume as these evaluate the progress made in this field since the discovery of Mohenjo Daro in the 1920s.

'Fifty years of Harappan archaeology' is a comprehensive review of the work carried out on the major aspects of the Harappan Civilization. Fresh and self-inspiring attempts have been made to study the archaeology of this civilization in the post-Independence India as the majority of the sites known till then became part of Pakistan. In 1947, only about 37 sites were known. Relentless survey conducted both in India and Pakistan during the last fifty odd years has thrown up a list of not less than 1,022 sites, distributed over an area of one million square kilometres. Of these, 406 sites are located in Pakistan while 616 are in India. About 96 of these sites have been excavated so far: 41 in Pakistan and 55 in India. The major credit for the progress made in India should go to the Archaeological Survey of India, followed by the M.S. University of Baroda at Vadodara, Kurukshetra University at Kurukshetra and Deccan College at Pune. The departments of Archaeology in the States of the Punjab, Rajasthan and Gujarat too have a substantial share in this. To the Archaeological Survey of India, which is nearing the centenary of its office (1902-2002), we owe our knowledge of the excavated sites of almost all the Mature Harappan phase located in India.

As many as 1,500 radiocarbon dates have been obtained for South Asian prehistoric sites. With the beginnings of settled life in South Asia, dated at 7000 BC, there is a long series of regional cultures that bridge the early Neolithic culture of Baluchistan with the Mature Harappan culture. The French excavations at Mehrgarh provided the first insight into the beginnings of settled life in the subcontinent. Our knowledge of this civilization has been drawn from the excavations carried out during the last three decades in India and Pakistan, with frequent international participation especially in Pakistan. The review summarizes the archaeological sequences and highlights the importance of the results of excavations. The sites described are Lothal, Kalibangan, Dholavira in India and Mohenjo Daro as well as Harappa in Pakistan. In the section on Harappan Civilization beyond South Asia, the emergence of Meluhha and excavations in Oman are discussed with implications for expansion of maritime activity. In the concluding section, an effective summary of paradigm shifts is given.

The 'geoarchaeological perspectives on Harappan sites' is a new and emerging field of inquiry in the archaeology of the Harappan Civilization. The Harappans developed interesting irrigation systems and they are believed to be the first—far earlier than the Romans, indeed—to have attempted to exploit the ground water. They also raised massive brick platforms for the dwellings of their 'ruling class' and other public buildings. There was an organized effort to grapple with the population pressure and resource stress, but the factors that brought about the decline of this civilization are still eluding explanation. Were there 'environmental changes generated by combined climatic, hydrographic, geological and human impacts' that brought about this dramatic change is the moot question. The answer might lie in the geoarchaeology which has so far remained an untapped area of investigation. Geoarchaeology provides a unique set of methods and techniques 'for tracking the preserved archaeological record from initial settlement and establishment to abandonment and preservation in sealed stratigraphies and landscape segments'. The review of geoarchaeological perspectives on Harappan sites provides the first comprehensive assessment of the current state of geoarchaeological research in the Indus heartland and also offers guidelines for further research. The paper goes into the geographical parameters governing the settlement location of the urban sites. It is observed that: (a) that the majority of the urban sites follow the lower course of the Indus, the Early Harappan sites being located in clusters to the north and west; (b) that the majority of sites are situated on floodplains or former floodplains at elevations below 1,200 m AMSL and that the hydrography of the Indus river is the 'key element explaining the variability as well as the chronology of site distribution'; (c) that the lower Indus channel changed course over a stretch of 25 km, and during the peak of the civilization it flowed close to Mohenjo Daro, as revealed by the fluvial remnants and the complex alignments of the primary Harappan sites and; (d) that in the upper Indus basin the Late Harappan settlements are clustered around the Ghaggar-Hakkra alluvial plain and the site desertion took place in response to river capture of the Sutlej during the Late Harappan times (*c.* 1500 BC). The upper Indus Basin is drained by the 'five rivers' and the lower Indus flows through the Sindh province. In each of these basins, the landscape units such as subrecent floodplains, recent floodplains, level bar uplands, undulating sandy terraces, bajadas and sandy deserts of Late Quaternary age have been recognized. Within these complexes are situated nearly 90 per cent of the known Harappan sites. It is observed that a chronostratigraphic reconstruction of these landform units are hindered by the lack of reliable Holocene soil chronologies. Despite this, an attempt has been made 'to link Harappan site clusters with discrete landform complexes in the upper and lower Indus Basin'. Further, this paper takes stock of research on the Late Quaternary tectonics and the drainage history of the Indus and also provides a synthesis of landscape records. An account of geoarchaeological profiles of key Harappan settlements, presented here for the first time, deserves to be specially noted.

Research on spatial archaeology of the urban settlements is only about two decades old. This aspect of research is not limited to the reconstruction of structure of individual settlements but also goes into the structures of their inter-connection within the given settlement network. More than 1,000 sites are found distributed over an area of one million square kilometres, making this civilization rank among the largest of the three early civilizations in the world. A review of the settlement patterns during the Mature Harappan phase exposes certain inadequacies in our studies and points out that in order to fully understand the hierarchic organization and the interconnectedness of the settlements, what kind of further settlement research is necessary. Mohenjo Daro was a major metropolis of which barely 10 per cent of the area occupied by it has so far been excavated. Large built-up areas of the city lie buried under the floodplain of the Indus; the city lies buried 7 m deep in the alluvium; its highest parts still rise more than 12 m above the floodplain. The urban dimensions of Mohenjo Daro present a large variety of architectural patterns, some of them monumental in nature. The entire settlement was laid out during a single stretch of time, implying that Harappans were in full command of the entire stretch of urban technology, and that such an extraordinary effort would have been possible only by those who had attained perfect mastery over the urban planning. The paper on 'settlement networks of the Indus Civilization' examines the geographical factors for the location of Mohenjo Daro, and from the perspective of centre-periphery model brings out the factors responsible for the rise of Mohenjo Daro, its uniqueness among contemporary largest cities of the time.

'The beginning of the Chalcolithic Culture in Gujarat' (Saurashtra, north Gujarat and Kachchh) can be traced back to the second half of the third millennium BC (pre-Harappan Culture in Gujarat). The excavations in Gujarat have brought to light evidence of the expansion of the pre-Harappan culture of Sindh into north Gujarat during this time period. There is also evidence of some non-Harappan ceramic traditions from the early stage onwards with the Mature Harappan phase in Gujarat. Distinctive features of the early Chalcolithic and the Non-Harappan traditions are reviewed in order to understand the early stage of the Integration and Consolidation of the Harappan Culture in Gujarat. This is based on the data recently found as well as reanalysis of earlier findings. The recent excavation at Datrana have brought to light very interesting evidence. Nagwada, Moti Pipli, Dholavira are the other sites which throw up Chalcolithic evidence of the late third millennium BC in Gujarat

'The Post-Urban phase in Gujarat' is characterized by the continuity of the cultural traits of the Mature phase, but it is devoid of urban propensity. This phenomenon appears to be the outcome of the normal process of cultural transformation in Harappan Culture caused by the general economic decline. This phase was indeed less organized, less differentiated and less specialized than the urban phase, and marks, perhaps, the beginning of decentralization and localization, making room for regional cultural expression. Against this background the archaeological sequence from a number of excavations carried out during the last five decades is described and the evidence for the post-urban phenomenon in Gujarat has been presented. Among the important sites excavated are Nageshwar, Rojdi, Kuntasi, Bhagasra, Orio Timbo, Padri, Ratanpura, Nagwada, Loteshwar, Moti Pipli, Santhli, Datrana, Zekhada, Surkotada and Shikarpur. The majority of these indicate an early penetration of Harappan Culture into Gujarat. The gradual transition from Mature Harappan to the Post-Harappan in most of these settlements has been seen as a degenerated phase. Among the distinctive features of the Post-Urban Harappan settlements in Gujarat is the general decline in material culture, a trait typical of the Urban phase. For instance, the characteristic shapes of Indus Goblets, beakers, and S-shaped jars almost disappear; the long chert blades of Sukkur (Pakistan) origin also vanish and the brick structures are discontinued. Lack of standardization and homogeneity in its material culture are other two notable features. On the basis of radiocarbon dates, the Post-Urban phase is dated to the beginning of the second millennium BC.

Notwithstanding finality of decipherment and the lack of related literary accounts elsewhere in the contemporary world, significant strides have been made to understand the socio-political and religious organizations of the Mature Harappans. The paper on Harappan social organization observes that during this phase a large number of urban settlements were established, for example, at Mohenjo Daro, Harappa, Ganweriwala, and Rakhigarhi, ranging in size between 200 and 80 hectares. These were located at major cross roads, along trade routes, integrating settlements, resource areas and production centres. Urbanism of the Indus people has been considered to be an important factor which favoured existence of a stratified society made up of occupational classes. Other determinants which support a structured socio-political and economic orders were specialized crafts, settlement layout, use of seals and writing, standard weights and various types of occupational specialization.

'The religion of the Harappan Civilization' as well as the issue of the Aryan-Dravidian dichotomy is the hot topic of the day. The historiography of the Harappan religion exposes the racial bias in our approach, for the authors of the civilization are thought to be immigrants from West Asia and that this civilization is stated to have been transplanted in its mature state. Later it was attributed to Aryans, who were also thought to have come from West Asia, a theory advanced by some Indologists. This led many to look for parallels either in Mesopotamia or in Egypt. Some of the Indologists, deeply rooted in Sanskritic and Vedic literature, looked at Harappan Civilization for the roots of Indian culture. The Aryan-Dravidian dichotomy is based on insufficient archaeological evidence and, that in spite of the fallacy of racial typology, as attested by bio-anthropological methods, the racial concept has survived to the day. Against the backdrop of such early notions the paper on 'Harappan religion: myth and polemics' makes an attempt to trace the history of this debate as well as the interpretation of iconographic representation, of terracottas and stone statuettes, and public structures as evidence of religious manifestations of the Harappans.

Terracottas have been found in large quantities at a number of sites in the Harappan province and these have been subjected to a study in order to understand their significance, both religious or craft technology. The paper on the terracotta figures from Mohenjo Daro draws attention to the current problem of terracotta studies; the arguments are partly based on research (including ethnographic data in India) and partly on the recent discoveries in Pakistan. The antiquity of terracotta art is now traced back to the seventh millennium BC on the basis of the evidence found at Mehrgarh in Baluchistan. The author directs her enquiry exclusively to the material evidence found at Mohenjo Daro, especially to the female figurines. Noting that the majority of the latter are found in association with other forms such as bulls, birds, dogs, monkeys, rams, male figurines, etc., he observes that holding them as merely symbols of fertility may be a gross simplification of their cultural significance. He feels that the ritual significance of these figurines needs to be understood in the light of ethnographic evidence.

Bio-anthropology of the Harappan skeletal series aims at answering questions such as: 'Who were these Harappans?' The question of Harappan identity has been tackled by focusing attention on the biological source material obtained from mortuaries. This formed a specialized study of the dentition, nonmetric variables, markers of pathological and occupational stress, indicators of growth and development pattern, and morphometric analysis of individual bones and skeletal regions, by a group of anthropologists in USA. Multivariate statistical analyses were also applied to determine the biological continuity of prehistoric population. The paper dealing with this subject examines the 'earlier morphometric and statistical analyses of the Harappan skeletons and demonstrates the value of a recent application of principal component analysis'. An important point which emerges from this study is that the modern scientific analysis does not support earlier schemes of racial typology and the concept of an 'Harappan race' is rather ill-founded.

Pastoralism, as a way of life in the prehistoric context, constitutes an important area of investigation and it is best understood against the faunal background. Because livestock management was vital to the food economy (both primary and secondary products), the archaeozoological investigations aim at reconstructing the evolutionary history of pastoralism, especially the role of domestic animals and of their management. The paper presented in this volume probes into the dawn of pastoralism; it is based on the faunal remains and, to a minor degree, on the iconographic evidence found in Baluchistan, (from Mehrgarh, the oldest Neolithic site in South Asia, dated in the seventh millennium BC) The main sites covered are Mehrgarh, Harappa and Dholavira. The authors also highlight the contributions of scholars and institutions who are responsible for the rapid advances made over the last five decades and draw attention to the lack of 'locally established tradition of the analysis of Holocene fauna from archaeological sites in Pakistan'. Besides highlighting the importance of Mehrgarh, which provides the earliest evidence of pastoralism in South Asia, this survey reveals that cattle domestication predominated over sheep and goat; there is lack of evidence to understand 'how the animals were husbanded and for what purpose they (were) kept'. It is also observed that farming and herding communities occupying the areas peripheral to the Harappan province, laid the foundation of later Chalcolithic cultures in peninsular India and that Harappan Civilization was not the source of these cultures.

As noted earlier, a large number of Harappan sites have been excavated in western India and archaeofaunal data have been obtained from several excavated sites during the last couple of decades, especially from those in Gujarat. Faunal assemblages from Kuntasi, Shikarpur, Orio Timbo, Surkotada, Nageshwar, etc., have revealed interesting information on the mode of subsistence. A large variety of animal species have been identified, though the collection is from a small number of sites. The majority of these animals, both wild and domesticated, were a part of their food economy. It has been found that about 80 per cent of the animal assemblage was domesticated. There is also evidence to believe exploitation of avian and aquatic species. A significant amount of animal protein was obtained from domestic animals such as cattle, buffalo, sheep, goat and pig. In this review, the author makes a particular point about the presence of horse and utilization of horse, camel and ass as beasts of burden from the evidence obtained from sites in western India. They have been connected with industrial and trade centres, where they are believed to have helped accelerated mobility of population. However, in the light of the present controversy regarding the Harappan horse, the equid remains from some of the sites need to be reinvestigated.

Discussion on Harappan archaeobotany is an important step forward for understanding the processes of food production in the Greater Indus Valley and beyond. The archaeobotanical evidence from Harappan sites and of their contemporaries in the adjoining regions has grown considerably since the first finds at Mohenjo Daro. Though the evidence obtained during the last two decades may help formulate some broad theories on Harappan agriculture, it is felt to be no sufficient enough to understand the entire area, especially the core areas like the river floodplains of Sindh. However, the casual samples collected so far help place our understanding of Harappan agriculture into an interregional context and also to assess its potential impact on broader historical patterns in South Asia. The archaeobotanical record for north-western South Asia is critically reviewed, bearing the likely geographical sources of particular crops and the periods and directions of their dispersal. This is followed by a discussion of the issues surrounding the introduction of African crops to South Asia, analysis of non-crop (weed) taxa in archaeobotanical samples, and a discussion on general agricultural issues such as irrigation and seasonality. Finally, some of the key issues and datasets of South Asian palaeoecology of the later Holocene are reviewed. An understanding of such issues and hypotheses relating to climatic change in South Asia is important for placing the agricultural evidence into its environmental context.

The Harappan script continues to haunt the decipherers and it still remains a major riddle. The majority of records being very short (the longest bearing only about 26 signs), is stated to be one of the major stumbling blocks in understanding these inscriptions, and unlike the Asokan record, there is no multi-lingual record to help us solve the Harappan script. Although the Finnish team led by Asko Parpola has made a remarkable breakthrough in deciphering the script, it remains to be widely accepted. The paper in this volume delves deep into this problem, provides an exhaustive survey of the attempts at decipherment and suggests alternative ways of attempting to solve this problem.

Harappan Technological Tradition is an area of research which is vital to our understanding of the trade and economy of the Mature Harappan phase. The focus of the paper on 'Some Important Aspects of the Harappan Technological Tradition' is craft technology during the Mature Harappan period (2600-1900 BC), which corresponds to the Integration Era. During this period, the proto-Urban cultures of the Indus Basin and of its periphery were organized into several regional states. During the period under consideration urbanism in the Indus valley reached its zenith affecting a parallel and equally impressive development of the industrial productivity. The process of integration also necessitated invention and adoption of specific styles in public and domestic architecture, ceramics, metallurgy, articles of adornment from a variety of raw materials, etc. The survey reveals the constraints involved in the study of craft traditions, such as undeciphered script and lack of problem oriented studies and theoretical models 'that go beyond evolutionary linearity and multi-linearity, centre-periphery, diffusion....'. However, a survey of the studies on craft technology in all its ramifications observes that these studies have kept pace 'with the fast transformation of the archaeological discipline all over the world. While in the past, the Indus region was thought to have been at the receiving end of technological diffusion from the West, it is becoming increasingly clear that it could be the other way round. This paper also discusses the theoretical and methodological issues that are being addressed to in the current research on craft production and technology. In presenting these issues, the authors highlight some of the recent discoveries about Harappan technologies that serve to distinguish this society in the context of other early state level societies.

In Harappan studies pottery has been used to construct a chronology and site-to-site relationship across the vast expanse of Harappan province. Apparently the interpretative potential of pottery has not yet fully been exploited. The variation occurring in the ceramics in terms of texture, colour, decoration or form or regional variation in the ceramic assemblages as well as a detailed picture of pottery styles, designs and technologies are yet to be fully understood. This review points out that social significance of pottery in Harappan studies is totally neglected. The author argues that a closer archaeological attention to pottery is desirable to reconstruct the socio-cultural and technological importance of ceramic wares. This chapter looks at the prospects for such an approach in the light of theoretical developments in ceramic studies.

S. Settar
Ravi Korisettar

Fifty Years of Harappan Archaeology: The Study of the Indus Civilization since Indian Independence

GREGORY L. POSSEHL

INTRODUCTION

Sir John Marshall's announcement of the discovery of the Indus Civilization on 20 September 1924 (Marshall 1924) forever changed the face of Indian archaeology (Fig. 1). There was international interest in this new civilization of the Bronze Age, which served to secure broad support for archaeological excavation and exploration in Sindh, Baluchistan, the Punjab and North-West Frontier in the 1920s and 1930s. Large scale excavations were undertaken at Mohenjo Daro from 1925 to 1931. There was parallel research at Harappa from 1920 to 1934. Sir Aurel Stein explored the North-West Frontier in 1927 (Stein 1929) and southern Baluchistan in 1927-8 (Stein 1931). N.G. Majumdar conducted his explorations and excavations in Sindh between 1927 and 1931 (Majumdar 1934).

The Great Depression of the 1930s eventually compromised the ability of the Government of India to support this research. World War II also inhibited archaeological digging. These combined conditions almost, but not quite, terminated work. Stein surveyed the Sarasvati in 1940 (Stein 1942) and excavated places like Kalepar and Kudwala Ther. M.S. Vats dug at Rangpur in Saurashtra in 1934-5 (Vats 1934-5) and Brigadier E.J. Ross investigated Rana Ghundai in northern Baluchistan from 1935 to 1940 (Ross 1946).

One of the early foreign archaeological projects in the subcontinent was conceived and sponsored by W. Norman Brown, a professor of Sanskrit at the University of Pennsylvania and the principal founder of the American Institute of Indian Studies. In the 1920s he was anxious to participate in the exploration of the newly discovered Harappan Civilization and visited Mohenjo Daro in 1928, where he met Ernest J.H. Mackay, then in charge of the excavations. Brown later recruited Mackay to be the field director of the American excavation at Chanhu Daro in Sindh. The excavation took place during the 1935-6 field season (Mackay 1943). It was funded by the Museum of Fine Arts in Boston, but it was Brown's project.

By the end of the North African campaign the Allies could see that the Germans were vulnerable to defeat, and had little hope of winning the War; although no one knew how long it might last. Nonetheless, confidence was buoyed, which allowed the government to think in slightly broader terms about public responsibility and heritage. This led them to seek out the services of R.E.M. Wheeler, then a Brigadier General serving in North Africa with an artillery regiment, as a Director General of the Archaeological Survey of

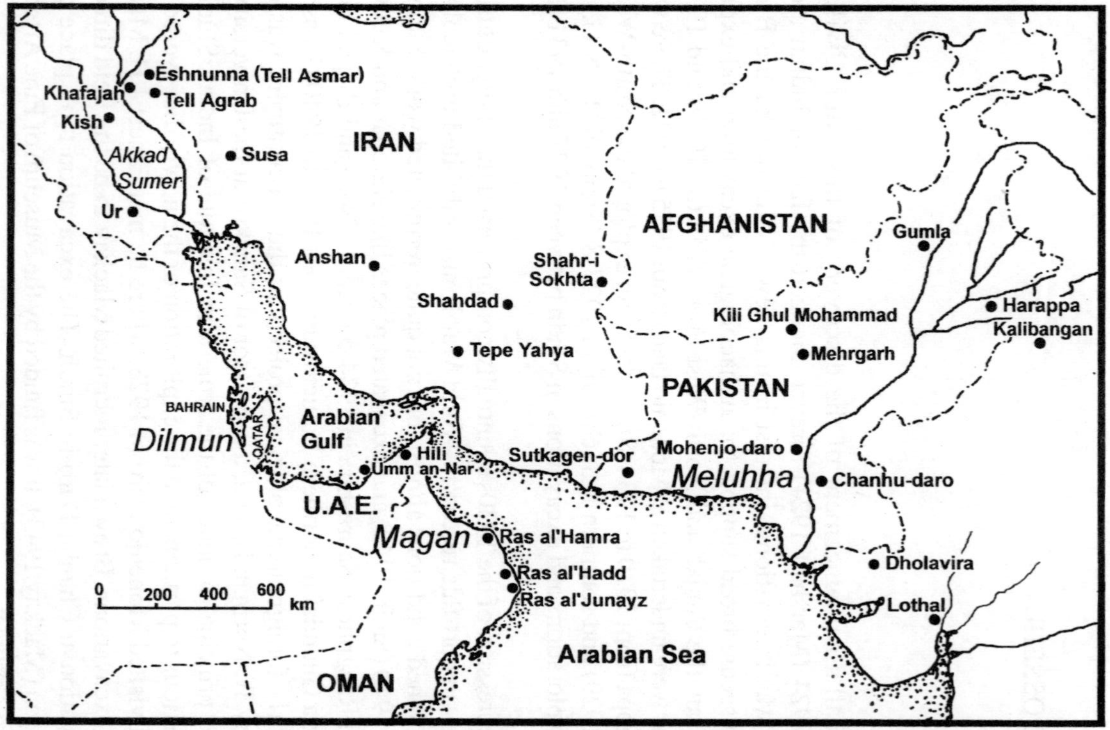

Fig. 1. The Indus region, the Gulf and Mesopotamia, with certain sites mentioned in the text.

India. Wheeler came to India in February 1944, and in some ways this can be seen as a harbinger of the future of archaeology in India.

World War II came to an end in 1945 and along with it came the Independence of India and Pakistan in 1947. Independence brought with it many changes, one of which was a reinvigoration of archaeological research, and the Archaeological Survey of India generally. There are several works that reivew the history of archaeological research in India and Pakistan till 1947 (Ghosh 1953a; 1961; Roy 1961; Chakrabarti: 1968).

HARAPPAN ARCHAEOLOGY ON THE EVE OF INDEPENDENCE

Knowledgeable archaeologists with the Archaeological Survey of India on the eve of Independence would have been well aware that the wealth of Mature Harappan sites, both excavated and unexcavated, were in Pakistan, along with huge collections. Most important were the two great cities: Mohenjo Daro (Marshall 1931; Mackay 1937-8) and Harappa (Vats 1940). In fact, there were only two excavated Harappan sites in the new India: Kotla Niahang Khan (Vats 1929-30) and Rangpur (Vats 1934-5), and there was dispute about Rangpur's cultural affiliation. There had been some digging at Kalibangan (Stein 1943: 49-52), but the cultural affiliation of that site was not recognized. K.N. Dikshit had also excavated at Ahichchhtra from 1940-4. It is a huge mound with a long culture historical sequence in the Ganga Valley (Ghosh 1989: 7-9). He did not find Harappan material there, but later digging did, at least for the Harappan Post-Urban (*IAR* 1964-5: 39-42).

A handful of unexcavated sites were known from Stein's work in Ganganagar district and other explorations in the north Punjab, in Roopnagar district, but the bulk of evidence for the Indus Civilization was in Pakistan, along with the two great cities. In an appendix to Sir Mortimer Wheeler's report on his 1946 excavations at Harappa, Donald E. McCown, in India on a John Simon Guggenheim Fellowship, compiled an authoritative list of Mature Harappan sites (McCown 1947). There were thirty-seven (Fig. 2). The past 50 years has seen this aspect of archaeology change, rather remarkably. The current documented record of Mature Harappan sites in my Gazetteer, are 1,022 settlements: 406 in Pakistan, 616 in India (Fig. 3). Of the 96 sites which are important to understanding the Mature Harappan have been excavated 41 are in Pakistan and 55 in India. There is a great deal of hard work implied in this reversal of positions and it began in 1947.

The leadership of the Archaeological Survey of India began with K.N. Dikshit who served from 21 March 1937 until the arrival of R.E.M. Wheeler in 1944. Wheeler handed the Director General's office to N.P. Chakravarti on 30 April 1948, who in turn relinquished it to M.S. Vats on 30 June 1950. A. Ghosh received charge from Vats on 2 March 1953 (Ghosh 1953a: 45-8). Things moved slowly, with planning and budgetary concerns. The only active project on Harappan archaeology in 1947 was the re-excavation of Rangpur by M.G. Dikshit of Deccan College (Dikshit 1950). In 1948, Beatrice de Cardi conducted a survey of Kalat State in Baluchistan (de Cardi 1983). Chakravarti allowed B.B. Lal to visit Bisauli and Rajpur Parsu, two Post-Urban Copper Hoard sites in the Ganga-Yamuna

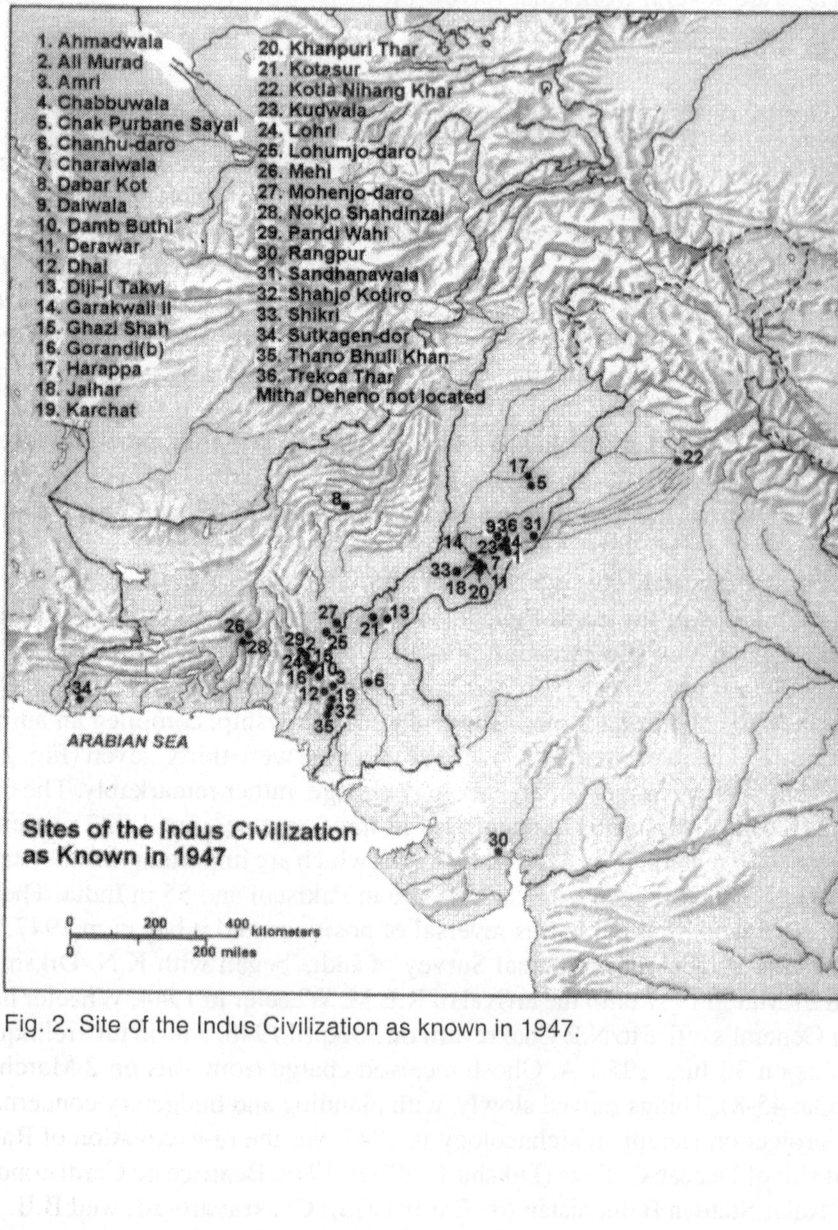

Fig. 2. Site of the Indus Civilization as known in 1947.

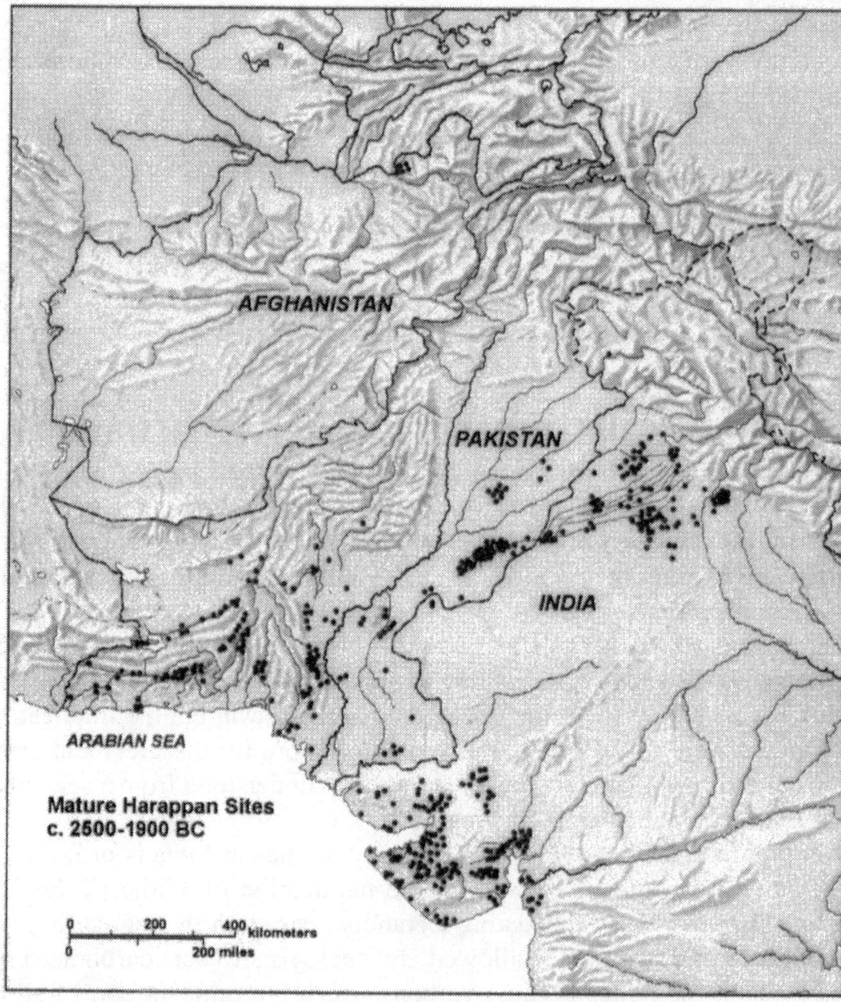

Fig. 3. Site of the Indus Civilization today.

Doab in 1949 (Lal 1951: 27-8, 37). Then in 1950-1 there was a spurt of activity. Wheeler went to Mohenjo Daro for one season (Wheeler 1950a, 1950b, 1950c; Alcock 1986). Walter A. Fairservis went to work in the Quetta Valley and began the discovery of the subcontinent's earliest domesticated plants and animals on which the Indus peoples based their economy (Fairservis 1956). B.B. Lal began his excavations at Hastinapura, with the Post-Urban Harappan, OCP material at the base, and defined the north Indian Early Iron Age in terms of the Painted Grey Ware (Lal 1954-5). A. Ghosh began his survey of the Sarasvati and revisited a number of Stein's sites, conducting test excavations at several of them (Ghosh 1952, 1953b).

PROGRESS IN CHRONOLOGY

The chronology of the earlier eras of Indian history was clouded by doubt and debate as India became an independent state in 1947. There was a strong sense that the Indus Civilization was contemporary with the Akkadian period in Mesopotamia, largely because of the presence there of Indus materials brought by the adventurous mariners of India who sailed into the Gulf and the port of Akkad. Sir Mortimer Wheeler's first edition of *The Indus Civilization* presented a long chronology for the Mature Harappan of 2500-1500 BC (Wheeler 1953: 4). There was also the journey of Alexander the Great into the Punjab in 326 BC and the historical cross-references that emerged between Indians and Westerners that helped, in some small way, to settle the chronology of the Mauryan dynasty. Finally, the discovery of Roman coinage at Indian sites, especially the megaliths of the south, were extremely important in establishing the antiquity of at least the later Megalithic monuments.

These chronologies were not precise and there were many gaps between periods and across the immense distances that span the regions of India. There were a few chronological points, as with Alexander the Great, that were known, but the implications that flowed from them were not always clear, providing room for disagreement among the experts. The chronology of ancient India was not well understood from a scientific point of view, but India was not alone in this regard.

The revolution in understanding the chronology of ancient India is probably, for the most part, thought to begin in 1948, with the publication of Willard Libby's *Radio carbon Dating* (Libby 1948). This dating technique, based on the regular decay of the radioactive isotope of carbon (^{14}C), allowed archaeologists to date carbonized or burnt organic materials in their sites because carbon is such a prominent part of all organic matter.

The first dates from the subcontinent come from Kili Ghul Mohammad and Damb Sadaat in Baluchistan, the result of the excavations of Walter Fairservis. They were run at the Lamont Laboratory affiliated to Columbia University in New York, using the early, crude, laboratory technique that dated the solid carbon directly. These dates showed that the early farming communities in the Baluchi hills were at least 6,000 years old and that Damb Sadaat, was partially coexistent with the Indus Civilization. Dates were also run at the University of Pennsylvania from archival samples from Mohenjo Daro and fresh excavations at Kot Diji, also in Pakistan. These confirmed the chronology that was derived from ties between Mesopotamia and the Indus Valley.

In the late 1950s it became apparent that India needed its own radiocarbon laboratory and D.P. Agrawal, a bright young archaeologist, was selected to make it a reality at the Tata Institute of Fundamental Research. This facility, which was later shifted to the Physical Research Laboratory in Ahmedabad, ran a series of dates on a host of excavations in the country. Date list number one had results from the following places: Ahar, Burzahom, Chandoli, Kalibangan, Lalitpur, Lothal, Navdatoli, Nevasa and Rajgir. These dates were the first leads to the true date for the Northern Neolithic of Kashmir (Burzahom) and surrounding valleys, the central Indian chalcolithic (Chandoli, Navdatoli, Nevasa, Ahar) and provided a cross-check on the chronology of the Mauryans (Rajgir). They also dated early Indian excavations on the Indus Civilization sites of Kalibangan and Lothal.

My list of over 1,500 dates from the subcontinent, includes 990 from India, 399 from Pakistan and 145 from Sri Lanka (Possehl 1989). Recent advances have added greater precision to the dating method and taken as a body, these dates have revolutionized our ideas concerning the chronology for prehistoric India. It is now known that the earliest food producing peoples of the subcontinent date to *c.* 7000 BC and that there is a long series of regional cultures that bridges the millennia between these early Neolithic folk and the Mature Harappan which can be securely placed at 2500-1900 BC. We know that the Bronze Age peoples of Malwa and the Deccan overlap with the later centuries of the Mature Harappan and continue on to the beginnings of the south and central India Iron Age. There are no historical gaps there. The same is true in north India where the transition from the later Harappan peoples can be dated to the introduction of iron technology, which began in India and many other parts of Asia, at 1100-1000 BC. There is a thorough review of chronology of Pakistan and Afghanistan (Shaffer 1992) as well as India (Possehl and Rissman 1992).

These chronological issues are dependent on the fundamentals of archaeology: careful excavation and detailed, intensive exploration. Excavation has grown to be a prominent and substantive pursuit in India, but archaeological exploration is not nearly as 'flashy' an undertaking and receives far less notice. It is, however, a very important tool for understanding the past through settlement patterns and an analysis of the size, density and longevity of human habitation.

ARCHAEOLOGICAL EXPLORATION

The greatest of the early archaeological explorers was Sir Aurel Stein. His work in Chinese Turkistan is a significant part of the history of archaeology, but his explorations in the North-West Frontier and Baluchistan were for decades the best source of information on the prehistoric peoples there. Stein was also a pioneer in the exploration of the ancient Sarasvati, which was pursued and expanded on by the great Director General of the Archaeological Survey of India, A. Ghosh, and even more recently by our Pakistani colleague M. Rafique Mughal.

In 1947, it is fair to say that India was poorly explored in terms of her archaeological heritage. Stein's work was there, but it was neither a dense area coverage, nor, by modern standards, was it systematic. Stein followed the well-worn roads and tracks of his exploration area, recording sites as he came upon them, which gives his work a linear quality, a distinct liability in the investigation of settlement patterns.

Over the years, in a patient programme of correcting this serious deficiency, India has been explored. The job is not yet done, and many districts have not been given the attention they will eventually receive, but substantial parts of the Punjab, Haryana, Rajasthan and Gujarat have been explored. Some of the credit for this exploration goes to the Archaeological Survey of India and devoted explorers like Jagat Pati Joshi and his team (Joshi et al. 1984), K.N. Dikshit, C. Marghabandhu and R.S. Bisht. Indian universities have been active in this area as well. Kurukshetra University has produced a number of dissertations and M.A. theses with taluka and district exploration as their theme. The same has been true for the M.S. University of Baroda and Deccan College, where dissertations based on exploration projects and the analysis of settlement patterns have led to giant strides being made in closing the gaps in this part of the archaeological record. In Pakistan, M.R. Mughal has done much exploration, especially in Cholistan (Mughal 1997). Mughal's research is a seminal contribution to our understanding of the Indus Civilization.

As August 1947 approached, Indian archaeologists became consciously aware that there were essentially no sites of ancient India's first civilization on their side of the Indo-Pakistan border. The premier sites of Mohenjo Daro and Harappa were in Sindh and the west Punjab. Corrective measures were soon taken. The Director General of the Archaeological Survey of India explored the now dry Sarasvati river system between 1950 and 1953. He found a large number of sites there, stretching back to Early Harappan times. The survey undertook excavation at a number of these, but the most important was at Kalibangan, where they worked for nine seasons, beginning in 1960. Another archaeologist from the Archaeological Survey of India, S.R. Rao began the exploration of Gujarat, looking for Mature Harappan sites there. M.S. Vats had excavated Rangpur in the old Limbdi State in 1934-5 and had determined that it had an affinity with Mature Harappan remains, although he thought this was a rather late manifestation. Rao started his work there, and then he found Lothal where he conducted the first of eight seasons in 1958. Thus, the Survey sprang to action when faced with the challenge of partition and was eminently successful in its exploration efforts, which were followed by strategic excavations. The ninety-six Mature Harappan sites have virtually all been excavated since 1947. Some of the excavations have been small, but some are a reflection of long term commitments with substantial resources at stake. The work at Kalibangan and Lothal was in this tradition. So too, is the research at places like Banawali (Haryana) and Dholavira (Kachchh). My own site of Rojdi in central Saurashtra (Rajkot district) has been the scene of nine seasons of work, two by the Gujarat State Department of Archaeology and seven by a joint team from there and the University of Pennsylvania, with much needed support from the American Institute of Indian Studies and the Government of India and Gujarat.

Publication of these materials is often perceived as a problem, and final reports are lacking on some of this work, but every site in my Gazetteer carries a bibliographic citation, so the explored sites have been published somewhere. Major excavation reports are missing for important places (e.g. Kalibangan), but there is a programme in place to publish them. Indian archaeologists are not alone in dealing with the gap between the closing of excavation work and the appearance of a written report. Good reports can take a decade, sometimes two, to write.

It was once thought that there was a 'Dark Age' in northern India that separated historical times from the later phases of the Harappan Civilization, the so-called 'Post-Urban Harappan'. This idea promoted the thought that the end of the ancient cities of the Indus was mysterious. It is now known that this perspective is not viable. Thanks largely to the explorations and excavations of Jagat Pati Joshi and his team from the Archaeological Survey of India , there is a complete culture historical sequence in the Punjab that connects the Mature Harappan with the Early Iron Age of the Painted Grey Ware. There is no 'Dark Age' in northern India, but there are new, important questions about the Early Iron Age and the peoples who made and used the Painted Grey Ware.

SPREADING THE RESPONSIBILITIES AND CREATING OPPORTUNITIES

Archaeology in India at Independence was primarily the domain of the Archaeological Survey of India. Over the years, with the growth of the Indian university system, and the presence of some very fine archaeologists on their faculties, opportunities for conducting serious archaeological research came to be shared. Indian universities, and state departments of archaeology have played an important role in the discipline, especially in Harappan archaeology. Of special note is the work of Deccan College in Gujarat, at Somnath (Dhavalikar and Possehl 1992), Kuntasi (Dhavalikar et al. 1996) and Padri (Shinde 1991, 1992; Shinde and Kar 1992). The work can be traced to the genius of India's foremost university based archaeologist, H.D. Sankalia. Sankalia's student, B. Subbarao went on to found the Department of Ancient History and Archaeology at the M.S. University of Baroda, which has conducted major excavations at many sites, including Somnath (Nanavati et al. 1971), Kanewal (Mehta et al. 1980), Nageshwar (Hegde et al. 1990). This faculty has also sponsored a number of important exploration programmes, often presented in the form of M.A. and Ph.D. theses. The Gujarat State Department of Archaeology has been active, as in my excavations at Rojdi (Possehl and Raval 1989) and Oriyo Timbo (Rissman and Chitalwala 1990). Indus archaeology and the Punjab and Haryana have been furthered in a significant way by the Punjab Department of Archaeology's excavations at Banawali (Bisht 1982) and Kunal (Khatri and Acharya 1995). The University of Kurukshetra has worked at a large number of sites, especially Mitathal (Suraj Bhan 1975), along with a long series of useful M.A. and Ph.D. dissertations on the archaeology of individual talukas and districts in Haryana.

Although the Centre for Historical Studies at Jawaharlal Nehru University is not known for its archaeological fieldwork, it is an immensely rich intellectual resource that has had an impact on Indus archaeology (Ratnagar 1981, 1991). Scholars working at the National Museum in New Delhi too have contribued (Gupta 1972, 1974, 1982, 1996; Asthana 1976, 1982, 1985).

Mention should be made of the work of the University of Peshawar and its explorations in the Gomal Valley (Dani 1970-1) and excavations at Rehman Dheri (Durrani 1988) as well as in Bannu (Khan et al. 1991). A.H. Dani, at one time a Superintendent with the Archaeological Survey of India, is the founding genius of this department.

This is not an exhaustive list of all that university and state departments of archaeology have done to further Indus archaeology in India, let alone archaeology generally. Many dedicated workers have been omitted from this brief encounter. The point to be made in this essay, is that in post-Independence times they have come to be invaluable, irreplaceable players in this intellectual endeavour.

THE MAJOR NEW EXCAVATIONS SINCE INDEPENDENCE

Most of the progress in Indus archaeology since Independence has been made from the excavations that have been conducted in both India and Pakistan. All of the important work cannot be summarized in a short essay, but several of the more important projects can be. In 1947 the beginning of food production and settled life, the 'neolithic', was obscure. No one knew where, let alone when, the 'neolithic' developed in the subcontinent. Archaeologists knew that the Harappans in Sindh and the Punjab were wheat and barley farmers, who kept cattle, sheep and goats, but the roots of this subsistence system had not been discovered. This began to change in 1952 with Walter Fairservis's excavations at Kili Ghul Mohammad (Fairservis 1956), but the real progress took place between 1974 and 1985 with the French excavations at Mehrgarh, under the direction of Jean-Francois Jarrige.

The Beginnings of Settled Life

The French excavations at Mehrgarh have given us our first in-depth insight into the beginnings of the village farming community and pastoral camp in the subcontinent. Through an interesting combination of chronological control and archaeological excavations Jean-Francois Jarrige and his team have pushed the beginnings of sedentism back to the seventh or eighth millennium, giving us an important insight into the food producing foundations of the Harappan Civilization.

Mehrgarh Aceramic, Chronology

Mehrgarh is a large, low, undulating site over 200 ha in size. It was established at the base of the Bolan Pass, on the northern Kachi plain (Fig. 4). Excavations there have shown that its large size is due to lateral stratigraphy and the inhabitants never occupied the entire area during any single period. The early settlement is in the north and the settlers, over time, generally moved south along the Bolan river. The latest work at the

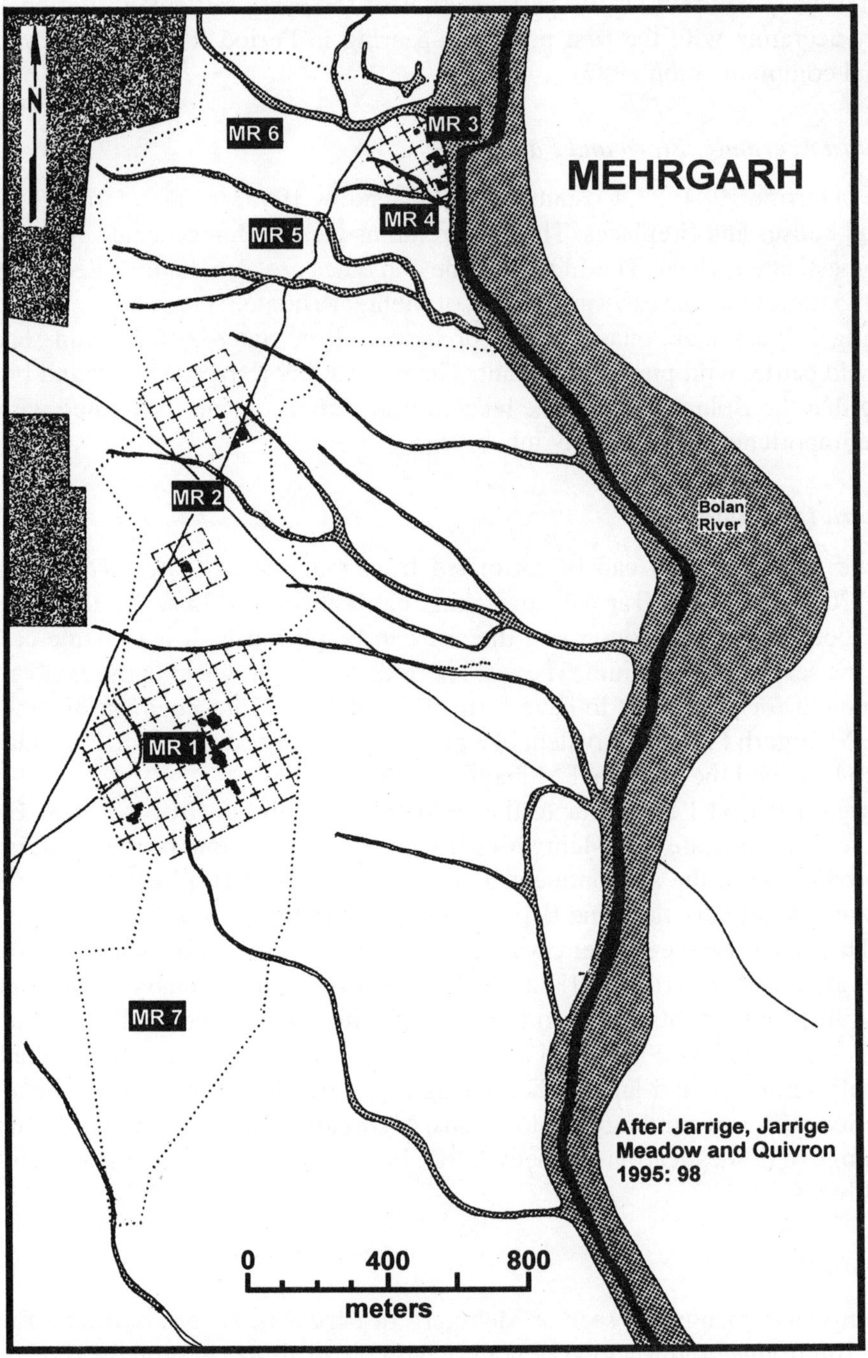

Fig. 4. Site plan of Mehrgarh (after the work of Jean-Francois Jarringe).

site, in 1996-7 has revised the periodization of the early settlement. Period I is now entirely aceramic with the first pottery appearing in Period II (Jean-Francois Jarrige: personal communication 1997).

Mehrgarh Aceramic, Flora and Fauna

Period I (Jarrige 1984: 23; Costantini 1984; Meadow 1993; see also Jarrige et al. 1995) has mud houses and fireplaces. The plant remains include domesticated and wild barley and domesticated wheat. The Indian jujube and dates are also documented. R. Meadow (1984: 35) notes that the early inhabitants of Mehrgarh hunted 'big game': gazelle, swamp deer, nilgai, blackbuck, onager, chital or spotted deer, water-buffalo, wild sheep, wild goat, wild cattle, wild pig and elephant. There are a few remains of fish and birds, suggesting that the Bolan river and the lake/swampy environments associated with it were of little importance to these early inhabitants.

Mehrgarh I: Chronology

The date of Mehrgarh I can be estimated from radiocarbon dates. They range from 9385±120 BP to 5530±180 BP with an average calibration of 5225 BC. Thus, the beginning of the food producing economy at the site can be placed with reasonable confidence within the seventh millennium. There are periods of abandonment in the excavated areas long enough for palaeosols to have formed, indicating a long segment of time for this period. Mehrgarh I is the equivalent of a general phase of occupation in Pakistan that has come to be called the Kili Ghul Mohammad Phase.

Mehrgarh Period I is similar to the Pre-pottery Neolithic B of the Near East. This would seem to indicate that Mehrgarh I is well removed in time from the beginnings of food production in the subcontinent. For example, Mehrgarh I has fully domesticated plants, of several varieties. The Period I village consisted of simple, multi-room buildings. The space between them was used for work areas and as a place for burial (Lechevallier and Quivron 1981: 72-85). Both primary and secondary burials were found in brick lined interments: some in the late aceramic have beads of shell and turquoise. There is one lapis lazuli bead and another of native copper (natural, unsmelted metal). The shell, turquoise and lapis indicate long range trade, travel, or some other form of interaction with surrounding peoples. Thus, Mehrgarh I does not seem to document the beginnings of domestication and settled life, but an early stage in the maturation of this way of life.

Mehrgarh II

Continuity and change are seen at Mehrgarh in Period II. A soft, buff, chaff tempered pottery is introduced. It is a kind of pottery with broad similarities on the Iranian plateau (e.g. Yahya Periods VII-V, Tepe Sialk, Belt and Hotu Caves), possibly as far west as the Zagros (Jarmo). This period at Mehrgarh might fit into a 'Chaff Ware Horizon' which would date to *c.* 5500 BC.

Better fired Plain Red Ware ceramics come in Period IIB, with continuity from older periods in other items of material culture. The dependence on domesticated animals continued to grow through this period, as did the reliance on cultivated plants.

> The charred seeds of wheat and barley belonging to the species *Triticum sphaerococcum* and *Hordeum sphaerococcum* that, according to L. Costantini, grow only on irrigated fields, also were collected from the ashy layers of Period II. (Jarrige et al. 1995: 318)

This is local irrigation, but its documentation so early in the food producing sequence at Mehrgarh is an important observation with regard to this technology.

The Remainder of the Mehrgarh Sequence

The remainder of the Mehrgarh sequence is also important because it traces the long history of a single settlement. There is work on these periods at other sites in Pakistan: Gumla (Dani 1970-1: 35-53), Kili Ghul Mohammad and Damb Sadaat (Fairservis 1956); Kot Diji (Khan 1965), Jalilpur (Mughal 1972), Balakot (Dales 1974, 1979), Rehman Dheri (Durrani 1988), Sheri Khan Tarakai, Islam Chowki and Lak Largai (F. Khan et al. 1991), Ghazi Shah (Flam 1993) and Lewan (Allchin and Allchin 1993). These excavations, and associated exploration, document the changing configurations of settlement prior to the Mature Harappan.

A. GHOSH AND THE MAJOR EXCAVATIONS AFTER INDEPENDENCE

A. Ghosh came to the Director Generalship with planning, a well trained core of officers, and governmental support. During his term, S.R. Rao conducted his important excavations at Rangpur (1953-4, 1954-5, 1956), published in Rao (1963a). The Survey initiated two of its most important post-Independence research projects in the Ghosh era; the work at Lothal, excavated from 1954-63 (Rao 1979, 1985) and at Kalibangan, excavated from 1960-9. Part of the motivation for these long-term projects was to document the presence of the Indus peoples in newly independent India and expand the geographical horizons of this civilization.

Lothal

The ancient site of Lothal is a town of the Harappan Civilization located near the head of the Gulf of Cambay in Gujarat (Fig. 5). Lothal is the southernmost of the major Mature Harappan settlements. The name can be interpreted to mean 'Mound of the Dead Men', the same as Mohenjo Daro, but both of these appellations are modern, we do not know the ancient name of either place. Lothal was discovered by S.R. Rao in 1954 and immediately came under excavation. Rao worked there for eight seasons, from 1954-5 to 1959-60 and 1961-2, 1962-3, the first two of which overlapped with his parallel excavations at neighbouring Rangpur.

Lothal was on the Mature Harappan frontier with peninsular India. It should be viewed

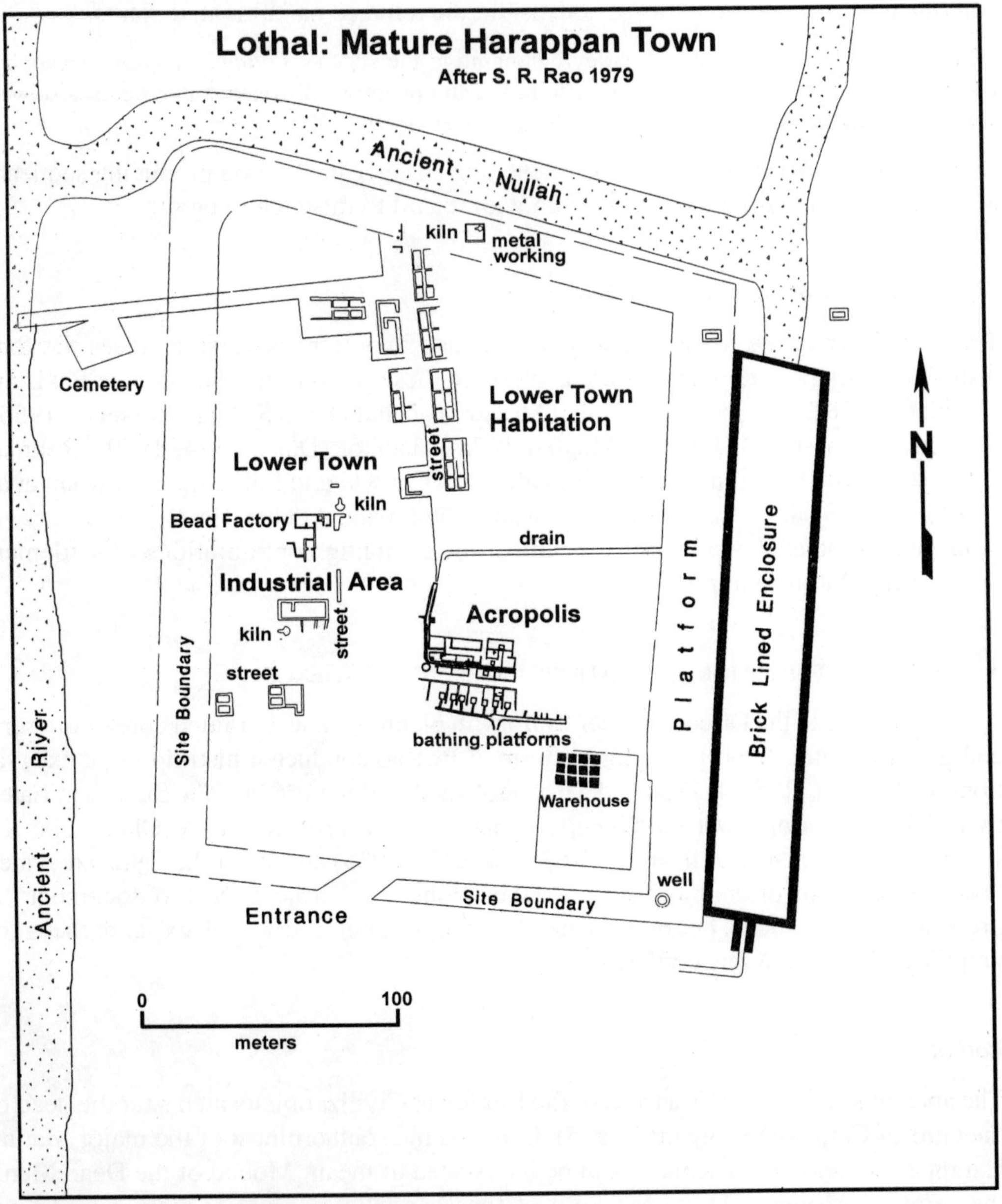

Fig. 5. Site Plan of Lothal (after the work of S.R. Rao).

as a border town, with important commercial relationships with non-Harappan peoples. Rao has claimed that Lothal was a port, a seat of maritime commerce linking ancient India with Mesopotamia. A large, brick-lined basin on the eastern side of the settlement is said to have been a dockyard or harbour for the ships involved in this commerce. This has been disputed by a number of scholars (e.g. Leshnik 1968; Possehl 1976).

The settlement was divided into three districts. An elevated mound is adjacent to the brick lined enclosure. On the summit is a building identified as a warehouse, a long building with bathing facilities and other structures of baked brick, a striking feature of Harappan architecture. The elevated portion of the site was also provided with a civil drainage system, another feature of the Harappan Civilization. To the north of this elevated platform were the domestic quarters of the town, with private houses. No formal market facilities have been documented. West of the platform was a manufacturing area, only a small part of which was excavated.

Whether Lothal was or was not a port, it was certainly a centre of craftsmanship. The excavations uncovered finished products and waste materials from a wide range of natural resources: copper, bronze, gold, carnelian, jasper, rock crystal and other semiprecious stones, ivory and shell. Many of these materials were associated with a bead making shop, similar to the installation at Chanhu Daro, another Harappan site. The bead making technology at Lothal, as documented by waste materials (beads broken in the process of being manufactured and drills), is the same as that documented at Mohenjo Daro, Mehrgarh and Shahr-i Sokhta in Seistan.

Typical Harappan seals and sealings were found at Lothal, most of which were the classic types. A number of more provincial glyptic objects were present as well. Perhaps the most important was a seal of Persian Gulf type, which was a surface find (Rao 1963b).

A small cemetery to the north-west of the site contained a number of interments, twenty of which were opened (Sarkar 1985). Four of the graves seem to have been cenotaphs, documented at Harappa as well. The rest were extended inhumations with modest grave goods. There was one double interment. The Lothal population was well within the range of variability for the Harappans; however, some biological features of the skeletons suggest that there was gene flow into this population from hunting and gathering peoples in this borderland (Kennedy et al. 1984).

Kalibangan

The second large, early excavation following Independence was undertaken at Kalibangan, along the ancient Sarasvati in northern Rajasthan (Fig. 6). It was first discovered in April 1917 by L.P. Tessitori (Tessitori 1918-19: 23) while he was working for the Archaeological Survey of India. In 1950 A. Ghosh revisited Kalibangan in the course of his exploration of the Sarasvati. He fully appreciated the site's archaeological potential and in his capacity as Director General of the Archaeological Survey of India undertook excavation there for nine seasons beginning in 1960-1 and ending in 1968-9. The field work was jointly directed by B.B. Lal and B.K. Thapar. The full excavation report on this work has not yet been published, but it is clear that work on this significant under-

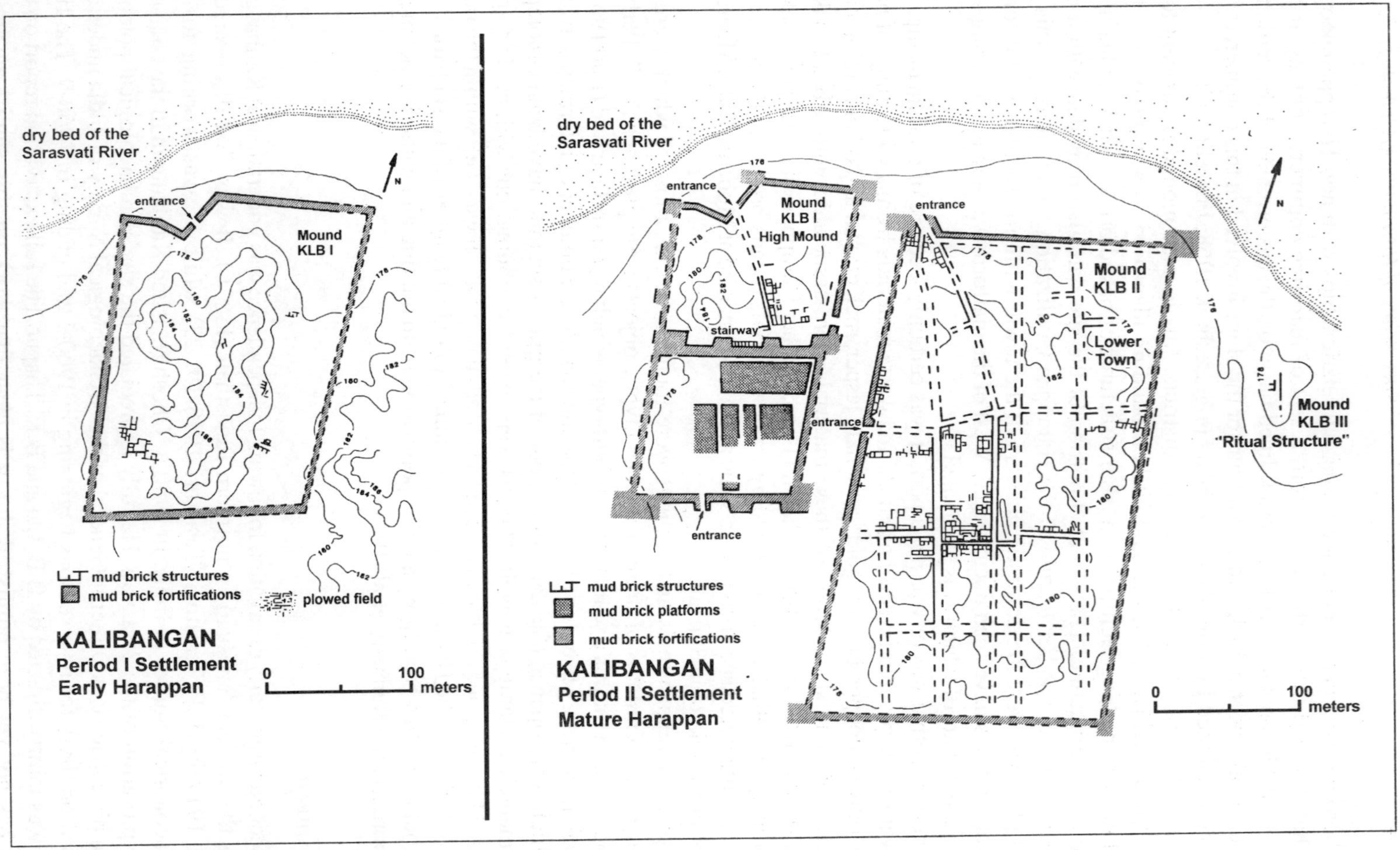

Fig. 6. Site plan of Kalibangan (courtesy of B.K. Thapar).

taking is proceeding at the Survey's facilities at Purana Qila in New Delhi. The best coverage of Kalibangan is found in Lal and Thapar (1967), Thapar (1973a, 1973b, 1975), Lal (1979, 1981). Kalibangan is a two period site with both an Early Harappan and a Mature Harappan occupation.

The Early Harappan Settlement

The Early Harappan settlement at Kalibangan is surrounded by a fortification wall in the shape of a parallelogram *c.* 250 x 170 m in extent. The first phase of the wall was made of mud bricks (30 x 20 x 10 cm) laid to a thickness of *c.* 1.90 m. A second phase of construction brought the thickness of this fortification up to 3 or 4 m, varying from place to place. The inner and outer faces of the fortifications were plastered with mud. Only one entrance, at the north-west corner, was excavated; other entrances were probably obscured by later Harappans. This opening has an interesting configuration as seen on the site plan and is cunningly designed for the protection of this vulnerable point.

The Early Harappan inhabitants of Kalibangan lived in well-made houses, oriented to the cardinal directions and made of the same small mud bricks used for their fortifications. The bricks were laid in English bond, with alternating rows of headers and stretcers. One house of the period had a drain made of baked bricks, a forerunner of later times. Baked bricks were never used in abundance at Kalibangan, as they were at Mohenjo Daro. The rooms of the houses were arranged around a courtyard and had domestic facilities including ovens. Above ground, closed ovens and the subterranean *tandoor* were found. The evidence for bread making is complemented by the presence of querns and mulling stones.

Direct and important evidence for cultivation was found in the form of a preserved plowed field, about 100 m to the south of the Period I settlement. It was covered by slump from the Early Harappan occupation and consisted of alternating furrows and hummocks in the earth. These were oriented to the cardinal directions and have a close ethnographic parallel in modern Rajasthani agricultural practice (Lal 1970-1).

The Transition between Periods I and II

There is an interesting and important transition between Periods I and II at Kalibangan. First, the excavators noticed cleavage and/or displacement of strata in the Period I levels. They have interpreted this as indicative of an earthquake (Lal 1979: 75) which may have led to the abandonment of the settlement. B.K. Thapar expresses it this way:

> This occupation continued through five structural phases, rising to a height of some 1.6 m, when it was brought to a close by a catastrophe (perhaps seismic), as evidenced by the occurrence of displaced (faulted?) deposits and subsided walls in different parts of the excavated area. Thereafter the site seems to have been abandoned, though only temporarily and a thin layer of sand, largely infertile, accumulated over the ruins. (Thapar 1973a: 87)

The upper levels of the Period I settlement were also eroded in some places. Whatever the reason for abandonment, and an earthquake is a good hypothesis, it was apparently complete, indicated by the presence of the infertile, windblown sand.

The Mature Harappan Settlement

When the Mature Harappans reoccupied Kalibangan their ceramics included many of the shapes and fabrics of the Period I occupation. This lasted for about one-half of Period II when it gave way to a more purely Harappan ceramic corpus (Thapar 1989: 196). Other sites in the north-eastern region of the Indus Civilization share this mixture of ceramics as seen at Kalibangan.

The Mature Harappan settlement plan of Kalibangan is significantly different from the original. There are two parts: the High Mound, designated KLB-1, is situated to the west, covering most of the abandoned Early Harappan settlement and to the east is the Lower Town, designated KLB-2, most of it on virgin soil. The old entrance in the north-western corner of the High Mound was once again in use. The Harappan settlers did another interesting thing; they used the old eastern wall of the original settlement (the Early Harappan site) as the northern part of the western wall of the new Lower Town. This reduced the width of the High Mound by about 60 m but created a High Mound that was exactly twice as long as it was wide, the same proportions employed at the Mound of the Great Bath at Mohenjo Daro. They also made good use of older building material, typical of our efficient Harappans.

The High Mound of Period II

During Period II the High Mound was well fortified, although the southern half was stronger than the north. There were two phases of construction and the wall was 3 to 7 m thick. In the earlier phase the Harappans used large bricks (40 x 20 x 10 cm); in the later phase they used smaller bricks (30 x 15 x 7.5 cm). Interestingly, the smaller size bricks were used throughout Period II for the construction of buildings.

The southern half of the High Mound, sometimes called the 'southern rhomb' (Lal 1979: 77), was equipped during Harappan times with a series of mud brick platforms on which ritual structures, connected with the use of fire and possibly animal remains, were located. These have been called 'fire-altars'. They are oval in plan, sunk in the ground and lined with mud plaster or bricks.

The southern rhomb contained several mud-brick platforms, oriented along the cardinal directions, on each of which stood a special structure. Although in most cases the details of these structures have disappeared owing to subsequent spoilation, there is reasonable evidence about their likely use. Thus, atop one of the platforms there lay a series of seven 'fire-altars' in a row. Behind these fire altars a wall ran in a north-south direction, which shows that the people had to face east while performing rituals at these altars. The altars were oblong on plan, sunk into the ground and lined with clay. They contained ash and charcoal, and a cylindrical or faceted clay (burnt or unburnt) stele standing up near the centre. Though in the series under discussion only fragments of what are called 'terracotta cakes' were obtained, elsewhere they were found in sufficient numbers showing that they formed some kind of an 'offering'. To the west of the fire-altars was the lower half of a jar embedded. It contained ash and charcoal and was evidently connected with the use of the fire-altars. Within a few meters of these altars was a well and a few bath-pavements suggesting ablutions before the performance of the ritual—a tradition still in vogue in India, among the Hindus (Lal 1979: 77).

The Lower Town of the Mature Harappan

Most of the people lived in the Lower Town of the Mature Harappan at Kalibangan. It was surrounded by a fortification wall that ranged in thickness between 3.5 and 9 m and had three or four phases of construction. This construction, just as with that of the High Mound, was plastered with mud and tapered from bottom to top. The fortifications protected a town laid out in a gridiron plan separating blocks of habitations. There were four streets running the full north-south distance of the settlement and three (possibly four) oriented east-west. It is interesting that the north-south streets do not run parallel to the fortifications, and two of them converge on the principal entrance to the Lower Town in the north-west corner of the settlement. Buildings at some intersections of these streets were equipped with wooden fenders to limit damage to, and done by, vehicular traffic. Lanes within the community blocks were *c.* 1.80 m wide and the other streets were multiples of this standard: 3.60, 5.40 and 7.20 m. There is some indication of habitation extending outside the fortifications in the protected area to the south of the High Mound and to the west of the Lower Town.

Kalibangan Harappan houses were of mud brick and consisted of rooms set around courtyards, many of which had their own wells. Roofs were flat, with wooden rafters supporting a covering of reeds and mud. There is only one building with stairs suggesting a second storey. Floors were of rammed earth, although there was some paving. Cooking was done in the open, generally in a corner of the courtyard.

> Most of the rooms were used for living purposes, which include their use as bedrooms, but some also served as stores. In one of the rooms many large jars were found embedded in the ground. These seem to have been used for the storage of grains. It further appears that in almost every house a room was reserved for the 'fire-altars' which had their characteristic shape and other features including the central stele. In a few cases these were lined with mud bricks. (Lal 1979: 85)

Some houses had narrow platforms along their exterior walls, on lanes and streets. These seem to be seating areas, similar to those in modern villages of the north-western subcontinent, used by the inhabitants to meet friends, exchange information and keep up with the day-to-day life of their community. A few baked bricks were used at Kalibangan in the Harappan period. They were pretty much reserved for use in ritual structures, drains, wells, bathing platforms and thresholds. Unlike Mohenjo Daro the drainage system was localized and discharged into large pots set in the ground.

Dholavira

The Archaeological Survey of India has been excavating Dholavira since 1989-90 (see *IAR* for yearly reports) (Fig. 7). This large, 60 ha site was discovered by Jagat Pati Joshi in 1967-8 (*IAR* 1967-8: 14-16). It is located on Khadir Island in the central part of the Great Rann of Kachchh. Dholavira is one of the five largest urban centres of the Harappan Civilization. Mohenjo Daro and Harappa are about 100 ha. Ganweriwala in Cholistan and Rakhighari in Haryana are both about 80 ha. The best bibliography on Dholavira is in Bisht (1989a, 1989b, 1991, 1994).

Seven years of large scale excavation have revealed that Dholavira was a planned settlement with an exquisite system of water storage and management. There is a long sequence of habitation there that begins during the Early/Mature Harappan Transition (*c.* 2600-2500 BC) and extends to the early centuries of the second millennium.

R.S. Bisht, the Director of the Dholavira excavations has defined seven periods of occupation, or stages, at the site. The first two fall within the Early/Mature Harappan Transition. Stages III, IV and V are Mature Harappan, the final two stages are post-Urban Harappan.

The earliest Stage I was the founding of the settlement on virgin soil. These pioneers knew the arts of copper working, bead-making, masonry and were careful planners of their architecture. The settlement of Stage I, located in the vicinity of the Citadel (Fig. 7), was surrounded by a substantial fortification, as thick as 11 m at its base. The houses were built of moulded mud bricks, with the Mature Harappan proportion of 4:2:1.

Stage II sees the widening and strengthening of the fortification wall and the enlargement of the settlement with building to the north. The early fortification wall was found to be plastered on both sides and parts of it were covered with a veneer of stone. The material culture of Stages I and II is similar, but there was an increase in the number of antiquities that were recovered. A boat-shaped crucible documents metal working at the site. The pioneer settlers of Stages I and II made ceramics with parallels to Amri Period II, Nausharo ID and Kot Diji Period I.

During Stage III Dholavira grew from a small settlement to a large town or city with two sets of fortifications, districts and a water storage system on a significant scale. This period marks the raising of the Citadel and Bailey, as seen on Fig. 7. Ceramics and small finds, including square Indus stamp seals, allow us to date this Stage to the early Mature Harappan. The stamp seals from Stage III at Dholavira do not bear Indus writing, but animal devices are present. Whether this is due to sampling or is a culture historical fact has not yet been determined.

The Stage II extension residential area was cleared, leveled and paved in Stage III which created an area of open ground that Bisht believes was a ceremonial ground. Farther to the north a large residential area was laid out, secured by the second fortification wall. The facility was provided with gates, bastions and drains. The new town was divided into residential areas with streets and lanes laid out in a gridiron pattern.

Toward the end of Stage III (Stage III B) Dholavira seems to have been struck by an earthquake of major magnitude, documented by slip faults in sections and the displacement of architectural features. This led to repairs within Stage III that are very large in

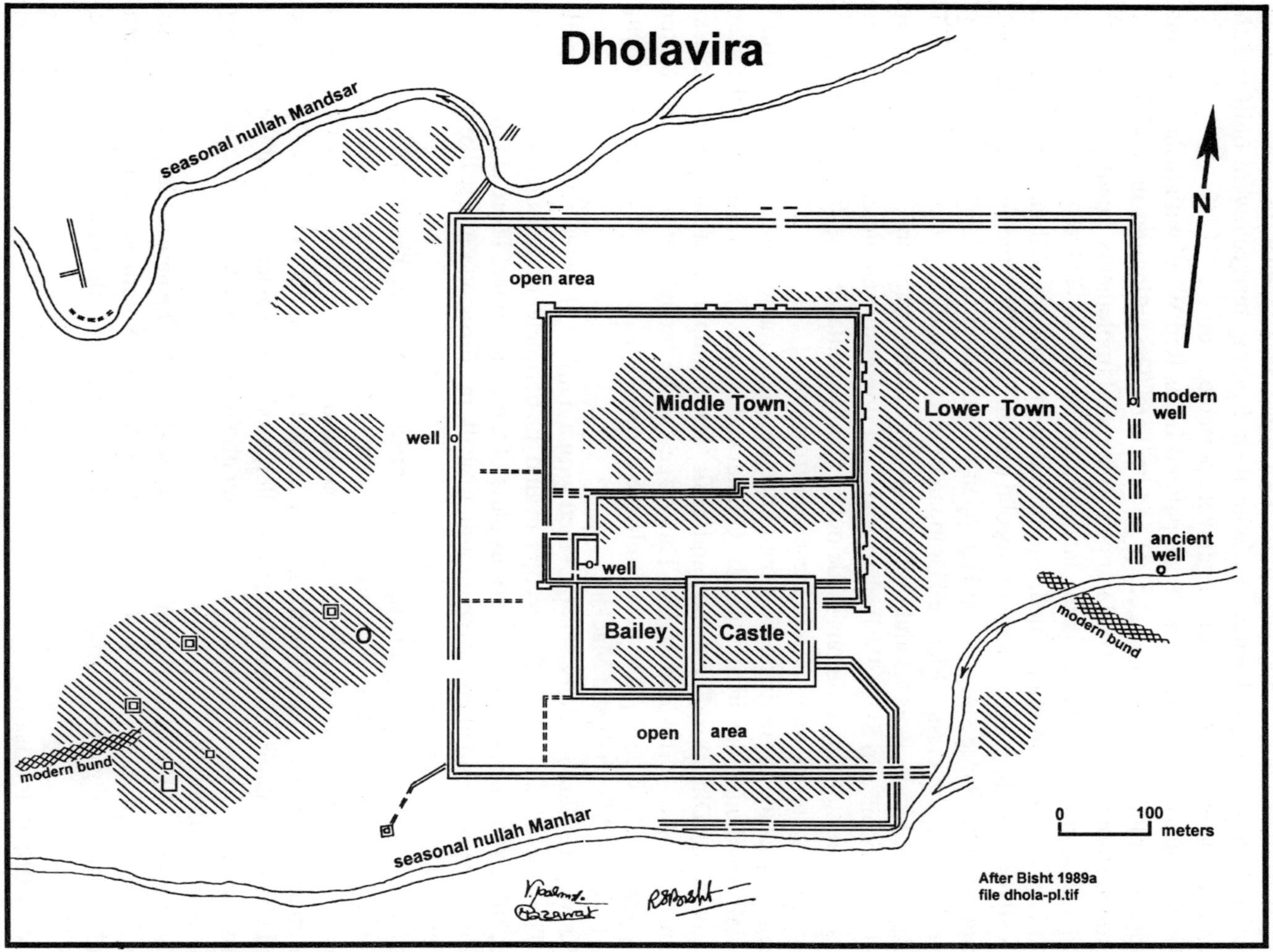

Fig. 7. Site plan of Dholavira (courtesy of R.S. Bisht).

scale. Parts of the Citadel and the residential areas were cleared of houses. Other residential areas were extended, especially to the east which necessitated the extension of the city wall. The monumental gateways, with their fronting terraces were built and the settlement reached its largest, best organized, perfected point.

The ceramics of Stage III is the black painted Indus Red Ware, with dishes on stand, Harappan storage jars, tea cups, goblets and beakers. The antiquities include the afòrementioned stamp seals, weights, Harappan style metal implements, beads and figurines.

Stage IV can be thought of as the later Mature Harappan. The city of Stage III was carefully preserved and maintained, and included the monumental gateways, fortification walls and the drainage system. Of special note in Stage IV is the now famous mosaic inscription of ten large signs of the Harappan script, found face down in a chamber of North Gate. All the classic Mature Harappan objects including pottery, seals now with writing, tools, beads, weights and other items of gold, copper, stone, shell and clay are found in abundance in Stage IV. Perhaps the most impressive architectural elements are pillars and free standing columns made out of locally available limestone. The so-called Harappan ring stones were used in these constructions.

Stage V sees the beginnings of a general decline in the maintenance of the city. This is especially evident in the urban core, the Citadel and Bailey. In contrast to this, the material culture of Dholavira, ceramics and seals, for example, continue in their classic Mature Harappan forms and styles. This stage can be thought of as the Late Mature Harappan, which would place it in a relative chronology as an equivalent of Mohenjo Daro Late I of Marshall and Mackay.

The Mature Harappan city was provided with a number of water management facilities. They included a series of reservoirs around the perimeter of the outer wall and stone lined, subterranean reservoirs in various parts of the civic centre. There are drains, some of which are stone lined and large enough to walk in. Terracotta pipes, like those from Mohenjo Daro are also known.

Stage V was followed by a temporary desertion of the site. The following Stage VI presents the Harappan cultural tradition in a form that is widely seen in Saurashtra, to the south. This represents drastic transformation and devolution of the Indus Civilization, with strong ties to the Late Sorath Harappan, and little contact with Sindh. The once grand city of Dholavira is now a much smaller, less diverse place, without the trappings of urbanization. Stage V comes to an end after about a century, with the second abandonment of the settlement.

The duration of the second abandonment is not known. The new settlers are much like their Stage VI predecessors, with clear ties to the Late Sorath Harappans. They built circular houses, engaged in limited craft activities and left little impression on the site.

EXCAVATIONS IN PAKISTAN

Important field work has been done in Pakistan on the Indus Civilization since Independence. Special mention should be made of the excavations by F.A. Khan at Kot Diji, which defined this cultural complex (Khan 1965). The Pakistan Department of Archaeology also excavated the Early Harappan site of Sarai Khola at the western end of the Taxila Valley (Halim 1972a, 1972b). The French work at Mehrgarh has already been noted, and they dug Amri (Casal 1964), Pirak (Jarrige and Santoni 1979) and Nausharo as well (J.F. Jarrige 1989; C. Jarrige 1994). The British have been working with the University of Peshawar in Bannu and surrounding areas (Khan et al. 1991; Allchin and Allchin 1992). Long term, large scale projects have also been undertaken at Mohenjo Daro and Harappa.

Mohenjo Daro

The research at Mohenjo Daro was begun in 1979 by Professor Michael Jansen of Aachen University (Fig. 8, Plan of Mohenjo Daro). The Aachen team worked closely for a time with another group of archaeologists from IsMEO in Rome, under the direction of Maurizio Tosi. There has been much good work done by these teams. Jansen has organized archives, discovered field notes from the Marshall and Mackay field seasons, reprinted and conserved photographs and has been responsible for many other small triumphs that taken together are a significant contribution to understanding Mohenjo Daro (Jansen and Urban 1984, 1985, 1987; Jansen and Tosi 1988; Jansen 1993). Jansen has also made a salient contribution to the history of research on the Indus Civilization (Jansen 1986).

Jansen has developed his own body of theory on Mohenjo Daro. First, he believes that the site was a 'founder's settlement' built at the beginning of the Mature Harappan as a kind of symbolic representation of the new civilization. This city was built on a series of platforms which elevated the settlement above the plain, protecting it from floods. He notes that the basic alignment of streets, lanes, drains and wells were laid out at the beginning and maintained through the span of the Mature Harappan. Much of the water management data are found in Jansen (1993). If Jansen is correct, and I like his ideas, Mohenjo Daro as a living city was approximately the size of the modern mounds that make up the archaeological site.

Many studies have spun off of the Aachen project at Mohenjo Daro. Alexandra Ardeleanu-Jansen has studied the sculpture, terracottas and excavated a well (Ardeleanu-Jansen 1984, 1992, 1993a, 1993b). Ute Franke-Vogt studies new glyptic material (Franke 1984; Franke-Vogt 1991a, 1991b). Several studies of Mature Harappan craft production were conducted (Halim and Vidale 1984; Vidale 1984, 1987; Tosi et al. 1984).

Based in large part on their research at Mohenjo Daro, Blackman and Vidale have produced some generalizations on Indus craft production. The first thought is that in some areas like Cholistan small settlements form a cloud of minor sites around an urban centre. Many of the smaller sites appear to have been specialized industrial localities (Blackman and Vidale 1992: 38). In other regions a different pattern emerges. For example, at Mohenjo Daro, Blackman and Vidale (1992: 38) note that:

> The surface survey of Mohenjo Daro shows that most of the heavy, polluting industries (e.g. ceramic and brick firing and metallurgical activities) are not represented in the urban compound. It must be presumed that these activities were carried out in a series of peripheral settlements (now invisible due to alluviation) that supplied the centre.

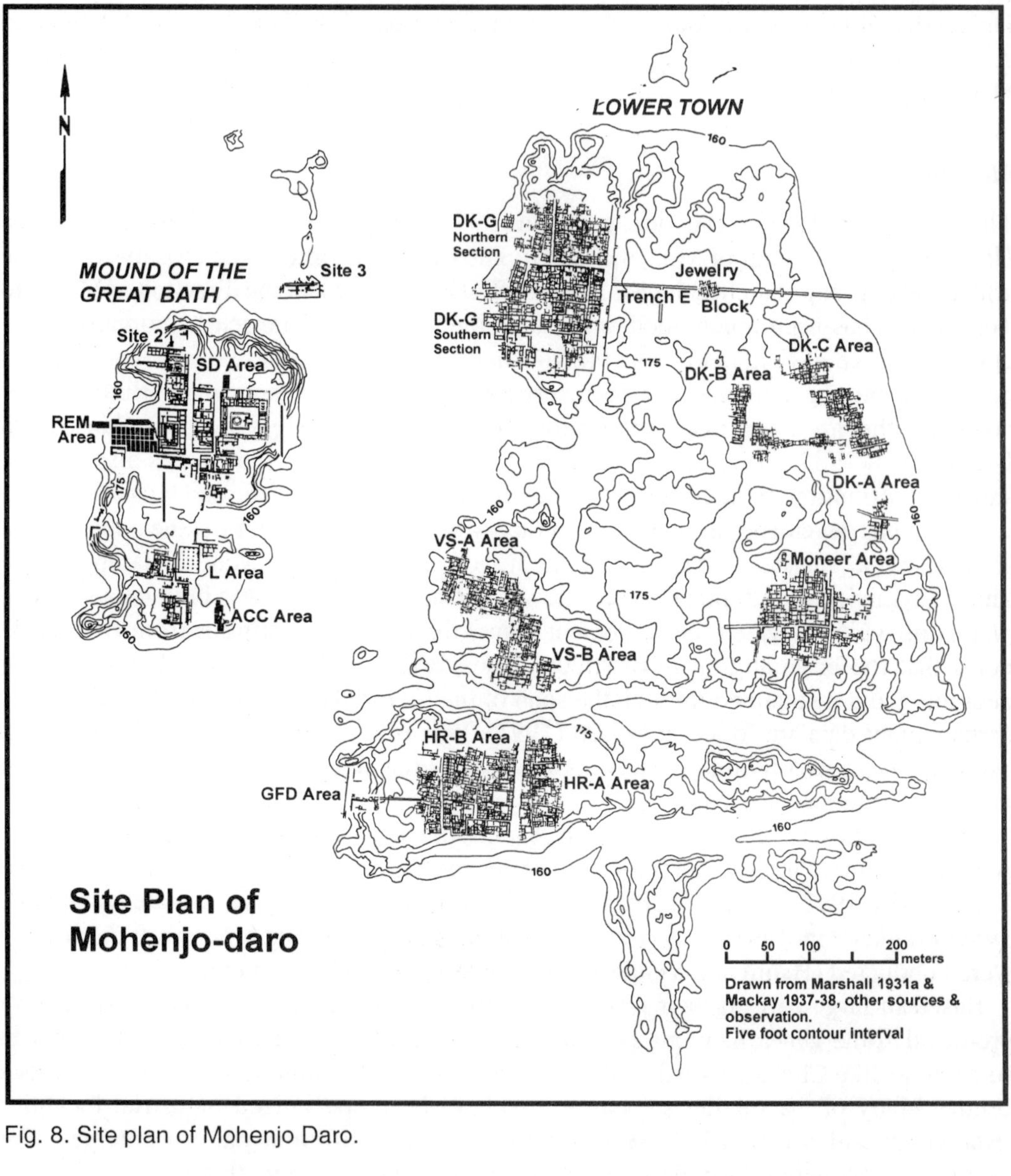

Fig. 8. Site plan of Mohenjo Daro.

This position can certainly be sustained for brick making, but for ceramics the case seems to be somewhat different.

Blackman and Vidale (1992: 38) go on to note that non-polluting industries were located within Mohenjo Daro. These industries were involved in the manufacture of things like seals, beads and shell ornaments, luxury and other prestige items, probably for consumption within the city.

The very high quality of Indus craftsmanship is also highlighted by these studies. As new work took place at Mohenjo Daro, a renewed investigation of Harappa, another of the urban centres of the Indus Civilization, was also formulated.

Harappa

The renewed work at Harappa was begun by George Dales in 1986. The accomplishments of this project have been many, including the training of a number of Pakistani students; all summarized in regular, substantial preliminary reports (see also Meadow 1991, and reports in *South Asian Archaeology*).

The research seems to have been most successful in defining the Early Harappan settlement at the southern end of the large AB Mound, extending to Mound E (Fig. 9). They have also found a phase of occupation prior to the Early Harappan (Kot Dijian) occupation. This appears to be related to the Hakkra wares of Cholistan, but it has some unique features as well. The excavations of the Mature Harappan levels have produced an impressive number of objects (seals, tokens, and others) with the Harappan script on them. The excavation team has spent a good portion of the most recent seasons excavating the south-eastern part of Mound E, and the gap between this Mound and ET (Fig. 9). They have found a very wide mud brick foundation and gateway in this corner of the city (Kenoyer 1993).

In the early years of the project many resources were devoted to excavating the Mature Harappan cemetery, known as R-37. Ninety skeletons were recovered and a team of Physical Anthropologists has analysed them. Their principal findings can be summarized as follows.

Most of the specimens were females. The age distribution of the sample is seen in Table 1.

The general health of this sample of the population of Mature Harappans was quite good. 'No cases of nutritional inadequacy, such as rickets, scurvy or anemia were identified: however there are three cases of arrested growth lines ...' (Dales et al. 1991: 210).

TABLE 1: AGE RANGE OF THE SKELETONS FROM CEMETERY R-37

Subadult	<16 years	15
Young Adult	17-34 years	35
Middle-aged Adult	35-55 years	27
Older Adult	>55 years	13
Total		90

This same report notes that there was a low incidence of traumatic injury or chronic infectious disease and no malignant neoplastic disease. Arthritis was the most common health problem identified in this skeletal series, most of it associated with the spinal column. 'There are several cases of severe arthritis in the neck, including fusion of adjacent elements. This could be associated with unusual stress on the neck vertebrae, such as would occur with carrying heavy loads on the head' (Dales et al. 1991: 210). This is, of course, one of the most common customs in South Asia today, especially among women, and this observation might indicate considerable time depth for this practice.

In the end this research tells us that the population of people interred in Cemetery R-37 were healthy agriculturists with biological affinities to later Indian populations.

The teeth from the Cemetery R-37 sample had a relatively high frequency of caries. This is in agreement with what would be expected from people who practiced an agricultural mode of existence (Dales et al. 1991: 212).

A statistical analysis of the crania suggests that the R-37 series is most closely related to other individuals interred in this cemetery and the two phases of Cemetery H, which indicated biological continuity from the Mature Harappan to the Post-Urban Harappan. Further biological continuity is suggested for north-western Pakistan because the R-37 individuals are also like those from the Iron Age cemetery at Timargarha.

These excavations, and other research have led to the reformulation of our understanding of the Indus Civilization. There are many more scholars studying these ancient peoples today than there were in 1947, and there is no single paradigm that has risen to the ascendancy. But, there are important new ideas about the Harappan Civilization.

THE HARAPPAN CIVILIZATION BEYOND THE INDIAN SUBCONTINENT

At the eve of discovery, in 1924, Sir John Marshall used the term 'Indo-Sumerian Civilization' to describe the culture of Mohenjo Daro and Harappa. It was reasonably clear that the finds were not related to Egypt, and Sumer gave researchers their only comparative material. There were also some Indus seals in the west, that indicated contact between the Indus Valley and Mesopotamia and the two regions are within striking distance of one another. But, by the end of the very large season of excavation in 1925-6 the term 'Indo-Sumerian' was dropped by Marshall:

> And here I may say parenthetically that I shall use the term 'Indus' henceforth to designate the particular culture of the Chalcolithic period which I have hitherto designated Indo-Sumerian, since the latter term is likely to imply a closer connection with Sumer than now seems justified'. (Marshall 1925-6: 75; see also Marshall 1926-7: 53)

Although Marshall attempted to make 'Indus Civilization', not 'Indus Valley Civilization', the standard, he was never quite successful. Some (e.g. E.J.H. Mackay and M.S. Vats) saw his term as parochial, and objected by noting that the civilization extended well beyond the confines of the Indus Valley, even if Marshall never intended a close geographical connotation for his name. Mackay preferred the notion of 'Harappa Culture' taking the archaeological tradition of using the 'type fossil' concept to name archaeological assemblages. G.R. Hunter, one of the early scholars working with the Indus script (Hunter 1929, 1932, 1934) seems to have coined the term 'Proto-Indian', a term also used by M.S. Vats, following his excavation at Rangpur (Vats 1934-5: 38). 'Proto-Indian' is still current with some scholars, more so in Russia, and particularly with those involved with the Indus script and other iconographic topics.

The presence of Indus artefacts, especially seals some with script, at Ur, Kish and other sites informed Marshall and his colleagues of some form of intercourse with the West (Fig. 1). This well known data set is reviewed in Ratnagar (1981) and Possehl (1996a). Large scale excavations at Ur and Kish were very important in this story and the leaders of these expeditions were destined to play a role in the history of archaeology in the subcontinent; Sir Leonard Woolley, of Ur, as a reviewer of the effectiveness of the Archaeological Survey of India (see below and Possehl 1993) and Stephen Langdon, an American Professor at Oxford, as a student of the Indus script (see below and Possehl 1996b: 79-80, 84, 90-100).

THE EMERGENCE OF MELUHHA

During the Early Dynastic Period a land known as Meluhha is first attested in the Mesopotamian cuneiform documents. There is also a reference in a boast by Sargon of Akkad (2334-2279 BC) which has been translated by Samuel N. Kramer (1964: 49).

The ships from Meluhha,
the ships from Magan,
the ships from Dilmun,
he made tie-up alongside the quay of Akkad.

We know from a number of pieces of evidence that Dilmun was the Island of Bahrain in the Arabian Gulf, and the near shores of the Arabian Peninsula. Magan was Oman, and perhaps part of the Iranian coast around the Straits of Hormuz. Meluhha then was a reference to the Greater Indus Region, including the Indus Civilization.

Evidence that accumulated through excavations first at Ur, Kish and Susa, then Tell Asmar, Tell Agrab and other places, provided information of undeniable trade between ancient India and Mesopotamia. How did the objects get there? Most archaeologists in the early decades of this century seem to have shared Ernest J.H. Mackay's view that contact was by sea and overland (Mackay 1937-8: 647).

It is now clear that by the early second millennium BC, the Mesopotamians had a significant interest in the Arabian Gulf, which they called the 'Lower Sea'. This was described by Leo Oppenheim in a paper, 'Seafaring Merchants of Ur' (1954) in which he outlined the maritime commerce in the Gulf and explored the locations of Dilmun, Magan and Meluhha. His essay was actually an extended book review of the report on cuneiform documents from Ur by H.H. Figulla and W.J. Martin (1953). These documents record the activities of a group of merchants involved in maritime commerce. They are called '*alak Dilmun*' and '... work hand in hand with enterprising capitalists in Ur to take garments to the island (of Dilmun) in order to buy large quantities of copper there' (Oppenheim 1954: 7). Because Dilmun (Bahrain) is not a source of copper ore and had little fuel for smelting, it was clear that it was a trading post: for Oppenheim a kind of 'window' into the eastern Gulf and beyond to the Arabian Sea.

Maritime trade in the Gulf, and Arabian Sea trade, was a source of state revenue because the palace levied taxes on the imports (Oppenheim 1954: 13). These imports were also important to the temple.

Travels to Telmun are repeatedly mentioned in a group of tablets which come patently from the archives of the temple of the goddess Ningal and list votive offerings, incoming tithe, etc. The contexts suggest that returning sailors were wont to offer the deity in gratitude a share of their goods (Oppenheim 1954: 7).

Ship's crews are known to have dedicated small silver boats in the temple as a sign of their respect for the god Ningal (Oppenheim 1954: 8, fn. 8).

This commercial activity can be classed as goal oriented behaviour, aimed at meeting demand and making a profit. The most prominent materials in the written record are copper, pearls, lapis lazuli, carnelian and exotic animals, not available to the common people in Mesopotamia. However, they were very much a part of the elite way of life there. The temple also needed many of them to build and maintain the cult system. So, the cuneiform record has its usual bias; it tells of the activities of the state and other elite institutions and individuals.

Meluhha was beyond Magan and is most frequently associated with the lands of the Harappan Civilization. Cuneiform documents composed before the time of Hammurabi contain 76 citations to Meluhha (Possehl 1996a).

The 'Meluhha Trade' was high value, state supported commercial activity aimed at satisfying the needs of an elite stratum of this ancient society. This is the stuff of ancient history, made alive by written documents. It provided a stimulus for archaeologists to go into the Gulf and find sites with evidence for this fascinating commerce that linked so many of the diverse cultures of Middle Asia in the third millennium BC. The work was pioneered by scholars such as Ernest J.H. Mackay (Mackay et al. 1929), Peter B. Cornwall (1944, 1946) and the Danish team that excavated on Bahrain Island just after World War II (Glob 1954, 1958a, 1958b; Bibby 1969). What they have discovered supports the cuneiform documents, and adds breadth to them. The current authoritative source on the archaeology of the Gulf region is by Daniel Potts (1990). Work is progressing so fast there that many new and important finds are not reported in that two-volume work.

RECENT ARCHAEOLOGICAL RESEARCH IN THE GULF AND OMAN

In the Gulf, archaeologists have discovered evidence of an early fisher-hunter-gatherer population with a distinctive maritime adaptation of their own at places such as Umm an-Nar and Ras al-Hamra. They exploited marine shells and fish for much of their livelihood. Sites on, or near, the sea coast are common throughout the third millennium, and dot the Island of Bahrain. In Oman there are also communities inland, some of which seem to have been the abodes of people exploiting the copper resources of the mountains, as well as engaging in farming and herding. Mature Harappan pottery is common at sites in Oman, the Emirates and on Bahrain itself. A number of Indus style cubical weights also occur, tying into the commerce noted in the cuneiform texts. The Harappan presence in the Gulf, as documented by ceramics and small finds, makes good Sargon's boast.

Complementing the evidence of the indigenous peoples of the Gulf and eastern Saudi Arabian coast is a site known variously as RJ-2 or Ra's al-Junayz (Fig. 9), located almost precisely on the easternmost point of the Arabian Peninsula. Excavations there, since the early 1980s, have revealed a small settlement at the water's edge. A series of long buildings with small rooms were found filled with trash, including an abundance of Mature Harappan fine Red Ware pottery, some with Indus graffiti scratched into it. A copper stamp seal of Indus type was also found. It is badly corroded, but seems to have the well known 'unicorn' motif. Of particular interest is the presence of about 300 pieces of bitumen. Some of these are hand shaped plano-convex 'loaves' or blocks. These have been interpreted as raw material shaped for storage or transport (Cleuziou and Tosi 1994: 749-50). Other pieces are usually small and three sided.

> The impressed objects are on average much smaller. Their weight ranges from 70 to 800 grams. The two main shapes are slabs and three-sided pieces. Slabs are squarish-shaped pieces with a flat section, 1-4 cm thick, the largest being some 25 cm long. They bear deep impressions on one side only, while the other is smooth. These impressions are either from mats or lashed reed bundles. Although an occasional string or a knot can be found associated with the mat impressions, most ropes are associated with bundles that were very tightly bound together.

Three-sided pieces are usually quite small in size. They originate from lumps of bitumen pushed between corner sections of bends in the bundle setting. They often bear impressions of knots and might be associated with the strengthening of the keel in critical parts. They may associate two faces with reed bundle impressions and one face with mat impressions. In one or two cases, some impressions can be interpreted as the product of coating against a piece of wood. An interesting case is lump 548 where a piece of wood is tied together by a rope to a cane from '*Phragmites* reed' (Cleuziou and Tosi 1994: 750).

About 20 per cent of the well preserved pieces have the impressions of barnacles, or the crustacean itself, on the smooth 'outer' side (Cleuziou and Tosi 1994: 751). It is reasonably clear that these were the caulking materials for locally maintained reed boats of antiquity.

Cleuziou and Tosi have attempted to identify the source of the bitumen. Using trace element analysis they conclude that the best fit for the signature is from bitumen sources in northern Iraq (Fattah, Kiffri), with Luristan as a less likely alternative (1994: 756).

Ra's al-Junayz is not in the Gulf, but on the Arabian Sea, and well down the coast from the point of entry into the Lower Sea of the Mesopotamians. The locality suggests that there was a second leg to the maritime activity of the Gulf, and that it extended down the coast and the Arabian Peninsula. This is part of the maritime activity that seems not to have been recorded by the Mesopotamian scribes. Serge Cleuziou (personal communication: 1990) has also noted that one senses from the Ra's al-Junayz finds the suggestion of a fishing village, not a port. It was a humble site of subsistence-based

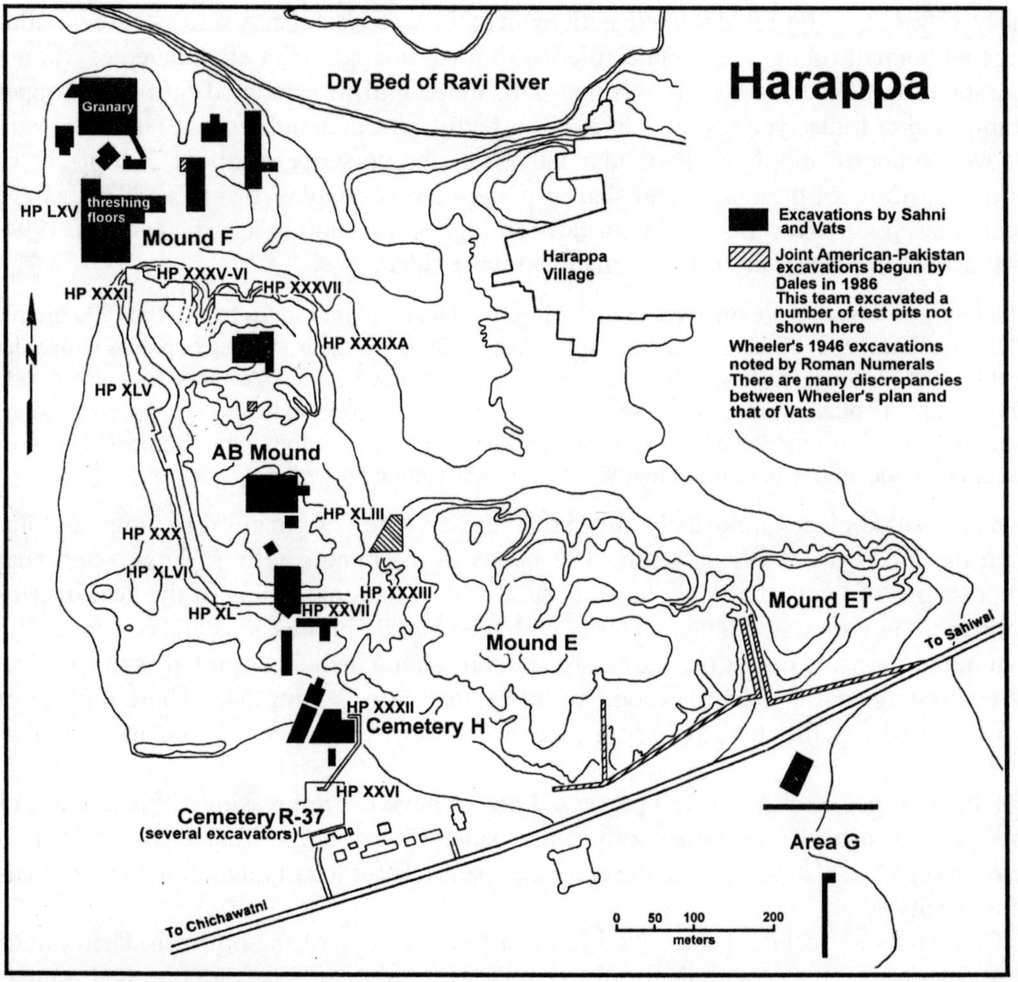

Fig. 9. Plan of Harappa.

fishermen, who seem to have visited there on a seasonal basis, possibly timed to coincide with fish runs.

Recent archaeological work in the Gulf and Oman shows that maritime trade reported in the cuneiform documents was only part of the maritime activity in the region. It was not all high value, profit oriented commerce, involving the state and religious institutions of Mesopotamian cities. There was also local, small-scale, subsistence level maritime activity, that involved trade, but was in a way different from the commerce of the documents (Woodburn and Crawford 1994). It can be thought of as two levels of activity, commercial and subsistence, remembering that the system as it should be reconstructed would have been much more complex, with many activities bridging the two levels.

AN EXPANDED GEOGRAPHY OF MARITIME ACTIVITY

The maritime activity was not restricted to the Gulf and the Asian coast, as far as the Indus river, or to dealings with Dilmun, Magan and Meluhha, the 'lands' mentioned in the cuneiform texts. The eastern and southern Omani sites, especially Ra's al-Junayz, are another leg of the maritime adaptation, not mentioned in the documents. This is important in many ways. From a methodological, critical point of view it is a good example of the limited sociocultural and historical contexts that ancient texts report, which is their profound bias no matter how useful they might be. It follows that archaeology can serve to complement and expand the information in ancient texts, easing and correcting that inherent bias. In terms of the African millets, Ra's al-Junayz and the other eastern and southern Omani sites seem to provide the connection between the subcontinent and the Horn of Africa via coastal trade to the mouth of the Red Sea, and possibly beyond.

It was adventurous sailors and probably sailing families seeking a livelihood who pioneered the route from the Gulf region to Africa. In 1952 Carl O. Sauer suggested that this coastal route '... may be a great lost corridor of mankind' (1952: 36). He was looking at the early dispersal of domesticated plants out of Africa into the economies of Arabia and South Asia. His could be one of those gifted insights that some scholars are able to articulate.

Although these sailing ventures were in African waters they would have come into contact with the foods of the local population. They may have brought food of their own, but the ships were small and drawing on local grain and meat would have made good sense. In this context the African millets were likely to have been taken on board ships and brought back north, to places such as Ra's al-Junayz and eventually to the subcontinent. Whether the millets were already fully domesticated remains to be settled, but the possibility exists that one or more were still morphologically wild, or in an intermediate state of cultivation, between the wild and fully domesticated form.

The African millets provide good, nourishing food. They are drought resistant and amenable to dry cropping. They are hardy and need little tending as they mature. They have large seeds on commodious seed-heads and can be productively and efficiently harvested. They also grow in hot weather, and were well adapted to the summer monsoon of the subcontinent. These appear to be the principal reasons for adoption by the ancient Indian farmer.

The third millennium pattern of maritime activity in the Gulf and Arabian Sea suggests how and by what route the African millets were introduced into the subcontinent. The Dilmun Trade of the cuneiform documents describes coastal trade from Gujarat to the head of the Gulf but recent archaeological discoveries document an additional leg to the maritime life of the times, extending down the Arabian coast at least as far as the mouth of the Red Sea. It was probably along this route that the millets reached the subcontinent

INDUS CIVILIZATION: PARADIGMS OF UNDERSTANDING

There has been tremendous change in our knowledge of, and perspective on, the Indus or Harappan Civilization over the past fifty years. Exploration, excavation and an expanded view of this fascinating ancient culture have revolutionized our thinking about this, the earliest phase of Indian history.

At Independence the interpretation of the civilization was guided by what has come to be called the 'Wheeler-Piggott Paradigm'. It began with the notion that the Harappan Civilization was the same wherever it was found. Everything was orderly and regulated, even a bit dull and more than a trifle lacking in the stimulus of individuality. Wheeler found, in Mohenjo Daro, an absence, even a suppression, of individual personality, and a strong sense of regimentation. He frequently recalled what he saw as the 'astonishing sameness' of the civilization and called this another quality of isolation.

Rather than thinking in terms of 'sameness' and 'isolation' recent research on the Harappan Civilization has defined regional 'polities' and interaction, and has sought to understand the long distance relationship between ancient India, the Horn of Africa, the Arabian Gulf, Central Asia, the Iranian Plateau and Mesopotamia. The regional mosaic of Early and Mature Harappan remains is seen as a proxy for ethnic diversity. The languages spoken by these people are not known, but there is a strong sense that the Early and Mature Harappan represent many kinds of people. There is also a growing sense that the Harappans in Saurashtra, north Gujarat and along the south Gujarat coast were quite different from their Sindhi and Punjabi contemporaries. They can be thought of as parts of a separate province or provinces of the Mature Harappan world. The same is true for the Mature Harappans to the east, beyond Kalibangan. This region also represents a Harappan world different from Sindh and the Punjab.

When Wheeler came to India he was determined to rethink the Harappan Civilization. This began in earnest with his first visit to Harappa in May of 1944. Wheeler approached the huge AB Mound in the early morning of May 1944 and immediately imagined it to have been a fortress to defend the inhabitants of the city from attack. Wheeler proposed that during times of peace the city's priests and god-head lived in this citadel. He used his knowledge of Mesopotamian society to interpret the Indian material because he believed that the Bronze Age of India recalled a social organization not altogether unlike that of the contemporary West.

It would be but natural to find that this similarity of supply and opportunity, combined with a roughly analogous equipment, produced in India a social organization not altogether unlike those of the contemporary West. And this, as we now begin to see more clearly than before, was actually the case. In Sumer, the wealth and discipline of the city-state were vested in the chief deity, i.e. in the priesthood or a priest-king. The civic focus was the exalted temple, centre of an elaborate and carefully ordered secular administration under divine sanction. About it were granaries and workshops, bakeries and breweries, manned by servile and semi-servile workers whose wage-lists or ration-lists are preserved to us.... Similarly, a cloth-factory employing ninety-eight women and sixty-three children was situated within the enclosure of the temple of the Moon God Nannar at Ur, and came within the administration of the city and the temple. Such cities were massively fortified, and the enwalled temple-tower arose as a sort of acropolis or citadel in their midst, symbol and stronghold of undivided religious and secular authority. In essence, the picture is one of a rigid and highly-evolved bureaucratic machine, capable of organizing and distributing surplus wealth and of defending it, but little conducive to the political liberty of the individual.

To this picture Harappa, amplified by Mohenjo Daro, begins to assume a significantly similar outline. The relatively small detached mound AB, highest on the site, stands aloof and heavily fortified, its defences carefully maintained. If its buildings, now pitifully wrecked, possessed anything of the distinction of those on the closely equivalent mound at Mohenjo Daro, it was marked by more than its defences. In its shadow, on the low ground between it and the former course of the river, lay blocks of barracks or cooly-quarters, serried lines of circular working-platforms, furnaces, and a notable series of store-houses, protected doubtless by a river-embankment or bund of which possible traces still exist.... The store-houses, with raised and ventilated floors, represent a type of granary familiar in many remote places and periods. They here stand in orderly array on a carefully-built podium with a battered retaining-wall of burnt brick, similar to that which revets the defences of the citadel....

It can no longer be doubted that, whatever the source of their authority—and a dominant religious element may fairly be assumed—the lords of Harappa administered their city in a fashion not remote from that of the priest-kings or governors of Sumer and Akkad. In other words, the social structure of Harappa conformed in principle with that of the three great riverine civilizations of the day. (Wheeler 1947: 73-4)

Stuart Piggott's position on Mature Harappan society is much the same, but he was a little more cautious in his treatment of Sumerian matters. In his book *Prehistoric India* (Piggott 1950) we find in the Harappan Civilization a state ruled by priest-kings, autocratically ruling the Harappan peoples from twin capitals of their vast empire. The whole was linked by the Indus and other rivers of the Punjab.

The idea that there were 'priest-kings' in the Indus cities has largely been abandoned as has the notion of citadels, although these concepts linger on in secondary literature. Archaeologists are now thinking in terms of a more decentralized political system, with loose alliances between the major urban environments and regions. But, there is no denying the presence of an artefactual style that covers about 10,00,000 sq km. It is now thought that the internal economics and trade of the Harappan Civilization was useful in promoting adherence to this style and that the style itself was deeply connected to the self-identification of the Harappan peoples. They used the style of their civilization, which we call the Mature Harappan, because it identified them as a certain kind of people.

Some progress has been made at defining the Early Harappan, the period that precedes the Mature Harappan. There are four Early Harappan assemblages: the Amri-Nal in southern Sindh and Baluchistan, the Kot Dijian in northern Sindh and the west Punjab; the Damb Sadaat in northern Baluchistan and the Sothi-Siswal in the Punjab, Haryana and northern Rajasthan. It is reasonably clear that the Mature Harappan is a 'fusion' of these peoples into a single civilization. How this fusion came about remains one of the topics of research. When it came about is somewhat better understood.

It is becoming increasingly clear that there was a Transitional Period between the Early and Mature Harappan (Shaffer and Lichtenstein 1989; Possehl 1990; Gupta 1996: 29, 77-8). Based on radiocarbon determinations this transition can be dated to *c.* 2600-2500 BC. It is within this one hundred years that we are beginning to see the beginnings of Harappan urbanization, the development of the system of writing, weights and measures, the evolution of the Mature Harappan style and, most important, the development of a social system with marked internal differentiation and structural specialization.

There is a current debate on whether or not the Indus Civilization was a state, or some other form of complex society. The principal players in this unresolved debate are S.C. Malik (1968), Jim Shaffer (1982), Walter A. Fairservis, Jr. (1986) and myself (1997b) vying for some alternative to the state. Those arguing for a more conventional state form of organization are: Jerome Jacobson (1986), Shereen Ratnagar (1991) and Mark Kenoyer (1994).

Sir John Marshall's essay on Indus religion is still a very good document (Marshall 1931b). But, some scholars have questioned his proposition that the famous horned seal is in fact a 'Proto-Siva' (e.g. Srinivasan 1984). Asko Parpola's efforts to decipher the Indus script has also led him to make a major statement of the Indus system of beliefs, which is best summarized in Parpola (1994).

Much remains to be learned about the Mature Harappan political system. It seems apparent from the archaeological remains that this was not a society where leadership led to personal aggrandizement as with the kings of Mesopotamia or the pharaohs of Egypt. There are still no Indus temples known to us, nor are there palaces. This has led me to think that the political system was segmented and lacked centralization (Possehl 1998b). In a major statement on the Mature Harappan political system Shereen Ratnagar has suggested that the Mature Harappan political system was based on kinship relations (lineages) with the 'state' organizing production; a dual system (1991).

This remains a topic suited for continued research. There appears to be better agreement on some aspects of the way in which the 10,00,000 sq. km of the Mature Harappan landscape might have been segmented. I have called these 'domains' to escape the notion of 'provinces' (Possehl 1992; Fig. 10). In an interesting coincidence the map prepared by Jagat Pati Joshi, for his political units (Joshi 1984) is largely coincident with my own.

There has been little progress in our understanding of the fabric of Mature Harappan society. Some potential insights have come from the study of the political system (Fairservis 1986; Ratnagar 1991; Possehl 1998b, see also Kenoyer 1992), but there is room for much more research on this important topic.

The 'eclipse' of the ancient cities of the Indus is still not thoroughly understood. There is no satisfactory explanation of the abandonment of Mohenjo Daro and many other settlements in Sindh and for the near abandonment of Harappa. An up-to-date review of the evidence is available (Possehl 1997). Wheeler's hypothesis that Aryan invaders brought the Indus Civilization to its knees is no longer thought to be tenable (1947: 78-85). First, Mohenjo Daro was abandoned by 1900 BC and there is no evidence for Aryans in the subcontinent at that time. Second, the locale for the Rigveda is the Punjab. There is no evidence for a battle, or battles at Mature Harappan sites in this region. The skeletons found in the late levels of Mohenjo Daro have no signs of trauma (Kennedy 1984), and Sindh is a distant echo in the *Rigveda*, so there is a bad historical mismatch there (Dales 1964).

The Raikes/Dales hypothesis that a dam flooded out Mohenjo Daro does not seem to hold much water (Raikes 1964, 1965; Dales 1966). This was thoroughly critiqued by H.T. Lambrick (1967). R.J. Wasson determined that the unconsolidated sediments of the Indus Valley would not have had sufficient structural integrity to hold back the river (Wasson 1984).

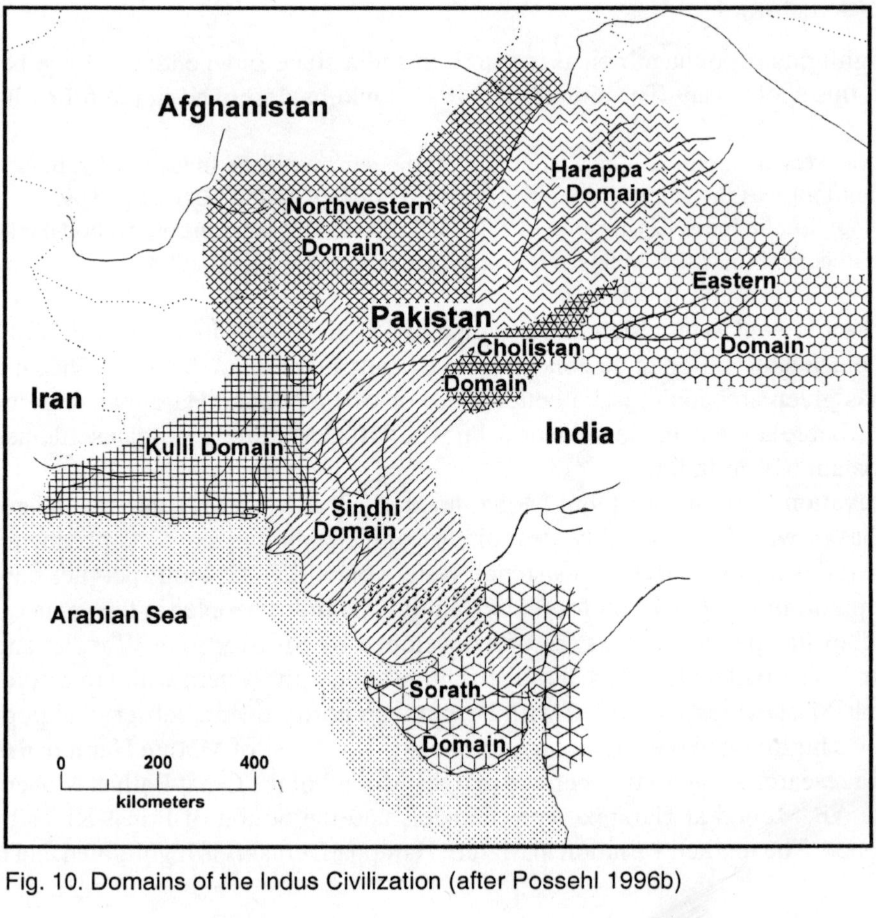

Fig. 10. Domains of the Indus Civilization (after Possehl 1996b)

There are some new data to be considered. First, it appears that the Sarasvati began to dry up at the opening of the second millennium, but that seems to have taken a lot of time. Second, there is regional continuity in Gujarat, Indian Punjab, Haryana and western Uttar Pradesh. The events in Sindh, especially at Mohenjo Daro, have no parallel in these regions. This calls into question the notion of an 'eclipse' at least in all of the 'domains' of the Indus Civilization. These points, and others, are made in Possehl (1997); but in the end an explanation of the changes to the Indus Civilization at the beginning of the second millennium eludes archaeologists.

It is not known what the Mature Harappan peoples called themselves, but the Sumerian word 'Meluhha' may have been their name for this civilization. The Indus writing system has been studied by a number of scholars, many of whom have claimed to read the script. To date, none of these decipherments can be shown to be valid and more work is needed on this important topic (Possehl 1996b), although there are new, valuable research tools (Mahadevan 1977; Joshi and Parpola 1987; Shah and Parpola 1991). The formulation of a programme of research, rather than the work of the individual 'genius decipherer,' is one of the current challenges to those who study the Indus Civilization.

CLOSING REMARKS

The highlights of archaeological research in India since Independence have been covered in this short essay. The situation in 1947 could be described in the following way:

> There was very poor chronological control over the remains of the Indus Civilization. The most important tool was the study of Mature Harappan artefacts in the Near East. This led to a long chronology for the Indus Civilization of *c*. 2500-1500 BC. The radiocarbon method has shortened and led to greater precision in this chronology which is now *c*. 2500-1900 BC.

Archaeological exploration in both India and Pakistan was incomplete in 1947. There is still much exploration to be done, but significant attention to this field since Independence has given archaeologists a better sense of where Mature Harappan sites are found and in what relative densities. We now know of 1022 Mature Harappan settlements: 406 in Pakistan; 616 in India.

Excavation, first at Kili Ghul Mohammad, then at Mehrgarh in post-Independence times has provided a reasonably clear picture of the beginnings of food production in the greater Indus region and the subsistence system on which the Indus peoples depended.

The predominant paradigm for understanding the Indus peoples in the years surrounding Indian Independence, was the one developed by Sir Mortimer Wheeler and Stuart Piggott. This invoked Citadels, a redistributive economic system with large civic granaries and Priest-Kings who ruled with despotic authority over a subservient population. They also highlighted the endless monotony and sameness of Mature Harappan remains. Modern researchers no longer believe that the Mound of the Great Bath at Mohenjo Daro and the AB Mound at Harappa were Citadels and the notion of Priest-Kings has been abandoned. The marked variation in Mature Harappan remains is highlighted and research that recognizes the diversity of Mature Harappan is on the ascendancy.

Major excavations during the post-Independence years in India at Lothal, Kalibangan and Dholavira, and scores of other sites, have documented the Harappan Civilization there and assisted in the abandonment of the older paradigms regarding the Indus peoples.

In 1947 the presence of Mature Harappan seals, beads and ceramics in Mesopotamia told of long-distance contact between ancient India and this region. The mechanism of this contact was not well understood. Today, primarily thanks to many excavations in the Arabian Gulf, we know of a definite Mature Harappan presence there and that seafaring peoples of Meluhha, the Akkadian name for the Harappan Civilization, were one of the means of contact. We also believe that Harappan seafarers sailed down the eastern coast of Saudi Arabia to the mouth of the Red Sea and brought African millets home with them where they were integrated into the Mature Harappan subsistence system as summer crops.

The Indus writing system was undeciphered in 1947 and it remains undeciphered today (Possehl 1996b). There has been little progress on this topic which cries out for rigorous research and teamwork.

In the end, a great deal has been learned about the Indus Civilization in the past 50 years. In spite of the fact that not everyone is happy with the names 'Indus Civilization' or 'Harappan Civilization' (Gupta 1996) progress on other fundamentals like chronology, settlement patterns and results from excavation are clearly apparent.

Indian archaeology in the United States is also healthy. In 1947 there were no prehistoric archaeologists with positions in American universities or museums dedicated to this study. By 1973 there were two, with two others in positions that were more general anthropological appointments. Today there are six appointments dedicated to the study of South Asian Archaeology in university departments in the United States with three additional appointments of professors with full qualifications in this topic, but who teach a more general archaeological curriculum.

Indian Independence has seen significant progress in understanding the prehistoric past in India. Most of this progress is attributable to the archaeological establishments in India: the Archaeological Survey, state departments of archaeology and their colleagues in Indian universities. The founding and growth of archaeology in Indian universities unfolded in the post-colonial era, but as yet there has been little written on this topic. It is hoped that the next fifty years will bring as much progress to understanding and international cooperation as that which has taken place since Indian Independence.

REFERENCES

Alcock, L. 1986. A Pottery Sequence from Mohenjo Daro: R.E.M. Wheeler's 1950 Citadel Mound Excavations, in *Excavations at Mohenjo Daro, Pakistan: the Pottery* (G.F. Dales and J.M. Kenoyer Eds.), pp. 493-551. Philadelphia: The University Museum.

Allchin, B. and F.R. Allchin 1993. Lewan: an Early Harappan Manufacturing Site in the Bannu

Basin, in *Harappan Civilization: a Recent Perspective* (G.L. Possehl Ed.), pp. 521-53. Delhi: Oxford-IBH and the American Institute of Indian Studies.

Ardeleanu-Jansen, A. 1984. Stone Sculptures from Mohenjo Daro, in *Reports on Field Work Carried out at* Mohenjo Daro, *Pakistan 1982-83 by the IsMEO-Aachen University Mission* (M. Jansen and G. Urban Eds.), pp. 139-57. Aachen-Rome: RWTH-IsMEO.

——— 1992. New Evidence on the Distribution of Artefacts: an Approach Towards a Qualitative-Quantitative Assessment of the Terracotta Figurines of Mohenjo Daro, in *South Asian Archaeology 1989* (C. Jarrige Ed.), pp. 5-14. Madison: Prehistory Press. Monographs in World Prehistory 14.

——— 1993. Who Fell in the Well? Digging up a Well in Mohenjo Daro, in *South Asian Archaeology 1991* (A.J. Gail and G.J.R. Mevissen Eds.), pp. 1-15. Stuttgart: Franz Steiner Verlag:

——— 1993. *Die Terrakotten in Mohenjo-daro: Eine Unterschung zur Keramischen Kleinplastik in Mohanjo-daro, Pakistan (c. 2300-1900 v. Chr.).* Aachen: Reinisch Westfalische Technische Hochschule.

Asthana, S. 1976. *History and Archaeology of India's Contacts with Other Countries, from Earliest Times to 300 B.C.* Delhi: B.R. Publishing Corporation.

——— 1982. Harappan Trade in Metals and Minerals: a Regional Approach, in *Harappan Civilization: a Contemporary Perspective* (G.L. Posseh Ed.), pp. 271-88. Delhi: Oxford-IBH and the American Institute of Indian Studies.

——— 1985. *Pre-Harappan Cultures of India and the Borderlands*. Delhi: Books & Books.

Bibby, T.G. 1969. *Looking for Dilmun*. New York: Alfred Knopf.

Bisht, R.S. 1982. Excavations at Banawali: 1974-77, in *Harappan Civilization: a Contemporary Perspective* (G.L. Possehl Ed.), pp. 113-24. Delhi: Oxford-IBH and the American Institute of Indian Studies:

——— 1989a. A New Model of the Harappan Town Planning as Revealed at Dholavira in Kutch: a Surface Study of Its Plan and Architecture, in *History and Archaeology: Professor H.D. Sankalia Felicitation Volume* (B. Chatterjee Ed.), pp. 397-408. Delhi: Ramanand Vidya Bhawan.

——— 1989b. The Harappan Colonization of Kutch: an Ergonomic Study with Reference to Dholavira and Surkotada, in *History and Art* (Krishna Deva and Lallanji Gopal Eds.), pp. 265- 72. Delhi: Ramanand Vidya Bhavan.

——— 1991. Dholavira: a New Horizon of the Indus Civilization, *Puratattva* 20: 71-82.

——— 1994. Secrets of the Water Fort, *Down to Earth* May: 25-31.

Blackman, J.M. and M. Vidale 1992. The Production and Distribution of Stoneware Bangles at Mohenjo Daro and Harappa as Monitored by Chemical Characterization Studies, in *South Asian Archaeology 1989* (C. Jarrige Ed.), pp. 37-44. Madison: Prehistory Press. Monographs in World Archaeology 14.

de Cardi, B. 1983. *Archaeological Surveys in Baluchistan, 1948 and 1957*. London: Institute of Archaeology. Occasional Publication 8.

Casal, J.-M. 1964. *Fouilles d'Amri*. Paris: Publications de la Commission des Fouilles Archaeologiques, Fouilles du Pakistan.

Chakrabarti, D.K. 1988. *A History of Indian Archaeology: from the Beginning to 1947*. Delhi: Munshiram Manoharlal.

Cleuziou, S. and M. Tosi 1994. Black Boats of Magan: Some Thoughts on Bronze Age Water Transport in Oman and Beyond from the Impressed Bitumen Slabs of Ra's al-Junayz, in *South Asian Archaeology 1993* (A. Parpola and P. Koskikallio Eds.), pp. 745-61. Helsinki: Annales Academiae Scientiarum Fennicae, Series B 271.

Cornwall, P.B. 1944. History of Bahrein Island Before Cyrus. Ph.D. Dissertation. Department of History: Harvard University.

——— 1946. On the Location of Dilmun, *Bulletin of the American Schools of Oriental Research* 103: 3-11.

Costantini, L. 1984. The Beginnings of Agriculture in the Kachi Plain: the Evidence from Mehrgarh, in *South Asian Archaeology 1981* (B. Allchin Ed.), pp. 29-33. Cambridge: Cambridge University Press.

Dales, G.F. 1964. The Mythical Massacre at Mohenjo-daro, *Expedition* 6(3): 36-43.

——— 1966. The Decline of the Harappans, *Scientific American* 214(5): 93-100.

——— 1974. Excavations at Balakot, Pakistan 1973, *Journal of Field Archaeology* 1: 3-22.

——— 1979. The Balakot Project: Summary of Four Years of Excavations in Pakistan, *Man and Environment* III: 45-53.

Dales, G.F., J.M. Kenoyer and Staff 1991. Summaries of Five Seasons of Research at Harappa (District Sahiwal, Punjab, Pakistan) 1986-1990, in *Harappa Excavations 1986-1990: a Multidisciplinary Approach to Third Millennium Urbanism* (R.H. Meadow Ed.), pp. 185-262. Madison: Prehistory Press. Monographs in World Archaeology 3.

Dani, A.H. 1970-1. Excavations in the Gomal Valley, *Ancient Pakistan* 5: 1-177.

Dhavalikar, M.K. and G.L. Possehl 1992. The Pre-Harappan Period at Prabhas Patan and the Pre-Harappan Phase in Gujarat, *Man and Environment* XVII (1): 71-8.

Dhavalikar, M.K., M.H. Raval and Y.M. Chitalwala 1996. *Kuntasi: a Harappan Emporium on West Coast*. Pune: Deccan College.

Dikshit, M.G. 1950. Excavations at Rangpur: 1947, *Bulletin of the Deccan College Research Institute* 11(1): 3-55.

Durrani, F.A. 1988. Excavations in the Gomal Valley: Rehman Dheri Excavation Report, No. 1, *Ancient Pakistan* 6: 1-204.

Fairservis, W.A. 1956. *Excavations in the Quetta Valley, West Pakistan*. New York: Anthropological Papers of the American Museum of Natural History 45(2).

——— 1986. Cattle and the Harappan Chiefdoms of the Indus Valley, *Expedition* 28(2): 43-50.

Figulla, H.A. and W.J. Martin 1953. *Ur Excavation Texts V: Letters and Documents of the Old-Babylonian Period*. London-Philadelphia: The British Museum and The University Museum.

Flam, L. 1993. Excavations at Ghazi Shah, Sindh, Pakistan, in *Harappan Civilization: a Recent Perspective* (G.L. Possehl Ed.), pp. 457-67. Delhi: Oxford-IBH and the American Institute of Indian Studies.

Franke, U. 1984. A Selection of Inscribed Objects Recovered from Mohenjo-daro, in *Reports on Field Work Carried out at Mohenjo-daro, Pakistan 1982-83 by the IsMEO-Aachen University Mission: Interim Reports* Vol. 1 (M. Jansen and G. Urban Eds.), pp. 117-38. Aachen-Rome: RWTH/IsMEO.

Franke-Vogt, U. 1991a. Die Glyptik Aus Mohenjo-Daro: Uniformitat und Variabilitat, in *Der Induskultur, Untersuchungen zur Typologie, Ikonographie und raumlichen Verteilung* 2 Vols. Mainz: Verlag Philipp von Zabern.

——— 1991b. The Glyptic Art of the Harappa Culture, in *Forgotten Cities on the Indus: Early Civilization in Pakistan from the 8th to the 2nd Millennium B.C.* (M. Jansen, M. Mulloy and G. Urban Eds.), pp. 179-87. Mainz: Verlag Philipp von Zabern.

Ghosh, A. 1952. The Rajputana Desert: Its Archaeological Aspect, *Bulletin of the National Institute of Sciences in India* 1: 37-42.

——— 1953a. Fifty Years of the Archaeological Survey of India, *Ancient India* 9: 29-52.

——— 1953b. Exploration in Bikanir, *East and West* 4(1): 31-4.

——— 1961. A Hundred Years of Indian Archaeology, *Cultural Forum* 4(2): 4-13.

——— 1989. Ahichchhatra, in *An Encyclopaedia of Indian Archaeology* (A. Ghosh Ed.), pp. 7-9. Delhi: Munshiram Manoharlal.

Glob, P.V. 1954. Temples at Babar, *Kuml* 4: 149-53.

——— 1958a. The Prosperity of Bahrain Five Thousand Years Ago: Solving the Riddle of the 100,000 Burial Mounds of the Island, *Illustrated London News* January 4: 14-16.

——— 1958b. Excavating a Bahrain Citadel of 5000 Years Ago and Seal Links with Ur and Mohenjo- daro, *Illustrated London News* January 11: 54-5.

Gupta, S.P. 1972. The Dichotomy of Harappan and Pre-Harappan Cultures, in *A Study of Harappan Pottery* (O. Manchanda Ed.), pp. 394-405. Delhi: Oriental Publishers.

——— 1974. Two Urbanizations in India: a Side Study in Their Social Structure, *Puratattva* 7: 53-60.

——— 1982. The Late Harappan: a Study in Cultural Dynamics, in *Harappan Civilization: a Contemporary Perspective* (G.L. Possehl Ed.), pp. 51-9. Delhi: Oxford -IBH and the American Institute of Indian Studies.

——— 1996. *The Indus-Saraswati Civilization: Origins, Problems, Issues*. Delhi: Pratibha Prakashan.

Halim, M.A. 1972a. Excavation at Sarai Khola (Part I), *Pakistan Archaeology* 7: 23-89.

——— 1972b. Excavations at Sarai Khola (Part II), *Pakistan Archaeology* 8: 1-112.

Halim, M.A. and M. Vidale 1984. Kilns, Bangles and Coated Vessels, in *Reports on Field Work Carried Out at Mohenjo-daro, Pakistan 1982-83 by the IsMEO-Aachen University Mission* (M. Jansen and G. Urban Eds.), pp. 63-97. Aachen-Rome: RWTH/IsMEO.

Hegde, K.T.M., K.K. Bhan, V.S. Sonawane, K. Krishnan and D.R. Shah 1992. *Excavation at Nageshwar, Gujarat: a Harappan Shell Working Site on the Gulf of Kutch*. Baroda: M.S. University of Baroda.

Hunter, G.R. 1929. The Script of Harappa and Mohenjo-Daro and Its Connection with Other Scripts. Ph.D. Dissertation. Oxford: Oxford University.

——— 1932. Mohenjo daro: Indus Epigraphy, *Journal of the Royal Asiatic Society of Great Britain and Ireland*: 466-503.

——— 1934. *The Script of Harappa and Mohenjo-Daro and Its Connection with Other Scripts*. London: Kegan Paul, Trench, Trubner & Co. Ltd.

IAR. Indian Archaeology—A Review. New Delhi: Annual Bulletin of the Archaeological Survey of India.

Jacobson, J. 1986. The Harappan Civilization: an Early State, in *Studies in the Archaeology of India and Pakistan* (J. Jacobson Ed.), pp. 137-73. Delhi: Oxford-IBH and the American Institute of Indian Studies.

Jansen, M. 1993. *Mohenjo-daro: Stadt der Brunnen und ynale (City of Wells and Drains), Wasserlexus vor 4500 jharan (Water Splendor 4500 Years Ago).* Dual German-English Text. Bergisch Gladbach, Frontinus-Gesellschaft e. V.

——— 1986. *Die Indus Zivilization: Wiederentdeckung Einer Fruhen Hochkultur*. Koln: DuMont Buchverlag.

Jansen, M. and G. Urban (Eds.) 1984. *Reports on Field Work Carried Out at Mohenjo-Daro,*

Pakistan 1982-83 by the IsMEO-Aachen University Mission. Interim Reports, Vol. 1. Aachen-Roma: RWTH-IsMEO.

——— 1985. *Mohenjo Daro: Report of the Aachen University Mission 1979-1985. Section One: Data Collection. Vol. I : Catalogue and Concordance of the Field Registers, 1924-38. Part One: the HR-Area Field Register, 1925-27*. Leiden: E. J. Brill.

——— 1987. *Reports on Field Work Carried Out at Mohenjo-Daro, Pakistan 1983-84 by the IsMEO-Aachen University Mission. Interim Reports*, Vol. 2. Aachen-Roma: RWTH-IsMEO.

Jansen, M. and M. Tosi, Eds. 1988. *Reports on Field Work Carried Out at Mohenjo-Daro, Pakistan 1983- 86 by the IsMEO-Aachen University Mission. Interim Reports*, Vol. 3. Aachen-Roma: RWTH-IsMEO.

Jarrige, C. 1994. The Mature Indus Phase at Naushạro as Seen from a Block of Period III, in *South Asian Archaeology 1993* (A. Parpola and P. Koskikallio Eds.), pp. 281-94. Helsinki: Annales Academiae Scientiarum Fennicae, Series B, Vol. 271.

Jarrige, C., J.-F. Jarrige, R.H. Meadow and G. Quivron 1995. *Mehrgarh: Field reports 1974-1985, from Neolithic times to the Indus Civilization*. Karachi: Department of Culture and Tourism of Sindh, Pakistan, Department of Archaeology and Museums, French Ministry of Foreign Affairs.

Jarrige, J.-F. 1984. Chronology of the Earlier Periods of the Greater Indus as Seen from Mehrgarh, Pakistan, in *South Asian Archaeology 1981* (B. Allchin Ed.), pp. 21-9. Cambridge: Cambridge University Press.

——— 1989. Excavation at Naushаro 1987-88, *Pakistan Archaeology* 24: 21-68.

Jarrige, J.-F. and M. Santoni 1979. *Fouilles de Pirak*. 2 Vols. Paris: Publications de la Commission des Fouilles Archaeologique, Fouilles du Pakistan, No. 2, Vol. 1.

Joshi, J.P. 1984. Harappa Culture: Emergence of a New Picture, *Puratattva* 13-14: 51-4.

Joshi, J.P., Madhu Bala and J. Ram 1984. The Indus Civilization: a Reconsideration on the Basis of Distribution Maps, in *Frontiers of the Indus Civilization* (B.B. Lal and S.P. Gupta Eds.), pp. 511-30 . Delhi: Books & Books.

Joshi, J.P. and A. Parpola 1987. *Corpus of Indus Seals and Inscriptions* (Vol. 1, Collections in India. Suomalainen Tiedeakatemia, Suomalaisen Tiedeakatemian Toimituksia). Helsinki: Annales Academiae Scientiarum Fennicae, Sarja, Series B, NIDE, Tome 239.

Kennedy, K.A.R. 1984. Trauma and Disease in the Ancient Harappans, in *Frontiers of the Indus Civilization* (B.B. Lal and S.P. Gupta Eds.), pp. 425-36. Delhi: Books & Books:.

Kennedy, K.A.R., J. Chimet, T. Disotell and D. Meyers 1984. Principal-Components Analysis of Prehistoric South Asian Crania, *American Journal of Physical Anthropology* 64 (2): 105-18.

Kenoyer, J.M. 1991. Urban Processes in the Indus Tradition: a Preliminary Model from Harappa, in *Harappa Excavations 1986-1990: a Multidisciplinary Approach to Third Millennium Urbanization* (R.H. Meadow Ed.), pp. 29-60. Madison: Prehistory Press. Monographs in World Archaeology 3.

——— 1992. Harappan Craft Specialization and the Question of Urban Segregation and Stratification, *The Eastern Anthropologist* 45(1-2): 39-54.

——— 1993. Excavation on Mound E, Harappa: a Systematic Approach to the Study of Indus Urbanization, in *South Asian Archaeology 1991* (A.J. Gail and G.J.R. Mevissen Eds.), pp. 165-94. Stuttgart: Franz Steiner Verlag.

——— 1994. The Harappan State, was It or wasn't It? in *From Sumer to Meluhha: Contributions to the Archaeology of South and West Asia in Memory of George F. Dales* (J.M. Kenoyer Ed.), pp. 71-80. Madison: Wisconsin Archaeological Reports 3.

Khan, F.A. 1965. Excavations at Kot Diji, *Pakistan Archaeology* 2: 11-85.

Khan, F., J.R. Knox and K.D. Thomas 1991. *Explorations and Excavations in Bannu District, North-West Frontier Province, Pakistan, 1985-88*. London: British Museum. Department of Oriental Antiquities, Occasional Paper 50.

Khatri, J.S. and M. Acharya 1995. Kunal: a New Indus-Saraswati Site, *Puratattva* 25: 84-6.

Kramer, S.N. 1964. The Indus Civilization and Dilmun, the Sumerian Paradise Land, *Expedition* 6(3): 44-52.

Lal, B.B. 1951. Further Copper Hoards from the Gangetic Basin and a Review of the Problem, *Ancient India* 7: 20-39.

——— 1954-5. Excavations at Hastinapura and Other Explorations in the Upper Ganga and Sutlej Basins 1950-52, *Ancient India* 10-11: 5-151.

——— 1970-1. Perhaps the Earliest Ploughed Field so far Excavated Anywhere in the World, *Puratattva* 4: 1-3.

——— 1979. Kalibangan and Indus Civilization. *Essays in Indian Protohistory* (D.P. Agrawal and D. K. Chakrabarti Eds.), pp. 65-97. Delhi: B.R. Publishing Corporation.

——— 1981. Some Reflections on the Structural Remains at Kalibangan, in *Indus Civilization: New Perspectives* (A.H. Dani Ed.), pp. 47-54. Islamabad: Quaid-i-Azam University.

Lal, B.B. and B.K. Thapar 1967. Excavations at Kalibangan: New Light on Indian Civilization, *Cultural Forum* 9(4): 78-88.

Lambrick, H.T. 1967. The Indus Flood-Plain and the Indus Civilization, *The Geographical Journal* 133: 483-94.

Lechevallier, M. and G. Quivron 1981. The Neolithic in Baluchistan: New Evidences from Mehrgarh. *South Asian Archaeology 1979* (H. Hartel Ed.), pp. 71-92. Berlin: Dietrich Reimer Verlag.

Leshnik, L.S. 1968. The Harappan 'Port' at Lothal: Another View, *American Anthropologist* 70(5): 911- 22.

Libby, W. 1948. *Radiocarbon Dating*. Chicago: University of Chicago Press.

Mackay, E.J.H. 1937-8. *Further Excavations at Mohenjo-daro*, 2 Vols. Delhi: Government of India.

——— 1943. *Chanhu-daro Excavations 1935-36*. New Haven: American Oriental Society, American Oriental Series 20.

Mackay, E.J.H., G. L. Harding, et al. 1929. *Bahrain and Hemamieh*. London: Publications of the British School of Archaeology in Egypt 47.

Mahadevan, I. 1977. *The Indus Script: Texts, Concordance and Tables*. New Delhi: Archaeological Survey of India.

Majumdar, N.G. 1934. *Explorations in Sind*. Delhi: Memoirs of the Archaeological Survey of India 48.

Malik, S.C. 1968. *Indian Civilization: the Formative Period*. Simla: Indian Institute of Advanced Study.

Marshall, Sir J. 1924. First Light on a Long Forgotten Civilization, *Illustrated London News* (20 September): 528-32, 548.

——— 1925-6. Exploration, Western Circle, Mohenjo-daro, *Annual Report of the Archaeological Survey of India, 1925-26*: 72-98.

——— 1926-7. The Indus Culture, *Annual Report of the Archaeological Survey of India, 1926-27*: 51-60.

——— 1931a. *Mohenjo-Daro and the Indus Civilization*. 3 Vols. London: Arthur Probsthain.

——— 1931b. Religion. *Mohenjo-daro and the Indus Civilization*, 3 Vols. London: A. Probsthain: 48-78.

McCown, D.E. 1947. Appendix B, Distribution of Harappa Pottery (in R.E.M. Wheeler, Harappa 1946: the Defenses and Cemetery R-37), *Ancient India* 3: 129-30.

Meadow, R.H. 1984. Notes on the Faunal Remains from Mehrgarh with a Focus on Cattle (*Bos*), in *South Asian Archaeology 1981* (B. Allchin Ed.), pp. 34-40. Cambridge: Cambridge University Press.

——— 1991. *Harappa Excavations 1986-1990: a Multidisciplinary Approach to Third Millennium Urbanism*. Madison: Prehistory Press.Monographs in World Archaeology 3.

——— 1993. Animal Domestication in the Middle East: a Revised View from the Eastern Margin, in *Harappan Civilization: a Recent Perspective* (G.L. Possehl Ed.), pp. 295-320. New Delhi, Oxford-IBH and the American Institute of Indian Studies.

Mughal, M.R. 1972. Excavation at Jalilpur, *Pakistan Archaeology* 8: 117-24.

——— 1997. *Ancient Cholistan: Archaeology and Architecture*. Lahore: Ferozsons.

Nanavati, J.M., R.N. Mehta, S.N. Chowdhary 1971. *Somnath—1956*. Baroda-Poona: Maharaja Sayajirao University Monograph No. 1, M.S. University and Deccan College.

Oppenheim, A. L. 1954. Seafaring Merchants of Ur, *Journal of the American Oriental Society* 74: 6-17.

Parpola, A. 1994. *Deciphering the Indus Script*. Cambridge: Cambridge University Press.

Piggott, S. 1950. *Prehistoric India to 1000 B.C.* Baltimore: Penguin Books.

Possehl, G.L. 1976. Lothal: a Gateway Settlement of the Harappan Civilization, in *Ecological Backgrounds of South Asian Prehistory* (K.A.R. Kennedy and G.L. Possehl Eds.), pp. 118-31. Ithaca: Cornell University South Asia Program. Occasional Papers and Theses 4.

——— 1986. African Millets in South Asian Prehistory, in *Studies in the Archaeology of India and Pakistan*. J. Jacobson. Delhi: Oxford-IBH and the American Institute of Indian Studies: 237-56.

——— 1989. *Radiocarbon Dates for South Asian Archaeology*. Philadelphia: University of Pennsylvania Museum.

——— 1990. Revolution in the Urban Revolution: the Emergence of Indus Urbanization, *Annual Review of Anthropology* 19: 261-82.

——— 1992. The Harappan Cultural Mosaic: Ecology Revisited, in *South Asian Archaeology 1989* (C. Jarrige Ed.), pp. 237-44. Madison: Prehistory Press. Monographs World Archaeology 14.

——— 1993. Sir Leonard Woolley Evaluates Indian Archaeology, *Harappan Studies* 1: 1-56.

——— 1996a. Meluhha, in *The Indian Ocean in Antiquity* (J.E. Reade Ed.), pp. 133-208. London: Kegan Paul International in Association with the British Museum.

——— 1996b. *Indus Age: the Writing System*. Philadelphia: University of Pennsylvania Press.

——— 1997. The Transformation of the Indus Civilization, *Journal of World Prehistory* 11(4): 1-11.

——— 1998a. The Introduction of African Millets to the Indian Subcontinent, in *Prehistoric Plant Exchanges* (H.D.V. Pendergast, N.L. Etkin, D. Harris and P.J. Houghton

Eds.), pp. 107-21. London: Kew Royal Botanic Gardens.

——— 1998b. Sociocultural Complexity without the State: the Indus Civilization, in *The Archaic State* (Feinmann M. Gary and J. Marcus Eds.), pp. 261-91. Santa Fe: School of American Research.

Possehl, G.L. and M.H. Raval 1989. *Harappan Civilization and Rojdi*. New Delhi: Oxford-IBH and the American Institute of Indian Studies.

Possehl, G.L. and P.C. Rissman 1992. The Chronology of Prehistoric India: from Earliest Times to the Iron Age, in *Chronologies in Old World Archaeology* 2 Vols. (R.W. Ehrich Ed.), pp. 465-90 and 447-74 . Chicago: University of Chicago Press.

Raikes, R.L. 1965. The Mohenjo Daro Floods, *Antiquity* 39: 196-203.

——— 1964. The end of the Ancient Cities of the Indus, *American Anthropologist* 66(2): 284-99.

Rao, S.R. 1963a. Excavations at Rangpur and Other Explorations in Gujarat, *Ancient India* 18-19: 5-207.

——— 1963b. A 'Persian Gulf' Seal from Lothal, *Antiquity* 37: 96-9.

——— 1979. *Lothal: a Harappan Port Town, 1955-62*. New Delhi: Memoirs of the Archaeological Survey of India 78(1).

——— 1985. *Lothal: a Harappan Port Town, 1955-62*. New Delhi: Memoirs of the Archaeological Survey of India 78(2).

Ratnagar, S. 1981. *Encounters: the Westerly Trade of the Harappa Civilization*. Delhi: Oxford University Press.

——— 1991. *Enquiries into the Political Organization of Harappan Society*. Pune: Ravish Publishers.

Rissman, P.C. and Y.M. Chitalwala 1990. *Harappan Civilization and Oriyo Timbo*. Delhi: Oxford-IBH and the American Institute of Indian Studies.

Ross, E.J. 1946. A Chalcolithic Site in Northern Baluchistan: Rana Ghundai, *Journal of Near Eastern Studies* 5(4): 291-315.

Roy, T.N. 1961. *The Story of Indian Archaeology: 1784-1947*. Delhi: Government of India.

Sarkar, S.S. 1985. Human Skeletal Remains from Lothal, in *Lothal: a Harappan Port Town, 1955-62* (S. R. Rao), pp. 269-304. Delhi: Archaeological Survey of India.

Sauer, C.O. 1952. *Agricultural Origins and Dispersals*. New York: American Geographical Society.

Shaffer, J. G. 1982. Harappan Culture: a Reconsideration, in *Harappan Civilization: a Contemporary Perspective* (G.L. Possehl Ed.), pp. 41-50. Delhi: Oxford-IBH and the American Institute of Indian Studies.

——— 1992. The Indus Valley, Baluchistan and Helmand Traditions: Neolithic Through Bronze Age, in *Chronologies in Old World Archaeology* 2 Vols. (R.W. Ehrich Ed.), pp. 441-64 and 425-46. Chicago: University of Chicago Press.

——— 1993. Reurbanization: the Eastern Punjab and Beyond, in *Urban Form and Meaning in South Asia* (H. Spodek and D.M. Srinivasan Eds.), pp. 53-67. Washington, D.C.: National Gallery of Art. Studies in the History of Art, 31.Center for Advanced Study in the Visual Arts Symposium Papers 15.

Shaffer, J.G. and D.A. Lichtenstein 1989. Ethnicity and Change in the Indus Valley Cultural Tradition, in *Old Problems and New Perspectives in South Asian Archaeology* (J.M. Kenoyer Ed.), pp. 117-26. Madison: Wisconsin Archaeological Reports 2.

Shah, S.G.M. and A. Parpola 1991. *Corpus of Indus Seals and Inscriptions* (Vol. 2: Collections in Pakistan. Suomalainen Tiedeakatemia, Suomalaisen Tiedeakatemian Toimituksia).

Helsinki: Annales Academiae Scientiarum Fennicae, Sarja, Series B, NIDE, Tome 240.

Shinde, V. 1991. A Horn-Headed Human Figure on a Harappan jar from Padri, Gujarat, *Man and Environment* XVI (2): 87-9.

——— 1992. Excavations at Padri—1990-91: a Preliminary Report, *Man and Environment* XVII (1): 79-86.

Shinde, V. and S.B. Kar 1992. Padri Ware: a New Painted Ceramic Found in Harappan Levels at Padri in Gujarat, *Man and Environment* XVII (2): 105-10.

Srinivasan, D. 1984. Unhinging Siva from the Indus Civilization, *Journal of the Royal Asiatic Society of Great Britain and Ireland*: 77-89.

Stein, Sir A. 1929. An Archaeological Tour in Waziristan and Northern Baluchistan. Calcutta: Government of India Central Publication Branch. Memoirs of the Archaeological Survey of India 37.

——— 1931. *An Archaeological Tour in Gedrosia*. Delhi: Memoirs of the Archaeological Survey of India 43.

——— 1942. A Survey of Ancient Sites Along the 'Lost' Sarasvati River, *The Geographical Journal* 99: 173-82.

Suraj Bhan 1975. *Excavation at Mitathal (1968) and Other Explorations in the Sutlej-Yamuna Divide*. Kurukshetra: Kurukshetra University.

Tessitori, L.P. 1918-19. Exploration, Bikaner, *Annual Report of the Archaeological Survey of India, 1918-19*: 22-3.

Thapar, B.K. 1973a. New Traits of the Indus Civilization at Kalibangan: an Appraisal, *South Asian Archaeology* (N. Hammond Ed.), pp. 85-104. Park Ridge: Noyes Press.

——— 1973b. Synthesis of the Multiple Data as Obtained from Kalibangan, in *Radiocarbon and Indian Archaeology* (D.P. Agrawal and A. Ghosh Eds), pp. 264-71. Bombay: Tata Institute of Fundamental Research.

——— 1975. Kalibangan: a Harappan Metropolis Beyond the Indus Valley, *Expedition* 17 (2): 19-32.

——— 1989. Kalibangan -1 and -2, in *An Encyclopaedia of Indian Archaeology* (A. Ghosh Ed.), pp. 194-6. Delhi: Munshiram Manoharlal.

Tosi, M., L. Bondioli and M. Vidale 1984. Craft Activity Areas and Surface Survey at Mohenjodaro, in *Reports on Field Work Carried out at Mohenjo Daro, Pakistan 1982-83 by the IsMEO-Aachen University Mission* (M. Jansen and G. Urban Eds.), pp. 9-38. Aachen-Rome: RWTH-IsMEO.

Vats, M.S. 1929-30. Kotla Nihang, *Annual Report of the Archaeological Survey of India, 1929-30*: 131-2.

——— 1934-5. Trial excavations at Rangpur, Limbdi State, Kathiawar, *Annual Report of the Archaeological Survey of India, 1934-35*: 34-8.

——— 1940. *Excavations at Harappa*, 2 Vols. New Delhi: Government of India.

Vidale, M. 1987. Some Aspects of Lapidary Craft at Mohenjo Daro in the Light of the Surface Record of the Moneer South East area, in *Reports on Field Work Carried Out at Mohenjo Daro, Pakistan, 1983-84* (M. Jansen and G. Urban Eds.), pp. 113-49. Aachen-Rome: RWTH-IsMEO.

Wasson, R.J. 1984. The Sedimentological Basis of the Mohenjo Daro Flood Hypothesis, *Man and Environment* VIII: 88-90.

Wheeler, R.E.M. 1947. Harappa 1946: the Defenses and Cemetery R-37, *Ancient India* 3: 58-130.

——— 1950a. Newly found at Mohenjo Daro: a Huge 4000-Year-Old Granary, *Illustrated London News* (20 May): 782-3.

——— 1950b. New Light on the Indus Civilization: the Mohenjo Daro Granary, *Illustrated London News* (27 May): 813-16.

——— 1950c. Man in 4000 Year Old Mohenjo Daro, *Illustrated London News* (3 June): 854-5.

Wheeler, Sir M. 1953. *The Indus Civilization*. Cambridge: Cambridge University Press.

Woodburn, M.A. and H.E.W. Crawford 1994. London-Bahrain Archaeological Expedition: 1991-2 Excavations at Saar, *Arabian Archaeology and Epigraphy* 5: 89-105.

Geoarchaeological Perspectives on the Harappan Sites of South Asia

JOSEPH SCHULDENREIN

INTRODUCTION

The archaeological record of the Indus or Harappan Civilization is arguably the most fragmentary of the major cultural heartlands. While the history of Indus site discovery extends as far back as the nineteenth century (Burnes 1834; Cunningham 1875; Dames 1886; Masson 1884; see discussion in Possehl 1991, also this volume), research has been largely centred on the major urban centres of Mohenjo Daro and Harappa. Over the past twenty years, there has been a proliferation of survey and excavation in the Indus heartland, and investigators are now beginning to appreciate the complexity of its settlement systems and networks. In conjunction with the broadened scope of archaeological explorations, palaeoenvironmental studies shed light on the Holocene ecology of South Asia. Reconstructions of ancient circulation, landscape, vegetation, and hydrographic systems have major but as yet untapped potential for understanding the dramatic, practically unprecedented emergence of complex societies in the Indus Valley in the third millennium BC.

Not surprisingly, geoarchaeology remains a largely neglected strategy in Harappan research. In the broad sense, geoarchaeology is concerned with changing landscapes and their impacts upon ancient sites. Geoarchaeology explores systematic relationships between individual sites and groups of sites using methods and techniques of the earth science (i.e. soils, sediments, drainage nets, topographic settings) (Butzer 1982; Waters 1999). Ultimately geoarchaeology provides a unique course for tracking the preserved archaeological record from initial settlement and establishment to abandonment and preservation in sealed stratigraphies and landscape segments. For complex societies such as those of the Indus, geoarchaeology is a powerful tool for understanding how environments and the resources they furnished were exploited and ultimately managed by societies coping with questions of population pressure and resource stress. In particular, the Indus Civilization is known to have featured water management and irrigation systems, complex mound construction, and use of domesticated plants and animals. The relatively sudden collapse of the Indus Civilization and its resource base has remained a mystery and would seem to be at least in part related to environmental changes generated by combined climatic, hydrographic, geological, and human impacts. Geoarchaeology is a potential means for sorting out these factors, linking them chronologically, and reconstructing those mechanisms that brought about monumental cultural transformations in South Asia during the Middle Holocene.

The purpose of this paper, is to critically assess the current state of geoarchaeological research in the Indus heartland and to offer some perspective and guidelines for expanding inquiry. Rapid and recent advances in South Asian palaeoenvironmental research is now providing much needed background for integrating archaeological records with landscape studies. Moreover, the scope of contemporary palaeoecological study in South Asia is as broad as it is dynamic, ranging from fluvial geomorphology to pollen work, and from palaeopedology to climatic modelling (see Wadia et al. 1995). Holocene environmental studies from across the subcontinent are beneficial in discerning the primary ecological shifts. While geoarchaeological approaches to Harappan studies remain the exception, the few site studies with palaeoenvironmental or earth science components afford limited windows on the site-landscape dynamic. Background sections of older site reports—especially at Mohenjo Daro and Harappa—can now be reassessed in light of the sophisticated palaeoecological models that have been advanced over the past decade.

CHRONOLOGY AND GEOGRAPHY OF HARAPPAN SITES

The Harappan or Indus Civilization has traditionally referred to the complex of sites centred on the Indus river and tributaries that culminated in urban adaptations between *c.* 3000 BC and 2000 BC (Allchin and Allchin 1982; Possehl 1997) (Fig. 1). While Harappan Civilization was most pervasive in the Indus Valley, its manifestations extended well into the eastern deserts of India (Thar) and may be culturally related to early agricultural communities in the western piedmont of Baluchistan (Jarrige and Lechevallier 1979). The Early Harappan stage lasted to *c.* 2500 BC, while the subsequent Mature Harappan was eclipsed by *c.* 2000 BC, and the civilization was in decline by 1750 BC. Modifications to the chronology have been advanced in recent years because of the larger sample of excavated sites, refinements to cultural stratigraphies, and a broader population of radiocarbon dates. Perhaps most significantly, the past decade has witnessed progressively more accurate calibration for Holocene ^{14}C determinations that have been able to accommodate the disjuncture between 'radiocarbon years' and 'solar years' (de Vries effects; see Stuiver et al. 1993; Taylor 1997). Accordingly, it is now possible to reliably pinpoint chronologies for Harappan sites that contain radiocarbon remains in secure stratigraphic context.

Figure 2 is a histogram depicting the distributions of 110 recently compiled radiocarbon dates from thirteen major Harappan sites including: Harappa; Mohenjo Daro; Kalibangan; Kot-Diji; Lothal; Surkotada; Rajdi; Daimabad; Bara; Mitathal; Sanghol; Banawali; and Hulas. It is noted, however, that 60 per cent of the total population of dates ($n = 66$) are derived from the urban centres of Harappan, Mohenjo Daro, and Kalibangan. All dates have been previously reported in several summary reports (Allchin and Allchin 1982; Kenoyer 1991a; Possehl 1997). Results show that the range of Harappan occupation spans the interval of the Middle to lower Late Holocene, with the highest site frequencies occurring between 4100 and 3500 BP (*c.* 2600-2000 BC, calibrated), the acknowledged

▲ = Early Harappan Sites

● = Mature Harappan Sites

Fig. 1. Distribution of Principal Early and Mature Harappan Sites.

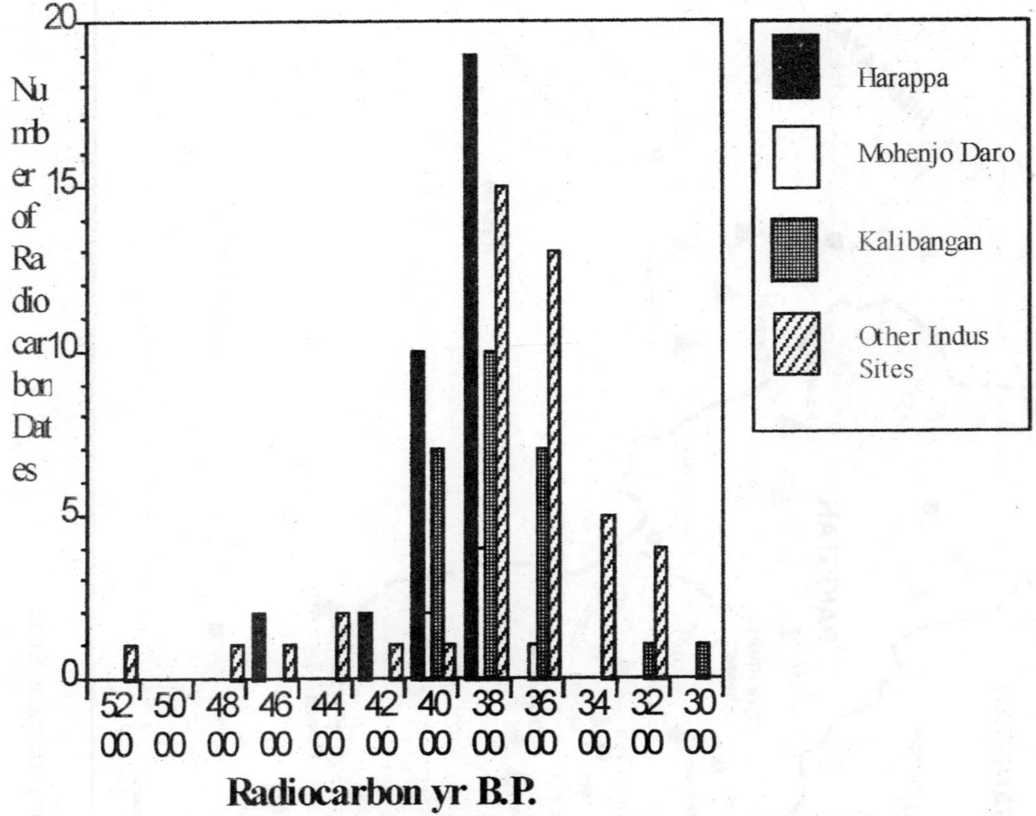

Fig. 2. Histogram depicting distribution of radiocarbon dates from Principal Harappan Sites (Sources: Kenoyer 1991; Possehl 1997; Allchin and Allchin 1982).

time frame of the Mature Harappan. The date distributions may also underscore several provocative trends:

(1) Across the Harappan heartland there is minimal evidence of occupation prior to 3000 BC: there are only four determinations from Harappa prior to that time and none from Mohenjo Daro and Kalibangan.
(2) The end of Harappan occupation is dramatic, given the fall-off in radiocarbon dates after 2000 BC; of the major sites only Kalibangan post-dates that period.
(3) Activity in both the northern and southern urban centres—represented by Harappa and Mohenjo Daro respectively—may have preceded the decline in satellite communities; the latter outlasted the two hub communities by 200-400 years.

It remains entirely possible that these dates are biased by preservation conditions and survey, collection, and excavation strategies pursued by investigators. Moreover, the data may not reflect cultural activities that may have taken place in heretofore undiscovered portions of sites. Finally, the continuous agricultural through Harappan sequences in Baluchistan and westward—at Mehrgarh and Mundigak—raise issues concerning the dramatic emergence of the Harappan Culture complex (Allchin and Allchin 1982; Jarrige and Lechevallier 1979). Nevertheless, the broad sampling of dates from across the Harappan heartland offers the possibility that these distributions represent pan-regional temporal trends.

The geography of Harappan settlement is closely linked to the alignment of the Indus Valley trunk and tributary drainages in the semi-arid regions of Pakistan, although more remote manifestations extend into piedmont and mountainous terrain in Afghanistan and east to desertic west-central and north-central India. It has been estimated that the Harappan territory encompasses nearly half a million square kilometres (Agrawal 1992). There is no unequivocal inventory of Harappan sites, in part because of disparate regional and local records, limited dissemination of much of the Pakistani and Indian literature, and lack of systematic documentation for inaccessible areas. Accordingly, it is not possible to present a settlement typology or profile for more restricted and diffuse Harappan occupations.

Figure 1 illustrates the configuration of the larger, most widely documented Harappan sites, assigned to Early or Mature stages. As shown, while the sites range from the upper Indus to the drainage's mouth at the Arabian Sea, the lower Indus is the major artery for Mature Harappan sites, while Early Harappan sites are more clustered to the west and north. Recent survey and testing has disclosed that the Punjab, is traversed by present, buried and ancient courses of the north-east—south-west flowing drainages that empty into the Indus (between the Jhelum and the Sutlej; Fig. 1), sustained extensive Indus satellite communities peripheral to Harappa (PAS 1998; Wright and Schuldenrein 1997, 1998). To date the majority of Harappan sites are located on floodplains, or former floodplain segments, at elevations below 1200 m.

The hydrography of the Indus is the key element explaining the variability as well as the chronology of site distributions. The Indus itself can be divided into two primary hydrographic reaches: the Upper Basin, north and east of the confluence of the 'Five Rivers' (Jhelum, Chenab, Ravi, Beas and Sutlej) in the Punjab, and the Lower Basin extending through Sindh to the stream mouth at the modern delta and coast (Fig. 1). In general, the rivers of the Punjab flow below the general levels of the adjacent floodplains. This is not so far the Indus. The two reaches are offset from one another primarily as a function of the collisional tectonics of the Himalayan orogen Tectonic maps show the Upper Basin positioned in the Sulaiman Foredeep and a zone of downwarp and platform slope, while the Lower Basin begins in the downwarp/platform zone and traverses a series of prominent fold belts aggrading onto the delta (Kazmi and Rana 1982; Haghipour et al. 1984; Biswas 1987). Both reaches cut through alluvial sediments of Tertiary-Holocene age. The Indus and its higher order tributaries differ from other rivers of the subcontinent insofar as channels are not classically or even continuously incised into their extensive alluvial plains. Lateral migration is characteristic of the courses of both reaches, such that metres upon metres of Late Quaternary sediment have accumulated and built up extensive, low relief alluvial plains. It is often impossible to differentiate buried channels as a result of the depth of sediment burial and the uniformity of sediment type; the latter is typically in the fine sand or silt loam size grade with the exception of localized reaches.

Hydrographic and sedimentological uniformity over broad segments of the Indus have obscured topography and complicated attempts to synthesize stream and valley history. As a result, it has been difficult to build settlement models based on alluvial histories. Recently, however, extensive geomorphological work along the channel of the lower Indus has produced systematic reconstructions of post-Pleistocene fluvial remnants associated with former stream courses. These have suggested that during Harappan times, the lower Indus channel was actually *c.* 25 km north-west of its present location on the flanks of the right bank of the river at Mohenjo Daro; river migration, encroachment, and attendant flood hazards to the site may have resulted in site abandonment (Flam 1993; Jorgensen et al. 1993). Lower Basin research has also demonstrated that progradation of the delta has built up the shoreline progressively south-westward into the Arabian Sea. While chrono-stratigraphic evidence documenting these geomorphic changes is lacking, the complex alignments of the primary Harappan centres south and west of Mohenjo Daro is consistent with arguments for progressive channel avulsion and shoreline displacements (see Fig. 1).

The Upper Valley drainage reaches (upstream of the 'five rivers confluence') have not been as extensively documented geomorphically and archaeologically, even for larger sites (compare site distributions north-east and south-west of the Basin divide in Fig. 1). Existing landscape models postulate that the higher order trunk streams have created a low-relief alluvial plain allowing for channel migration across an extensive terrain between the western mountains and the Thar desert. Floodplain morphology and depositional environments are virtually indistinguishable between one catchment and its adjacent hydrographic net across the drainage divide. With striking exceptions (i.e. the upper Ravi) upstream channel courses are mildly entrenched (i.e. by 2-3 m) into older Pleistocene alluvium, while downstream profiles feature thick accumulations of Holocene silts and sands (Abu Bakr and Jackson 1964). The relatively low density of sites is a function of a graded alluvial landscape in which diagnostic terraces and micro-environmental niches have been largely obscured by both gentle, uniform discharge, reduced base levels, and modifications to the natural hydrograhy by century old irrigation networks and their blanketing cover silts. However, a lack of systematic survey has also obscured knowledge of Harappan settlement in the Upper Basin. The recent Government of Pakistan survey of the Punjab (*PAS* 1998) and recent explorations along the buried bed of the Beas (Wright and Schuldenrein 1997, 1998) is expanding the site data base dramatically. To date, the densest and most extensive clusters of Upper Basin Late Harappan sites in the Punjab are those flanking the ancient course of the Ghaggar-Hakkra alluvial plain—the mythic Sarasvati and Drishadvati of the Rigvedic hymns—in the Cholistan south of the Sutlej (Fig. 1). The main site of this complex is Ganweriwala, which appears to have been a primary centre. Evidence for settlements extends semi-continuously *c.* 90 km to just west of Kalibangan (Possehl and Ravahl 1989; PAS 1998). Site abandonments in this reach appear to have been related to stream capture of the Sutlej during the Late Harappan (after 1500 BC), when the Indus and Ganga drainage divides began to assume their present configurations. The significance of such dramatic hydrographic realignments during the Late Holocene has been recognized by geographers (Seth 1978; Wilhelmy 1969). As elsewhere, however, the Ghaggar-Hakkra sites have not been the subject of intensive intra-site analysis (although see Mughal 1981, 1997); they have been the focus of critical palaeoenvironmental research (Courty 1995; Misra 1995; Possehl 1997; Shroder 1993).

Summarily, our understanding of Harappan chronology and geography has been enhanced in the past decade by an expanding radiocarbon data base and more sophisticated geomorphological methodologies. The latter facilitate reconstructions of landscape events and successions that begin to shed light trends on Harappan demographics and site preservation patterns. The absolute dates refine the time line and pinpoint that interval of the Middle-Late Holocene—*c.* 4500-3000 BP—in which evidence for landscape change is most crucial for explaining human ecological shifts. However, the utility of the geomorphic record remains limited by a lack of dates sub-surface stratigraphic evidence. In particular, there are few linked cultural and natural sequences—and especially buried soil chronologies—that can potentially separate intervals of Holocene landscape dynamism from those of stability.

HOLOCENE PALAEOENVIRONMENTS AND THE INDUS SITES

Palaeoenvironmental histories are typically synthesized from several lines of inquiry. For the Indian subcontinent in general and for the Indus in particular, the most productive research to date has included studies of: climate and circulation systems, geomorphology, and tectonics. An additional avenue of inquiry that is becoming increasingly critical is palaeo-biotic studies—palaeobotany, pollen analysis, and faunal research—but these have been largely centred on specific sites (especially at Harappa; see Meadow 1991; Belcher

1991; Miller 1991); the scopes of interpretations are generally focused on site catchments and meso-environments as well as on cultural bias in resource procurement. Pollen research is gaining momentum for the ancient lake basins in arid portions of the subcontinent (e.g. Kajale and Deotare 1997), and these will eventually be diagnostic when linked with geomorphic sequences and radiocarbon chronologies.

Current controversy surrounding the causes of emergence, florescence, and collapse of the Harappan Civilization centres on the relative roles played by climate and tectonics in affecting the flow patterns, landscape morphology, and ultimately the stability and agricultural reliability of the Indus and tributary floodplains (see Possehl 1997). Net effects of climatic and tectonic interaction are reflected in landscape relations (geomorphology). During much of the Holocene and alluvial system was affected by both mechanisms that collectively promoted the base level changes registered in continental and marine stratigraphic records. The Holocene data associated with climate and circulation, geomorphology, and tectonic factors is discussed below.

Present and Past Climate and Circulation Systems

The central component in the circulation patterns of South Asia is the monsoon. According to Ramage (1971), monsoon circulation is of thermal origin and blows through a continental heat low in summer and out of a cold continental anticyclone in winter. Regional variability in monsoon effects is in part due to the changing intensities of the summer and winter monsoons. Within the Asian monsoon regions, the Tibetan plateau is a critical landscape, since it anchors the summer heat low over northern India and east Pakistan, thus promoting the strongest monsoon inflow as the south-west monsoon. In winter, high pressure systems are intensified by outflow of Siberian air (from the north-west), blocked, by the Tibetan plateau but freely crossing into Eastern Asia. The Indian and Chinese monsoons are the most extensive and intense of the world's monsoon systems.

While the scale and extent of the contemporary Asian monsoon is well documented, the variability of monsoons behaviour in the past remains the subject of controversy. Wasson (1995) has argued that there is currently not sufficient proxy climatic data to conclude that Asian monsoons would not have had as strong and synchronous effects across both hemispheres in the Late Quaternary. Accordingly, he had marshalled evidence from palaeo-lake basins in northern Australia, India, Arabia, the Arabian Sea, Taiwan, Japan, and South-East Asia to conclude that a peak in available moisture occurred between 8000-6000 BP for all areas affected by monsoon circulation systems; in South Asia that peak is between 7000-5000 BP, based on records from the palaeo-lakes in Rajasthan (Wasson et al. 1984). Extending the chronology earlier in the Holocene, Kutzbach and Guetter (1986) claim that the interval 12,000-6000 BP corresponds to maximum amplitude solar season cycles in the northern hemisphere. This is clearly linked to intensified normal circulation generated by the strengthening of the East Asia summer monsoon. Fortification of that circulation pattern is enhanced by high evapotranspiration ratios in source areas (by higher temperatures). For much of the Early Holocene, the intensity of the greater monsoon was regulated by seasonal forcing (see also Bowler et al. 1995).

After *c.* 5000 BP there is considerably more variability between palaeo-lake records across monsoon impacted regions (from Arabia to South-East Asia and Australia). Generally, however levels drop, often precipitously, to *c.* 3000 BP. After that time the lake basins cease to provide evidence of synchronous trends.

Extrapolating palaeoclimatic impacts of the Asian monsoons on the fluvial systems of South Asia is a more controversial undertaking because of the unresolved chronology of Late Quaternary events and the effects of tectonics in the Himalayan belt on downstream locations. Relationships between monsoon rains and contemporary fluvial systems are just now beginning to be investigated. While it is accepted that modern floods in the subcontinent are more frequent during periods of accelerated monsoon rainfall, current studies are exploring the short and long term patterns of flooding in response to monsoon precipitation regimes. Palaeoflood records for streams clustered in drainage basins most strongly affected by high rainfalls are being correlated and the evolution of channel and floodplain geometry, hydraulics, and erosion is being linked to yearly variability in monsoon rainfall intensity (Baker et al. 1995).

Summarily, it is clear that there were some critical changes in monsoon circulation systems in the Holocene. The synchroneity of the various monsoon systems both spatially and temporally remains unresolved, in part, because investigations of appropriate palaeoenvironmental sites has been lagging. In South Asia, the best proxy climatic data of date come from the palaeo-lake basins in Rajasthan which reinforce interpretations in lake basins extending across the monsoon belts—from the Arabian Sea of Australia—for a major and pervasive moist period during the Early Holocene (McClure 1976; Swain et al. 1983). Desiccation, perhaps locally tempered by moist cycles, is indicated between 5000-3000 BP, after which variability between regions precludes generalization about climatic trends. There is considerable debate surrounding the role of palaeoclimatic forcing during the Middle and Late Holocene and the effects of circulation patterns on the Indus and Harappan adaptive strategies, as discussed below.

Geomorphology of the Indus Heartland

The alignment of larger sites of the Harappan Civilization in the Indus Valley and its margins necessitates a consideration of landscape relations, and their bearing on valley evolution and chronology. As noted, the 'five rivers divide' separates the drainage into two segments (Fig. 1). The Upper Basin is characterized by a series of high order tributaries comprising a low relief topography with mildly elevated interfluves, regionally referred to as *doabs* (whose names are combinations of the first parts of adjacent drainages), separated by laterally extensive alluvial basins (Khan 1991). The Lower Basin has sustained a more freely migrating stream-hemmed in between the Thar Desert and the Western Mountains—that eventually progrades into the coastal delta. Different hydrographic features of each reach are predetermined by their association with structural elements: chiefly the subsiding Sulaiman Foredeep for the Upper Basin, and southern uplift and the Kachi foredeep for the Lower Basin (Kazmie and Rana 1982; Shroder 1993).

The map of contemporary surface deposits provides critical insights into the Holocene history of Indus sedimentation, alluvial behaviour and ultimately, the distribution and preservation of Harappan sites. Mian and Syal (1986) undertook the first comprehensive mapping of landforms and surface across Pakistan, based on aerial photography and ground-truthing and integrated with earlier and reliable geological and soil maps. They grouped configurations of the country's land surface prior to identifying and assigning ages for alluvial and flanking landscape units (see Mian and Syal 1986: 26-42 with appended map).

For the Upper Basin, these primary landscape units are recognized (in order of decreasing area):

(1) *Subrecent Floodplains*. This unit encompasses most of the irrigated terrain immediately flanking the five rivers. Flooding is infrequent but a variety of meso-landforms are featured including level plains; basins and infilled channels; and levee remnants. Periodic sheet flooding and some catastrophic inundations account for most of the modification to this terrain in historic times. This terrain, regionally referred to as *bet*. (Khan 1991; Snelgrove 1967), is of Middle of Late Holocene age, and may be traversed by dunes of penecontemporaneous or later age (Figs. 3 and 4).

(2) *Level Bar Uplands*. These are the highest interfluves—also called 'tablelands'—and are considered to be of Pleistocene origin. Terraces are up to 9 m high but are generally on the order of 2 m. They are associated with downcut exposures in upstream reaches of the Chenab, Ravi, and Sutlej. As in the case of the Subrecent Floodplains, sheetflooding and monsoon rains have produced meso-landforms including level plains; broad basins; covered channel-levee remnants; and terrace scarps. Soil formation has been reported to be extensive across the better drained, higher elevation terraces.

(3) *Undulating Sandy Terraces*. Also of presumed Pleistocene origin, mapped outcrops are confined to a single, semi-continuous interfluve between the Jhelum and Indus north of Multan. High escarpments with undulating surfaces are typical. Evidence for post depositional processes include deflation (loess accumulations) and tectonics (surface boulders).

(4) *Bajadas*. The Piedmont Plain and slopes extend south-eastward from the foot of the mountains (Sulaiman Hills) to the alluvial basins. Distribution is limited to a series of coalescent aprons and fans paralleling the right bank of the Indus almost continuously into the lower valley. Sediment is generally stony and gravelly and age is Pleistocene to Holocene.

(5) *Recent Floodplains*. These are the most dynamic alluvial reaches and have been mapped for the proximal floodplains of the Indus and portions of the Chenab (specifically the Jhelum and Sutlej confluences). Reference is made to areas that are regularly inundated and sediment complexes that are periodically reworked.

(6) *Sandy Deserts*. These define the south-eastern margins of the Ghaggar plain in

Fig. 3. Dissected Harappan mound over looking Subrecent Floodplains landscape, Upper Indus Basin in Vicinity of buried bed of the Beas river.

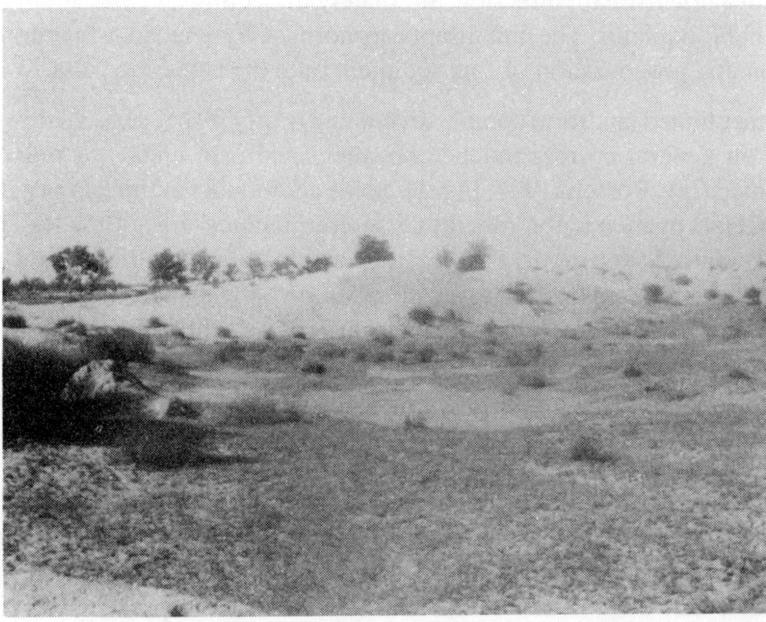

Fig. 4. Linear dune traversing Subrecent Floodplains near Khanewal, Upper Indus Basin.

Cholistan. The deserts include a complex of dune and terrace meso-environments, with topographic gradients strongly modified by tectonic activity and periodic intervals of deflation.

For the Lower Basin, the Indus grades from a partially incised to almost exclusively aggradational valley terrain and thence onto the prograded delta at the mouth of the Arabian Sea. Accordingly, the distribution of landscape units differs somewhat from that north of the divide. Lower Valley landforms are dominated by:

(1) *Subrecent Floodplains*. Since the trunk stream is no longer fed by extensive, higher order tributaries, the alluvial plain is somewhat narrower than it is in the upstream segment. However, between the confines of the Thar Desert and the Western Mountains the Indus itself has migrated more actively.
(2) *Bajadas*. South of Sibi there are extensive coalescent fans grading into the alluvial terrain.
(3) *Sandy Deserts*. The Thar Desert Margins are not widely known but landscapes are morphologically similar to those of Cholistan, albeit with greater relief.
(4) *Indus Delta Estuarine Plain*. The distal segment of the Coastal Plain is a complex of spill flats, basins, spill heads, meander bars and levees. A variety of sediment types are represented, with the level surfaces dominantly silty and the basins infilled with clays. Tidal flooding and riverine sedimentation attest to widely variable depositional regimes.
(5) *Recent Floodplains*. These become progressively more attenuated as the Indus channel avulses in a downstream direction, alternately dissecting and embanking against the Subrecent Floodplains. The unit disappears north of Hyderabad, a function of gradient reduction and progradation of fine sediment onto the estuarine dalta.

The aforementioned landform complexes contain nearly 90 per cent of known Harappan sites, based on general correspondence between landform units and most recent site distribution maps (i.e. Possehl 1997: Fig. 1). Some additional landforms may also preserve evidence of Harappan occupation, but site frequencies are either too minimal or depositional contexts too poorly understood to postulate landform and occupation equivalence. In some cases landforms are simply too young to preserve Harappan remains (i.e. contemporary Coastal Belt beyond the estuarine margin).

While Mian and Syal's (1986) geomorphic maps depict the landform groupings with a high degree of accuracy, the landscape sequences are not grounded in absolute (i.e. radiometrically based) chronologies. Even broad age designations (Pleistocene *vs.* Holocene) are largely inferential and appear to be based on relative landform elevations in alluvial settings and on scaled degrees of soil development on the more stable and older terraces. Thus in the 'five rivers' area (Upper Basin) the prevailing model projects alluvial surface ages on classic cut and fill models (Brinkman and Rafiq 1971; see discussion in Flam 1993). The level 'Bar Uplands'—the present interfluves—are considered to the Pleistocene terraces that were downcut and subsequently aggraded in the Early Holocene to create the 'Subrecent Floodplains'. A second cycle beginning with dissection of the 'Subrecent Floodplains', and culminating with construction of the 'Recent Floodplains' is assigned to the Late Holocene. Both cycles produced relatively shallow terraces, on the order of <1 m. Flam (1993: 269-70) has claimed that sediment degraded from the terraces during the presumed Early and Late Holocene erosional cycles was subsequently aggraded onto the accretionary floodplains of the Lower Valley. There is, however, an inherent paradox in his implicit invocation of Schumm's (1977) classic model of sediment transport model (postulating upstream erosion and downstream deposition), since Mian and Syal (1986) continue to map the Subrecent Floodplain unit well into the Lower Basin in Sindh. In the absence of more detailed mapping of low grade terrace surfaces bolstered by unit radiocarbon dates, these terrace chronologies remain uncertain and must be considered relative.

An additional factor inhibiting chrono-stratigraphic interpretations of landform complexes in both reaches of the Indus is the lack of comprehensive Holocene soil chronologies. Beg (1993: 258-63) has proposed a soil taxonomy for the terraces and Subrecent Floodplains that post-dates the landform chronology of Mian and Syal (1986). Hypothetically the pedogenic intervals are consistent with the landform history, as his chronology of soil formation post-dates deposition of respective alluvial units. Beg (1993) proposes a Mid-Late Holocene age for terrace soils and Late Holocene age for the Subrecent Floodplain soils. However, marker pedogenic horizons or characteristics are neither described in any detail nor dates. Soil stratigraphies remain a neglected area of Quaternary studies across the subcontinent in general despite their crucial role for separating periods of Holocene landscape stability from intervals of geomorphic dynamism (although see Pendall and Amundson 1990a, 1990b for assessment of the soils at Harappa).

Limitations on the precise ages of the landform complexes notwithstanding, it is still possible to link Harappan site clusters with discrete landform complexes in the upper and lower Indus Basins. The observations presented below are based on correlations between recorded site distributions (Fig. 1; Possehl 1997: Fig. 1) and geomorphic mapping units (Mian and Syal 1986). Given the unique settings of the Upper and Lower Valleys, it is instructive to consider the large scale landform/settlement trends for the Indus Valley generally and more regional manifestations that may have been controlled by the unique edaphic, climatic, and hydrographic features of each of the two valley reaches. Accordingly:

(1) There is a high density of Early Harappan sites on the Bajadas grading down from the Piedmont Plain. Major sites are generally associated with major drainages but smaller ones are not. Te coalescent alluvial fans upon which the latter sites are found are difficult to bracket stratigraphically, since such fans generally represent long-term sedimentation (spanning the Late Quaternary) along the Sulaiman Hills to the south-west.

(2) Markedly lower site densities in the Upper Valley (Punjab) may reflect the dynamism of the upper Indus drainage system and the dearth of systematic archaeological and geoarchaeological exploration of this region. The discrepancy in site frequencies between the Lower and Upper Valley is pronounced. The majority of known Punjab

sites are associated with the Level Bar Uplands (i.e. Harappa proper), although recent surveys indicate that the areas mapped as Subrecent Floodplains preserve significant Harappan mounds (Fig. 3) and the substrate are of Early Holocene age (Wright and Schuldenrein 1997, 1998).

(3) The preservation of extensive site complexes in the Sandy Deserts of Cholistan—Ghaggar-Hakkra plain—reflects a major palaeogeographic shift during the Holocene. The primary landscape modification involved stream capture and the westward migration of the drainage net, most dramatically the Sutlej, between *c.* 1500 BC and AD 1500. Both climatic and tectonic mechanisms have been invoked to explain attendant landscape overhauls (Shroder 1993; Wilhelmy 1969).

(4) The proliferation of lineally configured Late Harappan sites in the Lower Valley signifies pronounced channel avulsion along the downstream reaches of the Indus in the Middle and Late Holocene. The Indus flowed up to 25 km to the west of its present course at that time (Fig. 1). Sites span several geomorphic units, including the Subrecent Floodplains, Bajadas, and undifferentiated Piedmont segments. Former channel courses have been extensively mapped and relatively dated based on geomorphic features (Flam 1993; Jorgenson et al. 1993).

(5) Early and Late Harappan sites along the upper distributaries emptying into the mouth of the Arabian Sea, attest to extensive deltaic progradation during the Middle to Late Holocene. These are all associated with the mapped Estuary Plains and suggest that the Harappan Coast may have been tens of kilometres inland of its present location (Flam 1993; Lambrick 1975; Raikes 1964), although massive structural movements *c.* 60-120 m) and turbulent hurricanes during the Holocene may preclude legitimate estimates of coastal locations at specific points in time (Snead 1993a, 1993b).

Contemporary earth surface features provide indications as well as a relative chronology of past landscape relations. Potential for reliable palaeogeographic reconstructions for the Harappan period remain limited by an absence of pre- and post-occupation dates and a complex of external factors (tectonic, climatic, and anthropogenic) that have collectively restructured valley environments. Of these, the impacts of tectonics may be the most difficult to chronicle.

Late Quaternary Tectonics and the Drainage History of the Indus

Shroder (1993) has claimed that the landscape evolution of Pakistan is first and foremost a function of ongoing tectonism affecting the movements of the Indo-Pakistan plate into the Eurasian plate. It was the raising of the Qinghai-Tibetan plateau and the Himalaya that fashioned the antecedent drainages of the Indus and its tributaries, once trunk streams exited the Himalayan drainage heads. The fluvial landscape has been modified by non-structural processes during the Quaternary—i.e. erosion, slope failure, hydrography, climate—but these are considered to be secondary.

The chronology of the early orogeny is better understood than that responsible for sculpting the landscapes of Quaternary age. As noted, the drainage evolution of the Upper

Basin is somewhat known for the late Holocene through the efforts of Wilhelmy (1969) who reviewed texts of antiquity as well as extant maps depicting dried out channel courses. His efforts effectively tracked the north and westward migration of the Punjab drainages away from the Ghaggar-Hakkra between 4000 BP and the present. There were numerous avulsions and cross-divide stream captures between the Indus and Ganges stream nets. As recently as 500 years ago, the upper Indus had shifted *c.* 50 km to the west. While the westward migrations of the rivers has been assumed to be largely a function of pre- and early Quaternary tectonics—thus carving out ancient drainage lines—the preservation of the Harappan sites along the Ghaggar-Hakkra indicates that such climatic factors as local or regional desiccation and rainfall distribution patterns were equally significant in affecting erosion, sediment yield, and ultimately channel displacement. Systematic and sizeable dune fields and isolated distribution of aeolian features in the central and lower Punjab also argue for episodic circulation patterns. There are no comprehensive chronologies or accounts of structural modifications to the Holocene landscapes of the Punjab and at least one major researcher has not related structural relations to the changing geography of the Ghaggar-Hakkra plain (Courty 1995).

Landscape chronologies linked to structural events are somewhat better understood for the Lower Basin, although here, again, periods of regional drainage modification can only be dated in relative terms. Ancient Indus courses have been documented on the basis of relict channel features and boring logs that have exposed buried channel bottom sediments (Seth 1978; Kazmi 1984). Seth has proposed linking a visible channel displacement to the 1819 earthquake. The extreme tectonism on the Makran coast has caused contemporary displacements along the Indus delta on the order of 1.8-2.4 m. In 1945 a section of the coast near Pansi was uplifted by *c.* 4.5 m (Snead 1993a). Snead (1993b) has linked raised coastal and river terraces of up to 15 m with Upper Palaeolithic and Mesolithic surfaces. Uplift during the Late Holocene has been implicated for erosion of river beds into their own deposits (Flam 1993). Of greatest bearing of Lower Valley archaeological contexts, is the hypothesis that tectonic events accounted for the emplacement of a massive dam *c.* 40 m high and 80 m long) that backed up the lower Indus drainage and eventually flooded out Mohenjo Daro; the hypothesis was based on an analogue with a fault scarp created by the 1819 earthquake along the Kachchh (Kutch) Fault Zone that trapped waters at that time (Raikes 1965).

While tectonics were apparently pivotal in affecting the drainage and occupation histories of the Harappan countryside, the timing and magnitude of structural events remains difficult to calibrate. Jorgensen et al. (1993) note, for example, that while both the behaviour of the Indus river as well as relict landscape features along its reaches are unequivocal products of structural movements, it is probable that for segments of the Indus—especially in the downstream, aggradational catchment—modern rates of sedimentation probably exceed rates of tectonic deformation. Even though patterned channel behaviour (segmentation, alluviation, migration) represents the interaction of both hydrographic and structural elements, the relative effects of each has not yet been isolated chronologically across the Indus floodplain. To do so it is necessary to undertake detailed subsurface stratigraphic investigation and penetrating metres upon meters of homogeneous alluvium to isolate unconformable surfaces or vertical evidence indicative of structural disruption.

Synthesis of Landscape Records

The recent proliferation of Late Quaternary research across the subcontinent has exponentially increased the range and types of landscapes that inform for palaeogeographic purposes. A major emphasis has been placed on mountainous and glacial regions (e.g. the Himalayas; see Shroder 1993), but the record for lower-lying piedmont and valley terrain has expanded as well.

For present purposes, it is most appropriate to summarize the better documented landscape reconstructions that focus on:

(1) The semi-arid and arid Indus landscapes in which the Harappan sites are clustered;
(2) The critical later Middle Holocene period during which climatic and environmental changes bear most directly on Harappan settlement.

Table 1 presents a synopsis of Holocene landscape and palaeoclimatic trends across the Indian subcontinent antecedent, contemporaneous, and subsequent to the Harappan period; data sets associated with the Harappan period are highlighted (*c.* 5000-3000 BP). The types of settings for which information has been assembled include: aeolian mantled terrain; coasts (estuaries and drainage mouths); lake beds; fluvial features and valleys; buried soil (palaeosol) localities; and low-lying areas with evidence for structural movements (tectonics). The records have been abstracted from the published literature and are documented as appropriate for detailed reference. The shaded blocks without text in Table 1 refer to those time frames and data categories for which information is lacking.

In this connection, it is stressed that the documentation is neither comprehensive nor is it necessarily confined to regions in which major Harappan settlements are found. The most recent publications were consulted but many sources documenting environmental data are neither accessible nor published. In some cases geomorphic data sets were utilized from locations beyond core Harappan cultural regions, either because there is a dearth of evidence for Harappan environs or because specific distant locations are especially diagnostic of Middle Holocene palaeoclimatic signals. Thus, for example, reference is made to a palaeosol sequence in south-east India because of the extreme weathering in that soil that signified a climato-stratigraphic benchmark (Gardner 1995). The implicit assumption here is that since the overall mechanism driving climatic change across the subcontinent was the monsoon, both continental and littoral trends would have been registered across most geographic sub-divisions (although see Wasson 1995 for an alternative viewpoint).

In general, however, most of the key data sets were derived from Harappan regions, especially the Ghaggar-Hakkra plain for aeolian sequences (Courty 1995); the Makran

TABLE 1: SYNOPSIS OF HOLOCENE LANDSCAPE AND PALEOCLIMATIC TRENDS IN THE INDIAN SUBCONTINENT LANDSCAPE HISTORY

Years	Aeolian Activity	Coastal Changes	Lacustrine Record	Fluvial Sequences	Soil Chronology	Tectonics	Climate
BP 0				Reduction of swamps and channel activity; lowered water tables, Ghaggar; Incision in Deccan Uplands; aggradation exceeds subsidence in lower Indus		Upwarping promoting stream capture and westward drainage (lower Indus) with episodes of eastward avulsion	Reduced precipitation
1000	Moderate aeolian activity, Ghaggar	2 m regression in Saurashtra, accelerated pro-deltaic aggradation at mouth of Arabian sea (lower Indus)	Progressive desiccation and salinity: Didwana				High precipitation levels with contemporary rainfall patterns
2000				Peak flood stages-Narmada river; reduced seasonal flooding and siltation of channels, Ghaggar	Soil formation in Nepal		
3000				Sandy alluviation of Belan river; moderate aggradation in Deccan Uplands		Structural deformation leading to eastward and westward stream capture in Punjab (Ghaggar-Hakkra)	Generally decreased monsoonal precipitation punctuated by moister pulses
4000	Cessation of dune build-up; Thar Desert; localized sand dunes Ghaggar	Maximum sea level (+3 to +6m transgression)	Optimal fresh water influx and highest lake levels: Didwana	Reduction in aggradation and channel avulsion along lower Indus	Sultanpur soils at Harappa (Bk, Bw horizons)		
5000		Onset of marine transgression	Moderately deep fresh-water, Didwana				Stabilization and gradual decline of south-west monsoon intensity; high evapotranspiration
6000	Loess sedimentation, Ghaggar plain			Incision of Belan river into Pleistocene fills; reduced alluviation; slackwater formations, Ghaggar			Maximum winter monsoon

(contd.)

Years	Aeolian Activity	Coastal Changes	Lacustrine Record	Fluvial Sequences	Soil Chronology	Tectonics	Climate
7000		South-westward migration and sedimentation of Indus delta	Fluctuating dry/saline and deep/freshwater conditions, Didwana; high water levels and freshwater, Bap Malar, Thob	Rejuvenation of alluviation in valleys of Deccan uplands; massive seasonal flooding, Ghaggar plain	'Black Soils' form in Nevasa; soil formation in Nepal; Gamber, Lyallpur soils at Harappa (Bk, Bw, By horizons); weathering of E. Indian coastal 'red sands'		
8000	Limited extent and reduced rates of dune construction: Thar Desert						
9000				Rapid aggradation of lower Indus			Establishment of post-Pleistocene monsoon circulation
10000	Terminal loess deposition in interior Gujarat	Still-stands, submerged terraces in Goa (-92m, -85m, -75m and -55m)	Rising lake levels: Didwana	Alluviation at foot of Siwaliks			

REFERENCES: Lacustrine: Thar Desert and Didwana (Chawla et al. 1991; Misra, 1995; Singh et al. 1972, 1974, 1990; Singhvi et al. 1983, 1984 ; Wasson 1995); Kajale and Deotare (1997); Deotare et al. 1998.

Fluvial sequences: Narmada river (Baker et al. 1995); central India (Williams and Clark 1995); Pappu (1974; 1995); Korisettar (1979); Ghaggar plain (Courty, 1995); Indus (Jorgensen et al. 1993).

Soils: Nepal and Siwaliks (Corvinus 1995); Nevasa soils (Mishra 1995); 'red dunes' (Gardner and Martingell 1990); Pendall and Amundson (1990a, 1990b).

Aeolian: Gujarat loess (Chamyal and Merh 1995); Ghaggar (Courty 1995).

Sea levels: (Juyal et al. 1995); Sarma (1971); Marathe (1995); Flam (1993); Snead (1993a, 1993b).

Climate: Nigam and Hashimi (1995); Von Rad et al. (1999); Bryson (1996); Brinkman and Rafiq (1971); Singh et al. (1983); Wasson (1995).

Tectonics: Wilhelmy (1969); Jorgensen et al. (1993); Agrawal and Sood (1982).

(Pakistan) and west Indian coasts for littoral terrace chronologies and tectonics (Juyal et al. 1995; Snead 1993a, 1993b); the Thar Desert palaeo-lake chronologies from the well-known Didwana locality (Singh et al. 1974; Misra 1995; Wasson et al. 1984) and more recently from Bap-Malar and Thob (Kajale and Deotare 1997); fluvial sequences from the alluvial features and depressions in the Ghaggar-Hakkra (Courty 1995) and relict landforms from the lower Indus (Flam 1993; Jorgenson et al. 1993; Shroder 1993); soil sequences from Harappa (Amundson and Pendall 1991; Pendall and Amundson 1990); and tectonic chronologies from the lower Indus (Jorgenson et al. 1993; Snead 1993a, 1993b). Holocene climatic reconstructions were generated *primarily* from independent palaeo-circulation models (Bryson 1996; Swain et al. 1983; Wasson 1995) and *secondarily* from converging lines of interpretation from both the afore-referenced geomorphic and soils sequences and those from more distant localities. Finally a newly published source of critical palaeoclimatic information for the past 5000 years is the record of laminated (varved) sediments from marine cores taken off the Makran coast (von Rad et al. 1999) (Fig. 5).

Table 1 is instructive for several reasons. First, it surveys the state of Holocene palaeoecological research for each discipline. Second, it facilitates assessments of the reliability of palaeo-circulation models for particular time frames. Proxy climatic interpretations are either bolstered or refuted by reinforcing data sets. It follows that the more data sets that sustain particular environmental trends, the more reliable the palaeo-climatic interpretation for a particular Holocene interval. Finally, it is possible to judge whether or not sufficient palaeo-ecological data has been collected to test environmentally based hypotheses for the rise and fall of Harappan Civilization.

An overview of the individual data sets in Table 1 shows that for most categories, Holocene sequences are grounded on vertical successions at one or two sites. This is especially true for aeolian models, the lacustrine sequences of Rajasthan, and soil chronologies, the latter of which have been established largely at Harappa site and western Nepal (Corvinus 1995). Significantly, both the 10,000 year aeolian and lacustrine successions have been derived from the same general area (north-west India), but interpretations were generated in neighboring but unique (and contrasting) depositional settings. Sequences also cover the general sweep of Holocene time. Coastal and fluvial successions are recorded from a broad range of locations and provide evidence for climatic cycles in the form of discrete transgressive and regressive phases (coastal plains) and cut-and-fill episodes (fluvial behaviour). Finally, while the soil chronologies and tectonic records are incomplete for much of the Holocene, the reasons are different for each category. The literature suggests that minimal work has been done in the area of Holocene palaeopedology across the subcontinent. Quite the opposite is true for structural investigations. Extensive research has been done in the mountainous and piedmont sectors of Pakistan and India. However, the record for the alluvial valleys—and especially for the Early Holocene—is inaccessible because of the sheer volume of Holocene sediment that must be penetrated to reach stratigraphic evidence for structural displacements. An incomplete tectonic chronology impedes efforts is isolate thresholds of environmental change signalled by other indicators.

Unevenness between the individual categories notwithstanding, it is possible to discern converging lines of palaeogeographic evidence. Most striking is the evidence for Early Holocene moisture associated with the establishment of post-Pleistocene monsoon circulation. Reduction in aeolian activity (Ghaggar-Hakkra) is consistent with sequences for renewed alluviation and submerged coastlines for many regions of the subcontinent, highest lake levels in Rajasthan, and subsequent delta progradation as rising base levels reflect stabilization of transgressive coastlines. The formation of the most deeply weathered soil profiles at Harappa (Gamber and Lyallpur soils of Amundson and Pendall 1991) signifies that well drained surfaces flanked the major rivers of the Punjab at that time.

A gradual turn to desiccation, *c.* 7000-6000 BP, may be indicated by resumption of loess sedimentation in the Ghaggar plain, reduction in the scale of alluviation and incision in some of the main river valleys, and stabilization (and initial lowering) of lake levels. Soil chronologies have not been documented for this time frame, although it is not clear whether or not this is a function of increased erosion or insufficient research. Wasson (1995) infers that reduction in lake levels across the southern hemisphere's monsoon belts is proxy evidence for the decline of south-west monsoon intensity coupled with high evapo-transpiration ratios.

For the 2000 years of peak Harappan settlement in South Asia, the palaeo-environmental record is some-what ambiguous. Cessation of dune activity in the Ghaggar-Hakkra and optimal fresh water influx at Didwana and coastal transgressions (+3 to +6 m) may be measures of increased moisture, but such developments as channel avulsion, westward drainage displacement, and abandonment and desiccation of the Ghaggar-Hakkra plain midway through the interval, are more equivocal. Here again, the degree to which tectonics accounts for drainage realignment is both pivotal and uncertain. If extant reconstructions of channel desiccation are correct (Wilhelmy 1969), then the interval 4000-2500 BP resulted in net displacements of flow lines on the order of 100-50 km northward coupled with desiccation in abandoned channel lines. Even extensive structural dislocations should not have resulted in realignments of topography and drainage to such a degree that all signs of hydric conditions in the ancient depressions are absent. Courty's (1995) sedimentological study of the abandoned depressions in the Ghaggar plain argues for reduced seasonal flooding and dune encroachments and a turn to drier conditions, this argument is in opposition to widely held concepts to increased moisture budgets during the Harappan (Singh et al. 1974; Bryson and Swain 1981). Her position is that Harappan environments and rainfall distribution patterns were analogous to those of the present. The argument is compelling insofar as traditional landscape indicators of reduced moisture (i.e. lowered water tables, broader dune expanses) are linked to agricultural practices during the Harappan period. As noted earlier, a major concern in Courty's analysis is the absence of any consideration of tectonic influence as a mechanism accounting for the initial displacement of the drainage lines.

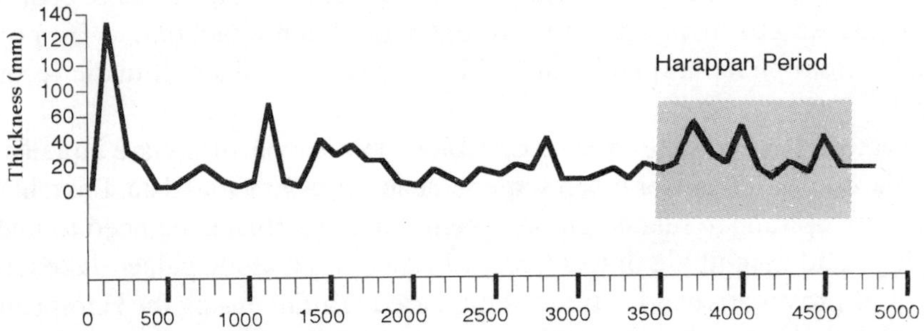

Fig. 5. Late Holocene climatic signals inferred from thickness of Turbidites in Oxygen Minimum Zone, off Pakistan Coast. Note Peaks in Thickness of Turbidite Beds for the Harappan Period (after von Rad et al., 1999).

Von Rad et al.'s (1999) coastal coring project offers new insights to the ambiguous climatic proxy data. The marine cores were used to infer palaeo-climatic conditions based on relative thicknesses of turbidite varves (i.e. continentally derived monsoon deposits); thicker varves signal greater precipitation while thin varve deposits denote less precipitation and drier circulation patterns. Figure 5 shows that during the Harappan period mean varve thickness spiked twice within the period 4000-3500 BP, suggesting that high and widely fluctuating levels of precipitation may have characterized the latter part of the occupation. This may also indicate that the distribution of rainfall or the frequency of overbanking would have accelerated at that time. It is not clear whether or not moister climates are implicated (i.e. varve thickness may also reflect human-induced mobilization of sediment), but precipitation intensities and regimes may have been different then than at any other time. Subsequently, a variety of sources suggest that lower precipitation and drier climates occurred (Table 1). It is therefore possible that increased rainfall may have disrupted water management systems of the Harappan populations and dictated changes to their adaptive strategies.

Depositional records of the past 3000 years suggests that the effects of human modifications to the landscape may have been as critical as any natural processes of sedimentation. Indeed, Courty (1995) notes that human impacts affected broad ecological balances 2000 years earlier (*c.* 5000 BP). The Late Holocene lake records suggest increased desiccation as water levels decrease, while reinitiation of dune activity also points to higher wind activity and less vegetation cover. Shoreline regression (by 2 m) is also consistent with the reduction in available moisture. Von Rad et al. (1999) imply that over the past few thousand years low precipitation values are characteristic and are interspersed with aperiodic surges that have minimal effects because of their limited durations. Palaeo-circulation models argue for high precipitation after 3000 BP, whose effects are tempered by the stabilization of contemporary seasonal rainfall distribution patters. Thus, despite increases in net moisture the distribution of precipitation may have had deleterious environmental effects—for example catastrophic inundations on the order of contemporary monsoon triggered storm floods—that might have been exacerbated by population increases and stress on natural landscapes. Here, again the palaeo-climatic record is not unequivocal.

Archaeologically based assessments of Holocene palaeoecology are equally divided concerning the conflation of Harappan settlement ad environmental data. Possehl's (1997) recent review of Harappan related environmental data reaffirms the need to understand the chronology and magnitude of tectonics, while noting that the palaeo-lake records, in particular, offer provocative indications of increased rainfall during the Harappan period. As discussed below, models of abandonment of Mohenjo Daro are as attributable to tectonically-triggered flooding as they are to climatic mechanisms. Possehl (1997) also notes that following the period of Harappan collapse (after 1750 BC) population expansion outside the Harappan heartland intensified, ironically during a period of presumed desiccation.

Recent research along the buried channel of the Beas river in the upper Indus is suggesting that an optimal method for sorting out landscape histories for the critical Middle Holocene—immediately antecedent to Harappan occupation—is to date and reconstruct alluvial chronologies sealed beneath Harappan mounds (Wright and Schuldenrein 1997, 1998). It is thereby possible to document changing thresholds in stream energy levels and floodplain morphologies, date them, and link them the length of contemporary drainage lines. In this way it may be possible to calibrate the relative impacts of tectonics and climatic mechanisms regionally, thus structuring chronologies for Holocene floodplain transformations.

In summary, the following working hypotheses can be generated Holocene palaeo-landscapes and circulation patterns for the greater Harappan countryside:

(1) Continental and littoral geomorphic histories and soil sequences converge around moister climates during the Early Holocene (*c.* 10,000-7000 BP), during which time post-Pleistocene monsoon circulation patterns were established; they stabilized towards the end of this period;
(2) There is more limited stratigraphic evidence for the lower Middle Holocene, although general indications are that south-west monsoon intensities diminish and drier climatic cycles are initiated (*c.* 7000-5000 BP);
(3) The record for the Middle Holocene contemporaneous with peak Harappan occupation (*c.* 5000-3000 BP) is ambivalent; mechanisms accounting for fluvial cut and fill cycles, moisture budgets, coastal terrace cutting, and aeolian events may reflect tectonic influences and human manipulation of alluvial and even perimeter environments (i.e. due to agricultural practices);
(4) The later Holocene stratigraphic record (< 3000 BP) preserves increasing evidence of anthropogenic sedimentation, underscoring human landscape manipulation; critically, present patterns of rainfall (seasonal precipitation) had been clearly established, although there are some indications of greater precipitation between 3000-2000 BP.

GEOARCHAEOLOGICAL PROFILES OF HARAPPAN SITES

As noted earlier, the scope of geoarchaeology extends beyond the reconstruction of natural environments contemporaneous with site occupation. Geoarchaeology is equally concerned with the processes of site formation itself and particularly with the circumstances surrounding site selection, construction and degradation. Across the Old and New Worlds, urban sites, such as those of the Harappan period, were typically selected for logistic advantages that enabled populations to exploit the broadest and most abundant selection of resources in optimal environments. Once selected, these initial urban sites became magnets for subsequent populations, provided that surrounding resource bases continued to be productive and/or sustain diverse subsistence environments. As archaeological sites, urban locations tended to expand horizontally across the landscape while building up vertically as stacked mounds. In the New World this pattern of site formation has been documented most widely in Mesoamerica and the North American mid-continent where sites are known as pyramids and mounds respectively. Across the Old World the most striking examples of such site development are the tells of the Near East and the mounds of the Indus Valley.

While the broad outlines of urban site morphologies and evolutionary histories have been widely known for years, it is only recently that systematic consideration has been given to rigorous and systematic reconstructions of the linked site formation chronologies, environmental successions, cultural sequences and abandonment histories. The details of site construction and destruction have been the subjects of a variety of recent studies of urban mounds (Davidson 1976; Kirkby and Kirkby 1976; Miller-Rosen 1986).

In the Indus Valley, ongoing excavations at the hub sites of Mohenjo Daro and Harappa have focused on site formation process, but largely within the context of understanding cultural sediments as cornerstones for reconstructing internal site function through time. The studies at Harappa have been especially comprehensive and have allowed for generation of well documented and dated sequences of changing site utilization (Kenoyer 1991a; Wheeler 1968). Investigations at Mohenjo Daro have been largely concerned with recording site architecture and manufacturing (Jansen 1980; 1984; Prachia et al. 1985). At both sites more limited efforts have been directed at addressing such human ecological issues as the environmental context of site selection and utilization. At Mohenjo Daro, however, the causes of site abandonment has been a focus of major research for over thirty years (see Jorgensen et al. 1993, and references).

Limited geoarchaeological methodologies have been applied at both sites and, as discussed below, they address questions in the following categories: (1) landscape chronology; (2) pedo-sedimentary history; (3) site formation models. Unfortunately, while general stratigraphic sequences have been developed for several of the other major Indus settlements, only minimal geoarchaeological work has been applied outside of the two hub settlements.

The following discussion provides a brief overview of the range of geoarchaeological themes that have been addressed at Mohenjo Daro, Harappa and other sites. The objective is to highlight the key questions addressed by investigators applying geoarchaeological methodologies and to assess the nature of their results. It is beyond the scope of this paper to review site excavation results, but these will be abstracted insofar as they bear on geoarchaeological interpretation.

Mohenjo Daro

Geoarchaeological investigations here have centred on two general questions. The first concerns the issue of site abandonment, since early investigators suspected that causes for the demise of Harappan Civilization were related to the precarious exposure of the settlement to the torrential floodwaters of the Indus river. A more recent application is the development of a macrostratigraphic model for the site using sedimentological parameters.

Circumstances surrounding the abandonment of Mohenjo Daro had fascinated researchers who suspected that either the site was flooded out by a series of floods that created a semi-permanent dam or lake or that channel avulsion resulted in lateral channel shifts, thus depleting soil moisture recharge and agricultural productivity of the fields fronting the existing flood plain. Arguments in support of the dam theory were given prominence in the 1960s and 1970s with the identification of alleged alluvial and paludal deposits ranging 8-12 m above the extant floodplain (Raikes 1964, 1965; Dales and Raikes 1977; Raikes and Dales 1977). The causes for this sedimentation pattern was damming of the lower Indus due to tectonism. An alternative hypothesis was proposed by Lambrick (1967) who initially questioned the field relations implicating the presence of the relict dam landform. He argued that the disposition of the deeply stacked fine sands, silts and clays was consistent with aeolian sedimentation. The Raikes' hypothesis has subsequently been questioned on a variety of grounds, most notably the likelihood that the impermeable source alluvium would not have been sufficiently permeable to retain the floodwaters and it would have failed.

Jorgensen et al. (1993) demonstrated that the dynamic of the Indus river was and has been such that channel avulsion is a much more logical explanation for site abandonment. Their arguments lend credence to the Lambrick (1967) interpretation. The identification of relict palaeo-channel forms and levee remnants in lower Sindh bolsters this hypothesis as well (Flam 1993). It is now thought that extensive meandering has resulted in long term displacement of the active Indus channel to its present position, *c.* 25 km south-east of its original course during peak Harappan occupation. As elsewhere, verification of this hypothesis must await both corroborative stratigraphic exploration as well as procurement of radiocarbon dates.

The second application of geoarchaeological methodologies pertains to the development of a working stratigraphy for the entire site. The need for such a sequence is underscored by the fact that culturally sterile deposits have still not been widely recorded at the site. Balista (1985) has undertaken a systematic drilling program to depths in excess of 10 m, and has proposed a limited tri-partite stratigraphy that consists of:

(1) *Low Alluvium*—a basal sediment that marks the interface between the youngest natural flood deposit and the oldest occupation levels.

(2) *Middle Alluvium*—Balista (1985) has postulated that this unit is the equivalent of Raikes' (1964, 1965) 'huge flood' deposits, based on stratigraphic and textural properties. Where this unit is absent the Low Alluvium is covered by alluvial fan or cultural sediments.
(3) *High Alluvium*—Texturally very similar to Low Alluvium and considered to be 'overbank deposits'.

Balista's (1985) focus on alluvial sedimentology led him to refute the Raikes' (1965) 'dam and flood' hypothesis because of a lack of correspondence between mound exposures and Raikes' characterization of 'interbedded flood and construction levels' (at the base of the succession in places). The fluvial sediment characteristics are consistent with those of streams that change course periodically and generally moves to a finer sedimentation regime (silts and clays) near the top of sequence.

Balista's (1985) tri-partite stratigraphy finally provides a provisional baseline for the complex sequence at Mohenjo Daro. However, critical data sets must be collected before a diachronic reconstruction for alluvial history can be assembled. There are few dates for the site as a whole and even fewer have been obtained from environmental samples (i.e. organic mats buried within the alluvium). There is minimal mention made of pedogenic horizons or even an acknowledgement of the need to link alluvial stratigraphies with soils and landforms and to generate a model grounded on converging lines of evidence.

Harappa

Explorations at Harappa began in 1926 and have been ongoing intermittently since that time (see Kenoyer 1991a and references). The site stratigraphy has been a centrepiece for the present series of investigations and it has been continuously updated. It has been known since early in the excavation's history that the site occupies a relict Pleistocene terrace overlooking an abandoned reach of the Ravi river (Whitehead 1932). Several master site sections (Kenoyer 1991a: Figs. 4.5, 4.10, 4.11, 4.14) document the depth of excavation into subcultural deposits in excess of 4 m. Further, preliminary interpretations of the alluvial nature of the contact deposits were proposed by Wheeler (1968) and radiocarbon samples for basal horizons, one of which may preserve a palaeosol, have been recently collected. Kenoyer (1991a) has noted the presence of tiny disc bead indicative of a possible Neolithic component at the site (perhaps equivalent to that a Mehrgarh), but corroborative evidence is lacking.

In addition to the exposure of the pre-Harappan floodplain, a robust of palaeosol mapping was undertaken in the vicinity of the site in the late 1980s by Amundson and Pendall (1991; Pendall and Amundson 1990a, 1990b). Their research produced a map of a series of Holocene soils that effectively ring the site and demarcate the ages and magnitudes of weathering environments radiating away from the mound proper (Amundson and Pendall 1991: Figs. 3 and 4). Their research determined that after stabilization of the Late Pleistocene terrace a succesion of soils formed on varied landscape segments and parent materials tied to the migrating behaviour of the channel and its surrounding floodplain. the oldest (Pleistocene) soils were recognized on the strength of diagnostic Bk soil horizons (with 'kankars') and dated to >7000 BP (albeit on the strength of a single, questionable determination on a carbonate nodule). Pedogenic horizons were utilized to isolate four progressively younger soils at 5000-15,000 BP; 2000-5000 BP; <4500 BP and Recent. Amundson and Pendall (1991) also undertook stable isotope analysis (for carbon and oxygen) offering the possibility that during Harappa times vegetation sustained more extensive tropical grassland covers and that cooler and moister climates may have prevailed.

As at Mohenjo Daro, there is a dearth of radiocarbon dates for the pre-occupation settings at Harappa. Additionally, the thoroughness of the palaeo-pedologic investigations is not paralleled by investigations of the depositional environments in the site vicinity. Thus, while there is an excellent baseline study of the surfaces contemporaneous and even pre-dating the Harappan occupation, there is no information on the changing stream environments during the Middle Holocene. More extensive geomorphological studies are warranted to develop a more comprehensive chronology.

Table 2 is a comparison of the types of geoarchaeological studies that have been undertaken at Mohenjo Daro and Harappa. As shown, research at each site has emphasized different aspects of the stratigraphic and geomorphic records. For example, geomorphic studies have been especially prominent at Mohenjo Daro addressing the questions of ancient hydrology and the impacts of channel migrations on site abandonment. Conversely, soil studies have been emphasized at Harappa, focusing more directly on climatic modelling and the duration of habitable environments contemporaneous with the various occupations of the site. Site formation studies must therefore be structured on the strength of baseline soil chronologies at Harappa and alluvial sequences at Mohenjo Daro.

Other Sites

There are several deep and extensive stratigraphic records for other Harappan sites in the Indus and tributary valleys. Most striking is the sequence from Mehrgarh, in the Kachi Plain, which houses a nearly continuous 8,000 year record of occupation beginning with the non-ceramic Neolithic (Jarrige and Lechevallier 1979). Deposits are preserved in over 11 of deposit including the mound itself and extend into the substrate below the surface of the present floodplain. Other stratified sites that either have Harappan components or contemporaneous deposits include Chirand in the Ganga Valley (>3.5 m of deposit); Balakot on the Makran Coast (>12 m of deposit); and Kot-Diji (4-5 m of alluvium with evidence of interdigitations of cultural fill and alluvium) (Allchin and Allchin 1982). Critical stratigraphic and geomorphic information is preserved at Kalibangan (Thapar 1973), and the Ghaggar-Hakkra complex (Ghosh 1973); for the latter deposits of the abandoned channels of the Sarasvati and Chautang (Drishadvati) have been examined sedimentologically (Courty 1995).

With the exception of the Ghaggar-Hakkra, only minimal geoarchaeological efforts have been undertaken at these site complexes. The varied geomorphic settings of these

TABLE 2: COMPARISON OF GEOARCHAEOLOGICAL STUDIES AT MOHENJO DARO AND HARAPPA

Site	Landscape Chronology	Pedo-sedmintary History	Site Formation Models	Geoarchaeological Assessment
Harappa	Single date pre-dating earliest Harappan remains; comprehensive radiocarbon chronology for site occupation sequence; relative chronology for Late Quaternary cut-fill cycles of Punjab drainages (focused on Ravi river)	Baseline pedological history of site; focus on stable environments punctuated by inferred periods of terrace and floodplain incision-aggradation (no geomorphic work); stable isotope studies for pre-occupation chronology with paleo-climatic implications	Can be inferred by linking Late Quaternary soil formation history with detailed models of site occupation across time and space; site-specific model not yet applied to regional environmental developments	Comprehensive model outlining periods of stability at site; lack of geomorphic reconstructions limits interpretations of Holocene dynamism and interpretations bearing on changing land use and demographics through time
Mohenjo Daro	Earliest absolute dates linked to Mature Harappan, but not tie to Indus alluvial history; no known environmental dates; model of channel migration and pro-deltaic coastal sedimentation of Lower Indus developed for period 4000-2000 BC.	Controversial history based on hydrogeologic models of channel migration and avulsion; direct links to tectonics and/or channel segmentation associated with damming, aeolian deposition; alluvial sediment histories developed; limited pedo-stratigraphy	Derived exclusively from alluvial histories; flooding regimes tied to and agricultural impacts during Late Harappan period; macro-scale models not linked to site-specific stratigraphies	Dominance of long-disputed geomorphic models centered on channel behaviour; no link to radiocarbon chronologies but inferred links to land use histories; very limited soil, sedimentological, and stratigraphic applications in support occupation histories

REFERENCES: Mohenjo Daro: Balista (1990); Cucarzi (1990); Holmes (1968); Flam (1963); Jansen and Urban (1987); Jorgensen et al. (1993); Lambrick (1967); Mackay (1945); Marshall (1931); Raikes (1965); Raikes and Dales (1977, 1986).

Harappa: Amundson and Pendall (1991); Greenman et al. (1967); Kenoyer (1991a, 1991b); Lambrick (1967); Mahr (1986); Mian and Syal (1986); Lambrick (1967); Mackay (1945); Marshall (1931); Raikes (1965); Raikes and Dales (1977, 1986).

sites, ranging from the coast to the interior Indus Plains make these sites optimal locales for comprehensive geoarchaeological investigation. Moreover, the lateral extent and vertical accumulation of debris from some of the key settlements suggest that optimal environmental and site formation information is preserved within the geogenic and anthropogenic sediment matrices associated with the sites and the depositional settings in their immediate environs.

Finally, as noted earlier, the recently published Punjab Survey (upper Indus Basin; *PAS* 1998) has considerable upgraded the data bank for sites in the five rivers vicinity. Ongoing investigations along the buried channel of the Beas emphasize the intimate relationships between site settlement and landscape (Wright and Schuldenrein 1997, 1998). Geoarchaeological research is directed towards reconstruction of ancient channel environments, beginning with subsurface testing of the alluvial deposits immediately underlying buried mounds. In this way, depositional settings as well as stable surfaces can be linked to the length of the drainageway to formulate models of environmental change for the periods leading up to initial settlement of the Punjab. Mound sediments are being examined to document activities and environmental information contemporaneous with occupation, and historic records are being consulted to register activities that resulted in present landscape configurations. A synthesis of these data sources will ultimately produce a systematic reconstruction of human and landscape relationships along this critical segment of the Harappan heartland.

DIRECTIONS FOR FUTURE RESEARCH

Recent advances of Late Quaternary research across the subcontinent have had a ripple effect in our understanding of Middle Holocene landscapes of the Harappan period. To date, most of the palaeo-environmental data has been derived from projects that are not archaeological in scope. While the understanding of Holocene environments has been vastly expanded, the data base remains uneven and the lack of radiometric controls impedes the potential to structure formal sequences.

Nevertheless, it is possible, at this stage, to prioritise those key issues and avenues of research that should be addressed in the immediate future:

(1) Concentrate efforts on reconstructing Middle and Late Holocene environmental events;
(2) Develop a comprehensive alluvial chronology and stratigraphy for the Indus Valley; this would include segmented studies for reaches along both the Upper and Lower basins;
(3) Address the question of climatic *vs.* tectonic forcing in explaining Holocene sequences in alluvial as well as littoral contexts;
(4) Undertake systematic geoarchaeological studies of site formation at Harappan sites flanking major trunk streams; cultural and geological sequences should be examined to isolate the impacts of human activity on Holocene alluvial and landscape stability;
(5) Document the changing balance between dynamic and stable landscapes through systematic studies of Holocene soil formation.

An emphasis on integrated geoarchaeological programmes is pivotal to realizing the research objectives of this programme. The future of Holocene studies across the subcontinent is contingent on inter-disciplinary cooperation between researchers concerned with the advancement of joint cultural and ecological studies.

ACKNOWLEDGEMENTS

I wish to thank individuals whose insights either stimulated or refined the themes presented in this paper. Rita Wright introduced me to broad issues surrounding the environmental archaeology of the Harappan period. Discussion with my colleagues Rafiq Mughal and Afzal Khan identified specific questions in the geoarchaeology of the Punjab that provoked a wider interest in site formation issues in the Indus Valley. I extend my appreciation to Don Thieme and Mark Smith of Geoarchaeology Research Associates for preparing the graphics. Finally, I would like to thank Ravi Korisettar for inviting me to contribute to this volume and for this persistent encouragement. Any shrotcomings are purely my own.

REFERENCES

Abu Bakr, M. and R.O. Jackson 1964. Geological Map of Pakistan. Government of Pakistan and United States Agency for International Development.

Agrawal, D.P. 1992. *Man and Environment in India Though Ages*. New Delhi: Books & Books.

Agrawal, D.P. and R.K. Sood 1982. Ecological Factors and the Harappan Civilization, in *Harappan Civilization: a Contemporary Perspective* (G.L. Possehl Ed.), pp. 223-31. New Delhi: Oxford-IBH and the American Institute of Indian Studies.

Allchin, B. and R. Allchin 1982. *The Rise of Civilization in India and Pakistan.* Cambridge: Cambridge University Press.

Amnundson, R. and E. Pendall 1991. Pedology and Late Quaternary Environments Surrounding Harappa: a Review and Synthesis, in *Harappan Excavations 1986-1990* (R. Meadow Ed.), pp. 13-27. Madison: Prehistory Press.

Baker, V.R., L.L. Ely, Y. Enzel and V.S. Kale 1995. Understanding India's Rivers: Late Quaternary Palaeofloods, Hazard Assessment and Global Change, in *Quaternary Environments and Geoarchaeology of India* (S. Wadia, R. Korisettar and V.S. Kale Eds.), pp. 61-77. Bangalore: Geological Society of India.

Balista, C. 1990. A New Solid-Core Drilling Campaign at Moenjodaro (1985/1986), in *Interim Reports*, Vol. 4 (G. Leonardi Ed.), pp. 69-113. Aachen and Rome: RWTH and IsMEO.

Beg, M.A.A. 1993. Surface Soils and Indus River Sediments, in *Himalaya to the Sea: Geology, Geomorphology and the Quaternary* (J.F. Shroder Ed.), pp. 251-64. London: Routledge.

Belcher, W.R. 1991. Fish Resources in an Early Urban Context at Harappa, in *Harappa Excavations 1986-1990* (R.H. Meadow Ed.), pp. 107-20. Madison: Prehistory Press.

Biswas, S.K. 1987. Regional Tectonic Framework, Structure, and Evolution of the Western Marginal Basins of India, *Tectonophysics* 135: 307-27.

Bowler, J.M., R, Jones and A. Zhisheng 1995. Climatic Change in Asia and the Western Pacific: Its Significance for Greenhouse Scenarios, in *Quaternary Environments and Geoarchaeology of India* (S. Wadia, R. Korisettar and V.S. Kale Eds.), pp. 1-21. Bangalore: Geological Society of India.

Brinkman, R. and M. Rafiq 1971. *Landforms and Soil Parent Materials in West Pakistan*. Lahore: Soil Survey Project of Pakistan.

Bryson, R.A. 1996. Proxy Indications of Holocene Winter Rains in South-West Asia Compared with Simulated Rainfall, in *Third Millenium* BC *Climate Change and Old World Collapse* (H.N. Dalfes, G. Kukla and H. Weiss Eds.), pp. 465-73. NATO ASI Series I. Vol. 49. Berlin: Springer-Verlag.

Bryson, R.A. and A.M. Swain 1981. Holocene Variations of Monsoon Rainfall in Rajasthan, *Quaternary Research* 16: 135-45.

Burnes, A. 1834. *Travels into Bokhara*, 3 vols. London: John Murray.

Butzer, K.W. 1982. *Archaeology as Human Ecology.* New York: Cambridge University Press.

Chamyal, L.S. and S.S. Merh 1995. The Quaternary Formations of Gujarat, in *Quaternary Environments and Geoarchaeology of India* (S. Wadia, R. Korisettar and V.S. Kale Eds.), pp. 246-57. Bangalore: Geological Society of India.

Chawla, S., R.P. Dhir and A.K. Singhvi 1991. Thermoluminescence Chronology of Sand Profiles in the Thar Desert and their Implications, *Quaternary Science Review* 11: 25-32.

Corvinus, G. 1995. Quaternary Stratigraphy of the Intermontane Dun Valleys of Dang-Deokhuri and Associated Prehistoric Settlements in Western Nepal, in *Quaternary Environments and Geoarchaeology of India* (S. Wadia, R. Korisettar and V.S. Kale Eds.), pp. 124-49. Bangalore: Geological Society of India.

Courty, M.A. 1995. Late Quaternary Environments Changes and Natural Constraints to Ancient Land Use (Northwest India), in *Ancient Peoples and Landscapes* (E. Johnson Ed.), pp. 105-26. Lubbock: Museum of Texas Tech University.

Cucarzi, M. 1990. An Integrated Programme of Geophysical Prospectings at Moenjodaro, in *Interim Reports,* Vol. 4 (G. Leonardi Ed.), pp. 13-49. Aachen and Rome: RWTH and IsMEO.

Cunningham, A. 1875. Harappa, *Archaeological Survey of India, Report 1872-73:* 105-8.

Dales, G.F. and R.L. Raikes 1977. The Mohenjo-daro Floods: a Rajoinder, *American Anthropologist* 70: 957-61.

Dames, M.L. 1886. Old Seals Found at Harappa, *The Indian Antiquary* 15: 1.

Davidson, D.A. 1976. Processes of Tell Formation and Erosion, in *Geoarchaeology: Earth Science and the Past* (D.A. Davidson and M.L. Shackley Eds.), pp. 255-66. London: Duckworth.

Deotare, B.C., M.D. Kajale, A.A. Kshirsagar and S.N. Rajaguru 1998. Geoarchaeological and Palaeoenvironmental Studies Around Bap-Malar Playa, District Jodhpur, Rajasthan, *Current Science* 75 (3): 316-20.

Flam, L. 1993. Fluvial Geomorphology of the Lower Indus Basin (Sindh, Pakistan) and the Indus Civilization, in *Himalaya to the Sea: Geology, Geomorphology and the Quaternary* (J.F. Shroder Ed.), pp. 265-87. London: Routledge.

Gardner, R.A.M. and H. Martingell 1990. Microlithic Sites and Their Palaeoenvironmental Setting, Southeast India: a Re-evaluation, *Geoarchaeology* 5: 1-13.

Ghosh, A. 1973. *The City in Early Historical India*. Simla: Indian Institute of Advanced Study.

Greenman, D.W., W.V. Swarzenski and G.D. Bennett 1967. *Geological Survey Water-Supply Paper 1608-H.* U.S. Government Printing Office.

Haghipour, A., M. Ghorashi and M.H. Kadjar 1984. *Seismotectonic Map of Iran, Afghanistan, and Pakistan.* Tehran: Geological Survey of Iran.

Holmes, D.A. 1968. The Recent History of the Indus, *Geographical Journal* 134: 367-81.

Jansen, M. 1980. Public Spaces in the Urban Settlements of the Harappa Culture, in *Art and Archaeological Research Papers*, Vol. 14 (D. Jones and G. Michell Eds.), pp. 11-19. London.

——— 1984. Architectural Remains in Mohenjo-Daro, in *Frontiers of the Indus Civilization* (B.B. Lal and S.P. Gupta Eds.), pp. 75-88. Delhi: Books & Books.

Jansen, M. and G. Urban (Eds.) 1987. *Interim Reports*, Vol. 2. Aachen and Rome: RWTH and IsMEO.

Jarrige, J.F. and M. Lechevallier 1979. Excavations at Mehrgarh, Baluchistan: Their Significance in the Prehistorical Context of the Indo-Pakistani Borderlands, in *South Asian Archaeology* 1977 (M. Taddei Ed.), pp. 463-535. Naples: Isituto Universitario Orientale.

Jorgensen, D.W., M.D. Harvey, S.A. Schumm and L. Flam 1993. Morphology and Dynamics of the Indus River: Implications for the Mohen Jo Daro Site, in *Himalaya to the Sea: Geology, Geomorphology and the Quaternary* (J.F. Shroder Ed.), pp. 288-326. London: Routledge.

Juyal, N., R.K. Pant, R. Bhushan and B.L.K. Somayajulu 1995. Radiometric Dating of Late Quaternary Sea Levels of the Saurashtra Coast, Western India: an Experiment with Oyster and Clam Shells, in *Quaternary Environments and Geoarchaeology of India* (S. Wadia, R. Korisettar and V.S. Kale Eds.), pp. 372-9. Bangalore: Geological Society of India.

Kajale, M.D. and B.C. Deotare 1997. Late Quaternary Environmental Studies on Salt Lakes in Western Rajasthan, India: a Summarized View, *Journal of Quaternary Science* 12 (5): 405-12.

Kazmi, A.H. 1984. Geology of the Indus Delta, in *Marine Geology and Oceanography of Arabian Sea and Coastal Pakistan* (B.U. Haq and J.D. Milliman Eds.), pp. 71-84. New York: Van Nostrand Reinhold.

Kazmi, A.H. and R.A. Rana 1982. *Tectonic Map of Pakistan.* Quetta: Geological Survey of Pakistan.

Kenoyer, J.M. 1991a. Urban Process in the Indus Tradition: a Preliminary Model from Harappa, in *Harappa Excavations 1986-1990: a Multidisciplinary Approach to Third Millennium Urbanism* (R.H. Meadow Ed.), pp. 29-60. Madison: Prehistory Press.

——— 1991b. The Indus Tradition of Pakistan and Western India, *Journal of World Prehistory* 5 (4): 331-85.

Khan, F.K. 1991. *Geography of Pakistan*. Oxford: Oxford University Press.

Kirkby, A. and M.J. Kirkby 1976. Geomorphic Processes and the Surface Survey of Archaeological Sites in Semi-Arid Areas, in *Geoarchaeology: Earth Science and the Past* (D.A. Davidson and M.L. Shackley Eds.), pp. 229-53. London: Duckworth.

Korisetter, R. 1979. Prehistory and Geomorphology of the Middle Krishna, Karnataka. Ph.D. Dissertation. Pune: University of Poona.

Kutzbach, J.E. and P.J. Gutter 1986. The Influence of Changing Orbital Parameters and Surface Boundary Conditions on Climate Simulations for the Past 18,000 Years, *Journal of Atmospheric Sciences* 43 (16): 17-26.

Lambrick, H.T. 1967. The Indus Flood-Plain and the 'Indus' Civilization, *The Geographical Journal* 133: 483-95.

——— 1975. *Sind: a Generation Introduction*. Hyderabad: Sindhi Akabi Board.

Mackay, D. 1945. Ancient River Beds and Dead Cities, *Antiquity* 19: 135-44.

Mahr, B.S. 1986. *Geomorphology of the Ravi River*. New Delhi: Inter-India Publications.

Marathe, A. 1995. Prehistory and Quaternary Sea Level Changes Along the West Coast of India: a Summary, in *Quaternary Environments and Geoarchaeology of India* (S. Wadia, R. Korisettar and V.S. Kale Eds.), pp. 405-13. Bangalore: Geological Society of India.

Marshall, J. 1931. *Mohenjo-Daro and the Indus Civilization*. London: Arthur Probsthain.

Masson, C. 1844. *A Narrative of Various Journeys in Baluchistan, Afghanistan and the Punjab*, 3 vols. London: Richard Bently.

McClure, H.A. 1976. Radiocarbon Chronology of Late Quaternary Lakes in the Arabian Desert, *Nature* 263: 755.

Meadow, R. 1991. Faunal Remains and Urbanism at Harappa, in *Harappa Excavations 1986-1990* (R.H. Meadow Ed.), pp. 89-106. Madison: Prehistory Press.

Mian, M.A. and M.N. Syal 1986. Geomorphology of Pakistan, in *Proceedings of the XII International Forum on Soil Taxonomy and Agrotechnology Transfer, Pakistan* (M. Ahmad, M. Akram, M.S. Baig, M.Y. Javed and Riaz-ul-Amin Eds). Lahore: Director General, Soil Survey of Pakistan.

Miller, H.M.L. 1991. Urban Palaeoethnobotany at Harappa, in *Harappa Excavations 1986-1990* (R.H. Meadow Ed.), pp. 121-6. Madison: Prehistory Press.

Miller-Rosen, A. 1986. *Cities of Clay: the Geoarchaeology of Tells*. Chicago: The University of Chicago Press.

Mishra, S. 1995. Prehistoric and Quaternary Studies at Nevasa: the Last Forty Years, in *Quaternary Environments and Geoarchaeology of India* (S. Wadia, R. Korisettar and V.S. Kale Eds.), pp. 324-32. Bangalore: Geological Society of India.

Misra, V.N. 1995. Evolution of Environment and Culture in the Rajasthan Desert during the Late Quaternary, in *Ancient Peoples and Landscapes* (E. Johnson Ed.), pp. 77-104. Lubbock: Museum of Texas Tech University.

Mughal, M.R. 1981. New Archaeological Evidence from Bahawalpur, in *Indus Civilization: New Perspectives* (A.H. Dani Ed.), pp. 33-42. Islamabad: Quaid-i-Azam University.

——— 1997. *Ancient Cholistan: Archaeology and Architecture.* Lahore: Ferozsons (Pvt.) Ltd.

Nigam, R. and N.H. Hashimi 1995. Marine Sediments and Palaeoclimatic Variations Since the Late Pleistocene: an Overview for the Arabian Sea, in *Quaternary Environments and Geoarchaeology of India* (S. Wadia, R Korisettar and V.S. Kale Eds.), pp. 380-90. Bangalore: Geological Society of India.

Pappu, R.S. 1974. *Pleistocene Studies in the Upper Krishna Basin*. Pune: Deccan College.

——— 1995. The Contribution of the East Sciences to the Development of Indian Archaeology, in *Quaternary Environments and Geoarchaeology of India* (S. Wadia, R. Korisettar and V.S. Kale Eds.), pp. 414-34. Bangalore: Geological Society of India.

PAS 1998. *Punjab Archaeological Survey.* Lahore: Government of Pakistan.

Pendall, E. and R. Amundson 1990a. Soil/Landform Relationships Surrounding the Harappa Archaeological Site, Pakistan, *Geoarchaeology* 5: 301-22.

——— 1990b. The Stable Isotope Chemistry of Pedogenic Carbonate in an Alluvial Soil from the Punjab, *Soil Science* 149: 199-211.

Possehl, G.L. 1991. A Short History of Archaeological Discovery at Harappa, in *Harappa Excavations 1986-1990: A Multidisciplinary Approach to Third Millennium Urbanism* (R.H. Meadow Ed.), pp. 5-11. Madison: Prehistory Press.

——— 1997. Climate and the Eclipse of the Ancient Cities of the Indus, in *Third Millennium BC Climate Change and Old World Collapse* (H.N. Dalfes, G. Kukla and H. Weiss Eds.), pp. 193-243. NATO ASI Series. Berlin: Springer.

Possehl, G.L, and M.H. Raval 1989. *Harappan Civilization and Rojdi.* New Delhi: Oxford-IBH.

Pracchia, S., M. Tosi and M. Vidale 1985. On the Type, Distribution and Extent of Craft Industries at Mohenjo-daro, in *South Asian Archaeology* 1983 (J. Schotsmans and M. Taddei Eds.), pp. 207-47. Naples: Istituto Universitario Orientale.

Raikes, R.L. 1964. The End of the Ancient Cities of the Indus, *American Anthropologist* 66: 284-99.

——— 1965. The Mohenjo-daro Floods, *Antiquity* 155: 196-203.

Raikes, R.L. and G.F. Dales 1977. The Mohenjo-daro Floods Reconsidered, *Journal of the Palaeontological Society of India* 20: 251-60.

——— 1986. Resposte to Watson's Sedimentological Basis of the Mohenjo-Daro Flood Hypothesis, *Man and Environment* X: 33-4.

Ramage, C.S. 1971. *Monsoon Meteorology.* New York: Academic Press.

Sarma, A.V.N. 1971. Decline of Harappan Culture: a Re-Look, in *K.A. Nilakantashastri Felicitation Volume*, pp. 288-98. Madras: Felicitation Committee.

Schumm, S.A. 1977. *The Fluvial System.* New York: John Wiley and Sons.

Seth, S.K. 1978. The Desiccation of the Thar Desert and its Environs During the Proto-Historical and Historical Periods, in *The Environmental History of the Near and Middle East* (W.C. Birce Ed.), pp. 279-305. London: Academic Press.

Shroder, J.F. 1993. Himalaya to the Sea: Geomorphology and the Quaternary of Pakistan in the Regional Context, in *Himalaya to the Sea: Geology, Geomorphology and the Quaternary* (J.F. Shroder Ed.), pp. 1-42. London: Routledge.

Singh, G., R.D. Joshi, S.K. Chopra and A.B. Singh 1974. Late Quaternary History of Vegetation and Climate of the Rajasthan Desert, India, *Philosophical Transactions of the Royal Society of London* B 267: 467-501.

Singh, G., R.D. Joshi and A.B. Singh 1972. Stratigraphic and Radiocarbon Evidence for the Age and Development of Three Salt Lake Deposits in Rajasthan, India, *Quaternary Research* 2: 496-505.

Singh, G., R.J. Wasson and D.P. Agrawal 1990. Vegetational and Seasonal Climatic Changes Since the Last Full Glacial in the Thar Desert, Northwestern India, *Review of Paleobotany and Palynology* 64: 351-8.

Singhvi, A.K., Y.P. Sharma and D.P. Agrawal 1982. Thermoluminescence Dating of Sand Dunes in Rajasthan, India, *Nature* 295: 313-15.

Snead, R.J. 1993a. Geography, Geomorphic Process and Effects on Archaeological Sites on the Makran Coast, in *Himalaya to the Sea: Geology, Geomorphology and the Quaternary* (J.F. Shroder Ed.), pp, 363-78. London: Routledge.

——— 1993b. Uplifted Marine Terraces along the Makran Coast of Pakistan and Iran, in *Himalaya to the Sea: Geology, Geomorphology and the Quaternary* (J.F. Shroder Ed.), pp. 288-326. London: Routledge.

Snelgrove, A.K. 1967. *Geohydrology of the Indus River, West Pakistan*. Hyderabad: Sindh University Press.

Stuiver, M., A. Long and R.S. Kra 1993. Calibration 1993, *Radiocarbon* 35: 1-244.

Swain, A.M., J.E. Kutzbach and S. Hastenrath 1983. Estimates of Holocene Precipitation for Rajasthan, India, Based on Pollen and Lake-Level Data, *Quaternary Research* 19: 1-17.

Taylor, R.E. 1997. Radiocarbon Dating, in *Chronometric Dating in Archaeology* (R.E. Taylor and M.J. Aitken Eds.), pp. 65-96. New York: Plenum Press.

Thapar, B.K. 1973. New Traits of the Indus Civilization at Kalibangan; an Appraisal, in *South Asian Archaeology 1971* (N. Hammond Ed.), pp. 85-104. London: Duckworth.

Von Rad, U., R. Schaaf, K.H. Michels, H. Schulz, W.H. Berger and F. Sirocko 1999. A 5000-yr Record of Climate Change in Varved Sediments from the Oxygen Minimum Zone Off Pakistan, Northeastern Arabian Sea, *Quaternary Research* 51 (1): 39-53.

Wadia, S., R. Korisettar and V.S. Kale (Eds.) 1995. *Quaternary Environments and Geoarchaeology of India Essays in Honour of Professor S.N. Rajaguru*. Bangalore: Geological Society of India.

Wasson, R.J. 1995. The Asian Monsoon During the Late Quaternary: a Test of Orbital Forcing and Palaeoanalogue Forecasting, in *Quaternary Environments and Geoarchaeology of India* (S. Wadia, R. Korisettar and V.S. Kale Eds.), pp. 22-35. Bangalore: Geological Society of India.

Wasson, R.J., S.N. Rajaguru, V.N. Misra, D.P. Agrawal, R.P. Dhir, A.K. Singhvi and K.K. Rao 1983. Geomorphology, Late Quaternary Stratigraphy and Palaeoclimatology of the Thar Dunefield, *Zeitschrift für Geomorphologie, Supplementband* 45: 117-51.

Wasson, R.J., G.I. Smith and D.P. Agrawal 1984. Late Quaternary Sediments, Minerals and Inferred Geochemical History of Didwana Lake, Thar Desert, India (1984), *Palaeogeography, Palaeoclimatology, Palaeoecology* 4: 345-72.

Waters, M.R. 1999. Book Review of Geoarchaeology: the Earth Science Approach to Archaeological Interpretation edited by George Rapp, Jr. and Christopher L. Hill 1998. Yale University Press, and Geological Methods for Archaeology edited by Norman Herz and Ervan G. Garrison 1997. Oxford University Press, *Geoarchaeology* 14 (3): 365-9.

Wheeler, M. 1968. *The Indus Civilization.* 3rd Edition. Cambridge: Cambridge University Press.

Whitehead, R.B. 1932. The River Courses of the Punjab and Sind, *Indian Antiquary* LXI: 163-9.

Wilhelmy, H. 1969. Das Urstromtal am Ostrand der Indusbene und das Sarasvati-Problem, *Zeitschrift für Geomorphologie, Supplementband* 8: 76-93.

Williams, M.A.J. and M.F. Clarke 1995.Quaternary Geology and Prehistoric Environments in the Son and Belan Valleys, North Central India, in *Quaternary Environments and Geoarchaeology of India* (S. Wadia, R. Korisettar and V.S. Kale Eds.), pp. 282-308. Bangalore: Geological Society of India.

Wright, R. and J. Schuldenrein 1997. Satellite Communities in the Harappa Countryside. Paper Presented at the 62nd Annual Meeting of the Society for American Archaeology.

——— 1998. Conditions of Growth and Settlement Interaction in the Indus Valley Civilization. Paper Presented at the 97th Annual Meeting of the American Anthropological Association.

Deciphering the Indus Script

R.A.E. CONINGHAM

INTRODUCTION

The three greatest obstacles facing any prospective decipherer of the Indus script are the absence of bilingual examples, the lack of knowledge of language which is depicted, and the shortness of individual extant examples—the longest being only 26 signs long. The known corpus consists of some 3,700 legible inscriptions distributed over an enormous area of southern Asia, from the Ganga-Yamuna Doab in the east to the Euphrates in the west, and from the Oxus in the north to Arabian Sea in the south, with an understandably higher concentration within the north-west of the Indian subcontinent—the heartland of the Indus Civilization itself (Fig. 1). The inscriptions between 170 and 220 consist of simple signs and between 170 and 200 composite signs and are found on a wide variety of raw materials ranging between steatite, marble, calcite, limestone, silver, copper, faience, terracotta, ceramic, shell, bone and ivory. Moreover, whilst some of the raw materials were inscribed with the Indus signs, others were stamped, or even cast, providing a bewildering variety. For example, there are examples of signs being both inscribed on ceramics before they were fired, as well as later being scratched on after firing. This variety is also found within the corpus of objects bearing the inscriptions. These objects range from inscribed seals, tablets, tools, vessels, bangles, ladles and other objects to sealings and mouldings. Perhaps the most remarkable recent addition to the corpus was the discovery of the Dholavira 'signboard', consisting of nine signs, each measuring 37 cm high and 27 cm wide (Bisht 1991). In addition to the signs many examples are provided with a single standing animal, whilst a smaller number appear to depict scenes of a more narrative nature. Some of the single animals are clearly recognizable as elephants, rhinoceros or bulls, whilst others are hybrid or composite. Apparently in general use for only 500 years, the complexity of the Indus script, combined with the three aforementioned obstacles, has bedeviled attempts at decipherment since its first discovery at the site of Harappa by Cunningham in 1872. Rather than describing each of these attempts, as has already been done elsewhere (Possehl 1996), the intention of this paper is, firstly, to identify common ground between such attempts, secondly, to discuss the controversial debate concerning the script's language, and, finally, to propose a common route forward.

THE COMMON GROUND

In 1994 Asoka Parpola, chief editor of the encyclopaedic *Corpus of Indus Seals and Inscriptions* (Joshi and Parpola 1987; Shah and Parpola 1991), published a book titled *Deciphering the Indus Script* (Parpola 1994). The result of over a quarter of a century's

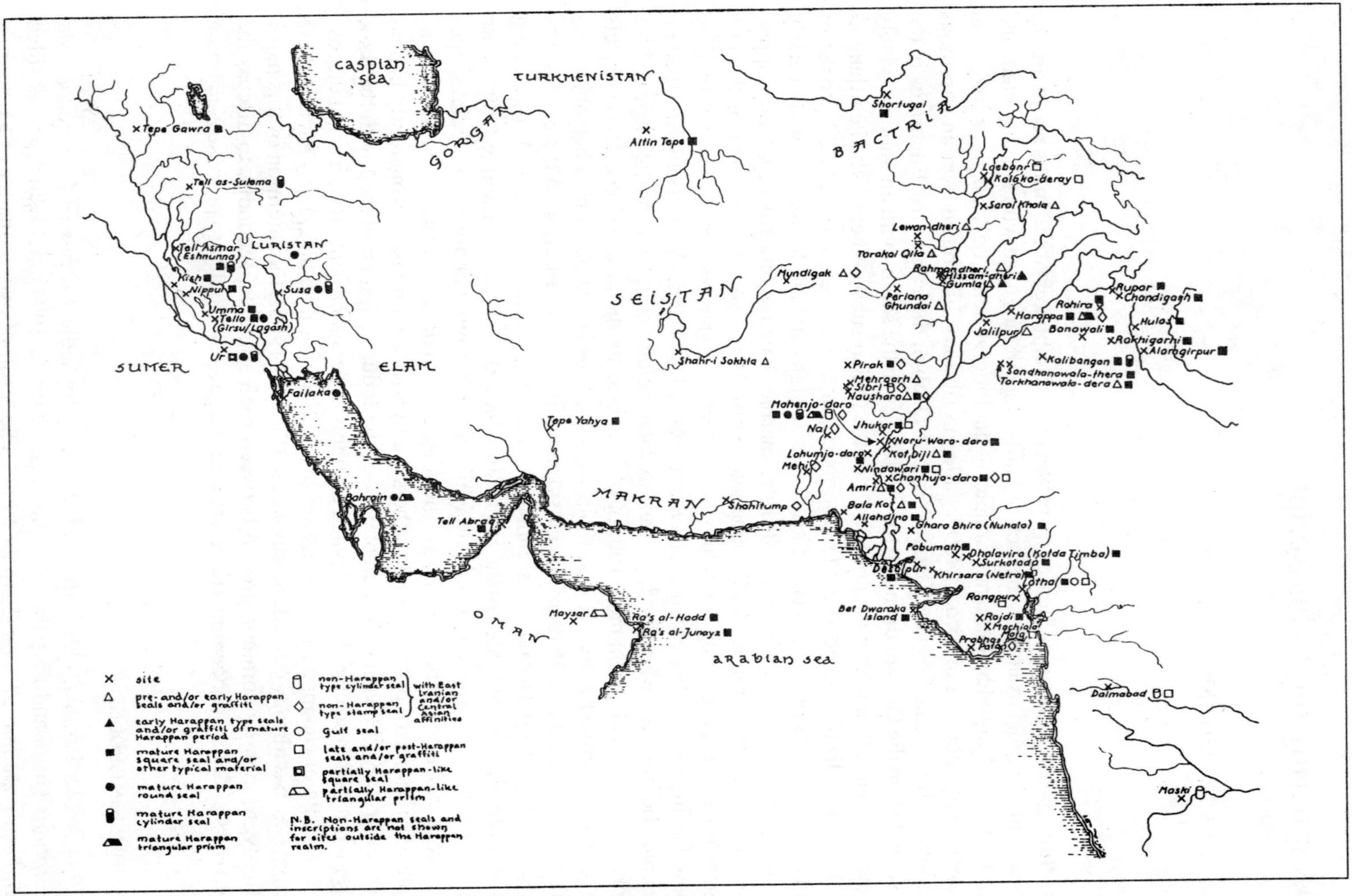

Fig. 1. Distribution map of Indus seals and inscriptions (after Parpola 1994:10).

research by a team of Finnish Vedic scholars, Assyriologists and computer scientists, it has been widely recognized by many reviewers as a major step towards the understanding of this previously undeciphered script (Coe 1995; Edens 1995; Mahadevan 1997). Although there is still debate as to the success of Parpola's 24 attempted readings, the book is extremely useful as it clearly defines a number of widely shared conclusions concerning basic typological features of the Indus script such as the direction of writing and recognition of numerals. One of the most generally accepted common points is that the script was written from right to left, although clearly stamps and moulds were written in reverse (Alekseev 1976; Gadd 1931; Hunter 1934; Lal 1966; Mahadevan 1977; Parpola 1994; Ross 1938; Zvelebil 1970). Evidence for such agreement is taken from the common cramping of signs at the left side of seals (Gadd 1931), the clear overlapping of signs on ceramic vessels inscribed prior to firing (Lal 1966) and the comparison between single-line and two-line sequences of identical inscriptions (Mahadevan 1977). It is apparent that the vast majority of examples are written from right to left, but it should be noted that almost 7 per cent are written from left to right (ibid.), a factor often interpreted a scribal error. It is generally agreed that numerical value signs are indicated by strokes, short in earlier examples and long in later ones (Fairservis 1992; Kinnier Wilson 1974; Mahadevan 1988; Mitchener 1978; Newberry 1980; Ross 1938; Wadell 1925) (Fig. 2), and as such strokes often occur with groups of semi-circles it has also been assumed that the latter represent 'tens' (Mahadevan 1988: 14; Parpola 1994: 82-3) (Fig. 3). Mahadevan has further suggested that whilst the largest identified numbers using this system are 35 and 76, it is possible that higher value signs have not yet been identified (Mahadevan 1988: 14). Whilst many would accept such value hypotheses, the underlying numerical system is still in debate. In the 1940s Ross suggested the presence of two numerical systems, one with a base ten and another with a base eight (Ross 1938:16), but Fairservis (1992) suggested a base eight (Fairservis 1992: 61) and Mahadevan a decimal base

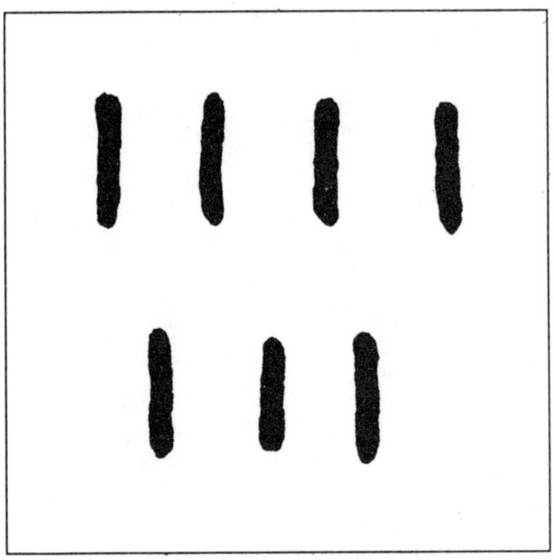

Fig. 2. Indus numerical value sign representing 7.

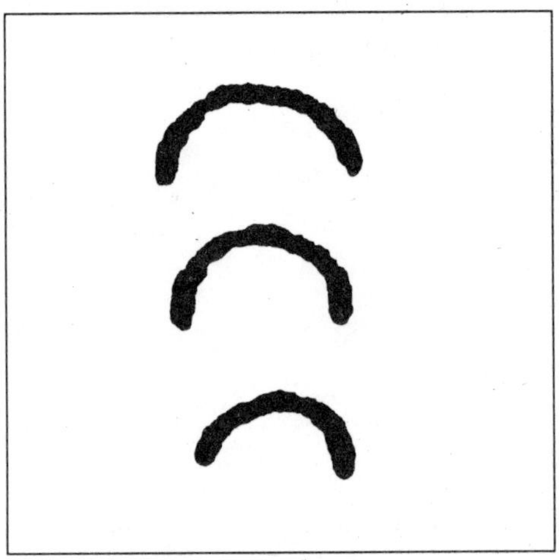

Fig. 3. Indus numerical value sign representing 30.

(Mahadevan 1988:14). Rather than any one suggestion being correct, it is quite possible that all are correct as Harappan weights indicate a mixed system, based upon binary, octonary and decimal bases (Marshall 1931).

Although some scholars have suggested that the Indus script was picto-phonographic (Heras 1953) or alphabetic (Rao 1982), Zvelebil has suggested that there is also broad support for the identification of the script as logo-syllabic possessing word-signs and phonetic syllables (Mahadevan 1988: 8; Parpola 1994:102; Zvelebil 1970: 195). One of the clearest explanations of such a suggestion is provided by Mahadevan (1988) (Table 1). He starts by identifying the four major types of ancient scripts, logo-graphic, logo-syllabic, syllabic and alphabetic (ibid. 5). The first used word-signs, the second used both word signs and phonetic syllables, the third either open syllables or open and closed syllables and the fourth single-sound signs. As such scripts are generally distinguished by the total number of signs used, he concludes that the Indus script's approximate 425 signs are logo-syllabic as logo-graphic used thousands of signs, logo-syllabic used between 900 and 400, closed and open syllabic between 200 and 100, open syllabic between 100 and 40 and alphabetic below 40 (ibid.). Even within this common ground there are a number of disagreements, for example, there is much debate as to the meaning of the signs, in that some may be phonographic and some pictograms may only be understood through the use of homophones—words pronounced the same but with different meanings (ibid. 14). Thus Parpola interprets the Indus fish sign (Fig. 4) through the use of the homophone that in Dravidian and *Proto-Dravidian languages the word fish, or **min*, also means star or planet (Parpola 1994: 180), a link already made by Heras (1953). Such debate may also be characterized by the different interpretations ascribed by different decipherers to the Indus sign (Fig. 5), number 342 of Mahadevan's concordance (Mahadevan 1977). This sign is the most commonly occurring within the Indus

TABLE 1: THE NUMBER AND TYPE OF SIGNS WITHIN ANCIENT SCRIPTS (after Mahadevan 1988: 5)

No.	Type of Scripts	Type of Signs	Total number of Signs	Examples
I	logo-graphic	word-signs	thousands	Chinese
II	logo-syllabic	word signs and phonetic syllables	900-400	Sumerian Egyptian Hittite
III	syllabic	(a) closed and open syllables	200-100	Elamite Cuneiform
		(b) open syllables	100-40	Linear B Old Persian
IV	alphabetic	single sound signs	< 40	Semitic Ugaritic Greek Latin

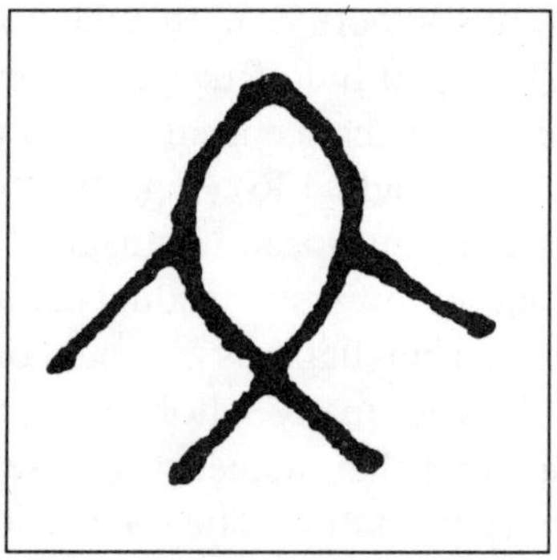

Fig. 4. Indus 'fish' sign.

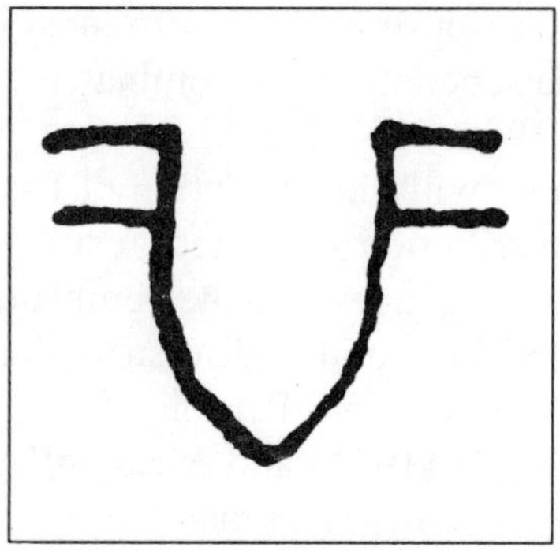

Fig. 5. Indus 'vessel' sign.

script and has been found in more than 1,000 examples and is thus a crucial element for our understanding of the script. Hrozny interpreted it as a sign for a vessel dedicated to a god or gods (Hrozny 1953: 175) and Lal agreed that it was probably derived from a portrayal of a vessel (Lal 1974: 176). Newberry, however, interpreted it as representing the western cardinal direction (Newberry 1980: 4-7), Kak as the sound 'sa' (Kak 1988: 138) and Fairservis as a third person singular honorific (Fairservis 1992: 173). Knorozov, following Heras (1953: 67), has interpreted the sign as a genitive and locative suffix (Knorozov 1976: 60), and Parpola interpreted this sign in 1969 as a ship (Parpola 1969: 21) and in 1994 as 'a title of respect commonly added to proper names, whether human or divine' (Parpola 1994: 97). He also suggested that such a hypothesis did not necessarily exclude the sign from representing a possessive marker (ibid.) and stated that it was probably derived from either the iconic meanings of 'bird', 'eagle', or 'to fly' (ibid.: 104) or a cow's head (ibid.)—for further interpretations see the excellent commentary by B.B. Lal (1979).

THE LINGUISTIC DEBATE

Whilst many of the above points are generally agreed, there is an underlying issue which has had powerful repercussions in terms of almost all studies of the Harappan or Indus Civilization—its language! Almost all the attempts at decipherment may be characterized into two main groups. Those who favour a Dravidian language (Heras 1953; Zide and Zvelebil 1976; Mahadevan 1988; Fairservis 1992; Parpola 1994) and those who favour an Indo-European one (Mitchiner 1978; Krishna Rao 1982, Rao 1982; Kak 1988; Priyanka and Manatunga 1988), notwithstanding earlier attempts to ascribe the script to a Sumerian language (Waddell 1925). It is also interesting to note that the selection of either of these two language families has been debated since the 1930s with Langdon attributing an Indo-Aryan language (1931) and Marshall a Dravidian one (1931) in the same volume. Respective decipherers have marshalled linguistic and archaeological evidence to support such claims with varying success. The linguistic evidence relies heavily upon two elements of data, firstly, the present distribution of these two language families in southern Asia, and secondly, a number of the typological characteristics of the Indus script. It is clear from most linguistic maps of southern Asia that the northern part of the subcontinent is dominated by a very broad sweep of Indo-European languages (Parpola 1994: 135) (Fig. 6) and that Dravidian languages are concentrated in the peninsular proper with the exception of Brahui in Baluchistan (ibid.: 136) (Fig. 7). That this overall distribution is a direct result of the influx of Indo-European languages forcing Dravidian languages into the peninsula and that Brahui represents a residual element of a once subcontinental-wide distribution of such Dravidian languages is accepted by most scholars (Heras 1953; Parpola 1994; Possehl 1996). Indeed, many scholars would also accept Stein's (1931) and Marshall's (1924) premise that they actually represented a fossil group of the Harappan Civilization itself, as Parpola states, 'The conclusion that the Brahui ... represent remnants of the language spoken by the descendants of the Early Harappan populations of Baluchistan is supported by the evidence' (Parpola 1994: 166-7). It has also been argued by a number of scholars that the Indus script has typological features, which are found in Dravidian languages but not within Indo-European ones (Parpola 1994; Zide and Zvelebil 1976; Mahadevan 1988; Fairservis 1992), thus strengthening the case for a Dravidian reading of the Indus script.

Such theories are, however, based upon two assumptions, firstly, the post-Urban Harappan arrival of Indo-Aryan languages, and secondly, the arrival of those languages in South Asia via the media of a diffusion of a new population. Evidence for the former assumption has clearly been seriously challenged by research conducted by Elfenbein, suggesting that far from representing a fossil remnant of a wider, Chalcolithic spread of Dravidian languages Brahui is most likely to be relatively late, first millennium AD language spread from western India (Elfenbein 1987). Furthermore, there have been a number of recent suggestions that there was a Neolithic, as opposed to a Chalcolithic, diffusion of Indo-European languages (Renfrew 1987). Renfrew's core hypothesis accepts the point made by most linguists and archaeologists that such an arrival of new languages brought by new people must be visible in the archaeological record, but argues that the most obvious discontinuity in the cultural record is the Neolithic rather than the Chalcolithic (Fig. 8). He thus argues that a Neolithic demic diffusion brought Indo-Aryan languages to South Asia (ibid.: 189-97), thus perhaps explaining the presence of apparent 'Vedic' elements within the Harappan Civilization such as the Kalibangan hearths, yogic postures and lingas (Allchin and Allchin 1982: 303). Most advocates of the Dravidian language hypothesis evaluate the possibility of an earlier presence of Indo-European languages within South Asia, but summarily dismiss the question of Austro-Asiatic and Sino-Tibetan language families (Parpola 1994: 137-42). However, both Bellwood and Higham have argued for a Neolithic demic diffusion from China into eastern and northern India as reflected in contemporary linguistic patterns (Bellwood 1995; Higham 1995). Parpola has dismissed the suitability of Austro-Asiatic as a candidate for the language of the Indus script as he states that it probably extended no further than the Ganga-Yamuna Doab (Parpola 1994: 140). He also postulates a link between the northern, or Kashmir-Swat, Neolithic with Sino-Tibetan languages (ibid.:142), suggesting that this language group was spoken across the entire northern edge of the Harappan Civilization from

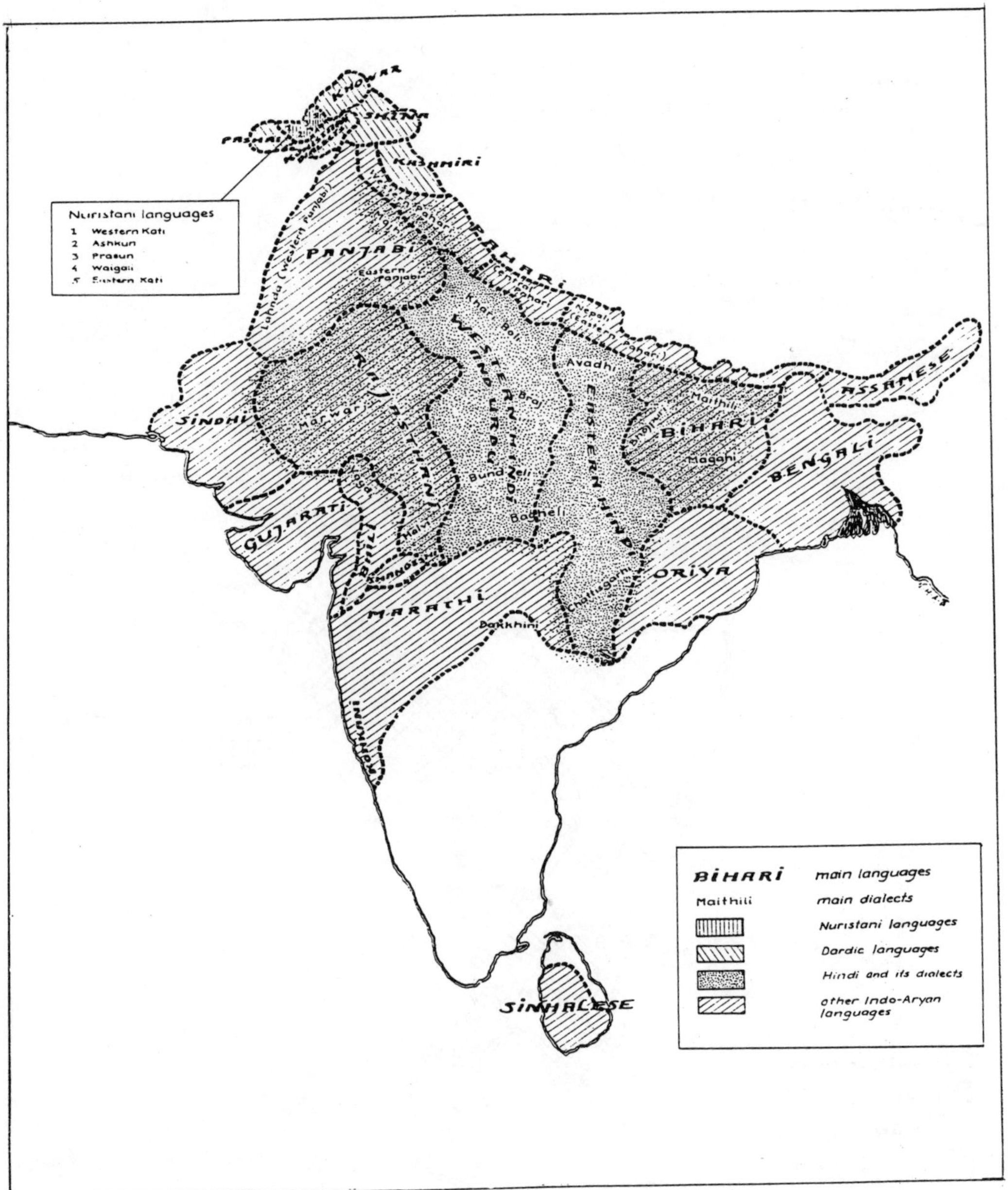

Fig. 6. Distribution map of Indo-European languages within South Asia (after Parpola 1994: 135).

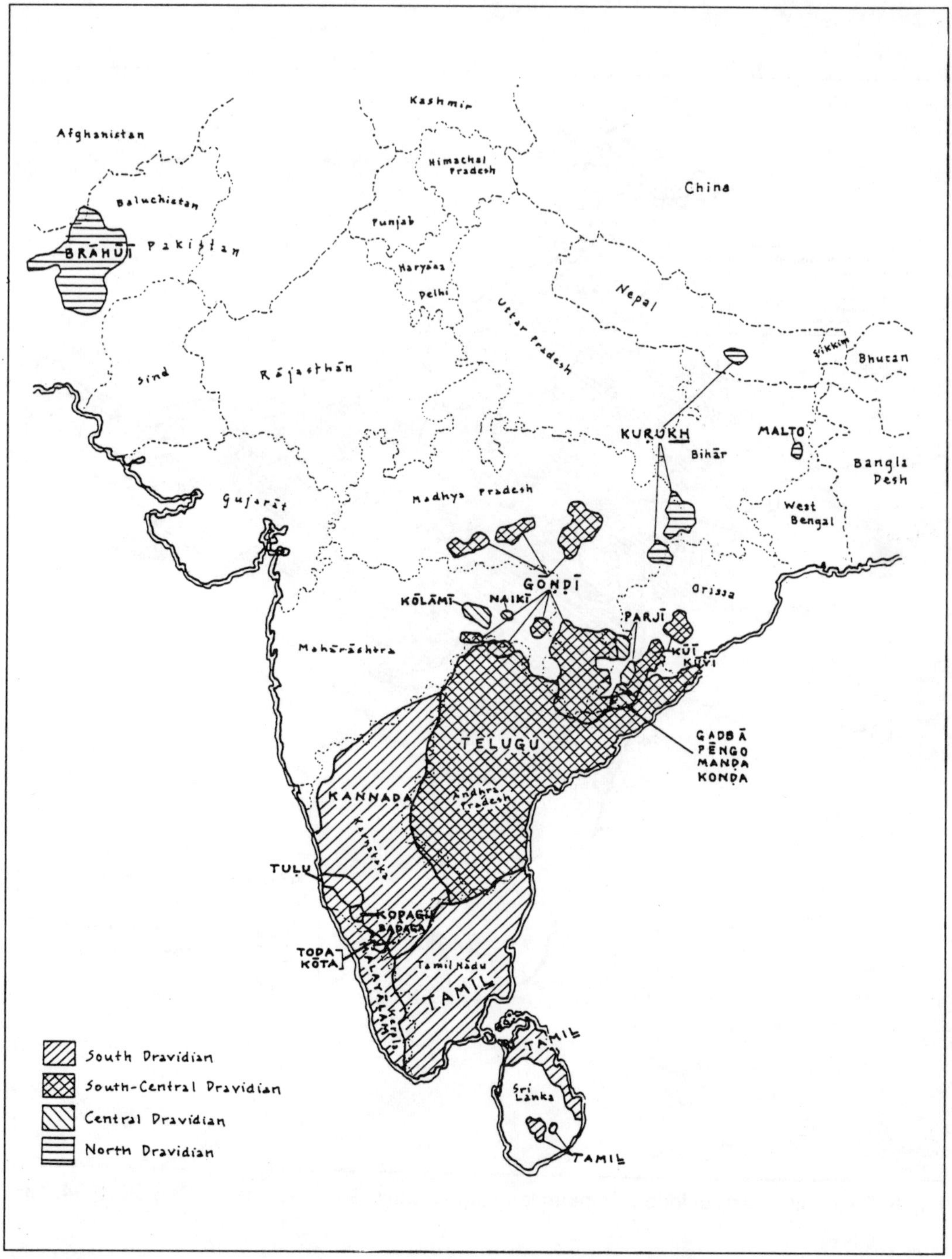

Fig. 7. Distribution map of Dravidian languages within South Asia (after Parpola 1994: 136).

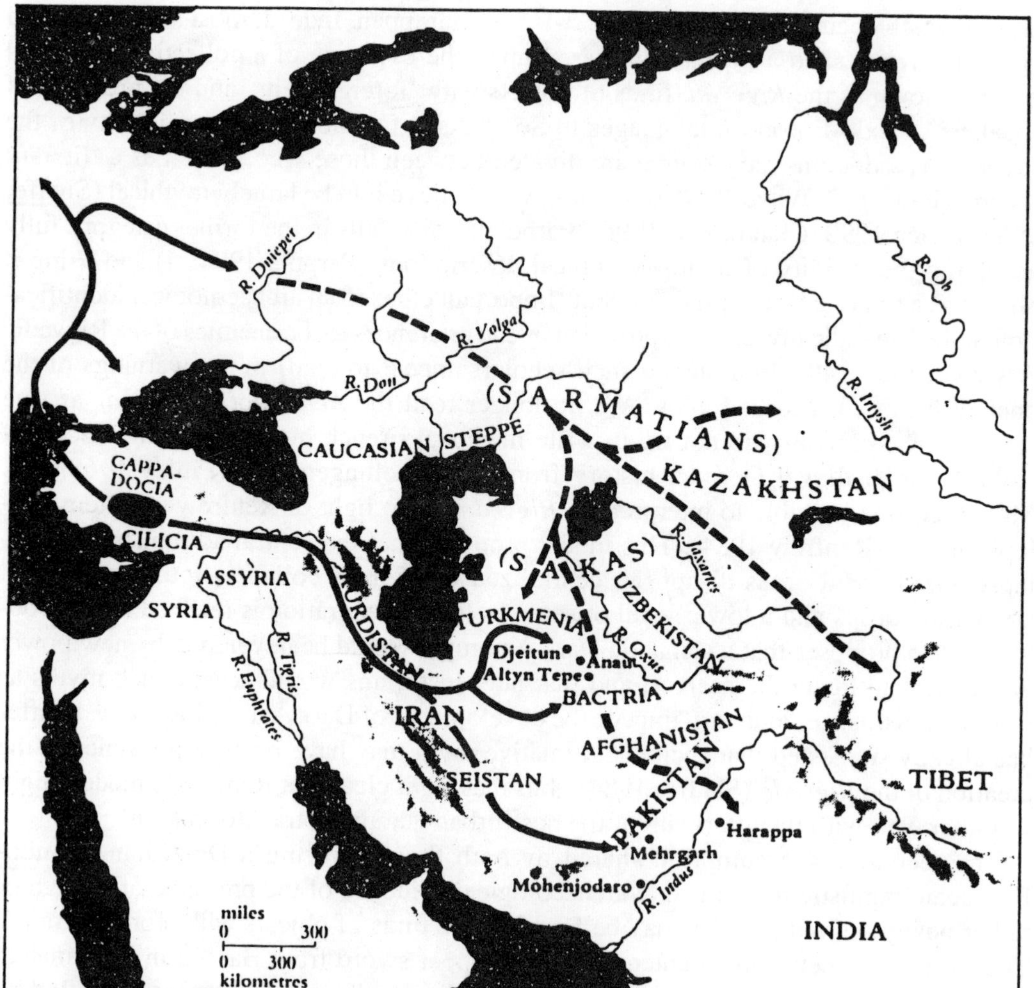

Fig. 8. Map showing the Chalcolithic diffusion of Indo-European languages (broken line) and the alternative Neolithic diffusion (bold) (after Renfrew 1987: 206).

Kashmir in the east to Swat in the west. Acknowledging contact between this group and the Harappan world, it is dismissed as a possibility in favour of a small pocket of Dravidian speakers who may have moved into the Indus system in mediaeval times!

The Dravidian hypothesis is also based upon the widely accepted concept of an arrival of one, or more, populations speaking new languages in South Asia from outside, an arrival which occurs during the late Post-Urban Harappan. Indeed, most scholars would cite support for such a mechanism based upon the evidence of a collection of sacred hymns known as the *Rigveda*, finds of objects with 'foreign-traits' and the presence of speakers of Indo-European languages in South Asia. Opinions on the reliability of the *Rigveda* as a documentary source are divided between those who view it as a 'literary record' (ibid.: 133; Witzel 1995) and those who believe it to be largely mythical (Shaffer 1984; Leach 1990; Chakrabarti 1995). Parpola clearly falls in the former category fully accepting the validity of its topographical descriptions (Parpola 1994: 5) and using it almost as a reliable historical document 'Important clues to an archaeological identification of the Rigvedic invasion are provided by the references to the enemies of the Rigvedic Aryans' (ibid.: 149). In doing so such scholars appear to confirm the warnings of the ancient historian, Moses Finley 'We no longer read the *Aeneid* or *King Lear* as true stories ... we certainly do not try to write medieval French history from the "Song of Roland" or medieval German history from the Nibelungenlied.' (Finley 1968: 36). Moreover, it is possible to interpret the *Rigveda* in the light of Renfrew's System Collapse model (Renfrew 1984). This model proposes that the central administration collapses, traditional elites disappear, centralized economies collapse, settlement shifts, population drops and a lower level of socio-political integration is reached (ibid.: 366-89). It also proposes that a romantic Dark Age myth would be developed by new power groups to legitimate themselves, and that later historians would accept such myths as truthful and this would in turn impede the development of Dark Age archaeology. Shaffer has already suggested that such a legitimative myth may have been responsible for the creation of the *Rigveda* (Shaffer 1984), thus making it clear that Renfrew's model might fit rather well with the aftermath of the post-urban Harappan transformation!

The second key assumption shared by both those favoring a Dravidian or Indo-European linguistic model is that archaeological evidence of the presence of foreign or rather newly arrived peoples may be found in the finds of objects with 'foreign-traits'. The similarities between an antennae-hilted copper sword from Bactria in Afghanistan and a similar example from Uttar Pradesh in India are thought to 'suggest that "Indian Dasas" may have introduced some artefact types found in the Copper Hoards of the upper Ganges Valley' (Parpola 1994: 154), a point supported by Allchin (1980). Similarly, Falk has suggested that it is possible to draw further analogies between certain objects within the 'Copper Hoard Culture' and objects described within the *Rigveda* (Falk 1994) and Mallory identified the Gandhara Grave complex and Painted Grey Ware as further Indo-European indicators (Mallory 1989) (Fig. 9). The Megalithic sites of Peninsular India are also interpreted as the result of a further diffusion of people 'All this evidence suggests the introduction of the Megalithic culture into India by horse-riding and warring

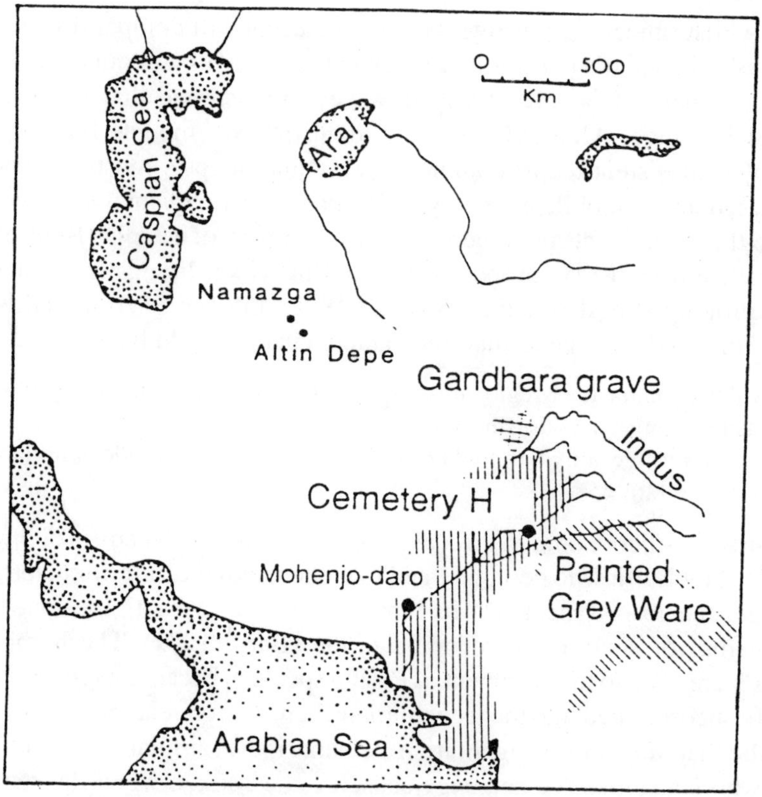

Fig. 9. Map showing archaeological culture-complexes identified as Indo-European speakers by Mallory (Mallory 1989: 592).

nomads, probably speaking an Aryan language' (Parpola 1994: 172)—a view also shared by others (Allchin 1980). These interpretations suggest the simple equation that 'material culture = people = language' and are rather reminiscent of some of Childe's culture historical frameworks (Childe 1956). Processual and post-processual developments in archaeological theory have surely enabled us to abandon such crude equations and to acknowledge that the dynamics of material culture, ethnicity and language are far more complex? Indeed, even Parpola concedes that 'the correspondence between language and culture is not always one to one' (Parpola 1994: 137). Objects do not necessarily need to be carried by a single group from one location to another, objects are traded and if one imagines a down the line exchange one can observe an object travelling hundreds of miles whilst its human carriers themselves only travel tens of miles. As a number of scholars have demonstrated the continuity between the Harappan and the Early Historic periods (Coningham 1995; Shaffer 1993), an alternative interpretation of these objects would be therefore that a transformation of Harappan systems of socio-political integration led to the introduction of new systems of integration. In such a scenario it seems likely that the arrival of these new systems would be accompanied by the arrival of new prestige objects and concepts. The population would thus remain by and large stationary whilst objects of prestige, being the currency of competition, would change.

Having established the possibility that objects can travel without necessarily the long-distance movement of people, it will now be demonstrated that the same is possible for language change. Although Renfrew identified six models for linguistic change (demographic-subsistence, elite dominance, systems collapse, constrained population displacement, sedentary-mobile boundary shift; and donor-recipient population system) they all include the permanent movement of large numbers of people (Renfrew 1987: 121-37). Sherratt, however, has proposed a model in which linguistic replacement occurs through a prolonged trade contact (Sherratt 1988: 458-63; Sherratt and Sherratt 1988) (Fig. 10). This model suggests that trade and exchange could have:

> created new demands for inter-regional communication, especially between elites. These would have provided circumstances for the formation of pigins and creoles, which because of their association with prestige activities could have slowly gained much wider currency in pre-literate communities. (Sherratt: 458-63)

As discussed earlier (Coningham et al. 1996) the complex dynamics of linguistic change are illustrated by Barth who demonstrated that one language, inferior in terms of numbers and prestige, can absorb speakers of a more populous and prestigious one because of the different nature of socio-political organization (Barth 1972). The number of Baluchi speakers is increasing to the detriment of Pushtu speakers because it is easier for a disgraced Pathan to be incorporated into the inegalitarian client-patron relationship of a neighbouring Baluch tribe than into a more egalitarian Pathan tribe. A similar argument is put forward by Ehret who states that 'A language ceased to be spokęn when the sense of separate ethnicity with which it was bound up had ceased to be relevant or functional.' (Ehret 1988: 570). Furthermore he has suggested that such changes can be set off by 'merely local disparities' (ibid.) and that 'language and ethnic shift can take place without radical change in the material particulars of life and with an amount of change in the human gene pool so small as to be for all practical purposes undetectable' (ibid.: 571). One should also take serious note of Robb's model for the mechanisms of such disperals within Eurasia (Robb 1991). Taking the premise that often 'random, directionless processes can add up to directed results' (ibid.: 287), Robb created a computerized simulation model for the random diffusion of language. Assuming that individual communities 'grow, dwindle, fuse, merge or go extinct for reasons as varied as intermarriage, disease, demographic change, ecological shift, internecine conflict, economic stress, external political pressure, opportunism, or the assimilation of refugees, immigrants or captives' (ibid.), Robb demonstrated that random microchange within territories often led to recolonization, both social and linguistic, by immediate neighbours. Starting with 64 language groups evenly distributed within the overall test area—Eurasia (Fig. 11), in each territory was generated a random number with each turn (ibid.: 288). If the generated number fell below a pre-set level the territory was assumed to have undergone linguistic change through a colonization by one of its neighbours, which was randomly selected. The turn ended when a new number had been calculated for each square within the test area and a new linguistic map generated. Within 30 turns 16 language groups had become extinct (Fig. 12), a number which rose to 36 within 60 turns (Fig. 13), culminating in the successfully colonization of the entire test area by two language families by the 1550 turn (ibid.: 289) (Fig. 14). It is important therefore to note that firstly, a general pattern can be created through minute random changes and secondly, that areas can be re-colonized by the same language family (ibid.: 288). In summary, it is therefore suggested that attempts to understand the meaning of the Indus script should concentrate on the study of the archaeological context of the Indus script itself, rather than trying to assume what the language of the script was and then set out to decipher it. Clearly from Robb's model the language of the Indus script could have been Indo-Aryan, Dravidian, Sino-Tibetan or even a language since lost!

DISCUSSION AND CONCLUSION

Now, of course, the question is how can we possibly approach the question of the decipherment of an unknown script of an unknown language? The answer is easier than might first appear; to decipher can also mean 'to make out the meaning of', and this surely we can do at a certain level without knowing the script or the language. We may approach this problem with reference, not to the Harappan script itself, but to the use of graffito in the Early Harappan period through Quivron's exemplary study of inscribed and painted marks at Mehrgarh and Nausharo (Quivron 1997) (Fig. 15). A number of scholars have studied the similarities and differences between such marks present within the Early Harappan and signs within the later Indus script, and have suggested that there may have been some degree of continuity (Lal 1974; Durrani 1984). However, Parpola suggests such continuity is unclear stating that 'nowhere do we find clear evidence of a gradual progress toward real writing in the Early Harappan period' (Parpola 1994: 53), a view also shared by Possehl (Possehl 1996: 57). Quivron studied a corpus of 1265 marks from vessels recovered from excavations at Mehrgarh and Nausharo which provide a sequence from 3600 to 2500 BC (Quivron 1997: 45). All the marks were made before firing, presumably when the vessel was drying, and most were made on the underside of the base. The key corpus is provided by a failed open kiln, dating to Mehrgarh period VI (*c.* 2700 BC), which contained a large number of abandoned vessels, many of which were inscribed with different signs (ibid.: 53). A further large collection of vessels, one hundred, was recovered from storage room CXVIII belonging to Mehrgarh period VII, of which 33 were incised with a total of 16 different signs (ibid.). Quivron assumed that as there was no apparent link between sign and vessel type within room CXVIII, the purpose of the inscribed signs was during the manufacturing cycle (ibid.: 55). Furthermore he noted that the frequencies of such signs increases and peaks at *c.* 2700 BC and then decreases, and these marks are then mainly post-firing graffito, and makes the comment that this may be indicative of the increasing centralization of ceramic production during the mature Harappan period (ibid.: 61). In an end note Quivron also suggests that the 'marks were perhaps used to avoid confusion of ownership during firing in cases where the vessels were fired in communal kilns' (ibid.); this surely is the key point of this study. Clearly, it would make greater economic sense for individual potters to spread the risk of a failed

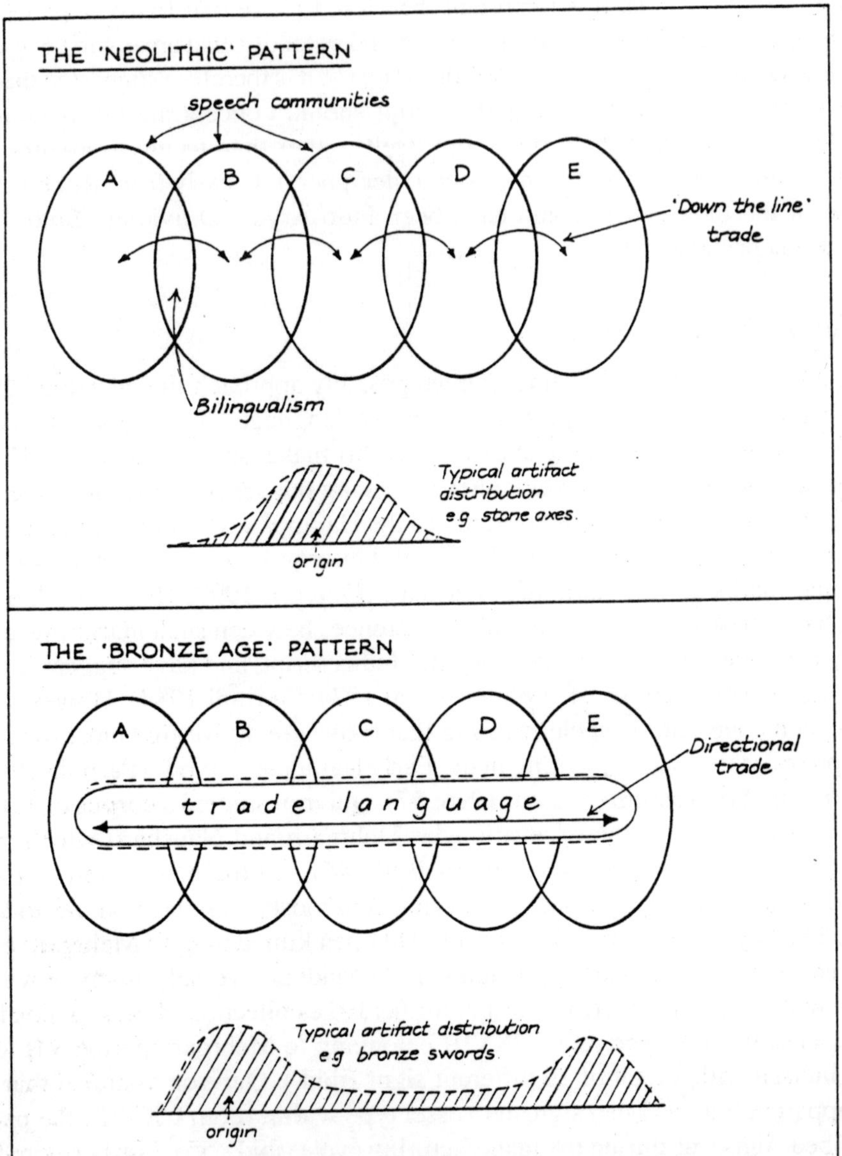

Fig 10. Diagrams showing contrasting models for the diffusion of language (Sherratt and Sherratt 1988: 592).

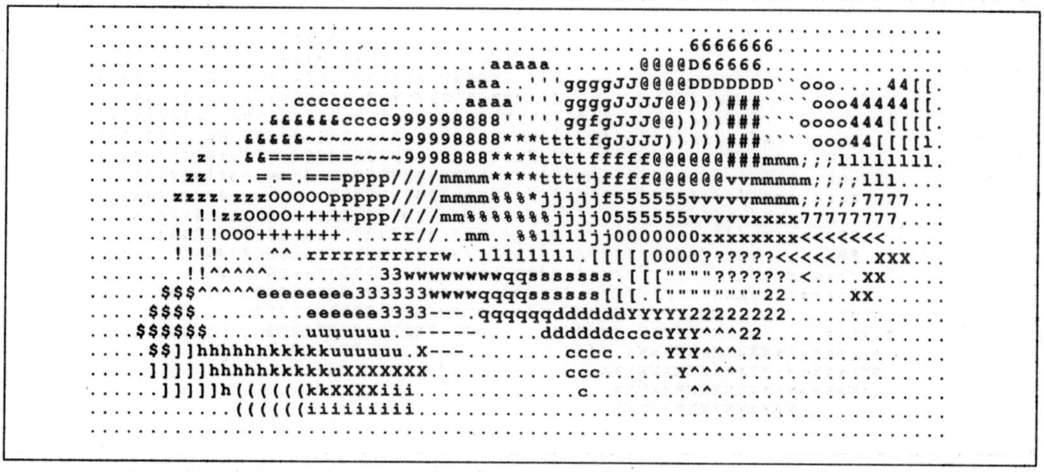

Fig. 11. Simulated Eurasian language distribution at start of program (after Robb 1991: 288).

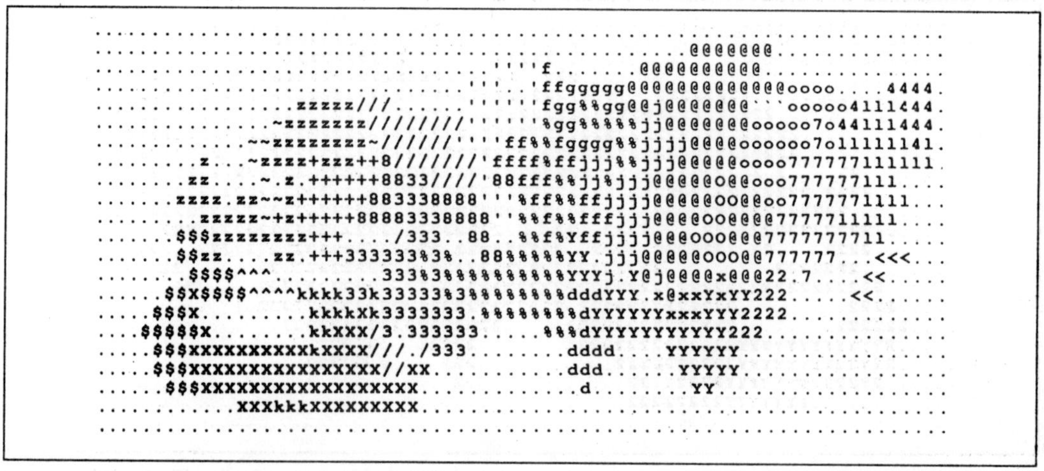

Fig. 12. Simulated Eurasian language distribution after 60 turns (after Robb 1991: 289).

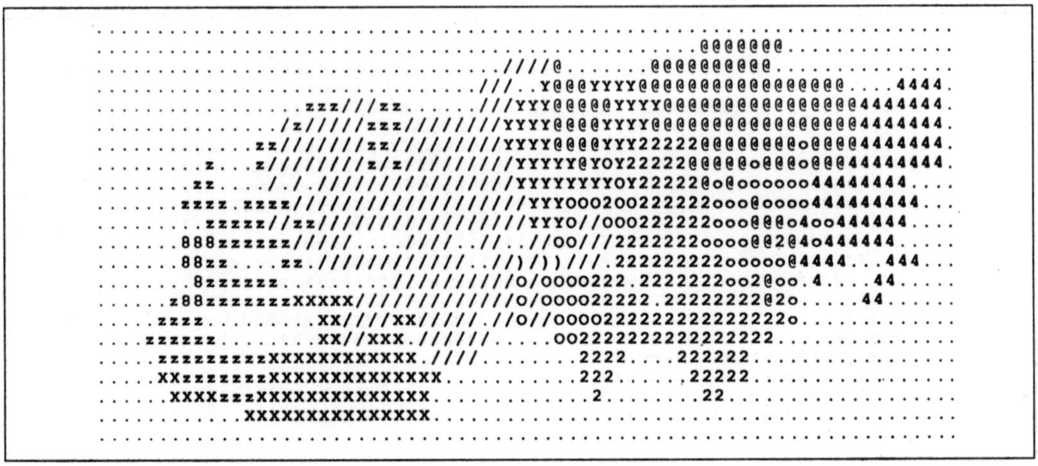

Fig. 13. Simulated Eurasian language distribution after 340 turns (after Robb 1991: 290).

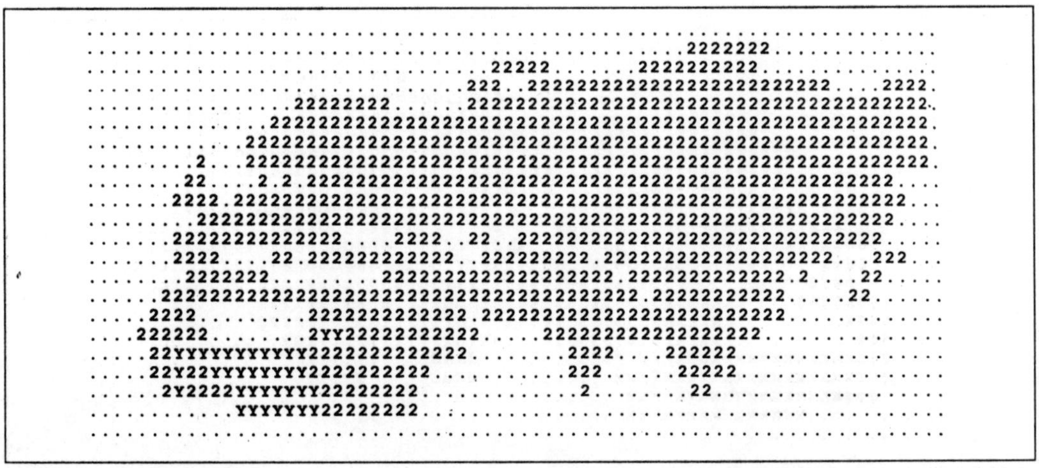

Fig. 14. Simulated Eurasian language distribution after 2000 turns (after Robb 1991: 290).

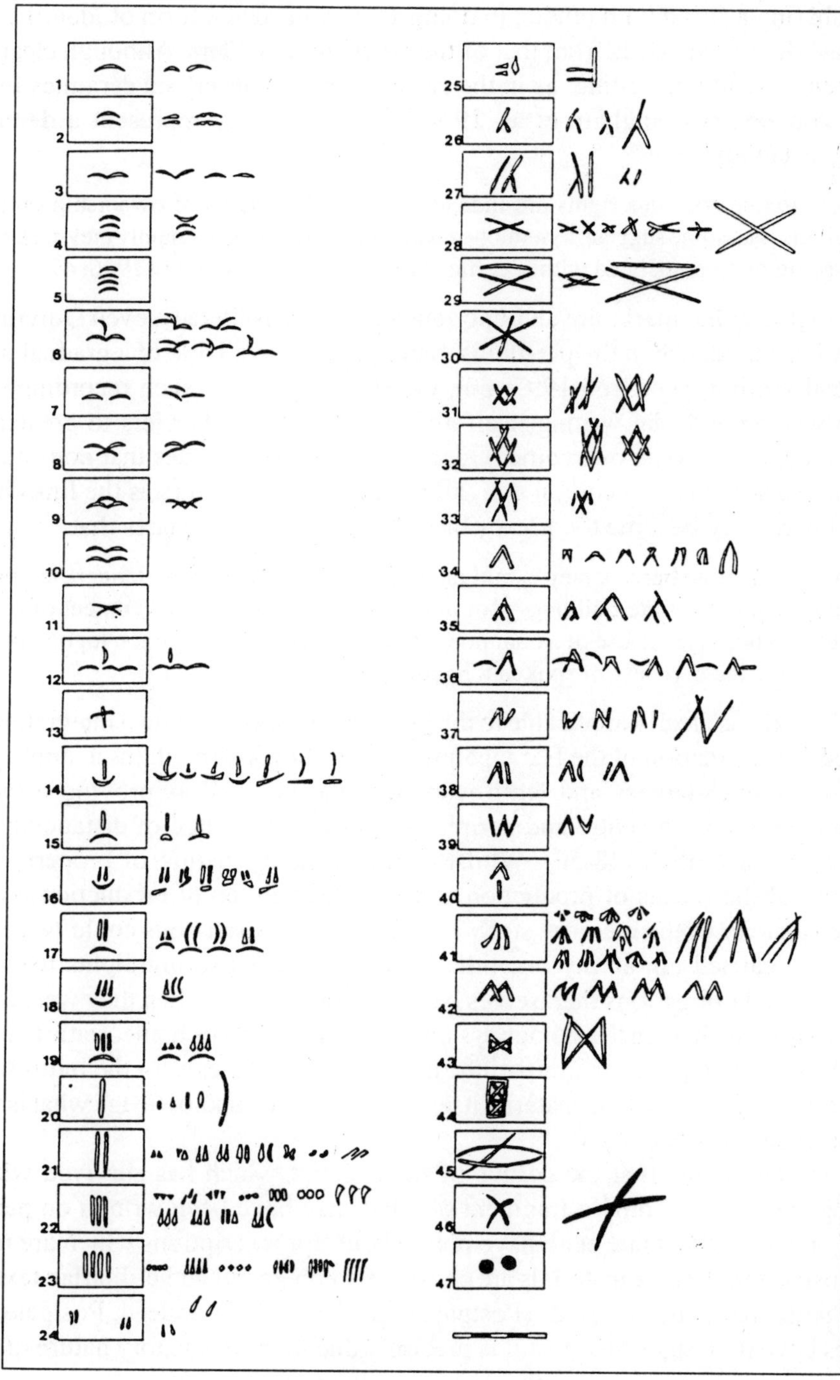

Fig. 15. Master sign list of pot marks from Mehrgarh and Nausharo (after Quivron 1997: 47).

firing by sharing a firing with others; in doing so they needed a form of identification to differentiate their own goods from that of the other share holders. Although clearly such developments are not in writing, as in the case for graffito-inscribed ceramics from late Iron Age contexts (Coningham et al. 1996; Lal 1960), they represent a demand for recording, as Goody states:

> In some non-literate societies rights are indicated by graphic marks of ownership on pots and livestock, giving rise, some suggest, to semiotic codes of limited scope. Certainly they are embryonic forms of writing often associated with specific claims to property. (Goody 1986: 47)

Whilst such graphic marks are an important step towards literacy, even Quivron states that 'there is no evidence in the pre-Indus material so far available of a gradual progress towards real writing' (Quivron 1997: 60). Goody concurs that such recording systems are not in writing and that writing itself allows a number of barriers to greater socio-economic integration to be overcome (Goody 1986). Goody argues that non-literate societies can expand only to a certain size, after which fission occurs as the links between centre and periphery become too great (ibid.: 111), however, he states that:

> The presence of a literate bureaucracy ... mitigates against those fissiparous tendencies, providing a consolidating factor in state building—not only because of the fact and content of communication ... but also because the use of a common written language or a common logographic script helps to overcome the diversity of spoken tongues and dialects. (ibid.: 112)

Goody's model is clearly applicable to the processes of socio-political integration which culminated in the creation of the Harappan world. Writing also contains a number of key elements such as exactness and legitimacy and that, as well as proving a means of communication between centre and periphery, it also is a method of distancing oneself from direct contact (ibid.: 48-50). Whilst enabling the alienation of property and the organization of the means of production and the organization of production it also expands 'the capacity of the memory store ... so that more transactions could be kept track of, and hence carried on, at any one time' (ibid.: 78). He also highlights the fact that 'reciprocities and obligations themselves became more precise when they were set down in writing than being held in the storage system of the brain with its homeostatic tendencies' (ibid.: 82). If we are to recover similar information and hypothesis for the Indus script we have to return the context of the material itself, and indeed to acknowledge what is missing from the archaeological context.

Many scholars agree that the corpus of Indus script which has survived within the archaeological record is only a fragment of what may have been written on perishable materials, indeed as Postgate et al. have pointed out 'for inscriptions which are meant to last, expensive and durable materials are chosen, for ephemeral and utilitarian texts cheap and perishable materials are used' (Postgate et al. 1995: 464). Indeed, Postgate and his colleagues have now suggested that it is precisely due to this transitory nature of utilitarian inscriptions that we are left with a top heavy view stating that:

> A popular, long-held and much-published view is that writing was developed for ceremonial

purposes. However, recent evidence from Egypt and elsewhere suggests instead a utilitarian, administrative origin. (Postgate et al.: 478)

One might also include in this process the new evidence for the existence of pre-Asokan Brahmi as represented by fourth century BC inscribed sherds from Anuradhapura (Coningham et al. 1996). Having acknowledged that the objects which have survived in the archaeological record may have been exceptional rather than common examples we may now begin to identify some of the key elements for further study. The first point must be to concentrate on an analysis of the structural context in which these inscriptions have been found. It is highly striking, for example, that little research has actually been carried out in such an area. Interpretations for the use of the Indus script have remained at very general levels (Ratnagar 1991), and unless we understand more fully about the

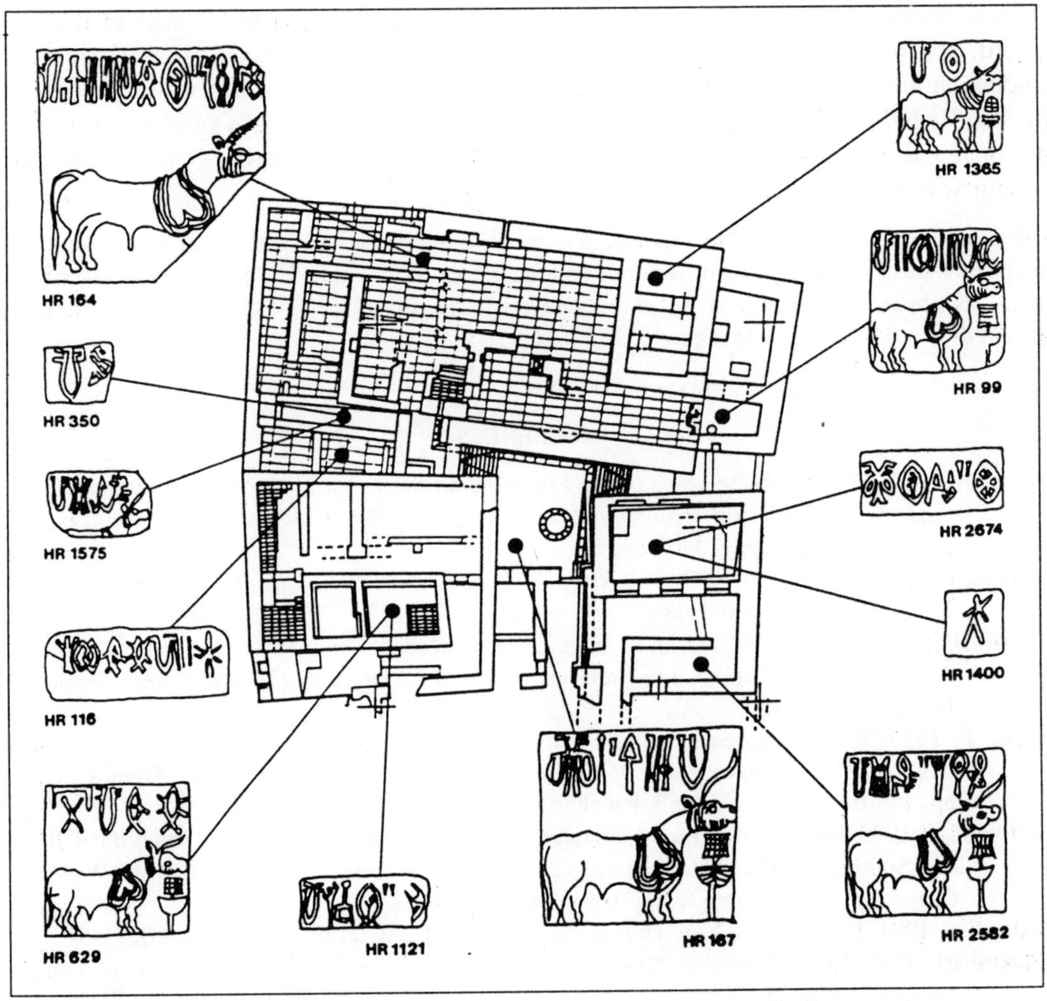

Fig. 16. Distribution of seals within House AI, Block I, HR area at Mohenjo Daro (after Jansen 1987: 160).

site formation process in action which created the fills of those actual rooms we are unlikely to create more specific models. For example, the discovery of twelve seals in house I in area HR of MohenjoDaro has been rather underplayed by many scholars (Parpola 1994: 118; Possehl 1996) (Fig. 16). Of the seven seals which depicted an animal, all depicted the same animal—the unicorn. As Jansen, as Wheeler before him (1968), has identified this building as one of special architectural function, perhaps a temple (Jansen 1987), is it not likely that the 'unicorn' motif which links the seals together may not represent the resident deity? Whilst such hypothesis are difficult to test, as the material was excavated well over half a century ago, the current excavations at Harappa are yielding very detailed evidence.about the use of the script, and more importantly, its archaeological context (Meadow and Kenoyer 1997). Indeed of their 130 inscribed objects from the 1994 to 1995 seasons, a number appear to have been made with exactly the same moulds as those recovered from other parts of the city in the 1930s. The study of such examples afford, as Meadow and Kenoyer suggest, 'contemporaneity of occupation as well as soicoeconomic and perhaps ritual interaction between inhabitants of distinct sectors of the city' (ibid.: 157), a wider study utilizing such a methodology would allow intra-regional and inter-regional patterns to be studied. In conclusion perhaps then we should concur with the statement by Meadow and Kenoyer:

> Using modern archaeological techniques of excavation combined with technical and contextual analyses should enable us to gain a better understanding of the cultural domain of the inscribed items, as opposed to knowledge of the actual language, decipherment of which still seems a distant dream. (Meadows and Kenoyer 1997: 163)

REFERENCES

Alekseev, G.V. 1976. Characteristics of the Proto-Indian Script, in *The Soviet Decipherment of the Indus Valley Script: Translation and Critique* (A.R.K. Zide and K.V. Zvelebil Eds.), pp. 17-22. The Hague: Mouton.

Allchin, B. and F.R. Allchin 1982. *The Rise of Civilization in India and Pakistan*. Cambridge: Cambridge University Press.

Allchin, F.R. 1980. Archaeological and Language-Historical Evidence for the Movement of Indo-Aryan Speaking People into India and Pakistan, *Journal of the K.R. Cama Research Institute* 48: 68-102.

Barth, F. 1972. Ethnic Processes on the Pathan-Baluch Boundary, in *Directions in Socio-linguistics: the Ethnography of Communications* (J.J. Gumperz and D. Hymes Eds.), pp. 454-64. New York: Holt, Rinehart & Winston.

Bellwood, P. 1995. Early Agriculture, Language History and the Archaeological Record in China and Southeast Asia, in *Archaeology in Southeast Asia* (C-T Yeung and B. Li Wai-ling (Eds.), pp. 11-22, Hong Kong: University of Hong Kong.

Bisht, R.S. 1991. Dholavira: a New Horizon of the Indus Civilization, *Puratattva* 20: 71-82.

Chakrabarti, D.K. 1995. Review of 'Deciphering the Indus Script', *Journal of the Royal Asiatic Society* 5: 428-30.

Childe, V.G. 1956. *Piecing Together the Past*. London: Routledge & Kegan Paul.

Coe, M.D. 1995. On Not Breaking the Indus Code, *Antiquity* 69: 393-5.

Coningham, R.A.E. 1995. Dark Age or Continuum?: an Archaeological Analysis of the Second Emergence of Urbanism in South Asia, in *The Archaeology of Early Historic South Asia: the Emergence of Cities and States* (F.R. Allchin Ed.), pp. 54-72. Cambridge: Cambridge University Press.

Coningham, R.A.E., F.R. Allchin, C.M. Batt and D. Lucy 1996. Passage to India? Anuradhapura and the Early Use of the Brahmi Script, *Cambridge Archaeological Journal* 6 (1): 73-97.

Durrani, F.A. 1984. Some Early Harappan Sites in Gomal and Bannu Valleys, in *Frontiers of the Indus Civilization* (B.B. Lal and S.P. Gupta Eds.), pp. 505-10. Delhi: Books & Books.

Edens, C. 1995. Tackling Torquemada, *Nature* 374: 223-4.

Ehret, C. 1988. Language Change and the Material Correlates of Language and Ethnic Shift, *Antiquity*, 62: 564-74.

Elfenbein, J.H. 1987. A Periplus of the Brahui Problem, *Studia Iranica* 16: 215-33.

Fairservis, W.A. 1992. *The Harappan Civilization and Its Writing: a Model for the Decipherment of the Indus Script*. Lahore: Vanguard Books.

Falk, H. 1994. Copper Hoard Weapons and the Vedic Vajra, in *South Asian Archaeology 1993* (A. Parpola and P. Koskikallio Eds.), pp. 193-206. Helsinki: Annales Academiae Scientiarum Fennicae, Series B, Vol. 271.

Finley, M.I. 1968. *Aspects of antiquity*, London: Chatto & Windus.

Gadd, C.J. 1931. Sign-List of Early Indus Script: Some External Features of Its Writing, in *Mohenjo-daro and the Indus Civilization* (J.H. Marshall Ed.), pp. 406-14. London: Arthur Probsthain.

Goody, J. 1986. *The Logic of Writing and the Organization of Society*. Cambridge: Cambridge University Press.

Heras, H. 1953. *Studies in Proto-Indo-Mediterranean Culture*. Bombay: Indian Historical Research Institute.

Higham, C.F.W. 1995. Lingnan and Southeast Asia in Prehistory, in *Archaeology in Southeast Asia* (C-T Yeung and B. Li Wai-ling Eds.), pp. 23-39. Hong Kong: University of Hong Kong.

Hrozny, B. 1951. *Ancient History of Western Asia, India and Crete*. Prague: Artia.

Hunter, G.R. 1934. *The Script of Harappa and Mohenjo-daro and Its Connection with Other Scripts*. London: Kegan Paul, Trench, Trubner & Co.

Jansen, M. 1987. Mohenjo-daro—a City on the Indus, in *Forgotten Cities on the Indus* (M. Jansen, M. Mulloy and G. Urban Eds.), pp. 145-66. Mainz: Philip Von Zabern.

Joshi, J.P. and Parpola, A. 1987. *Corpus of Indus Seals and Inscriptions: Vol. 1*. Helsinki: Suomalainen Tiedeakatemia, Soumalaisen Tiedaeakatemian Toimituksia Annales Academiae Scientiarum Fennicae, Sarja Series B, NIDE Tome 239.

Kak, S.C. 1988. A frequency Analysis of the Indus script, *Cryptologia* 12 (3): 129-43.

Kinnier Wilson, J.V. 1974. *Indo-Sumerian: a New Approach to the Problems of the Indus Script*. Oxford: Oxford University Press.

Knorozov, Yu. V. 1976. The Characteristics of the Language of the Proto-Indian Inscriptions, in 1976, *The Soviet Decipherment of the Indus Valley Script: Translation and Critique* (A.R.K. Zide and K.V. Zvelebil Eds.), pp. 55-62. The Hague: Mouton.

Krishna Rao, M.V.N. 1966. *Indus Script Deciphered*. Delhi: Agam Kala.

Lal, B.B. 1960. From the Megalithic to the Harappan, Tracing Back the Graffiti on the Pottery, *Ancient India* 16: 4-24.

——— 1966. The Direction of Writing in the Harappan Script, *Antiquity* 40: 52-5.

——— 1974. Some Aspects of the Archaeological Evidence Relating to the Indus Script, *Puratattva* 7: 20-4.

——— 1979. On the Most Frequently Used Symbol in the Indus Script, *East and West* 29: 27-35.

Langdon, S.H. 1931.The Indus Script in *Mohenjo-daro and the Indus Civilisation* (J.H. Marshall Ed.), pp. 423-55. London: Arthur Probsthain.

Leach, E.R. 1990. Aryan Invasions Over Four Millennia, in *Culture Through Time* (E. Ohnuki-Tierney Ed.), pp. 227-45. Stanford: Stanford University Press.

Mahadevan, I. 1977. *The Indus Script: Texts, Concordance and Tables*. New Delhi: Memoirs of the Archaeological Survey of India 77.

——— 1988. What Do We Know About the Indus Script? *Neti Neti* ('Not This Nor That'), Indian Historical Congress, 49th Session, Section V, Dharwad.

——— 1997. An Encyclopedia of the Indus Script, *International Journal of Dravidian Linguistics* XXVI (1): 107-22.

Mallory, J.P. 1989. *In Search of the Indo-Europeans: Language, Archaeology and Myth*. London: Thames and Hudson.

Marshall, J.H. 1924. First Light on a Long Forgotten Civilisation, *The Illustrated London News* (20 September): 528-32.

——— 1931. *Mohenjo-daro and the Indus Civilisation*. London: Arthur Probsthain.

Meadow, R.H. and J.M. Kenoyer 1997. Excavations at Harappa 1994-5: New Perspectives on the Indus Script, Craft Activities and City Organisation, in *South Asian Archaeology 1995* (F.R. Allchin and B. Allchin Eds.), pp. 139-72. New Delhi: Oxford-IBH.

Mitchiner, J.E. 1978. *Studies in the Indus Valley Inscriptions*. New Delhi: Oxford-IBH.

Newberry, J. 1980. *Indus Script of the Mohenjo-daro Shamans*. Victoria: John Newberry.

Parpola, A. 1994. *Deciphering the Indus Script*. Cambridge: Cambridge University Press.

Possehl, G.L. 1996. *Indus Age: the Writing System*. Philadephia: University of Pennsylvania Press.

Postgate, N., T. Wang and T. Wilkinson 1995. The Evidence for Early Writing: Utilitarian or Ceremonial, *Antiquity* 69: 459-80.

Priyanka, B. and A. Manatunga 1988. *Studies in the Decipherment of the Harappan Script and Harappan seals*. Colombo: Archaeodocumentation.

Quivron, G. 1997. Incised and Painted Marks on the Pottery of Mehrgarh and Nausharo-Baluchistan, in *South Asian Archaeology 1995* (F.R. Allchin and B. Allchin Eds.), pp. 45-62. New Delhi: Oxford-IBH.

Rao, S.R. 1982. *The Decipherment of the Indus Script*. Bombay: Asia Publishing House.

Ratnagar, S. 1991. *Enquires into the Political Organisation of Harappan Society*. Pune: Ravish.

Renfrew, A.C. 1984. *Approaches to Social Archaeology*. Edinburgh: Edinburgh University Press.

——— 1987. *Archaeology and Langauge: the Puzzle of Indo-European Origins*. London: Jonathan Cape.

Robb, J. 1991. Random Causes with Directed Effects: the Indo-European Language Spread and the Stochastic Loss of Lineages, *Antiquity* 65: 287-91.

Ross, A.S.C. 1938. *The Numerial Signs of the Mohenjo-daro Script*. New Delhi: Memoirs of the Archaeological Survey of India 57.

Shaffer, J.G. 1984. The Indo-Aryan Invasions: Cultural Myth and Archaeological Reality, in *The People of South Asia* (J.R. Lukacs Ed.), pp. 74-90. New York: Plenum Press.

——— 1993. Reurbanisation: the Eastern Punjab and Beyond, in *Urban form and Meaning in*

South Asia: the Shaping of Cities from Baluchistan to Precolonial Times (H. Spodek and D.M. Srinivasan Eds.), pp. 53-67. Hanover: University Press of New England.

Shah, S.G.M. and A. Parpola 1991. *Corpus of Indus Seals and Inscriptions: Volume.* Helsinki: Suomalainen Tiedeakatemia, Soumalaisen Tiedaeakatemian Toimituksia Annales Academiae Scientiarum Fennicae, Sarja Series B, NIDE Tome 240.

Sherratt, A. 1988, Review of 'Archaeology and Language', *Current Anthropology* 29 (3): 458-63.

Sherratt, A. and S. Sherratt 1988. The Archaeology of Indo-European: an Alternative View, *Antiquity* 62: 584-95.

Stein, M.A. 1931. *An Archaeological Tour in Gedrosia.* New Delhi: Memoirs of the Archaeological Survey of India 43.

Waddell, L.A. 1925. *The Indo-Sumerian Seals Deciphered.* London: Luzac & Co.

Wheeler, R.E.M. 1968. *The Indus Civilisation.* Cambridge: Cambridge University Press.

Witzel, M. 1995. Rigvedic History: Poets, Chieftains and Polities, in *The Indo-Aryans of Ancient South Asia: Langauge, Material Culture and Ethnicity* (G. Erdosy Ed.), pp. 307-54. Berlin: Walter de Gruyter.

Zide, A.R.K. and K.V. Zvelebil (Eds.) 1976. *The Soviet Decipherment of the Indus Valley Script: Translation and Critique.* The Hague: Mouton.

Zvelebil, K.V. 1970. *Comparitive Dravidian Phonology.* The Hague: Mouton.

Settlement Networks of the Indus Civilization

MICHAEL JANSEN

With more than 1,000 known sites within a territory of over 1 million sq km, the Indus Civilization is the largest of the early civilizations known to man. In the light of research during the past 20 years a clearer view of its development is emerging. Thereby one of the key questions regarding the Harappan society pertains to its spatial distribution and the changes over time as identifiable by archaeological artefacts. Of concern are not only the individual settlement structures, but also the structure of their interconnection within the settlement network.

If one considers a culture to be a phenomenon which is manifest in time and space, then at different times different states of expansion may be observed. Analogous to the (traditional) classification of cultural processes into an early, middle, and late phases (with the 'middle' being the most important one), we often can observe a contractional movement before or parallel to the early phase, an expansion for the middle and a reduction or disintegration for the late phase.

'Settlement network', therefore, has not only a synchronic but also a diachronic dimension. Analogous to a normal net, the 'knots' in the settlement network are the settlements themselves and the 'strings' are communication lines which may be material (e.g. transport lines like land, water or airways, etc.) or also immaterial (e.g. acoustic, optical, electronic ones).[1] Since without communication 'culture' does not exist, an investigation into settlements of a culture would be incomplete without also considering the settlement network.

The connecting road system is a key factor for the settlement nets of the Indus Civilization. Since the 1960s first investigations into settlement networks in archaeology were carried out by anthropologists in the USA. In those days Robert McC. Adams (1965) and later together with Hans Nissen (1972) developed a new approach towards regional analyses of settlement networks for the Diyala Region based on the German Walter Christaller's 'Central Place Theory' (1933) (Fig. 1). This method soon was adopted by other scholars and expanded (Johnson 1972; Kohl 1979). To the Indus Civilization it was at least indirectly introduced by Louis Flam in his Ph.D dissertation (Flam 1981) (Fig. 2).

The first vague interpretations with regard to dependencies between and evaluations of settlements came to light as early as the 1930s. Later, from Piggott (1950) and then especially from Sir Mortimer Wheeler (1953) the hypothesis arose of an Indus Imperium with Harappa and Mohenjo Daro as the twin capital cities (see Mughal 1990). Since the mid 1960s (Agrawal 1964, 1971; Allchin and Allchin 1968; Dales 1962, 1968, 1973; Fairservis 1961, 1967, 1971), movement entered the otherwise static state of research which was dominated monolithically by Wheeler's interpretation which understood the

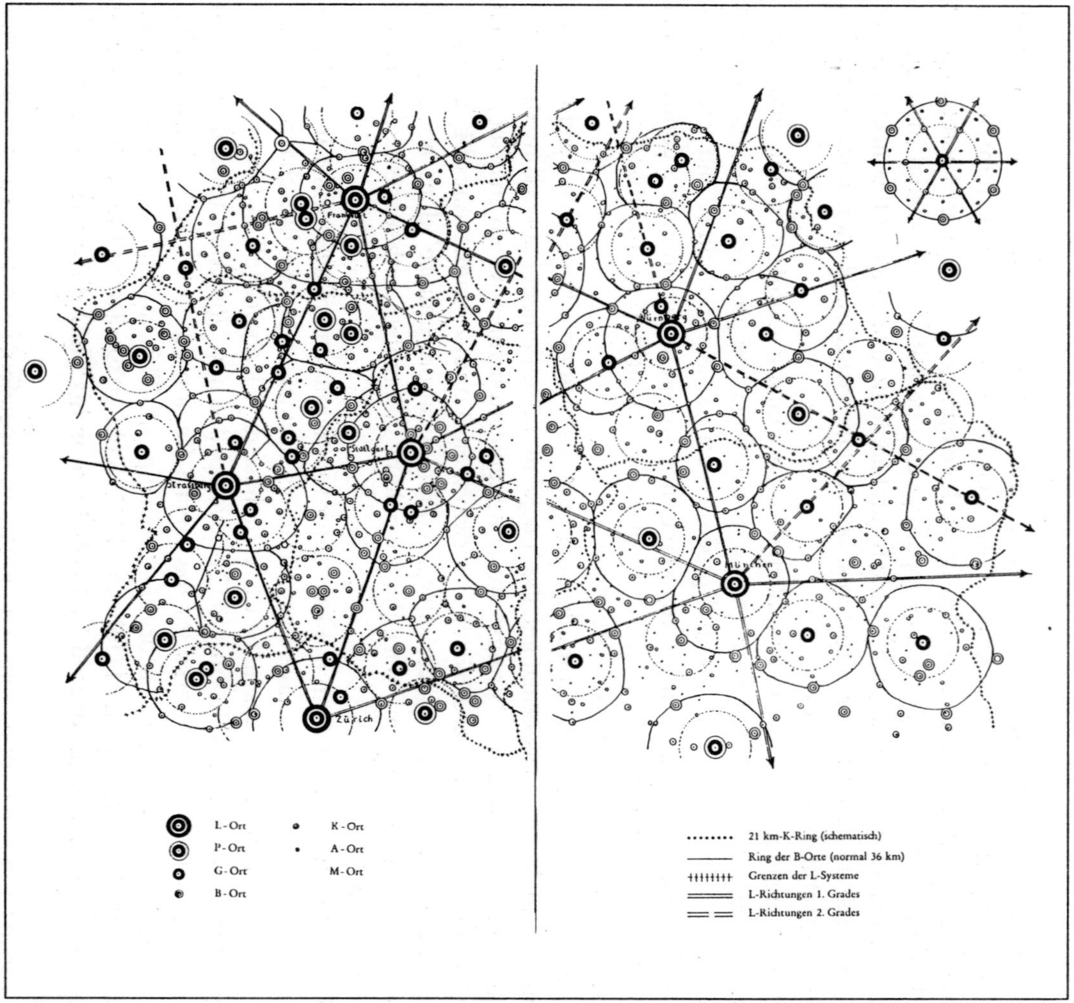

Fig. 1. The system of central places in South Germany (Christaller 1933: Karte 4).

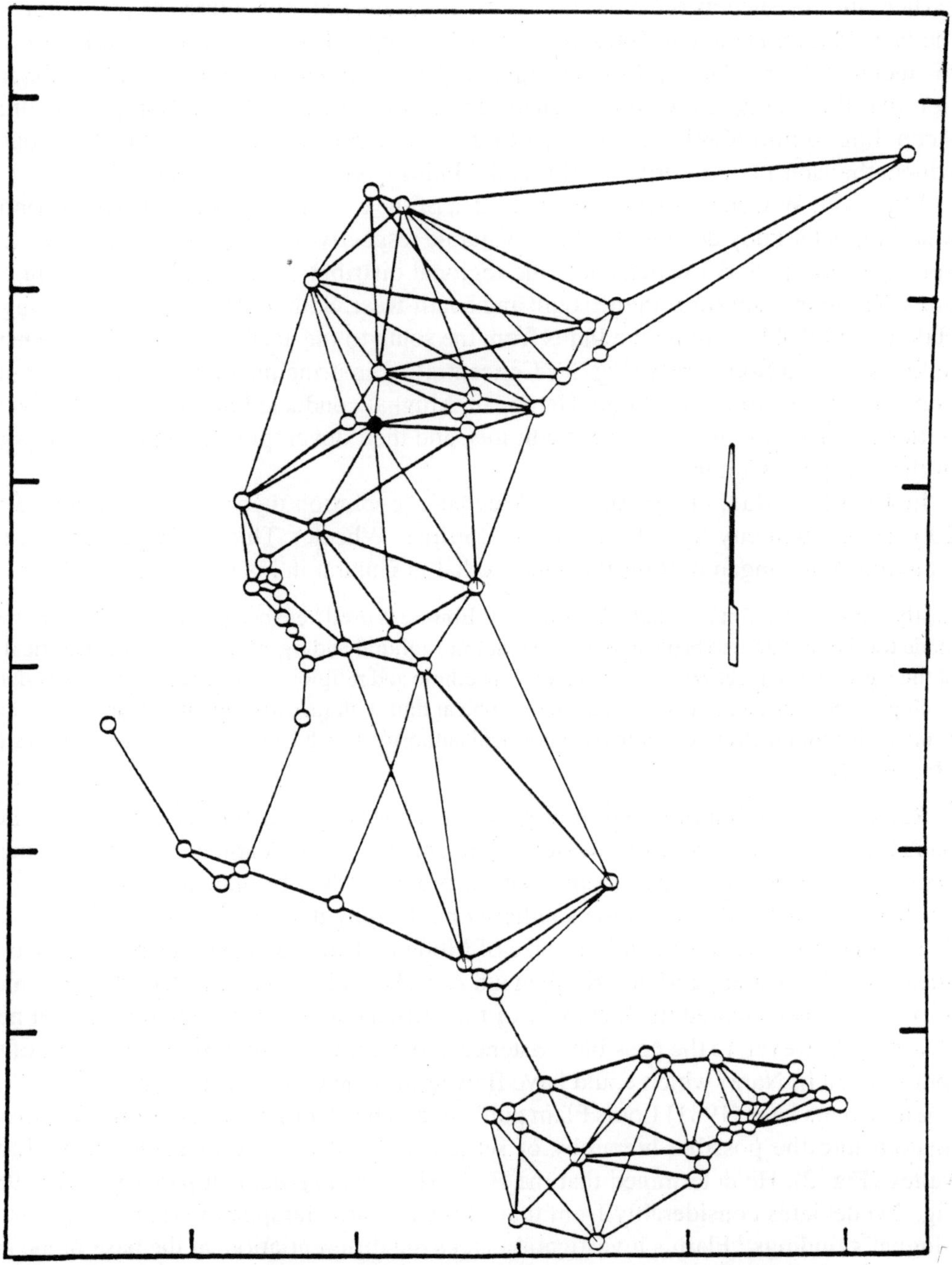

Fig. 2. Diagram of the Harappan Settlement Pattern (Black Circle is Mohenjo Daro) (Flam 1981: Fig. 72).

earlier cultures such as the Kot Diji, Amri, and (later) Sothi Cultures as pre-cultures to the later Mature Harappan (Jansen 1994). Opposing Wheeler and greatly influenced by his mentor, George Dales, Rafique Mughal (1971) expressed the notion in his dissertation that these cultures were the genetic forerunners of the Mature Harappan Culture. According to him Kot Diji, Amri and Sothi were type-sites of regional cultures out of which, the later mature (urban) culture, the Indus Civilization developed.

Moreover, Wheeler believed that the 'idea of the city' was imported from Mesopotamia. Mughal's study dealt with all the available respective archaeological materials (and not especially pottery) which show the regional distribution limits of the different cultures. These include Amri in the south and south-west, Sothi in the north-east (Ghaggar-Hakra), and Kot Diji along the Indus from the south to the north including the extension in the Amri and Sothi areas (Fig. 3). Concentrating in principle on the (material) transition between the Early to Mature Harappan, Mughal conducted no investigations on the settlement network of the different cultures, and their development into the urban phase of the Harappan Culture.

In 1973 S.R. Rao, an opponent of Mughal's 'evolution theory', also disavowed the 20 year old twin city hypothesis of Sir Mortimer Wheeler. This was a consequence of including Kalibangan in Rajasthan and Lothal in Gujarat in his list of 'capitals'.

> Lastly I must also point out, that the term Indus Empire is used here because a serious attempt was made for the first time to bring about the economic, cultural and by inference, political unification of the various provinces despite the underlying ethnic and religious differences of the inhabitants. Each province formed a well-defined geographical unit with its own capital, but appears to have come under administrative control of a political authority which had its focus in the Indus Valley. (Rao 1973:4)

Rao divided the 'empire' into four provinces, a western, central, eastern and southern one (Fig. 4), each, except the western, Baluchistan, with a capital, whereby Mohenjo Daro and Harappa belonged to the central province, Kalibangan was assigned to the northern province and Lothal the southern one. Hereby it seems worthwhile to mention that Lothal is only one fifteenth the size of Mohenjo Daro (Mohenjo Daro encompasses atleast 100 ha; Harappa 45 ha; Kalibangan *c.* 12 ha and Lothal < 10 ha). Unfortunately Rao neither investigated the hierarchy of the settlements nor their communication nets. He refers, however, to the possible existence in the third millennium of a river east of the Indus (western Nara) which could have flowed into the Gulf of Kachchh.

Eight years later (1981) Louis Flam published in his doctoral dissertation a first investigation into the possible hierarchy of settlements and their connections in the Indus Valley (Fig. 2). He determined that the Early Harappan settlement pattern (Flam 1981: Fig. 26) deviates considerably from that of the Mature Harappan period, in contrast to Mughal's findings.[2] Flam's investigation lacks the differentiation, at the base of the survey studies, e.g. that of Adams and Nissen. He proposed neither a concept of a hierarchy of the settlements, nor one for their interconnections.[3]

Mughal (1990-4) attempted one of the most recent comparative studies of settlements and their links to each other.[4] His classification of settlements rests essentially on the

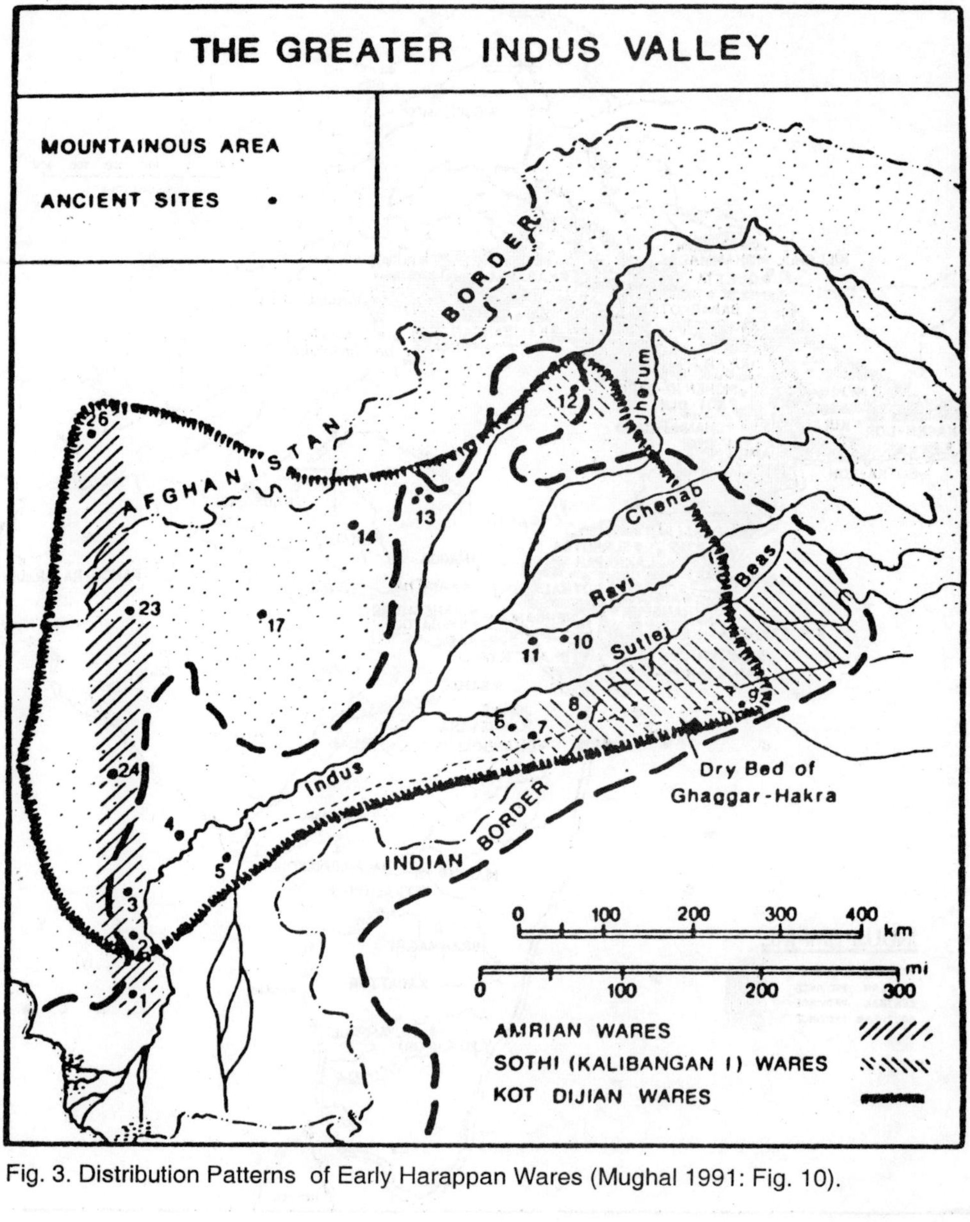

Fig. 3. Distribution Patterns of Early Harappan Wares (Mughal 1991: Fig. 10).

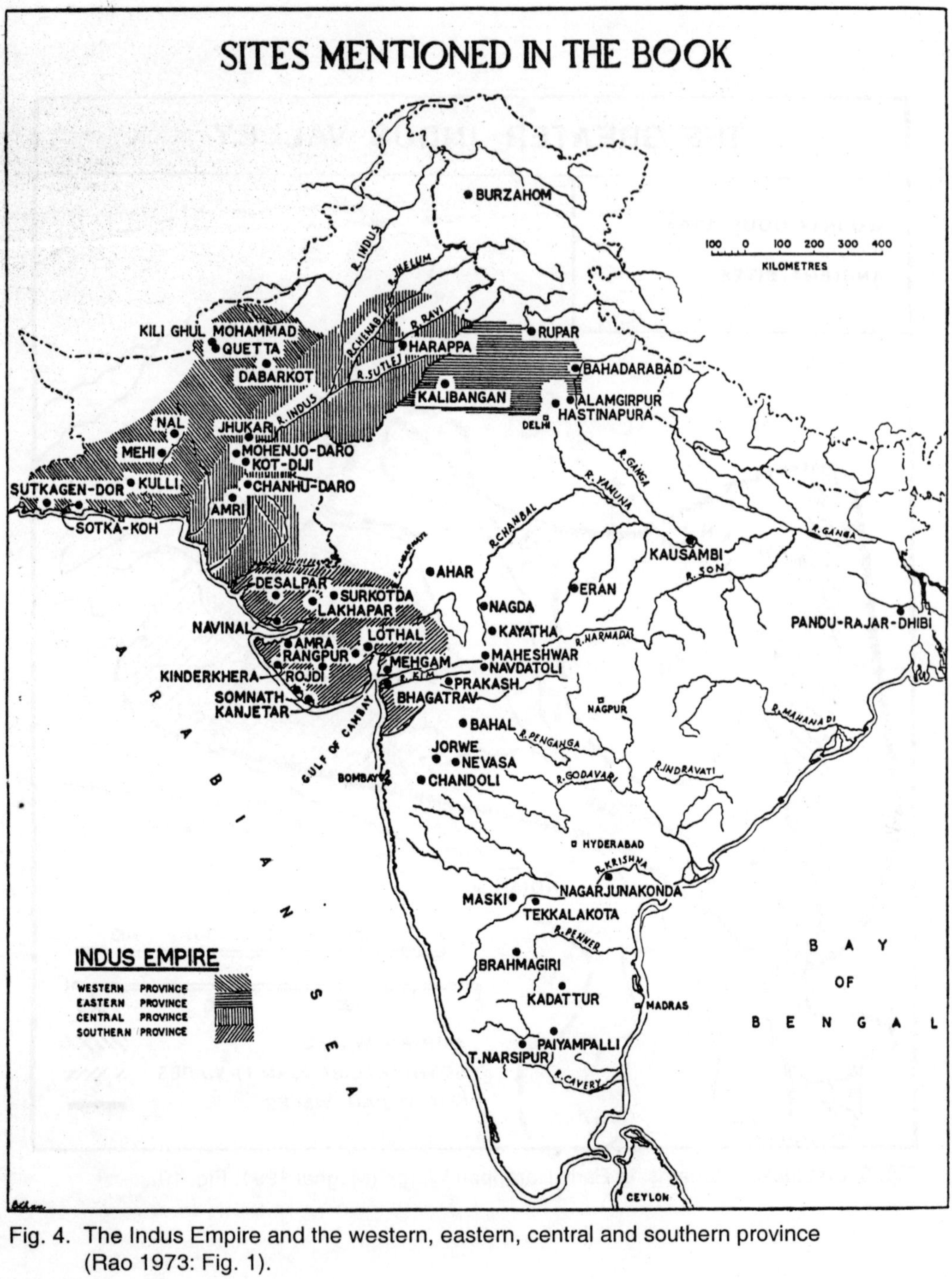

Fig. 4. The Indus Empire and the western, eastern, central and southern province (Rao 1973: Fig. 1).

parameter size (1990:7).[5] Thus, a 'city' is defined as a settlement equal, larger than 30 ha, a 'town' between 10 to 30 ha, and a 'village' up to 10 ha. In a later study he assigned settlements exceeding 80 ha[6] to a fourth category.

Mughal's investigation as to settlement size led to the conclusion that large settlements (Dholavira, Ganweriwala, Harappa, Kot Diji and Lothal) lay far apart from each other—*c.* 400 km (Fig. 5). This phenomenon, which he considers to be unique, replaces the 'twin city theory' of Harappa and Mohenjo Daro (Mughal 1994).

In order to carry out a comprehensive study of the settlements, including their hierarchical relations and their interconnections, further settlement research is necessary. Inspite of these constraints and based on further unpublished observation at Mohenjo Daro and studies of the Indus settlements, a further attempt may be risked here.

In 1987 during work with the UNESCO project one of the new spurs (21/4) attached to the Indus bunds was built to protect the site against flooding by the river. During the foundation works 2 m below the present-day surface (at that site approx. 44 m AMSL), extensive settlement walls came to light[7] (Figs. 6 and 7) and so it can be assumed that Mohenjo Daro extends below the present surface alluvium in areas as far as 1.5 km from the centre. With the help of borings around Mohenjo Daro we know that the city beneath the present-day surface extends far to the south and east, also somewhat to the north, but not to the west (Jansen 1999, in press) (Fig. 8-9). With an estimated minimum of 200 ha, Mohenjo Daro clearly overshadows all known settlements of the Indus Civilization. In terms of its size,[8] this city is the centre of the civilization. But Mohenjo Daro distinguishes itself not only by its size! No other settlement contains so many unique architectural structures (especially the Great Bath, Fig. 10), so many buildings made of baked brick, and so many drains and wells (See Jansen 1993b). In size and wealth no other settlement is comparable.[9] Thus, it seems, Mohenjo Daro was first in the hierarchy of all the other settlements known up to now.

Many indications point towards a founding and building of the first urban 'Mohenjo Daro' in a rather short time (see Jansen 1995). If this assumption is right then the builders of this monumental project would have been already fully in control of the entire spectrum of building technology (prefabrication of normed bricks, walls in block-bond [so-called English bond], the levelling of the water canals, the sinking of wells down to over 20 m in depth, etc.). Moreover, they would have been able to plan and organize the construction of a city of more than 200 ha in a short time on top of a protective earthern substructure up to 7 m high in the middle of the alluvial Indus Valley plain (Fig. 11) despite the danger of annual floods! The foundation structures alone which finally protected the buildings on top of it against the annual floods could have occupied for example 5,000 workers for several years.[10] These extraordinary efforts would have been possible only by a highly developed spirit of planning, the necessary population potential, and a corresponding economy. Above all, there must have existed the necessity for such an extraordinary effort.

Recent excavations at Harappa reveal beneath the Mature Harappan layers extensive Early Harappan ones. Mark Kenoyer and Richard Meadow along with their team point

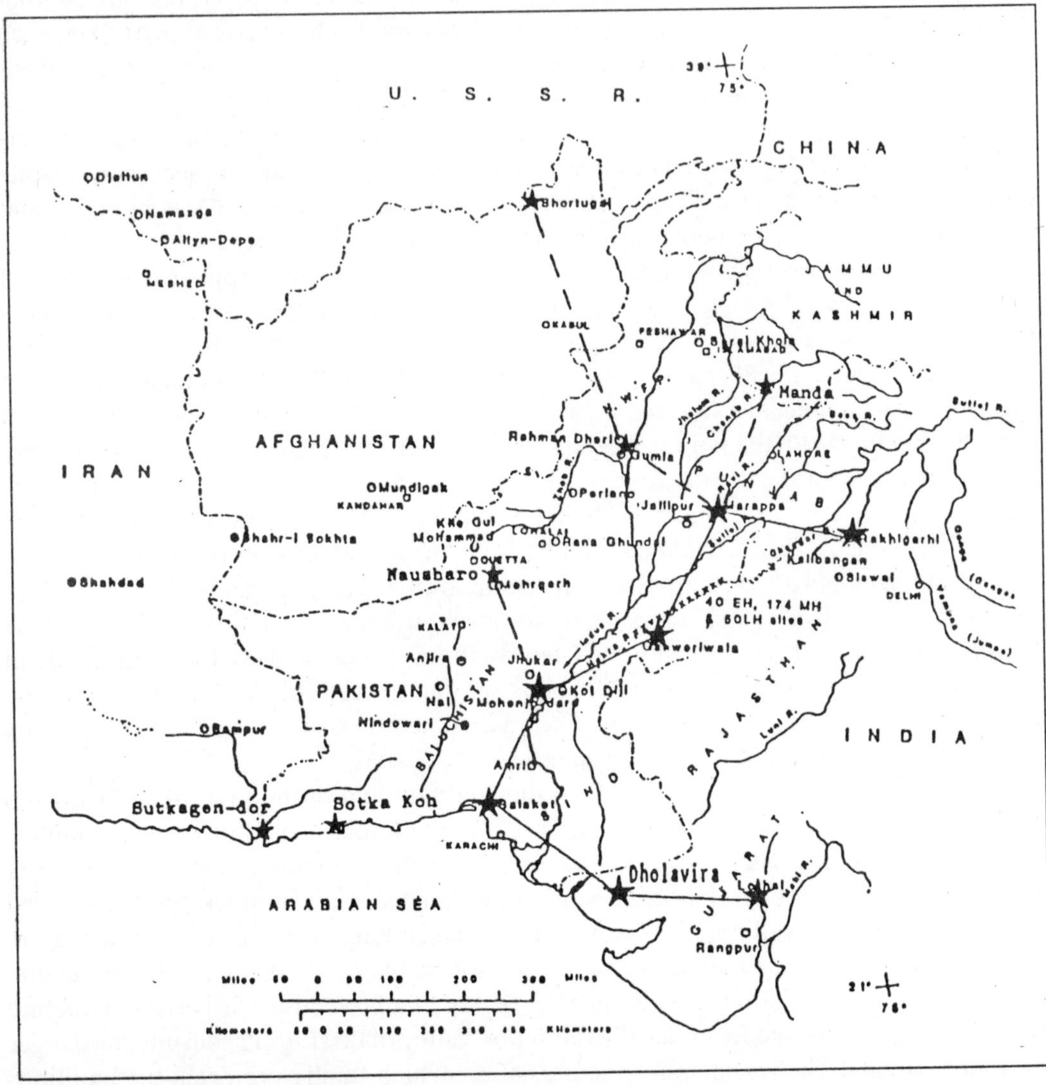

Fig. 5. Principal cities of the Indus Civilization showing almost equidistant locations (Mughal 1994: Map 2).

Fig. 6. Foundation trench of spur 21/4 near Mohenjo Daro showing Mature Harappan structures (Jansen 1987, RWTH).

Fig. 7. Details of a partly excavated well with Late Mature Harappan lining on top (Jansen 1987, RWTH).

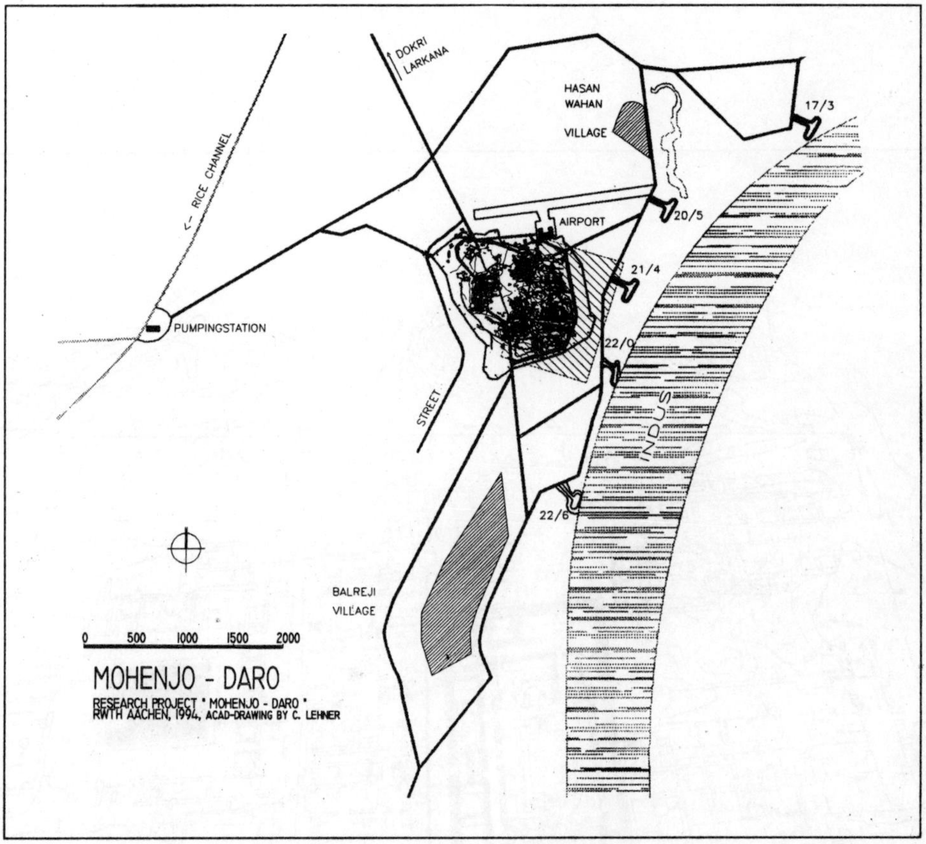

Fig. 8. Regional map of Mohenjo Daro with protective bunds, airport and spurs.

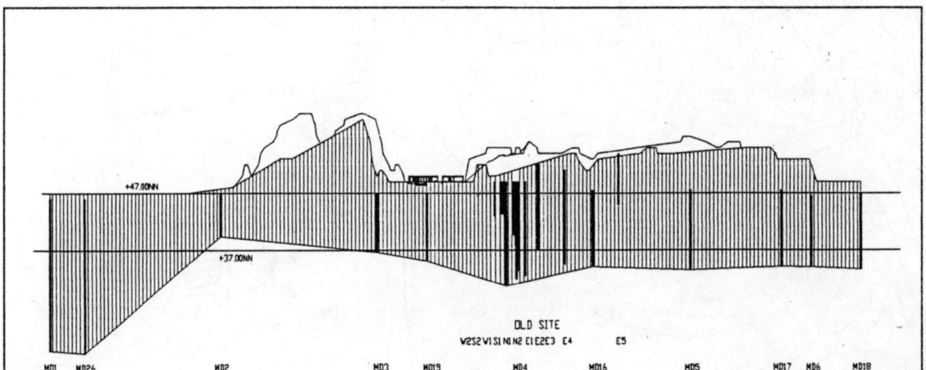

Fig. 9. Computer cross-section (W-E) according to drilling profiles with clear indication of deep depression in the west (Jansen 1995, RWTH).

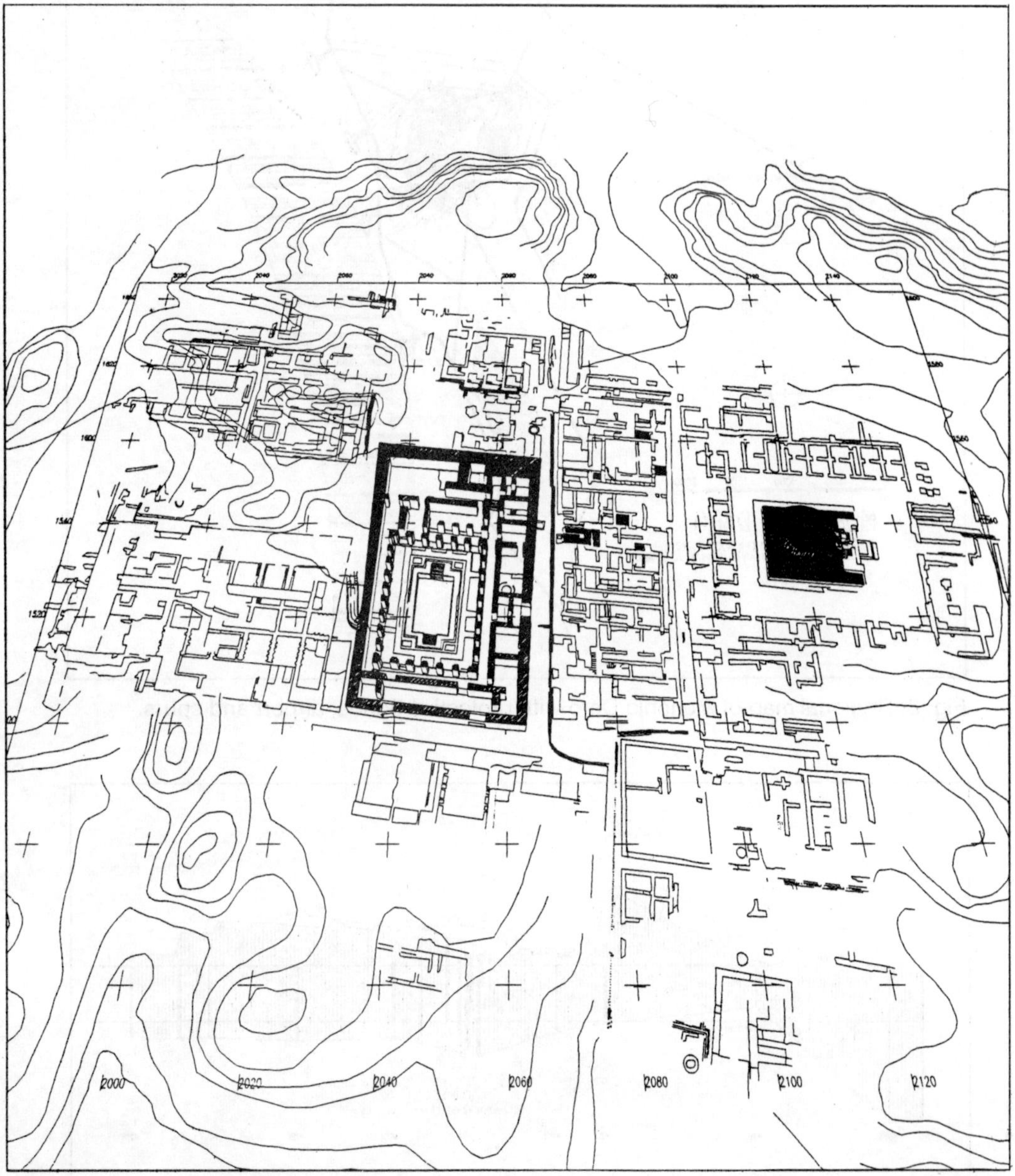

Fig. 10. Northern part of Citadel in preudo-3-D bird's-eye view (Jansen 1997, Langer RWTH).

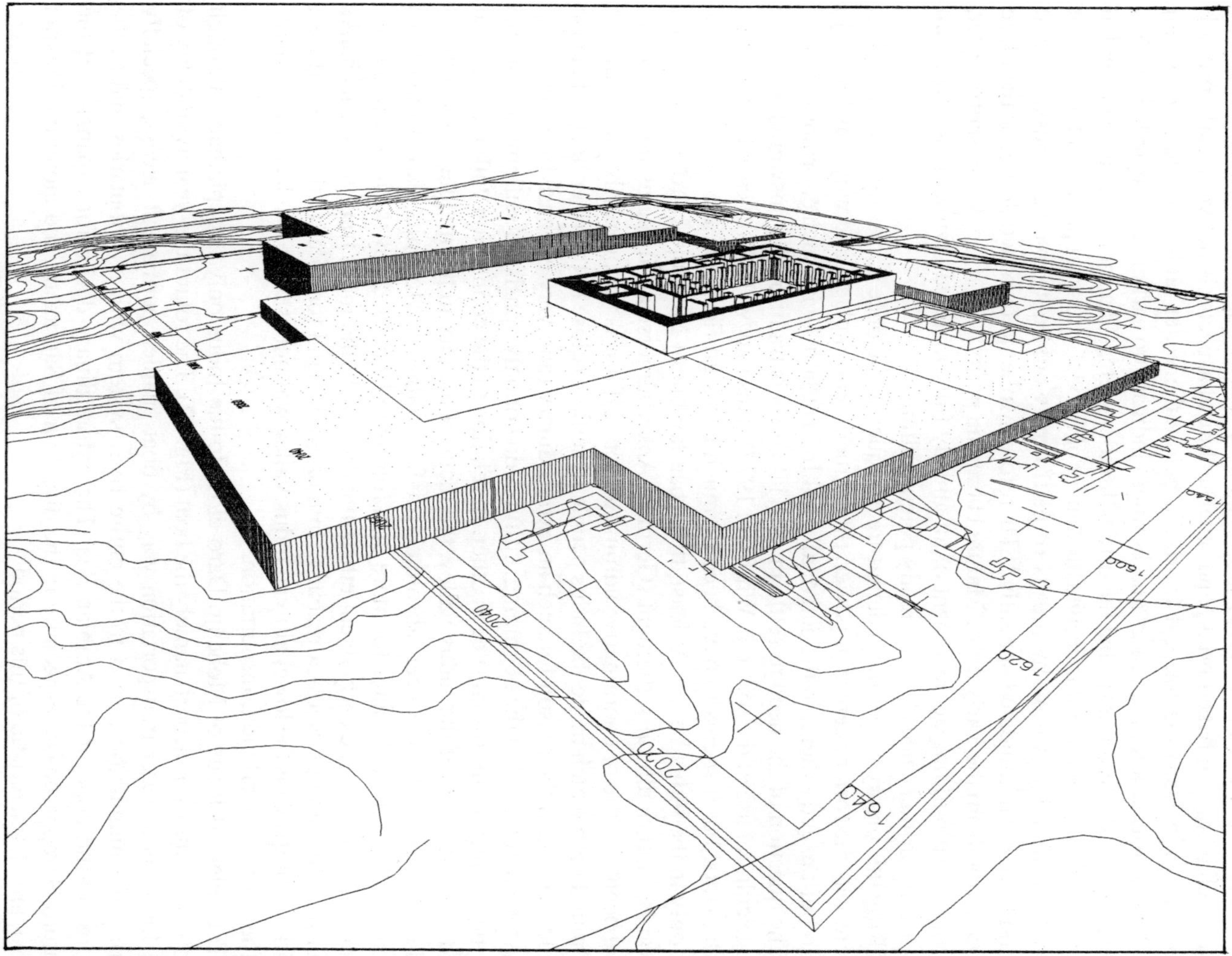

Fig. 11. Systematic illustration of the Citadel platform system (Jansen 1997, Langer RWTH).

out that the transition between the two was not abrupt, though the transition to writing and specially to the Mature Harappan technical standard (circular wells, drains and other water architecture in baked brick, and other technical aspects) is not yet clearly proved.

At Mohenjo Daro the deepest levels lie below the water table. But up to now[11] all available information (soundings and borings) indicate no earlier settlement below this. This supports the hypothesis that the original settlers selected a spot on alluvial ground in the direct vicinity of the Indus despite the danger of floods. An earlier permanent settlement without artificial elevation by means of platforms would not have been possible as it would have been inundated annually.[12] Therefore, Mohenjo Daro would not be the place of transition from the Early to the Mature Harappan period, but it would be, shortly after, the first great building achievement of an already fully matured civilization—the result of an extraordinary need of an already potent culture.

Using this theory as a point of departure, the question at once comes up that if existing, where was the former centre of power, the former 'central place' and why was Mohenjo Daro built exactly there, in the active alluvial Indus Plain[13] with such enormous efforts?

The question of the need to settle in alluvial zones is traditionally answered by virtue of agricultural use of the soil (e.g. Wittfogel 1977). This may well be the case for Neolithic settlements, but it seems to have become much less significant for the bronze age city, not only in the Indus Valley. At least, the urban lay-out of Mohenjo Daro does not point towards an agricultural settlement (German: Ackerbürgerstadt) it seems much more to have been a centre of coordinative administration.[14] If it was not primarily the fertility of the inundation which made the Indus people to settle so close to the river itself what else could have been the reason for such an extraordinary (and very expensive!) effort?

As we mentioned in the beginning, cultures do not only consist of settlements but also by their connections amongst each other. In relation to the connection with the potential land route systems of the Indus Valley, the locus of the city in the middle of the alluvial Indus Plain would have been absolutely disfavourable as Mohenjo Daro would have been cut off from land routes for more than four months per year by the inundating river. Then and as late as the early twentieth century annually the Indus transgressed its banks after mid-July and in its lower reaches[15] inundated the land for miles to the east and west (Aitken 1909). Thus the lower alluvial Indus Valley was not usable for at least four months in the year for overland transportation.[16]

The selected locus of Mohenjo Daro close to the Indus only is explainable through another means of transport, namely the boat (Fig. 12). The round-the-year availability of the Indus as a water transportation way by boat enabled permanent access, specially during the inundation period to the entire river system with its tributaries and to the entire coastal zone of the Arabian Sea. The extraordinary desire for expansion of the Mature Harappa phase, especially in the direction of Saurashtra and along the Makran coast, are characteristic of this period.

In the light of all this, the selection of the locus for the centre so close to a dangerous river system is understandable. But it anticipates not only the extensive use of the boat before the existence of Mohenjo Daro but also the exploitation of the Greater Indus

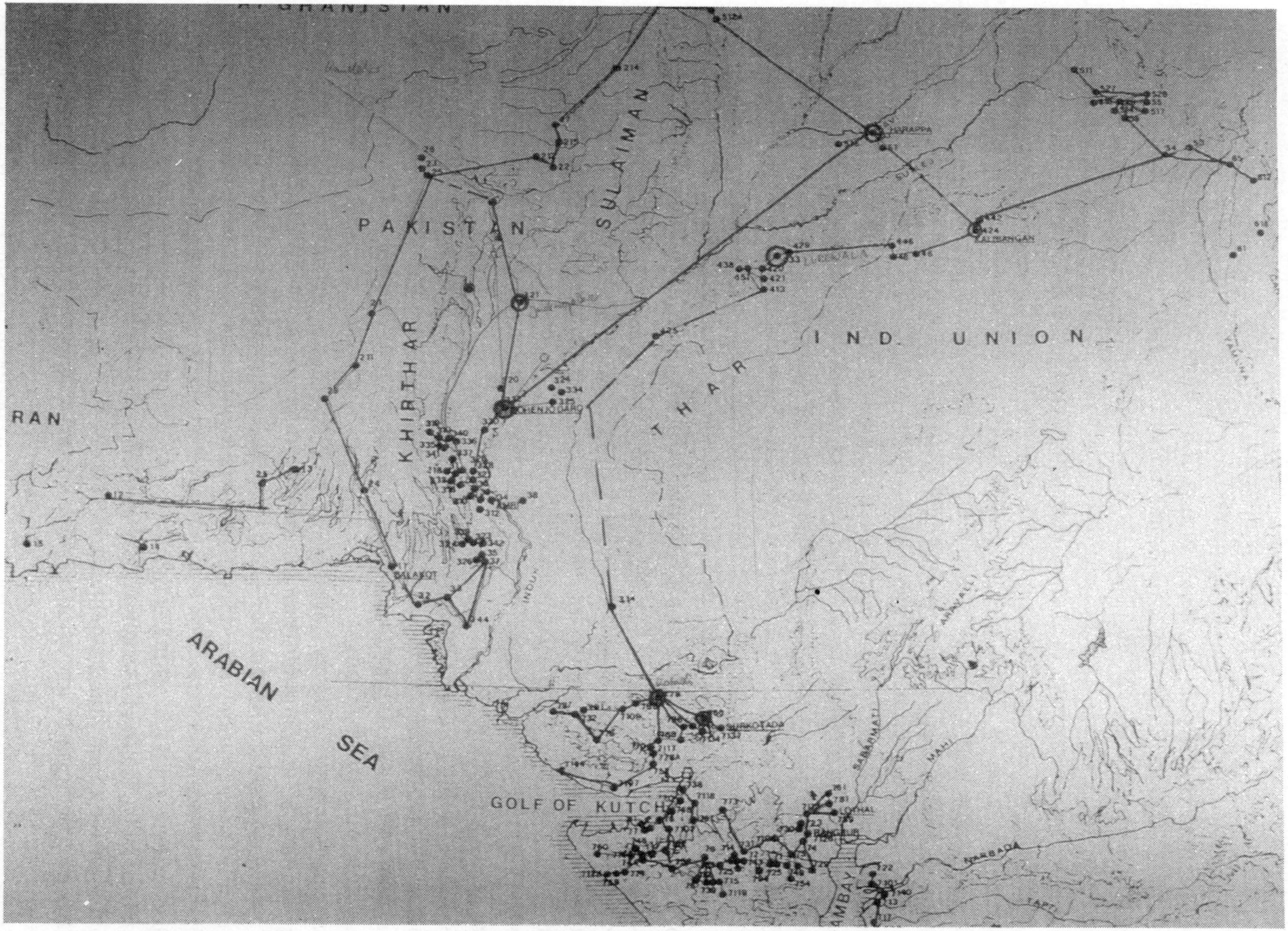

Fig. 12. Communication network of the Greater Indus Valley with land route to the west and water routes in the centre and east (Ghaggar-Hakkra).

Basin. The boat must have already been known and used during the Early Harappan period, most probably by the Kot Diji Culture people.

For the selection of the locus of Mohenjo Daro the crossing of two transport systems must have been responsible: the water system of the Indus itself and the west-east[17] land route from the Quetta Valley (Mundigak and further on to Mesopotamia) along the Bolan River to Kot Diji and the western Nara. At Kot Diji, for example, the richest flint mines of the Rohri Hills were long exploited.

If this hypothesis is true, then the Indus Civilization was controlled from Mohenjo Daro primarily by means of water transport.[18] Therefore, the 'settlement net' would not consist of hexagons or circles like those developed by Christaller and Adams but of a more linear structure along the water transport routes. Therefore, simple linear connections as demonstrated by Flam or Mughal would not reflect the individual situation of the Indus Civilization. If there existed sub-centres, they would exist within the settlement-net structure marked by the peculiar interconnection of accesibility.

Once we establish a settlement net with hierarchic settlement structures for the Mature Harappan period, we should look for the potentials of interconnection and hierarchy for the Early and Late Harappan periods. For those nets it might become clear that they were much less dependant on the water transport and more oriented towards land transport (like the Amri system in the mountains against the Hakkra system or the Kot Doji one). Regarding the hierarchy of settlements the interesting question would be: 'Where were the "central places"(if existant) of those cultures?'

For the Mature Harappan period we have to raise the question: 'From where did the population come to fill a city like Mohenjo Daro and to "run" this civilization?' The population of Mohenjo Daro has been estimated to be around 40,000, which for an area of at least 100 ha seems to be too high.[19] But it may be appropriate for the newest data of a size of at least 200 ha.

To fill all Harappan settlements with settlers the calculation would be somewhat more difficult! Taking the more than 1,000 known settlements and supposing 600 inhabitants per settlement (about 100 families) on the average,[20] then without the great cities a total population of 6,00,000 results.

At least two hypotheses are current to identify the region of origin of the civilization. One assumes the area around Harappa, and the other around Mohenjo Daro. Wherever this area was located, it seems likely that the people must have lived in the direct vicinity of the Indus river system, where they, without being periodically endangered, could study the Indus and extensively travel on it with boats. Also the irrigation of the fields—probably the prerequisite for the levelling of the drains in Mohenjo Daro—must have been known. Manchhar Lake, south of Mohenjo Daro, as well as the Kachi Plain are areas with a long tradition of settlement, the Manchhar Lake shows an early tradition of the use of boats, the Kachi a tradition of irrigation. Neither of these aspects seems to be found around Harappa.[21]

Therefore, in my opinion, the former seems to be the most suitable area for such an early development. Many settlements as far west as the Quetta Valley were abandoned in the first half of the third millennium perhaps in order to settle the people at Mohenjo

Daro. Essential elements of the Indus Civilization are present in the Kot Diji culture, not to mention the fact that it occupied a large area of the Indus Valley. This leads one to the assumption that already at this time boats were in use, even if not as intensively as during the succeeding period. Wherever the area of the final development towards the great cities took place, one must assume the development of well-technology (wedge-shaped bricks, development towards the cylindrical form, construction from top to bottom, etc.), of masonry technology, and the development of writing. According to the extensive distribution of settlements within the Indus Valley, at the end of the Early Harappan period a society must have developed which converted itself (or was converted) into a system which we designate as the Mature Harappan period or the Indus Civilization. Soon it was organizationally and financially in a position to build Mohenjo Daro as its (first?) monumental expression. Considering all of the contexts, it is clear that Mohenjo Daro was not a centre of production but rather an administrative one. It was the new centre on the main line of communication, the Indus.

OUTSIDE, INSIDE

When considering the Indus Civilization, we must also take note of the non-Indus cultures. What was there where the Indus Civilization was not located and how did the two relate to each other?

First we must consider the West. In the direct vicinity lie the mountains of Baluchistan, the Khirtar and Sulaiman ranges. The Bolan river system rises in the uplands of Quetta, flows through the Bolan Pass, and picks up one of the main west-east axis which aims directly toward Mohenjo Daro. Traversing the Indus at Kot Diji, a centre for flint mined in the adjacent Rohri Hills, this axis ends here, if not at nearby Mohenjo Daro. The Quetta Valley is linked further to the west to the important settlement Mundigak. The latter in turn is integrally linked with the Helmand and Namazga cultures as well as with the area of Elam and there with with Mesopotamia.

This transportation corridor was especially important in the first half of the third millennium BC, as Tosi (1983) has shown. In the second half of the third millennium this overland connection collapses. In its place evidently a sea route develops along the Makran coast leading to the Umm an Nar culture of south-eastern Arabia and onto Dilmun. Overland trade seems to have been replaced by marine trade. The motivation may have been similar to that when in 1492 Columbus discovered the New World in trying to trace a sea route to India and in 1498 with Vasco da Gama who found it around Africa: The blocking of the land route (here by the Turks through the conquest of Constantinople in 1453) and the shift to a new transport medium, the more secure water. Following the decline of the Mature Harappa Culture around 2000 BC new and intensive influences came from the West and from Central Asia (for example in Merhgarh VIII) and afterwards from 1400 with the coming of the Aryans.

One phenomenon should be singled out here: the settlement Shortugai. Although during the Mature Harappan period no settlement of this culture is known in the highlands of Baluchistan, what is striking is the trading station for lapis lazuli Shortugai in

Badakhshan. Evidently in control of the lapis mines, this settlement from 2500 BC is Mature Harappan. The presence of a population from the Indus Valley correlates with the shift from a land to sea trade. Thus, lapis must have been transported first to the Indus Valley, then by sea route to the Arabian Peninsula, before perhaps reaching a final destination in Egypt. This is a challenging statement. The *Periplus Maris Erythraei* informs us that lapis belonged to the most important trade goods from the Indus during the Roman Empire, a tradition which reached back to as early as the third millennium BC.

The replacement of land with sea trade made the Indus system more dependent on the outside world. The interruption of sea contact with the West also would have constituted a reason for a break of general contacts which might have also supported the later decline.

To the east, the Thar desert separates the Indus Plain from the remaining subcontinent. Only in the north from the Delhi gates and to the south from Saurashtra were there communication paths with the neolithic-megalithic cultures of the interior. To what extent coastal trade on the west and south coasts took place has not yet been investigated. Lothal has been understood as a 'gate-way' settlement which communicated with the outside world. Contact with the north over the passes of the Himalaya (Karakorum) towards Tibet are very limited at this time.

The south is delimited by the Arabian Sea of which we know that together with the Indus it forms an important means of transportation for coastal ships. Many of the border settlements to the west may well be border forts. Often they lie in defendable situations (for example, Suktagen Dor) and are heavily fortified. To the west there seems to have existed a territorial defense system against attack from the mountains (e.g. Gaj Naig) which could explain why Mohenjo Daro as an 'inland' city had hardly any fortification.[22]

Centre - Periphery

The Indus Civilization obviously did not begin with Mohenjo Daro but rather produced this city. Mohenjo Daro, situated on the axis of the east-west trade route Quetta, Kachi, and Indus, as well as within reach of the open sea[23] was a new foundation: the result of necessity and experience.

With the founding of Mohenjo Daro, the Indus Civilization continued its great *floruit* being also marked by an extraordinary expansive thrust, understandable in light of the fact that with the exception of clay the Indus Valley contains no raw materials. While the alluvial Indus Valley itself remained thinly settled,[24] the ecological niches at the flanks were heavily populated. These include the area of the Manchhar Lake, Kachi Plain, Gomal Plain, Punjab, the area of the upper Sutlej, the Ganga-Yamuna Doab, the old river system of the Ghaggar including Cholistan, its continuation to the south in the area of eastern Nara, down to Saurashtra (Fig. 13).

Several considerations (e.g. Ratnagar 1991; Mughal 1997) show that the peripheral areas supplied different raw materials. A survey of Cholistan and Bahawalpur revealed these as production areas as opposed to Saurashtra where only cotton was grown. To

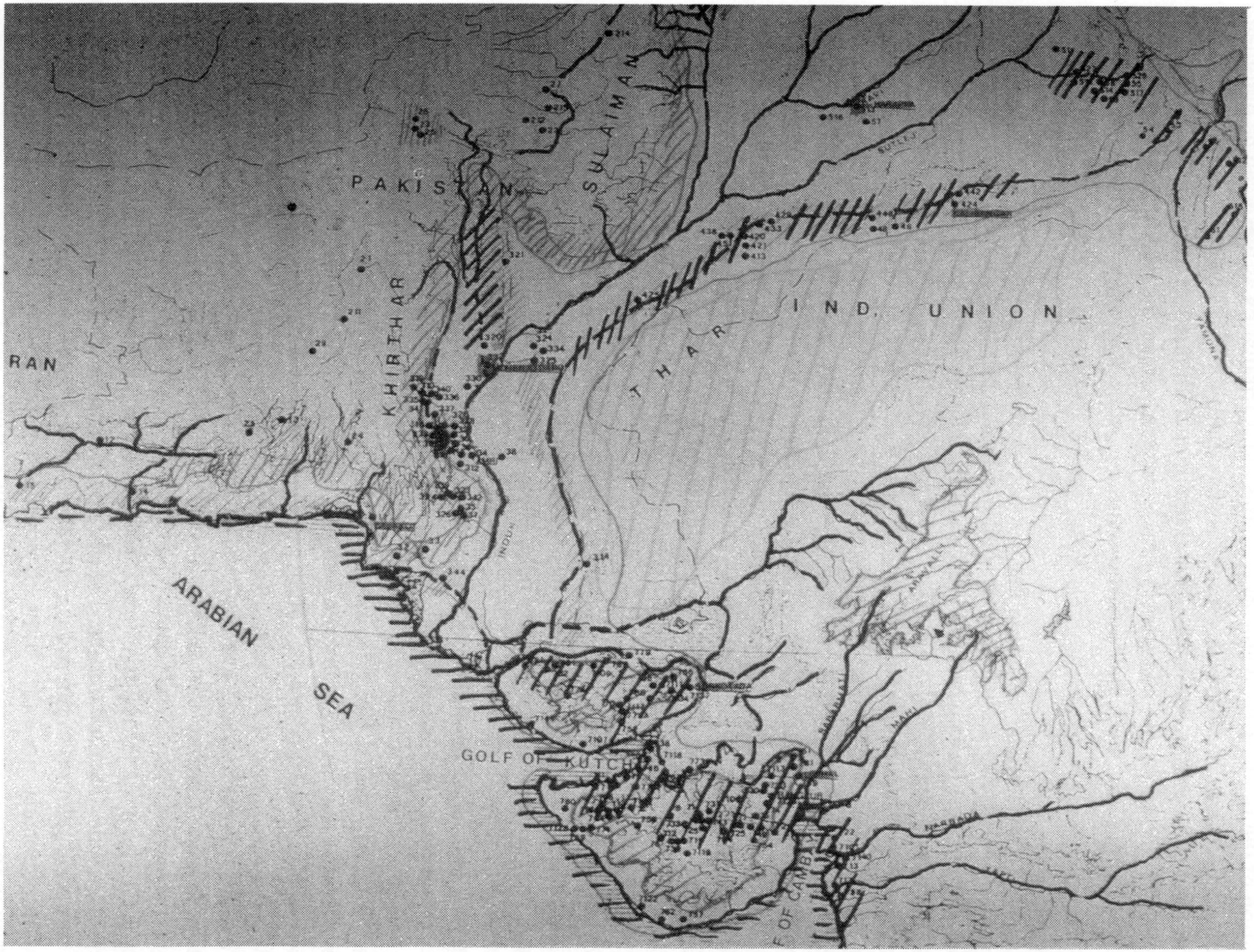

Fig. 13. Peripheral 'niches' to the central Indus system with the Kachi and Gomal plains to the west and the Ganga-Yamuna Doab, the Ghaggar-Hakkra and the Kachchh area to the east.

what extent the alluvial Indus Plain was used for intensive agriculture is not yet known. Irrigation of the fields is thinkable only in the Indus tributaries as these can be dammed and thus controlled. The Indus itself never was controllable.[25] The only traditional cultivation form is the *rabi* where at the end of the annual inundation the moist soil was (and is) used for cultivation. In addition, we know nothing about the relation of the different regions among each other, and with the centre.

Road System

The present work has shown that the cultural development within the settlement networks of noth-west India was directly linked with the form and change of communication lines. Thereby the shift in the means of transport from a land to a marine way played an important role. This is understandable since for five months of the year the lower Indus Valley is inaccessible for land transportation. From here old roads lead off to the west over the highlands of Sindh-Kohistan. The Indus Plain was either flooded or following the retreat of the annual floods, still marshy. There were only a few months in spring and early summer where the lower Indus Plain was accessaible. To the east roads which lead off to the north and south are not known. Thus, the western highlands and their piedmont were themselves even till recently important communicational areas. In Harappan times they were, at least partly for the Indus Civilization system, substituted by the water transport on the Indus.

Within the Kot Diji complex [26] the river transport seems to have begun. The extension of this material complex suggests early contact with the alluvial core area of the Indus Valley. The centre could easily have been Harappa in Punjab,[27] but the area of the Gomal Plain, with mighty settlements such as Rahman Dheri (first half of the third millennium BC), and the Manchhar Lake also come in question, with the advantage that the latter is not only the largest sweet water reservoir on the subcontinent, but also settlements are located from the end of the fourth millennium which could have existed only with the help of boats. Here the origin for the development of the boat can be sought. Such boats, as they are known even today with the Mohana, have a flat hull, and are designed to ply on shallow water. Parallel to them the Sothi Culture developed east along the Ghaggar.

That the communication ran essentially north-south has been mentioned by several authors. It seems essential that apparently parallel to and east of the Indus with the Ghaggar and further south with today's eastern Nara, a second axis north-south existed which was much more heavily settled than that of the Indus and ended in the Rann of Kachchh, where hundreds of settlements are located on the peninsulas of Kachchh and Saurashtra. The temporal relation to the Indus axis seems to be given. Understandable is the heavy population density since this river system was smaller and more easily controllable in relation to the water household than the Indus system.

A similarity of the north-south axial settlement network in the Indus Valley and the Ghaggar/eastern Nara is higly probable:

Hypothetical Stages of the Network

- Fourth millennium: Land routes through the highlands parallel to the alluvial Indus Valley;
- Beginning of third millennium until *c.* 2500 BC: In addition to the land routes decentralized use of Indus waterways;
- From *c.* 2500 BC onwards: Intensive use of Indus waterways;
- From *c.* 2300 to 1900 BC in addition: Intensive use of the Ghaggar-eastern Nara water system; expansion along the Makran Coast up to Oman.

During the blossoming of the Indus Civilization, the complex settlement net system was directed from Mohenjo Daro. How and under what circumstances this happened is part of forthcoming investigations.

NOTES

1. New kinds of access, such as internet, are progressive, and can only be mentioned here in passing. They bring with them completely new possibilities. The city of Bangalore as a new seat of the electronic industry can be considered due to its data highway connections with the rest of the world as a 'First World' city within 'World' India. Qualities are no longer assigned solely through the geographic position, but rather by means of communication.
2. This observation is not convincing because the graphic representation in question possesses little informational value.
3. Looking into the bibliography the 'Central Place Theory' seems not to have played a major role here.
4. Another attempt by G. Possehl (1997) is not significant.
5. 'Size' cannot be applied as the only parameter to qualify for a 'city' or a 'settlement' (see, e.g. Weber 1921)
6. I wonder how the Harappans knew the measure 'hectare' to identify their cities.
7. In those days an emergency excavation was carried out by the Department of Archaeology, Karachi which is not yet published.
8. Which should not be the only parameter!
9. It might be added that through its destruction in the nineteenth century Harappa suffered to such an extent that it is difficult to compare it today with Mohenjo Daro. The most recent investigations offer further data (M. Kenoyer and R. Meadow). In any case Harappa seems to be smaller than Mohenjo Daro.
10. With an annual production of about 300 cu m mud bricks per person and a total volume of approximately 5,60,000 cu m for the citadel and at least 5 million cu m for the lower city.
11. R. Mughal saw in some pottery from Wheeler's excavation in 1950 Early Harappan material which could not be proved (see, e.g. M. Jansen ....). The unpublished drawings and photographs of Wheeler's excavation are with the author.
12. See reports on traditional settlement behaviour in Sindh, e.g. *The Gazetteer of Sind* 1909.
13. Our drilling profiles clearly show that in those days the Indus flowed close to the west of the citadel (see Fig. 8, and M. Jansen 1999). There must have been deviations from this course during the more than 500 years of its existence. To investigate into these phenomena further sedimentological studies have to be carried out. Here a sound test could be made along Wheeler's deep sounding of 1950, as we have horizontal alluvial deposits of over 4,500 years against the vertical Harappan retaining wall (including the colluvium). Wheeler's original drawings are with the author.
14. Neither the street system (small lanes, etc.) nor the lay out of houses favours an agrarian system. In

addition, our surface surveys have clearly shown that the site was not a production centre. Production centres seem to have been in the periphery as in Cholistan.

15. The behaviour in the upper Indus Valley seems to have been different.
16. Therefore the roads there traditionally do not pass through the alluvial Indus Valley, but rather through the western elevated plain of Sindh-Kohistan. Only as a result of the damming of the Indus by the British, the alluvial valley was settled and developed with roads. In 1857 a railroad was built along the mountains and on the elevated terraces.
17. Coming down the Kachi plain to Mohenjo Daro in N-S direction.
18. One of the few exceptions is the location of Shortughai in north Afghanistan which could only be reached by land route. Otherwise the overwhelming amount of settlement in the Mature Harappan period lies within the reach of the water transport (see, the change during the Late Harappan period in Saurashtra).
19. This figure was calculated by Walter Fairservis based on the comparative study with settlements of the nineteenth century in this area and similar size.
20. This is a rather speculative approach based on average size of 3 ha or settlement and approximately 50 sq m/ inhabitants. In fact, we have no idea of the density and how the composition of the individual population within a settlement was. Were there only 'Harappans' and what does this term actually mean? Or was there a mixture between the locals and the 'invaders'. Here we will face problems also archaeologically speaking, because traditionally one went primarily for the 'Harappan' artefacts and neglected the 'non Harappan' ones (see e.g. Kalibangan).
21. I am aware of my provocative position.
22. The dispute between Childe and Wheeler about the fortifications in the Indus Valley sites was an ideological one. At least the 'fortifications' unearthed at Mohenjo Daro are none, as they do not mark the limit of the citadel but according to our present knowledge structures more than 7 m are above the former alluvial plain.
23. The coast was *c.* 100 km closer to Mohenjo Daro than now.
24. Several authors explain the apparent thin population as a result of the burial of the ancient settlements below the Indus alluvium.
25. Until the building of the Sukkur Barrage in 1932. It would be absurd to explain the existence of Mohenjo Daro as a result of agricultural development.
26. Although this culture is named after the site Kot Diji, certainly it is not the 'central place' of the culture.
27. The most recent excavations by my American colleagues reveal Harappa to be a centre of the Kot Diji Culture since the distribution of this culture was identified primarily by the similarity of pottery, and the pottery in such a characteristic form is primarily found at Harappa, which could be the former centre of this culture. But the (hypothetical) use of the boat and the need to expand require further explanation.

REFERENCES

Adams, R.McC. 1965. *Land Behind Baghdad*. Chicago: University of Chicago Press.

Adams, R.McC and H. Nissen 1972. *The Uruk Countryside: the Natural Setting of Urban Societies*. Chicago: University of Chicago Press.

Agrawal, D.P. 1964. Harappa Culture: New Evidence for a Shorter Chronology, *Science* 143: 950-2

——— 1971. *The Copper Bronze Age in India*. New Delhi: Munshiram Manoharlal.

Aitkin, E.H. (Compiler) 1907. *Gazetteer of the Province of Sind*. Karachi.

Allchin, B. and F.R. Allchin 1968. *The Birth of Indian Civilization*. Harmondsworth: Penguin Books.

——— 1997. *Origins of a Civilization*. New Delhi: Penguin India Ltd.

Christaller, W. 1933. *Die zentralen Orte in Süddeutschland. Eine Ökonomisch-Geographische*

Untersuchung über die Gesetzmäßigkeit der Verbreitung und Entwicklung der Siedlungen mit städtischen Funktionen. Jena: Zeiss.

Dales, G.F. 1962. Harappan Outposts on the Makran Coast, *Antiquity* 36: 86-92.

——— 1965. Recent Pre- and Proto-historic Researches in Pakistan and Afghanistan, *Expedition* 7 (4): 10-19.

——— 1973. Recent Pre- and Protohistoric Researches in Pakistan and Afghanistan, in *Radiocarbon and Indian Archaeology* (D.P. Agrawal and A. Ghosh Eds.), pp. 118-30. Bombay: Tata Institute of Fundamental Research.

Fairservis, W.A. Jr. 1961. The Harappan Civilization—New Evidence and More Theory, *Novitates 2055.* New York: American Museum of Natural History.

——— 1967. The Origin, Character and Decline of an Early Civilization, *Novitates 2302.* New York: American Museum of Natural History.

——— 1971. *The Roots of Ancient India.* New York: Macmillan.

Flam, L. 1981. The Paleography and Prehistoric Settlement Patterns in Sind, Pakistan (*c.* 4000-2000 B.C.). Ph.D. Dissertation. Philadelphia: University of Pennsylvania.

——— 1993. Fluvial Geomorphology of the Lower Indus Basin (Sindh, Pakistan) and the Indus Civilization, in *Himalaya to the Sea. Geology, Geomorphology and the Quaternary* (J.F. Shroder Ed.), pp. 265-87. London-New York: Routledge.

Jansen, M. 1993a. Mohenjo Daro: Type Site of the Earliest Urbanization Process in South Asia, in *Urban Form and Meaning in South Asia: the Shaping of Cities from Baluchistan to Precolonial Times* (H. Spodek and D.M. Srinivasan Eds.), pp. 35-52. Washington, D.C.: National Gallery of Art.

——— 1993b. Pre, Proto, Early, Mature, Urban, Late, Post Harappan: Linearity, Multilinearity: 'Babylonian Language Confusion' or Ideological Dispute?, in *South Asian Archaeology 1991* (Adalbert J. Gail and Gerd J.R. Mevissen Eds.), pp. 135-48. Stuttgart: Franz Steiner Verlag.

——— 1998 CD-Rom Mohenjo Daro Photographic Data Bank. Aachen.

——— 1999. Mohenjo Daro and the River Indus, in *Indus River: Biodiversity, Resource, Humankind* (A. and P.S. Meadows, Eds.), pp. 355-86. Karachi: Oxford University Press. Published for the Linnian Society of London.

Johnson, G. 1972. A Test of the Utility of Central Place Theory in Archaeology, in *Man Settlement and Urbanism* (P. Ucko, R. Tringham and G. Dimbley Eds.), pp. 769-85. London: Duckworth.

Kohl, P. 1979. The 'World-Economy' of West Asia in the Third Millennium B.C., in *South Asian Archaeology 1977*(M. Taddei Ed.), pp. 55-85. Naples: Instituto Universitario Orientale.

Meadows, A. and P.S. Meadows 1999. *Indus River: Biodiversity, Resource, Humankind.* Published for the Linnian Society of London. Karachi: Oxford University Press.

Mughal, R. 1971. The Early Harappan Period in the Greater Indus Valley and Northern Baluchistan (*c.* 3000-2400 B.C.). Ph.D. Dissertation. Ann Arbor, Michigan : University of Pennsylvania.

——— 1990a. The Harappan Settlement Systems and Patterns in the Greater Indus Valley (*c.* 3500-1500 B.C.), *Pakistan Archaeology* 25: 1-72.

——— 1990b. The Harappan 'Twin Capitals' and Reality, *Journal of Central Asia* XIII (1): 155-62.

——— 1990c. Further Evidence of the Early Harappan Culture in the Greater Indus Valley: 1971-90, *South Asian Studies* 6: 175-99.

——— 1991. The Cultural Patterns of Ancient Pakistan and Neighbouring Regions *c.* 7000-1500 B.C., *Pakistan Archaeology* 26: 218-37.

——— 1994. Ancient Cities of the Indus, *Lahore Museum Bulletin* VII (1-2): 53-9.

——— 1997. *Ancient Cholistan: Archaeology and Architecture.* Lahore: Ferozsons.

Panhawar, M.H. 1977. Source Material on Sind. Jamshoro.

Piggott, S. 1950 (Reprint 1961). *Prehistoric India to 1000 BC.* Harmondsworth: Penguin.

Possehl, G. (Ed.) 1993. *Harappan Civilization: a Recent Perspective.* New Delhi: Oxford-IBH and the American Institute of Indian Studies.

Possehl, G. 1997. The Transformation of the Indus Civilization, *Journal of World Prehistory* 11 (4): 425-72.

Rao, S.R. 1973. *Lothal and the Indus Civilization.* Bombay: Asia Publishing House.

——— 1979. *Lothal, a Harappan Port.* New Delhi: Memoirs of the Archaeological Survey of India 78 (1).

——— 1985. *Lothal 1955-62.* New Delhi: Memoirs of the Archaeological Survey of India 78 (2).

Ratnagar, S. 1991. *Enquiries into the Political Organization of Harappan Society.* Pune: Ravish.

Schroder, J. 1993. *Himalaya to the Sea. Geology, Geomorphology and the Quaternary.* London-New York: Routledge.

Weber, M. 1921. *The City* (Edited and Translated by D. Martindale and G. Neuwirth [1958]). New York-London: The Free Press

Wheeler, Sir M. 1953. *The Indus Civilization.* Cambridge: Cambridge University Press.

Wittfogel, Karl A. 1977. *Die Orientalische Despotie.* Köln: Eine vergleichende Untersuchung totaler Macht.

The Pre-Harappan Cultures of Gujarat

P. AJITHPRASAD

The origin of Indus Valley Civilization evokes considerable curiosity and discussion even after more than seventy years of continuous research and study. One reason for this is the apparent absence of sites showing a cultural change gradually leading towards the urban way of life in the valley of Indus and its tributaries. There seems to be an abruptness in the emergence of urban ethos of the Harappan Civilization in the Chalcolithic cultural arena during the middle of the third millennium BC. This has led many scholars since the 1930s to invoke a Mesopotamian inspiration in the origin of the Indus Valley Civilization (see Mackay 1938; Wheeler 1960). However, for many researchers this has been a proposition simply untenable in the cultural process, especially after the discovery of a number of village farming Chalcolithic settlements predating the Harappan Culture in Sindh, Baluchistan and in Rajasthan. Thus, in the 1960s, while passionately advocating the claim of Sothi Culture, the remains of which had then recently been located in the Drishadvati Valley in Rajasthan, as an antecedent stage (Early/Pre-Harappan) in the making of the Harappan Culture, A. Ghosh wrote: '... while death from unidentified source is understandable natural birth is an unnatural phenomenon' (Ghosh 1965). This, succinctly describes the awkwardness of an abrupt, inspirational origin of the Harappan Culture.

Historically speaking this was the first emphatic appeal for recognizing a direct antecedent stage of the Harappan Culture and its indigenous origin. Since then, extensive studies in the Harappan cultural domain especially in the Indus and the Ghaggar-Hakkra systems and in the Baluchistan region in Pakistan by M.R. Mughal (1970, 1982, 1990) have helped immensely to define and delineate the Early Harappan sub-stratum of the Harappan Civilization. His efforts have been largely instrumental in bringing together not only the disjointed cultural assemblages from Kot Diji, Amri and Kalibangan but also from a number of Chalcolithic settlements in the respective regions. One important result of these studies has been the acceptance of a new model in recent years which describes the Harappan urbanism as the culmination of a process started much earlier than it actually manifested (Possehl 1977, 1990).[1] Thus, recent excavations at Nausharo in Baluchistan (Jarrige et al. 1995) or Dholavira in Kachchh (Bisht 1991) describes the Pre-Urban, Urban and Post-Urban cultural traits as different stages in the beginning, culmination and decline of a cultural continuum.[2]

Thus, Baluchistan, the lower and upper Indus Valley in Sindh and Punjab, the dried up beds of Hakkra, Ghaggar and Sarasvati rivers in Bikaner and Rajasthan are all believed to have been teaming with a number of Chalcolithic village farming communities eventually forming a stable base for the emergence of Harappan urbanism. But, the picture emerging from Gujarat, till very recently, seems to be slightly different from the above one. It has traditionally been assumed that it was the immigrant Harappans, who established their settlements in different parts of Gujarat with a view to expanding their industrial base during the Mature/Urban phase, responsible for the introduction of Chalcolithic village farming life in Gujarat. And, according to this view, while the Harappans with their superior technology migrated from north, Gujarat was inhabited by Stone Age hunter-gatherer communities using microlithic blade tools (Possehl 1980). Hence, possibilities of coming across indigenous Chalcolithic settlements in Gujarat predating the Harappan immigration was never taken as a serious proposition. Consequently, until very recently Bronze Age/Chalcolithic settlement in Gujarat was synonymous with the Harappan Culture. So strong is this paradigm in the research programmes in Gujarat, that many researchers have bent over backwards in their attempt to accommodate incongruous evidence into the above conceptual model.[3]

S.R. Rao in the 1960s for the first time described the possible existence of an indigenous Chalcolithic population at Lothal prior to the Harappan occupation (Rao 1963). Prior to this the excavation at Somnath (Prabhas Patan) in 1955-6 had resulted in the identification of Prabhas Ware, a Non-Harappan ceramic tradition contemporary to the Harappan Culture in the southern coast of Saurashtra (Subbarao 1958).[4] In spite of this, in their enthusiasm to establish a concrete presence of the Indus Civilization in the newly found political boundaries of India, most of the researchers over the years have almost completely ignored the indigenous Chalcolithic cultures in Gujarat. No wonder, therefore, that the Harappans with their loud cultural idioms have been dominating research programmes dealing with the Chalcolithic archaeology in Gujarat.

It is refreshing to see host of new data that are coming up in recent years from new discoveries and also from the reanalysis of already reported remains for understanding the Pre-Harappan or early Non-Harappan Chalcolithic cultures of Gujarat. This in the process have been instrumental for understanding the development and spread of Harappan Culture itself and its social configuration vis-à-vis the indigenous traditions of Gujarat. Recent excavations, especially at Nagwada in north Gujarat (Hegde et al. 1988; *IAR* 1985-6 to 1989-90) and Dholavira in Kachchh from 1989 onwards (Bisht 1991) have brought to light interesting Early Harappan assemblages from stratigraphic contexts that can be confidently assigned to a date prior to the Harappan occupation. The significance of these new discoveries was reviewed by Dhavalikar and Possehl (1992) in the backdrop of the Pre-Prabhas assemblage from Somnath with a view to understanding the Pre-Harappan substratum of Chalcolithic Gujarat. This was later followed by a review of Pre-Harappan and Non-Harappan assemblages reported from different parts of Gujarat incorporating new data from Loteshwar in Mehsana district, north Gujarat and from Padri in Bhavnagar district, Saurashtra coast by Sonawane and Ajithprasad in 1994.

In addition to the above, recent excavations in 1994 and 1995 at Datrana in Banaskantha district, north Gujarat by the M.S. University of Baroda have brought to light further interesting evidence of a new Pre-Harappan assemblage which shows close correspondence with the Pre-Prabhas assemblage reported from Somnath (Ajithprasad et al. 1995). Some amount of overlapping of this assemblage with the Anarta ceramic tradition and the pottery from the Chalcolithic burials of north Gujarat is also evident at the site.

Important features of the newly discovered Pre-Harappan assemblage from Datrana and its stratigraphical and chronological position with other Pre-/Non-Harappan Cultures of north Gujarat and Saurashtra are discussed in this paper.

The criteria we may follow here for designating early Non-Harappan or Pre-Harappan cultures are simple: (a) they should be distinct from the Harappan in their material culture, and (b) they should have an independent existence chronologically/stratigraphically prior to the beginning of Harappan occupation in the region under study. Following these criteria it may not be difficult to delineate the features of Pre-Urban Chalcolithic Cultures; however, it becomes complicated when these traits become part of the Urban Harappan with little or no modification. Identification of such Non-Harappan traits in the Harappan ethos in different regions are therefore important in understanding the social configuration of the Harappan society (Ajithprasad and Sonawane, in press).

A cursory look at the radiocarbon dates from the Harappan and other Chalcolithic sites in Gujarat may indicate that a majority of dates for the Urban Harappan settlements fall within the time bracket, *c*. 2500 to 2000 BC (Table1). But, there are a few sites like Prabhas Patan, Padri and Loteshwar which show dates earlier than 2500 BC. The dates are fairly consistent and reliable and therefore they can be easily classified as Pre-Harappan. In addition to these, the Early Harappan assemblage from Dholavira, the burial pottery assemblages from north Gujarat and to some extent the Micaceous Red Ware of Saurashtra certainly show a stratigraphic precedence over the Harappan assemblage (Table 2). Material assemblages from all these sites are distinctly different from the Harappans and therefore call attention in light of new discovery from Datrana. Since the Non-Harappan pottery from Datrana and the Pre-Prabhas pottery exhibit close similarity, a detailed description of the latter may form a proper backdrop for understanding the Datrana assemblage.

PRE-PRABHAS AND PRABHAS ASSEMBLAGES

Historically, this is the first Non-Hârappan assemblage unearthed in Gujarat in the mid 1950s excavation from Prabhas Patan (Somnath) (20°53' N: 70°24' E) in Junagadh district (Fig. 1) on the southern coast of Saurashtra (*IAR* 1956-7; Subbarao 1958). However, its Pre-Harappan status was recognized only in the early 1990s (Dhavalikar and Possehl 1992). The site is located at the mouth of the Hiranya river, hardly 3 km away from the sea shore. Excavations starting from the 1950s by the State Archaeology Department together with the M.S. University of Baroda (*IAR* 1955-6), followed by State Archaeology Department (*IAR* 1956-7) and finally by Deccan College, Pune in association with the State Archaeology Department in the 1970s (*IAR* 1971-2), have brought to light a fivefold cultural sequence. Among these the early three periods belonged to a Chalcolithic culture affiliated to the Harappan Civilization and the later two belonged to the Historic period (Dhavalikar 1984).

Among the three Chalcolithic periods, the Period I and II, designated as Pre-Prabhas and Prabhas respectively, are important in the present context as these two incorporated distinct ceramic assemblages that are different from the Harappan. Period III on the other

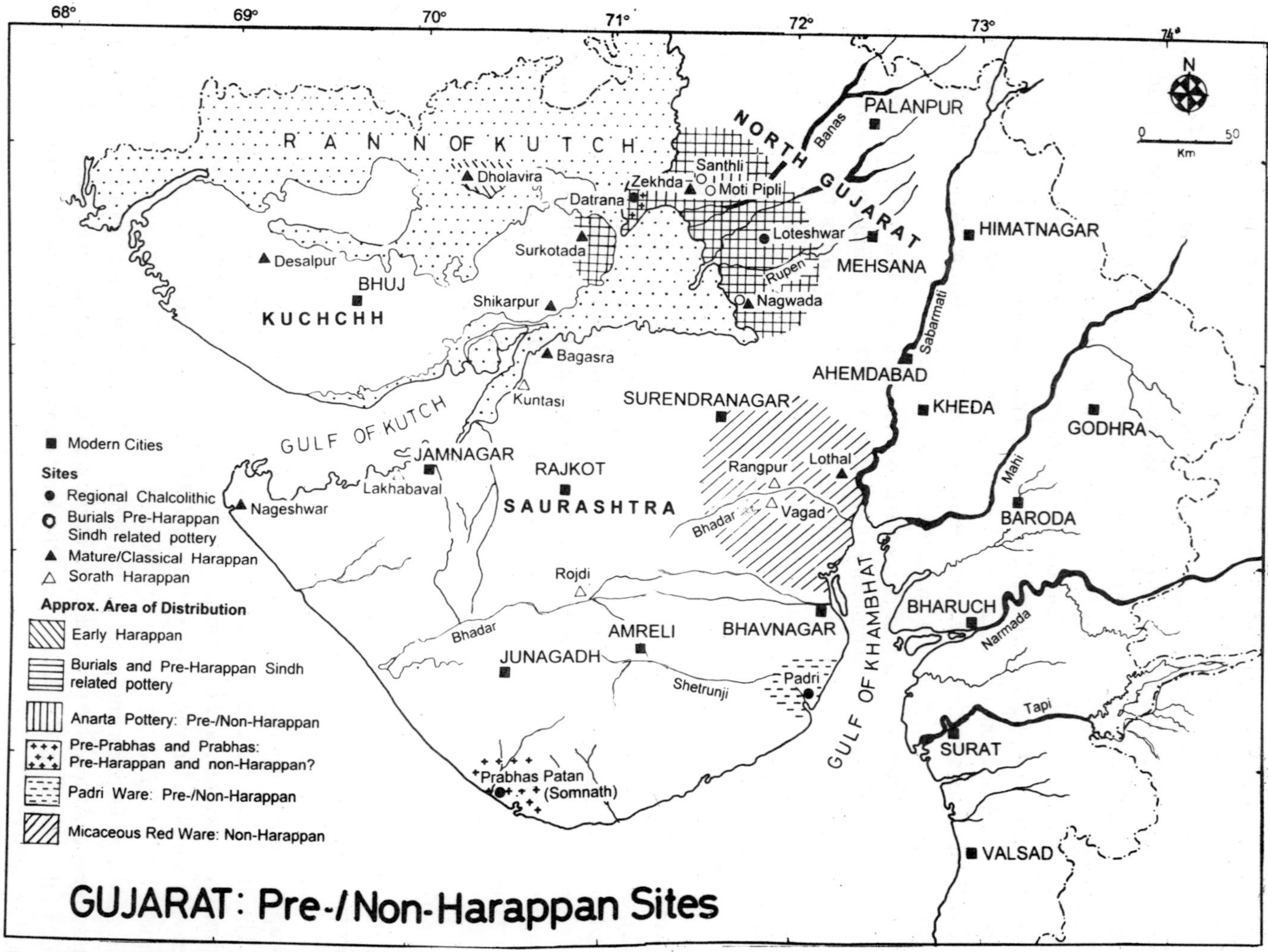

Fig. 1. Pre-/Non-Harappan sites in Gujarat.

TABLE 1. RADIOCARBON DATES FROM HARAPPAN AFFILIATED CHALCOLITHIC SITES IN GUJARAT

Site & Sample No.	Cultural Affiliation	Date BC / BP	Calibrated date Half life 5730
Lothal	Urban Harappan		
TF 136	Lothal A, Period IA	2080±135 BC	2461 Cal. BC
TF 22	Lothal A, Period IIIB	2010±115 BC	2328 Cal. BC
TF 27	Lothal A, Period IIIB	2005±115 BC	2315 Cal. BC
Surkotada	Urban Harappan		
TF 1305	Period IA, early levels	2055±100 BC	2455 Cal. BC
TF 1301±	Period IA	2005±135 BC	2315 Cal. BC
TF 1295	Period IB	1945±100 BC	2202 Cal. BC
Rojdi	Urban Harappan		
PRL 1284	Rojdi A	2325±115 BC	2699 Cal. BC
PRL 1093	Rojdi A	2090±115 BC	2462 Cal. BC
TF 200	Rojdi B	1975±115 BC	2283 Cal. BC
PRL 1088	Rojdi B	1935±125 BC	2198 Cal. BC
Nagwada	Urban Harappan		
A 4555	Period IB,	1860±80 BC	2133 Cal. BC
Prabhas Patan	Pre-Harappan		
PRL 90	Period I, Pre-Prabhas	2415±115 BC	2892 Cal. BC
TF 1287	Period I, Pre-Prabhas	2460±110 BC	2911 Cal. BC
	Urban Harappan		
PRL 92	Period II, Prabhas	1995±100 BC	2299 Cal. BC
TF 1282	Period II, Prabhas	1755±95 BC	1953 Cal. BC
Loteshwar	Pre-Harappan		
PRL 1564	Period II, Anarta	2510±110 BC	2921 Cal. BC
PRL 1565	Period II, Anarta	3100±110 BC	3698 Cal. BC
Padri	Pre-Harappan		
PRL 1785	Period II	4520±90 BP	3049 Cal. BC
PRL 1787	Period II	4960±100 BP	3680 Cal. BC

Dates from Possehl 1993; Supplied by V.S. Shinde (personal communication).

hand is characterized by the presence of Lustrous Red Ware and therefore belonging to the Post-Urban phase of the Harappan Culture in Gujarat.

Period I at the site is represented by a thin deposit lying directly above the natural sediments. According to Subbarao (1958), it is characterized by the occurrence of a 'corrugated or broadly incised Ware with typical blade industry of Agate and Chalcedony with crested ridge'. In addition to this, excavations in the 1970s have revealed a few more pottery types which were different from the Harappan pottery belonging to this period. These are: (1) Coarse Red-Grey Ware, (2) Red Slipped Ware, (3) Black and Red Ware and (4) Incised Red Ware (*IAR* 1971-2; Dhavalikar and Possehl 1992). Wide mouthed jar, basins with flat bottom, small carinated *handies* and some vessels with ring base are the important vessels in this assemblage. The fabric of all the above pottery was predominantly coarse and they were all handmade. However, the external surface is smooth and even shows fine burnishing. The Black and Red Ware on the other hand is made of relatively fine clay and has a bright red slip on the exterior. It is well burnished on both interior and exterior. The Incised Red Ware with surface colour varying from drab red to grey also has a coarse fabric. The incised designs which mostly consists of bold strokes were probably executed by a rather blunt instrument. A similar decoration consisting of incised oblique lines are common on the Black and Red Ware vessels at the flaring out rim (Dhavalikar and Possehl 1992). This peculiar incised design seems to be a characteristic feature of the Pre-Prabhas pottery. A few Harappan pottery especially those of dish-on-stand, steatite micro-beads and segmented faience beads are also reported from this deposit.

Two radiocarbon dates, 2983 ± 65 BC and 2869 ± 80 BC (Table 1), from this deposit show that, this early Chalcolithic occupation goes back to the beginning of third millennium BC; about three to four hundred years earlier than the beginning of Urban Harappan in Gujarat. It is interesting to note that the Pre-Prabhas pottery is not reported from any of the sites in Saurashtra so far. P.P. Pandya reports about a Corrugated Grey Ware, similar to the one from the Pre-Prabhas levels, found from Rojdi in Rajkot district (*IAR* 1957-8). If this is true it may show the spread of Pre-Prabhas traits into neighbouring Chalcolithic sites although there seems to be some time-lag between them. What is more interesting however, is the discovery of an almost similar ceramic assemblage in a recent excavation by the M.S. University of Baroda from Datrana in north Gujarat. We may discuss that in detail later.

Period II, that follows Period I, is marked by a new set of ceramic assemblage known as the Prabhas Ware.[5] The Prabhas Ware is characterized by hemispherical bowls with slightly incurved and beveled rim; and medium size jars/pots with an everted short rim, incipient neck, wide shoulder and globular body. Prabhas Ware is made of fine clay and treated with a thin greenish grey slip. It is decorated with faint violet or purple pigment. The decorative patterns, generally geometric forms like horizontal and vertical lines, dots and other forms, were executed in horizontal panels or registers at the rim or at the shoulder (Nanavati et al. 1971). Besides, the assemblage includes Black and Red Ware, stud-handled bowls and Harappan pottery in this period.

Remains of several extensive stone structures, a few copper implements including a small celt, steatite and faience beads, and a carved stone seal bearing images of several stylized deer indicate the unmistakable Harappan influence. Radiocarbon dates show that this period belongs to the last phase of the Mature/Urban Harappan Culture. Prabhas pottery has a wide distribution in Saurashtra, as it is reported from Rojdi in Rajkot district, Amra and Lakhabaval in Jamnagar district. Most of these are isolated finds indicting mere contact and contemporaneity of sites.

PRE-HARAPPAN ASSEMBLAGES FROM NORTH GUJARAT

North Gujarat is the corridor which connects Kachchh with Saurashtra and the mainland Gujarat. The southern and western parts of it, partially bordering the two Ranns of Kachchh, are a vast undulating plain mainly formed of alluvial formations and fossil sand dunes. The north-eastern part is dotted with several small hillocks and the attendant reddish soil covering the piedmont. Although bordering the Rajasthan desert at its north and falling into the semi-arid climatic zone it is a region where rich Mesolithic sites are found on top of stabilized fossil sand dunes (Sankalia 1955; Bhan 1994). Nevertheless, till very recently it has been believed that the region is inhospitable for Chalcolithic peasant communities to settle down (Rao 1963; Leshnik 1967). Explorations during the last two decades by the M.S. University of Baroda have brought to light more than 100 Chalcolithic sites in this region (Hegde and Sonawane 1986; Bhan 1994; Ajithprasad and Sonawane 1993). Subsequent excavations in the 1980s and 1990s have resulted in the identification of three distinct early Non-Harappan or Pre-Harappan assemblages. The most important among these which shows a regional identity in terms of geographical spread is the Anarta pottery tradition excavated from Loteshwar and Nagwada (Sonawane and Ajithprasad 1994). The second one is a group of pottery initially reported from several burials at Nagwada (Hegde et al. 1988) and later from Santhli and a few other sites. It shows a general resemblance with the Pre-Harappan pottery of Sindh. And the third Pre-Harappan assemblage is a set of unique pottery unearthed in the excavation at Datrana in 1994 which shows close resemblance to the Pre-Prabhas pottery.

PRE-HARAPPAN ASSEMBLAGE FROM DATRANA

The Chalcolithic site at Datrana (23° 46' 30" N: 71° 06' 30" E) in Banskantha district is located about 2 km south-west of the village on a large crescentic stabilized sand dune (Fig. 1). The site measuring about 40 ha is a large blade industry site and shows several discrete clusters of artefact-spread including pottery, large amount of lithic blade industry debitage and bone fragments. Excavations at the site in 1994 and 1995 by M.S. University of Baroda have revealed a twofold cultural sequence: Period I and Period II. In a total of 75 to 90 cm deposit, Period I is represented by microliths and other Mesolithic relics; and Period II by Chalcolithic relics including pottery and copper implements. No stratigraphic break between the two are noticeable at the site.

The Chalcolithic occupation at the site is characterized by several distinct types of pottery belonging to different Non-Harappan traditions. They can be classified into three distinct categories: (a) a unique group of pottery resembling the Pre-Prabhas type, (b) the Anarta type, and (c) the Early Harappan pottery reported from the burials at Nagwada and Santhli (Sonawane and Ajithprasad 1994). Among these the most abundant pottery is the Pre-Prabhas type which includes four different types (Figs. 2 and 3). These are:

(a) Fine Red Ware with a bright red slip and broadly corrugated exterior (Fig. 3. 20, 21). These are generally sherds of large pots with a smooth surface finish. Another variety of this pottery shows a series of roughly horizontal or oblique incised lines as a decorative pattern (Fig. 3. 25, 26). The incisions are different from the usual incised decorations using a sharp tool. These are, in fact, broad and shallow incised lines produced by using the smooth rounded end of cylindrical rod.

(b) Coarse Grey or Red Ware, generally represented by medium size open mouthed vessels, basin and squat pots with a flat base and thick walls. The exterior is smoothly burnished and decorated in a similar manner with obliquely incised lines in horizontal registers (Fig. 2. 13, 14, 15; Fig. 3. 24, 27).

(c) Fine Grey Ware, small carinated pots (*handi*) generally with thin walls and showing almost a similar incised decoration as above (Fig. 2. 10, 11, 12; Fig. 3. 23).

(d) The fourth variety is Black and Red Ware. They are made of fine clay and have bright red slip. Both exterior and interior are burnished and smooth. An open mouthed deep basin with flaring out rim and narrow bottom of vessel with a ring base are the two vessels found in this type (Fig. 2. 5-9). The basin shows a similar obliquely incised lines at the rim in the interior. Black and Red Ware sherds showing corrugated exterior are also abundant (Fig. 3. 17-19)

It is obvious that the above pottery types are analogous in shape and in incised decoration with the Pre-Prabhas pottery reported from Period I of Somnath.[6] Therefore, by interpolating the date of Pre-Prabhas, a date *c.* 2900 to 3000 BC can be assigned to the beginning of Chalcolithic occupation at Datrana. The two other Pre-/Non-Harappan ceramic types, the Anarta pottery and the Pre-Harappan Sindh related pottery associated with the Chalcolithic burials of north Gujarat,[7] are found only in the upper levels close to the surface indicating that these two ceramics came into contact with the above community in Datrana only at the last stage of its existence.

It is indeed not easy to give a proper explanation for the striking resemblance between artefacts from sites located at such far away places of disparate environmental setting; Datrana is situated in dissolute semiarid north Gujarat whereas Somnath is at the sea coast in Saurashtra separated by about 400 km. While certain general resemblance in pottery style may arise by sheer accident or by contact, a one to one similarity may certainly indicate a common origin and probable migration. None of the sites so far located in north Gujarat shows a ceramic industry similar to that of Datrana.

It is interesting to note that the authors of this pottery were expert stone knappers who had produced a number of long blades using crested ridge technique on local chalcedony and jasper and even produced small circular beads of carnelian employing their own ingenious method (Ajithprasad et al. 1995). Long blades of Rohri chert are found in the upper layers associated with the Pre-Harappan burial pottery and the Anarta pottery. Whatever it may signify, a good Chalcolithic blade industry on locally available agate was found with the Pre-Prabhas assemblage too. Copper implements found from this period included a small curved knife-blade and a very fine punch point which may have been used in the production of lithic blades. Although distinct areas of activity could be identified, no remains of any kind of structures could be identified in the excavation.

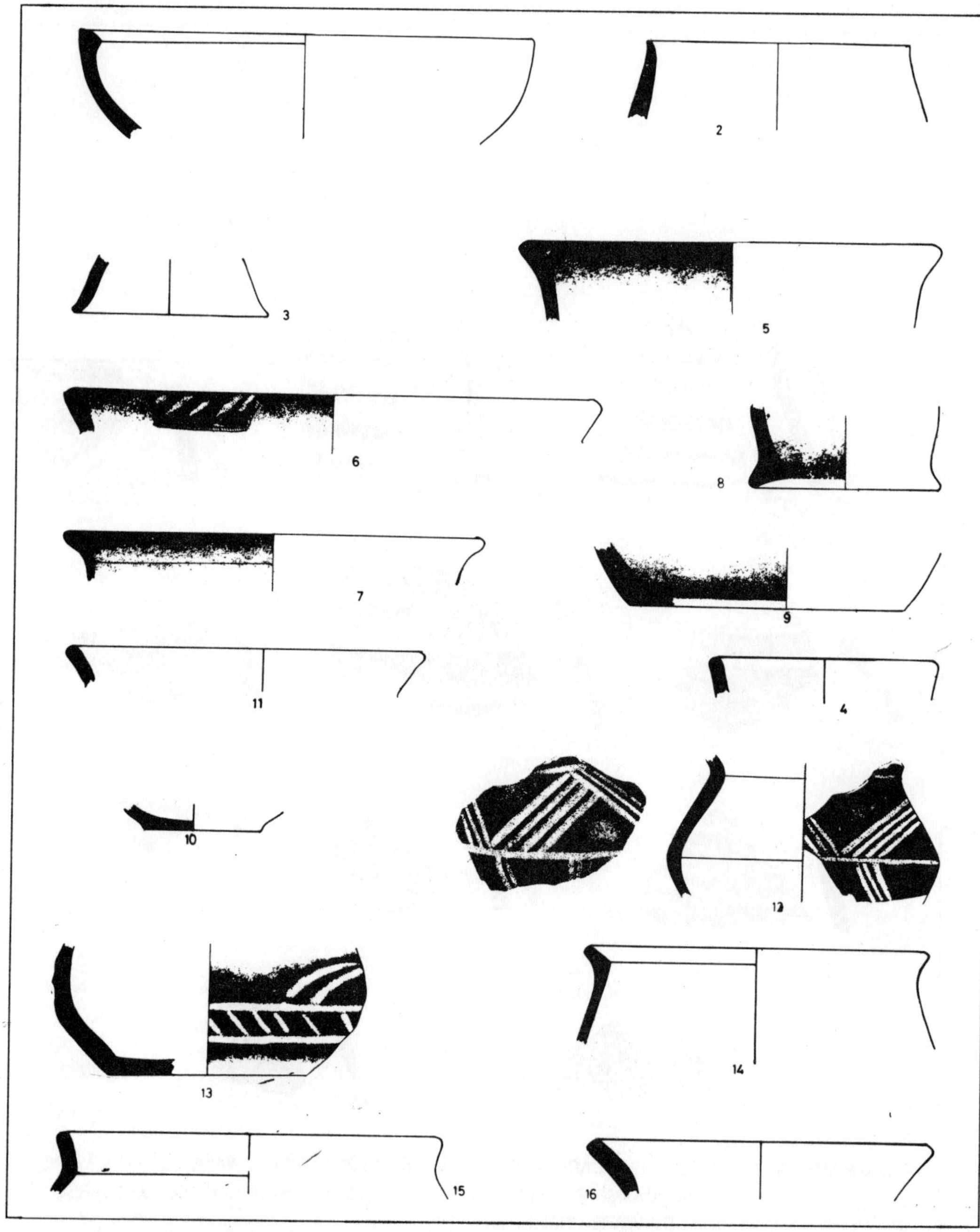

Fig. 2. Pre-Harappan pottery from Datrana: 1, 2, 3 Pre-Harappan Sindh related burial pottery: Fine Red Ware; 4-16 Pre-Harappan pottery resembling Pre-Prabhas (4 Red Ware, 5-9 Black and Red Ware, 10-12 Grey Ware, 13-16 Coarse Grey Ware, 15 Coarse Red Ware, 6, 12, 13 incised decoration).

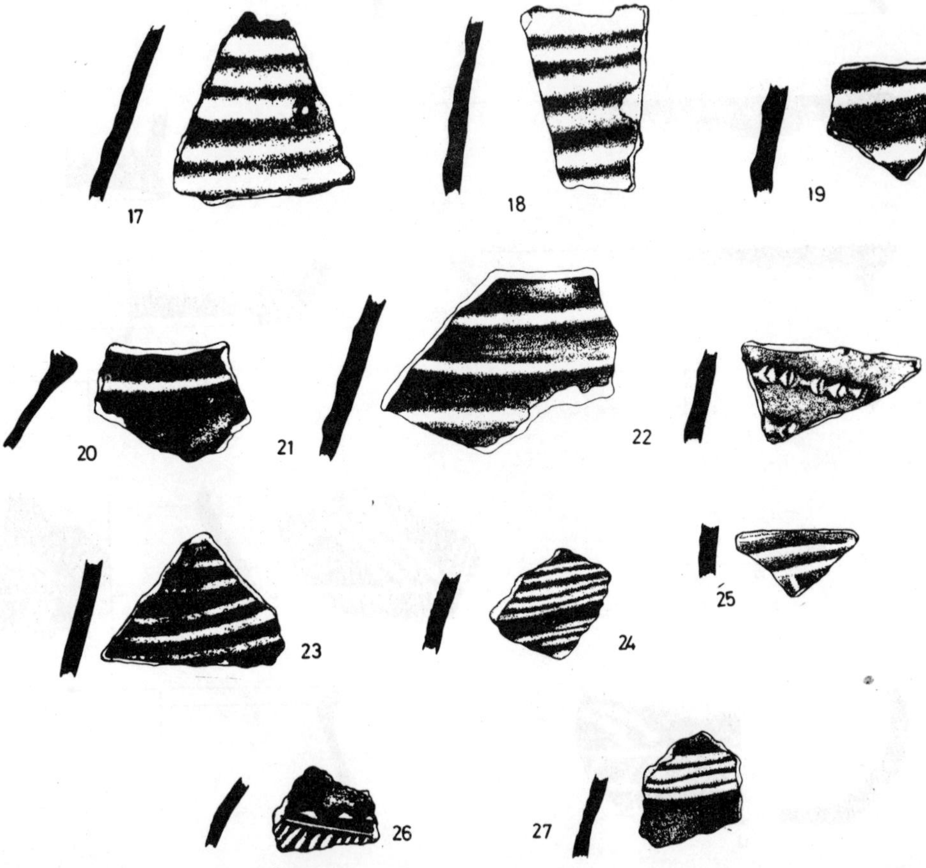

DATRANA-IV. FIG. 2. 17, 18, 19 BLACK AND RED WARE, 20,21,22 RED WARE 23 GREY WARE, 24 COARSE RED WARE (INCISED), 25,26 RED WARE (INCISED), 27 COARSE GREY WARE (INCISED).

Fig. 3. Pre-Harappan pottery resembling Pre-Prabhas from Datrana: 17-19 Black and Red Ware; 20-2, 25, 26 Red Ware; 23 Grey Ware; 24 Coarse Red Ware; 27 Coarse Grey Ware (17-21 corrugated exterior, 22-7 incised decoration).

Therefore, it seems, this was a site of short duration belonging to the early centuries of the third millennium BC.

ANARTA PRE-/NON-HARAPPAN ASSEMBLAGE

The Anarta chalcolithic tradition of north Gujarat is one of the better researched Pre-/Non-Harappan assemblages in Gujarat. A detailed description of the cultural idioms of this tradition and its regional aspect has already been attempted (Sonawane and Ajithprasad 1993; Ajithprasad and Sonawane 1993). It is identified mainly on the basis of a group of pottery which are distinctly different from the Harappan. The pottery was first recognized in 1985 in the excavation at Nagwada in Surendranagar district where it was found associated with the Mature Harappan elements. However, its personality as an independent Pre-Harappan ceramic tradition of north Gujarat was established only after the excavation at Loteshwar in Mahesana district in 1991-2 (Mahida 1992). A few more sites showing its independent existence have been reported from this area in the Rupen estuary (Ajithprasad and Sonawane 1993).

Most of our understanding of the above Pre-Harappan Culture comes from the excavations at Loteshwar (23°36'00" N: 71°50'20" E) and Nagwada (23°18'15" N: 71°42'30" E) both located in the Rupan estuary (Fig. 1). Loteshwar in Sami Taluka, Mahesana district on excavation revealed a twofold cultural sequence; the earliest of which was represented by a rich Mesolithic occupation and the later one belonging to the regional Chalcolithic Culture. The Chalcolithic deposit is characterized by an assortment of Pre-Harappan ceramic types (Figs. 4, 5, 6). Four important types are identified in this assemblage: (a) Gritty Red Ware, (b) Fine Red Ware, (c) Burnished Red Ware, and (d) Burnished Grey/Black Ware. Among these the Gritty Red Ware is the most dominant type with two sub-types and it is followed by the Fine Red Ware. The other two types are relatively rare.

In the case of Gritty Red Ware the vessels are either hand modelled or made on a slow turntable. The clay used in their production was insufficiently elutriated and contained a lot of sand and other tempering materials. Small and medium sized pots/jars with a flaring rim, constricted neck and bulbous body, large pots (Fig. 4), bowls with straight or convex sides with slightly incurved rim and basins with a thick flaring out rim and a blunt carination below it (Fig. 5) are the important forms in this category. They are either treated with a red slip of varying hue or with a thin wash of the slip. Unevenly smeared chocolate slip on bowls and small jars is also common. Many of these vessels show a bichrome decoration as they are painted with varying shades of black or red pigments on a white or cream background. White, either in a black background or directly over the slip was also used for decorating pottery. Sets of simple horizontal, vertical and wavy lines, latticed circles and squares and intersecting loops or a combination of all these executed around the rim, shoulder and body, especially in the case of pots are some of the decorative patterns on the vessels. In the case of bowls the paintings are set in panels confined to the rim. In general the vessels have a clumsy appearance even after the application of slip and decoration.

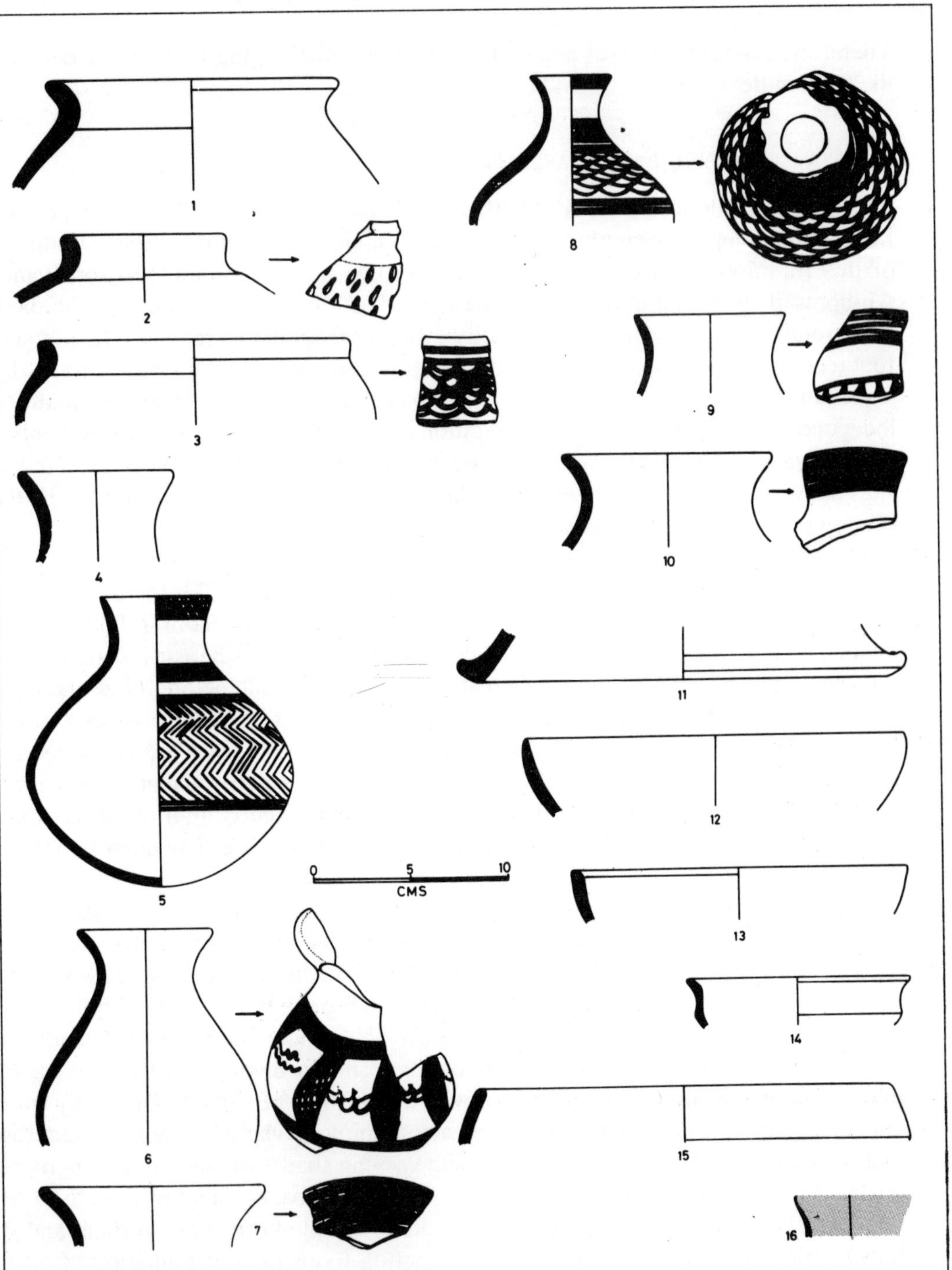

Fig. 4. Anarta pottery from Loteshwar: 1 Coarse Red Ware; 2 Coarse Grey Ware; 3, 4, 6, 10 Gritty Red Ware; 5, 7-9 Fine Red Ware (Bichrome: black on white); 11 Fine Red Ware; 12-15 Black and Red Ware, 16 Burnished Grey/Black Ware.

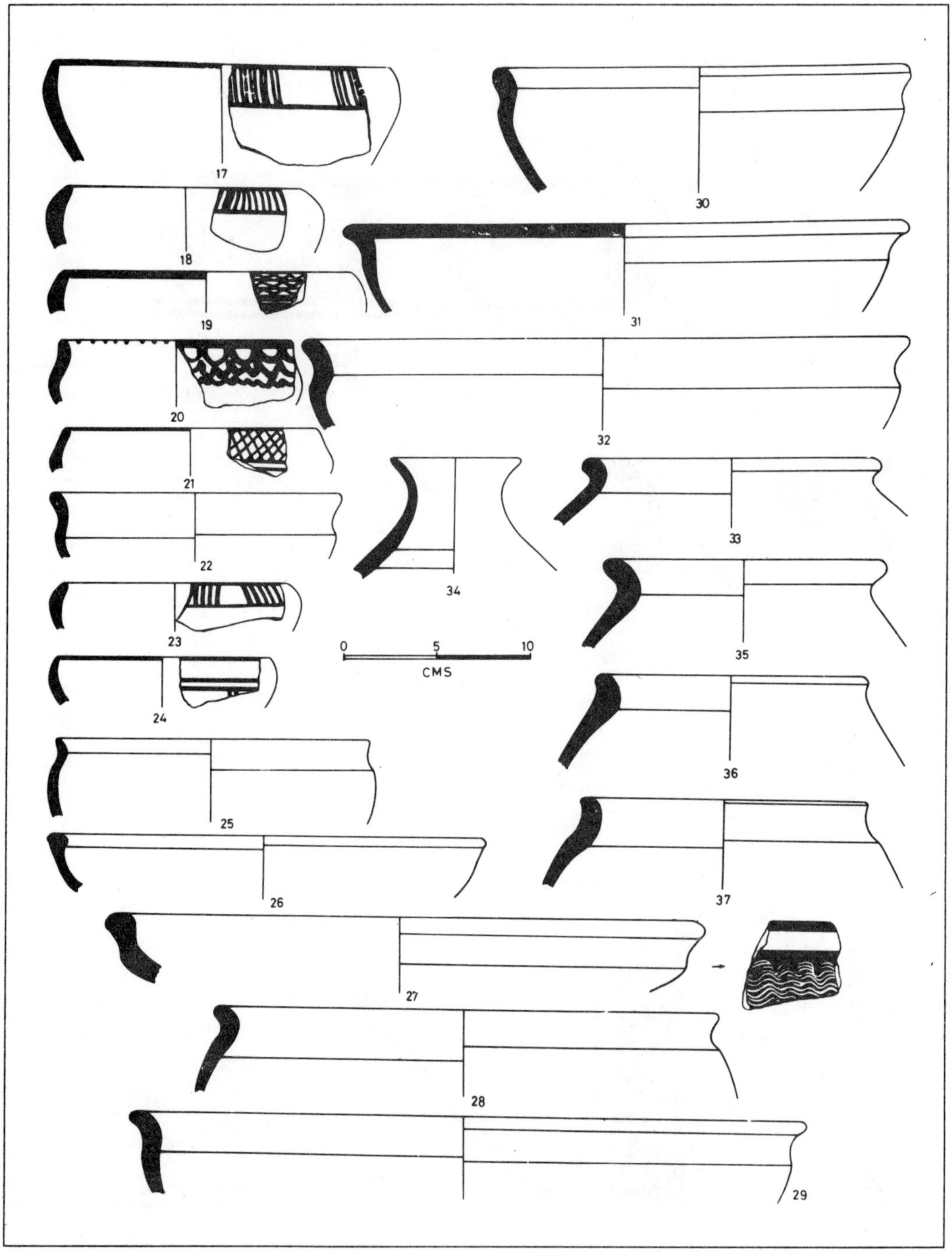

Fig. 5. Anarta Pottery from Loteshwar: 17, 18, 20-2, 28-30, 32-6 Gritty Red Ware; 19, 23-7, 31 Fine Red Ware (19 bichrome: black on cream, 23 cream slip, 24 chocolate slip, 27 reserved slip); 37 Coarse Red Ware.

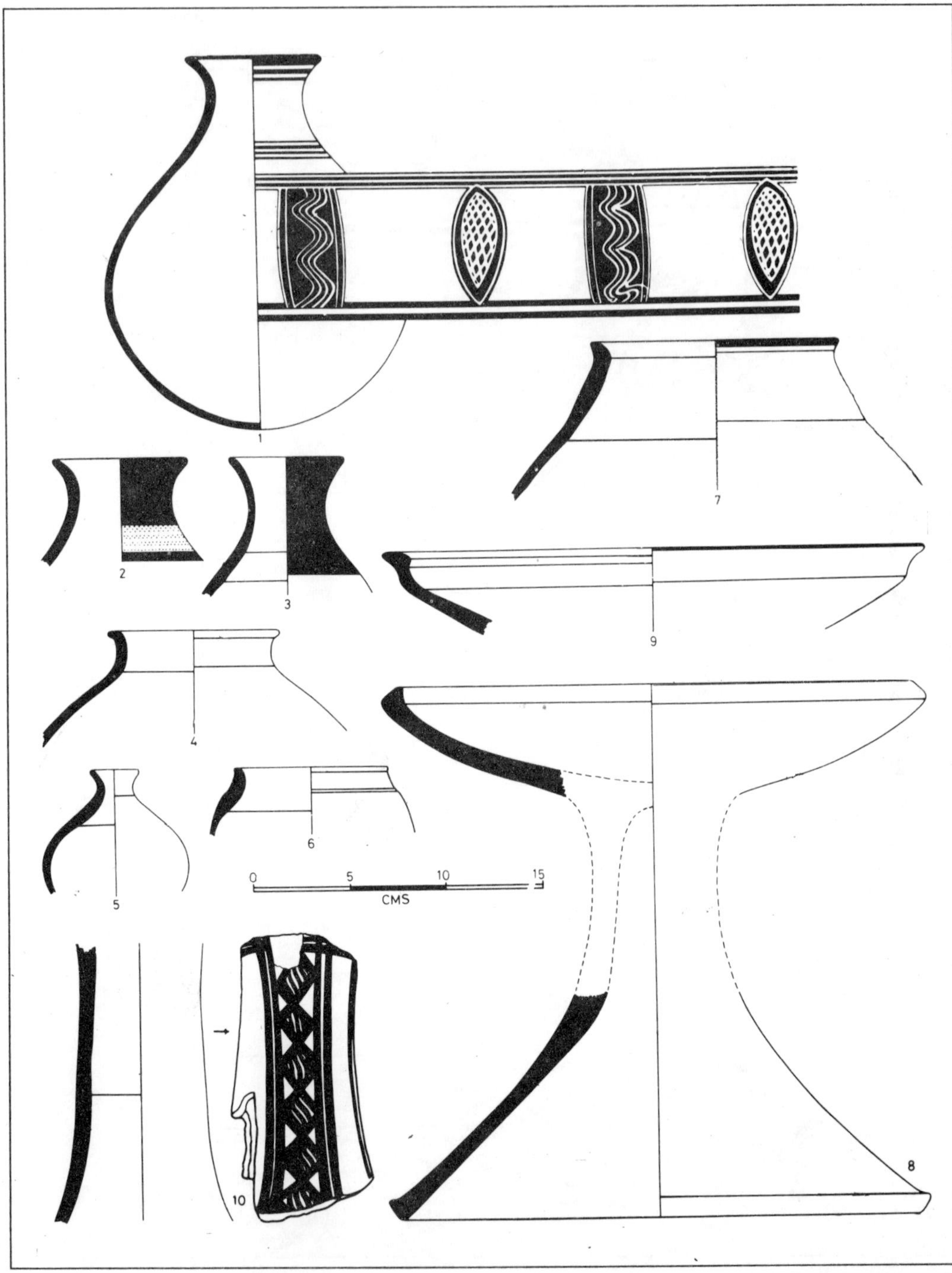

Fig. 6. Nagwada: 1 Burnished Red Ware; 2, 3, 9 Fine Red Ware (1, 2 Bichrome); 4 Burnished Grey Ware; 5, 6, 10 Coarse Gritty Red Ware; 7 Red Ware; 8·Grey Ware (1-6, 9, 10 Anarta pottery, 9 Imitation of the Harappan form, 7, 8 Burial pottery).

The Fine Red Ware, the second important pottery is made from a well elutriated clay containing a fair amount of fine mica particles. It is similar to the Gritty Red Ware in other features like the vessel forms and decoration. The Burnished Red Ware and the Burnished Grey/Black Ware on the other hand are represented by small pots or jars with a flaring rim, constricted, elongated neck and bulbous body (Fig. 6). These are thin walled vessels made of relatively fine clay on a slow, turntable. They have a well burnished smooth surface. The Burnished Red Ware is painted with parallel and wavy lines in panels using a white or bluish grey pigment on a black background over a bright red slip (Fig. 6. 1). The Burnished Grey/Black Ware is painted with a fugitive white colour, similar to the white painting that appears on the Harappan Black and Red Ware.

All the above pottery types have common vessel forms and they share several common features in their pattern and scheme of decoration suggesting that they all belong to a single pottery tradition. Apart from this, the Loteshwar assemblage has yielded a thin walled pottery decorated with simple incised decorations (Fig. 4. 2) and a variety of Reserved Slip Ware which is different from the varieties usually found in the Harappan context . The latter one is of a shallow dish having a fine red body applied with a red first slip and a black second slip (Fig. 5. 27). The black second slip was removed in the typical reserved slip technique forming a zigzag pattern. This and the incised pottery are not reported so far from other excavated sites belonging to this cultural tradition.

Two radiocarbon dates from Loteshwar indicate a very early origin of this ceramic tradition in the Rupen Valley of north Gujarat dating back to the beginning of third millennium BC, if not earlier (Table 1). The use of white and cream pigment either as a background for painting decorative patterns in shades of red and black or use of white as pigment directly over black as well as red is a widely spread Pre-Harappan tradition in decorating pottery in many sites in the Indus Valley and Rajasthan. In this respect the Gritty Red Ware can be compared with the bichrome pottery of Jalilpur (Mughal 1974), Fabric A of Kalibangan (Thapar 1975) and to a certain extent the Early Harappan pottery from Dholavira (Bisht 1991).

The maximum habitation deposit at Loteshwar, including that of the Mesolithic, is 85 to 90 cm. In this the Chalcolithic deposit was hardly 30 cm and in many places at the site it was as thin and flimsy as 10 to 20 cm. A similar flimsy deposit was found at Santhli too. Several pits with dimensions ranging from 2 m to 0.50 m in depth as well as in diameter are found at both these places. They are generally filled with a lot of ash and debris of Chalcolithic habitation. The function of these pits has not yet been properly understood. Pits of similar nature but smaller in size have also been excavated from the early levels at Nagwada where the Anarta pottery is found associated with the Mature/Classical Harappan remains. In addition to the pits a few post holes and rubble stone foundations of structures are also reported from the early levels at Nagwada (Hegde et al. 1988).

They certainly knew about the use of copper as a few copper pins, rods and fragmentary wires were recovered from Loteshwar and other sites. Similarly they have also used steatite micro-beads, beads of semiprecious stones and shell. Their contact at a later stage with the Harappan is reflected in the introduction of Harappan technology and use of typical Harappan material. At Nagwada they even imitated several Harappan vessel forms like the dish-on-stand with incised decoration, perforated jar and beakers in the Anarta pottery.

A study conducted for ascertaining the geographical extension and cultural context of this pottery indicate that its spread is mainly confined to north Gujarat and south-eastern parts of Kachchh adjacent to north Gujarat (Ajithprasad and Sonawane in 1993). While at Loteshwar it is found independently, at Nagwada in Surendranagar district, it is associated with Mature Harappan assemblage in Period IB. The site has yielded most of the type-fossils of the Harappan Culture including an inscribed terracotta sealing, agate weights, etched carnelian beads, Rohri chert blades, shell objects, disc beads of gold, several semiprecious stone beads, coppers celts, etc. (Hegde 1989). However, more than 80 per cent of the ceramic assemblage belonged to the Anarta pottery indicating its predominance. In the same Mature Harappan context it is also reported from Zekhda (Momin 1983), about 100 km north of Nagwada, in Banskantha district and from Surkotada in Kachchh.

The Gritty Red Ware and the Fine Red Ware of the Anarta tradition are analogous with the Non-Harappan Coarse Red Ware, Polychrome and Bichrome Wares reported from Surkotada and the Coarse Red Ware from Lothal (Hegde et al. 1988). The above Non-Harappan pottery types occur at Surkotada in the earliest levels, Period IA, dated to *c*. 2500 BC along with Mature Harappan relics (Joshi 1972). In the succeeding Period IB, the Non-Harappan Coarse Red Ware outnumbers the Harappan pottery indicating its remarkable influence over the Harappan Culture at the site. A painted Coarse Red Ware similar to the Gritty Red Ware reported from Lothal along with the Micaceous Red Ware and the Harappan Wares (Rao 1985: 393-407) may probably suggest the interactive sphere of this regional Chalcolithic tradition.

The tradition seems to have survived the Urban Harappan in north Gujarat as at several sites it is associated with the so called Late Harappan or Rangpur IIB, IIC and rarely with Rangpur III affiliated sites. However, the Burnished Red Ware and the bowls with panel design and the bichrome decoration disappear in the later period while other pottery continued without much of a change.

CHALCOLITHIC BURIALS AND PRE-HARAPPAN POTTERY

This is another group of pottery belonging to the Pre-Harappan reported mainly from the burials and a few habitation sites in north Gujarat. It was first reported from Nagwada in the 1985 excavation by the M.S. University of Baroda. The excavation revealed a single period of occupation divisible into two sub-periods: Period IA and Period IB (Hegde et al. 1988). Period IA is represented by a number of burials belonging to the earliest occupation at the site. The succeeding Period IB, as has been described above belonged to the Mature/Urban Harappan but showing a strong presence of the Anarta Chalcolithic assemblage. This sub-period has been dated to *c*. 2200 BC. What is surprising here is the conspicuous absence of the burial pottery types in the Period IB habitation deposit.

Two distinct types of burials are found at Nagwada. These are: (a) extended inhumation burials and (b) symbolic pot burials containing no skeletal remains. The extended burials invariably contained a few pottery vessels of different size and shape as burial goods. The symbolic pot-burials on the other hand are represented by a group of vessels arranged in an oval pit. The number of vessels found in them varied from six to ten. Red Ware, a pinkish Buff Ware, and Grey Ware are the important ceramic types found in the burials. They are different from the Harappan pottery and are not reported from the succeeding Mature Harappan, Period IB, deposit. The clay used in their production was well elutriated and they were slipped[8] painted even though the slip and painting had almost completely peeled off.

Characteristic shapes in the burial pottery are a large bulbous pot, flasks or beaker-shaped vases with sides converging into a rather narrow opening, beakers with slightly flaring rim, dish-on-stand with up turned rim, dish with no carination and shallow bowls (Figs. 6 and 7). The large bulbous pot has a narrow flat base, a short and straight neck and a flat rim. It is painted at the rim with a thick dark band and at the shoulder with horizontal and wavy lines. A stylized pipal leaf motif on one of the large pots is also noteworthy (Fig. 7).

These shapes and the decorations do not resemble the shape and decoration of the Harappan pottery; rather they resemble similar vessels recovered from the Pre-Harappan levels at Kot Diji, Amri, and Balakot (Hegde et al. 1988; see Khan 1965; Casal 1964; Dales 1974). Besides, similar pot-burials were found in association with Pre-Harappan sites at Nal and Damb Bhuti (Piggott 1952). Besides, the 'burial pottery' discovered from north Gujarat is similar to the pottery, especially the beakers, flask like vases, large pots and jars and dish-on-stand with up-turned rim, excavated in the 1970s from the pot-burials in the cemetery at Surkotada (Joshi 1990). Even though their general Pre-Harappan features were alluded to in the description, he included them in the general Harappan category and thereby missed the importance of the assemblage in understanding the Early Harappan settlements in Kachchh and north Gujarat. It now becomes apparent that the movement of early Chalcolithic communities had started much earlier than the Harappans and the Pre-Harappan settlements in Sindh and Baluchistan had extended further southwards into north-west Gujarat prior to the times of the Mature Harappan (Hegde et al. 1988).

Subsequent exploration in north Gujarat revealed several sites yielding a similar assemblage of pottery. Most of these are small ephemeral sites showing scanty deposit probably indicating temporary occupation. Two of these sites, Santhli-II (23° 54' N: 71° 29' 10" E) and Moti Pipli in Banaskantha district (Fig. 1) were subjected to excavation for ascertaining their content and stratigraphic context. Excavation at Santhli, a site showing discrete clusters of artefact concentration each measuring not more than 30 x 20 m on a large stabilized sand dune, revealed a 20 cm Chalcolithic deposit lying over an equally flimsy Mesolithic occupation. The Chalcolithic deposit incorporated two extended burials containing pots as burial goods. These pots and a few sherds collected from the flimsy habitation debris are similar to the pottery found in the burials at Nagwada. One of this

Fig. 7. Nagwada: Burial pottery: 1 Buff Ware; 2-4, 6-8, 10-11 Red Ware; 5, 9 Grey Ware; 12,13 Gritty Red Ware (1, 2 Extended burial, 3-11 Pot-burial, 12,13 Urn-burial).

was a double burial interred in a rectangular pit containing five pots, including the large pot with bulbous body, flask or beaker shaped vase with sides converging to a constricted rim, a small beaker, dishes and a dish-on-stand.

In contrast to the above, the excavations at Moti Pipli in 1993 brought to light a good habitation deposit and other interesting evidence of this Chalcolithic community. The Chalcolithic occupation at Moti Pipli was largely confined to the southern half of a reasonably large mound measuring approximately 600 x 120 m. The excavation has revealed a twofold cultural sequence: the Mesolithic followed by the Chalcolithic. About 50 cm deep Chalcolithic deposit incorporated the above Pre-Harappan ceramics and the Anarta pottery. This ceramic assemblage not only included all the vessel forms reported from the burials at Nagwada, Surkotada and Santhli but also a number of new shapes especially large pots with a prominent flange below the rim at the shoulder with a thick black band at the rim, dish-on-stand with polychrome painted design (Figs. 8, 9), etc., which show a very close resemblance with the Early Harappan Kot Diji pottery (Majumdar and Sonawane 1996-7). They were all found from regular habitation deposit; and no burial was found at the site in the excavation.

The community used several copper implements like small rods and wires and copper fish hooks and lithic tools made on long blades of Rohri chert. No evidence of permanent structures, except a few clay lumps with reed impressions probably remains of wattle and daub structures are found at the site. This, in fact, is the only site in this region showing prolonged occupation and relatively good amount of cultural deposit belonging to the Pre-/Early Harappan period. Most of the other sites show very small area of surface-spread and scanty deposit. Dhavalikar and Possehl (1992) have postulated a mechanism of episodic movement of Pre-Harappan nomads in search of pastoral land from Sindh towards south into north Gujarat as an explanatory model for understanding formation process of these Chalcolithic settlements. While this may be true for the initial expansion, the excavation at Moti Pipli indicates that the site was a long period settlement of the Pre-Harappans. It also shows interaction with the indigenous Anarta Chalcolithic communities of this region. Therefore, several small sites of the above nature which are located within the vicinity of Moti Pipli may reflect strategies, including pastoralism, adopted for exploitation of resources by the Pre-/ Early Harappan community at Moti Pipli.

As none of these assemblages has been dated by radiocarbon we need to depend upon ceramic analogy and stratigraphic seriation for dating them. Similar vessels reported from several Early Harappan sites in Sindh, Baluchistan and upper Indus Valley have been dated from the middle of fourth millennium BC. to the early centuries of third millennium BC (Possehl 1993). At Moti Pipli, Santhli, Datrana and a few other sites in north Gujarat it is found associated with the regional Anarta pottery which has also been dated to the beginning of third millennium BC. Moreover, at Datrana this pottery is found associated with a ceramic assemblage comparable to the Pre-Prabhas assemblage in the upper levels which has also been dated to the beginning of third millennium BC It therefore follows that this Pre-Harappan Chalcolithic assemblage may be dated to the beginning of the third millennium BC.

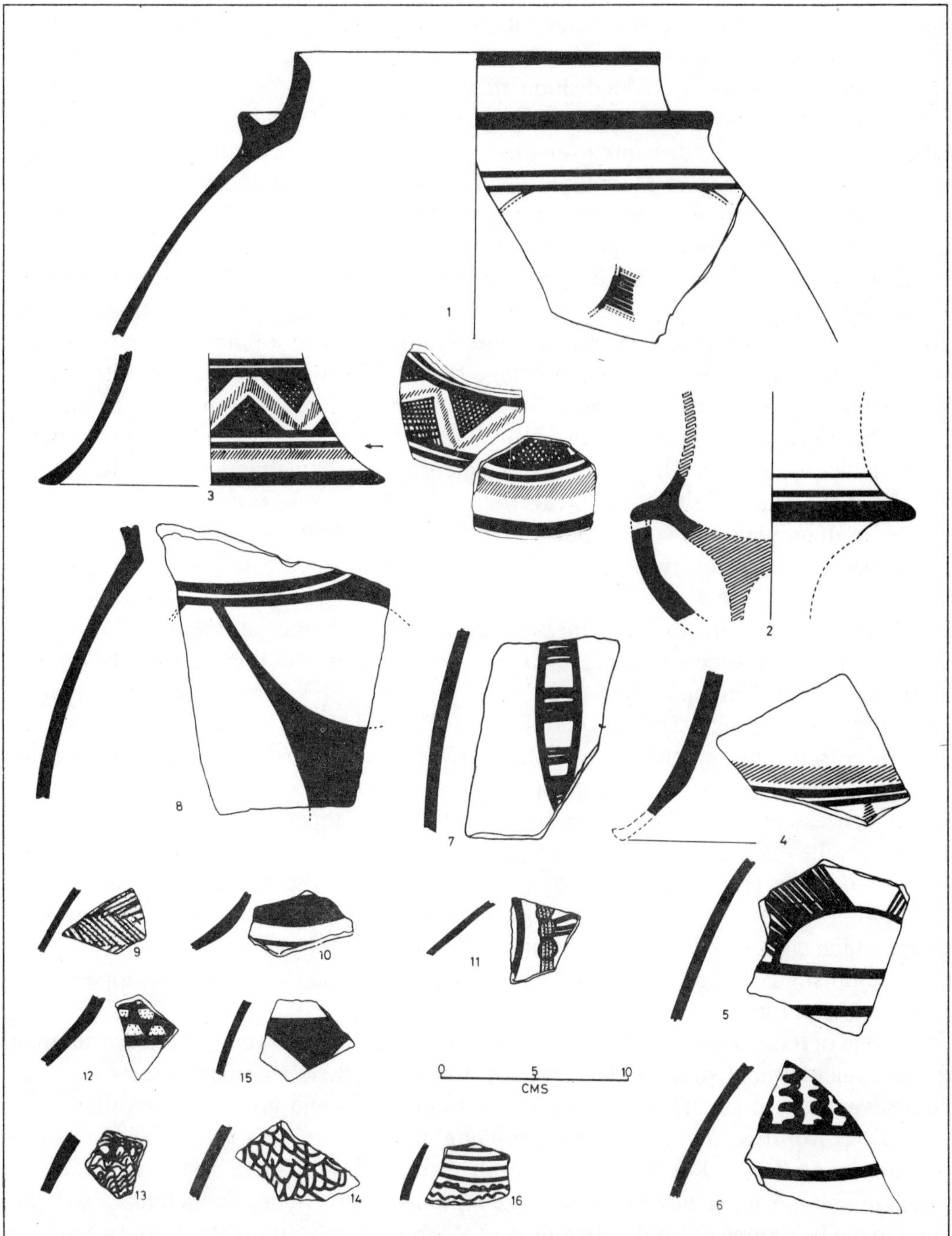

Fig. 8. Moti Pipli, Pre-Harappan pottery: 1- 8 Fine Red Ware (4, 6-8 Buff Slip; 3 Polychrome: black and red on cream); 9-14 Red Ware (9, 11, 12, 14 Bichrome: black on cream); 15 Burnished Red Ware (9-15 Anarta); 16 Reserved Slip Ware.

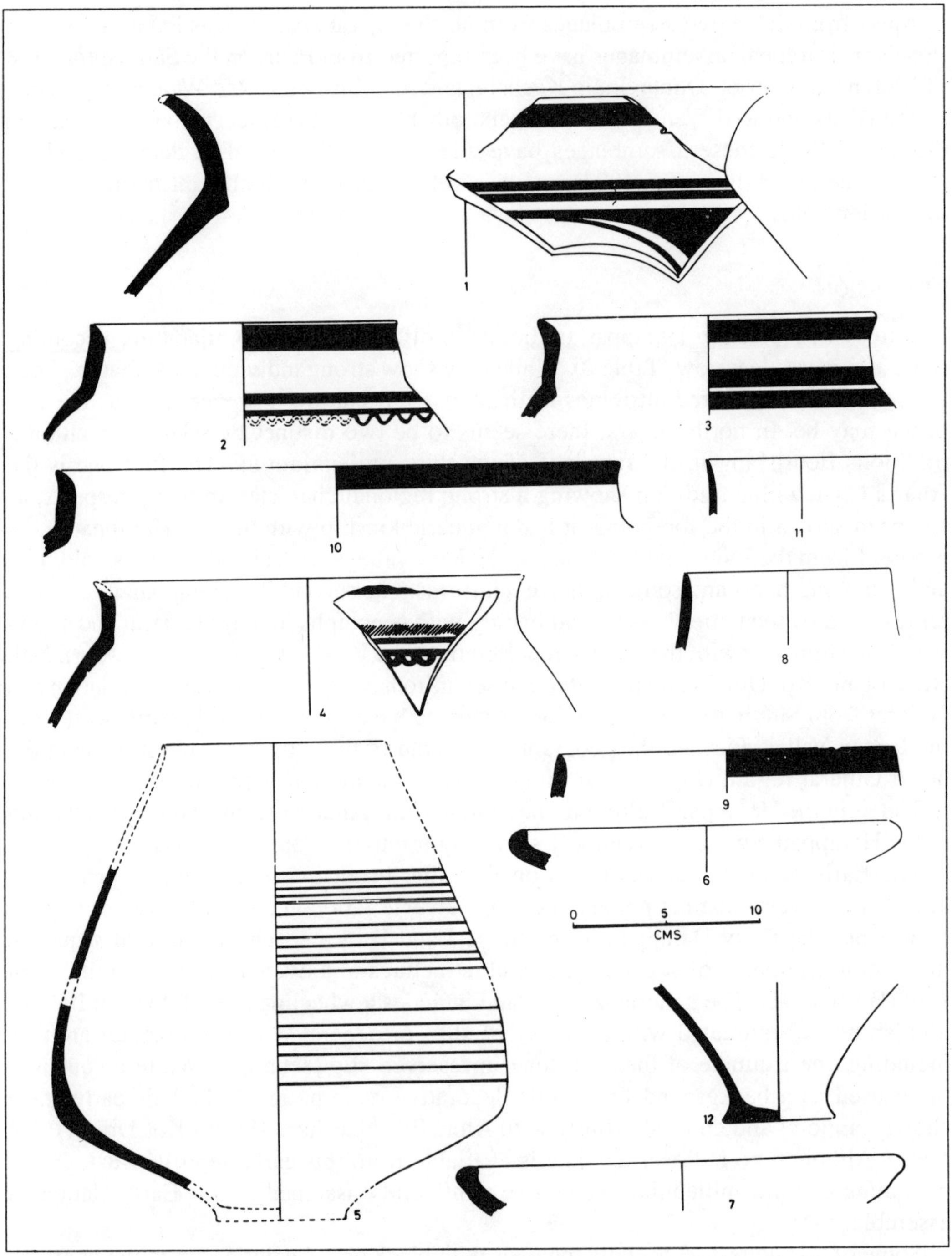

Fig. 9. Moti Pipli, Pre-Harappan pottery: 1-5 Fine Red Ware; 6-9 Red Ware; 10, 11 Buff Ware; 12 Gritty Red Ware.

Apart from the above assemblages from north Gujarat and Prabhas Patan, important Pre-/Non-Harappan assemblages have been reported from Padri on the Saurashtra coast of Bhavnagar district, Dholavira in Kachchh and the Micaceous Red Ware and the associated Black and Red Ware from Lothal and other sites in the Bhal region of Saurashtra (Table 2). Since these assemblages have already been reviewed in detail elsewhere (Sonawane and Ajithprasad 1994), we may refer only their significant features in the discussion below.

DISCUSSION

Features of several Pre-Harappan traditions in different parts of Gujarat are becoming more and more clear now (Table 2). While they show strong individualistic features they also show certain shared attributes in their material culture however tenuous the evidence may be. In north Gujarat there seems to be two distinct Pre-Harappan cultural traditions flourishing in the first half of the third millennium BC. The first one is the Anarta Chalcolithic tradition showing a strong regional character. In many respects, as has been shown in the foregoing, it had a generic kinship with the Pre-Harappan traits reported from the Indus and the Ghaggar-Hakkra valleys, especially in the use of white and cream pigments and some of the vessel forms. The second Pre-Harappan tradition is represented by the pottery associated mainly with cenotaphs in north Gujarat and showing close similarity with the pottery reported from the Pre-Harappan levels at Amri, Nal, Balakot and Kot Diji. While the latter one seems to have spread towards south into north Gujarat from Sindh, the Anarta tradition seems to have spread towards north-west from the Rupen Valley. Further, the geographical spread of these two are coterminous in the north Gujarat region (Fig. 1) indicating a strong interaction between the two. This is reflected in the Harappan Culture in the region as the Anarta ceramics quickly adapting to the Harappan ethos and eventually surviving it into the Post-Urban phase.

The Early Harappan at Dholavira on the other hand reveals a different picture. In addition to several distinct pottery showing 'diverse fabric and equally diverse surface treatment', the Early Harappan in the Stage-I and II of a sevenfold cultural sequence incorporates remains of several mud brick structures and even a massive fortification wall (Bisht 1991). The ceramic assemblage includes a wheelmade Red Ware of light or pinkish red tones treated with a variety of slips or decorated with horizontal grooves including one example of incision done in reserved slip technique. White colour was often used as a background for simple decorative patterns in black. This early stage shows temporal and cultural affinity with Amri IIB, Nausharo ID and Kot Diji I (Bisht 1993). Although no radiocarbon date is available from this early deposit, a date in the beginning of third millennium BC can be confidently assigned to this Early Harappan assemblage.

Some of this pottery, especially the ones with black or red paintings in white or cream background, are similar to the bichrome decorated Gritty Red Ware and Fine Red Ware of Anarta tradition. However, there is no similarity between the Fine Red Ware vessels of the two traditions. Similarly, although the Early Harappan assemblage from Dholavira

TABLE 2. PRE-HARAPPAN SUB-STRATUM IN THE CULTURAL SEQUENCE OF SOME OF THE SITES

Date	Padri	Lothal	Somnath	Datrana
AD 400 AD 00	Period I Early Historic		Period V Early Historic	
00 300 BC			Period IV Early Historic	
1500 BC			Period III: Post-Urban: Lustrous Red Ware, Black & Red Ware	
		Lothal B: Phase V Post-Urban		
2000 BC	Period II Sorath Harappan + Padri Ware	Lothal A: II, III, IV Urban Harappan Inscribed seals + Harappan Wares + Micaceous Red + Black & Red Ware	Period II Prabhas Ware, Black & Red, Harappan Wares, Faience, Steatite Beads, Structures	
2500 BC		Lothal A: Phase I Harappan + Micaceous Red Ware + Black & Red Ware		
3000 BC	Padri Ware + Harappan? + copper + Lithic/ blade tools		Period I Pre-Prabhas Faience, Steatite Incised Red, Black & Red and Corrugated Red Wares; Crested ridge blade	Period II Pre-Harappan Anarta + Burial pottery + Black & Red, Incised Red/Grey and Corrugated Wares + copper + beads Rohri chert blades
<3500 BC				Period I Mesolithic

and the pottery associated with the Chalcolithic burials of north Gujarat may belong to the general Pre-Harappan traditions of Sindh, the resemblance between the two are meagre and negligible. So far, it appears that no site in the region shows a ceramic assemblage comparable to the above. It therefore calls for a detailed examination of Chalcolithic assemblages in this region for understanding the mechanism of integration.

Another Pre-/Non-Harappan assemblage showing a similar geographic isolation is the Padri Ware reported from Padri (22°22' N: 72°55' E) in the Saurashtra coast of Bhavnagar district. The Padri Ware in Period II is found associated with the urban Sorath Harappan deposit resembling Rojdi B dating about 2200 BC (Shinde 1991). However, a 1 m thick substratum in the Period II in later excavations have showed a predominance of Padri Ware and few Harappan sherds (Shinde: personal communication). Radiocarbon dates from this deposit show a very early date going back to the second half of the fourth millennium BC (Table 1), suggesting that it was one of the earliest Chalcolithic settlements in Gujarat.

Padri Ware vessels are either hand modelled or made on a slow turn-wheel and are treated with thick slip. Bowls with convex or straight sides and small or medium size globular pots are the only two vessel forms found in this pottery. They are made from a coarse clay and decorated with linear patterns sometimes in a panel of horizontal lines. The paintings in black are done carelessly and show a creative clumsiness (Shinde and Kar 1992). Cultural equipments apart from pottery of this early Chalcolithic occupation are not very clear. However, there is evidence to indicate that people during this early phase lived in houses built of dense clay and made use of copper implements and lithic blade tools exploiting the locally available raw materials.

It is not sure whether the Padri Ware is reported from any other Chalcolithic sites in the region around Padri. Due to its early date and distinct features one would expect Padri Ware to be a Chalcolithic tradition bearing a regional identity. This can only be ascertained by tracing its geographical distribution in Saurashtra.

While the Early Harappan assemblage at Dholavira and the pottery from Chalcolithic cenotaphs of north Gujarat indicate the expansion of divergent Early Harappan traditions from Sindh towards south, the Anarta pottery represents the distinct Non-Harappan regional tradition of north Gujarat. In this cultural mosaic the Pre-Harappan assemblage resembling the Pre-Prabhas ceramics from Datrana appears to be standing in isolation. The one to one similarity of the Pre-Prabhas assemblage from Somnath and that of Datrana may indicate migration and movement of this tradition; the direction of which is not very clear at present. As these assemblages show the earliest date for the Black and Red Ware, it is tempting to ask whether this has anything to do with the spread of Black and Red Ware towards further north-east along the Banas Valley into Ahar and other sites in southern Rajasthan, especially now that, the Banas Chalcolithic has been dated to *c* 2600 BC at Balathal in Udaipur district, Rajasthan (Misra et al. 1997).

For answering this question we may have to address the chronological position of Black and Red Ware and Micaceous Red Ware reported from several sites in the Bhal region of Saurashtra. Micaceous Red Ware in this low-lying region between the Gulf of Cambay and the Nal depression in the north is found associated with Black and Red Ware. It is represented by characteristic hemispherical bowls with and without a stud handle and pots or jars with flaring rim. The vessels are made from very fine clay containing a high concentration of mica particles. However, what makes it a strong contender for one of the early Non-Harappan regional Chalcolithic traditions of Saurashtra is its stratigraphic position and geographic distribution. Stratigraphically it is found from the lowermost layer at Lothal dating back to earlier than 2450 BC. Although no separate substratum exclusively of the Micaceous Red Ware and the Black and Red Ware was not found in spite of several efforts, according to Rao (1985), the Micaceous Red Ware increases in quantity in the early levels; the bottom of this could not be reached due to water logging. He, therefore, presumed that the Micaceous Red Ware folks were the original indigenous settlers at Lothal and it was the Micaceous Red Ware people who introduced inverted firing and the Black and Red Ware in Gujarat (Rao 1963).

Dhavalikar and Possehl (1992) on the other hand rightfully point out that its Pre-Harappan character can be proved only if we are able to resolve the issue whether the Micaceous Red Ware was adopted by the Harappans from the indigenous population or was it an innovation of the Harappan potters at Lothal. The first proposition seems to be more close to the truth for many reasons. To begin with, bowls are not at all popular in the Harappan Culture in the Indus Valley proper or in Rajasthan and Punjab. On the contrary, convex sided bowls, including the stud-handled variety are one of the type-fossils of Harappan sites in Saurashtra. While stud-handled bowls first appear in the Micaceous Red Ware, simple bowls with straight or slightly incurved rims are a common shape in the Pre-/Non-Harappan Padri Ware, and in the Anarta pottery of north Gujarat. The Harappans introducing a totally new vessel form, that too using a clay paste different from what they have been acquainted to while they were busy settling down at Lothal appears a little over stretched.

Secondly, if we admit that the Micaceous Red Ware was an innovation by the Harappans, it follows that the Black and Red Ware also was introduced by the Harappans, for both of them were found together at the earliest level from Lothal. But we now know that the Black and Red Ware had a much earlier origin in the Pre-Prabhas assemblage. It is highly improbable that the Harappan may have reinvented it about three or four centuries later in the same region.

Moreover, well made Black and Red Ware vessels are found in a variety of shapes from Pre-Prabhas assemblage at Somnath and from Datrana. Some of the forms have no parallel in other associated pottery, for example the ring based pot/jar, indicating that the Pre-Prabhas folks were proficient enough in the Black and Red Ware technique. In contrast the Black and Red Ware unearthed from Lothal mostly imitates the vessel shapes of the Micaceous Red Ware indicating a mere adoption of the technology. The Black and Red Ware, therefore, appears to be firmly footed in the Pre-Prabhas assemblage rather than in the Micaceous Red Ware.

On the other hand, the presence of Black and Red Ware in the Micaceous Red Ware assemblage and the appearance of hemispherical bowls resembling the Micaceous Red Ware bowls later in the Prabhas period at Somnath may probably indicate a long standing interaction of the two traditions. These are hypothetical propositions which need further investigations to test their veracity. Future studies in Saurashtra should therefore focus on understanding the Pre-Harappan status of Micaceous Red Ware and the interactive spheres of Micaceous Red Ware and Pre-Prabhas assemblage including the Prabhas pottery.

Two broad distinct groups of Non-Harappan assemblages predating the Harappan occupation in Gujarat can be identified from the foregoing. The first one is a set of assemblages forming the Early Harappan or Pre-Urban reported from Dholavira and to some extent the ceramic assemblage from Moti Pipli and from several burials including Nagwada and Santhli in north Gujarat and Surkotada in Kachchh. These two have a general resemblance with the Early Harappan ceramics reported from sites in Sindh and Baluchistan and therefore indicate the extension of the Early Harappan communities of that region into Kachchh and parts of north Gujarat prior to the Urban Harappan.

The second group comprises an assortment of Chalcolithic village farming communities in diverse geographical regions. They show a certain amount of individuality at least in their ceramic industry and at the same time show remarkable adaptive flexibility. It is noticeable that none of these Pre-/Non Harappan settlements, in fact, anticipates an urban way of life, as is the case at Dholavira or at Kalibangan where we come across evidence of rudimentary planning and architecture even in the Pre-Harappan period. In contrast these were small rural farming settlements affording flimsy structures mostly of wattle and daub or similar nondescript materials. However they did have the knowledge of copper metallurgy and produced pottery vessels and lapidary stone beads.

TABLE 3. IMPORTANT CHALCOLITHIC SITES IN GUJARAT

Loteshwar	Nagwada	Moti Pipli	Dholavira
			Stage VI, VII: Post-Urban
	Period IB: Anarta, Harappan pottery Inscribed sealing Copper + Shell + Lithic beads		Stage V: Terminal Urban Harappan Stage IV Urban Harappan Inscribed Seals, Citadel
			Stage III Early Hr. + Hr. (Transition)
Period II Anarta Pre-Harappan Gritty Red Ware, Burnished Red , Reserved Slip and Incised Red Ware Copper + Steatite beads	Period IB: Burials Pre-Harappan Pottery	Period II Anarta Pot. + Pre-Harappan burial Pottery (Kot Diji type). Rohri chert blades + Copper	Stage I, II Early Harappan Red ware, Grey Ware, Bichrome decoration + long blades, Copper, Fortification wall
Period I Mesolithic		Period I Mesolithic	

It is apparent that the Harappan Culture incorporates all these indigenous strands in the structure and fabric of its society. Besides, it is futile to think that two distinct cultures living in close geographical proximity can live a long period of time without getting influenced by each other. In fact, it is this interaction that may have given rise to the distinct cultural patterns which we see in the Harappan Culture in Gujarat. It does not certainly mean a complete surrendering of identities; it only means adapting themselves to a new set of sustainable norms related to production and consumption. The effect of this interaction depends directly upon the intensity of interaction which is determined by several physical and social variables. Several trajectories indicating the integration of the two traditions are evident both in the urban and rural economic level. For example, the continuation of Micaceous Red Ware and the Black and Red Ware with little or no change in the Harappan context from Lothal indicates their integration in an urban centre. On the other hand, the predominance of Anarta pottery in Period IB at Surkotada and its association with a few clearly classical Harappan relics including seals and sealings at Nagwada may bespeak the level of integration in a quasi-urban as well as in rural settlements.

The focus so far has been to establish the antecedent stages and to understand the role of Pre-Harappan cultures in the emergence of the Urban Harappan economy in Gujarat. But, there is yet another issue which needs immediate attention; that is, the regional Chalcolithic cultures themselves. For instance, how do we account for the existence in terms of origin, development and interaction of these Chalcolithic traditions. Were they intrinsically disparate groups or were they different expressions of the same cultural strand in different regions? What was the nature of their interaction network? These are some of the aspects which demand new deductive inquiries for understanding not only the regional diversity but also, as we stated earlier, the social and economic configuration of the Harappan Culture.

ACKNOWLEDGEMENTS

Most of the data regarding the Chalcolithic settlements of north Gujarat were collected through a series of explorations in that region which were supported by the Ford Foundation Research Grant to the Department of Archaeology, the M.S. University of Baroda. I thank Professor V.H. Sonawane and Professor V.S. Parekh for allowing me to use data from recently excavated sites, especially Datrana, Loteshwar and Moti Pipli in north Gujarat.

NOTES

1. See Shaffer (1982) for a good discussion on the 'cyclic model' of development of Harappan Culture.
2. For an early application of a similar model see Dales' (1965) scheme of cultural development in which he gives emphasis on looking at the entire history of Chalcolithic Cultures of South Asia into a number of distinct 'Phases' designated alphabetically. Also see Fairservis (1967) for a corresponding scheme visualizing the entire food producing Pre-Harappan and Harappan cultural succession in the Indus system and Baluchistan comprising five successive 'Stages'.

3. The best example for this is the scant attention the Pre-Prabhas assemblage from Somnath received in spite of the two radiocarbon dates indicating an early third millennium date for its beginning.
4. See the comments of Rao (1965) and Dhaky (1965) on the antecedent stages of Harappan Culture, especially in Gujarat.
5. It is interesting that, initially it was the Prabhas assemblage which received all attention as a Non-Harappan Chalcolithic tradition or a sub-Indus Culture within the large cultural domain of the Harappan Culture. This may be due to the fact that even though a thin Pre-Prabhas substratum was identified in the 1950s, its stratigraphical and chronological contexts were firmly established much later, only in the 1970s (*IAR* 1971-2). And secondly, a date going back as early as 2900 BC for this deposit was not fitting well in the conceptual model which visualized the Harappans introducing the Chalcolithic way of life in Gujarat. Thus, its Pre-Harappan status was recognized only in the 1990s after the discovery of several Chalcolithic assemblages in Gujarat predating the Harappan Culture.
6. The similarities between the Datrana pottery and the Pre-Prabhas pottery were first pointed out by G.L. Possehl who had seen the Datrana assemblage in one of his visits to the M.S. Univeristy.
7. Features of these two Pre-Harappan ceramic traditions are discussed in the next few pages.
8. In addition to these two, a very large pot of the Gritty Red Ware found in the excavation is believed to be an urn burial.

REFERENCES

Ajithprasad, P. and V.H. Sonavane 1993. Harappan Culture in North Gujarat: a Regional Paradigm. Paper Presented at the Seminar in the Harappans in Gujarat: Problems and Prospects at Deccau College, Pune.

Ajithprasad, P., V.H. Sonawane, V.S. Parekh and P.C. Chaudhari 1995. Datrana: a Chalcolithic Blade Industry Site in North Gujarat. Paper Presented in the XXII Annual Conference of the ISPQUS at Gorakhpur (Unpublished).

Bhan, K.K 1994. Cultural Development of the Prehistoric Period in North Gujarat with Reference to Western India, *South Asian Studies* 10: 71-90.

Bisht, R.S. 1991. Dholavira: a New Horizon of the Indus Civilization, *Puratattva* 20: 71-82.

——— 1993. Dholavira Excavation: a Brief Note (Unpublished Paper).

——— 1994. Urban Planning at Dholavira: a Harappan City. Paper Presented at the Seminar on 'The City and the Stars: Cosmic Urban Geometries of India' at Indira Gandhi National Centre for the Arts, New Delhi.

Casal, J.M. 1964. *Fouilles D'Amri*, 2 vols. Paris, Publication De La Commission des Fouilles Archaeologique. Fouilles de Pakistan: Figs. 38, 39, 62.

Dales, G.F. 1965. A Suggested Chronology for Afghanistan, Baluchistan and the Indus Valley, in *Chronologies in the Old World Archaeology* (R. Ehrich Ed.), pp. 257-84. Chicago: The University of Chicago Press.

——— 1974. Excavations at Balakot, Pakistan 1973, *Journal of Field Archaeology* 1: 3-22.

Dhavalikar, M.K. 1984. Sub-Indus Cultures of Central and Western India, in *Frontiers of the Indus Civilization* (B.B. Lal and S.P. Gupta Eds.), pp. 243-51. New Delhi: Books & Books.

Dhavalikar, M.K. and G.L. Possehl 1992. The Pre-Harappan Period at Prabhas Patan and the Pre-Harappan Phase in Gujarat, *Man and Environment* XVII (1): 72-8.

Fairservis, W. 1967. Origin, Character and Decline of an Early Civilization, *Novitiates* 2302. New York: American Museum of Natural History.

Ghosh, A. 1965. The Indus Civilization: Its Origin, Authors, Extent and Chronology, in *Indian*

Prehistory: 1964 (V.N. Misra and M.S. Mate Eds.), pp. 113-50. Poona: Deccan College.

Hegde, K.T.M. 1989 Boom Town: Harappa, *The Future Perfect 2001* (December): 19-22.

Hegde, K.T.M. and V.H. Sonawane 1986. Landscape and Settlement Pattern of the Harappan Culture Villages in the Rupen Estuary, *Man and Environment* X: 23-31.

Hegde, K.T.M., V.H. Sonawane, D.R. Shah, K.K. Bhan, P. Ajithprasad, K. Krishnan and S. Pratapachandran 1988. Excavations at Nagwada—1986-87: a Preliminary Report, *Man and Environment* XII: 55-65.

IAR. Indian Archaeology —A Review. New Delhi: Archaeological Survey of India.

Jarrige J, F., G. Quiviron and C. Jarrige 1995. Excavation at Mehrgarh and Nausharo (MS) French Archaeological Mission in Pakistan 16th to 20th Session, 1990-4.

Joshi, J.P. 1972. Exploration in Kutch and Excavation at Surkotada and New Light on Harappan Migration, *Journal of the Oriental Institut* 22 (1-2): 98-144.

——— 1990. *Excavations at Surkotada 1971-72 and Exploration in Kutch.* New Delhi: Memoirs of the Archaeological Survey of India 87.

Khan, A.R. 1965. Excavations at Kot Diji, *Pakistan Archaeology* 2: 11-85.

Leshnik, L.S. 1968. Prehistoric Exploration in North Gujarat and Parts of Rajasthan, *East and West* 18 (3-4): 298-310.

Mackay, E.J.H. 1938. *Further Excavations at Mohenjo Daro*, Vol. I. Delhi: Government of India Press.

Mahida, Bhamini. 1992. Chalcolithic settlements of North Gujarat: a Study of Regional Tradition in the Rupen Estuary. M.A. Dissertation. Vadodara: the M.S. University of Baroda.

Majumdar, Abhijit and V. H. Sonawane 1996-7. Pre-Harappan Burial Pottery from Moti Pipli: a New Dimension in the Cultural Assemblage of North Gujarat, *Pragdhara* 7: 11-17.

Misra V.N., Vasant Shinde, R. K Mohanty, Lalit Pandey and Jeevan Kharakwal 1997. Excavation at Balathal, Udaipur District, Rajasthan (1995-97), with Special Reference to Chalcolithic Architecture, *Man and Environment* XXII (2): 35-59.

Momin, K. N. 1983 Excavation at Zekhada, *Puratattva* (12): 120-5.

Mughal, M.R. 1970. The Early Harappan Period in the Greater Indus Valley and Northern Baluchistan (*c.* 3000-2400 BC). Ph.D. dissertation. Philadephia: University of Pennsylvania.

——— 1974. New Evidence of the Early Harappan Culture from Jalilpur, *Pakistan Archaeology* 27 (2):106-13.

——— 1982. Recent Archaeological Research in the Cholistan Desert, in *Harappan Civilization: a Contemporary Perspective* (G.L. Possehl Ed.), pp. 85-9. Delhi: Oxford-IBH.

——— 1990. Further Evidence of the Early Harappan Culture in the Greater Indus Valley, *South Asian Studies* 6: 175-99.

Nanavati, J. M., R.N. Mehta and S.N. Chaudhary 1971. *Somnath-1956.* Vadodara: Department of Archaeology, Gujarat State and the M.S. University of Baroda: 18-41.

Piggott, Stuart. 1952. *Prehistoric India.* Hammondsworth: Penguin Books.

Possehl, G.L. 1977. The End of State and the Continuity of Tradition, *Realm and Religion in Traditional India* (Richard Fox Ed.), pp. 234-54. Durham: Carolina Academic Press.

——— 1980. *Indus Civilization in Saurashtra.* Delhi: B.R. Publishing Corporation.

——— 1990. Revolution in the Urban Revolution: the Emergence of Indus Civilization, *Annual Review of Anthropology* 19: 261-82.

——— 1993. Radiometric Dates from South East Asia: Compiled by G.L. Possehl.

Rao, S.R. 1963 Excavations at Rangpur and Other Explorations in Gujarat, *Ancient India* 18-19: 5-207.

——— 1965. Comments on A. Ghosh's 'The Indus Civilization: Its Origin, Authors, Extent and Chronology', in *Indian Prehistory: 1964* (V.N. Misra and M.S. Mate Eds.), pp. 129-31. Poona: Deccan College.

——— 1985. *Lothal: a Harappan Port Town 1955-62*. New Delhi: Memoirs of the Archaeological Survey of India 78 (2).

Sankalia, H.D. 1955. Excavations at Langhnaj, Gujarat, *Man* 55: 26.

Shaffer, Jim G. 1982. Harappan Culture: a Reconsideration, in *Harappan Civilization: a Contemporary Perspective* (G.L. Possehl Ed.), pp. 41-50. New Delhi: Oxford-IBH.

Shinde, Vasant 1992. Excavations at Padri—1990-91: a Preliminary Report, *Man and Environment* XVII (1): 79-86.

Shinde, Vasant and S.B. Kar 1992. Padri Ware: a New Painted Ceramic Found in the Harappan Levels at Padri in Gujarat, *Man and Environment* XVII (2): 105-10.

Sonawane, V.H. and P. Ajithprasad 1994. Harappan Culture and Gujarat, *Man and Environment* XIX (1-2): 129-39.

Subbarao, B. 1958. *The Personality of India*. Baroda: M.S. University of Baroda. M.S. University Archaeology Series 3.

Thapar, B.K. 1975. Kalibangan: a Harappan Metropolis Beyond the Indus Valley, *Expedition* 17 (2): 19-32.

Wheeler, R.E.M. 1960. *The Indus Civilization*. Cambridge: Cambridge University Press.

Post-Urban Harappan Culture in Gujarat

V.H. SONAWANE

INTRODUCTION

Culture transformation or change is a continuous process with a varying degree of intensity. It involves factors like human adjustments to prevailing environmental and social conditions of the region. Culture change is also multidirectional and the degree and nature of change vary in time and space. Precisely, therefore, the beginning, growth and decline of the Harappan Culture, like other cultures, has been categorized into separate phases termed differently by various scholars (Rao 1963; Mughal 1970; Possehl 1977, 1980, 1984, 1993). In order to eliminate the confusion created by the indiscriminate use of the terms Pre and/or Early Harappan and the often misused notion of Late Harappan, Possehl (1992a: 118) has proposed an alternative terminology for the Harappan cultural tradition using the terms Pre-Urban, Urban and Post-Urban phase indicating socio-cultural and technological development in various stages of the Harappan occupation. In this system too, although the Urban phase is rather well defined through type-fossils and several other settlement features, the Pre-Urban and the Post-Urban phases are not so clearly defined. There seems to be a lack of consistency in the material relics from different sites of both the Pre-Urban and Post-Urban phases. Moreover, it must be noted that these three divisions are not necessarily time brackets applicable throughout the entire Harappan region (Sonawane and Ajithprasad 1994: 130).

Before going into the details of the Post-Urban phase, it is pertinent to note the various aspects which led scholars to define the Urban phase of Harappan Civilization. These broad parameters include large size settlements, monumental architecture, long distance trade, craft specialization, class hierarchy, state organization as well as diagnostic artefacts such as Indus seals, ceramic forms like goblets, perforated cylindrical jars and jars with 'S' profiles often decorated with intricate or naturalistic painted motifs. In addition, triangular terracotta cakes, kidney shaped inlays, long chert blades of Rohri origin, etc., also suggested by Childe (1950) and Wheeler (1968: 63) are characteristic features of the Harappan settlements associated with the Urban/Mature phase. However, with renewed research on the above mentioned aspects of Urban/Mature Harappan phase, it is clear that the presence or absence of these features would depend on multiple factors like location and nature of the settlements.

The entire gamut of the Harappan Civilization in its Mature phase is thought to be urbanized giving an impression that all the settlements during this phase are of urban character. In fact, in this context, it is observed that the number of small settlements representing rural aspects of Harappan Culture are far more in number than the urban centres. It is a well-known fact that urban centres cannot exist without a strong rural base. A glance at the settlement pattern reveals that even during the Mature Harappan phase, village or rural settlements existed in clusters around the primary urban settlements demonstrating a symbiotic relationship between the two (Sonawane and Mehta 1985: 38). It would, therefore, be far-fetched to expect all the features of urbanism from any single site representing the mature cultural phase. One of the first casualties in the wake of these new studies is the concept of Harappan homogeneity. This observation is especially true when it comes to the regional diversities within the Harappan Civilization, particularly in the far flung areas of its expansion.

POST-URBAN PHASE

The very term 'Post-Urban' phase indicates that it does not mark the end of a cultural tradition but suggests the termination of an Urban phase within it as a process of localization and invariably marks the collapse of a flourishing civilization. The preceding Urban/Mature phase was, perhaps, more in line with the concept of civilization while the Post-Urban phase was a poor reminder of this glorious past. This phase is identified with the archaeological assemblages which follow the earlier Urban/Mature phase thereby showing a cultural continuity but appears only when the Harappan cultural ethos started declining. This phenomenon appears to be the outcome of the normal process of cultural transformation in Harappan Culture due to a general economic decline that brought in changes in the internal interaction of the society. Obviously, this feature explains why the material culture of the deurbanized phase becomes poor when the urban fabric of a culture disintegrates. It also witnessed a general decline in the civic standards and marks this devolutionary trend or stage. Infact, this cultural phase represents the reversal of all the abstract criteria of urbanization as laid down by Childe (1950) and discussed by Adams (1966: 10-11). Ghosh has identified this cultural phase with those which are later than the Mature Harappan but still have affinities with it in a degenerated form (Dikshit 1981-3: 55). Dales observed that with the decline of this civilization, the sophisticated Harappan traits were watered down by mingling with the impoverished local cultures, until what was once distinctively Harappan was diluted to the point of non-existence (Dales 1966). Possehl, in the context of Gujarat, believes that the level of socio-cultural attainments which existed throughout its Mature phase was slowed down in its later stage. It was centrally less organized, less differentiated and less specialized than the Urban phase (Possehl 1980: 20). According to Allchin what is probably important in understanding the cultural development of the Post-Urban phase is that throughout every province of the Indus Civilization societies survived which, while losing the distinctive characteristics of the settlement, nonetheless retained a broadly 'Harappan' tradition in other respects (Allchin 1990). Whereas, in the light of recent studies, Shaffer considered it as a process of decentralization and localization which gave rise to regional cultural expressions rather than extinction (Shaffer 1992). This stage is the result of the breakdown of the urban fabric of the Harappa Civilization and therefore, represents a stage of readjustment by an urban system to a rural setting without losing its basic ethos (Gupta 1993: 58). Chitalwala remarks that the existence of both cognate and extraneous cultural strains which are easily identifiable and have not metamorphosed into a wholly new cultural entity showing Harappan affinity even in its barest outlines could be regarded as Post-Urban (Chitalwala 1985: 58). On similar lines, Lal has tried to define the term Late Harappan as a culture which has transformed itself from the Mature Harappan, while losing some of the latter's traits and evolving some new ones, but still identifiable as having been derived from the latter (Lal 1997: 263).

The idea of devolution and therefore, a Post-Urban phase of the Harappan Civilization was first expressed by N.G. Majumdar in 1928 at the site of Jhukar by identifying a pottery type which was in certain ways different from the Mature Harappan. The cultural strata representing the Jhukar type of pottery show occupational and cultural continuity of the earlier Mature Harappan tradition at the site (Majumdar 1934: 154). Similar situations also prevailed at Amri, Chanhu Daro and Mohenjo Daro; however, the material culture indicating the lifestyle of the people advertantly reflected the adverse economic conditions. Mackay later pointed out that the structural data from the late levels of Mohenjo Daro are relatively poor in comparison to the preceding levels (Mackay 1938).

These observations, in turn, evoked speculations for the causes of these changes towards the deterioration and the end of the Harappan Civilization. Catastrophic climatic changes, floods (Marshall 1931), vagaries of the Indus river (Mackay 1938: 6), Aryan invasion (Wheeler 1947), violent tectonic uplifts in the lower reaches of the Indus resulting in the pooling of flood waters (Raikes 1964; Dales 1966; Misra 1984), an overly taxed subsistence system (Fairservis 1967), and over-all decline in the international trade in the beginning of the second millennium BC were some of the proposed explanations. These explanations mainly depend upon models of diffusion and culture change to explain the deterioration and abandonment of the cities of this civilization; however, no single cause can be isolated as an explanation to the process of change or end. Infact, all these theories point towards a cultural devolution rather than an abrupt end. In cultural devolution also, one could observe that its rate and configuration varied from region to region, depending on a number of local factors. The discovery of a large number of Post-Urban settlements spread over in different parts of the entire domain of Harappan Civilization has removed the last lingering doubts about the continuity of the Harappan tradition even after the decline of the major urban centres. The current research, thus, shows that the Harappan Culture did not end abruptly as was thought before (Possehl 1980: 13).

The Post-Urban phase of the Indus Civilization is an integral part of the total spread of this culture beginning from the Afghan area in the extreme north to the Godavari Basin in the south and from the Makaran coast in the west to western Uttar Pradesh in the east. This area comprises a large portion of the territory of the Indian subcontinent and includes Sindh, Punjab, Baluchistan, Kashmir, Haryana, Rajasthan, western Uttar Pradesh, Gujarat and northern Maharashtra. Practically, a large number of sites representing Post-Urban Harappan phase have been noted from these different regions which formed a part of the Harappan Culture zone.

GUJARAT: BACKGROUND

Before going into the details of the Post-Urban Harappan phase, it is imperative to review the nature of Pre-Urban and Urban phases in Gujarat for a proper understanding of the process of deurbanization in terms of the Harappan legacy. The Harappan concept, derived from the findings at major sites in the Indus Valley significantly influenced the interpretations of the discoveries in Gujarat. Initially M.G. Dikshit's (1950) and B. Subbarao's (1958) work recognizing Chalcolithic or regional phenomena at some of the Harappan settlements of Saurashtra were neglected or even opposed. Against this background, Rao in his renewed excavations at Rangpur in 1953 tried to ascertain the nature of the material relics and was able to identify the Harappan character by following the type-fossil analogy method. Nevertheless, he had also observed that much of the materials at the site was at variance with the true Harappan material and stratigraphically these 'Sub-Indus' elements predominantly came from the upper levels (Rao 1963). This led to the threefold division of the Harappan Culture in Gujarat into Mature, Late and Post Harappan. The merit of this division is that for the first time the three phases of the Harappan Culture were clearly defined in terms of ceramic and other cultural indices at a time when Harappan studies were growing into a jumble of confusion (Ajithprasad and Sonawane 1993). This division was essentially chronological, based on stratigraphy and to a large extent, ignored other aspects of cultural variation. Initially, this unilinear evolution of cultural material helped to categorize sites within this broad framework. However, subsequently the same criteria continued to be used ignoring other factors that can contribute to variations in the material culture.

During the last two decades, with the involvement of several institutions and application of new field methods, studies in the Harappan Culture in Gujarat have become more problem-oriented and region-specific. Thus major areas of Harappan occupation in Gujarat such as the coastal region of Saurashtra, central Saurashtra, western part of north Gujarat and Kachchh attracted more attention and became separate areas for intensive study. As a result, there have been a number of explorations and many small and large-scale excavations at a few sites in each of these regions from 1980 onwards. Important excavated sites among these are Nageshwar (Jamnagar district), Rojdi, Kuntasi and Bagasra (Rajkot district), Oriyo Timbo and Padri (Bhavnagar district), Ratanpura, Nagwada, Loteshwar, Moti Pipli, Santhli, Datrana and Zekhada (north Gujarat) and Surkotada, Dholavira and Shikarpur (Kachchh). These recently excavated sites have brought to light several interesting aspects of the Harappan Culture and its cultural dynamism. When these aspects are considered as a whole, an important point that emerges is the recognition of Non-Harappan Chalcolithic traditions contemporary with, if not earlier than, the Harappan Culture in Gujarat. Radiocarbon dates (calibrated) from a few of these sites go back to the second half of the fourth to the beginning of the third millennium BC making them more than half a millennium earlier than the beginning of the Harappan Culture. In this regard, it is worth noting that the region of Saurashtra and north Gujarat has revealed sites of the Pre-Urban phase showing the existence of indigenous regional Chalcolithic cultural traditions involving Non-Harappan pottery types such as Pre-Prabhas Ware

(Dhavalikar and Possehl 1992), Padri Ware (Shinde and Kar 1992), Micaceous Red Ware (Rao 1985: 393-5; Herman and Krishnan 1994), Black and Red Ware (Rao 1979: 24) and Anarta Ware (Ajithprasad and Sonawane 1993) prior to the penetration of the Harappans in this area (Sonawane and Ajithprasad 1994: 130-6).

Equally important evidence has been brought forth recently from Nagwada and Santhli regarding the early penetration of Harappans in north Gujarat. The pottery found from the extended inhumation and symbolic pot burials as burial goods do not show similarities with the classic Harappan pottery; it rather resembles the vessel forms recovered from the Pre-Harappan levels at Kot Diji (Khan 1965), Amri (Casal 1964) and Balakot (Dales 1974). Analogous pottery types have been reported from secondary fractional and pot burials from the cemetery at Surkotada. These too are comparable with the Pre-Harappan burials of Sindh and Baluchistan (Joshi 1990). Stratigraphically, the burials at Nagwada are found below the Mature Harappan levels. Therefore, it signifies that the elements of the Pre-Harappan Culture of Sindh and Baluchistan extended further southwards as far as north Gujarat (Sonawane and Ajithprasad 1994). The archaeological data recovered from the lower levels of Dholavira is also suggestive in this context. Therefore, one has to view the development of Urban and Post-Urban Harappan phase of Gujarat in light of its antecedent Pre-Urban phase.

Subsequently, Possehl and Raval (1989) claimed regionality of the Harappan Culture after a systematic analysis of the excavated materials from Rojdi. Although some of the classical Harappan traits such as weights and measures, etched carnelian beads and copper implements of definite Harappan type, without seals, are found at Rojdi, the ceramic assemblage has nothing in common with classic Harappan pottery as represented in Kachchh and Sindh in Urban Harappan phase. However, the new radiocarbon dates indicate that the early levels at Rojdi were contemporaneous with the Mature/Urban phase of the Harappan Culture. Thus 'Sorath Harappan', a regional manifestation of the Harappan Culture in Saurashtra as distinct from the 'Sindhi Harappan' was proposed as an explanatory model. This has drastically changed the traditional picture about the existence of sites in Saurashtra during Urban Harappan phase (Possehl 1992b). The ceramic assemblage at Rojdi could be classified into a 'threefold' scheme: Rojdi A, B and C. This scheme by and large follows Rao's general sequence of Rangpur IIA, IIB and IIC (Possehl and Raval 1989). The 'Sorath Harappan' is a powerful conceptual model explaining changes in its material relics and their integration into the larger Harappan cultural frame. Though its chronological position is well defined, the cultural aspects are yet to be clarified further and hence, caution has to be exercised before attempting to reclassify the Harappan sites in Gujarat (Bhan 1989: 235-42; Possehl 1992a; Bhan 1992: 181-8).

In this context, it is imperative to note that in more than 500 Harappan site scatters, associated with different levels of Harappan affiliation during the third and second millennium BC in Gujarat, the settlements representing Mature/Urban Harappan phase (Sindhi Harappan) are few and far between. Out of the 25 settlements of this phase, 15 are situated in Kachchh while the rest are sparsely distributed in other parts of the region. Based on site character, it is hypothesized that these settlements were either engaged in some kind of specialized craft production as industrial/manufacturing centres or served as trading cum administrative centres or both. These sites, locationally can be broadly categorized as coastal and territorial settlements. The first category of settlements are situated on the sea coast or on the margins of the Ranns, which are hypothesized as being originally forming an arm of the Arabian Sea, while the territorial sites are situated in the hinterland regions surrounded by considerable land mass. From the site distribution, it appears that the second group of sites are more frequent in the eastern parts of Kachchh whereas the first one are confined to the coastal area of Saurashtra including the margins of the Ranns. Locational aspects of these sites make them economically related and inter-dependent. It has been noticed that the territorial sites are never as large and economically as developed as the coastal ones. Besides, coastal sites have a more relevant connotation so far as overseas trade relationships with settlements of the Western world, especially the Middle East, are concerned. The symbiotic relationship between these sites played an important role in establishing link with inter-regional and international trade network which was in some respect vital to their prosperity (Chitalwala 1988-9: 340). The locational set up of these settlements amply demonstrate that these were developed mainly for trade and access to raw materials of specific commodities and to facilitate their flow towards the areas of demand especially the nucleus Harappan urban centres.

The discovery of Lothal, Nageshwar, Padri, Kuntasi and Bagasra in Saurashtra, Nagwada and Zekhada in north Gujarat and Dholavira, Shikarpur, Surkotada and Pabumath in Kachchh, located on the coast or along the margins of the geomorphological features like the Ranns amply demonstrated that these settlements were engaged in the manufacture of specialized items of semi-precious stones, steatite, faience, chank shell, ivory, copper, etc., for the purpose of trade. Of these, regional centres like Lothal and Dholavira definitely acted as trading and administrative stations, demonstrating the dependence of the central Indus urban centres on the outlying resource area of Gujarat. This very fact clearly indicates that the hinterland region, particularly of Saurashtra and the mainland Gujarat, was not accessed or exploited by the immigrant Harappans during its Mature/Urban phase. The absence of Mature/Urban Harappan settlements in the interiors of Saurashtra particularly corroborated this view. On the contrary, territorial settlements of Kachchh such as Surkotada, Pabumath and Khirasara acted as garrison defence outposts in order to control the resource areas of further south and east. It is worth noting that quite a few of these are strongly fortified.

From the aforesaid data, it is quite clear that the southward expansion of Harappan Culture into Gujarat during its Mature/Urban phase was marked by the acceleration of the process of utilizing natural resources by colonizing selective ecological regions keeping an eye on its resource potentials exclusively for trade of varying degrees rather than acquiring the entire territory for political dominance (Sonawane 1992: 169), like the initial European colonies in India during the seventeenth century.

Prior to the arrival of the Harappans in Gujarat, this land was already inhabited by the local/indigenous regional Chalcolithic communities, with whom the immigrant Harappans interacted for effective exploitation of the local resources in order to sustain their specific needs. This has resulted in the amalgamation of more than one cultural trait in the material inventory at most of the Harappan settlements during its Mature/Urban phase. Such a coexistence suggests a symbiotic relationship between two divergent cultural communities. Many a time, Non-Harappan elements are found more predominant than the Harappan at most of the sites. Ceramic assemblage recovered from the earliest levels at Lothal (Rao 1979: 28-9) and Nagwada IB (Sonawane 1994-5: 5) would corroborate this assumption.

The excavated sites such as Desalpur, Surkotada, Pabumath, Shikarpur and Dholavira in Kachchh; Lothal and Bagasra in Saurashtra and Nagwada in north Gujarat have most of the diagnostic elements of the Mature Indus Civilization such as the typical ceramic with fossil forms, metal tools, architecture with the standard brick size, uniform weight system, seals and sealings with writing, variety of ornamental beads including etched carnelian, long parallel sided chert blades of Rohri origin, terracotta triangular cakes, etc. On the other hand, sites like Nageshwar, Kuntasi, Padri, Rangpur in Saurashtra and Zekhada in north Gujarat because of their specific function cannot be expected to possess all the parameters as distinctive markers of the Urban phase found elsewhere in contemporary settlements. While the Rojdi A and B occupation, fall within the Urban phase at least in date, the material inventory is quite different in detail from that of the Urban phase Harappan as represented in Kachchh and Sindh (Possehl 1992a: 129).

The drainage network of Kachchh, Saurashtra and the mainland of Gujarat is complex and varied from region to region. The spread of Harappan Culture was therefore conditioned by areas of attraction. These features partly explain the regional diversities even within Gujarat in the manifestation of the Harappan Culture. Unlike the fertile tracts of the Indus Valley in Sindh, none of the rivers in Gujarat, particularly of Harappan eco-zones, lend themselves for irrigational use with ancient technology. Agriculture here is entirely dependent on dry farming techniques. Therefore, alternative subsistence strategies were adopted by the Harappan and allied Chalcolithic communities to suit the environmental setting. As a result, most of these sites account for a complex system of occupational diversity. What emerges is a complicated picture of the varying interrelated aspects of sedentism, pastoralism, hunting and many other diversified resource exploitation strategies. In order to compensate for dry scarcity and to minimize the risks of periodic rainfall fluctuation, we can hypothesize an extensive land use pattern which took advantage of the region's total available subsistence potentiality. A wide range of site locations, thus, not only highlights the adaptive skills of the enterprising Harappans but also throws light on how it gave rise to the regional phenomenon called the 'Sorath Harappan'.

POST-URBAN HARAPPAN PHASE

In the absence of an abrupt end to the Mature/Urban phase, the continuity has been seen in the form of a degenerated phase at most of the Harappan settlements in Gujarat. Therefore, keeping in view the radiocarbon determinations from different known sites and reanalysis of the excavated data it has been felt that the occupations during Lothal B, Rangpur IIC and III, Rojdi C, Kuntasi II (Dhavalikar et al. 1996), Padri IIIB (Shinde 1992), Prabahs Patan II and III (Dhavalikar 1995: 27), Vagad IB and IC (Sonawane and Mehta 1985) and Dholavira stage VI and VII (Bisht 1997: 17) marked the onset of the Post-Urban Harappan phase in Gujarat. Apart from these above cited excavated sites, where habitational strata have shown continuity in Harappan occupation from Urban to Post-Urban phases, the excavations at Kanewal (Mehta et al. 1980), Nesadi (Mehta 1984), Ratanpura (Sonawane 1994-5) and Oriyo Timbo (Rissman and Chitalwala 1990) demonstrate an independent existence of this Post-Urban Harappan phase. In the archaeological literature explored sites based on Rangpur sequence, particularly sites related to Rangpur IIB and IIC are clubbed together, though culturally both the phases are not alike. Long ago, Misra made a sharp, critical review and argued that culturally Rangpur IIB is part of Rangpur IIA itself (Misra 1965: 45-6). This can even be further tested with the Rojdi sequence. Since culturally Rojdi A and B are correlated with Rangpur IIA and IIB as Urban Harappan, logically or even otherwise, Rojdi C and Rangpur IIC are prone to be featuring Post-Urban. Unless good cultural and chronological markers are found in the explored material, the precise number of sites in each period will remain unknown. Therefore, for better analytical interpretation only excavated sites have the potential to offer more reliable evidence.

Among the distinctive features of the Post-Urban Harappan settlements in Gujarat, the first and foremost is the general economic decline in material culture which causes a gradual process of deurbanization. Since the prosperity of the Urban Harappan settlements was dependent on foreign or long distance trade, they suffered a decline as soon as the trade began to dwindle at the beginning of the second millennium BC. This is the reason why some of the Mature/Urban sites do not survive during the Post-Urban phase, Nageshwar, Nagwada Surkotada, etc., to name a few, are good examples to explain such adverse effects. Shift in climatic conditions causing increased aridity is also regarded as another responsible factor for this change.

It is clear from the fact that certain forms like 'Indus goblets', beakers and 'S' shaped jars almost disappear, other characteristic ceramics, including perforated jar, continue with slight changes in shape and decoration; however, the fabric became coarser and in painted design linear patterns became common in contrast to the diagnostic Mature Harappan naturalistic decorations. The convex-sided bowls developed a blunt or even sharp carination at the shoulder. The stud of the handled bowl which became longer at Rangpur did not undergo any change at Rojdi, where long and short handles occur at all levels. The stem part of the dish-on-stand became squat while the projected dish acquired a beaded rim. Lustrous Red Ware, characterized by high polished red slip, which is actually introduced in the upper levels of Rangpur IIC, became the prominent ceramic type during Period III. The white painted Black and Red Ware also became more conspicuous by its presence. The Prabhas Ware, distinct from Lustrous Red Ware, treated with pinkish or orange wash with purple or dark brown painted designs mostly set in panels and registers suggest regional innovations. Graffiti on pottery, some of which resemble the signs of the Harappan script also occur, reminding us of the continuity of the earlier tradition, though in a reduced frequency. Although the classical Reserved Slip Ware totally disappeared, its crude variant as an imitation was found lingering at a few sites. Some elements of Jhukar pottery were also observed in the ceramic assemblage in its upper strata at Dholavira.

This transformation is not reflected in ceramics alone. Among other artefacts, long chert blades, a material that had been imported from the Sukar Rohri Hills of Sindh, Pakistan, was no longer available because of the steep fall in trade and were substituted by smaller blades of locally available chert and chalcedony. Perhaps for the same reason, the cubical chert/agate weights, so diagnostic of the Urban phase are no longer found, and are replaced by truncated spherical weights of sandstone and similar material. Though terracotta beads become common, simple varieties of semi-precious stone beads and shell objects did continue to some extent because of the local availability of the required raw material. The absence of steatite micro and disc beads inspite of local availability of raw material in certain parts of the region again reflects on the restricted movement of the people. In addition, there are stray occurrences of terracotta triangular cakes and sporadic finds of stamped seals with only inscriptions, devoid of the usual animal or other figure depictions. The overall decline in the material culture of this phase is also reflected in the use of metal objects.

The deterioration in settlement pattern is also very explicit as compared to the earlier phase. The acropolis, warehouse and dockyard at Lothal were abandoned. Even the house floors were now made of brickbats collected from earlier constructions. The situation of Rangpur is not much different. At Dholavira, during phase VI and VII, the one-time city shrank into a small settlement confined to the Citadel and the southern margin of the Middle Town where they delimited it by raising a wall of an entirely different workmanship. Like Lothal, there was no control over planning of the settlement. Ordinary type of circular residential structures without use of bricks again suggest the adverse economic conditions of the people. Stone structural remains found at Rojdi, Kuntasi and mud constructions at Prabhas Patan and Padri reflects on the overall decline in the Harappan planning of the settlement. The archaeological data recovered from these sites witness clear signs of shrinkage in the size of settlements during this cultural phase.

The other category of settlements exhibiting non-durable architectural features comprising simple round huts with wattle-and-daub walls as seen at Kanewal, Vagad, Ratanpura and Nesadi, are far more in number. These have been interpreted as small rural village or dry season pastoral camps, where people were engaged in agricultural and pastoral subsistence activities. In this context, it is interesting to note that anthropologists like Flannery (1972) and Binford (1990) have come to the conclusion that a round hut generally suggests seasonal occupation. In this case, it can be inferred that there was a considerable component of semi-nomadic population during the Post-Urban Harappan times (Varma 1991).

Intensive surveys carried out by Chitalwala (1979), Momin (1979), Possehl (1980), Bhan (1886), and by a team of archaeologists from the M.S. University of Baroda (Ajithprasad and Sonawane 1993), particularly in Saurashtra and western part of north Gujarat revealed that most of the sites representing Rangpur IIB (Urban phase) continued during Period IIC; however there is a marked decline in the number of settlements thereafter which are associated with Rangpur III—Lustrous Red Ware (Bhan 1992). Any study based on settlement patterns faces a great number of interpretation hurdles. Therefore, a critical evolution of the investigative process remains critical. However, the recently discovered sites in north Gujarat offer a good example of the dispersed type of settlement pattern in contrast to that of the linear-dendritic pattern of Saurashtra. The pattern of settlements in Saurashtra are mostly controlled by various river systems, whereas in north Gujarat it was based on locational variables of relict sand dunes associated with inter-dunal depressions forming ponds, rather than rivers. While the majority of the Saurashtrian sites are attributed to a shift in the pattern of land use from *rabi* to *kharif* crops (Possehl 1980: 54), the western part of north Gujarat, because of its typical ecological and environmental factors, favoured pastoral activities. The availability of excellent grassland, water, patchy appearance of thin cultural deposits and large frequency of animal bones suggests that sites in north Gujarat may have served as temporary or seasonal camps involved in pastoral activities (Bhan 1992: 175-9; Sonawane 1994-5: 8-10). An important feature of these settlements is that there are small clusters of two or three sites and the average distance between two such clusters is not more than 10 km. The migration of present-day pastoralists from Saurashtra and Kachchh to north Gujarat and the seasonally marshy areas of the region is a well known phenomenon. These pastoralists particularly the Bharvad and Rabari communities visit these areas during seasons when sufficient fodder is available. They return to the same region repeatedly, establishing short term camps. This pattern would account for the thin patchy habitational debris (Bhan 1992: 178-9). This fact very well reflects on the carrying capacity of the restricted catchment area in the makeup of the settlements. On the other hand, only ten sites of this phase have been reported from Kachchh so far. It seems, after having served as a corridor during the Urban/Mature phase, most of the sites in Kachchh were abandoned, most probably because of the inhospitable terrain and climate. Here, in Kachchh during this phase except for Dholavira, the rest of the sites are not located at places where the Mature Harappans lived.

In fact, there is believed to have been a gradual shift in the subsistence strategy from farming to herding towards the closing centuries of this phase (Varma 1991), in which nomadic pastoralism seems to have played a significant role. This brought them into contact with the neighbouring Chalcolithic communities of the Banas Valley and Malwa. Such contacts are explicitly observed at Jokha (Mehta et al. 1971), Dhatva (Mehta et al. 1975) and Ratanpura (Bhan 1989: 231; Sonawane 1994-5: 9). The presence of Lustrous Red Ware in Navdatoli phase III and Ahar IC also support this assumption.

Considering the chronological position of Rojdi C and the absence of urban elements after *c*. 1900 BC, it is clear that Rojdi C and Rangpur IIC mark the beginning of the Post-Urban Harappan phase in Gujarat. Therefore, the time bracket can be proposed on the basis of available dates from some of the sites in Gujarat besides those of Lustrous Red Ware bearing deposits at Ahar and Navdatoli. These radiocarbon determinations place this phase into a bracket of *c*. 1900-1400 BC (Table 1).

TABLE 1. RADIOCARBON DATES FROM IMPORTANT SITES UNDER REVIEW

Site	Number	5568 BP	5730 BC	Calibrated	Cultural Period
Loteshwar	PRL 1564	4460 ± 110	2510 ± 110	2921 BC	Period II - Anarta Tradition
Loteshwar	PRL 1565	5050 ± 110	3100 ± 110	3698 BC	Period II - Anarta Tradition
Padri	PRL 1785	4390 ± 90	4520 ± 90	3048 BC	Period I - Padri Ware
Padri	PRL 1787	4820 ± 100	4960 ± 100	3680 BC	Period I - Padri Ware
Prabhas Patan	PRL 90	4240 ± 110	2415 ± 115	2892 BC	Period I - Pre Prabhas
Prabhas Patan	TF 1287	4280 ± 105	2460 ± 110	2911 BC	Period I - Pre Prabhas
Rojdi	PRL 1284	3810 ± 100	1960 ± 105	2283 BC	Period A - Sorath Harappan
Rojdi	PRL 1093	3920 ± 110	2090 ± 115	2462 BC	Period A - Sorath Harappan
Rojdi	PRL 1085	4020 ± 110	2190 ± 115	2573 BC	Period A - Sorath Harappan
Rojdi	PRL 1091	4150 ± 110	2325 ± 115	2867, 2699 BC	Period A - Sorath Harappan
Rojdi	PRL 1282	3470 ± 140	1620 ± 145	1866, 1772 BC	Period B - Sorath Harappan
Rojdi	PRL 1088	3770 ± 120	1935 ± 125	2198, 2149 BC	Period B - Sorath Harappan
Rojdi	TF 200	3810 ± 110	1975 ± 115	2283 BC	Period B - Sorath Harappan
Lothal	TF 27	3840 ± 110	2005 ± 115	2315 BC	Period A - Urban Harappan
Lothal	TF 22	3845 ± 110	2010 ± 115	2328 BC	Period A - Urban Harappan
Lothal	TF 136	3915 ± 130	2808 ± 135	2461 BC	Period A - Urban Harappan
Lothal	TF 19	3650 ± 135	1810 ± 140	2034 BC	Period B - Post-Urban Harappan
Kuntasi	PRL 1371	3650 ± 140	1810 ± 145	2014 BC	Period I - Urban Harappan
Kuntasi	PRL 1370	3710 ± 160	1870 ± 165	2135, 2050 BC	Period I - Urban Harappan
Kuntasi	BS 567	3870 ± 90	2035 ± 95	2451, 2356 BC	Period I - Urban Harappan
Nagwada	A 4555	3700 ± 80	1860 ± 80	2133, 2067 BC	Period IB - Urban Harappan
Vagad	BS 752	3625 ± 100	1780 ± 105	2170 BC	Period IA - Urban Harappan
Vagad	BS 751	2320 ± 100	1470 ± 105	1775 BC	Period IB - Post-Urban Harappan
Ahar	TF 32	3400 ± 105	1550 ± 110	1733-1697 BC	Period IC - Banas Chalcolithic
Navdatoli	P 204	3449 ± 127	1600 ± 130	1749 BC	Phase III - Malwa Chalcolithic

CONCLUSION

Thus, the cultural variables seen in subsistence and settlement pattern show a lack of standardization and homogeneity in its material culture during this Post-Urban Harappan phase. The small size of settlements with a non-descriptive architectural pattern, reduced number of items of material culture and thin habitational deposits corroborate this assumption. Although, there was certainly a decline in the material prosperity, a basic continuity of the Harappan tradition was still observed in the form of some lingering features of the Harappan Culture transforming the urban way of life into a rural one.

In the present state of our knowledge, based on available radiocarbon dates from different Harappan sites, it appears that the onset of the overall decline or deurbanization of Harappan Culture overall took place after the beginning of the second millennium BC (Lal 1997: 238-54). Though the causes of this decline are not yet precisely known, it is certain that each of the different regions within the Indian subcontinent has its own particular problem. Climatic changes, tectonic movements and shifts in hydraulic regime can be regarded as homogeneous. All do, however, share the common features of deurbanization, i.e. the relative smallness of the settlements, lack of monumental buildings and the absence of long distance trade as summarized by Ghosh (1993: 383). As a result, the social fabric of the Post-Urban Harappans became weak and economic conditions were geared more to meet the subsistence requirements than to gain any surplus. Because of weak political power, it witnessed a process of decentralization and localization, giving rise to regional cultural expressions. To a certain extent, this process of deurbanization can be equated with the indigenization process (Malik 1968: 120-1) and the idea of various cultures '... influencing each other' (Subbarao 1958: 151-2).

REFERENCES

Adams, R.M. 1966. *The Evolution of Urban Society*. Chicago: Aldine.

Ajithprasad, P. and V.H. Sonawane 1993. Harappa Culture in North Gujarat: a Regional Paradigm. Paper Presented at the Conference on the Harappans in Gujarat: Problems and Prospects. Pune: Deccan College.

Allchin, F.R. 1990. The End of Harappan Urban Phase and its Aftermath, *Ancient Ceylon* 4 (10): 25-40.

Bhan, K.K. 1986. Recent Explorations in the Jamnagar District of Saurashtra, *Man and Environment* X: 1-21.

——— 1989. Late Harappan Settlements of Western India, with Specific Reference to Gujarat, in *Old Problems and New Perspectives in the Archaeology of South Asia* (J.M. Kenoyer Ed.), pp. 219-43. Madison: Prehistory Press. Wisconsin Archaeological Reports 2.

——— 1992. Late Harappan Gujarat, *The Eastern Anthropologist* 45 (1-2): 173-92.

Binford, L.R. 1990. Mobility, Housing and Environment: a Comparative Study, *Journal of Anthropological Archaeology* 46: 119-52.

Bisht, R.S. 1997. Dholavira Excavations: 1990-94, in *Facets of Indian Civilization: Recent Perspectives* (J.P. Joshi Ed.), pp. 107-20. New Delhi: Aryan Books International.

Casal, J.M. 1964. *Fouilles D'Amri*, 2 vols. Paris:Publication de la Commission des Fouilles Archaelogique, Fouilles de Pakistan.

Childe, V.G. 1950. The Urban Revolution, *The Town Planning Review* 21 (1): 3-17.

Chitalwala, Y. M. 1979. Harappan and Post-Harappan Settlement Patterns in the Rajkot District of Saurashtra, in *Essays in Indian Protohistory* (D.P. Agrawal and D.K. Chakrabarti Eds.), pp. 113-21. Delhi: B.R. Publishing Corporation.

——— 1985. Late Harappan Culture, in *Recent Advances in Indian Archaeology* (S.B. Deo and K. Paddayya Eds.), pp. 57-64. Poona: Deccan College.

——— 1988-9. Harappan Settlements in Kutch and Saurashtra: Problems and Perspectives, *Bulletin of the Deccan College Post-Graduate and Research Institute* 47-8: 339-2.

Dales, G.F. 1966. The Decline of the Harappans, *Scientific American* 214 (5): 92-100.

——— 1974 Excavations at Balakot, Pakistan 1973, *Journal of Field Archaeology* 1: 3-22.

Dhavalikar, M.K. 1994. *Cultural Imperialism: Indus Civilization in Western India.* New Delhi: Books & Books.

Dhavalikar, M.K. and G.L. Possehl 1992. The Pre-Harappan Period at Prabhas Patan and the Pre-Harappan Phase in Gujarat, *Man and Environment* XVII (1): 72-8.

Dhavalikar, M.K., M.R. Raval and Y.M. Chitalwala 1996. *Kuntasi: a Harappan Emporium on West Coast*. Pune: Deccan College.

Dikshit, K.N. 1981-3. Late Harappan Cultures: a Reappraisal, *Puratattva* 13-14: 55-61.

Dikshit, M.G. 1950. Excavations at Rangpur: 1947, *Bulletin of the Deccan College Research Institute* 11 (1): 3-55.

Fairservis, W.A. 1967. The Origin, Character and Decline of the Early Civilization, *Novitates* 2055. New York: American Museum of Natural History.

Flannery, K.V. 1972. The Origin of the Village as a Settlement Type in Meso-America and the Near East, in *Man Settlement and Urbanism* (P. Ucko, R. Tringham and G.W. Dimbleby Eds.), pp. 23-53. London: Duckworth.

Ghosh, A. 1993. Deurbanization of the Harappan Civilization, in *Harappan Civilization: a Recent Perspective* (G.L. Possehl Ed.), pp. 381-4. New Delhi: Oxford-IBH and the American Institute of Indian Studies.

Gupta, S.P. 1993. The Late Harappan: a Study of Cultural Dynamics, in *Harappan Civilization: a Recent Perspective* (G.L. Possehl Ed.), pp. 51-9. New Delhi: Oxford-IBH and the American Institute of Indian Studies.

Herman, C.F. and K. Krishnan 1994. Micaceous Red Ware: a Gujarat Proto-Historic Cultural Complex or Just Ceramic? in *South Asian Archaeology 1993*, Vol. I (Asko Parpola and Petteri Koskikallio Eds.), pp. 225-43. Helsinki: Annales Academiae Scientiarum Fennicae, Series B, Vol. 271.

Joshi, J.P. 1990. *Excavations at Surkotada 1971-72 and Exploration in Kutch*. New Delhi: Memoirs of the Archaeological Survey of India 87.

Khan, F.A. 1965. Excavations at Kot Diji, *Pakistan Archaeology* 2: 11-85.

Lal, B.B. 1997. *The Earliest Civilization of South Asia: Rise, Maturity and Decline*. New Delhi: Aryan Books International.

Mackay, E.J.H. 1938. *Further Excavations at Mohenjo-daro*. New Delhi: Government of India.

Majumdar, N.G. 1934. *Explorations of Sind*. New Delhi: Memoirs of the Archaeological Survey of India 48.

Malik, S.C. 1968. *The Formative Period of Indus Civilization: a Study of Archaeology as Anthropology*. Simla: Indian Institute of Advanced Study.

Marshall, John 1931. *Mohenjo-daro and the Indus Civilization*. London: Arthur Probsthain.

Mehta, R.N. 1984. Valabhi—a Station of Harappan Cattle-Breeders, in *Frontiers of the Indus Civilization* (B.B. Lal and S.P. Gupta Eds.), pp. 227-30. Delhi: Books & Books.

Mehta, R.N. and S.N. Chowdhary 1971. *Excavation at Jokha*. Baroda: the Maharaja Sayajirao University, Archaeology Series 11.

——— 1975. *Excavation at Dhatva*. Baroda: the Maharaja Sayajirao University, Archaeology Series 12.

Mehta, R.N., K.N. Momin and D.R. Shah 1980. *Excavation at Kanewal*. Baroda: the Maharaja Sayajirao University, Archaeology Series 11.

Misra, V.N. 1965. Review of 'Ancient India, Bulletin of the Archaeological Survey of India 18-19 (1962-62)', *The Eastern Anthropologist* 18 (1): 44-52.

——— 1984. Climate, a Factor in the Rise and Fall of the Indus Civilization—Evidence from Rajasthan and Beyond, in *Frontiers of the Indus Civilization* (B.B. Lal and S.P. Gupta Eds.), pp. 461-89. Delhi: Books & Books.

Momin, K.N. 1979. Archaeology of Kheda District (Gujarat) upto 1500 A.D). Ph.D. Dissertation. Baroda: the M.S. University of Baroda.

Mughal, M.R. 1970. The Early Harappan Period in the Greater Indus Valley and Baluchistan. Ph.D. Dissertation. Philadelphia: University of Pennsylvania.

Possehl, G.L. 1977. The End of a State and the Continuity of a Tradition: a Discussion of Late Harappan, in *Realm and Region in Traditional India* (Richard Fox Ed.), pp. 234-54. New Delhi: Vikas Publishing House.

——— 1980. *Indus Civilization in Saurashtra*. New Delhi: B.R. Publishing Corporation.

——— 1984. Archaeological Terminology and the Harappan Civilization, in *Frontiers of the Indus Civilization* (B.B. Lal and S.P. Gupta Eds.), pp. 27-38. Delhi: Books & Books.

——— 1992a. The Harappan Civilization in Gujarat: the Sorath and Sindhi Harappans, *The Eastern Anthropologist* 45 (1-2): 117-54.

——— 1992b. The Harappans in Saurashtra: New Chronological Considerations, *Puratattva* 22: 25-9.

——— 1993. The Harappan Civilization: a Contemporary Perspective, in *Harappan Civilization: a Recent Perspective* (G.L. Possehl Ed.), pp. 15-28. New Delhi: Oxford-IBH and American Institute of Indian Studies.

Possehl, G.L. and M.H. Raval 1989. *Harappan Civilization and Rojdi*. New Delhi: Oxford-IBH.

Raikes, R.C. 1964. The End of the Ancient Cities of the Indus, *American Anthropologist* 66 (2): 179-93.

Rao, S.R. 1963. Excavations at Rangpur and Other Explorations in Gujarat, *Ancient India* 18-19: 5-207.

——— 1979. *Lothal: a Harappan Port Town 1955-62*. New Delhi: Memoirs of Archaeological Survey of India 78 (1).

——— 1985. *Lothal: a Harappan Port Town 1955-62*. New Delhi: Memoirs of Archaeological Survey of India 78 (2).

Rissman, Paul C. and Y.M. Chitalwala 1990. *Harappan Civilization and Oriyo Timbo*. New Delhi: Oxford-IBH.

Shaffer, J.G. 1992. The Indus Valley, Baluchistan and Helmand Traditions: Neolithic Through Bronze Age, in *Chronology of in Old World Archaeology*, Vol. 1 (R. Ehrich Ed.), pp. 441-64. Chicago: University of Chicago Press.

Shinde, V.S. 1992. Padri and the Indus Civilization, *South Asian Studies* 8: 55-66.

Shinde, V.S. and S.B. Kar 1992. Padri Ware: a New Painted Ceramic Found in the Harappan Levels at Padri in Gujarat, *Man and Environment* 17 (2): 105-10.

Sonawane, V.H. 1992. Fresh Light on the Specialized Crafts of the Harappans in Gujarat, *The Eastern Anthropologist* 45 (1-2): 155-72.

——— 1994-5. Harappan Settlements of Rupen Estuary, Gujarat, *Pragdhara* 5: 1-11.

Sonawane V.H. and P. Ajithprasad 1994. Harappa Culture and Gujarat, *Man and Environment* XIX (1-2): 129-39.

Sonawane, V.H. and R.N. Mehta 1985. Vagad: a Rural Harappan Settlement in Gujarat, *Man and Environment* IX: 38-44.

Subbarao, B. 1958. *The Personality of India*. Baroda: Maharaja Sayajirao University, Archaeology Series 3.

Varma, Supriya 1991. Villages Abandoned: the Case for Mobile Pastoralism in Post Harappan Gujarat, *Studies in History* (New Series) 7 (2): 279-300.

Wheeler, R.E.M. 1947. Harappa 1946: the Defenses and Cemetery R-37, *Ancient India* 3: 58-130.

Harappan Social Organization

M.K. DHAVALIKAR

The epoch making discovery of the Indus Civilization revealed to the world that there flourished in India some four thousand years ago a glorious civilization which was in several respects more advanced than some of its contemporaries. Recent research has brought to light over a thousand settlements of this great civilization of which a vast majority (over 700) are in India and the remaining in Pakistan. Its origins go back into the latter half of the fourth millennium and its main focus was the Saraswati Valley (present Ghaggar in Rajasthan). Quite a few sites have been excavated and they demonstrate the nature of its urban centres; and Mohenjo Daro is supposed to be the largest city of the ancient world. The overall settlement pattern of Harappan towns and cities shows that it was a class structured society. But our knowledge of the Harappan social organization is almost next to nothing. This lacuna is in the main, due to the general presumption that we cannot dig out the social organization of a prehistoric community. Hawkes (1954: 61-2) had made a list of those aspects of prehistoric cultures about which we will never know and had included 'social organization' among them, but it has now become possible to do so if we follow the new paradigms in archaeology.

> It has often been suggested that we cannot dig up a social system or ideology. Granted we cannot excavate a kinship terminology or a philosophy, but we can and do excavate the material items which functioned together with those more behavioral elements within the approriate cultural sub-systems. The formal structure of artifact assemblages together with the between element of contextual relationships should and do present a systematic and understandable picture of *the total extinct* cultural system. (Binford 1962: 218-19)

When the major sites like Mohenjo Daro and Harappa were excavated in the early twenties of this century, the technique of excavation and the methods of data recovery were not advanced as they are today. But even in the post-Independence period, when several Harappan sites were excavated, no one indulged in this sort of exercise. Casual observations were made, as for instance, that the Harappan society was a stratified society and that some sort of hierarchy existed in this class structured society (Malik 1979; Chitawala 1984; Kenoyer 1989, 1991; Lal 1993). Some scholars are bold enough to pronounce that caste system was prevalent in the Harappan society (Ratnagar 1991: 18-19; Kenoyer 1991, 1992). These views were apparently based on the existence of twin mounds of a major Harappan sites which represented the citadel on the left and the lower city on the right, some times both enclosed by circumvallations. It was therefore obvious that the rulers lived in the citadel area and the common people in the Lower Town. Wheeler (1968) emphasized this particular feature of the Harappan town planning which suggested that it was a ranked society (Kenoyer 1989: 188-9). Furthermore, it was presumed that the same situation prevailed even in the Early Harappan times as some sites of this culture too have double mounds (Flam 1984: 81).

There seems to be a general unanimity that the Citadel in all probability served as the residence of the ruling chief/chief priest; possibly both the functions were combined in one person. A very impressive building was exposed in the Citadel at Mohenjo Daro to the east of the Great Bath. It consisted of an open courtyard surrounded by spacious rooms and corridors. It has been identified as the residence of the Chief Priest. Close by is the Great Bath which may have been used for rituals. It reminds us of the 'Pushakarini' at Caishali which belongs to the third-second century BC. The literary evidence suggests that it was used for ritual bath. Mention may also be made in this context of a stele found in the Gulf region which depicts a ruler being given a ritual bath in such a structure. Lal (1993, 1997: Chapter 12) has given a detailed description of the Citadel at Kalibangan and has convincingly shown that it was most probably the residence of the Chief Priest. The Citadel, in sharp contrast to the Lower Town, did not have a pattern of grid-iron planning. It was divided into two sectors, one on the north and the other on the south. There were no residential structures in the northern part, but instead there were several large and high platforms in the north-western part where on one such platform there was a row of fire altars. Close to them was a brick-lined well and a brick paved bathing floor. On another platform there was a brick lined sacrificial pit. Lal (1984) has presented a graphic picture of the rituals that might have been taking place in this area of the citadel. In the northern part were encountered residential structures for the occupants of the citadel.

The general impression still persists that the Harappan townships were divided only in two parts, the Citadel and the Lower Town. However, Lal (1997: 229 ff) has now noted that at Kalibangan the habitation was distributed in three distinct localities. Of these the Citadel and the Lower Town were fortified. Lal therefore infers that there was a threefold division of the society: (1) a priestly class living in the Citadel, (2) an agriculturist-cum-merchant class living in the Lower Town, and (3) a workers' class living outside the two fortified areas. Recent evidence, however, shows that there were not three but four localities, distinctly marked and properly segregated, in a Harappan city. At Mohenjo Daro, the Lower Town was separated from the Citadel by 150 m and the same was the case at Harappa whereas at Kalibangan, a smaller town, the distance between the two was 40 m. It is highly likely that there was water in this area as suggested by the evidence from Dholavira.

It is highly probable that large Harappan urban centres were divided into four localities as the evidence from Dholavira clearly establishes. Bisht's (1991) excavations at Dholavira are underway and the structures so far uncovered have led him to infer, and rightly, that the city was clearly divided into four parts: the citadel which was occupied by the rulers; the bailey or the Noblemen's quarters; the Middle Town for the agriculturists, merchants, craftsmen and traders; and the Lower Town for manual workers and landless labourers. The most noteworthy feature of this fourfold division was that all these sectors were separated from each other into water tight compartments by circumvallations, making them sort of 'Ghettos' as in mediaeval Europe. Even at Harappa four such localities can be identified; besides the Citadel (area AB) and the Lower Town (Mound E), there is area G which is now being subjected to excavation, as also area F (Dales 1992).

This fourfold division of the society into four classes is no doubt significant as it remind us of the *varna* system prevalent in the Hindu society today. It would not therefore be proper to blame it on the Aryans. Moreover, if the Aryans came to India from outside, they should have introduced it in those lands where they went as in Greece; and if they were indigenous, then they in all probability may have followed the system which already was in vogue during the Harappan times. Some scholars go a step further and have argued in favour of the prevalance of even the caste system during the Harappan times. It has been observed that the caste system promotes stability and continuity and is conducive to social stability for the handing down of technology within endogamus groups (Ratnagar 1991: 18-19; Kenoyer 1991, 1992). In this context it is significant that the late Professor Iravati Karve, a renowned sociologist, was of the opinion that the caste system existed in India even in pre-Vedic times.

> It is probable that something very like castes were in India even before the Aryans as a conquering people placed their three *varnas* at the head of the whole indigenous society. (Karve 1991: 57)

She further adds:

> The author feels that the '*jati*' system which allowed innumerable different endogamus groups to live separately is entirely different from the *varna* system which divided all society into four ranks. The *jati* organization or something very like it was in existence in India for a very long time, the author thinks, even prior to coming in of the Aryans. In course of time, the *varna* system was modified and the *varna* and the *jati* were interwoven together to form a very elaborate ranking system. (Karve 1991)

Karve has advanced very forceful arguments in support of her view. According to her, *varna* should not be taken to mean colour, as is generally supposed only because the Aryans were white and the authochthonous dark, but means rank in a given hierarchy, a sort of sequential position, or order of precedence as in *varna-mala* (alphabet). She has rightly pointed out that one can change his *varna* but not his *jati*. For instance, the Kayasthas of Uttar Pradesh were declared by the Allahabad High Court as *Kshatriyas* whereas those of Bengal were declared *Sudras* by the Calcutta High Court (ibid.: 45). It was sometime in the fifties of this century that the *Malis* (gardners) of Maharashtra who wanted to be Kshatriyas applied to the Bombay High Court, but their petition was dismissed and they remained Sudras. Similarly the Kunbis (cultivators) of Maharashtra, who formely claimed that they were Kshatriyas, now again want to be Sudras because of the Mandal Commission report. Hence Iravati Karve states:

> It is wrong to suppose that the *varna* system arose out of consciousness of racial distinction as indicated by skin colour. The Aryan world was made up of the three classes of priests, noblemen and commoners. All the people worshipped the same gods and underwent the same rituals from birth to death. (Karve 1991)

The recent excavations at Harappa by the University of California are very significant in this context. The evidence points to the segregation of different groups in the society. The excavation on Mound E, which was not formerly excavated, has yielded evidence pointing to the fact that it was occupied in the Mature Harappan phase by craftsmen, particularly those engaged in pottery manufacture, shell cutting, flint knapping, etc. There was clear evidence of craft specialization indicating that 'these crafts were extremely complex and involved technologies that would have been known only to a limited segment of the urban population' (Kenoyer 1992: 47). The same seems to be the case with the HR area at Mohenjo Daro where there was evidence of localized crafts as also occupational specialization (Mackay 1938). It is noteworthy that at Harappa itself, in the earlier excavation, Wheeler (1968: 31ff) found a whole street with stone mortars for dehusking grain and pounding it into flour. Piggott (1952: Chaps. VI, VII) identified the area as that of slave quarters, or place of government enterprise where slaves pounded cereals. To Irawati Karve (1991: 58), it was 'a street lived in by a caste-like group who specialized in pounding rice'. It is interesting to note in this context that similar evidence is also available in Buddhist literature. A Jataka story described a street in a city in Buddha's time (sixth century BC) as being occupied by carpenters, or the story of Vidubha, the son of Prasenjit, a king of Kosala, who was a contemporary of Buddha, and in whose capital was a street where only labourers lived. This tradition continues till today in our villages where different caste groups, especially the craftsmen, live in separate areas as far as possible. Kenoyer (1989: 189) is justified in his observation that

> 'given the size and socio-economic complexity of the Indus cities, it is not unlikely that some form of socio-economic ranking was present', and that 'this inequality may have been maintained through a centralised authority as is done presently under the *Jajmani* system'.

Some sort of ranking also existed even in Pre-Harappan times as the recent evidence from Harappa would indicate. There are over thirty Pre/Early Harappan sites of which at least fifteen are represented by two mounds, and there may be many more. Since the Early Harappans substantially contributed to the making up of the Harappan Civilization, it is highly likely that the Early Harappan society was also characterized by ranking. The excavation of Mound E at Harappa as revealed evidence indicating that even in the Early Harappan times craftsman had occupied that locality. This would reflect the hereditary nature of craft specialization. Kenoyer (1992: 49) is therefore justified in concluding that

> the potters were involved in producing specific types of vessels and were not producing the entire corpus of pottery vessels used at the site and the 'localisation' of production in one area of the city without any direct control by an external authority.

It is worth noting that even today in India certain potters make only certain types of pots (Karve 1991: 26).

There is now adequate evidence pointing to the prevalence of a fourfold division of the society and some scholars are inclined to infer the existence of caste system durign the Harappan times without, however, advancing supportive evidence. Shereen Ratnagar states that stability and continuity of material culture is striking and it may be said that a caste organization was conducive to social stability; to the handing down of technology within hereditary occupational groups and the spread of technique through marriages within endogamous caste groups. (Ratnagar 1991: 18)

Such an organization must have promoted hereditary craftsmanship within occupational groups which in course of time developed into an endogamous class in the historical period. This in a way approximates to the class system which has become a distinguishing feature of the Hindu society. It is pertinent to note that the most important difference between the *varna* (class) system and the caste (*jati*) system is that in the former it is the profession of a person which determines his *varna* whereas in the latter, the birth determines his profession. As the evidence from Vedic literature shows, there must have been freedom for a person to choose the craft of his liking. This, in hereditary succession, may have helped in developing and refining his craft. It has been observed that 'castes occupying the same rank in the same region are not necessarily similar in physical appearance and measurements nor do castes occupying different levels in the social status show necessarily physical differences' (Karve 1991: 60). Karve has established it by the fact that physical measurements have failed to show any difference between the Marathas and Kunbis, Kshatriyas and Sudras repectively in Maharashtra (ibid.: 20). This observation is significant in the light of evidence of skeletal remains from Harappan sites. According to Kennedy (1984: 102):

When multivariate studies are made using data for populations of the Mediterranean, Western Asia and the area influenced by the ancient Harappans in South Asia, a biological continuum extending over some five millennia is demonstrable. In short, the ancient Harappans are markedly different in their skeletal biology from the present day inhabitants of north-western India and Pakistan which, in turn, share a high frequency of phenotypic characters with both ancient and living peoples of Afghanistan, Iran and the lands bordering the Aegean and Mediterranean.

Within the subcontinent itself the evidence of skeletal biology indicates that the Harappan population was as cosmopolitan as that of India today, that is, the Harappans in Punjab and Sindh resembled the present-day Punjabis and Sindhis and those of Gujarat, Gujaratis of our own times. Sarkar (1964) maintians that the Harappans were not different from the present ethnic types living in their respective areas. Moreover, Sen (1964-5: 178ff) has observed that the ethnic stock of Cemetery R-37 and that of Cemetery H appears to have been the same. This is significant in view of the fact that the recent excavations at Harappa have revealed that there is an appreciable overlap between the Mature Harappan phase and Cemetary H (Meadow 1991).

There may not be much difference between the Harappan social organization of the Mature and Late Harappan times. The latter is marked by degeneration because of drastic climatic changes such as tectonic movements (Courty 1994) in Sindh and Punjab, changes in hydraulic regimes of rivers in Rajasthan; a marked shift towards aridty in Rajasthan and Gujarat (Dhavalikar 1997) and lowering of the sea levels (Sarma 1971) which made the ports inoperative with consequent loss of trade. This environmental change was not confined to India only, but was almost global in character. All this led to deurbanization of Harappan cities, and what we have are just large and small villages, the main occupation being subsistence agriculture, cattle-keeping, hunting and fishing. This is clearly evident in Saurashtra where numerous Late Harappan settlements have been found and a few of them have been excavated also. Among these mention should be made of Zekada, Kanewal and Sai-no-Tekdo where the Late Harappans lived in round huts which are indicative of a seasonally settled life. Anthropologists have observed that:

> We note immediately a strong set of relationships between mobility pattern and house plan. Fully nomadic people tend to construct houses with a circular or semi-circular plan, as do semi-nomadic people, while semi-sedentary and fully sedentary people favour rectangular house plans, although semi-circular house plans continue as a secondary plan. (Binford 1990: 123)

A large chunk of population may have resorted to pastoral nomadism in the Late Harappan period. Possehl (1979) too has argued in favour of a considerable pastoral element in the Harappan society and there cannot be two opinions about it, for even today pastoral nomadism is, as a mode of life, pursued by some 10 per cent of the population in India.

POLITICAL ORGANIZATION

It is really disheartening that in spite of the vast data from Harappan urban centres, not much can be said about the social organization of the Indus Civilization in the absence of contextual evidence. However, of late quite a few scholars have directed their attention to the political organization of this great civilization. There is little doubt that there was in all probability a strong central authority which sustained the Harappan Kingdom or 'empire' as some would call it. Sir Mortimer Wheeler once observed that the Indus Civilization was 'the vastest political experiment before the advent of the Roman empire'. It may however be stated that there is a great divergence of opinion ranging from the lack of political authority, to chiefdom, and primary and secondary statehood. Moreover, there is a difference of opinion whether there was a single political authority at the centre or whether different regions were independant. According to Malik (1979: 194-9), the absence of a supreme god, unusual monumental architecture, lack of rich mortuary remains, are all indicative of the absence of a strong central authority. Piggott (1952: 153) is of the opinion that it was a theocratic organization, in which the Chief Priest was himself the ruler. Some scholars prefer to consider it as chiefdom society. Fairservis thinks that it was not a state society but a chiefdom.

> Can one call the Harappan chieftainship(s) a civilization? If we define true civilization as something beyond mere technological accomplishment, an efficient organization with a literary memory bank reflective of a concern for human condition, as existed in San dai Chang, Sumero-Akkadia and Old Kingdom Egypt, then the Harappan culture does not qualify. India's first civilization appears sometime in the Vedic Age, according to that criterion. (Fairservis 1991: 108)

Shaffer (1982: 49) also held a similar view, for in his opinion a technologically advanced urban literate culture was achieved without the usually associated social organization based on hereditary elites, centralized political government and warfare.

The Harappan political organization must have been quite complex, and it is highly likely that it was a state in the accepted sence of the term. Several theories of the origin of state have been propounded and various criteria have been proposed. There is very convincing archaeological evidence to demonstrate that the invention of agriculture led to surplus food production, creating division of labour which in turn made craft specialization possible. This resulted in the social and political integration, uniting a number of previously independent units into a state. This entire process is delineated by Jacobson (1986), Sudeshna Guha (1989) and Shereen Ratnagar (1991). They are all unanimous in their verdict that the Harappans were organized into a state society.

It is pertinent to examine the sine qua non of a state society. In this respect the anthropological paradigms are of great help. Anthropologists have demonstrated that human societies evolve from band organization into a state society through chiefdom (Service 1975; Fried 1967). Urbanization was once throught to be a pre-requisite of a state society (Wheatley 1972) but has to be rejected because it has been shown that there are nomadic states as in Central Asia (Krader 1978) and the early states of Scythians; even Egypt has been described as a civilization without cities (Davis 1955).

The chief criteria of a state society include monumental architecture, a bureaucracy, coercive power to enforce its decisions on its subjects, biological evidence indicating differences in subsistence system and differences in mortuary remains showing difference in statuses, a well defined territory characterized by a four-tiered settlements hierarchy and a large population (Steponaitis 1981). According to Redman (1968: 280) a state society is characterized by concentration of economic power, organization along political and territorial lines, hierarchical and differential access to basic resources and monopoly of force. It will be seen that very convincing evidence is available from the excavation of Harappan sites that meets all these criteria and there should therefore be no hesitation in identifying the Harappan Civilization as a state society. It can further be averred that it was a secondary state and the Early Harappans were organized into a primary state.

The Harappan Civilization fulfils all these criteria in ample measure. It had a well defined territory, a large population, an efficient bureaucracy to enforce its decisions on the populace, a regular surplus to maintain the apparatus of the state, a stratified social organization, a common ideology legitimizing the authority of the ruling class, and finally a standing army. The Harappan territory was more extensive than that of my other contemporary civilization and the population was quite large, about 4,00,000 (Jacobson 1986: 147). The metorpolitan centres at Harappa and Mohenjo Daro had a population of about 50,000 each (Fairservis 1967). It is not difficult to compute for other centres, given the recent methods of doing it (Chakrabarti 1979: 210-12). The four tiered settlement hierarchy has been clearly established by Jacobson (1986: 153-5). There were large metropolitan centres like Harappa, and Mohenjo Daro, towns like Lothal and Kalibangan, large and small villages and even pastoral camps as at Oriya Timbo (Gujarat).

There must have existed a very strong bureaucracy which was rigorously authoritarian (Piggott 1952: 140) or else there would not have been such a striking uniformity in their material culture over such a vast area. The standard brick size, weights and measures, town planning, drainage system, etc., all presuppose that the rules and regulations were rigorously enforced. In the words of Wheeler (1968: 4) it was a highly evolved bureaucratic machine, for 'behind so vast a uniformity must lie an administrative and economic discipline, however exercised, of an impressive kind'. The surplus must have been considerable as flourishing trade with West Asia was in our favour. The stratified social organization is evident from the ghetto-like town planning at Dholavira. Although there are no impressive edifices like the Ziggurat or pyramids, the fortified urban centres, more particularly the stone built citadel of Dholavira, are nothing if not monumental. Evidence for a standing army with defensive measures too is available (Dhavalikar 1994: 179) or else the invasion of Rimush, the Akkadian King (2315-2307 BC) could not have been repelled (Sarkar 1975-6).

In his recent work Lal (1997: Chap. 12), has raised a certain question: Was the Harappan organization still at the stage of petty chiefdoms based primarily on kinship, or was there a state in the real sense of the term? In the latter case, further questions might be asked, i.e. was it an empire covering the entire known area of the Mature Harappan Civilization—from Sutkagen Dor in Baluchistan in the west to Alamgirpur in the east and from Manda in Jammu and Kashmir in the north to Daimabad in Maharashtra in the south or were there many small states?

After examining the evidence and various views, particularly that of Possehl (1993: Fig. 2), who has divided the entire Harappan region into six or seven 'provinces' which were probably autonomous.

Province	Capital
1. Sindh	Mohenjo Daro
2. Punjab	Harappa
3. South-east Punjab (Cholistan)	Ganweriwala
4. Baluchistan	Sutkagen Dor
5. Haryana	Banawali/Rakhigarhi
6. Rajasthan	Kalibangan
7. Gujarat	Dholavira

Lal invokes the analogy of the early historical period which witnessed the emergence of sixteen city states (mahajanapadas). Alternatively, he suggests that a city like Mohenjo Daro or Harappa may have emerged a leader through trade and commerce, overpowered other states and established an empire. This raises further questions: Were there kings in each sate or an emperor, and further where were their palaces? The Citadel may have been their residence and it may be noted that many medieval chiefs palaces were modest structures, as for instance the Peshwa's palace in Pune which was not much different from the 'wadas' of their *sardars*.

Another suggestion which has not received serious attention is that offered by Piggott (1952: 153) who hypothesized the presence of a 'priest king' and postulated an almost theocratic government. This however was in the realm of conjecture and no evidence was adduced in support of the Great Bath at Mohenjo Daro having an upper storey which was supposed to have been occupied by priests, and even at Kalibangan the Citadel probably served the residence of chief-priests. Beyond this one cannot say anything about the religious organization. The possibility is that religion probably was not organized as, for instance, Christianity and Islam are; on the other hand it was in all likelihood similar to Hinduism today with each person having his own personal deity which was placed in a small niche in his house. This would also explain as to why there is no structure so far unearthered at any Harappan site which can be identified as religious—a temple or a prayer house—save that in the HR area at Harappa (Wheeler 1968: 52-3; Dhavalikar and Atre 1989).

The foregoing discussion amply brings into sharp focus how sketchy is our knowledge of the Harappan society. It is therefore very necessary that all future excavations are carried out with special emphasis on contextual evidence. Considerable work has been done in the Western world on prehistoric social organization by employing anthropological paradigms which we should employ too.

REFERENCES

Allchin, B. and F.R. Allchin 1997. *Origins of a Civilization: the Prehistory and Early Archaeology of South Asia.* New Delhi: Viking-Penguin Books India.

Binford, L.S. 1962. Archaeology as Anthropology, *American Antiquity* 28: 215-25.

——— 1990. Mobility, Housing and Environment: a Comparative Study, *Journal of Anthropological Archaeology* 46: 119-52.

Bisht, R.S. 1991. Dholavira—a New Horizon of Indus Civilization, *Puratattva* 20: 71-82.

Chakrabarti, D.K. 1979. The Size of Harappan Settlements, in *Essays in Indian Protohistory* (D.P. Agrawal and D.K. Chakrabarti Eds.), pp. 205-15. Delhi: D.K. Publishers.

Chitalwala, Y.M. 1984. The Problem of Class Structure in Indus Civilization, *Frontiers of the Indus Civilization* (B.B. Lal and S.P. Gupta Eds.), pp. 197-201. New Delhi: Books & Books.

Courty, M.A. 1994. Spatial and Temporal Analysis of the Late Third Millennium Climatic Change and Socio-Economic Collapse: Problem, Evidence, Skepticism and more Question, Paper Read at III World Archaeology Congress, New Delhi (unpublished).

Dales, G.F. 1992. Recent Excavations at Harappa, *The Eastern Anthropologists* 45: 21-38.

Davis, K. 1955. The Origin and Growth of Urbanisation in the World, *American Journal of Sociology* 61: 430-9.

Dhavalikar, M.K. 1994. *Cultural Imperialism: Indus Civilization in Western India.* New Delhi: Books & Books.

——— 1997. *Indian Protohistory.* New Delhi: Books & Books.

Dhavalikar, M.K. and S. Atre 1989. The Fire Cult and virgin: a Harappan Ritual, in *Old Problems and New Perspectives in the Archaeology of South Asia* (J.M. Kenoyer Ed.), pp. 193-206. Madison: University of Wisconsin. Wisconsin Arch. Reports 2.

Fairservis, Walter A. 1967. The Origin, Character and the Decline of an Early Civilization, *Novitales 2055.* New York: American Museum of Natural History.

——— 1991. Review of G.L. Possehl and M.R. Raval, *Harappan Civilization and Rojdi, Journal of the American Oriental Society* 111: 108-13.

Flam, Louis 1984. Palaeogeography and Prehistoric Settlement Patterns of the Lower Indus Valley, Sind, Pakistan, in *Studies in the Archaeology and Palaeoanthropology of South Asia*, (K.A.R. Kennedy and G.L. Possehl Eds.), pp. 77-82. New Delhi: Oxford-IBH and the American Institute of Indian Studies.

Fried, M.H. 1967. *The Evolution of Political Society*. New York: Random House.

Guha, Sudeshna 1989. Evolution of the Harappan State. Ph.D. dissertation. Pune: University of Poona.

Hawkes, Christopher 1954. Archaeology Theory and Method: Some Suggestions from the Old World, *American Anthropologist* 56: 155-68.

Jacobson, Jerome 1986. The Harappan Civilization: an Early State, in *Studies in the Archaeology of India and Pakistan* (J. Jacobson Ed.), pp. 137-73. New Delhi: Oxford-IBH and the American Institute of Indian Studies.

Karve, Iravati 1991 (Reprint). *Hindu Society: a Reinterpretation*. Pune: Deccan College.

Kennedy, K.A.R. 1984. A Reassessment of the Theories of Racial Origins of the People of the Indus Valley Civilization from recent Anthropological Data, in *Studies in the Archaeology and Palaeoanthropology* of *South Asia* (K.A.R. Kennedy and Gregory L. Possehl Eds.), pp. 99-107. New Delhi: Oxford-IBH.

——— 1992. Biological Anthropology of Human Skeletal Remains from Harappa 1928-88, *The Eastern Anthropologist* 45: 55-85.

Kenoyer, Mark J. 1989. Socio-Economic Structures of the Indus Civilization: a Summary, *Paleorient* 10: 49-63.

——— 1991. The Indus Valley Tradition of Pakistan and Western India, *Journal of World Prehistory* 5: 331-85.

——— 1992. The Harappan Craft Specialization and the Question of Urban Segregation and Stratification, *The Eastern Anthropologist* 45: 49-54.

Krader, L. 1978. The Origin of State Among the Nomads of Asia, in *The Early State* (H.J.M. Classen and P. Skalmik Eds.), pp. 93-107. The Hague: Mouton.

Lal, B.B. 1984. Some Reflections on the Structural Remains at Kalibangan, in *Frontiers of the Indus Civilization* (B.B. Lal and S.P. Gupta Eds.), pp. 55-62. New Delhi: Books & Books.

——— 1993. A Glimpse of the Social Stratification and Political Set up of the Indus Civilization, *Harappan Studies* 1: 63-71.

——— 1997. *The Earliest Civilization of South Asia.* New Delhi: Aryan Books International.

Mackay, E. 1938. *Further Excavations at Mohenjodaro*. Delhi: Government of India.

Mackay, E. 1979. Changing Perspective of Archaeology, in *Essays in Indian Protohistory* (D.P. Agrawal and D.K. Chakrabarti Eds.), pp. 197-204. New Delhi: D.K. Publishers.

Malik, S.C. 1979. Changing Perspectives in Archaeology, in *Essays in Indian Protohistory* (D.P. Agrawal and D.K. Chakrabarti Eds.), pp. 187-204. New Delhi: D.K. Publishers.

Meadow, Richard (Ed.) 1991. *Harappa Excavations 1986-90: a Multi-Disciplinary Approach to Third Millennium Urbanism*. Madison: Wisconsin University Press. Monograph in World Archaeology 3.

Piggott, Stuart, 1952. *Prehistoric India.* Harmondsworth: Penguin Books.

Possehl, G.L. 1979. Pastoral Nomadism in Indus Civilization: a Hypothesis. *South Asian Archaeology 1977* (M. Taddei Ed.), pp. 537-51. Naples: Instituto Universitario Orientale.

——— 1993. *Harappan Civilization—a Recent Perspective.* New Delhi: Oxford-IBH and the American Institute of Indian Studies.

Ratnagar, Shereen, 1991. *Enquires into the Political Organisation of Harappan Society.* Pune: Ravish.

Redman, Charles 1968. *Rise of Civilization: from Early Farmers to Urban Society in the Near East.* San Fransisco: W.H. Freeman.

Sarkar, H. 1975-6. The Conquest of Meluhha by Rimush (2315-2307 BC): a Hypothesis, *Puratattva* 8: 157-8.

Sarkar, S.S. 1964. *Ancient Races of Punjab, Sind, and Baluchistan* Calcutta: Book Land Pvt. Ltd.

Sarma, A.V.N. 1971. Decline of Harappan Culture: a Re-Look, in *K.A. Nilkanta Sastri Felicitation Volume,* pp. 280-96. Madras: Professor K.A. Nilakanta Sastri Felicitation Committee.

Service, Elman 1975. *Origins of State and Civilization.* New York: Norbon.

Shaffer, Jim G. 1982. Harappan Culture: a Reconsideration, in *Harappan Civilization: Contemporary Perspective* (G.L. Possehl Ed.), pp. 41-50. New Delhi: Oxford-IBH and the American Institute of Indian Studies.

Steponaitis, V.T. 1981. Settlement Hierarchy and Political Complexity in Non-Market Societies, *American Anthropologist* 83: 320-63.

Wheatley, P. 1972. The Concept of Urbanization, in *Man, Settlement and Urbanism* (P.J. Ucko, R. Tringham and D.W. Dimbleby Eds.), pp. 601-37. London: Duckworth.

Wheeler, R.E.M. 1968. *Indus Civilization*. Cambridge: Cambridge University Press.

Harappan Religion: Myth and Polemics

SHUBHANGANA ATRE

INTRODUCTION

The religion that is followed by a large section of Indian population and which is generally termed as Hinduism, is an amorphous motley of varied patterns of religious practices and philosophies and unlike other major religions is not known to have a tradition of prophets. Despite this, it surprisingly holds a common array of basic mythological beliefs and ideological paradigms as to what 'religion' is! Given the geographical expanse of a country and the diversity of Indian culture, it is amazing that the unity and uniqueness of beliefs and practices which form the basics of 'Hinduism' are maintained without being affected by all external, mainly historical, temporal and geographical factors.

Naturally, one begins to wonder about the roots and evolutionary processes of Hinduism. The curiosity to know its origin is quite common among Indians from all walks of life. Hinduism, which was known to our ancients as Sanatana Dharma, i.e. the one which has been always there implies that it has no known origins in terms of a specific point of time. The common notion, howsoever inadvertently formulated—in academic and non-academic minds alike—carries the faith that Hinduism is a cognate development of Vedic religion. It is a supposition which inevitably furthers a straight equation of the Aryan connection.

The Aryan-Dravidian dichotomy has much to add to the complexity of the problem. The modern historiography, on the one hand taught us to glorify our ancient past and especially the so-called Aryan culture and on the other taught us to put the entire culpability of the inherent social injustice on the tenets of the same cultural system. This position reflects overwhelmingly in the ambiguous understanding of our past and present social realities. Even scholars with an objective point of view do not seem to have totally escaped the intellectual bias created by it. Susceptibility to a particular hypothetical situation on conscious or sub-conscious level, on the part of the scholar, has also added to this spectrum of conflicting premises. As a result we have various subtle divides like Vedic/non-Vedic, Aryan/Dravidian, Orthodox/non-Orthodox, Brahmin/non-Brahmin, north/south, etc., which are proving to be major influencing factors, creating at least a partial blindness to reality. Speculative and analytical statements alike, made by various scholars regarding 'Harappan Religion' can be taken up as an apt illustration of the predicament.

The Harappan Civilization as the most ancient of the Indian subcontinent is naturally looked upon as the primary source of many of our cultural traits and as having potential to provide answers to many of our questions. However, almost every aspect of this civilization has held some unresolved mysteries and religion is no exception. The religion of the Harappans is one subject which has been handled in an arbitrary manner by a large number of scholars because of various reasons.

The major factor responsible for this is the inaccessibility of the written records recovered from the Harappan sites. It is a well known fact that the Harappan inscriptions mainly occurring on seals remain to be deciphered yet. Scholars are also aware that even if we succeed in doing so, the inscriptions are of such short length that they would not provide much information beyond names of some deities or individuals, or perhaps some sketchy records.

In the absence of substantial written evidence, the archaeological data are always viewed as incapable of justifiably projecting abstract social facts, especially those which relate to ideological manoeuvres. Thus, 'Religion' is last on the list of an archaeologist studying the Harappan Civilization. However, they would not choose to maintain a complete silence either, because deep down the awareness is alive that religion has always remained an inseparable part of the social as well as the personal life of individuals in all ancient societies.

But the task of determining the racial and cultural identity of the Harappans, which in turn can provide a clue to the understanding of their religious beliefs, is another bottleneck. The skeletal remains are expected to enlighten us on the matter of supposed racial affinities but they have not proved to be of much help. There is hardly any literature available and as already seen the extant inscriptions are not still deciphered. Therefore, their cultural identity also remains open to anybody's and everybody's guess. Academicians have been engaged in this guess work ever since the discovery of Harappan Civilization.

The early excavators, especially the Western scholars, were conclusively convinced that the Harappans were aliens on the land, most probably coming from the west, i.e. Mesopotamia. But the so-called Aryans, the creators of the Vedas—the earliest literature of the subcontinent known so far, were also thought to have come from the west. In a nation which was then ruled by the British, strangers to the land and its culture, and also where the first generation of natives had entered the academics after completing education under the Western system, the issue of India's ancient past had assumed altogether different dimensions.

British scholars trained in modern historiography generally believed, very firmly, that Indian civilization never promoted a sense of proper history and India's history cannot be traced to a period earlier than Alexander's invasion, i.e. fourth century AD. The discovery of the Harappan cities—Harappa and Mohenjo Daro, changed the scenario in a flash and suddenly it dawned upon people that India had a history going back at least to third millennium BC; as old and glorious as Mesopotamia and Egypt, and given the belief that Indian history cannot be older than fourth century AD the European scholarship was quick to portray the Harappan Civilization as being transplanted in a state of maturity. This notion got strongly entrenched then because the probable native antecedents had still not been unearthed at that time.

This is, in brief, the background of the beginnings of the early attempts to visualize the most ancient civilization that flourished on the Indian subcontinent. Archaeologists, at their end, began to look for parallels in Mesopotamian and Egyptian civilizations while Indologists with their own perspective attempted to tally the archaeological information with linguistic and literary evidences. Indologists then were mainly engrossed with Sanskrit as one of the Indo-European language group, and studying Vedic literature with major stress on this aspect. To them it appeared as the foundation of all classical traits of Indian culture. Archaeologists, on the other hand, were aware of various folk practices, which sometimes may even represent a complete deviation from the Vedic traditions, that formed essential components of the extant popular culture including religion. When it came to interpreting material remains with regard to religious practices of the Harappans the respective positions of scholars were bound to reflect.

The first of the interpretative statements regarding Harappan religion, of course, comprise those by Sir John Marshall and his team which also included E. Mackay. It is very obvious that they drew parallels from the clusters of varied religious practices that could be collectively designated as 'Hinduism', and they also attempted to relate their deductions to the basics of Indian philosophical tenets. Thus, the picture created could at the most be a working hypothesis. However, in the ensuing arguments, perhaps this fact was either totally forgotten or disregarded by the archaeologist and Indologist alike. Hence, what we get to see of Harappan religion is a fuzzy picture. It gives an impression letting us believe that the Harappans who otherwise comprised a very organized urban population were least concerned with organizing their religious life.

It is apparent that Marshall based his deductions on the basis of extant religious practices of the Hindus, although his initial premise was that of a non-Aryan origin of the Harappan people as there was hardly any material evidence to conjecture the presence of either the Vedic sacrificial system or worship of Brahmanic deities at both Harappa and Mohenjo Daro. This premise was further strengthened by another view held firmly by archaeologists that the Vedic Aryans must have arrived in the north-west provinces of the Indian subcontinent at about 1500 BC and the Harappan chronology stands to be much earlier.

Large scale massacre was inferred on the basis of skeletal remains found interred collectively at various places (Marshall 1931, Vol. I: 79-80). Mackay also regarded these skeletons as belonging to the Late Indus Valley period and felt that they probably represented individuals 'killed by raiders when they were attempting to escape from the city and were subsequently buried' (1937: 614).

Wheeler helped to perpetuate this theory by asserting that the evidence at Mohenjo Daro confirmed large scale massacre and it corroborated the descriptions of the battles Aryans had to fight with the earlier non-Aryan settlers of the land who dwelt in fortified cities. Indra, the Vedic god, was eulogized for his valour and endowed with the epithet *Puramdhara* which means destroyer of the fortified cities. On this basis Wheeler proclaimed, 'Indra stands accused' (1968: 132). It was almost unanimously accepted in the academic sphere that these non-Aryan residents of the fortified cities were of Dravidian origin and thus was cemented the notion of Dravidian affinities of the Harappans.

Notwithstanding, the general notion of Dravidian affinities of the Harappans and the Aryans being outsiders arriving much later on the scene, there are quite a few Indian scholars who believe at any instance that the Aryans were autochthonous. Besides, a number of scholars would also like to believe that the Aryans had arrived on the sub-continent at least a couple of millennia earlier than the archaeological tradition projects. Thus, we can detect certain undercurrents influencing the individual mien of scholars which in turn predetermines the projection of the reconstruction of any given aspect of the Harappan Civilization.

Reverting once again to the problem of Harappan script, it might be illustrated how true the above situation is. The futility of various attempts and claims of successfully deciphering the Harappan script is best described by Zide (1970: 7) long ago, a statement which holds true till today:

> ... except for methodical evaluations ..., the 'decipherment' have been based on untenable hypotheses, lack of chronological accuracy, unsound reconstructions because of linguistic naïveté and in general preconceptions of the language of the inscriptions which were not based on any systematic or rigourous evaluations but on *a priori* and untenable assertions.

It has to be borne in mind, that the task of deciphering any script that has become defunct depends on the ascription of distinct phonetic value to the alphabetic letters or syllables or pictographs, as the case may be. In the instance of the Harappan script, scholars differ as to the very basic nature of the script, i.e. which of these three categories it represents. This and other computable issues related to the script apart, the truly perplexing issue is to decide the sound embodied by each component of the script.

This problem in the instance of decipherment of other ancient scripts could be solved because of inscriptions executed in multiplescripts which may or may not be multilingual. Unfortunately, so far, no such multilingual or multiscript inscriptions have been discovered which could provide a key to the Harappan script. Scholars have come up with their own individual notions regarding the identity of the Harappans and accordingly the probable language encoded in the script. Thus, scholars who would like to read Sanskrit in the Harappan inscriptions would orient their attempts accordingly.

We have now a long enough tradition of integrated indological and archaeological studies which should induce us to cross the barriers of the Aryan/Dravidian or Vedic/non-Vedic dichotomy. More so, when scientists are now assuring us of the fallacy of racial division on the basis of physical types! Indeed, the very concept of 'race' is now considered to be obsolete, but Indian historiography seems to have preferred to remain oblivious of this fact, and by and large the terms 'Aryan' and 'Dravidian' continue to be perceived as racial denominations based on physical types.

The only substantiation offered for this supposition is Vedic references describing the people calling themselves 'Arya', who were tall, fair complexioned, with aquiline nose, and so on. The same people described their rivals, whom they called 'Dasyus', as people with dark skin, snub nose and with improper speech. Frequent citations of these descriptions have only helped to perpetuate stereotypes perceived as two distinct races—'Aryan' and 'Dravidian'; the 'Dasyus' invariably being perceived as the 'Dravidians'. It is remembered by very few that these terms denote only two lingual groups.

HARAPPAN RELIGION—A MATTER OF THEORIZING VERILY AS ONE SEES IT

In the light of the above discussion, the random approach is evident, by archaeologists and others, often adopted as a result of their personal inclinations in reconstructing the religious phenomenon as part of the socio-cultural life of the Harappans. With the help of a few representative examples the resultant chaotic scenario shall emerge very clearly in this section.

The following quotation may amply illustrate the indecisive state of present scholarship. It is stated, 'If religion is taken into account they were more Aryan than Dravidian and if racial affinities alone are considered there was an admixture of "Aryan" and other elements' (Rao 1973: 251). Of course, it is not to say that this statement is without substantiation, but the tenuous character of such substantiation needs to be considered carefully.

The anthropological, i.e. the skeletal data have been studied from the site of Lothal and it is said that three racial types have been identified on the basis of nine crania. The three racial types as identified are (ibid.: 146-7):

akin to the proto-Nordic or Caucasoid type,
akin to the proto-Mediterranean type,
akin to the Alpino-Armenoid type.

Thus, apparently the conclusion of racial admixture based on physical types might be justified, unless the basic fact is grossly overlooked that the terms 'Aryan' and 'Dravidian' only denote lingual groups. Even if hypothetically one has to presume that the proto-Nordic or Caucasoid type is to be associated with 'Aryan', one cannot forget that any other type is not yet identified as definitive of 'Dravidian'. The identification of the 'Dravidian' remains simply based on the only assumption of their not being characteristic of the supposed 'Aryan' group. The fallacious nature of such a contention for scientific method need not be stressed.

It is interesting to note Mackay's cautious comments regarding the composition of Harappan population at Mohenjo Daro, based on physical types. As he aptly pointed out 'mixing of blood for a considerable time and individuals possessing different combinations of characters were not uncommon' (1937: 632). The cosmopolitan composition of Harappan population is a well acknowledged fact now which essentially leaves the Aryan/Dravidian controversy redundant and calls for an awareness of the exclusive lingual connotation of the terms. He also assured that the term 'Mediterranean' as descriptive of the majority type was retained, 'because of its general acceptance and association with the culture with which the civilization of the Indus Valley had so much in common until a more acceptable term is put forward' (1937: 632). However, the association of terms defining physical types with lingual terms like 'Aryan' and 'Dravidian' appears to have nowhere been suggested.

It brings us back to the first half of the above cited statement of Rao that Harappans were 'more Aryan than Dravidian' as far as their religion is concerned. This supposition is claimed to have been substantiated, perhaps by the presence of sacrificial altars and a sacrificial pit belonging to Phase III at Lothal (ibid.: 218). It is also brought out that horse bones have been reported from the mature levels of Lothal and Surkotada, and rice from the mature levels of Rangpur and Lothal (ibid: 219). Thus, the equation of Harappans being non-Aryan, because they did not know horse and rice is refuted.

The general absence of typical female figurines at Harappan sites in Gujarat and Rajasthan, and also the non-conformity of those few found at Lothal have been pointed out. Also the fact that any image resembling the so-called Mother Goddess does not appear on seals is taken to be evidence enough for the Mother Goddess worship restricted to being a household cult, popular only with a section of Harappan society and not a subject of state cognizance (ibid. 214-15). Existence of widely divergent religious practices (ibid.: 220) is also recognized despite the guess of Harappans being more Aryan than Dravidian.

The roots of the factors involved in such a tightrope-walk lies in the tussle between the position a scholar has assumed and the established academic faith kept up since the beginnings of Harappan studies. John Marshall carried out the initial task of analysing Harappan material in order to understand the religious aspects of Harappan Culture. Most of his views have continued to be accepted except by a few scholars suggesting slight variations as to the identification of the so-called proto-Pasupati, and some intermittent assertions of finding Vedic analogies. As mentioned earlier while interpreting the Harappan artefacts Marshall essentially presumed the non-Aryan identity of the Harappan Culture,

In Marshall's own words:

> All the material of religious nature recovered at Mohenjodaro and Harappa appears to be characteristically Indian. Although, relatively meagre in proportion to the extent and importance of the sites, this material is sufficient at any rate to make it clear that iconic and aniconic cults existed side by side, and were just as compatible five thousand years ago as they are in Hinduism today. It exhibits to our eyes, on the one hand the worship of the mother goddess, who still occupies a foremost place among the teeming village population of India; and side by side with a god whom we have seen a good reason to recognize as the ancestor of the historic Siva, the principle male deity of the Hindu pantheon. On the other hand, it shows us the worship of animals and trees and inanimate stones or other objects in much the same form as it meets us in the historic times in semi-human, at others in syncretic and fabulous shape. Trees, too, are worshipped in their natural state, but their indwelling spirits are already completely anthropomorphised. The *lingam* and *yoni*, both have their places in religious scheme, as they have in Saivism and along with these emblems are other stones, apparently of a baetylic nature. Chremanthism exemplified in the worship of the sacred 'incense-burners', amulets and charms are common, attesting to the existence of the demonophobia with which Hinduism has always been incurably afflicted. And there is evidence that Yoga was always playing its part as a religious practice. (1931, Vol. I: 76-7)

Thus it is obvious that Marshall based his analysis on drawing parallels from the religious practices of the larger population of India using 'Hinduism' as a general term for all. Hence, 'Hinduism' as a term in this instance spells out a certain disparity of comprehension when confronted either by scholars brought up in the Indian tradition or those who are practising Hinduism on the one hand, while on the other to a Western mind it might convey only an ancient, unorganized or even worse, a 'primitive' religion full of voodoo. This undertone is plainly insinuated in Marshall's comment on the chremanthism attesting demonophobia, 'with which Hinduism has always incurably afflicted'.

Some of Marshall's loud thinking, perhaps contributed categorically to the presumption of non-Aryan characteristics of Harappan pantheon. After asserting the supposed male deity of the Harappans as proto-Siva, he pondered,

> whether, like Siva, this pre-Aryan[1] god of Mohenjodaro was associated with the mountains, whether he had an orgiastic side of his nature, and whether he was already regarded as a supreme but essentially personal deity, are points that must be left to future research to determine. (1931: 56)

The faint hint of the typical western bias towards the religious practices of Hindus is reflected in the seemingly naive, innocent musings when Marshall wonders regarding 'an orgiastic side' of the god's nature.

The dilemma of the Western scholarship undoubtedly resounds in such observations. On one hand, it highly admired the philosophical abstractions of the Vedas and the Upanishads, and on the other, the practices based on sympathetic magic were dismissed as pagan and orgiastic. This undertone is evident in a number of western writings about pre-Christian and Oriental religious practices. The very fact that these practices were always referred to as 'cults' and not as a religious system itself shows the strong bias. This Western bias is responsible for associating everything related to the 'higher consciousness' with the Vedas—implying 'Aryan', and the rest with the lower stratum of religiosity—implying non-Aryan. Indian scholars, to a large extent are no exceptions to this.

The intellectual thrust of the postulated interpretation of the existence of a proto-Siva inherently led to presume a cult of phallic worship, and thus conical objects and ring-stones of varied sizes were frequently referred to as *lingam* and *yoni* respectively. Further it was pointed out that as 'emblems of creation', they are 'indissolubly connected with worship of Siva' (Marshall 1931: 256). Along with the presence of a male deity as the presiding god,[2] worship of a Mother Goddess was also presumed on the basis of terracotta female figurines, thought to be typically representative of the goddess.

Deductions based on these assumptions of proto-Siva, Mother Goddess and presence of *lingam* and *yoni* as emblems of their creative powers drew Marshall's attention to the Indian philosophy of dualism known as *Sankhya Darshan*, which led him to believe that the Harappan proto-Siva and the Mother Goddess manifested the abstract concepts of *Puruṣa* and *Prakṛti* of a much later philosophical thought.

Despite the hotchpotch of a religion presented to us as Harappan, Marshall and other early scholars are not to be blamed for the eternal confusion present in the academic field of Harappan religion. The later scholars threw overboard every caution that was presented by the early scholars. For instance, Marshall very clearly cautions that 'it is necessary to guard against the mistake seeing phallic meaning in sacred stones where none in reality exists' (1931: 58).

> Since in India itself baetylic stones, such as those which guard the fields and crossways, are just as numerous as phallic ones and are common objects of worship with the primitive tribes, among whom they are specially associated with the Mother Goddess. (1931: 61)

At another place, regarding the female figurines, he recalls that the correspondence between them and those found in Western Asia 'is such that it is difficult to resist the conclusion' that the Harappan figurines 'also represented a Mother or Nature Goddess and served the same purpose as their counter parts in the West' (1931: 50).

This particular conjecture regarding the figurines being of votive nature is the finest example among Marshall's number of cautious observations which have been conveniently and continually overlooked. It is almost unquestionably accepted that the terracotta female figurines represent icons of the Mother Goddess.

So far, it has been attempted to bring out the roots of the presently mystifying range of scholarly interpretations regarding Harappan religion. There are many such interpretations available today, which need not be enumerated one by one. Most of the subsequent publications to Marshall and Mackay's are devoted either to re-establish or re-examine his theories and a few can be classed as attempts to branch off. They can be broadly classified into three groups.

(i) Studies concentrating on the iconographic features of Harappan deities, e.g. K.A.N. Shastri (1957 and 1965) did not dispute the masculinity of the deity identified as proto-Pasupati by Marshall but differed so far as the morphological analysis of the iconographic characteristics were concerned. He argued that this god was neither three faced nor even human-faced. To him, 'his, whole form, though apparently human, is cunningly contrived to be a combination of various animals'. He also emphasized on the Vedic traditions as the exclusive source of Harappan religion and identified the god as the presiding male deity of the *Asvattha.*

(ii) Studies involving the Aryan-Dravidian controversy. The academic claim of Dravidian or non-Vedic/Aryan affinity of the Harappans and their origin has been glanced over, so far. However, there is a very strong stream of thought believing that the Aryan/Vedic people were no strangers to this land and now a still stronger opinion is emerging which would strongly suggest their identity as proper Harappans and none else.

Its roots are to be found in a sincere disbelief in the idea of Aryan/Vedic as nomadic people arriving into a land where an urban culture, in a much advanced state, was already in existence. To them such advanced culture could not possibly belong to a people for whom Vedic people had expressed extreme disdain.

A number of scholars also vouch for exact parallels in Vedic descriptions to match Harappan artefacts and structural remains. To illustrate, we may cite the attempts of identifying Harappa with *Hariyūpiya* on the banks of *Parusni*. Geographically and phonetically this identification seems to be most plausible, unless one is reminded of the association of the name, 'Hadappa' with the mound of dead and it not being a corruption of any city name of the ancient times. The scholars assuming Hadappa to be the ruins of

Vedic *Hariyūpiya*, neither account for this fact, nor do they offer any justification for their assertion.

It has to be pointed out at this juncture that the studies concentrating on grasping the nature of religious practices among the Harappan society, by and large, take into account the archaeological material recovered from Hadappa, Mohenjo Daro and to some extent Lothal, Kalibangan, etc. However, in the post-Independence period many other Harappan sites in the Indian territory have been excavated and excavators of sites like Dholavira, Rakhigarhi, etc., are more and more inclined to equate Harappan socio-religious phenomena with that of the Vedic system.

(iii) Studies basically attempting to decipher the Harappan script which incidentally cover some religious aspects.

It is not meant to deride or to demean any of the attempts of drawing Vedic parallels to study the religious phenomena of the Harappans but it is simply intended to attract the attention of the scholarly world to the need of treating it as a complete system in its own right which unmistakably reflected the intellectual and psychic make-up of an immaculate society. This, of course, cannot be done on the basis of one's beliefs, however earnest they are.

In other words, an objective approach to the subject requires that we treat the 'Harappan' as an inseparable part of the ancient world that flourished with an economy combining various strategies, of which agriculture formed an innate base. 'Fertility' was the major, or perhaps the only concern behind all the overt manifestations of their religiosity; Vedic people were also no exception. Hence, it is inevitable that we stumble on illusive parallels, if we proceed without caution, blindfolded by preconceived notions.

Anthropologists, all over the world have confirmed that the early human societies revered the 'feminine' as the very source of all creation and in that capacity they established the 'goddess' by various names as their presiding deity. It is also asserted that it was only much later, when men emerged as the only political force because of their military prowess, that the reign of 'goddesses' was either totally annihilated or they were subdued to a negligible, secondary role.

The 'Vedic' is unhesitatingly acknowledged as the patriarchal and militaristic society recognizing no major 'goddess'. However, there is no explicit evidence yet to confirm the Vedic/non-Vedic identity of the Harappans; nor any to prove a 'god' on the pantheon and the sacrificial system akin to the Vedic. Hence, it would be prudent to treat the subject more objectively, i.e. perceiving it as a full-fledged religious system, commissioned to achieve the goal of bountifulness, and not as a random search for deities that we find familiar and thereby acceptable.

HARAPPAN RELIGION—AS PERCEIVED SO FAR

As has been discussed so far, it is apparent that the understanding of 'Harappan Religion' has remained entrapped in controversies and a clutter of academic perspectives treating individual components of the system by isolating them, especially in the pursuit of searching Vedic parallels.

For a general revision of the available literature dealing with Harappan pantheon and the respective position assumed by scholars, as to the Vedic/non-Vedic origin, following aspects have proved to be of much concern to them:

—Identification of the male deity seated on a dais in yogic posture.
—Mother Goddess worship and the female figurines.
—Phallic objects.
—Unicorn and the cult-object.
—Other animal motifs.
—Fire worship and sacrifice.

It is neither possible nor necessary to include each and every work highlighting the above aspects within limits of this paper, but a few representative studies may be adequate, if reviewed, to gain an insight into the general academic trend in the field.

MALE DEITY SEATED ON A DAIS IN YOGIC POSTURE

As we have already seen that when Marshall identified this deity appearing on the much publicized seal (no. DK 5175) as the prototype of historic Siva, it was accepted almost readily. A few divergent suggestions were forwarded but the basic thesis of Marshall that the god was basically of pre-Aryan/non-Aryan, by implication 'Dravidian' origin prevailed and was also sometimes strengthened by subsequent studies.[3]

For instance, the title of an article, 'Siva—his pre-Aryan origins' speaks for itself (Ghosh 1936). The strong notion of the arrival of the Aryans later to the Harappans, and their taking to the ways of the latter was enhanced by the writings of scholars like Fr. Heras and Karmarkar. Fr. Heras (1943) concluded that Aryan religion adopted the monotheistic dogma of the Dravidians; they especially took to the worship of Siva, named so after a Dravidian tribe who worshipped the god. Aryans who worshipped Siva came to be known as Anu. Karmarkar (1942a, 1942b, 1944, 1945) in his writings strongly propagated that the nude god identified as Siva and the associated cult practices like phallic worship and human sacrifice were of pre-Aryan origin, traceable to Harappan Culture.

This trend has continued till date without significant changes to a great degree, though there have been sporadic attempts to divert. However such attempts could hardly attract attention. There are a number of scholars who accepted the identity of the deity as a male but not exactly as 'Siva'. Bhandarkar (1937) identified it as 'Vedic Rudra'. Saletore (1939) proposed that the god represented by the Mohenjo Daro seal was 'Vedic Agni', whose three main attributes are his three faces, the horns and his eastern origin. Shastri (1957 and 1965) did not accept the morphological analysis offered by Marshall, stating that the god is neither three faced, nor even human faced, but 'a combination of various animals'. To him the supreme god of Harappa was the deity of the *Asvattha* (*Ficus religiosa*) and the Harappan religion did not reflect anything that was out of Vedic traditions.

Among some rare attempts to sound a ring of caution was an article by Jyotirmayee

Bose (1940) who accepted in principle the iconographic similarities between the attributes of Siva and the Harappan god but felt that one must wait for further discoveries before its absolute identity is established as Siva. Dorothy Srinivasan (1976-7) after reviewing the criticism on Marshall's views offered by various scholars opines that, 'none of these identifications, to judge from a series of important and relevant works published in the last decades have replaced Marshall's suggestions'. She has tried, with the help of archaeological and Vedic evidence to argue that it goes, 'strongly against the possibility of a tricephalic proto-Siva'. She has expressed the likelihood, 'that the figure represents a divine bull-man, possibly a deity of fertility and abundance.' During Caspers (1985), Hiltebeitel (1978) refuted all the characteristics identified as those of Siva in the instance of Mohenjo Daro seal and claimed that the god should be identified as Mahisasura of the Puranas. Aravamuthan (1948), in addition to Pasupati, identified some other Brahmanic gods in the Harappan pantheon with the help of other seals. The list included Brahma, Karttikeya, Agni and seven Krittikas.

The most radical among the attempts to break away from Marshall's thesis was by Sullivan (1964), who was the first and the only one for a long time, to dare to identify the deity as a female. Even Mackay (1938, Vol. I: 335-6) who had perceived such a possibility did not pursue it any further. The wheel remains largely unturned since Marshall's time; rather it is almost being brought to a stand-still with new archaeological finds being interpreted in the same line. Shinde (1991) has identified the horned figure on a jar recovered during the excavations at Padri in Gujarat, a Harappan site, as Pasupati.

Apart from these, Parpola's comments regarding Harappan religion, which came as the result of his prolonged research on Harappan script should also be mentioned here (1985); especially his detailed elucidation regarding the robe with trefoil design, worn by the so-called priest-king. He identifies the robe as the *tarpya* garment of Lord Varuna and feels that it helps to establish the continuity between Harappan and Vedic rituals as many Vedic rituals originated in Harappan traditions. He points out that the trefoil motif was basically embedded with astral and also fertility symbolism thus establishing close association between the functions assumed by Varuna and Siva.

MOTHER GODDESS WORSHIP AND FEMALE FIGURINES

By now, it is quite clear that the concept of a male deity as the presiding god of Harappan religious organization has kept the scholars so preoccupied that even those who accepted in principle that goddess worship was an equally important feature in the Harappan religious system, did overlook the fact that it is pertinent to search for iconographic portraits of her which were executed with similar norms and through the same medium, i.e. the seals.

Usually the typical terracotta female figurines, wearing a short skirt, a fan-shaped head-dress and multiple bead strings around the neck are presumed to be the icons of a Mother Goddess. It was, of course, Marshall (1931, Vol. I: 49-50 and 339) who suggested the possibility of their being sacred images, representing the Great Mother Goddess, because he could detect a certain correspondence between these figurines and those found all over West Asia. The identification of these figurines as images of the Mother Goddess is generally accepted, occasionally with minor differences. For instance, Mode (1961) suggested closer Syrio-Cretan association than the other West Asian specimens. He, especially pointed out to the characteristic association of dove with the Mother Goddess cults of Harappa, Mohenjo Daro and Crete (Puri 1940-1).

Although the question of proper identification of the representations of the Mother Goddess has not received an overwhelming response unlike the case of the so-called proto-Pasupati, there have been a handful of scholars who have considered it. More remote seems to have remained the question of either refuting Marshall's identification of the female figurines or searching among the seal motifs for any iconographic representation of the goddess. Dasgupta (1935) identified a seal motif of a female figure in birth giving posture, with a plant issuing forth of her womb as the Earth Goddess, while some scholars based on seal motifs suggest the Harappan goddess to be the prototype of either Durga or Nana-Amba. For instance, based on a composite seal motif bearing a female figure with a half human and half animal who is probably attacking a tiger, Hiltebeitel (1978) suggested it to be the prototype of Durga. Durga, as far as her iconography is concerned, is thought to have been influenced by various iconographic traits of the goddess Nana. It is no wonder if any scholar had perceived the Harappan goddess to be exhibiting similar traits and compared the two, as has been done by Puri (1940a and b, 1943, 1943-4). Gordon (1943) refuted Marshall's assumption of the divinity of any figurines other than horned male ones and thought the female figurines to be votive in nature. Chaudhuri (1950, 1951) also rejected the idea of female figurines being images of the Mother Goddess and thought them to be either toys or votive figurines.

PHALLIC OBJECTS

That the people of Harappan Civilization were non-Vedic, worshipped a Lord of Beasts and a Mother Goddess are the concepts which have to be associated unfailingly with the cult of phallic worship represented by phallic objects. Marshall classified the aniconic objects into three types:

> The first class comprises those of the type illustrated in Plates XIII, 3 and XIV, 2, 4 and 5. Two of these are unquestionably phallic, more or less realistically modelled and proved conclusively that phallism in India had a pre-Aryan origin, thus disposing once and for all of the fantastic theory that it was introduced into India by Greeks and other Western invaders. Further evidence of the same kind—one a *linga* or phallus (Pl. XIII, 1) and the other a *yoni* or vulva (Pl. XIII, 7) which Sir Aurel Stein found in Chalcolithic sites in northern Baluchistañ, the former at Mughal Ghundai. The other objects in this class (Pl. XIII, 3 and XIV, 5) are more conventionalized in shape and their character, therefore is not so obvious. They vary in size from half an inch to a foot or thereabouts in height and are made generally of limestone or alabaster, but the miniature ones are also made of shell, faience and paste, the last mentioned being sometimes coloured to simulate carnelian. These miniature specimens might have served as gamesmen but the larger specimens and their shape does not suit them for use as weights; nor is there any other utilitarian purpose that can be suggested

for them. Indeed, the only explanation applicable to them all is that they were sacred objects of some sort, the larger ones surviving as aniconic agalmata for cult purposes, the smaller as amulets to be carried on the person, just as miniature *lingas* seem highly probable from their shape, which in spite of its conventionality, inevitably calls to mind the *linga* from Mughal Ghundai (Pl. XIII, 1). (1931, Vol. I: 59-60)

However, Marshall did not hold this identification as absolute. Mackay was also quite apprehensive about accepting it. This was apparent when he commented,

> Some of the stone objects included here amongst the gamesmen are thought by Sir John Marshall to be *lingas*, similar to those carried by Saivites (Lingayatas) at the present day. This may have been the case with some of the plainer ones, but a great number of these objects could hardly have been used for any other purpose than for a game. (1948, Vol. I: 570)

The identification of ring-stones as *yoni* was also purely hypothetical which Marshall thought to be reasonable and maintained it just because that was 'the only one yet advanced' which adequately explained them. However, he also cautioned not to infer each holed stone to be the same (1931, Vol. I: 63). Mackay had suggested that these ring stones were perhaps some sort of architectural components (1948, Vol. I: 595-8; 1948: 29-30, 62). There have been a few scholars in the subsequent period who have either questioned or completely refuted the identification of the supposed phallic objects. Sankaranand Swami pointed out that Marshall's theory of phallic worship practiced by the Harappans based on the identification of certain stone objects as phallic was incorrect because he felt that most of such objects were imported and so he emphasized that cones and rings were not at all associated with phallic worship (1957: 32-5).

Dales has dealt with this matter systematically and refuted the concept of *linga* and *yoni* stones completely. He pointed out in the first place that these so-called *linga* and *yoni* stones were never found together. He also pointed out that there was no other evidence, except an unidentified photograph of a realistic phallic object in Marshall's report (Pl. XIII, 3), to presume that phallic worship comprised an important element of Harappan religion (1984: 109-15).

UNICORN AND THE CULT-OBJECT

The myth of unicorn was always associated with India and it was firmly entrenched in the popular mind by the avowed description of the animal by Greek writers. It is obvious that the composition of the Harappan unicorn motif is of a mythical kind though some scholars would believe that it might have been a realistic animal. It is also dominated by the symbolism of male virility by the emphasis on its male member and the single horn. The so-called cult-object is almost invariably associated with it. It would have been extraordinary if the motif had not attracted frequent attention of scholars. However, in this instance also scholars seem to have been caught up in the web of Vedic/Brahmanic/non-Vedic significance of the symbol rather than understanding the mythical-cultural-artistic components of its theme. Dave (1969a, 1969b), with the help of texts eulogizing god Vishnu claimed that the unicorn represents Lord Vishnu and his origin is earlier than

Siva-Pasupati. Mahadevan (1984) identifies the cult object as the strainer for Soma juice and points out that all the five essential elements of a Soma sacrifice are present here, viz., the strainer (*pavitra*), sieve (*anvi*), zigzag lines indicating the flow of Soma juice (*pavamana*), droplets of the juice (*indu*) and the bull/unicorn (*vrsan*).

OTHER ANIMAL MOTIFS

Besides unicorn the other animal appearing on Harappan seals is the *Brahmani* bull with its majestic stance. Another species of the bull depicted realistically on the seals is the short-horned, humpless bull in front of a feeding tub. The ubiquitous terracotta bull figurines are also present in the Harappan repertoire. However, not much has been said about these animals beyond presuming the existence of a bull cult, especially as associated with the worship of Pasupati. In an article entitled, 'Sacred cows,· Sacred Places: Origins and Survivals of Animal Homes in India', Lodrick (1981) suggests a cattle cult among the Harappans and the bull as the symbol of masculinity. Apparently nothing should seem unwarranted in this hypothesis except the fact that the cows never formed a subject matter of animal depiction either on the Harappan seals or any other artefacts. The bull chariot and the ithyphallic deity of Daimabad have been linked with the Harappan Pasupati and the bull by Dhavalikar (1970, 1978). The present author has attempted to analyse the association of Harappan ideology with the Harappan animal motifs among which the Brahmani bull seems to have a special significance, perhaps as the fecundating agent of the Mother Goddess (Atre 1989a).

FIRE WORSHIP AND SACRIFICE

Fire Worship was not conceived as part of the Harappan religion as represented by the evidence recovered from Punjab and Sindh. However, the evidence of the fire-altars public as well as domestic, claimed to have been recovered from sites like Kalibangan and Lothal brought a change in the scenario which was puzzling for those who believed in the rigid uniformity. The question was once again focused on the Vedic/non-Vedic dichotomy with regards to the origin and nature of the Harappan fire worship and the sacrificial practices indicated by those altars. Rao (1986) has projected the evidence as indicative of Vedic sacrificial practices comparable to the ancient Iranian fire cult. Rao (1985) also feels that the cult object associated with the unicorn represents the fire-altar. Dhavalikar and Atre (1989) concur with this type of identification, but on the basis of objective analysis of the seal motifs alone.

HARAPPAN RELIGION—MAKING SENSE OF THE DISORDERLY SCENARIO

One thing is certain that the Harappan inscriptions do not offer any substantial help in resolving the mysteries associated with the civilization because of the inaccessibility of the script. Comparisons drawn from the Vedic literature remain grossly subjective.

The only sensible way left is to subject to scrutiny minute details of the composition of artefacts of religious usage, various motifs on seals, and the spatial relationship of structural remains. They are obviously the visible manifestations of deeply rooted mythological and ritualistic traditions.

Once the analysis at this level is complete, analogies from any accessible literary and anthropological sources may be drawn without any bias to any single culture. That is because, it is a well acknowledged fact that basic human religiosity has often displayed an inclination towards creating common idioms irrespective of the spatial and temporal distance.

As far as the artefacts are concerned, a number of pots of ceramic and metal ought to signify ritualistic function. However, it is not without ambiguity because frequently pots meant for regular use may be converted into ritualistic ones with or without sanctification. In the Harappan assemblage, besides pottery used as grave goods, only the perforated jars indicate some probability of having been used for extra-mundane purpose, i.e. for transporting the sacred fire between the household and public altars (Atre 1987: 197; Dhavalikar and Atre: 1989)

Similarly the objects of plastic art including terracotta figurines, especially the so-called typical Harappan Mother Goddess figures form an important part of the religious assemblage of Harappan artefacts. Again, there is no justification ever offered by archaeologists for naming female figurines of almost every style and class generally as 'Mother Goddess' figurines. A closer scrutiny would oblige them to differ from this set trend (Atre 1985-6).

From prehistoric time man has created female representations, many a time with opulent physiognomy and with an emphasis on their generative organs. That was perhaps the basic reason to reckon them as Mother Goddess. However, there may be times when simple logic is defeated and erroneous appellations continue to be in use. Calling prehistoric female figures summarily as 'Venuses' is an eloquent example.

The terracotta figurines from Harappan assemblages can be divided into two categories, viz., the so-called typical Mother Goddess figurines and others. As Marshall put it, the most common type of female figurines, i.e. the semi-nude type wearing the peculiar fan-shaped head-dress with pannier-shaped appendages, are sacred images and probably represented the Great Mother Goddess. He could detect a certain correspondence between these figurines and those found all over West Asia (1931, Vol. I: 49-50 and 339).

The observation by Sircar (1980) regarding female figurines, though in the context of the historic period, may prove significant. He thought that the terra cotta figurines were valued for their protective aspects. The very fact that the Harappan figurines were found as 'cast-aways' points to the possibility of their being used for a similar purpose and being discarded because they broke eventually, or the purpose was over. It has also been suggested that such figurines were used for ritual enactment in ancient cultures (Gimbutas 1975: 117-42). This may be true in the instance of Harappan figurines, especially those of the second category. We may also postulate that figurines of both kind were of votive nature.

There is good reason to class the figurines with fan-shaped head-dress as votive figurines and not as Mother Goddess icons. Basically, if one has to assume that they were icons of a deity of central importance along with a male deity, then the question arises why the two of them were represented in different modes; the first in the medium of terracotta and the latter only as an iconographic depiction on seals. The rule does not seem to break even accidentally. The disparity in the frequency of their occurrence is also significant (Atre 1985-6: 8).

It does not fit into the general pattern of Harappan Culture which revealed a high tendency towards standardization in every other sphere of life. Most probably the terracotta figurines were of votive nature and not icons as their 'cast-away' status, and in some instances the reporting of soot marks inside the pannier-shaped appendages would confirm.

Curiously enough, archaeologists and consequently others seem to have been obstinate in defining the main iconographic attribute of the so-called proto-Pasupati figure, as *urdhva-retas* (ithyphallic). Their was one exception, however, of Sullivan (1964) who dared to suggest that this deity could have been indeed a female. On the basis of a partly broken seal on which the same deity is depicted in a slightly changed position and thereby showing a long plait, even Mackay found himself in a pondering mood as to the gender of the so-called proto-Pasupati figure (1938, Vol. I: 335-6).

However, he managed to shrug off his doubts by stating, 'Possibly both male and female deities were represented with pigtails on occasion; I cannot think that the figure on seal 235 is that of a female deity'. It should be noted that Mackay did not give any explicit reasons for this particular 'feeling' against identifying it as a female deity. Indeed, the pigtail has proved to be a major signifier of the feminine gender of the deity (Dhavalikar and Atre 1989; Atre: 1998).

Thus it seems that the goddess was endowed with very defined iconographic attributes and had a full-fledged cult organization forming the core of the Harappan religion. A comprehensive approach to Harappan seal motifs confirms this further. To drive the point home we need to understand a number of common features of Mother Goddess cults present at various places, at various times. They are as follows:

—The concept of fertility lies at the base and accordingly a reenactment of the vegetation cycle forms the main goal of all ritual practices because they are based on sympathetic magic. A score of mythological stories act as guidelines in delineating the procedures of such rituals.
—The iconography of the goddess is usually predominated by therianthropic physical attributes.
—Either a tree, a column or a pillar, also water, fire, different kinds of wild as well as domesticated birds—especially dove—are among her cognizance.
—The goddess as Mother Earth is either self-generative or is associated generally with the solar principle for its fecundity. However, it is not always necessary that the male principle should be present either as a male deity of equal status or as her legitimate consort.

—There is always room for minor additions or omissions in individual cults.

We have already referred to K.A.N. Shastri (1957) who pointed out the combination of various animal features in the iconographic composition of the so-called Pasupati figure. However, his Vedic bias kept him from realizing its true significance. Scholars like D. Srinivasan (1976-7) also acknowledged its half-human, half-animal composition but because they studied the seal figures in isolation, the possibility of proper identification escaped them. Sullivan (1964) rightly perceived that even the arms which were described as being ornamented with number of armlets were, in fact, insect-like. Often when the same deity appears in a standing posture her legs appear to have hoof-like ends. These factors accentuate the therianthropic aspect of the goddess' iconography.

The tiny space available on the seals for the portrayal of the deity makes it difficult to be very explicit in depicting the female attributes with pronounced strokes, but on one seal where she is engaged in a fight with the tiger, the feminine contours are unmistakable (Atre 1985-6, 1987). The goddess is the unchallenged 'Mistress' of the world of animals as is clear from the various scenes depicted on the seals (Atre 1987: 194-6, 1989a).

The goddess as the ruler of wild-beasts and vegetation of course originated in primitive times, her antiquity going beyond the pastoral, agricultural phase of human history. Neumann (1974: 270, 272) demonstrated that despite the tendency of correlating the worship of the Great Mother with 'agriculture and the economic dominance it gave to woman', it should be attributed to the collective psychology of the unconscious. This matriarchal significance of the feminine is far older than the agricultural phase.

Association of phantasmal animals, including unicorn, of trees and columns, wells and water, crocodiles and snakes and also birds confirm the relatedness of ideology with goddess cults of other cultures. Fire worship, and along with it human and animal sacrifice, has been almost always associated with goddess cults everywhere. Evidence for animal and probable human sacrifice is not lacking.

The structural remains within the citadels at Mohenjo Daro, Harappa, Kalibangan and now Dholavira comprise a number of large public structures, but none has been so far undoubtedly identified as a temple. Perhaps, we have been searching in vain for closer parallels to match the present-day concept of temple architecture.

A scholar familiar with village settlement patterns would naturally know that often the temples there have a very humble appearance, not much different from an ordinary house or a hut. It is most likely that a shrine may not be enclosed at all, especially those of the tutelary deities. It is also true that more often than not the tutelary deity happens to be a goddess. Her shrine would be generally located on the outskirts of the village, at an isolated spot and would stand open to the sky. Remarkably, the goddess would be without any male partner. She is self-generative and in that capacity she is the mother and yet a virgin. However humble the shrine may be, it would be unfailingly associated with a sacrificial altar or a mere spot dedicated to the purpose and a hearth and a water-place.

The urban Harappans, with their advanced town planning, perhaps would not leave their shrines in such a humble state, but we would certainly not expect them to keep up with temple architecture of historic and modern periods. There have been many attempts to identify a temple at Mohenjo Daro but none has been proved to be convincing. However, if we stop looking for extraordinary structures for temples then their might be one claimant for identification of a temple.

This particular structure (Marshall 1931, Vol. I: 202 and Vol. III: XXXIX) appears to have very regular plan (62' x 50') with alignments in right angles. The rooms surrounding the central courtyard are evenly placed leaving the courtyard perfectly rectangular. In the centre of the courtyard there were four piers which perhaps supported a canopy. There were staircases almost in every alternate room leading to the roof, perhaps to reach a huge fire altar (Dhavalikar and Atre 1989).

If it was, as the circumstantial evidence indicates, a place of public ritual, then its location in the quarter full of imposing residential houses in the Lower Town and not being in the Citadel, becomes all the more significant. That would imply that the priestly authority had to conduct at least some of their ritualistic operations from this centre in the Lower Town. It also implies that people certainly had some autonomy as far as their routine religious life was concerned.

The evidence for regional variations in the religious manifestations were perhaps the result of constant expansion of Harappan activities towards its peripheral regions and one may infer that while Mohenjo Daro was the main centre of religious activities of the Harappans, Kalibangan proceeded to evolve as another and perhaps the major one in later period (Atre 1989b). The ideological contents remain the same but the symbols seem to be changing in these regions, with structural fire altars replacing the cult object and reducing the significance of seal images and terracotta figurines.

Thus only if we prepare ourselves to seek academic freedom from the preoccupation of pinning down the racial/cultural identity and finding out a known name for the Harappans, it would be possible to get a pragmatic picture of their religious behaviour and to establish some link with our own past. The journey is to reach beyond myths and polemics rather than to get into it.

NOTES

1. It should be clear by now that pre-Aryan was essentially non-Aryan to Marshall and his contemporaries, especially the Western scholars.
2. Marshall was not very emphatic about the presiding status of the God, considering the parallels of the goddess cults where the goddess is usually associated with a minor god.
3. Identification of proto-Siva as the Harappan god was based on its supposed ithyphallism. This assumption was based on the term *Sisnadevah* used by the Vedic people to refer to non-Vedics. This term was interpreted as 'people worshipping a phallic god'. However, Pusalkar (1954) has pointed out that this interpretation cannot be accepted as the term refers to noncelibates among Aryans.

REFERENCES

Aravamuthan, T.G. 1948. More Gods of Harappa, *Journal of the Bihar Research Society* 34 (3-4): 31-82.

Atre, Shubhangana 1985-6. The Lady of Beasts: the Harappan Goddess, *Puratattva* 16: 7-13.

——— 1987. *The Archetypal Mother: a Systemic Approach to Harappan Religion*. Pune: Ravish.

——— 1989a. Harappan Seal Motifs: the Animal Retinue, *Bulletin of the Deccan College Post-Graduate and Research Institute* 49: 43-9.

——— 1989b. Towards an Economico-Religious Model for Harappan Urbanism, *South Asian Studies* 5: 49-58.

——— 1999. The High Preistess: Gender Signifiers and the Feminine in the Harappan Context, *South Asian Studies* 14 (in press).

Bhandarkar, D.R. 193[illegible]. Siva of Pre-Historic India, *Journal of the Indian Society of Oriental Art* 5: 74-110.

Bose Jyotirmayee 1940. The Proto-Type of Siva in the Prehistoric Age, *Calcutta Review* 76 (1): 75-81.

Chaudhuri, N.M. 1950. The Worship of the Great Mother in the Indus Region, *Calcutta Review* 117 (3): 151-67.

——— 1951. The Worship of the Great Mother in the Indus Region, *Calcutta Review*118 (1): 1- 17.

Dales, George F. 1984. Sex and Stone at Mohenjo-daro, in *Frontiers of the Indus Civilization* (B.B. Lal and S.P. Gupta Eds.), pp. 109-15. New Delhi: Books & Books.

Dasgupta, C.C. 1935. Female Fertility Figures, *Man* 35: 95.

Dave, S.S. 1969a. A Note on the So-called 'Cult Standard' on Indus Seal, *Proceedings of the Indian History Congress* 30: 30.

——— 1969b. Visnu: Earliest Deity at Mohenjo-Daro, *All India Oriental Conference (Summaries of Papers)* 25: 153-4.

Dhavalikar, M.K. 1970. A Prehistoric Deity of Western India, *Man* (New Series) 5 (1): 131-2.

——— 1978. Proto-Pasupati in Western India, *East and West* 28 (1-4): 203-11.

Dhavalikar, M.K. and Shubhangana Atre 1989. Fire Cult and Virgin Sacrifice: Some Harappan Rituals, in *Old Problems and New Perspective in the Archaeology of South Asia* (J.M. Kenoyer Ed.), pp. 193-205. Madison: Prehistory Press. Wisconsin Archaeological Reports.

During Caspers, E.C.L. 1985a. Hindu Mythology and Harappan Religion, *Itihas Patrika* 5 (3): 66-72.

Ghosh, A. 1936. Siva—His Pre-Aryan Origin, *Indian Culture* 2.

Gimbutas, Marija 1974. *The Gods and Goddesses of Old Europe: 7000-3500* BC London: Thames and Hudson.

Gordon, D.H. 1943. Early Indian Terracottas, *Journal of the India Society of Oriental Art* 11: 136-96.

Heras, H. 1943. The Anu in India and in Egypt, *Proceedings of the Indian History Congress, Hyderabad* 5: 92-101.

Hiltbeitel, Alf 1978. The Indus Valley 'Proto-Siva' Re-examined Through Reflections on the Goddess, the Buffalo, and the Symbolism of Vahanas, *Anthropos* 73: 767-97.

Karmarkar, A.P. 1942a. Some Nude Gods in Hindu Pantheon, *Annals of the Bhandarkar Oriental Research Institute* 23: 214-23.

——— 1942b. An Early Attempt of the Aryans Against the Naga Cult, *New Indian Antiquary* 5: 184-9.

——— 1944. Human Sacrifice in Proto-India, *Annals of the Bhandarkar Oriental Research Institute* 25: 109-15.

——— 1945. The Linga Cult in Ancient India: Its Proto-Indian Origin and Early Development, in *B.C. Law Commemoration Volume*, pp. 456-68.

Lodrick, Daryck O. 1981. *Sacred Cows, Sacred Places: Origins and Survivals of Animal Homes in India*. Berkeley: University of California Press.

Mackay, E.J.H. 1937. *Further Excavations at Mohenjo-daro*. New Delhi: Government of India.

——— 1948 *Early Indus Civilizations* (Second Edition). London: Luzac and Co.

Mahadevan, Iravatham. The Cult Object on Unicorn Seals: a Sacred Filter?, *International Congress of Humanistic Studies in Asia and North Africa* 31: 1021-4.

Marshall (Sir), John 1931. *Mohenjo-daro and the Indus Civilization*. London: A. Probsthain.

Mode, Heinz 1961. *The Harappan Culture and the West*. Calcutta: Sree Saraswati Press Ltd.

Neumann, Erich 1974. *The Great Mother: an Analysis of the Archetype* (Ralph Manheim Translator). Princeton: Princeton University Press.

Parpola. A. 1985. *The Sky Garment: a Study of the Harappan Religion and Its Relation to the Mesopotamian and Later Indian Religions* (Studia Orientalia 57). Helsinki: Finnish Oriental Society.

Puri Baij Nath 1940-1. Nana the Mother Goddess of India and Western Asia, *Indian Culture* 7: 225-8.

——— 1940-1. Further Evidence on the Goddess Nana as Mother Goddess Amba, *Indian Culture* 7: 492-3.

——— 1943. The Mother Goddess at Mohenjo-daro Identified, *Proceedings of the 5th Indian History Congress*: 101-2.

——— 1943-4. Can We Identify the Mother Goddess Cult at Mohenjodaro?, *Quarterly Journal of the Mythic Society* 34 (2-3): 159-64.

Pusalkar, AD 1954. Sisnadeva in *Rgveda* and Phallus Worship in the Indus Valley, in *Sarup Commemoration Volume*, pp. 49-54.

Rao, S.R. 1973. *Lothal and Indus Civilization*. Bombay: Asia Publishing House.

——— 1985. Language and Religion of the Indus Valley Civilization, *Bharati* (New Series) 3: 1-19.

——— 1986. Concept and Evolution of Sacrifice in the Indus Civilization and Vedic Period. Summaries of Papers, Seminar on Sacrifice in India, Bombay University.

Sankaranand, Swami 1957. Phallic Emblems of the Indus Valley, *Proceedings of Indian History Congress* 20: 32-5.

Saletore, B.A. 1939. Identification of a Mohenjo-daro Figure, *New Review* 10: 28-35.

Sircar, D.C. 1980. Aspects of Cult of Indian Mother Goddess, *Journal of Indian Museums* 36: 9-20.

Shastri, K.A.N. 1957. *New Light on the Indus Civilization: Religion and Chronology*, Vol. I. Delhi: Atma Ram and Sons.

——— 1965. *Disposal of the Dead: the Aryan Problem and the Atharva Veda*, Vol. II. Delhi: Atma Ram and Sons.

Shinde, V.S. 1991. A Horn-Headed Human Figure on a Harappan Jar from Padri, Gujarat, *Man and Environment* XVI (2): 87-9.

Srinivasan Dorothy 1976-7. The So-Called Proto-Siva Seal from Mohenjo-daro: an Iconological Assessment, *Archives of Asian Art*: 47-58.

Sullivan, H.P. 1964. A Re-examination of the Religion of the Indus Civilization, *History of Religion* 4 (1): 115-25.

Wheeler, (Sir) R.E.M. 1968. *The Indus Civilization*, Supplementary Volume to *The Cambridge History of India*. Cambridge: Cambridge University Press.

Zide, A.R.K. 1970. A Brief Survey of Work to Date on the Indus Valley Script, *Journal of Tamil Studies* 2 (1): 1-12.

The Terracotta Figurines from Mohenjo Daro: Considerations on Tradition, Craft and Ideology in the Harappan Civilization (*c.* 2400-1800 BC)

ALEXANDRA ARDELEANU-JANSEN

BACKGROUND

Of all the products of Harappan craftsmanship, the terracotta figurines form one of the most interesting groups. These figures may represent either human beings or animals, or even composite creatures combining both human and animal characteristics. They have been found in large quantities in many sites all over the Indus Basin, and appear to have belonged to the trappings of everyday Harappan life. Yet their frequent occurrence has not made them less puzzling to the modern scholar, and indeed they have remained a continuous subject of research and speculation ever since their first discovery. The old obstacle complicating our understanding of the Indus Civilization as a whole and of certain classes of artefacts in particular is that we are faced with purely material phenomena which we have to interpret against our personal academic background, which in turn is moulded by manifold factors such as time, environment, culture, society, etc.

No written texts have come down to us, either from the Indus Valley people themselves or from contemporary neighbouring cultures, from which we could glean information on Harappan society, their social system, political order or religious beliefs. As a result, all the conclusions drawn to date about this ancient culture are in fact interpretations based on indirect deductions rooted in the individual background of the scholars concerned. Presuming that our intellectual background differs fundamentally from that of the Harappans *c.* 4,000 years ago, we are confronted with the old dilemma of how to approach our subject: while we consider the artefact remains to be related to certain functions and ideological concepts which we are eager to understand, we seem at the same time to be incapable of finalizing a standard methodological procedure for interpreting the evidence. Besides the glyptic art, the terracotta figurines constitute the most numerous and varied class of artistic subjects of the Indus Civilization. As far as our present knowledge is concerned, monumental art of any kind was unknown to the Harappans—a fact which might indeed have a significance of its own. Apart from the very interesting stone images of human and animal forms which were found exclusively at Mohenjo Daro (Ardeleanu-Jansen 1984, 1987), a variety of small stone, bronze, and shell statuettes have been brought to light. But no matter how conclusive these artistic expressions might be, none of these groups shows such a great variety in subject and style as the terracottas. The ceramic figurines therefore could yield much potential information which, as pointed out before, only accentuates the problem of adequate interpretation. In order to find out the function and meaning of the figurines, a scientific investigation must include as many different aspects of their nature as possible. In the case of our assemblage from Mohenjo Daro this involves several independent fields of research which, when their findings are compared, might result in a clearer picture about the terracotta figurines themselves and eventually also about their original functions.

Two of these approaches have already been mentioned in the title of this paper: tradition and craft can, in fact, reveal indicative clues as they are both closely linked and have a direct impact on the products a society chooses to create. Another important aspect, which has never been doubted by any scholar dealing with this subject-matter, is the iconographical dimension in relation to the occurrence of certain motifs in space and time. But the silent archaeological record can provide further information if the evidence is analysed according to the context of objects found, viz., the association of terracotta figurines within their group and in relation to other artefacts and to the structural remains.

In the following pages I will give a brief outline of the current problems and results which are based partly on recent archaeological discoveries in Pakistan and partly on my preliminary research on the terracotta figurines from Mohenjo Daro.

TERRACOTTAS FROM MEHRGARH: THE EARLY EVIDENCE

Recent archaeological investigations in north-western Pakistan have revealed that terracotta figurines have a long tradition in the subcontinent which goes as far back as the seventh millennium BC.

In Mehrgarh, a Neolithic settlement close to the Bolan Pass in the Kachi plain of north-west Baluchistan, the French Archaeological Mission, CNRS Paris, in collaboration with the Department of Archaeology, Government of Pakistan, has unearthed several successive strata which bear witness to seven distinct periods of occupation dating from the seventh millennium to the mid-third millennium BC. Right from Period Ia onwards which belongs to the aceramic Neolithic phase (Jarrige and Lechevallier 1979: 471ff.), crudely modelled human figurines of unbaked clay were found. They represent in abbreviated form, sitting figures with outstretched legs and accentuated buttocks (C. Jarrige 1984: 133).

In their 'foot-shaped' appearance, these figurines can today be regarded as the forerunners of a progressive development in the terracotta art of northern Baluchistan which culminates around 3000 BC in thousands of very sophisticatedly modelled, sitting female statuettes with elaborate coiffures and delicately modelled bodies (C. Jarrige 1984: 133; J.F. Jarrige 1981: 103). These terracotta figurines give testimony to the long tradition in subject and style which held sway throughout three millennia, but they also show how the technological achievements of a society have a direct impact on its artistic expression. The figurines are thus the result of a highly developed ceramic technology which evolved in Mehrgarh as a result of a growing specialization within the pottery craft.

In Period VII, during the first half of the third millennium BC just before the Indus

Civilization makes its appearance, the Mehrgarh terracotta figurines change in style: they are rendered for the first time in an upright position, and the hairstyles and jewellery become increasingly diversified (C. Jarrige 1987: 1).[1]

Furthermore, their production increases dramatically (J.F. Jarrige 1981: 104) and it is also during this period that male terracotta figurines begin to appear (C. Jarrige 1987: 98).

As far as I can tell today, the emergence of male statuettes is a phenomenon which arises on the subcontinent for the first time in Mehrgarh Period VII and in the Kulli Complex (Possehl 1986: 3) where formative stage has also to be related to the first half of the third millennium BC.

This innovation seems to be a milestone in the development of terracotta art. Catherine Jarrige suggested recently that the emergence of new and different types of human representations should not be regarded as just 'the result of the decorative fantasy of the potters' (C. Jarrige 1984: 133) but rather as a consequence of a more complex iconography which seems to be the product of an increasingly refined ideology. This implies that the production of hitherto unknown figurine types, namely male statuettes, might be taken as an indication of 'a more and more complex symbolic system' (C. Jarrige 1984: 134), itself the result of the growing cultural integration within the greater Baluchistan region (C. Jarrige 1984: 133).

It is interesting to note that at this particular period the animal representations also become more varied. Besides cattle figurines, birds, dogs and boars turn up during Mehrgarh Period VII, while in the 'Kulli Complex' the well-known bull figurines of the Kulli type are now joined by birds (Stein 1931: Pl. XXIX; Piggott 1952: 106), rams (Stein 1931: Pls. XXXI, XXVIII), dogs (Stein 1931: Pl. XXXI), toy carts (Piggott 1952: 110) and even bull figurines designed to be mounted on wheels (Stein 1931: Pl. XXVII).

Since all of these iconographic motifs recur in the mature phase of the Harappa Culture, one is inclined to think that the huge diversity, of the Indus Valley terracotta art was partly an offshoot of the development which took place in the first half of the third millennium in north and south Baluchistan. However, the variety of figurine types within the Indus Civilization, or at least within its western urban centres, is so great that one might expect an even broader 'cultural integration' than that apparent between the Indo-Iranian borderlands.

TERRACOTTAS FROM MOHENJO DARO: A STUDY

The following consideration of the terracotta figurines of the Indus Civilization will focus mainly on the specimens from Mohenjo Daro, as this body of data provides a large enough base for preliminary observations and some provocative hypotheses.

Since the publications of Marshall and Mackay in the 1930s, it is well known that most of the human figurines from this site represent females (Marshall 1931: 49). However, neither Marshall nor Mackay included statistics on the frequency of particular iconographic subjects. A preliminary analysis of the inventory of the excavation conducted by Hargreaves in a residential quarter situated in the Lower Town of Mohenjo Daro (the

HR-Area) showed that nearly 80 per cent of the recovered anthropomorphic statuettes belong to this category. At present the mission is bringing out all further data on CD-Rom.[2]

Yet this does not mean that female or even human terracottas necessarily belong to the artefact assemblage of every site identified as a Harappan settlement. This intriguing phenomenon has already been observed by a number of scholars (e.g. Gupta 1980: 176; During Caspers 1985: 268; Asthana 1985: 198). In Kalibangan, for example, human representations seem to be completely absent (Thapar 1973: 101; Bisht and Asthana 1979: 230) while in Lothal only comparatively few (13) have been found so far (Rao 1985: 476). To date, Banawali Ther in Haryana seems to be the only site on the Indian side of the subcontinent where female terracotta figurines have been found in large numbers (Bisht and Asthana 1979). All the other known Harappan sites beyond the Greater Indus Valley yielded terracotta animals only.

How this presence and absence of evidence is to be interpreted is not yet clear. However, it certainly warrants a detailed analysis which holds promise of a deeper insight into the geographical and/or historical complexities of Harappan society.

Still, what we understand from the corpus of terracotta figurines from Mohenjo Daro forms a highly diversified picture. Apart from the great variety of animal terracotta art, anthropomorphic figurines represent so many different subject types that only a few can be dealt with here.

Even within the group of female statuettes the variety is so great that it is hard to ascribe certain features to one specific type of figurine alone. Although it is possible to make a superficial classification according to distinctive subjects, such as the youthful, slim woman ornamented with rich jewellery and a fantastic headdress (Fig. 1) or the matronly looking, pot-bellied female (Fig. 2), an attempt to single out specific details such as jewellery, headdress and clothing and to attribute them to certain types is ultimately impossible. We are forced with the fact that more variations than expected are possible and that only a painstaking restudy of all the iconographical details could furnish a better picture. At the same time, however, it cannot be overlooked that some of the figurines have so many details in common that one is inclined to think they were produced by the same hand.

The youthfully slim female type (Fig. 1) is shown standing upright with the upper half of the body generally naked except for heavy jewellery adorning the neck and perhaps also the arms and ankles. She is clad in a short loincloth or mini skirt held by a broad belt. The fan-shaped headgear is frequently so monstrous and cumbersome that it is hard to imagine it was modelled after types actually worn, but then this was also the case with the exaggerated heaps of curly hair decorating the figurines from Mehrgarh Period VI (J.F. Jarrige and Lechevallier 1979: Fig. 25).

As dark stains were still discernible on some of the pannier-like appendages on either side of the heads when they were found, their excavators, Mackay and Wheeler, concluded that they had served as little containers for the burning of oil or incense (Mackay 1938: 260; Wheeler 1968: 91).

Fig. 1. A group of female terracotta figurines.

Fig. 2. A general type of female terracotta representation.

Fig. 3a. A group of male terracotta figurines.

Fig. 3b. A male representation on a seal.

Another general type of female representation mentioned above is the pot-bellied matron mostly devoid of jewellery and completely naked, but sometimes also wearing a girdle, necklaces, even anklets and a headdress or turban. Certain specimens of this type hold a baby in their arms (Fig. 2), but an infant may also occur as an attribute of the slim type. It is probable that the corpulent bodies of these figurines were intended to represent pregnancy, the corollary to the motherhood aspect of fertility.

Another important feature of the matronly type of figurine is that it can actually stand without support, while the youthful slim type could only be put standing against a wall, laid down or stuck into the ground. This slim figurine type was most probably intended to be seen from the front only as the back is almost always flat and carelessly modelled.

Other statuettes are represented lying on a bed or *charpoy* while another group carries some form of requisite, in one case a fruit platter, in another something that might be taken to be a drum. But these variations are comparatively rare.

The male representations are invariably naked and clearly distinguishable either by their separately applied sexual organs, a beard and/or little pellets of clay as nipples which are too small to be mistaken for female breasts (Fig. 3a). In general, their jewellery is much less elaborate than that of their female counterparts, but some of them wear fillets tied around the head. A necklace, either plain or with one or more pendants also occurs fairly frequently. Rare, however, are bangles adorning the arms in much the same manner as those of certain individuals depicted on particular seals (Fig. 3b).

Most probably because of their narrative character, these engraved seal scenes referred to have already given rise to much speculation on their cult significance. In general, it does not seem unlikely that they incorporate hidden clues to the ideology of the Harappans. Assuming then, that the naked individuals on these seals are engaged in some kind of ritual, then indeed, especially with regard to the nakedness of the male terracotta figurines, we could impute a cult connotation to this particular subject.

The ideological significance of certain other male statuettes is further emphasized by the fact that some of them wear a headdress akin to cattle or buffalo horns in almost the same manner as that depicted on the seals. Even though we cannot be sure about a religious connotation some kind of magical practice might in all probability be inherent in them.

Other, much simpler male figurines are represented in a pose which strongly suggests a gesture of adoration. There is another striking example which is rendered in a comparable pose (Fig. 4). This bearded figure is wearing both a necklace and a headband. Although the workmanship is rather poor, the representation shows strong similarities to the full-length stone sculptures which have been found in Mohenjo Daro (Fig. 5). This resemblance has already been pointed out by Wheeler who thought that the stone images represent deities (Wheeler 1968: 91).

In a previous article (Ardeleanu-Jansen 1984), I suggested that the steatite bust of the so-called 'Priest-King' should be viewed in relation to this group of kneeling males which were all retrieved from Late Harappan contexts at Mohenjo Daro. Because of the angles at which the missing arms of the fragmentary bust are held, I paralleled it with the more

Fig. 4. A male terracotta in a kneeling posture.

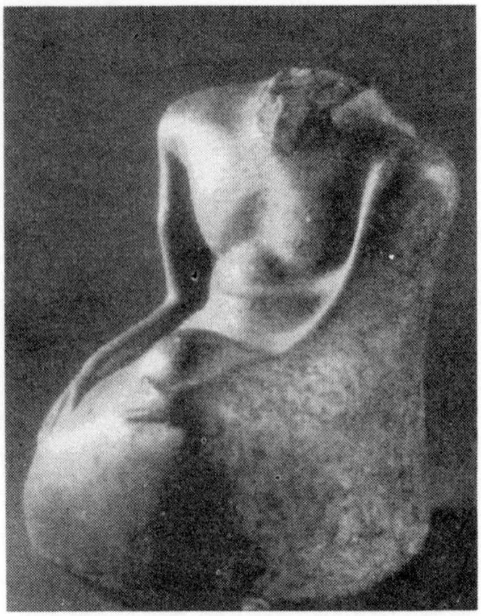

Fig. 5. A stone sculpture.

complete examples whose statuesque sitting postures convey tranquility and meditation suggesting a ritual significance.

The statue of the 'Priest-King', however, has more important characteristics which make a unique connotation possible. These are first of all the trefoil ornamentations on the figure's cloak but also the fillet which is tied around the head and falls down the back in two strands. Certain stone sculptures from Mohenjo Daro and from Bronze Age cultures of adjacent areas indicate that these devices could be taken as signs of sovereignty. Thus the clay band laid around the head of the terracotta figurine described above might, in addition to the characteristic posture, be taken as a further allusion to the stone images, indicating that the small statuette had, despite its comparatively poor quality, a votive significance.

Whereas most of the female statuettes have been related to a fertility cult which venerated the reproductive powers of the female in the form of an image of the 'Great Mother Goddess', with familiar parallel in a conceptual tradition which seems to have been widespread in Neolithic and Chalcolithic societies, most of the other Harappan figurines, in particular those which are crudely modelled, were thought to be children's toys.

Let me quote Mackay himself:

> The great majority were without doubt made as toys for children, and judging by the roughness of their workmanship were frequently the handiwork of children themselves. (Marshall 1931: 346)

And commenting on the male terracottas he wrote:

> The comparative paucity of male figurines is significant. For some reason they were not popular in clay, excepting the few rough examples made by children obviously as playthings. (Marshall 1931: 340)

This view of Mackay, later partly shared by Wheeler (Wheeler 1968: 91), was already rejected by some scholars in the 1930s. D.H. and M.E. Gordon (1940a and b), for example, stated that:

> It is just conceivable that children might make clay figures, but that their elders would have troubled to fire them does not appear to us to be in the least degree credible. (Gordon and Gordon 1940: 5)

Apart from the manufacturing process, which admittedly was no longer as sophisticated in Harappan times as it was at the beginning of the third millennium BC in Baluchistan, it is indeed hard to imagine that children should have been able to model clay figurines which would not warp during firing.

As During Caspers observed,

> ... as a rule human terracottas consist of a prefabricated, roughly violin-shaped core with stump-like protuberances for the attachment of head and arms, whereas the legs, consisting of two small rolls of clay, were moulded against the uneven and flattish base of this central core piece. (During Caspers 1985: 281)

This modelling method seems to hold true for most of the Harappan terracotta figurines as it does also for certain types which Dani[3] found at Gumla (Dani 1970-1: 24, 3, 5). This indicates that the technique of manufacturing the figurines is based on a tradition which was followed by many figurine makers in the Greater Indus Valley. Thus here we have a further argument against the theory that children manufactured their own toys, since it is very unlikely that children would have been so confirmative in their modelling technique.

In a recent publication H. Mode brought forth fresh arguments concerning the toy and non-toy dispute. Apart from the fact that the abundance of terracotta figurines in the Indus Valley sites would imply—if they were just simple toys—that children played a major role in that society (Mode 1987: 931), he reviewed the toy hypothesis in the light of a specific group of figurines, namely, the wheeled terracotta animals. Mode's criticism was that especially animal figurines on wheels were, merely because they were so easily movable by children, almost always interpreted as children's toys (ibid.).

The initially provocative hypothesis of his article is that these animal statuettes should rather be regarded as cult images akin to later examples from Daimabad, where bronze images of animals on wheeled platforms (elephant, rhinoceros, buffalo and two bulls harnessed to a chariot driven by a male individual) were recovered (Mode 1987: 926, 929). These bronze animals can most probably be dated to the middle of the second millennium BC (Dhavalikar 1978: 207) or might even be related to a Late Harappan occupation attested at this site (ibid.: 211).

An echo of the Harappan Tradition of wheeled terracotta animals can also be observed in the second millennium site of Pirak, in Kachi district, where wheeled camel figurines were found (Jarrige and Santoni 1979: 168, Pl. XLII, B).

For the historic period, Mode referred to specimens from Taxila, Nagda, Mathura and Bhita (Mode 1987: 936). He considered these examples in the light of the still living tradition of chakras and rathas on the Subcontinent (Mode: 937ff.). In the case of the Daimabad bronzes, this comparison was already drawn by M.K. Dhavalikar when he resumed his observations on the pieces concerned[4] (Dhavalikar 1978: 210f.):

> Since the objects are thus movable it is not unlikely that they were meant to be taken out in a procession. Such a procession of animals can be seen on a seal from Mohenjo Daro. Religious processions play an important role in Hinduism and there is no doubt that they are the survivals of ancient traditions. (Dhavalikar 1978: 210-11)

Although Mode's view that the wheeled animal terracottas from the Harappan Culture represent cult images might still be regarded with scepticism, I would like to support his position by drawing attention to a particular type of terracotta animal from Mohenjo Daro (Marshall 1931: CLIII, 24), Kalibangan, Mithatal (Bhan 1975: Pl. XX) and other Harappan sites as well as from the post-Harappan period at Jhukar (Majumdar 1934: Pl. XVI, 14) which were obviously intended to be put on wheels. These little statuettes combine the body of a pot-bellied bird with the attributes of ram's horns and muzzle, thus representing a hybrid which can only be the result of a flight of fantasy into the world of myths. This makes it all the more improbable that these movable animals were merely simple toys for children.

It is interesting to note at this point that in other third millennium cultures also, e.g. in the Diyala region of Iraq comparable terracotta objects on wheels came to light. Although H. Frankfort regarded the figurine of a wheeled animal from an Akkadian house in Tell Asmar (Frankfort 1933: 39, Fig. 6) as a toy, he stated that

> the wheeled terracotta object in the form of a house with two containers and a surmounted 'dish-on-stand' (Fig. 6), rescued from the Sin temple in Khafaje, might have been a cult carriage which was used to consecrate water, grain and oil ... put in the receptacles ... and brought before the god. (Frankfort 1935: 46-8)

Further he states that:

> I am attracted by another explanation, and should tentatively suggest that the carriage is a contrivance used in eliciting that particular class of omen in which the divine will becomes manifest in the figures formed by drops of oil floating on water. This would actually happen in the bowl, while the two vessels below would contain the consecrated ingredients, oil and water. (Frankfort 1935: 46-8)[5]

Against the background of the fact that Harappan-related material was found in the Diyala region it seems not unlikely that the moveable terracotta items represent a widespread phenomenon which was known during the later half of the third millennium BC in many areas of the Near East and the neighbouring regions of Asia.

But there are also other indications which could be used as arguments against the view that the terracotta figurines of the Harappans were mostly simple toys.

Other less sophisticated statuettes from Mohenjo Daro depict small quadrupeds with human faces. Some of them have beards, others have horns or both. In view of the large

Fig. 6. The wheeled terracottas (after Frankfort 1933).

assortment of hybrid creatures depicted on the seals, however, these chimerical representations are not all that surprising, but it is very unlikely that they represent just fantasy animals without any deeper symbolic meaning.

Also preserved is a sizeable number of small terracotta masks which, without exception, were cast from moulds so that many identical examples of each type could be produced. These masks also combine human faces with animal horns and ears, and a hole pierced through on either side of the face before firing shows that the masks were intended to be attached to something with a string. What this something was we do not know, unfortunately, but we can at least conjecture that the fantastic mixture of human and animal feature symbolizes apotrophaic or supernatural powers.

Within the group of natural animals, bovines predominate but dogs, birds, rams or goats, water buffaloes, rhinoceroses, pigs, rabbits, elephants, monkeys and many more species were also depicted.

The predominance of bulls has given rise to the theory that the Indus Valley people also subscribed to some kind of bull cult, perhaps a manifestation of the fertility symbolism which played an essential role in many other early societies dependent on their agricultural and stock-breeding skills. With regard to the frequent depiction of bulls, either the Indian zebu or the humpless, so-called 'unicorn' on the steatite seals, it is indeed hard to refrain from the conclusion that cattle played a major role for the Harappans.

This impression is backed by the fact that bulls outnumber all the other animal representations in clay and also by the particular occurrence in Mohenjo Daro of a very sophisticatedly modelled variety of terracotta bull (Fig. 7). It is not unlikely that the heads of this type were produced in moulds with the ears and horns added later (During Caspers 1985: 279).

The rather artistically modelled bull statuettes were carved out of steatite (Mackay

Fig. 7. The famous terracotta bull.

1938: Pl. LXXIX, 24) or shell (*Xancus pyrum*) (Mackay 1938: Pl. LXXIX, 28) or were cast in bronze (Thapar 1985: Pl. 9). One fragmentary steatite figurine (Ardeleanu-Jansen 1989) even demonstrates that the trefoil ornament, a very selectively applied symbolic motif of the third and second millennium BC cultures of the Indus Valley, adjacent south Turkmenia and Mesopotamia is associated with a bull representation. It seems that this clover-leaf design spread eastwards from Mesopotamia where it had an astral significance connected with the so-called Bull of Heaven (Wolkstein and Kramer 1983: 157).

Admittedly it is difficult to assess the extent of iconological parallels between the Sumerian and Harappan cultures without written sources, but the evidence of the abundance of cattle representations in terracotta as well as on seals, and also on pottery throughout the millennia, strongly suggests that the bull played a major role in the economy and ideology of the subcontinent.

It would definitely go beyond the scope of this paper to describe the whole repertoire of terracotta figurines from Mohenjo Daro, but some further examples are worth mentioning for the picture they give of the flora and fauna of the Indus Valley *c.* 4,000 years ago.

Thus it would seem, for instance, that the rhinoceros was indigenous to the Greater Indus Valley region in Harappan times, a circumstance which may indicate a change in climate during the course of the millennia. The rhinoceros is also depicted, though not very frequently, on the seals and likewise in terracotta. In the 1987 field season, the French 'Mission de l'Indus' recovered rhinoceros bones from an excavation context of the mature Harappan period in Nausharo (J.F. Jarrige: personal communication). This find can thus be interpreted as more concrete evidence of such environmental changes, if one discounts the possibility that the Harappans imported the animal.

One of the animals represented astonishingly often in the corpus of terracotta animals from Mohenjo Daro is the dog. Some terracotta dogs are shown wearing collars, an indication that they were kept as pets. It is also not unlikely that they were even used by the Indus peoples as retrievers in the hunt, as clay figurines of dogs with the kill in their mouths illustrate.

But apart from these figurines, there are other indications of the role terracotta dogs might have played in the Indus Valley. Texts from Ur, for example, relate how the ruler Ibbi-Sin (2028-2004 BC) was presented with a symbolic red dog from Meluhha, i.e. a pottery figurine of a dog from the Indus Valley. We know from Mesopotamia that from the time of Ibbi-Sin right up to the Neo-Babylonian periods apotrophaic terracotta figurines were used in a variety of magical rituals of exorcism (Lamberg-Karlovsky 1980: 389). Clay dogs, for example, were modelled specially to be buried as protectors of a house against evil spirits (Gurney 1935: 31-2; Rittig 1977: 145ff). Although we still cannot be sure about similar practices in the Indus Valley, it is interesting to learn from the above mentioned text that this particular symbolic tradition of the Mesopotamians was known to the Harappans, since it was a person from Meluhha who offered Ibbi-Sin the red-dog as a gift. (Lamberg-Karlovsky 1980: 389). And in fact this should not surprise us, as written texts point to the acculturation of Meluhhan traders in Mesopotamia in the late third millennium (ibid.).

CONCLUSION

At present, we cannot draw a final picture of the significance the terracotta figurines had in the Harappan Culture. No doubt, we still have to penetrate deeper into their iconographical and distributional patterns which can only be achieved by a careful examination of the sites where terracotta statuettes have been found and by an exhaustive compilation of the various motifs according to their regional and temporal distribution.

With the help of the field inventories[6] of the later excavators of Mohenjo Daro and their photographic documentation[7] a considerable amount of terracotta figurines have already been re-evaluated and their archaeological association reconstructed. However, it has to be admitted at this point that even the most careful analysis of the field records runs the risk of failing to distinguish between a secondary trash deposit and an original setting of artefacts left behind by the inhabitants of that ancient town.

Yet the preliminary analysis seems to indicate that most of the figurines in Mohenjo Daro were found smashed in secondary locations, and that none was found in a context which could be interpreted as a shrine, altar or temple. The latter fact had already been mentioned by Marshall and Mackay (Marshall 1931: 340) and was most probably the reason for Marshall's assumption that they served as votive offerings rather than as cult images for household shrines (Marshall 1931: 50).

Broken terracotta figurines were, according to the observations of the French Mission in Mehrgarh, also in the majority throughout all periods of the Mehrgarh settlement (C. Jarrige 1984: 133), and this could actually mean that the fragile models were only intended for short-term use after which, when accidentally broken, they were simply thrown away.

If we consider the diverse practices connected with terracotta figurines in the rural areas of India today, the smashed state of the idols should not surprise us and various explanations seem possible,

According to the findings of ethnographic studies, the production and use of terracotta figurines is often 'governed by a strict seasonality' (Blurton 1985: 67) indicating a yearly 'ritual cycle' (Jayaswal n.d.: 10) in which terracotta figurines are used on special occasions. 'Some of the household rituals of Bihar and Uttar Pradesh', for example, require 'women devotees to prepare simple ... clay figurines for domestic worship' (Jayaswal n.d.: 6), while the Bhils in Gujarat buy their votive terracotta idols from the potters after the harvest has been brought in and offer them to the gods through their deposition at the base of a tree (Blurton 1985: 76).

Fischer and Shah published a report about an apotrophaic ceremony called *bhagtai* (Fischer and Shah 1973: 51) against ghosts and evil spirits which they witnessed in the Chodri tribe in Gujarat (ibid.: 51ff.). In order to drive out evil spirits and disease in a patient, a tribal priest or shaman called *bhagata* (also called *bhagatai*) performs a ceremony during which he models clay figurines. They are meant to be substitutes for the spirits and after food has been offered to them in order to placate the spirits the figurines are deposited in a field far away from the village (ibid.).

Besides their function as toys, there is a great deal of evidence that terracotta figurines are traditionally used in India as votive offerings and images representing deities. They are used on special occasions and often little attention is paid to their actual physical quality as their value lies solely on the votive level (Gupta 1980: 174).

V. Jayaswal recently drew attention to the fact that the 'literary evidence from the historical period testifies ... to the use of clay figurines for certain ritual performances ...' in substitution for live animal sacrifices (Jayaswal n.d.: 7) in the performance of *sraddha* ceremonies (ibid.). Thus we find here another indication of the significance of clay images being confined exclusively to the ritual in which they play a role, after which they lose their purely ceremonial importance.

So far, the evidence gained through the re-interpretation of the field inventories from Mohenjo Daro suggests that the majority of the terracotta figurines were not isolated finds but were usually associated with other terracotta images. Thus the female figurines were found together with animal representations such as bulls, birds and dogs, but also with monkeys, rams and other female or male figurines.

This evidence could indicate that the female representations have to be seen in a broader context than generally proposed. Thus the interpretation according to which they are merely to be regarded as idols of the 'Great Mother Goddess' symbolizing the procreative aspects of womanhood (and the idea of fertility) in general appears to be too simplified.

From the results gathered so far, it is apparent that we have to base our interpretation on a combination of two main factors, namely, the iconographical diversity of the female figurines themselves and the range of other human and animal terracotta figurines associated with them. Taken together, these factors indicate an ideological sophistication which goes far beyond the familiar fertility and maternity complex.

Another factor to be considered is that the range of representational subjects and iconographical diversity is complemented by the contemporaneous use of different figurine types. The figurines may have been regarded as substitute symbols for conception in a complex pantheon. We should not forget that a whole cosmos of conceptions regarding divine beings emerged from the subcontinent.

Finally, it should also be remembered, that apart from the diversity in the terracotta art from Mohenjo Daro, it is still an interesting and perhaps significant point of evidence that no temples or other monumental effigies of a monumentalized ideology have been found so far.

As the majority of the terracotta figurines were rescued from the habitational areas of the settlement, it is conceivable that the ideological practices connected with them were mostly the private concern of the townspeople.

The same might hold true for another aspect of Harappan ritual activity, namely, personal cleansing. On the architectural evidence, it seems very likely that water-related functions played a role in the ideology of the Indus people. The sheer dimensions of the Great Bath in Mohenjo Daro can be taken as proportional to the importance of ritual cleanings in the life of the town. The frequency of bathing platforms in the dwelling-houses of the 'Lower Town' would suggest that such ritual cleansings were so inherent to Harappan society that they were likewise primarily the private domestic concern of the inhabitants, the Great Bath being reserved either for more formal, ceremonial occasions or for a particular population group.

These observations lead us to wonder whether comparable structures existed to manipulate the ideological convictions of the Harappans, much as the popular ideology of the contemporary Mesopotamians and Egyptians was used as a political and economic tool in the hands of the controlling class. But here we already find ourselves trespassing on areas which belong to the field of future research.

NOTES

1. These so-called 'zhob-figurines' were already known since Sir A. Stein encountered them in the 1920s at numerous sites in northern Baluchistan (Stein 1931). Stray finds at centres like Mundigak (Casal 1961: Pl. XLI, 8 and 9) and Shahr-i Sokhta (Tosi 1983a: Fig. 61)indicate that they might even have been exported from Baluchistan to Afghanistan and Iranian Seistan (J.F. Jarrige 1981: 10-11).
2. This inventory was entered into a personal computer and programmed by the German Research Project at Mohenjo Daro, Aachen University. It was published in 1985 under the title *Mohenjo Daro, Report of the Aachen University Mission 1979-1985*. Data Collection Vol. 1, Part 1, The HR-Area Field Register 1925-7, Jansen and Urban (Eds.), Leiden.
3. Type (c), the so-called 'cobra-type' which was the most dominant type at Gumla occurring from Gumla Period III onwards, which Dani connected with the 'pre-Harappan Kot Diji levels' (Dani 1970-1: 65, 68).
4. 'Since the objects are thus movable it is not unlikely that they were meant to be taken out in a procession. Such a procession of animals can be seen on a seal from Mohenjo Daro. Religious processions play an important role in Hinduism and there is no doubt that they are the survivals of ancient traditions.' (Dhavalikar 1978: 210-11).
5. Tell Asmar (Frankfort 1933: 50).
6. Fieldbooks of the Mohenjo Daro excavations 1924-38, courtesy of the Department of Archaeology and Museums, Government of Pakistan. See also footnote 2.
7. Sindh volumes of the phototheque of the Archaeological Survey of India 1902-40, courtesy of the Department of Archaeology and Museums, Government of Pakistan and the Archaeological Survey of India, New Delhi.

REFERENCES

Ardeleanu-Jansen, A. 1984. Stone Sculptures from Mohenjo-Daro, in *Reports on Field Work Carried out at Mohenjo-daro, Paksitan 1982-83 by the IsMEO-Aachen University Mission: Interim Report 1* (M. Jansen and G. Urban Eds.), pp. 139-57. Aachen-Roma: RWTH-IsMEO.

——— 1989. A Short Note on a Steatite Sculpture Fragment from Mohenjo-Daro, in *South Asian Archaeology 1985* (K. Frifelt and P. Sorensen Eds.), pp. 196-210. London: Curzon Press, Scandinavia Insititute of Asian Studies, Occasional Paper 4.

——— 1987. The Theriomorphic Stone Sculpture from Mohenjo-Daro Reconsidered, in *Interim Reports 2* (M. Jansen and G. Urban Eds.), pp. 59-68. Aachen-Roma: RWTH-IsMEO

Asthana, S. 1985. *Pre-Harappan Cultures of India and the Borderlands*. Delhi: Books & Books.

Bhan, S. 1975. *Excavation at Mitathal (1968) and Other Explorations in the Sutlej-Yamuna Divide*. Kurukshetra: Kurukshetra University.

Bisht, R.S. and S. Asthana 1979. Banawali and Some Other Recently Excavated Harappan Sites in India, in *South Asian Archaeology 1977* (Taddei Ed.), pp. 223-40. Naples: Instituto Universitario Orientale.

Blurton, R.T. 1985. Tribal Terracotta Figurines in Gujarat: the Technology of Their Production, *South Asian Studies* 1: 67-77.

Casal, J.M. 1961. *Fouilles de Mundigak*, 2 vols. Paris: Memories de la Delegation Archaeologique Francais en Afganistan, Tome 17. Librairie C. Klincksiek.

Dani, A.H. 1970-1. Excavations in the Gomal Valley, *Ancient Pakistan* 5: 1-177.

Dhavalikar, M.K. 1978. Proto-Pasupati in Western India, *East and West* 28 (1-4): 203-12.

During Caspers, E.C.L. 1985. Sundry Technical Aspects of the Manufacture of Indus Valley Terracotta Art, in *Orientalia Losephi Tucci Memoriae Dicata* (G. Gnoli and L. Lanciotti Eds.), pp. 267- 85. Rome: IsMEO.

Fischer, E. and Haku Shah 1976. Treatment Against Ghosts and Spirits. The Bhagtai-Ceremony of the Chodhri Tribe in Gujarat, in *German Scholars on India, Contributions to Indian Studies* Vol. II (Cultural Department of the Embassy of the Federal Republic of Germany Ed.), pp. 51- 60. Bombay: Nachiketa Publications Limited.

Frankfort, H. 1935. *Oriental Institute Discoveries in Iraq, 1933-34: Fourth Preliminary Report of the Iraq Expedition*. Chicago: The University of Chicago Press.

Frankfort., J. 1933. *Tell Asmar, Khafaje and Khorsabad. Second Preliminary Report of the Iraq Expedition*. Chicago: The University of Chicago Press.

Gordon, D.H. and M.E. Gordon 1940a. Survivals of the Indus Culture, *Journal of the Royal Asiatic Society of Bengal* 6: 61-72.

——— 1940b. Mohenjo-Daro: Some Observations on Indian Prehistory, *Iraq* VII: 1-12.

Gupta, S.P. 1980. *The Roots of Indian Art*. Delhi: B.R. Publishing Corporation.

Hurney, O.R. 1935. Babylonian Prophylactic Figures and Their Rituals, *Annals of Archaeology and Anthropology* XXII: 31-96.

Jarrige, C. 1984. Terracotta Human Figurines from Nindowari, in *South Asian Archaeology 1981* (B. Allchin Ed.), pp. 129-34. Cambridge: Cambridge University Press.

——— 1987. Die Terrakotta figurinen aus Mehrgarh, in *Vergessene Stadte am Indus: Ausstellungskatalog Aachen 1987*, pp. 95-101. Mainz: Verlag Philipp von Zabern.

Jarrige, J.F. 1979. Excavations at Mehrgarh, Baluchistan: Their Significance in the Prehistorical Context of the Indo-Paksitan Borderlands, in *South Asian Archaeology 1977* (M. Taddei Ed.), pp. 463-536. Naples: Instituto Univesitario Orientale.

Jarrige, J.F. and M. Santoni 1979. *Foullies de Pirak*. 2 vols. Paris: Publication de la Commission des Fouiles Archaeologiques, Fouilles du Pakistan.

——— 1981. Economy and Society in the Early Chalcolithic and Bronze Age of Baluchistan, in *South Asian Archaeology 1979* (Hartel Ed.), pp. 93-114. Berlin: Dietrich Reimer.

——— 1984. Chronology of the Earlier Periods of the Greater Indus as Seen from Mehrgarh, Pakistan, in *South Asian Archaeology 1981* (B. Allchin Ed.), pp. 21-8. Cambridge: Cambridge University Press.

——— 1986. Excavations at Mehrgarh-Nausharo, *Pakistan Archaeology* 10-22: 63-130.

——— 1987. Die fruhesten Kulturen in Pakistan und ihre Entwicklung, *in Vergessene Stadte am Indus: Ausstellungskatalog Aachen*, pp. 50-66. Mainz.

Jayaswal, V. n.d. Socio-Ritual Significance of Ancient Terracottas in the Gangetic Plains: the Ethno- archaeological and Literary Evidence. Paper Read in the Conference on South Asia, 6-8 November 1986, Madison, Wisconsin.

Kohl, P. (Ed.) 1980. *Soviet Anthropology and Archaeology: the Bronze Age Civilization of Central Asia: Recent Soviet Discoveries,* Vol. XIX (1-2). New York: Armonk.

Lamberg-Karlovsky, C.C.1980. Afterword, in *Soviet Anthropology and Archaeology: the Bronze Age Civilization of Central Asia: Recent Soviet Discoveries,* Vol. XIX (1-2) (P. Kohl Ed.), pp. 386-97. New York: Armonk.

Mackay, E.J.H. 1938. *Further Excavations at Mohenjo-Daro.* New Delhi: Governement of India.

Majumdar, N.G. 1934. *Explorations in Sind.* New Delhi: Memoirs of the Archaeological Survey of India 48.

Marshall, Sir J. 1931. *Mohenjo-Daro and the Indus Civilization.* London: Arthur Probsthain.

Mode, H. 1987. Der Chakra-Bildtradition, Symbol, Funktion, in *Orientalia Losephi Tucci Memoriae Dicata* (G. Gnoli and L. Lanciotti Eds.), pp. 925-42. Rome: IsMEO.

Piggott, S. 1952. *Prehistoric India.* Harmondsworth: Penguin Books.

Possehl, G. 1986. *Kulli: an Exploration of Ancient Civilization in South Asia. Centres of Civilization.* Durham: Carolina Academic Press.

Rao, S.R. 1985. *Lothal 1955-62.* New Delhi: Memoirs of the Archaeological Survey of India 78 (2).

Rittig, D. 1977. Assyrisch-Babylonische Kleinplastik Magischer Bedeutung vom 13.-6 Jh. v. Chr. Münchener Universitats-Schriften. Phil. Fachbereich 12, Münchener Vorderasiatische Studien, Vol. 1, (B. Hrouda Ed.). München: Verlag Uni-Druck.

Stein, Sir A. 1931. *An Archaeological Tour in Gedrosia.* New Delhi: Memoirs of the Archaeological Survey of India 48.

Thapar, B.K. 1973. New Traits of the Indus Civilization at Kalibangan: an Appraisal, in *South Asian Archaeology 1971* (N. Hammond Ed.), pp. 85-104. London: Duckworth.

Thapar, B.K. 1985. *Recent Archaeological Discoveries in India.* Paris-Tokyo: UNESCO.

Tosi, M. 1983a. Development, Continuity and Cultural Change in the Stratigraphical Sequence of Shahr-i-Sokhta, in *Prehistoric Sistan 1* (M. Tosi Ed.), pp. 127-80. Rome: IsMEO.

——— 1983b. *Prehistoric Sistan I.* Rome: IsMEO.

Wheeler, Sir M. 1968. *The Indus Civilization.* Cambridge: Cambridge University Press.

Wolkstein, D. 1983. *Inanna, Queen of Heaven and Earth: Her Stories and Hymns from Sumer.* New York: Harper Row Publishers.

Some Important Aspects of the Harappan Technological Tradition

K.K. BHAN, M. VIDALE and J.M. KENOYER

INTRODUCTION

This paper will discuss some aspects of the current research on craft production in the Harappan phase of the Indus tradition. In this phase (*c.* 2600 to 1900 BC) corresponding to the Integration Era (defined in Shaffer 1991 and Kenoyer 1991a), the proto-urban communities of the Indus basin and the surrounding regions (Fig. 1) appear to have been organized into several regional states (probably city states) (Kenoyer in press) which over the course of seven centuries, appear to have attained some form of political unification (Jacobson 1986; Kenoyer 1991a). From approximately 2600 to 1900 BC, we observe the growth to a maximum extent of the first urban centres of South Asia. The development of large cities affected a parallel and equally impressive development of the industrial sector, in agreement with one of the most foresighted interpretations of V.G. Childe (1950). An important aspect of this process of integration was the invention or the adoption of specific styles in material culture, namely, in public and domestic architecture, ceramics (including pottery and refined personal ornaments such as faience and stoneware bangles), metallurgy, steatite, agate and shell ornaments. To a large extent, the ancient crafts of the Indus society have been studied only within the urban contexts of cities and towns. Unfortunately, suburban or rural industrial sites, such as those reported in Cholistan area (Mughal 1980, 1982), in Sindh (Flam 1986) and throughout Kachchh, Saurashtra and Haryana, etc. (S. Bhan 1973; K.K. Bhan 1986, 1992; Bisht 1982, 1990; Dikshit 1981; Joshi 1972) are still awaiting study and excavation. In other cases, it appears that geomorphological processes of site formation have made it difficult to survey and excavate the periphery of the ancient mounds that are buried in several metres of alluvium (for example, at Mohenjo Daro and Balakot).

In studying the craft traditions of the Harappan phase we are hampered by the fact that the Indus script has not been convincingly deciphered and there are no graphic representations of the organization of crafts. This means unlike Egypt or Mesopotamia, we have no written records or graphic illustrations with which to compare and test our interpretations of the organization of craft traditions. On the other hand, this handicap has led to a development of more rigorous methods of recording and analysis of the archaeological materials, which have opened up totally new spheres of investigation and interpretation. Some of the important themes that have been the focus of recent work include the segregation and control of production and political control, and the question of part-time and full-time specialists. It has also led to the development of specialized ethnoarchaeological

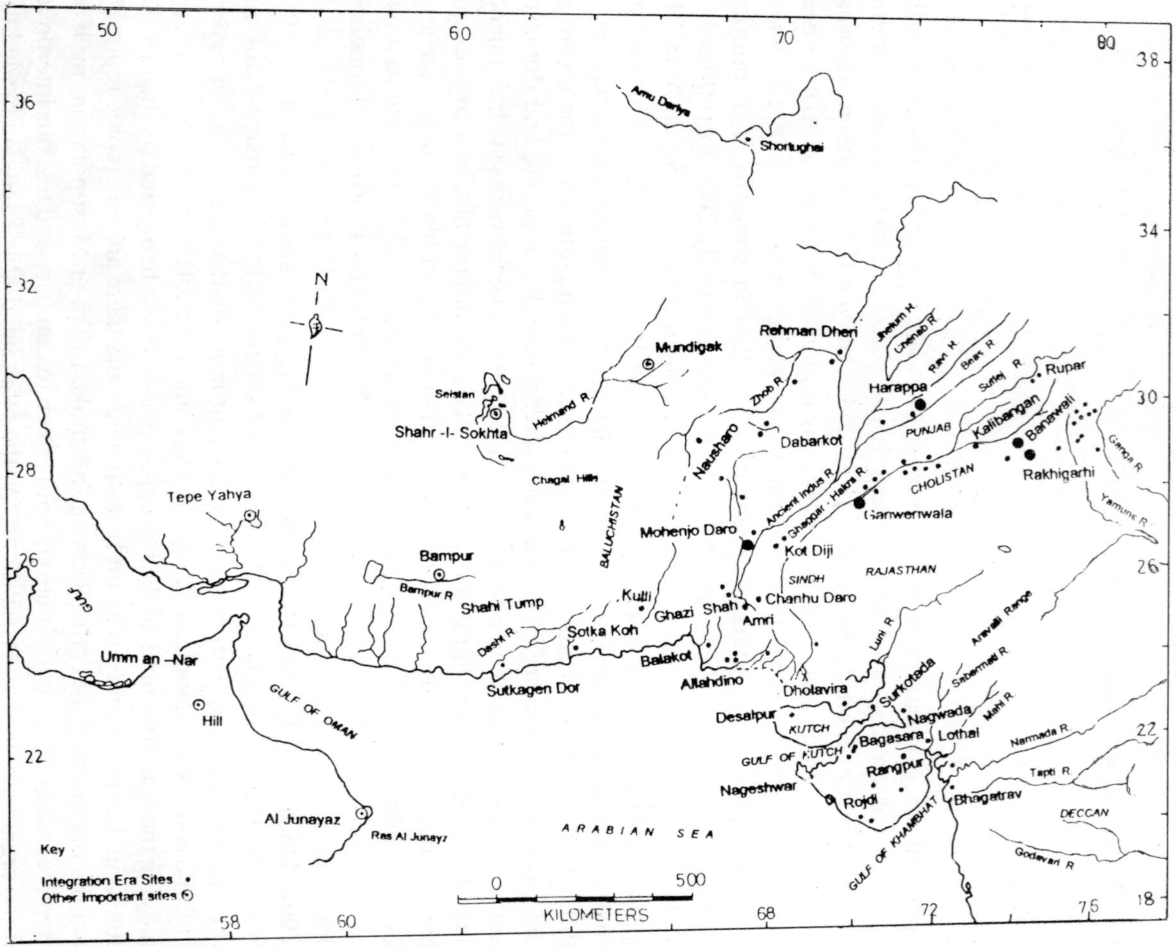

Fig. 1. Major Sites of the Integration Era, Harappan Phase.

and ethnoexperimental studies of traditional crafts that can be used to develop more appropriate research strategies and interpretive models (see Sinopoli 1991a).

At present, the archaeologists with interest in Harappan crafts are burdened with the major responsibility of extending research into every facet of material culture production and interpreting the new data into more complex interpretive models. This requires the refinement of data recovery through survey and excavation, methods of laboratory conservation and analytical techniques. It also requires the development of problem oriented studies and new theoretical models that go beyond evolutionary linearity and multilinearity, centre-periphery, diffusion, simple hierarchies or stratification, and the limited nature of dichotomy. This entails the reconstructing of the academic processes of model building and testing to allow for non-Western (or, realistically, less-Western) approaches to the difficult epistemological and ideological problems of craft studies.

The industrial debris left by artisans is a reliable marker of one of the most important dimensions of social differentiation. In Harappan studies, archaeologists have been more successful in identifying and reconstructing major aspects of production than, for example, religious or administrative practices. Presently, from a strictly archaeological viewpoint, the most direct method for understanding social stratification and segregation in Harappan society is through the ancient craft organization. The division of labour in the Indo-Pakistan subcontinent is a key variable for the interpretation of society since it is closely related to the ritual organization of the society, as well as the socio-political structure. Professional specialization in ancient India is far from being a 'neutral' field of inquiry. However, interpretive models for the organization of Harappan crafts are derived from two different sources. Scholars favouring the idea of a substantial cultural gap between the Harappan and later cultures often dismiss any relationship between prehistoric and historic periods and use models derived from modern observation or ancient parallels outside the subcontinent (Wheeler 1968). On the other hand, proponents of an overall cultural continuity in the subcontinent interpret the archaeological evidence in the context of occupational specialization and hereditary caste organization that is present in the later urban cultures of the Early Historic period (beginning 600 BC).

SEGREGATION AND CONTROL OF PRODUCTION

The first major issue has been the interpretation of archaeological patterning of craft indicators using models developed in other regions of the world and for different social contexts. The traditional interpretation of the presence of highly specialized crafts in Harappan cities and towns is indicative of a centralized political control of production and distribution. This hypothesis supports the idea of a substantial degree of socio-economic stratification and class differentiation in Harappan society.

It is evident that the 'model', or part of it, was in the past at the root of influential and long-lasting interpretations of Harappan society. Vat's idea of 'workmen's quarters' at Harappa (1940: 61-3), as comparable with similar 'workmen's village' at Tell-el Amarna in Egypt clearly demonstrates its 'Western' background. Actually, besides the architectural layout of these poorly preserved houses, nothing supported such an interpretation. On the contrary, the discovery below the floor of a house of a rich jewelry hoard would point to relationships with an elite context.

Another evidence of craft production at Harappa was observed above the 'workmen's quarters'(i.e. in later phases of occupation), as the site appeared to have been resettled by craftsmen using many highly vitrified kilns and perhaps living in thatched huts (Vats 1940: 470: Wheeler 1968: 32). Unfortunately, no stratigraphic section of this deposit was published, and we have no detail on the original stratigraphy of the site or its dynamics of formation. In terms of political control, the implication of a process of squatting across the ruins of an abandoned architectural compound do not necessarily coincide with those of a 'craftsmen quarter' managed by central authorities. Furthermore, although these kilns are interpreted as metalworking facilities, this idea was based on very little or no evidence at all (Kenoyer and Miller, in press), and they could have been simply pottery kilns. Wheeler's interpretation of the famous rows of circular structures as specialized installation for pounding cereals is based on a single published section which could be interpreted in many ways, and does not appear to be conclusive (Wheeler 1947). It shows how biased and forceful has been the attempt to frame the archaeological evidence of Harappan cities within a pre-existing Near Eastern interpretation imposed from the West.

Kenoyer stresses that part of the difficulty in applying this 'model' lies in its lack of epistemological coherence, and in its abstraction from the reality of the Indo-Pakistani subcontinent.

> While this model may seem quite straightforward, a theoretical jump has been made in assuming that segregation of specialized crafts can be attributed to centralized control and to socio-economic stratification. Ethnoarchaeological studies of specialized crafts indicate that there is no direct correlation between the craft activities and the control of production or socio-economic stratification. (Kenoyer 1992: 42)

What we perceive as material evidence for urban segregation may reflect different phenomena. On a purely archaeological ground, the selective location of large amounts of industrial debris may be due to the growth of large dumps within the settlements, having little relationship with the place where manufacture took place. So, particularly during surface survey, large concentrations of craft residues do not necessarily indicate workshops and craft quarters. The permanence of a large group of potters in the same area for a short time might produce a large amount of waste abandoned on the spot, while a well organized potters quarter might have required efficient forms of maintenance of the space, with the consequent growth of dumps far from the workshops. Furthermore, as observed, for example at Mohenjo Daro , Harappa and Nagwada large amounts of industrial residues were removed and displaced all over for architectural purposes. Only a careful evaluation of the stratigraphy below the surface spreads of industrial refuse can provide safer grounds for interpretation.

On the other hand, segregation may reflect the need of craft groups to live in close proximity for exchanging resources and services, or for obeying rules of behavior shared by the whole society; or the intentional organization of the craft groups into hierarchic segments by a central urban authority. Kenoyer (1992) cites as an example contemporary pottery production in India and Pakistan, which is decentralized, being organized along kin-based networks and depending upon reciprocal obligation and exchange transactions between potters and non-potters. Part of the pottery so produced and distributed is fairly standardized in shape and decoration, as it must conform to the aesthetic standards of large, loosely spread kin or ethnic groups. In many contemporary urban contexts pottery making also appears to be spatially segregated but this localization of production does not reflect any active purposeful interference from state. In spite of the limited amount of research so far accomplished, the first models derived from ethnoarchaeology can already be considered better candidates for explaining some forms of Harappan craft organization than old models plainly derived from Egypt or Mesopotamia.

ORIGINATION OF CRAFT PRODUCTION AND POLITICAL COMPLEXITY

In traditional Near-Eastern archaeology, iconography and written records of transactions between craftsmen and institutions help in understanding the growth of political complexity. In Harappan archaeology, we have to rely on less direct approaches. While hypotheses of urban segregation need to be tested upon the base of a careful evaluation of archaeological record of craft production, there are some aspects of the relationship between craft production and political complexity which can be monitored on the basis of the archaeometric study of the industries alone. In order to understand better the nature and the context of political control possibly exerted on ancient craftsmen and the role of this control in the development of early states in South Asia, it might be useful to differentiate and discuss various crafts in categories or types.

For example, in discussing the emergence of urban societies in the ancient Near East, Nissen (1988: 49-51) classifies craft professions along two axis: frequency of demand for a given class of commodities *versus* the amount of technological know-how required for manufacturing. In this way, following Nissen, we may be able to recognize three broad groups of crafts: first, food production, depending upon a constant widespread demand, but requiring a limited technological know-how; second, a group of 'basic' crafts such as plaster or pottery making depending on a demand relatively constant in time, but not on daily base like the first group, and involving a higher amount of technological knowledge; and third, crafts whose performances were frequently required, such as production of ornaments, pigments and the like, and distinguished by very specific and complex know-how.

Nissens's model may be valid as far as it is based upon a generic correlation between demographic and settlement growth, political complexity and processes of occupational specialization. A relatively direct correlation between the development of political complexity (in particular, the evolution of early states and empires) and institutionalized form of craft specialization has been demonstrated in an important paper by J.E. Clark (1990). But out of this order of generic correlations, Nissen's model presents several problems. For example, the relationships between demand and technological know-how is far from simple and linear. Nissen furthermore does not explain the relationship between the growth of occupational specialization and the evolution of political organization. His reference to an abstract 'demand' as a key factor directly promoting specialized production seems to take for granted that these professions could have had an 'independent' character, or that their emergence was simply a byproduct of improved economic conditions. In contrast, many studies show the fundamentally political role played by crafts specialists in the process of growth of early states (see Claessen and Skalnik 1978; Brumfiel and Earle 1987; Peregrine 1991; Vidale 1989; Kenoyer 1989, 1992 and many others).

Kenoyer (1989, 1992) has proposed a useful classification of ancient craft professions in prehistoric societies based upon two lines of inquiry: the local *versus* non-local availability of raw material and the simple or complex character of the technologies involved. On this basis, Kenoyer divides Harappan craft into 4 categories.

—local raw material and simple technologies-wood working, terracotta ceramic production, house building;
—non-local materials and simple technologies-stone working, flint knapping;
—local raw material and complex technologies-stoneware bangle production, other elaborated ceramic industries, inlaid woodwork;
—non-local raw material and complex technologies-agate bead manufacture, seal production, metalworking, etc.

Kenoyer argues that categories depending upon complex technologies (categories 3 and 4) would involve standardization, while the other categories would be expected to show a higher degree of regional variation. Political control on craft production could assume the form of control on technological know-how, on labour, on access to rare raw materials, on distribution, according to the pattern to be contextually investigated in archaeological record (1992: 44-5). Unlike Nissen's parameters, the criteria proposed by Kenoyer can actually be monitored (at least partially) in archaeological record; technology can be reconstructed by studying artefacts, and provenance studies are probably the most developed branch of archaeometry.

In general, cross cultural research has shown that political elites of chiefdom patronize the production of luxury goods manufactured with raw material that are non-local, rare or difficult to obtain, and are transformed through massive investments of labour in the form of simple technologies (Clark 1990; Peregrine 1991). 'Classic' example of these types of craft production are the production of polished stone axes by the Trobriand islanders (defined as a case of 'technical hypertrophy' by Malinowski 1922), the manufacture of ornaments and status signs in native copper by native American populations of the northern plains and the north-eastern coast, or the production of feather caps in the Hawaii Islands (see Clark 1990, and Brumifel and Earle 1987 for bibliography).

On the other hand, some state-level societies show a radical shift, sponsoring the production of ornaments and status signs whose raw materials were relatively common or easy to obtain but required very elaborate technologies. 'Instead, it appears that raw materials for personnel ornaments are more likely to come from a local source than a non-local one as societies become more politically centralized' (Peregrine 1991: 8). Very often, a key element in these elaborate technologies is the intervention of pyrotechnological processes. A good example of this trend is the production of luxury wares such as the famous Arretine in Roman times, made with plain, ubiquitous local clays but through exceedingly complex firing techniques. The importance of this option is immediately evident: if institutionalized elites of a state-level society needed to mark their status with luxury items, control of labour and technological know-how allowed a clear-cut, immediate differentiation from commoners which did not depend upon external sources or agents.

FULL-TIME *VERSUS* PART-TIME CRAFT SPECIALIZATION

The traditional way of understanding the development of craft sectors in early urban societies is to think that craftsmen were gradually involved in projects and institutions ruled by political leaders. In the beginning, this process would have affected groups of farmers in the period of suspension of agricultural activities. In time, these part-time craftsmen would have been progressively and systematically enrolled full-time by central institutions such as temples, palaces, and attached manufacturing units. This development would have been accompanied by a growing coercion and centralization of some aspects of economy, including redistribution of food rations to specialists, supported by the use of writing for administration and specialized schools for training elites of official scribes (see Liverani 1988: 107-40; Chapple and Coon 1942; Wenke 1980, and others see also some implications of the model proposed in Rice 1981).

This model might actually reflect a main evolutionary trend of Near-Eastern and other societies. Claessen and Skalnik, for example, found statistical correlation between state organization and full-time craft specialists (1978: 544). But this idea seems often to involve another theoretical jump, which more or less openly implies that a part-time specialist would be less 'efficient' than his full-time counterparts. For example, some north American archaeologists think that full-time craft specialization is a necessary component of craft specialization or the only possible form of specialization (Yerkes 1983).

Again, one should be aware that similar statements cannot be adequately controlled in the archaeological record. The only way of archaeologically detecting forms of attached craft specialization is through the identification of workshops or manufacturing areas within the precinct of temples, palaces or elite houses (see, for example, Henrickson 1982) or through the analysis of literary texts or administrative devices showing taxation. But even in these cases it might be exceedingly difficult to distinguish part-time craft production. The manufacturing residues of a part-time specialist would not be easily differentiated from those of a full-time craftsman in terms of technological performance (Kenoyer et al. 1991). Eventually, proofs of full-time craft specialization could be sought for in the realm of stratigraphy, i.e. in terms of stratigraphic formation processes (for example, understanding the maintenance of the workshop floors and correlating stratigraphically working and dumping areas). But the type of excavation which were carried out in the past did not record the detailed stratigraphy of floors and dumping areas we need for such purposes.

Our ethnoarchaeological research at Khambhat suggests that part-time specialization may be the subject of a strong hierarchic control, exactly like full-time specialization; it appears as a very dynamic solution, compatible with complex forms of labour organization. Here, craftsmen distinguished by an extreme level of specialization (a single stage of manufacturing for single type of bead) such as drillers are engaged in manufacturing on a part-time basis, when agricultural season is slow. In spite of this part-time organization, drillers live in a suburban village traditionally associated with the craft. Archaeologically, if the faint evidence left by the drilling process would be recognized in archaeological record, it would represent a good case of 'urban segregation' of a specific craft, even if the selective location of drillers is now due to family and caste traditions and to the relative social connections than to coercion.

Thus, part-time specialization seems to be advantageous both for agate dealers that control the industry and for the drillers, who are paid small amounts of extra cash, very difficult to obtain with their normal agricultural activities. It is tempting to assume that part of the problem in recognizing traditional forms of centralized control on production in Harappan cities is the systematic employment of part-time craft specialists, hosted for short time within the urban structure or decentralized manufacturing sites (Pracchia et al. 1985). Part-time specialization actually could have been in itself not an 'imperfect' evolutionary stage towards a full-time schedule, but an important factor for the emergence of social stratification and development of state-level societies in itself.

As this paper will show, while some important crafts of the Integration Era are in course old study, and we are able to reconstruct in detail some technological aspects, the general picture is unclear; there are substantial gaps in our understanding of several important manufacturing cycles. In future, when more information will be available, it will be very interesting to observe in this light the transition of different protohistoric technologies from Regionalization to the Integration Era, and finally to the later context of the Localization Era in the second millennium BC.

ETHNOARCHAEOLOGICAL STUDIES

The proliferation of the so-called 'ethnoarchaeological' studies in South Asian archaeology has resulted in a confusion regarding the use of the term and the validity of many archaeological interpretations. There is no need to repeat the numerous cautionary tales about the indiscriminate use of analogies. They abound in the Western journals, but we must recognize that even though South Asia has very long cultural continuities in technology, as well as in social and ritual organizations, we need to define strong theoretical and methodological framework for each and every study that is undertaken. Ethnoarchaeology is a broad field of inquiry that encompasses all aspects of human adaptation, from the selection of raw materials to the ideological basis for specific symbols. Nevertheless, it is important to emphasize that not all ethnographic observations of traditional or modern crafts are ethnoarchaeological studies. To be effective, ethnoarchaeological research must be undertaken in a rigorous and well defined manner to address specific aspects of material culture patterning that is preserved archaeologically. Also, it is not sufficient to say that there are similarities or differences, but it is necessary to define why they are significant and how they can be used to make more reliable archaeological interpretations.

During the last two decades ethnoarchaeological research on craft production has made significant advances, especially in the context of Harappan studies. Sinopoli (1991a) has presented an important overview and critique of the most important publications and highlighted some of the theoretical and methodological issues. A discussion of specific Harappan crafts below will provide examples of how ethnoarchaeological studies have contributed to more reliable interpretations and how they are of help in developing more meaningful research on the larger questions of urbanism and the character of the Indus socio-religious and political systems.

THE ARCHAEOLOGICAL RECORD OF HARAPPAN CRAFT PRODUCTION

Lithic Industries

The study of chipped stone or lithic industries of the Harappan phase is still in its infancy, partly because of the emphasis given to other categories of objects made from bronze, semi-precious stone, shell, etc. Nevertheless, several important studies have identified the direction for future research and set out a range of methodologies that can be applied to morphological studies of Harappan lithic technology in the urban context (Biagi 1990; Bulgarelli 1986; Hoffman and Cleland 1977; Cleland 1997; Inizan and Lechevallier 1985; Inizan 1985, 1990; Kenoyer 1984a; Lechevallier 1979, 1984; Vidale 1985, 1987d, 1990c). It is clear that Harappans used chert implements and other types of chipped and ground stone tools for specific technological and subsistence activities which could not be undertaken with metal tools. The lithic repertoire of the Harappans included both blade and flake technologies to produce specialized forms of drills, scrapers, cutting tools and sickle components as well as unmodified blades and flakes. These tools were used directly for subsistence activities as well as processing other materials in specialized crafts such as lapidary and the manufacture of objects from soft stone, wood, shell, ceramics and possibly even for metal working (for example, engraving and drilling).

Most of the techniques used for making chert flakes and blades are well known from the earlier periods; heat treatment of some chert and almost all other types of cryptocrystalline silicates, direct hammer percussion, indirect percussion using punch, bipolar flaking, backing retouch, pecking, grinding and polishing. Pelegrin has proposed that some form of pressure techniques (shoulder or chest punch or possibly a lever punch) would have been necessary for the production of the long parallel sided blades characteristic of the Harappan phase (Pelegrin: personal communication). On the other hand, replicative studies conducted by Kenoyer, both at Khambhat and at Harappa, have identified the use of inverse percussion for blade production, for the manufacture of chert weights and chert burnishers and for the production of bead blanks. Hand held pressure flaking has been identified only on the final retouch of drills and final trimming of the long carnelian bead blanks from Chanhu Daro.

Due to the fact that it is very difficult to differentiate many of these techniques it has been necessary to develop more highly refined recording systems for characterization of lithic debitage and flaking pattern (Kenoyer and Meadow 1992; Kenoyer et al. 1994). Much of the study is closely related to the study of stone bead manufacture and has been undertaken in the course of research on bead chipping experts of Khambhat (Kenoyer et al. 1991). It is not unlikely that many different techniques were being used to produce very similar if not identical types of blades and finished tools. These techniques may result from individual specialists or they may reveal regional or chronological patterns. It is hoped that the excavation of chert manufacturing areas in Rohri (Biagi: personal communication) and the recent collections of-large quantities of chert and micro-crystalline silicates manufacturing debris and finished tools from Harappa and many excavated sites of Gujarat will provide important new data on the details of Harappan lithic technology.

LAPIDARY: AGATE, CARNELIAN AND OTHER DECORATIVE STONES

Agate and particularly carnelian bead making was probably the first craft to reveal the impressive standards of Harappan technology. At the site of Chanhu Daro, Mackay came across large amounts of industrial refuse from bead making workshops, including defective or discarded carnelian nodules, roughouts and beads, raw materials for drill manufacture, and debitage for drill making (Mackay 1937, 1943). Other scattered evidence of bead making, although not concentrated within isolated workshops, were discovered at Mohenjo Daro (Mackay 1938; Vidale 1984) and by Vats (1940) and Meadow and Kenoyer (1992) at Harappa. Similarly a limited amount of finished beads (11 agate items out of 1050 beads in various materials) has been reported from the excavations at Surkotada (Joshi 1990: 313-37). When we compare the bead making areas of Chanhu Daro and Mohenjo Daro with the so-called 'bead factory' at Lothal, we have to conclude that it could probably not be considered an actual manufacturing site. In particular, the inventory of finds does not correspond with what one would expect: chert bladelets and chert knapping debitage, agate flakes and their exhausted cores, constricted and tapered drills are conspicuous by their absence. Inspection of the nearby surface during several visits by the authors failed in revealing any waste dumps. Rather, the building might represent a warehouse where beads in various stages of manufacture were stored by merchants. For Lothal, unfortunately, so far no technological detail is given on the many unfinished and finished beads of the two hoards reported by Rao (1979: 118-20).

In recent times, agate bead technology has been the focus of new research, both on ethnoarchaeological and archaeological sides. The present city of Khambhat in Gujarat has been the subject of much research both in previous and more recent times (Arkell 1938; Trivedi 1964; Janaki 1980; Possehl 1981; Francis 1982; Kenoyer 1986). Documentation of the contemporary bead technology in Gujarat has provided important clues for the study of a craft which appears to have maintained several ancient forms.

Furthermore, recent studies are focusing on the relationships between technology, formation of different types of deposits and assemblage of craft indicators, and various forms of organization of production. The information may be used to interpret Harappan archaeological contexts of bead production (Kenoyer et al. 1991; Vidale et al. 1992; Roux and Pelegrin 1990).

Recently, new bead making sites referable to the Indus tradition were identified at sites such as Lewan in Bannu Basin, N.W.F.P., Pakistan (Allchin et al. 1986: 81-7), Gazi Shah in Sindh (Flam 1992), Rehman Dheri (Durrani 1988; Durrani et al. 1991), Banawali (Bisht 1982; Sonawane 1992), Nagwada (Bhan 1986; Hegde et al. 1988). Datrana (Ajithprasad et al. 1995) and Bagasra (Sonawane et al. 1996) in Gujarat.

At Lewan, a site referable to the Regionalization Era, local and non-local semiprecious stones (jasper, quartz, 'striped and speckled metamorphic and igneous rocks', corralline limestone, serpentine, quartzite) were exploited for the production of beads and other larger artefacts in ground stone. Indicators of this craft appear in localized areas. Bead making tools are considered as connected with a local microlithic tradition, and in particular, drills are manufactured out of very small blades and belong to the 'constructed' type of drill (as defined in Kenoyer and Vidale 1993).

Nagwada, a site belonging to the Integration Era has revealed several traces of bead making activities, found loosely scattered across the excavated trenches (majority of the times coming from secondary contest). Stone used for making beads include carnelian, agate, amzonite, jasper, while large lumps of steatite suggests the presence of other craft technologies. Unfinished beads reported in the form of roughouts, blanks and beads are broken in drilling and heating. Tools include stone hammers and grinders and used and unused 'tapered cylindrical' drills (Bhan 1986; Hegde et al. 1988).

In order to understand better some aspects of Harappan bead technology it is mandatory to go back to the evidence gathered by Mackay at Chanhu Daro (1943). At this site he was able to reconstruct the broad outline of the manufacturing sequence of carnelian beads including the beautiful long bicone specimens well known from Harappan hoards, possibly the subject of long-distance trade with Early Dynastic Mesopotamia (Chakrabarti 1982). Interestingly, no evidence of these luxury beads were reported from Mohenjo Daro surface survey and in the excavations at Nagwada. The long beads produced at Chanhu Daro required a difficult and expensive manufacturing sequence, probably involving multiple cycles of firing, sawing with metal tools, chipping, smoothing on various types of grinding stones, and multi-stage drilling processes with highly specialized drills. These drills are of a specific Harappan type, and are labelled as 'constructed cylindrical' in order to distinguish them from the more common 'tapered cylindrical drills' of the Regionalization Era of the Indus Valley and earlier third millennium cultural complexes of South Asia (Kenoyer and Vidale 1993: Fig. 2).

In 1993-4 J.M. Kenoyer and K.K. Bhan carried out a preliminary inspection of Mackay's bead collection from Chanhu Daro and beads from Ur in the Museum of Fine Arts in Boston, British Museum and University Museum, University of Philadelphia. Preliminary results from their studies indicate that while many long carnelian beads found at Ur appear to have been produced in the Indus Valley, other examples, made with Indus drilling technology and Indus raw material may have been produced in Mesopotamia in unique forms for Mesopotamian elites. It is possible that these beads were in fact made by migrant Indus artisans residing in Mesopotamia and these artisans may have been members of the so-called Melluhan minority that are documented in Mesopotamian texts (Parpola et al. 1977).

The preliminary inspection of the long carnelian beads has also indicated in some cases the use of three drills of different diameters for drilling the same bead. Evidently the professional drillers of Chanhu Daro manufactured and/or were endowed with sets of drills of grading diameters for the various phases of work. Drills used for agate and carnelian at Harappa, Chanhu Daro, Mohenjo Daro and Bagasra were made with a very distinctive rock, for which we still do not have a proper name. Visually it is composed of a yellowish-brown matrix with inner dark mottling (Vidale 1984: Fig. 57-67; Kenoyer and Vidale 1993: Fig. 3, 8-13).

In this context one should mention an old terminological problem which continues to generate confusion. When cylindrical drills were discovered in the workshop area of Shahr-i-Sokhta (Piperno 1973, 1976, 1981) the raw material used for production, a greenish-gray hard stone, was defined as 'Phtanite'. Since then, as tapered cylindrical drills of Shahr-i-Sokhta, Mehrgarh (Jarrige 1981) and other sites were compared with the constricted drills of the Harappan phase, the rock name 'Phtanite' has been also used for the drills found at Chanhu Daro, and Mohenjo Daro (Vidale 1984). This name seems to have come in general use, although no analytical determination supported the identification. In a recent paper (Kenoyer and Vidale 1993), we rejected the term 'Phtanite' because of lack of chemical analyses and as a non-universally accepted scientific term, but V. Francaviglia of Italian C.N.R pointed to Vidale that phtanite is actually the name given to a group of clayey schists produced by concentration of silica generated by living organisms (Fourmarier 1949: 41, 720, 721, 737). Recently, phtanite has been probably identified by X-ray diffraction at least in a bead from Mundigak in Afghanistan; XRD spectra showed quartz and clay minerals, probably illite (Bouquillon and Barthelemy 1992). Thus, it appears that we should correct our previous views and to accept the term phtanite as a distinctive type of rock; but it appears highly inprobable that rock containing quartz and clay minerals would have been selected for drilling agate or carnelian, as it would be softer than quartz. Actually, XRD analysis of samples of greenstones, respectively from Mehrgarh and Shahr-i-Sokhta, turned out to be vesuvianite (calcium magnesium aluminum silicate hydroxide) and an unidentified iron magnesium silicate nothing to do with phtanite (Kenoyer and Vidale 1993).

Going back to the raw material Harappans used for drill-making, this distinctive rock was found in angular blocks at Mohenjo Daro, Chanhu Daro and Harappa. These blocks were grooved and split in bars which were pressure-flaked to form drill roughouts. These were later finely ground and polished; the upper part was ground into a carefully faceted shaft, probably to grant a good centring. The point was shaped into a distinctive constricted shape. Another feature of the drill is a distinctive circular depression on the tip, whose nature was not fully understood. Drill manufacture required specialized skills which could be transmitted only through long periods of apprenticeship (Kenoyer and Vidale 1993: Fig. 3).

This rock can easily scratch quartz but cannot scratch beryl, as its hardness is between 7 and 8 on Moh's scale. SEM and microprobe analysis showed that the stone is an aluminium silicate with iron titanium component. X-ray diffraction analysis showed the presence of quartz and sillimanite or/and mullite (these two minerals are very difficult to distinguish by XRD, also because there are some intermediate mineral phases). In prehistory, metamorphic rocks containing sillimanite have been used for the production of hard tools in Europe, in the Arabian peninsula (V. Francaviglia: personal communication) as well as in the New World. Waiting for a final identification, we decided to call this stone 'Ernestite' in honour of the seminal research of E.J.H. Mackay (Kenoyer and Vidale 1993).

In order to understand the drilling properties of this rock, we effected a series of experiments using the drilling apparatus nowadays used at Khambhat. Drills were made with different materials and tested by Kenoyer on similar heat-treated carnelian beads. The drilling rate of 'Ernestite' averages 2.37 mm per hour, about three times the rate of a common jasper, and higher than that of a copper drill with corundum. During perforation the drill tips were resharpened by flaking and grinding. By replicating this process we were able to recreate the circular depression on the tip of the drill, showing that this is a byproduct of friction and not an intentional feature. Our results suggest that in Harappan times the use of copper drills with abrasives is unlikely. Harappan beadmakers selected the best possible material, and distributed it across long distances in the major urban centers. A more precise identification of 'Ernestite' should allow us to trace out the possible source of this material and its routes of trade across Harappan lands.

Substantial new evidence on bead making craft was brought to light with the Aachen-IsMEO survey of the workshop areas of Mohenjo Daro (Vidale 1984). In the so-called Moneer South-East Area, it was possible, among other industries, to map the surface and collect thousands of flakes of semi-precious stones, defective bead roughouts, broken drills, both used and finished, the debitage left by the manufacture of drills, agrinding stone for smoothing the beads and an unfinished cubic weight in chert from Rohri Hills. Some fragments show the use of copper saw for cutting hard metamorphic rocks.

Quantitative analysis of the varieties of semi-precious stones exploited on this site included in the first place chalcedony, i.e. agate in various colours, mainly varieties of red, followed by a translucent apple-green stone that we called 'serpentine', but also a green variety of grossular (Vidale: personal observation), jasper, bloodstone, rock crystal, and to finish with, a few flakes of lapis lazuli, turquoise and other unidentified stones. Grossular is a distinctive green semi-precious stone which is found in several areas of the Indo-Pakistani subcontinent, such as Malakand, Quetta, Gujarat and Chennai areas, and it seems to have been exported to Mesopotamia for making seals at least in Neo-Assyrian and Neo-Babylonian times (Sax 1991). This list of semi-precious stones is definitely varied. The most important technological feature of agate working in this site is a very skilful exploitation of a relatively poor material. Instead of the beautiful, massive and transparent carnelian used at Chanhu Daro, the Moneer bead makers used an opaque fibrous white to redness agate, whose red was enhanced by firing. The fibrous agate is distinguished by inner diaclastic planes which run orthogonally to the direction of the stone's radial fibres. Bead roughouts were detached by percussion exploiting the stone structure, as squared blocklets of multi-layered agate, which could be ground into attractive beads with eye-like patterns (Vidale 1984: 140-2). Equally skillful and specialized appears the manufacture of ornaments in the stone possibly identified as grossular (Vidale 1984: Fig. 35).

In summary for the Integration Era (or Harappan Phase) of the Indus tradition, we have at present detailed information on two manufacturing sites. the Chanhu Daro 'workshop' and the Moneer South-East Area of Mohenjo Daro. Both sites show efficient and very specialized techniques for transforming semi-precious stones into beads. At Chanhu Daro we witness the application of standardized techniques for the production of large quantities of valuable beads of rare, high quality transparent carnelian. In contrast, in the Moneer site different techniques were used, on a much limited scale for the production of smaller beads with a wide range of raw materials. In another paper Kenoyer et al. (in press) have hypothesized, on the basis of preliminary comparisons with ethnoarchaeological evidence from Khambhat, that these two production contexts could represent two different forms of organization, namely, centralized production controlled by possible state institutions or important merchants connected with elites, *versus* a more flexible independent production. Only the extension of research to other Harappan bead-making areas will help a proper testing of this idea.

STEATITE AND STEATITE BASED CRAFTS

> Steatite is a natural ceramic material. Instead of going through the laborious process of mixing clay throwing on wheel, and finishing, functional articles such as cups, bowls, plates and spoons can be carved directly in soapstone and then fired. This is done in India today. ... (Ritchie 1973: 48)

The term 'steatite' or 'soapstone' in archaeology of the subcontinent indicates various types of soft rocks which appear to be rather common both in the metamorphic belt of Baluchistan, the Aravallis and the Deccan plateau. Apparently, the commercial label may be applied to rocks containing talc (magnesium silicate) and other minerals, pyrophillite (a rarer aluminum silicate, never reported from prehistory of the subcontinent) and sometimes rocks of chlorite group (aluminum magnesium iron silicates).

It is difficult to overestimate the role of this rock and minerals (particularly talc) and their geographical distribution in the development of Harappan crafts. Harappan craftsmen were able to make steatite ornaments by complex manufacturing techniques including carving, glazing, painting, powdering, mixing the powder into an artificial paste and firing. It is well known that talc stands high temperatures without much chemical change, and undergoes the first transformations somewhere around 1000 °C, to change into enstatite and cristobalite as the temperature approaches 1200 °C. According to Ritchie (1973) the hardness of steatite may be raised by baking in an electric kiln from 1 to 5.5 to 6.5 on Moh's scale, and according to other scholars even to 7 (Hegde et al. 1982: 242; see also Vidale 1987c: 113). As a matter of fact, the properties of talc as a very efficient natural refractory have been universally appreciated in different times and different cultures (for example, Tite and Bimson 1989; Wilson 1973).

The earliest bead workshop we know for the prehistory of the subcontinent is a disc-bead manufacturing area excavated at Mehrgarh and dating to the fifth millennium BC (Jarrige 1981; Vidale 1993). At this site, steatite beads were manufactured besides shell discs, and the two types were probably strung together in contrasting patterns. A preliminary set of XRD analysis of samples identified this rock as composed of talc and calcite. The results are being currently compared with other XRD analysis of ethnographic 'steatite' and soapstones from Pakistan and archaeological samples form Mohenjo Daro (Vidale: personal communication), which have been variously identified as pure talc and talc with quartz or dolomite. This stage of mineralogical identification is needed before finer analytical techniques are applied. The mineralogical variability of these rocks in Pakistan and India is probably very high and it will take a lot of work before mineralogical or chemical groups could be defined and the source areas of specific rocks singled out.

The manufacturing sequence of talc disc beads at Mehrgarh included the shaping of rod like blanks having polygonal sections, slicing of these rods into polygonal blanks, and their bi-polar perforation with chert drills made of bladelets. Then, the perforated discs were probably strung on a fiber and ground in series into fine grained abrasive stones. Vidale has reconstructed the various stages of the manufacturing sequence by microscopic observation of the manufacturing traces, experimental replicas and scanning electron microscopic (SEM) observation of both archaeological and experimental samples (1993).

Any talc-cutting or grinding operation produces large amounts of a white shiny powder (Vidale and Shar 1990). Perhaps this powder became in time the base material of a totally new technology. According to the 'classic' excavation reports of the 1930s many 'steatite' ornaments of the Indus tradition were made through a ceramic process employing talc powder as base material (see Vidale 1987c for a review). In particular, Mackay (1937: 10-12; 1943: 212-13) hypothesized that some 'artificial' steatite 'paste' was the base material for production of Harappan microbeads. This suggestion was confirmed by Hegde and his colleagues (Hegde et al. 1982), when they analysed some microbeads found in the so called pot-hoard found below the floor of a circular Harappan house at Zekhda in Gujarat. Chemical analysis showed that the beads were made of silica and magnesia, with traces of alumina and iron oxide. Analysed with X-ray diffraction (XRD), the beads turned out to be composed of cristobalite, the high temperature modification of quartz (stable from 1470 to about 1700 °C and enstatite (anhydrous magnesium silicate). Both cristobalite and enstatite are known as transformation products of talc affected by pyrotechnological treatment (Hegde 1983:70). Micro-morphological analysis of manufacturing traces at the optical microscope showed cutting marks and spiral oriented traces which suggested a ceramic manufacturing process through extrusion. The conclusion of Hegde and his colleagues is that the base material for the microbeads was powdered steatite treated in plastic form from a special extruding device and then fired. Aluminium and iron, according to the reconstruction, were present in the beads as natural components of some kind of a not well defined 'talcose steatite' from Aravalli belt, and not because clays were purposefully added to the mixture. However, it should be noted that, in the samples of talcose rocks from Harappa, Mohenjo Daro and Mehrgarh, Vidale was unable to observe aluminum with EDS. There is a strong possibility that the alumina-iron components are actually due to addition of a fairly low percentage of clay material to the talc powder. The presence of enstatite and cristobalite seems to be further confirmed by preliminary research by D. Straham on a *parure* of microbeads found in the graveyard of Harappa (Straham: personal communication).

Less controversial are the manufacturing techniques of Harappan disc beads, the most distinctive and ubiquitous artefacts of the Integration Era. Basing himself upon the discovery at Chanhu Daro of a concentration of thin, perforated plates of dark steatite, Mackay thought that the manufacturing sequence had to include the shaping of the sheets, perforation, firing/hardening and then rounding (1937: 13). Vidale has observed a square perforated blank whitened by firing that would partially support his reconstruction (Vidale 1987a; Pl. IVc). Moreover, in at least two areas of Mohenjo Daro we found perforated blanks, square in section, which could represent unfinished disc-beads, square in shape (Vidale 1987). Therefore, it is possible that disc-beads were manufactured by shaping long cylindrical blanks (perhaps) perforating the blanks, and finally separating the thin disks with a very fine copper-bronze saw. Disc-beads were then fired at a relatively high temperature, because preliminary XRD analyses of samples from Harappa and Mohenjo Daro show the presence of enstatite and cristobalite (Vidale: personal observation).

Another type of beads very common in Harappan and Early Harappan contexts are the so-called 'paste' beads. They resemble disc-beads in their colour and surface features, but they are thicker, with regular short cylindrical body and an equally even, cylindrical hole. They often show along the edges coarse cutting marks suggesting that these beads too were somehow carelessly sawn out of long cylindrical blanks (see Vidale 1989a). In 1992, we began to study with SEM-EDS some white thick cylindrical beads from Harappan sites and other contemporaneous contexts. Some beads from Harappa would appear to be covered with a glaze (Vandiver and Vidale: personal observation), and where the glaze had been bleached out, it was possible to observe the core of the bead. It appeared to be composed of a chaotic body of broken sheet-like particles. Anyhow, as natural talc has a rather chaotic 'cardhouse' sheet structure, it is not immediately easy to differentiate solid stone beads from artificial ceramic mixture. Chemically, the core showed mainly peaks of silicon and magnesium, indicating talc. Additional XRD analyses, including the use of a Gandolfi camera, are being currently run by Vandiver and Vidale to test the hypothesis that these beads were actually made with a ceramic process. The glaze shows the presence of aluminum, calcium, potassium and iron.

This technology represents a very promising line of inquiry. Steatite and, in general, talcose rocks would have been available to the Harappans in a wide range of geological contexts, from the Baluchistan belt to the Aravali and various areas in the north of the Deccan plateau. The procurement of steatite would have depended upon medium-long distance trade routes. Judging from the amazing amounts of steatite and steatite-related ornaments unearthed at any Harappan site, this trade must have been massive. Harappans could have used high quality talc rocks for making sophisticated goods such as seals and glazed beads and might have recycled the powder for mass-producing large amounts of beads and microbeads found in the cities and in the graveyards.

SHELL WORKING

Shell working is the industry for which we have the clearest picture of urban segregation and about the sequential stages of manufacture of various types of objects. The study of shell, which is one of the most durable materials found in the archaeological context has helped us to reconstruct the trade network within the Indus Valley and adjoining regions. Some shell species have a very isolated or limited distribution along specific coastal regions and by determining the ancient source areas of these species, we have been able to gain a new perspective on the trade networks and exploitation of marine resources by prehistoric coastal population (Kenoyer 1983, 1984c, 1985; Bhan and Kenoyer 1984; Bhan 1991).

Although many different species of marine and fresh water mollusca have been reported from most of the major Harappan sites, the shell of only a few species: *Turbinella pyrum, Chicoreus ramosus, Fasciolaria trapezium, Lambis truncata. Tivela damaoides,* etc, were actually used for the manufacture of shell objects such as bangles, inlays, ladles, rings, beads, figurines, etc. (natural shell that have been simply perforated for use as ornaments, e.g. dentallium shell are not included in the present discussion).

Kenoyer's study on the shell industry of Indus Civilization has indicated that three areas were being exploited for the procurement of raw material (1983). *Turbinella pyrum* and various other secondary species were being obtained from the western coast (Karachi and Makran region), while *Chocoreus ramosus* and *Fasciolaria trapezium* were obtained from the eastern coast (Gulf of Kachchh and Gulf of Khambhat). *Lambis truncata* and *Fasciolaria trapezium* could have been obtained form the coast of Oman. On the basis of the distribution of different species originating from these distinct source areas and the nature of shell manufacturing at specific Harappan sites, Kenoyer (1983) postulated a complex hierarchy of interaction spheres and systems within the Greater Indus Valley region.

Shell industry of the Harappan period also reflects the stratification in the trade of raw material and the movement of finished objects. At Mohenjo Daro, Chanhu Daro, Harappa, Nagwada and Lothal we see a wide variety of objects being primarily produced for the markets within the sites and the nearby sites. On the other hand small rural or coastal sites like Allahdino, Balakot and Nageshwar produced a limited range of artefacts. At Balakot the intensive production of *Tivela damaoides* bangles appears to have oriented towards a regional market along the western coast. At Allahdino, bangles appear to have been specifically for local inhabitants (Kenoyer 1983: 255). Nageshwar, however, seems to have been a specialized centre in the production of bangles and ladles primarily for regional and extra-regional markets (Bhan and Kenoyer 1984; Bhan 1991). In contrast to specialization between sites, the manufacturing technology was quite standardized. A specific technique for chipping and cutting shell was evident in all distinct workshops and even the width of copper/bronze saw blade was identical. A detailed study carried out by Kenoyer (1983) has indicated that the saw used for cutting shell had a long convex cutting edge, that was extremely thin, between 0.4 and 0.6 mm, and might have been bi-directionally denticulated. Several convex saws have been reported from excavations, but none of them fit the requirements indicated by the study of shell wasters. Although there was some regional variation in the widths of bangles, they were all incised with the 'V' chevron motifs and the tradition continued throughout the Integration Era.

The intensive surface survey followed by excavations at Nageshwar has revealed a segregation of the activity area: one such location that with assurance could be assigned to shell working and pottery making was near the north-western periphery of the site (Bhan 1991: Fig. B2). This area stands out for two types of craft indicators. The first type of indicator is provided by *T. Pyrum* during the preliminary chipping stage for perforating the tip of the apex of the gastropods and loosening of the internal septa (Bhan 1991: Pls. V and VI). The manufacturing waste of the subsequent stages in the bangle manufacture was not obtained from this area, thereby suggesting that the shell sawing location was different. Kenoyer (1984: 107) located a similar surface indicator at a low peripheral mound, several hundred metres north-east of the Moneer Area at Mohenjo Daro. Based on the ethnographic observation from shell manufacture in modern Bengal, Kenoyer is of the opinion that the operation was necessary to remove the body of the animal in order to clear the shell for further operation and usually the odorous task is carried out away from the habitation area. Later the same area seems to have been used by potters for pottery manufacture. The surface survey and subsequent excavation of the area revealed a pottery kiln and kiln wasters, over fired and deformed vessels and a pottery mould. A significant find of this area related to this craft was a terracotta anvil usually referred to as dabber in archaeological literature.

Another shell working location at Nageshwar was found associated with the manufacture of ladles and bangles from *C. ramosus*. It is situated on the south-west of the site (Bhan 1991: Fig. B1 and B2). A large number of *C. ramosus* wasters discarded during ladle manufacture and a number of sawn shell sections forming unworked blanks of the ladle were recovered (Bhan 1991: Pl. XIII). Besides, a large number of *C. ramsous* wasters related to bangle production—which could be easily identified by the presence of unperforated sawn apexes and anterior portion of shell of this species have also been found (Bhan 1991: Pls. XI-XII).

A dump consisting of 714 sawn anteriors, 430 outer margin of lips and 11 apex portions of *T. pyrum* were located in G9 square (Bhan 1991: Figs. B1 and B2) occupying an area of 1.36 x 1 m. Kenoyer, who has the experience of working at Nageshwar (Bhan and Kenoyer 1984) as well as at Mohenjo Daro (1984) is of the opinion that the shell found in this square are much more than those reported from the entire site of Mohenjo Daro. This is a very significant observation and pointing towards the intensity of shell manufacturing being carried out at this small rural Harappan site. These shell fragments are typical wasters that are produced during the manufacture of bangles. This primary dump appears to be purposefully and carefully saved by the shell craftsmen to be reused to produce beads, rings or inlay. The absence of any inlay ring or bead wasters in this area suggested that this area was a bangle manufacturing location. The subsequent excavation in the near by area revealed another neatly kept heap of 413 columella of *T. pyrum* on a rammed floor and it further substantiated the above observation.

In studying the relative frequency of the finished and unfinished objects to the manufacturing waste obtained during surface survey and excavation at Nageshwar, we see a pattern of immense quantity of waste and relatively a small number of objects, thereby suggesting that the site was primarily a manufacturing centre specialized in the production of bangles, ladles and supply of raw material for trade to regional and extra-regional markets. However, at Nageshwar, where intensive shell working was being carried out, it is conceivable that a group of divers-collectors may have been engaged at least part-time supplying raw material to the workshop.

The most common shell object at most of the major Harappan sites is represented by shell bangles. These bangles were produced almost exclusively from *T. pyrum*, using a variety of specialized and unspecialized tools. The manufacturing sequence begins with the preparation of shell for sawing by hollowing out the interior and breaking the thick columella (Fig. 2). A stone or metal hammer was used to perforate the apex and metal pick was used to break the internal septa. This stage of manufacture leaves distinct indicators in the form of the tip of the apex and chipped fragments of septa (Bhan 1991: Pls. V and VI). The hollowed shell was then sawn diagonally to avoid aperture and remove anterior. This stage of bangle production also leaves archaeologically recognizable indicators (Bhan 1991: Pls. VII and VIII). The remaining hollow spire was sawn diagonally into rough circlets of desired width. These circlets thus produced were ground on the interior using cylindrical pieces of sandstone or some other type of abrasive tool, while the exterior was probably ground on a flat sandstone slab (Fig. 3). Most of the finished bangels were perhaps incised with a motif in the form of a chevron 'V'.

In addition to *T. pyrum*, two more species: *C. ramsous* and occasionally *Puglina buchephala* were used for manufacturing bangles (Kenoyer 1984). In the preparation of *C. ramosus*, first spine were sawn and remnant parts of spine on the shell were ground to produce a smooth exterior surface for sawing the body of the shell. Then instead of hollowing out the shell from the apex, the septa and hollow columella were broken by chipping from the large orifice of the shell. Once it was hollowed out the shell was sawn like *T. pyrum*, to produce rough circlets, which were further processed as described above for *T. pyrum*. The bangle manufacture from *C. ramosus* also leave very recognizable wasters in the form of unperforated apexes and columella portions (Bhan 1991: Pls. XI and XII). Although the difference in the procedure did not affect the finished product, it does exemplify the ingenuity and technical skill of the Harappan craftsmen.

Differences in shell morphology, however, do affect the form of the finished bangles,

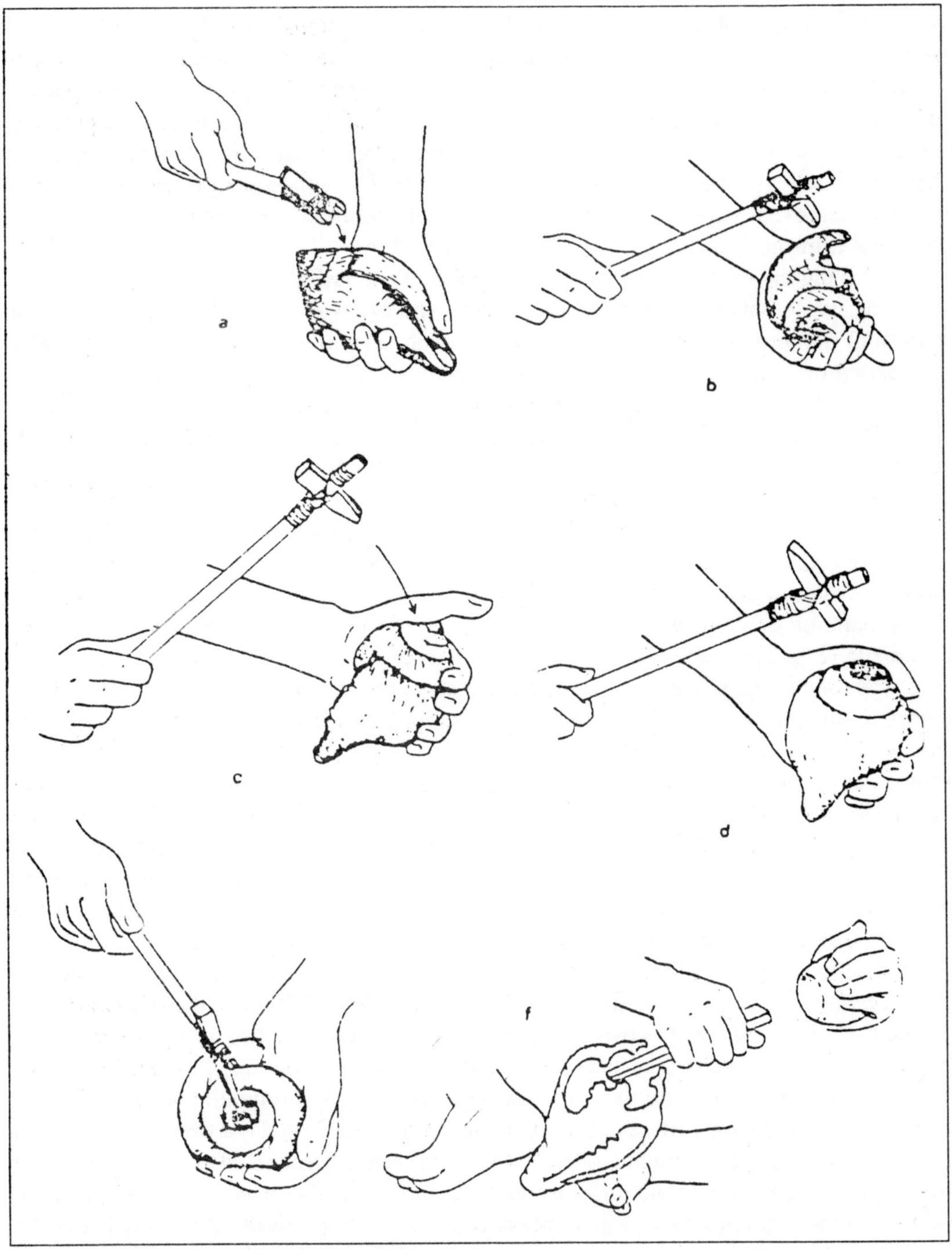

Fig. 2. Bangle Manufacture with *Turbinella pyrum*. Preliminary chipping and removal of internal columella (a to f), after Kenoyer 1983, Fig. 3-6.

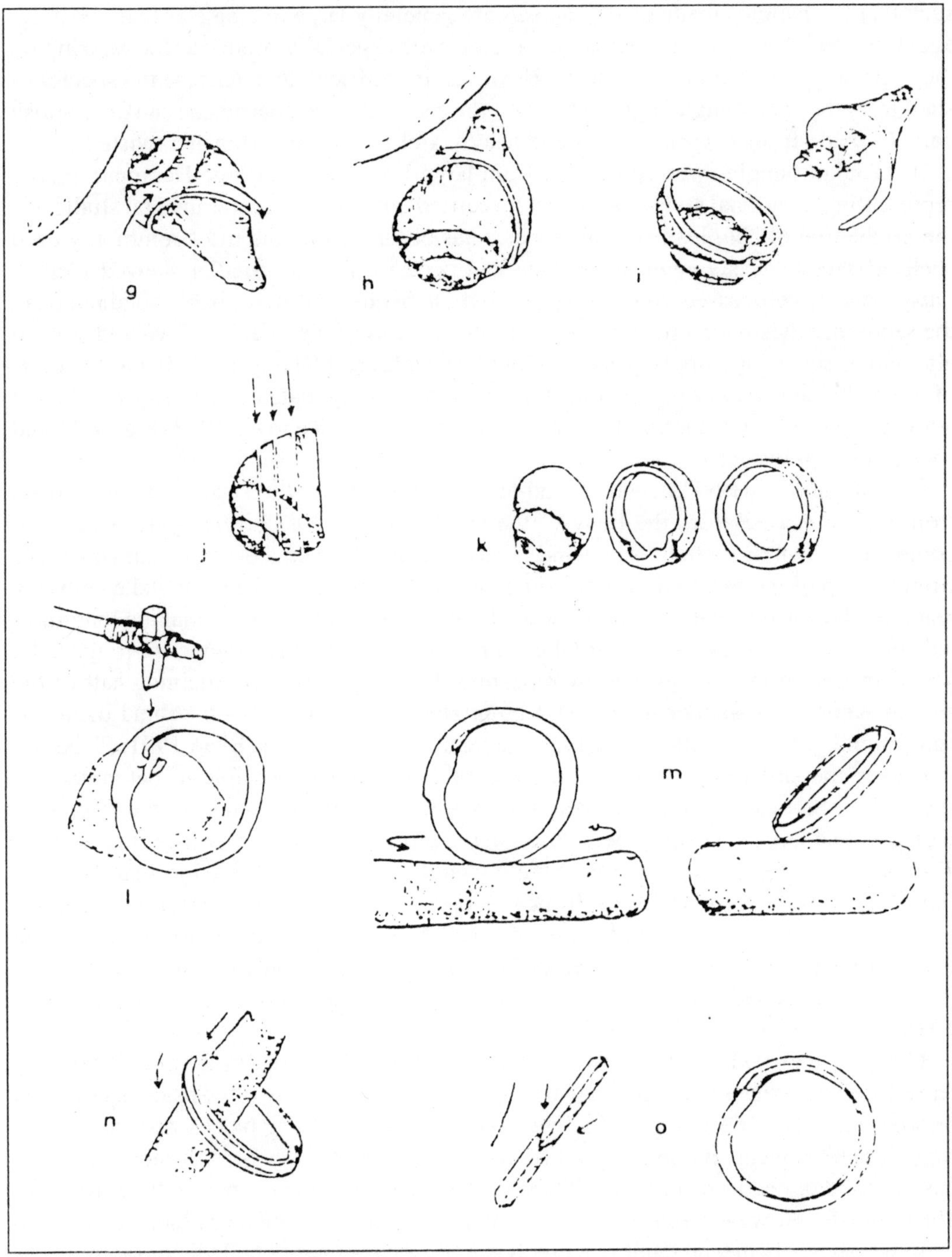

Fig. 3. Bangle Manufacture with *Turbinella pyrum.* Sawing shell circlet (g to k), finishing shell blank (i to n), and final incising (o), after Kenoyer 1983, Fig. 3-6.

such that the bangles made of *C. ramosus* are generally large in diameter than the average *T. pyrum*. It is possible that large bangles were especially produced for wearing on the upper arms or as ankle ornaments. However, it is difficult to determine the species of shell from the shell bangle fragments, but if the shell suture is present one can distinguish bangles made from *T. pyrum* (thick and heavy) and *C. ramosus* (thin and twisted).

At Balakot bangles were produced from large bivalves during the Harappan phase, representing a regional style. Kenoyer who carried out extensive experimental studies on the production of bangles from this species has observed that the most commonly used shell at Balakot was *Trivial damaoides*, but occasionally the smaller skewed *Calista impar* was also processed. According to him these bivalves were probably obtained from the sandy beaches on the nearby coast and the process of manufacture involved several alternating stages of chipping and grinding (see Dales and Kenoyer 1977). On the basis of a detailed analysis of the manufacturing waste and replicate experiments conducted ten basic stages of production have been recognized (see Kenoyer 1983: Fig. 3-21 and for detailed discussion).

One of the distinctive utensils found at Harappan sites is the large shell ladle made from *C. ramosus*. Before the body of the shell could be cut, all the spines were first completely sawn or partially sawn and later chipped off. Then a diagonal cut was made from the top of the main whorl extending around both sides of the shell and eventually reaching the narrow anterior end of the shell. A handle was formed by making longitudinal cuts from the anterior tip toward the main body whorl. In this manner, the rough ladle was detached from the shell and by repeating the process on the remaining half of the shell a second but smaller ladle could be produced (Fig. 4), leaving behind the apex, spine along with columella as a distinctive manufacturing waste (Bhan 1991: Pl. XIII).

Due to the small size of most inlay pieces, it is often impossible to determine the species of shell used to make a particular piece, but a study of shell waste fragments indicates that large gastropods were used in the production of inlay. Waste fragments of *T. pyrum* and *C. ramosus* left from bangle manufacture were recycled to make various flat designs. Kenoyer (1984: Fig. 9) has reported that *Fasciloaria tapezium* may have been used solely for the manufacture of inlay. Numerous examples have been found from Mohenjo Daro, and more recently from Bagasra, where only the thick body whorl were sawn, chiselled, and drilled to produce various geometric shapes (Kenoyer 1984: 104).

The craftsmen of Indus Civilization were extremely skilled at working shell and they chose different species to produce a wide range of objects that were often made in terracotta or other material. These objects include cone, cylinders gaming pieces, spheres, 'wavy rings', 'cap', toy cart frames, animal figurines and liberation vessels. Kenoyer has discussed the manufacturing process of these objects and need not be repeated here (Kenoyer 1984: 104-5). However, Kenoyer recovered a very important shell artefact, at Mohenjo Daro which needs special mention here. It is a broken fragment of a ladle or sawn waster that fits in the palm of a hand and has numerous shallow depressions in the concave portion of this piece. He assumes that it must have been used by bead drillers as backing

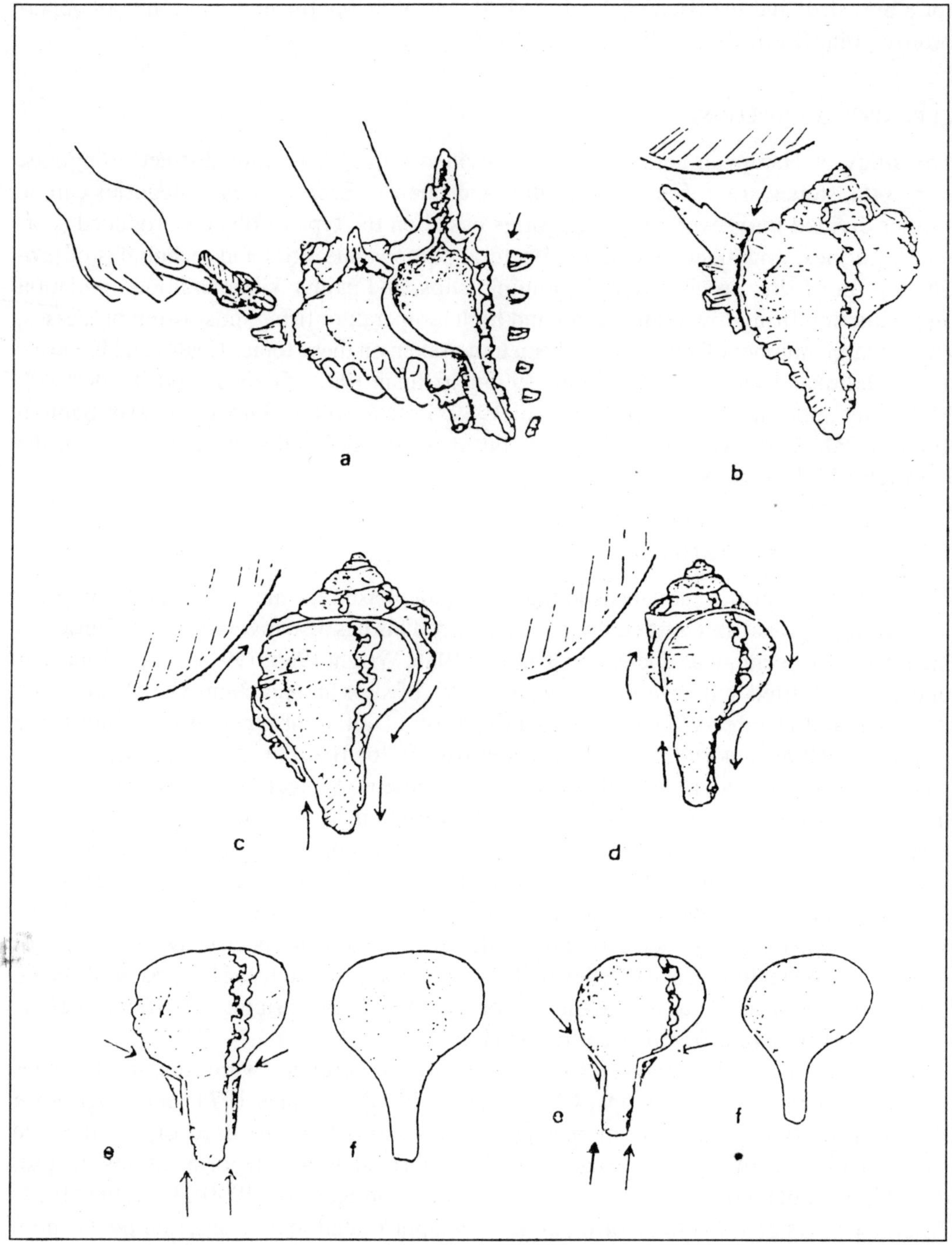

Fig. 4. Ladle Manufacture with *Chicoreus ramosus* (after Kenoyer 1983, Fig. 3-7).

for a bow drill and the back of the drill shaft was probably tipped by a stone or copper/bronze point (Kenoyer 1983: 193, Fig. 3-13).

CERAMIC TECHNOLOGY

The study of Harappan ceramics can be divided into at least four distinct groupings; terracotta, stoneware, refractory ceramics and faience. Each of these categories can be further divided into several sub-categories based on the type of objects produced (pottery, figurines, ornaments, tools, architectural components, etc.) and techniques of production (pre-firing process, temper, joining, slips, and paints, kiln condition, oxidation and reduction firing low temperature and high temperature firing, post firing processes, etc.). A large number of studies have been undertaken on these topics (Dales and Kenoyer 1986; Halim and Vidale 1984; Jenkins 1995; Krishnan 1992; Krishnan and Hegde 1987; McCarthy and Vanidver 1990; Panjwani 1989; Praccia 1985; Sinopoli 1991b; Santoni 1989; Vidale 1990; Wright 1989, 1991) but it is possible to discuss only a few of the highlights in the context of this article.

Terracotta Pottery Production

One of the most critical advances in the Harappan phase ceramic studies is the progress in defining regional styles of ceramic production. This has also involved the definition of manufacturing techniques (Dales and Kenoyer 1986; Wright 1989, 1991), material analysis of clays, both fired and unfired (Panjwani 1989), of slips and pigments (Krishnan 1992; Krishnan and Hegde 1987) and the identification of different types of kilns and firing techniques (Pracchia 1985; Dales and Kenoyer 1986; Bhan et al. 1991). Many more studies currently underway will make the statement 'typical Harappan ceramics' a meaningless phrase, as there is considerable variation in the production at the major urban centres as well as that being produced at regional centres and rural sites. Eventually, when the types of ceramics being produced at specific site are defined more precisely it will be possible to undertake studies on intra-regional trade of ceramics through the sourcing of specific clays and through the identification of site specific uses of temper or manufacturing techniques. At the level of a single urban site such as Harappa or Mohenjo Daro it will be possible to define the movement of ceramics originating from a specific kiln or workshop to different areas of the city.

Where as distinctive categories of kilns for firing ceramics were identified at sites such as Mohenjo Daro, Harappa, Chanhu Daro, Balakot (Dales 1974) and Nageshwar (Bhan et al. 1991), only the more recent excavations have focused on the detailed stratigraphic accumulations of manufacturing debris and the categories of vessels produced in a single workshop (Pracchia 1985; Dales and Kenoyer 1990). Pracchia (1985) reports a series of six pottery firing kilns with a perforated grate supported by a central pillar from the excavation of Lal Shah (*c.* third quarter of the third millennium BC). On the basis of stratigraphical analysis, Pracchia suggested that the kilns were not used simultaneously, and probably used seasonally for a period of 10-15 years.

At Mohenjo Daro, in the late levels there is evidence for potters setting up workshop in various habitation areas (Pracchia et al. 1985), indicating changing activity patterns in different chronological phases. Similar patterns were reported from Mound F at Harappa (Vats 1940), but more recently, the excavations of a series of kilns on the north-western corner of Mound E have revealed the presence of pottery workshops that may indicate long term hereditary craft activities in a segregated area of the city (Dales and Kenoyer 1990). This suggests that while some ceramic production may have shifted to different areas of the city, other workshops remained in the same locality for hundreds of years.

In terms of ceramic production sequence, current studies at the type site of Harappa (Wright 1991: personal communication) along with experimental reconstruction and analytical studies are beginning to shed new light on the complexity of manufacturing techniques which with eventually allow for the identification and differentiation of workshops within larger urban centres. Changes in production stages between Early Harappan and Harappan Phase as well as during the course of the Harappan Phase itself are critical for a more complete documentation of the transformation of the Indus Valley ceramics over a passage of time.

One of the most important studies of Harappan ceramics is seen in the study of stoneware bangle production and the use of high temperature reduction firing techniques.

Stoneware Bangle Manufacture

Harappan stoneware bangles are high-quality ceramic ornaments that are unparalleled in ancient as well as modern world. While stoneware vessels have been found in the ancient Near East (see Schneider 1989), no stoneware bangles were made outside the Harappan cities. Harappan bangles of good quality although unglazed, fully meet the standards of current definition for this category of ceramics. Possibly, this industry was developed before the Harappan Phase, as Vidale observed many partially sintered grayish bangles on the surface of Juderjo Daro, and Thomas (1986) describes similar bangles from the site of Lewan that dates to Regionalization Era. Kenoyer also noticed thin, heavily reduced ceramic bangles in the Early Harappan levels at Harappa. He also found in Mound E a small kiln dateable to Period II where small ceramic objects and possibly bangles could have been fired in reducing conditions (Kenoyer 1991a and b).

It should be remarked that, so far, Harappan stoneware bangles were positively reported from Mohenjo Daro and Harappa. These ornaments therefore seem to be exclusively associated with the elites of the urban centres of the Harappan world. At Mohenjo Daro, the area where stoneware bangles were fired (and most probably also formed) were identified on surface by Aachen-IsMEO surface survey programme. The results of these studies on this peculiar Harappan craft have been reported in several papers (Halim and Vidale 1984, 1987a, 1989, 1990a; Blackman and Vidale 1993) and thus will not be described at length.

About 100 ceramic samples connected with this industry were chemically analysed by Blackman and Vidale (1993) by Neutron Activation. These samples include fragmentary stoneware bangles, kiln fragments and pieces of firing containers from Mohenjo Daro, and more clay and bangle samples from Harappa. This research showed that clay from Mohenjo Daro and Harappa are relatively easy to distinguish in terms of chemical composition. A possible reason for this difference is that the Indus clays at Mohenjo Daro, and to Sindh in general, would show major concentration of elements deposited in the forms of soluble salts, due to the higher rate of cumulative evaporation of river waters along its course (C. Balista: personal communication).

Although, so far, no workshop area has been identified at Harappa, we establish that the stoneware bangles were manufactured with local clays both at Harappa and Mohenjo Daro. The composition of a single bangle does not fit either with the chemical groups of Harappa and Mohenjo Daro, and must have come from another source at a still unidentified site. It would be interesting to analyse bangles from other major sites such as Ganeriwala, Kalibangan, Rakhigarhi and Dholavira. Curiously, the majority of stoneware bangles found at Harappa appear to have been made at Mohenjo Daro, where as no bangle with the Ravi river clays distinctive of Harappa has been found at Mohenjo Daro. The relationship between the two sites is therefore asymmetrical, and, given the fact that both cities had their stoneware workshops, it is difficult to explain this pattern of distribution in terms of trade.

Although specimens available for study show a certain degree of variation, these bangles are generally made with highly refined clays. After firing, the greatest temper inclusion does not exceed 20 microns in many cases. Comparison with latter porcelain technologies could suggest that such a fineness was obtained with complex and long techniques of decantation, but most probably in the large alluvial plains of the Indus Basin it was relatively easy and inexpensive to select clay fractions which could be kept in suspension within tanks, jars or simply in holes dug in the ground. The experiments conducted by Kenoyer and a local potter (Mohammad Nawaz) have been able to replicate the types of fine clay used in stoneware bangle production using decantation (Kenoyer 1994c).

Most probably, stoneware bangles were formed by throwing on the wheel clay cylinders and trimming them in series with sharp pointed tools which left on their surface distinctive, very fine parallel marks. This reconstruction is supported by Xeroradiographies of some bangles and experimental replicas of the forming process carried out by a professional potter in collaboration with Vidale. This technique would explain the extremely regular fashion of the bangles, the asymmetry of their section (egg-shaped to triangular) as well as their high degree of dimensional standardization. We disagree with Schneider's (1984) suggestion that these objects were formed with mouds.

The manufacturing operation performed in the workshop identified at Mohenjo Daro included also the fabrication of small firing containers or saggers in which 2 or 3 bangles were inserted, or larger saggers in which the smaller ones with the bangles were piled, of different types of pottery lids, and the production of thousands of coarse terracotta rings which were used for separating the bottom of large saggers from the kiln's floor (Fig. 5) (Halim and Vidale 1984; Vidale 1987). A limited surface clearing of a kiln area at Mohenjo Daro (Pracchia and Vidale 1993) suggests that the kilns were large rectangular structures,

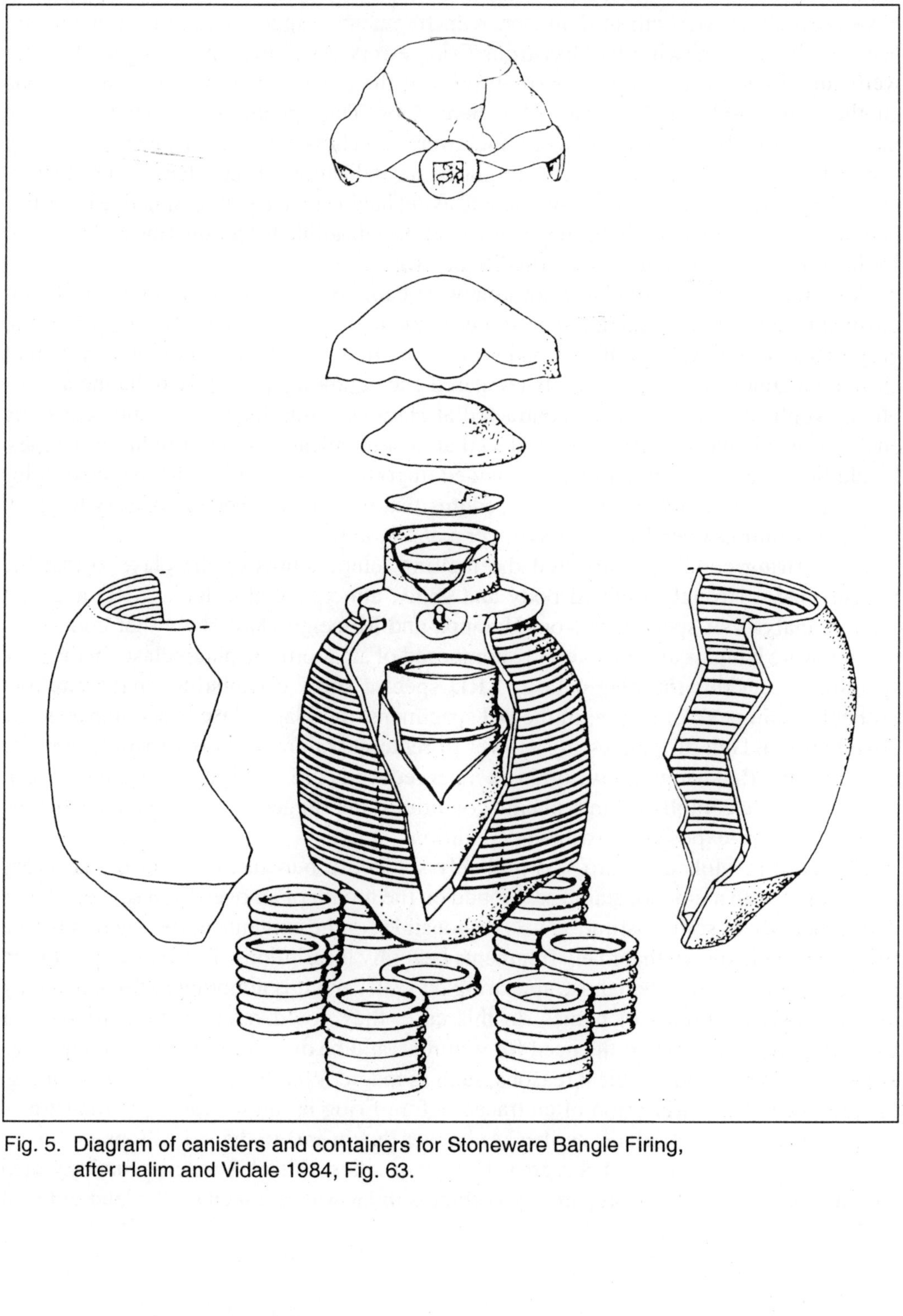

Fig. 5. Diagram of canisters and containers for Stoneware Bangle Firing, after Halim and Vidale 1984, Fig. 63.

about 3 x 1.5 m, with thick, chaff-tempered suspended grid. The grid holes appear to have been about 8-10 cm in diameter. Kiln fragments, saggers and other remains are heavily vitrified, showing the disastrous firing errors. As in the small saggers, bangles were superimposed in couples or small piles of three. During firing they stuck to one another, and later had to be separated by percussion. This operation left on the surface of the bangles rough breakage surfaces which were somehow concealed by coarse grinding and polishing. We believe that this might be an indication of an intensive production cycle that salvaged whatever was possible to avoid having to make the distinctive inscribed bangles a second time. Perhaps they were meeting a deadline for production and the need for bangles was more crucial than quality control.

Two major categories of Harappan stoneware bangles have been identified, one distinguished by a bright red, and another, more frequent at Mohenjo Daro, having pinkish to grey-black colour. At least this second group was fired within a very complex system of closed containers coated with chaff-tempered clay, granting a strongly reducing atmosphere. Replicative experiments conducted at Harappa using local clays and goat dung enclosed inside the saggers have produced almost identical colours of reduced bangles. In addition, these experiments have provided important new insights on the type of kilns that may been used and the firing procedures that would have been necessary to reach high temperatures over 1000 °C (Kenoyer a and b, in press).

These firing conditions lowered the melting temperatures of the clay, so that the bangles had a strongly sintered body and shiny, almost metallic look. XRD and thin section analysis of specimens from Harappa and Mohenjo Daro show that both types of stoneware bangles are substantially composed of an anorthitic plagioclase. In the grey specimens, besides the plagioclase, XRD spectra show cristobalite, magnetite and probably main peak of augite; in the red specimens, the plagioclase is accompanied by cristobalite and quartz (suggesting a lower firing temperature or shorter firing), hematite and diopside. Red bangles have often an inner reduced core, and this might suggest that, sintering was accomplished in reducing conditions, the saggers were opened, so that the bangles were re-exposed to oxidizing conditions.

This craft at Mohenjo Daro was probably subject to bureaucratic control, as a very fine sealing with a unicorn stamp seal found on the mouth of an over-fired sagger, shows that somebody or some institution was responsible for the contents of the saggers before firing. It is well known that many fragments bear tiny inscriptions. These inscriptions, on an average, are shorter than those appearing on seals, and it is tempting to think that they report names or initials of names. In this case, they could refer to the craftsmen or workshop, or to the owner; the need for writing could be due to administrative purposes as well as unknown ideological reasons, such as magic. Whatever the possible meaning, the presence of an inscription often traced before firing on these bangles demonstrates the presence and the work of 'scribes' (whoever they were) in the workshops.

After the abandonment of the great Harappan cities, this elaborate technology died with its social context, and apparently nothing similar was resumed by the later elites of the Early Historic cities.

FAIENCE TECHNOLOGY

By 2600 BC, like Egyptian and Mesopotamian, Indus Valley artisans also created a glassy or vitreous paste commonly referred as 'faience' (Vandiver 1982). It reached a high level of production and approached the quality of early glass (MacCarthy and Vandiver 1990; Kenoyer 1994a, 1994b). While many techniques were similar, each cultural region developed its own style of ornaments and technologies for producing them.

A wide variety of faience ornaments including beads, bangles and jewellry have been retrieved from the major ancient cities of Mohenjo Daro, Harappa, Chanhu Daro, Dholavira and Bagasra (Marshall 1931; Mackay 1938, 1943; Vats 1940; Dales and Kenoyer 1991; Sonawane et al. 1996). Recent excavations at Harappa have revealed the faience beads from the early levels (recent excavations have uncovered a settlement dating to 3300 BC), but the production of elaborate faience ornaments, figures and vessels are more prevalent during the Harappan phase (Dales and Kenoyer 1991; Kenoyer 1991).

The ancient artisans of the Indus Civilization appear to have almost exclusively utilized efflorescence, a technique wherein the colour of the glaze is strongly bonded with the underlying body. Recent studies show that efflorescence itself has variations and can be divided into two processes based on how quartz is prepared. In one process, the faience paste is made from powdered quartz combined with both flux and colourant. In the second process, the powdered quartz is partially melted with a colourant to produce *frit* and then reground to very fine powder. This fine glassy powder, already coloured, is mixed with additional flux to prepare faience paste. Adding fine ground quartz increases the volume, but also results in a reduction of colour homogeneity. Faience objects made by the first process tend to have larger quartz grains (50 to 100 microns) and on close examination a speckled colour distribution. Under low magnification (20X) its granular character is discernible in objects where the glaze is eroded or where a broken edge reveals the objects interior core. This paste produced small tokens as well as a wide variety of beads. A similar coarse grained faience was commonly made in Egypt and Mesopotamia (Kenoyer 1994a).

Most faience objects—bangles, tiny beads, miniature vessels and animal figurines—were produced using the second process, resulting in a homogenous, compact structure with a high percentage of glassy matrix. No other region of the ancient world is known to have produced this type of glassy faience referred as compact faience (McCarthy and Vandiver 1990). It is made of extremely fine evenly coloured glassy powder that has a high percentage of glass and fine grains of unmelted quartz, with grain size less than thirty microns (very few had particles larger than 50 microns). When quartz is ground to this size, the texture resembles talcum powder.

The discovery of white rock quartz and quartzite fragments at Harappa and more recently from Bagasra suggests that it may have been a major source for silica powder used in making faience objects. Other minerals found in Harappan faience included alumina, sodium and potassium, and since these are not found in large quantities in natural quartzite, they must have derived from the adhesive, flux or colorants that were mixed with the silica (McCarthy and Vandiver 1990). The sodium and potassium probably came from two types of flux that are still used for glazing and glass production in South Asia (Kenoyer 1994c). In the traditional glazed tile technology and glass production in South Asia, the primary flux for melting silica is an alkaline ash derived from the burning of desert plants generally referred to as camel-thorn [Urdu *sajji* or *khar*; *Haloxylon recurvum*; *H. multiflorum*, *Sal-sola foetida*, *Suaeda fructicosa* (Rye and Evans 1976)]. Experiments carried out by Kenoyer (1994c) with fine ground frit and *sajji* demonstrated that no additional adhesive or gums are necessary for forming difficult objects such as bangles or tiny vessels. Another type of flux used in glazing is naturally occurring sodium carbonate/bicarbonate, commonly referred as natron (Urdu *reh*). Traces of calcium in some Harappan faience may be due to calcinated bone or calcium phosphate, also a flux and probably a component of white faience, since *sajji* or *khar* creates a greenish-grey glaze.

Copper, iron or manganese are also found in minute traces in Harappan faience and although they help to lower the fusion point of silica, their primary function appears to have been for colour. Most faience of the ancient world, including the Indus cities, was coloured with copper minerals to produce blue-green glazes. However, the Harappans developed special techniques to produce glazes of pure white (from calcium), deep azure (from copper minerals), black (from manganese), yellow, brown and red-brown (from iron minerals) and brilliant red (colourant unknown). These glazes were usually used with one or more colours and reflect an intimate knowledge of the temperatures needed to melt silica as well as the atmosphere (oxidizing or reducing) for obtaining specific colours (Kenoyer 1994c).

One of the important questions about faience technology is the type of adhesive used to hold the ground quartz together during forming process. In recent experiments conducted by him Kenoyer (1994c) tried numerous adhesives which included honey, mustard oil, clay, gum of *shisham* tree (*Dalbergia latifolia*) and gum tragacanth. *Shisham* gum proved to be one of the best adhesives since it did not shrink. He is of the opinion that it is possible that the Harappans used no adhesives at all because of the extremely fine powder that was used and when combined with water and the soapy alkaline mixture of *sajji* and natron, the fine quartz was malleable enough to from delicate shapes. Even during drying, the paste remained quite strong and it is possible to scrape and incise the surface with intricate designs.

The technique of making compact faience continued after the Indus Civilization ended and set the foundation for the development of glass technology of later Early Historic period (*c.* 600 BC). The famous *meena-kari*, enamel on gold and silver, which is still practiced throughout South Asia, may also have roots in the early experiments with glazed faience inlay in gold.

REFRACTORY CERAMICS

Although not much work has been undertaken on the refractory ceramics produced by the Harappans, it is clear that this category of ceramics was crucial to technologies such as steatite firing, stoneware bangle production, faience production and metallurgy

(Kenoyer and Miller, in press; Miller 1994). Refractory clays appears to have been produced by the inclusion of chaff, grog and sand tempers. Cooking vessels at many sites have refractory slips on the exterior to protect the vessels from thermal shock. Saggers for stoneware firing were coated with a thick layer of chaff tempered clay to keep the interior saggers from melting under the intense heat of the kilns. Crucibles to melt frit for faience making, for firing steatite, and also for melting of copper and bronze were made from special clays and selected vegetable and mineral tempers. Refractory ceramic vessels are closely associated with primary production areas and are important for understanding the organization of these technologies and their role in the socio-economic structure of Indus cities. This field of research is extremely important because it is connected to some of the most important technologies that were controlled and exploited by elite communities of the urban centres.

HARAPPAN METALLURGY

The Harappans had a well developed and highly specialized metal technology, but oddly enough it is one of the least studied craft traditions. Although we have numerous metal objects, ranging from gold and silver to copper and bronze, few objects have been subjected to metallurgical or compositional analysis (Agrawal 1971; Piggott et al. 1989; see Kenoyer and Miller, in press, for a comprehensive summary). Few analyses have been done on the ores, slags, ingots from Indus sites. The study of ores from a variety of possible sources available to the Indus metalsmiths have also been neglected. However, a few studies on the smelting procedures and the source of silver, lead and copper of Rajasthan have been undertaken though the dates of the earliest use of these mines is uncertain (Agrawala 1984a; Craddock et al. 1989; Hegde and Ericson 1985; Mehta 1998; Bhan et al., forthcoming).

The earliest evidence of metal in the form of copper ornaments comes from Neolithic levels (Period IB), *c.* 6000 BC (Jarrige 1983, 1985). How this technology evolved is still unclear, since no evidence for processing of copper metal has been found from this site. Nevertheless, by the fourth and third millennium the mining and smelting of ores was being carried out at many locations throughout Baluchistan and Afghanistan (Dales and Flam 1969; Fairservis 1952; Jarrige and Toss 1981; Stech and Pigott 1986). The use of crucible for melting copper comes from Period III, *c.* 4000-3000 BC at Mehrgarh (Jarrige 1985). The evidence from Mehrgarh and other early sites clearly demonstrate that pyrotechnological innovations of Neolithic and Chalcolithic periods set the technological background for the complex metallurgical tradition of the Harappan phase (Jarrige 1985; Jarrige and Lechevallier 1979). Besides, the sites such as Nausharo (Jarrige 1990), Balakot (Dales 1979), Gazi Shah (Flam 1993), Rehmandheri (Durrani 1988) and Kalibangan (Agrawala 1984a; Lal and Thapar 1967) have shown the evidence of the use of copper in a period prior to the Harappan phase, along with corresponding changes in other technologies. Another important data which however still remains to be understood is the Ganeshwar-Jodhpura culture of Rajasthan (Agrawala 1984a). Agrawala reported one thousand objects from unknown or surface finds and later excavations by Kumar (1986) have not been able to clear up the question of its chronological affinities (Kenoyer and Miller, in press). The copper objects from Ganeshwar and northern Aravalli are extremely important for a complete understanding of the copper metallurgy.

METAL ORES

A. Copper

After very careful analysis of the analytical data Kenoyer and Miller (in press) have proposed three possible major regions that could have supplied the copper ore or processed metal to the smiths of the Indus Valley. They suggested that the first region could have been the combined area of Baluchistan and Afghanistan, to the west of Indus, extending from coastal Makran to the highland Badakshan. In this region numerous copper working areas have been reported (Dales and Flam 1969; Fairservis 1952) along with cultural material of Helmand tradition, *c.* 2600-2500 BC (Shaffer 1991). The copper smelting activity, therefore, was contemporaneous with Early Harappan or the Harappan phase of the Indus tradition. The most pressing question regarding copper smelting sites in Baluchistan and southern Afghanistan (often referred to as Gardan-i-Reg), concerns the specific elemental composition of metal smelted from different ores (Kenoyer and Miller in press). Each copper mining area has a slightly different range of trace elements. Copper and iron ores that are rich in arsenic are found in limited distribution in Baluchistan (Agrawal 1971; Ullah 1940) and the Iranian plateau (Pigott 1989), but it is not clear if these ores were being exploited continuously or only during specific chronological periods. Actual arsenic ores may have been traded to the smelting areas or even to the major cities of the Indus region for use in copper metallurgy (Kenoyer and Miller, in press).

The second region is to the east of the Indus and Ghaggar-Hakkra Valley, comprising the north-south oriented Aravalli mountain ranges of Rajasthan. Mughal (1980) reported many Harappan sites in the modern desert region of Cholistan, Pakistan, along the dry bed of Ghaggar-Hakkra river. Many of the sites Mughal reported have kilns that appear to him to have been used for 'firing pottery, clay objects, bricks and perhaps copper smelting' (Mughal 1980). Although this region is close to the copper source of Rajasthan, these sites cannot be classified as copper smelting sites in the absence of other indicators like ores, slag heaps and smelting furnaces (Kenoyer and Miller, in press).

Nevertheless, the low incidence of arsenic from the finished objects at Lothal and Rangpur could be taken as circumstantial evidence for the exploitation of the Aravali copper ores by Gujarat Harappans. However, Rao insists that arsenic-free Rangpur and Lothal copper comes from Oman, rather than from Rajasthan (Rao 1963, 1979, 1984). Omani copper ores are similar to those of the Aravalli region. Both these areas have little or no arsenic, but have cobalt, vanadium and chromium (Agrawal 1971: 152, Table 20; Berthoud and Cleuziou 1983). Besides, at this point there is no direct evidence for Harappan mines or smelting sites in the Aravalli copper resource areas even though these areas have been repeatedly explored by various scholars. The earliest well dated copper smelting slags comes from Ahar dated to the second millennium BC (Hegde and Ericson 1985). Although Hegde and Ericson assumed that the smelting furnaces they found in the Aravalis are from third millennium BC they have not been dated either by radiocarbon or associated artefacts (1985). If these sources were exploited by the Harappans, it is possible that Harappans themselves were not involved in mining and smelting, but such activities were undertaken by local communities of the Aravali region and the Ganeshwar culture, and Aharians may have been one of these groups (Agrawala 1984).

The third and fourth potential source suggested by Kenoyer and Miller (in Press) is the inland mountain range of modern Oman and eastern Iran, but so far there are no clear indications that the Indus metalsmiths used Iranian metal. Within the availability of at least three different major resource areas within easy reach, Kenoyer and Miller proposed that it is not unlikely that larger urban centres used copper from more than one source over 800 years of the Harappan era. However, only future systematic studies will provide the necessary data.

B. Tin

Relatively pure copper objects have been found at all Harappan sites, where copper objects have been analysed and comprise the largest percentage of objects. Tin-bronze comes second and arsenial bronze third, depending upon how one defines alloys (see Kenoyer and Miller [in press] for a very useful discussion). The major source of tin during the Harappan times, if tin was added as a separate metal to from the alloy, were probably derived from western and northern Afghanistan, near the ancient lapis lazuli mines (Kenoyer and Miller, in press). The most important Harappan phase site Shortugai is located in a strategic position near these resources having evidence of lapis lazuli and gold working, but it is not clear if the site was indeed trading in tin also (Frankfort 1989). Although small quantities of tin ore deposits are known from Hazaribagh, Ranchi, Gaya in Bihar, Banaskantha in Gujarat, Dharwar greenstones in Karnataka and Bhilwara in Rajasthan (Agrawal 1971), there is also no indication of old mines and it is likely that the stream tin might have been used for alloying (Ullah 1940)

C. Lead

Numerous lead objects have been found at Harappan sites and it is clear that unlike tin, lead was used as a separate metal. Lead may have been deliberately added to a copper object, as the addition of lead causes molten copper to flow more easily. The lead ore, cerrusite and galena have been reported form Nal in Baluchistan and Mohenjo Daro respectively. Besides, small masses of lead were found in the excavation at Chanhu Daro. The ores of lead (cerrusite and galena) are found in many regions of Baluchistan and Rajasthan (Ajmer) (Marshall 1931). Craddock et al. (1989) describe in detail lead, silver and zinc ores of the Aravallis.

D. Silver

Silver objects are not common at the Harappan sites. However, only two examples of silver have been analysed from Mohenjo Daro and they contain significant amounts of copper and lead (Ullah in Mackay 1938: 599). Although the source of silver is not known, on the basis of copper and lead traces Sana Ullah suggests that most of silver was extracted from argentiferous galena. Sir Edwin Pascoe (Marshall 1931) notes the numerous silver mines in Baluchistan and Afghanistan. Craddock et al. (1989) describes the silver deposits of Aravallis, but there is no evidence of its exploitation until after the Harappan period.

E. Gold

Gold ornaments or flakes of gold leaf have been reported from most of the sites. Like copper there has been much discussion on the possible origin of gold. Some scholars have preferred to consider the Kolar gold mines as a major source area. However, there is no conclusive evidence of trade between Indus and the Kolar gold producing areas of south India. The most obvious source of alluvial gold is in the upper reaches of the Indus Valley itself and the streams of northern Afghanistan (Marshall 1931). Indications of gold working have been found at Shortugai during the Harappan phase occupation. Significant quantities of gold are also found in the tributaries of Amu Dariya and the Kokcha river (Kenoyer and Miller, in press). Sonawane (1992: 165) has identified the site of Nagwada with the production of gold caps to be mounted on the beads, but there is no other conclusive evidence of gold working at the site.

Not much gold recovered from the Harappan sites has been subjected to chemical analysis. Two gold objects from Lothal revealed 33.45 per cent and 41.48 per cent of silver (Lal 1985). Lal concludes that a high percentage of silver and the absence of lead indicates that these items were made of electrum, rather than an artificial mixture of silver (derived from galena) and gold. Recent analysis to determine the over all ratio of gold to silver, of a few gold samples from Harappa, has indicated the proportion of gold to silver to be between 91 per cent and 94 per cent (Kenoyer and Miller, in press).

METAL PROCESSING

A. Smelting

As mentioned above neither much metal ore, nor accumulated manufacturing debris—slag, vitrified masses of silica and other fused material, which accumulates in conspicuous mounds near smelting furnaces—have been recovered from any of the Harappan sites. On the basis of quantity and type of slag from Harappan sites, Kenoyer and Miller (in press) have suggested that it represents melting rather than smelting. However, a survey similar to the one undertaken by Lowe (1989a, 1989b) in south India to locate working sites may prove useful, if undertaken in the region around Gardan-i-Reg, and the Aravalli region.

Plano-convex disc-shaped ingots have been recovered from Chanhu Daro (Mackay 1943: 188), Lothal (Rao 1979), and Harappa. Many of the ingots recently rediscovered by Kenoyer in the reserve collection at Harappa and Mohenjo Daro have been found smashed and broken in half or smaller wedge shaped fragments, apparently to facilitate further processing (Kenoyer and Miller, in press). Therefore in view of this evidence, Mackay, Kenoyer and Miller, are of the opinion that most of the copper was imported in ingot form, and little or no smelting was done at the major sites of Indus tradition (Mackay 1938: 45; Kenoyer and Miller, in press).

B. Melting of Metal

Not many substantial indicators, to define various stages in metal processing have been recovered from Harappan sites. The analysis of 'crucibles' from Lothal have revealed traces of copper (Lal 1985: 601). Nevertheless two 'crucible' fragments from Mohenjo Daro (Vats 1940: 471) and one from Harappa (Ullah 1931: 485) have been reported from the excavations. Recently, Kenoyer and Miller (in press) have reported a few crucibles with copper prills and slagging from the surface survey at Harappa and Mohenjo Daro. After a careful re-examination of the data on the kilns from Mohenjo Daro, Harappa; and Lothal, Kenoyer and Miller (in press) have suggested that there are no metal processing kilns from any of the Harappan sites. However, their on going research in this direction has started to produce the type of data needed to define copper processing kilns. Dales and Kenoyer (1989) have recovered a few kiln wall fragments with embedded copper prills, on the southern slope of Mound E at Harappa, while Vidale also reports the discovery of small circular kiln (approximately 0.8 to 1 m in diameter), surrounded by hundreds copper prills and over fired pieces of clay with traces of copper at Mohenjo Daro between VS and Moneer Area.

OBJECTS OF PRODUCTION

A. Casting

Metals can be shaped in two ways: casting and fabrication. Casting is done when the metal is molten. The only published 'moulds' from Harappan sites are from Lothal. Rao identifies two grooved stones as 'open moulds' for casting pins/rods at Lothal (Rao 1979: 557, 569, Fig. 121: 3 and 4; Pl. CCLIIb). Similar stones with large parallel groves are usually associated with agate bead manufacturing areas and have been reported from Harappan sites like Harappa, Chanhu Daro, Mohenjo Daro and Dholavira. Another problem with the identification as pointed out by Kenoyer and Miller (in press) is that the groves are not straight along their length and sides, taper off in depth at the end, and are much larger than the types of pins and rods found at the Harappan sites.

At present, no convincing example of metal casting moulds of any kind have been reported from Indus tradition sites. Paradoxically, the metallographic analyses have indicated that some copper objects from Harappan sites were definitely made by open or bivalve casting (Agrawal 1971; Pigott et al. 1989; Ullah 1940; Wraight 1940). The presence of cast objects and the absence of moulds could be taken as an indicator of the import of finished metal objects, but this is very unlikely. Many of the cast Harappan metal objects, particularly the figurines, are definitely Harappan in style, corresponding to the morphology and subject matter of objects in other materials such as faience, stone and ceramic. There is no evidence for Harappan-style metal objects from sites outside the Harappan area. Yale (1985b) notes that Harappan metalware is very different from contemporaneous products in other areas. Recent ethnoarchaeological studies carried out have indicated that the absence of moulds could be because of the use of sand moulds, which leaves very ephemeral remains for archaeologists. This is very well suited for flat objects such as celts, axes, adzes, knives or spears. It may even leave a characteristic bivalve line on the objects (Mehta 1998; Bhan et al., forthcoming), often taken to be an indication of the use of stone or terracotta bivalve moulds.

Besides, the materials used to make 'lost model moulds' are also quite ephemeral. Lost model casting employs a more cohesive sand clay to retain the complex three-dimensional features of the cast object to be cast. Lost model casting, which has a wide spatial distribution and long ethnohistoric continuity in the subcontinent, often employs several grades of material. First, the model of wax, resin, tar, etc., is coated with a fine sandy clay. This inner coat will form the details of the mould. The crucible containing the metal can be built into the mould, as is also done in Africa (see Mehta 1998; Bhan et al. forthcoming; Horne 1990, 1965; Fox 1988; Reeves 1962). An essential component of the lost model process is the use of a sandy clay that will not sinter under high temperature. Thus, in addition to the fact that moulds are broken to remove the cast object, such moulds also break down quickly when exposed to weathering. Perhaps with increasing awareness of these methods archaeologists will began to look more closely at patches of sand for the tiny fragments that may retain the contours of the cast object.

B. Fabrication

Fabrication involves the direct shaping of metal. The tools and techniques of casting and fabrication overlap to some degree, and ancient smiths may have been involved in both. Fabrication of metal objects include all the various forms of modification of non-molten metal: forging, cutting, joining finishing vis filling, polishing and detailing. The metal can be worked while hot or cold, but at a heat below the molten state. Ingots (either secondary or smelting ingots) can be worked either into small sheets or to form directly into finished objects. Cast semi-finished objects, such as those found by Mackay at Chanhu Daro (1943: 175) also would be subsequently worked to form the finished objects.

Forging

Forging is the mechanical stretching of metal, usually by hammering the metal on anvil or stake. The main source of evidence of forging comes from metallographic examination of artefacts. Forging not only shapes the object, it also hardens it and so forging is an important step in the manufacture of edge tools. Forging can be done while the metal is hot or cold. Annealing is reheating of an object after working and most of the metal-working involves cycles of annealing and hot and cold forging. There is evidence for forging during the Harappan phase, both finds of tool, marks and from metallograhic studies (Agrawal 1971; Mackay 1938; Pigott et al. 1989).

Sheet Manufacture

Sheet manufacturing is also a form of forging and fragments of copper, silver and/or gold sheets have been found at Chanhu Daro (Mackay 1943), Harappa (Vats 1940), Lothal (Rao 1979), Mohenjo Daro (Mackay 1938; Marshall 1931) and Nagwada. However, the method of sheet manufacture is unknown, and there are no published anvils or hammers. Sinking and raising to form vessels from metal is also a form of forging. As the name implies, sinking is the forming of metal by hammering from the interior of the object into a depression on an anvil, while raising employs hammering from the exterior of the object over a shaped stake. The Harappans seem to have raised the vessels (Mackay 1938: Chap. XIII; Vats 1940), and also appear to have made some jewelry by similar forming techniques, particularly the gold 'cones' (Kenoyer and Miller, in press). The decorative use of forming includes the use of stamps or punches, hammering of thin metal sheets (often gold) into or over patterns, and chasing. Simple circular punch marks were used in the decoration of gold objects and fillets (e.g. Mackay 1938: 525, no. 4; Marshall 1931 Vol. 3, Pl. CXVIII, 14) and sheet metal was beaten out from one side to make designs (Vats 1940: 64, (d) no. 8).

Wire Production

Although there are abundant examples of copper and silver wire production their production has not been studied at all. Wires were used to make rings possibly for adorning the fingers, toes and ears as well as for other purposes. Some stone beads have pieces of copper wire inserted through the hole, possibly in imitation of the method seen with the gold wire, so that the beads could be hung as pendants form a larger composite necklace. Occasionally, reports of copper 'drill bits' found stuck in bead may be such fragments of corroded copper (Kenoyer and Miller, in press). Traditionally copper wire is produced by passing a carefully hammered copper rod through a steel *drawplate*, which has a series of progressive small holes. It is perfectly possible to draw copper or copper alloys through the *drawplate* of the same material (Bhan et al., forthcoming).

Cutting

Harappans seem to have cut many of the metals. Cutting was probably done for the most part with chisels (Mackay 1938, Chap. XIII). In addition there are some saw marks in the metal objects (Mackay 1938: 368, 452, 475, 583). From the evidence of both chisel and saw marks, the usual procedure seems to have been to cut a groove in metal mass on one or more sides, then snap the piece.

JOINING

The number of identified Harappan methods of joining metal is very limited. There are a few examples of cold joining, comprising primarily the use of a rivet to attach handles to metal vessels (Marshall 1931). Hot joining is represented by evidence for soldering of gold and silver (Ullah 1940; Rao 1979) and one example of pouring molten copper over a joint to attach the handle to a copper vessel (Mackay in Marshall 1931: 489).

FINISHING

There are only a few discussions of Harappan metal finishing techniques (Mackay 1938). More precise information on finishing and manufacturing techniques in general, would benefit greatly from a restudy of all the objects in a standardized fashion, using Xeroradiography of the objects and selected metallography.

It is apparent that the study of the Indus tradition metal processing is still far from understood and faces numerous challenges. The search for metal processing sites, both in sites and the resource areas, should particularly get high priority. Given the fumes, smoke and fire associated with metal processing, the most likely location of melting and casting metal-working areas would not be found on the high mounded portion of the settlements but may be buried beneath the alluvium or at the edge of the site. It is also possible that the infrastructure of Harappan craft production encouraged the establishment of 'villages' of specialized producers, such as the site of Chanhu Daro, which seems to be a specialized lapidary production site and Nageshwar, a small shell working site on the Gulf of Kachchh. The currently unexcavated sites of Cholistan may supply evidence for a great deal of metalworking , as hinted at by large-scale surface surveys (Mughal 1982).

CONCLUSION

Harappan artisans developed elegant objects out of bronze, gold and silver, terracotta, glazed ceramics and semi-precious stones. Many of the exquisite objects are extremely small, often made from raw materials that were transformed through complex techniques of manufacture. Their craftsmanship demonstrated a total control of the medium and ability to capture the essence of a symbol or figure with a few delicate strokes. The small scale of Indus objects suggests that craftsmanship and technical qualities were more desirable than gross monumentality. The legacy of the Indus arts and crafts is still seen reflected in the modern cities and villages of India and Pakistan (see Kenoyer 1998 for a very useful discussion).

As has been demonstrated in the above sections, studies of Harappan crafts are not only keeping pace with the fast transformation of the archaeological discipline all over the world, but they are in fact defining significant variables for the discussion of crafts in the earliest urban societies (Kenoyer 1989; Vidale et al. 1992; Sinopoli 1991a). However it should be noted that there are many other technologies that are being studied but could not be covered in this paper. The production of plasters and mortar for extensive architecture at Harappan sites is an area of study that has caught much attention. Another area of obvious interest is carving and transport of massive ringstones and architectural components discovered at Mohenjo Daro, Harappa and Dholavira. Specific technologies to produce tools and weapons for fishing and hunting, shipping and transport are all sadly underrepresented in the literature and need further work.

As scholars continue to unravel the complex features of Harappan technology we will be able to define the role of these industries in the rise and maintenance of urban centres and compare these patterns with those found in Western Asia. While in the past, the Indus region was thought to have been at the receiving end of technological diffusion from the west, it is becoming more and more apparent that this is an inadequate model. Current investigations of information exchange and control of knowledge are gradually breaking away from the bonds of directionality that dominated the diffusion model in the past. The comparison of faience manufacture, lapidary, metal processing techniques, etc., between culturally very distinct regions known to have communicated with each other to some degree will add considerably to our knowledge. Furthermore, the comparison of production techniques and use of finished objects within the Indus Tradition itself will be extremely important. Through such approaches we will begin more meaningful discussions of independent and derived invention, shared and restricted knowledge, and the adoption of technological style, including the deliberate choice of methodologies as a component of ethnic identity.

ACKNOWLEDGMENT

K.K. Bhan would like to acknowledge the Ancient Iran Trust, the Charles Wallace India Trust and the Ford Foundation for providing the grants to carry out research on this paper. Our collective research on bead manufacture has been supported by grants from Smithsonian Institution Foreign Currency Program. Short Term Fellowships at the Conservation Analytical Laboratory have been provided to both M. Vidale and J.M. Kenoyer to conduct research on various technologies discussed above. J.M. Kenoyer has carried out much of his research on ancient technologies through a National Science Foundation Presidential Young Investigator Award and M. Vidale has received support through IsMEO and NATO Fellowship. Additional support for excavation at Harappa has been provided by the National Geographic Society, the Peabody Museum and private contributors. We would like to acknowledge the support of our respective institutions for providing funds and the necessary facilities for undertaking our research on ancient technologies. Finally we would like to acknowledge (without mentioning the names) all of the stimulating discussions with our colleagues and artisans that have helped us to refine our discussions and understand specific technologies better.

REFERENCES

Agrawal, D.P. 1971. *The Copper-Bronze Age in India*. New Delhi: Munshiram Monoharlal.

——— 1984. Metal Technology of the Harappans, in *Frontiers of the Indus Civilization* (B.B. Lal and S.P. Gupta Eds.), pp. 163-8. New Delhi: Books & Books.

Agrawala, R.C. 1984. Aravalli, the Major Source of Copper for the Indus and Indus-Related Cultures, in *Frontiers of the Indus Civilization* (B.B. Lal and S.P. Gupta Eds.), pp. 157-62. New Delhi: Books & Books.

Ajithprasad, P., V.H. Sonawane, V.S. Parekh and P.C. Chaudheri 1995. Datrana: a Chalcolithic Blade Industry Site in North Gujarat. A Paper Presented at the XXIII Annual Conference of the ISPQUS at Gorakhpur University, Gorakhpur, U.P.

Allchin, Bridget (Ed.) 1994. *Living Traditions: Studies in the Ethnoarchaeology of South Asia*. New Delhi: Oxford-IBH.

Allchin, F.R., B. Allchin, F.A. Durrani and M.F. Khan (Eds.) 1986. *Lewan and the Bannu Basin*. Oxford: BAR International Series 310.

Anderson-Gerfaud, P., M.L. Inizan, M. Lechevallier, J. Pelegrin and M. Pernot 1989. Des lames de silex dans un atelier de Potier Harappéen: Interaction de Domaines Techniques, *Comptes Rendues de l'Académie des Sciences* 308(II): 443-9.

Arkell, A.J. 1936. Cambay and the Bead Trade, *Antiquity* 10: 292-305.

Balista, C. and G. Leonardi 1984. A Preliminary Research on the Degradative Evolution of the Deposits and the Dislocation of the Archaeological Indicators of Craft Activities on the Surface of Mohenjo-daro, in *Interim Report*, Vol. 2 (M. Jansen and G. Urban Eds.), pp. 91-104. Rome-Aachen: IsMEO-RWTH.

Berthoud, T. and S. Cleuziou 1983. Farming Communities of the Oman Peninsula and the Copper of Makkan, *Journal of Oman Studies* 6 (2): 239-45.

Bhan, Kuldeep K., 1986. Recent Exploration in the Jamnagar District of Saurashtra, *Man and Environment* 10: 1-21.

——— 1989. Late Harappan Settlements of Western India with Specific Reference to Gujarat, in *Old Problems and New Perspectives in the Archaeology of South Asia* (J.M. Kenoyer Ed.), pp. 219-42. Madison: Wisconsin Archaeological Reports 2.

——— 1991a. Shell Industry, in *Excavation at Nageshwar: a Harappan Shell Working Site on the Gulf of Kutch.* Vadodara: the M.S. University, Archaeology Series 18.

——— 1992. Late Harappan Gujarat, *The Eastern Anthropologist* 45 (1-2): 173-92.

——— 1994. Cultural Development of the Prehistoric Period in North Gujarat with Reference to Western India, *South Asian Studies* 10: 71-90.

Bhan, Kuldeep K. and J.M. Kenoyer 1980-1. Nageshwar: an Industrial Centre of the Chalcolithic Period, *Puratattva* 12: 115-20.

——— 1984. Nageshwar: a Mature Harappan Shell Working Site on the Gulf of Kutch, *Journal of the Oriental Institute* 34 (1-2): 115-20.

Bhan, Kuldeep K., K. Krishnan and V. H. Sonawane 1992. Pottery, in *Excavations at Nageshwar: a Harappan Shell Working Site on the Gulf of Kutch*. Vadodara: the M.S. University, Archaeology Series 18.

Bhan, Kuldeep K., Massimo Vidale and J.M. Kenoyer 1994. Harappan Technology: Theoretical and Methodological Issues, *Man and Environment* XIX (1-2): 141-57.

Bhan, Kuldeep K., Nikita Mehta and K. Krishnan (forthcoming). A Preliminary Ethno-archaeological Study of Copper Working at Dariyavad, Western India.

Bhan, S. 1973. The Sequence and Spread of Prehistoric Cultures in the Upper Sarasvati, in *Radio-carbon and Indian Archaeology* (D.P. Agrawal and A. Ghosh Eds.), pp. 252-63. Bombay: Tata Institute of Fundamental Research.

Biagi, P. and M. Cremaschi 1990. Geoarchaeological Investigations on the Rohri Hills (Sindh, Pakistan), in *South Asian Archaeology 1987* (M. Taddei and P. Callieri Eds.), pp. 31-42. Rome: IsMEO.

Bisht, R.S. 1982. Excavations at Banawali, 1974-7. in *Harappan Civilization: a Contemporary Perspective* (G.L. Possehl Ed.), pp. 113-24. New Delhi: Oxford-IBH.

——— 1990. Dholavira: New Horizons of the Indus Civilization, *Puratattva* 20: 71-82.

Bisht, R.S. and S. Asthana 1979. Banawali and Other Recently Excavated Harappan Sites in India, in *South Asian Archaeology 1977* (M. Taddei Ed.), pp. 223-40. Naples: Istituto Universitario Orientale.

Blackman, J.M. and M. Vidale 1993. The Production and Distribution of Stoneware Bangles at Mohenjo-daro and Harappa as Monitored by Chemical Characterization Studies, in *South Asian Archaeology 1989* (C. Jarrige Ed.), pp. 37-44. Madison: Prehistory Press.

Bondioli, L., M. Tosi and Massimo Vidale 1984. Craft Activity Areas and Surface Survey at Mohenjo-daro, in *Interim Reports*, Vol. 1 (M. Jansen and G. Urban Eds.), pp. 9-37. Aachen-Rome: RWTH-IsMEO.

Bondioli, L. and Massimo Vidale 1986. Architecture and Craft Production Across the Surface Palimpsest of Mohenjo-daro: Some Processual Perspectives, *Arqueologia Espacial* 8 (2): 115-38.

Bulgarelli, M.G. 1986. Remarks on the Mohenjo-daro Lithic Industry, Moneer South East Area, *East and West* 36 (4): 517-20.

Bouquillon, A. and B. Barthelemy 1992. *Analyse de Materiaux. Elements de Parures de Mundigak. Musee des Arts Asiaques-Guimet.* Paris: Ministére Culture N 1941.

Brumfiel, E.M and T.K Earle (Eds.) 1987. *Specialization, Exchange and Complex Societies.* Cambridge: Cambridge University Press.

Chakrabarti, D.K. 1982. Long Barrel-Cylinder Beads and the Issue of Pre-Sargonic Contact Between the Harappan Civilization and Mesopotamia, in *Harappan Civilization* (G.L. Possehl Ed.), pp. 265-70. New Delhi: Oxford-IBH and the American Institute of Indian Studies.

Chapple, E.D. and C.S. Coon 1942. *Principle of Anthropology*. New York: Holt & Co.

Childe, V.G. 1950. The Urban Revolution, *Town Planning Review* 21: 3-17.

Claessen, H.J.M and P. Skalnik (Eds.) 1978. *The Early State*. The Hague: Mouton.

Clark, J.E. 1990. Craft Specialization and Cultural Complexity, *Research in Economic Anthropology* 12: 289-346.

Cleland, J.H. 1977. Chalcolithic and Bronze Age Chipped Stone Industries of the Indus Region. Ph.D. dissertation. Virginia: Virginia University.

Craddock, P.T., I.C. Freestone, L.K. Gujjar, A. Middleton and L. Willies 1989. The Production of Lead, Silver and Zinc in Ancient India, in *Old World Archaeo-metallurgy* (A. Hauptmann, E. Pernick and G. Wagner Eds.). Bochum: Selstverlag des Deutschen Berbau-Museum.

Dales, G.F. 1974. Excavation at Balakot, Pakistan 1973, *Journal of Field Archaeology* 1 (1-2): 1-22.

——— 1979. The Balakot Project: Summary of Four Years of Excavation, *Man and Environment* III: 45-53.

——— 1991. Some Specialized Ceramics Studies at Harappa, in *Harappa Excavations 1986-1990: a Multidisciplinary Approach to Third Millennium Urbanism* (R.H. Meadow Ed.), pp. 61-9. Madison: Prehistory Press.

Dales, G.F. and L. Flam 1969. On Tracking the Wooly and the Like, *Expedition* 12 (1): 15-23.

Dales, G.F. and J.M. Kenoyer 1977. Shell Working at Ancient Balakot, Pakistan, *Expedition* 19 (2): 13-19.

——— 1986. *Excavation at Mohenjo Daro, Pakistan: the Pottery*. Philadelphia: University Museum Press.

——— 1990. Excavation at Harappa-1988, *Pakistan Archaeology* 23: 68-176.

——— 1992a. Harappa 1989: Summary of the Fourth Season, in *South Asian Archaeology 1989* (C. Jarrige Ed.), pp. 57-68. Madison: Prehistory Press.

——— 1992b. New Investigations at an Ancient City, in *Harappan Civilization: a Contemporary Perspective* (G.L. Possehl Ed.), pp. 469-520. New Delhi: Oxford-IBH and the American Institute of Indian Studies.

Dikshit, K.N. 1981. The Excavations at Hulas and Further Excavations of the Upper Ganga-Yamuna Doab, *Man and Environment* V: 70-6.

Durrani, F.A. 1988. Excavations in the Gomal Valley: Rehman Dheri Excavation Report No. 1, *Ancient Pakistan* 6: 1-232.

Durrani, F.A., G. Erdosy and Ihsan Ali 1991. Excavation at Rehman Dheri 1991, *Ancient Pakistan* 7: 63-151.

Embers, M. 1963. The Relationship between Economic and Political Development in Nonindustrial Societies, *Ethnology* II: 228-48.

Emmerich, A. 1965. *Sweat of the Sun and Tears of the Moon: Gold and Silver in Pre-Columbian Art*. Seattle: University of Washington Press.

Fairservis, W.A.1952. *Preliminary Report on the Prehistoric Archaeology of Afghan-Baluchi Area. Novitiates1587.* New York: American Museum of Natural History.

——— 1961. Archaeological Studies in the Seistan Basin of Southwestern Afghanistan and Eastern Iran in the Zoab and Loralai Districts, West Pakistan, *Anthropological Papers of the American Museum of Natural History* 48 (1): 1-128.

Feinman, G.M., S. Upham and K.G. Lightfoot 1981. The Production Step Measure: an Ordinal Index of Labor Input Ceramic Manufacture, *American Antiquity* 46 (4): 871-84.

Flam, L. 1986. Recent Exploration in Sind: Paleography, Regional Ecology and Prehistoric Settlement Pattern, in *Studies in the Archaeology of India and Pakistan* (J. Jacobson Ed.), pp. 65-89. New Delhi: Oxford-IBH.

——— 1993. Excavation at Ghazi Shah, Sindh, Pakistan, in *Harappan Civilization: a Recent Perspective* (G.L. Possehl Ed.), pp. 457-67. New Delhi: Oxford-IBH and the American Institute of Indian Studies.

Fourmarier, P. 1949. *Prinicipes de Géologie*. Paris: Tome Premier.

Fox, C. 1988. *Asante Brass Casting: Lost-Wax Casting of Gold Weights, Ritual Vessels and Sculptures, with Handmade Equipment*. Cambridge: Cambridge University African Studies Centre.

Francis, P. 1982. Indian Agate Beads, *The World of Beads Monograph Series.* Lake Placid: Lapis Route Books.

Frankfort, H.P. 1984. The Harappan Settlement of Shortugai, in *Frontiers of the Indus Civilization* (B.B. Lal and S.P. Gupta Eds.), pp. 301-10. New Delhi: Books & Books.

——— 1989. *Fouilles de Shortugai Recherches sur L'Asie Centrale Protohistorique*. Paris: Diffusion de Boccard.

Halim, A. and M. Vidale 1984. *Kilns, Bangles and Coated Vessels: Ceramic production in Closed Containers at Mohenjo daro*, in *Interim Report.* Vol. 2 (M. Jansen and G. Urban Eds.), pp. 63-97. Aachen-Rome: RWTH-IsMEO.

Hegde, K.T.M. 1965. Chalcolithic Period Copper Metallurgy in India. Ph.D. Dissertation. Baroda: the M.S. University of Baroda.

——— 1983. The Art of Harappan Microbeads. Archaeology, *Archaeology News*: 70-2.

Hegde, K.T.M., R.V. Karanth and S.P. Sychanthavong 1982. On the Composition and Technology of Harappan Microbeads, in *Harappan Civilization* (G.L Possehl Ed.), pp. 239-44. New Delhi: Oxford-IBH.

Hegde K.T.M., Kuldeep K. Bhan and V.H. Sonawane 1984-5. Excavations at Nageshwar 1984: a Preliminary Report, *Journal of the M. S. University of Baroda* 33-34 (1): 3-12.

Hegde, K.T.M and J.E. Ericson 1985. Ancient Indian Copper Smelting Furnace, in *Furnace and Smelting Technology in Antiquity* (P.T. Craddock and M.J. Hughes Eds.), pp. 59-70. London: British Museum Research Laboratory. British Museum Occasional Papers 48.

Hegde, K.T.M., V.H. Sonawane, D.R. Shah, Kuldeep K. Bhan, Ajithprasad, K. Krishnan, Pratapchandran 1988. Excavation at Nagwada, 1986 and 1987: a Preliminary Report, *Man and Environment* XII: 55-65.

Hegde, K.T.M., Kuldeep K. Bhan, V.H. Sonawane, K. Krishnan and D.R. Shah 1992. *Excavation at Nageshwar : a Shell Working Site on the Gulf of Kutch*. Vadodara: the M.S. University of Baroda.

Henrickson, E.F. 1982. Functional Analysis of Elite Residences in the Early Dynastic of the Diyala Region: House D and the Walled Quarter at Khafaja and the 'Palaces' at Tell Asmar, *Mesopotamia* XVII: 5-33.

Hoffmann, M.A. 1974. The Social Context of Trash Disposal in an Early Dynastic Egyptian Town, *American Antiquity* 39: 34-50.

Hoffmann, M.A. and J. Cleland 1977. *Excavations at Allahdino II, the Lithic Industry*. New York: American Museum of Natural History.

Horne, Lee 1990. A Study of Traditional Lost-Wax Casting in India, *JOM* October: 46-7.

Inizan, M.L. and M. Lechevallier 1985. La Taille du silex par Pression à Mehrgarh, Pakistan: La Tombe d' un Tailleur? *Paleorient* 11 (1): 111-18.

——— 1990. A Techno-economic Approach to Lithics: Some Examples of Blade Pressure Debitage in the Indo-Pakistani Subcontinent, in *South Asian Archaeology 1987* (M. Taddei and P. Calleri Eds.), pp. 43-59. Rome: IsMEO.

Jacobson, J. 1986. The Harappan Civilization: an Early State, in *Studies in Archaeology of India and Pakistan* (J. Jacobson Ed.), pp. 137-73. New Delhi: Oxford-IBH.

Janaki, V.A. 1980. *The Commerce of Cambay from Earliest Period to Nineteenth Century*. Vadodara: the M.S. University of Baroda Geographic Series 10.

Jarrige, J.F. 1981. Economy and Society in Early Chalcolithic/ Bronze Age in Baluchistan: New Perspectives from Recent Excavations at Mehrgarh, in *South Asian Archaeology 1979* (H. Hartel Ed.), pp. 93-114. Berlin: Dietrich Reimer.

——— 1983. New Trends in the Archaeology of Greater Indus in the Light of Recent Excavations at Mehrgarh, Baluchistan. Paper Presented at International Seminar of Peshawar.

——— 1985. Continuity and Change in the North Kachi Plain (Baluchistan, Pakistan) at the Beginning of the Second Millennium BC, in *South Asian Archaeology 1983* (J. Schotmans and M. Taddei Eds.), pp. 35-68. Naples: Istituto Universitario Orientale.

——— 1990. Excavation at Nausharo 1987-8, *Pakistan Archaeology* 24: 21-67.

Jarrige, J.F., and M. Lechevallier 1979. Excavations at Mehrgarh, Baluchistan: Their Significance in the Prehistoric Context of the Indo-Pakistan Border Lands, in *South Asian Archaeology 1977* (M. Taddei Ed.), pp. 463-536. Naples: Istituto Universitario Orientale.

Jarrige, J.F. and M. Tosi 1981. The Natural Resources of Mundigak, in *South Asian Archaeology 1979* (H. Hartel Ed.), pp. 115-42. Berlin: Dietrich Reimer.

Jenkins, Paul C. 1994a. Continuity and Change in Ceramics Sequence at Harappa, in *South Asian Archaeology 1993* (Asko Parpola and Petteri Koskikaillo Eds.), pp. 315-28.

Helsinki: Annales Academiae Scientiraium Fennicae, Series B, Vol. 271.

——— 1994b. Cemetery R-37: a Re-examination of Pottery, in *From Sumer to Meluhha: Contribution to the Archaeology of West and South Asia in Memory of George F. Dales* (J.M. Kenoyer Ed.), pp. 105-12. Madison: University of Wisconsin.

Joshi, J.P. 1973. Exploration in Kachchh and Excavation at Surkotada and New Light on Harappan Migration, *Journal of the Oriental Institute* 22: 98-144.

——— 1973. *Excavations at Surkotada*, in *Radiocarbon and Indian Archaeology* (D.P. Agrawal and A. Ghosh Eds.), pp. 173-81. Bombay: Tata Institute of Fundamental Research.

Kenoyer, J.M. 1983. Shell Working Industries of the Indus Civilization: an Archaeological and Ethnographic Perspective. Ph.D. dissertation. Berkley: University of California.

——— 1984a. Shell Industries at Mohenjo-daro, Pakistan, in *Interim Report* Vol. 1 (M. Jansen and G. Urban Eds.), pp. 99-115. Rome-Aachen: RWTH-IsMEO.

——— 1984b. Chipped Stone Tools from Mohenjo-daro, in *Frontiers of the Indus Civilization* (B.B. Lal and S.P. Gupta Eds.), pp. 117-36. New Delhi: Books & Books.

——— 1984c. Shell Working Industries of the Indus Civilization: a Summary, *Paleorient* 10 (1): 9-63.

——— 1985. Shell Working at Mohenjo-daro, Pakistan, in *South Asian Archaeology 1983* (J. Schotsmans and M. Taddei Eds.), pp. 279-344. Naples: Istituto Univerrsitario Orientale.

——— 1986. The Indus Bead Industry: Contributions in Bead Technology, *Ornaments* 10 (1): 18-23.

——— 1989. Socio-Economic Structures of the Indus Civilization as Reflected in Specialized Craft and the Question of Ritual Segregation, in *Old Problems and New Perspective in the Archaeology of South Asia* (J.M. Kenoyer Ed.), pp. 183-92. Madison: Wisconsin Archaeological Reports 2.

——— 1991a. The Indus Valley Tradition of Pakistan and Western India, *Journal of World Prehistory* 5 (4): 331-85.

——— 1991b. Urban Process in the Indus Tradition: a Preliminary Model from Harappa, in *Harappa Excavations 1986-1990: a Multidisciplinary Approach to Third Millennium Urbanism* (R.H. Meadow Ed.), pp. 29-60. Madison: Prehistory Press.

——— 1992 Harappan Craft Specialization and the Question of Urban Segregation and Stratification, *The Eastern Anthropologist* 45 (1): 39-54.

——— 1994a. Faience from the Indus Valley Civilization, *Ornament* 17 (3): 36-9, 95.

——— 1994b. The Harappan State. Was it or wasn't it ? in *From Sumer to Meluhha: Contributions to the Archaeology of West and South Asia: Essays in Memory of George F. Dales Jr.* (J.M. Kenoyer Ed.), pp. 71-80. Madison: University of Wisconsin.

——— 1994c. Experimental Studies of Indus Valley Technology at Harappa, in *South Asian Archaeology 1993* (A. Parpola and P. Koskikallio Eds.) Helsinki: Annales Academiae Scientiraium Fennicae, Series B, Vol. 271.

——— (in press). Early City-States in South Asia; Comparing the Harappan Phase and the Early Historic Period, in *The Archaeology of City-States: Cross Cultural Approaches* (Deborah L. Nichols and Thomas H. Charlton Eds).

——— 1998. *Ancient Cities of the Indus Valley Civilization*. Karachi: American Institute of Pakistan Studies and Oxford University Press.

Kenoyer, J.M. and R.H. Meadow 1992. *Harappan Archaeological Project 1992*. Madison: Wisconsin and Harvard University.

Kenoyer, J.M. and M. Vidale 1993. A New Look at Stone Drills of the Indus Valley Tradition, in

Material Issues in art and Archaeology III (P. Vandiver, J.R. Durzick, G.S. Wheeler and I. Freestone Eds.), pp. 495-518. Pittsburg: Materials Research Society.

Kenoyer, J.M. and H.M.L. Miller (in press). Metal Technologies of the Indus Valley Traditions in Pakistan and Western India, in *The Ancient Metallurgy of the Asian Old World* (V. Piggott Ed.). Philadelphia: The University Museum, University Monograph 89.

Kenoyer, J.M., M. Vidale and Kuldeep K. Bhan 1991. Contemporary Stone Bead Making in Khambhat, India: Patterns of Craft Specialization and Organization of Production as Reflected in the Archaeological Record, *World Archaeology* 23 (1): 44-63.

——— 1994. Carnelian Bead Production In Khambhat, India: an Ethnoarchaeological Studies in *Living Traditions: Studies in the Ethnoarchaeology of South Asia* (B. Allchin Ed.), pp. 281-306. New Delhi: Oxford-IBH.

Krishnan, K. 1992. An Analysis of Decorative Pigments on Harappan Pottery from Gujarat, *South Asian Studies* 8: 125-32.

Krishnan, K. and K.T.M. Hegde 1987. Chemical and Petrographic Studies in Pottery of Harappa Culture in Gujarat, *Journal of the M.S. University of Baroda* 35-6: 27-56.

Kumar, V. 1986. Excavation at Ganeshwar, District Sikar. *Indian Archaeology—A Review 1983-84*: 71-2.

Kuttruuff, J.T. 1991. The Interpretation of Textile Production and Use by High and Low Status Caddoan Groups, in *Material Issues in Art and Archaeology* (P.B. Vandiver, J. Druzik and G.S. Wheeler Eds.), pp. 777-83. Pittsburg: Materials Research Society.

Lal, B.B. 1985. Report on the Chemical Analysis and Examination of Metallic and Other Objects from Lothal, in *Lothal: a Harappan Port Town (1955-62)*, Vol. 2 (S.R. Rao), pp. 651-66. New Delhi: Memoir of the Archaeological Survey of India 78.

Lal, B.B. and B.K. Thapar 1967. Excavation at Kalibangan: New Light on the Indus Civilization, *Cultural Forum* 9(4): 78-88.

Lechevallier, M. 1979. L' Industrie Lithique D' Amri, Pakistan, *Paleorient* 5: 281-95.

——— 1984. The Flint Industry at Mehrgarh, in *South Asian Archaeology 1981*(B. Allchin Ed.), pp. 45-51. Cambridge: Cambridge University Press.

Leonardi, G. 1989. *Mohenjo-daro: from Surface Evaluation to Ground Testing, in Interim Report*, Vol. 3 (M. Jansen and M. Tosi Eds.), pp. 7-70. Aachen-Rome: RWTH-IsMEO.

Liverani, M. 1988. Antico Oriente, Storia Societa, *Economia,* Editori Laterza.

Lowe, T.L. 1989a. Refractories in High-Carbon Iron Processing: a Preliminary Study of the Deccani Wootz-Making Crucibles, in *Ceramics and Civilization IV: Cross Craft and Cross Cultural Interpretations in Ceramics* (P.E. McGovern and M.D. Notis Eds.), pp. 237-51. Westerville, Ohio: The American Society Inc.

——— 1989b. Solidification and the Crucible Processing of Deccani Ancient Steel, in *Principles of Solidification and Material Processing*, Vol. 2 (R. Trivedi, J.J. Sekhar and J. Mazumdar Eds.), pp. 729-40. New Delhi: Oxford-IBH.

Mackay, E.J.H. 1937. Bead Making in Ancient Sind, *Journal of the American Oriental Society* 47: 1-5.

——— 1938. *Further Excavations at Mohenjo-daro*. New Delhi: Government of India.

——— 1943. *Chanhu-daro Excavations 1935-36*. New Haven, CN: American Oriental Society.

Malinowski, B. 1922. *Argonauts of the Western Pacific*. London: Routledge & Keagan Paul.

Marshall, Sir J. 1931. *Mohenjo-daro and the Indus Civilization*. London: Arthur Probsthain.

Mehta, Nikita 1998. Preliminary Ethnoarchaeological Studies of Traditional Copper/Brass Casting in Western India. M.A. Dissertation. Vadodara: the M.S. University of Baroda.

McCarthy, B. and P.B. Vandiver 1990. Ancient High Strength Ceramics: Fritted Faience Bangle Manufacture at Harappa (Pakistan), *c.* 2300-1800 BC, in *Material Issues in Art and Archaeology*, Vol. 2 (P. B. Vandiver, J. Druzik and G.S. Wheeler Eds.), pp. 495-510. 185. Pittsburg: Materials Research Society.

Miller, Heather M.L. 1994a. Pakistan Indus Tradition Craft Production: Research Plan and Preliminary Results of Surveys Assessing the Distribution of Manufacturing at Harappa, in *Sumer to Meluhha: Contributions to the Archaeology of West and South Asia in Memory of George F. Dales* (J.M. Kenoyer Ed.), pp. 81-104. Madison: University of Wisconsin.

——— 1994b. Metal Processing at Harappa and Mohenjo-daro: Information from Non-metal Remains, in *South Asian Archaeology 1993* (Asko Parpola and Petteri Koskikallio Eds.), Helsinki: Annales Academiae Scientiraium Fennicae, Series B, Vol. 271.

Mughal, M.R. 1980. New Archaeological Evidence From Bahwalpur, *Man and Environment* IV: 93-8.

——— 1982. Recent Archaeological Research in Cholistan Desert, in *Harappan Civilization* (G.L. Possehl Ed.), pp. 86-95. New Delhi: Oxford-IBH for the American Institute of Indian Studies.

Nissen, H.J. 1988. del Vicino Oriente, a Curadi, M. Liverani, *Editori Laterza,* Bari.

Panjwani, P.A. 1989. Petrography of Harappan Pottery from Lothal, *Man and Environment* XIII: 83-6.

Parpola, S., A. Parpola, R.H. Brunswig 1977. The Meluhha Village: Evidence of Acculturation of Harappan Traders in Late Third Millennium Mesopotamia? *Journal of the Economic and Social History of the Orient* 20 (2): 9-165.

Peregrine, P. 1991. Some Political Aspects of Craft Specialization, *World Archaeology* 23 (1): 1-11.

Pigott, V.C. 1989. Bronze in Pre-Islamic Iran, in *Encyclopedia Iranica.* Vol. IV, pp. 457-71. London: Routledge and Keagan Paul Ltd.

Pigott, V.C., S. Fleming, E. Reistroffer 1989. Preliminary Research on Copper-Base Metallurgy at Harappa; the PIXE Analysis and Metallography. University of Pennsylvania: *MASCA*.

Piperno, M. 1973. Micro-drilling at Shahr-i-Sokhta: the Making and Use of Lithic Drill-heads, in *South Asian Archaeology 1971* (N. Hammond Ed.), pp. 119-29. London: Duckworth.

——— 1976. Grave 77 at Shahr-i-Sokhta: Further Evidence of Technological Specialization in 3rd Millennium BC, *East and West* 26: 9-12.

——— 1981. Bead Making and Boring Techniques in 3rd Millennium Indo-Iran, in *Prehistoric Sistan* I (M. Tosi Ed.), pp. 319-25. Rome: IsMEO.

Possehl, G.L. 1981. Cambay Beadmaking, *Expedition* 23 (4): 39-47.

Pracchia, S. 1985. Excavation of a Bronze-Age Ceramic Manufacturing Area at Lal Shah, Mehrgarh, *East and West* 35 (4): 458-86.

——— 1987. Surface Analysis of Pottery Manufacturing Area at Mohenjo-daro, The 1984 Season, in *Interim Report*, Vol. 2 (M. Jansen and G. Urban Eds.), pp. 151-66. Rome-Aachen: IsMEO-RWTH.

Pracchia, S., M. Tosi and M. Vidale 1985. On the Type, Distribution and Extent of Craft Industries at Mohenjo-daro, in *South Asian Archaeology 1983* (M. Taddei Ed.), pp. 207-47. Naples: Istituto Universitario Orientale.

Pracchia, S. and M. Vidale 1991. Understanding Pottery Production Through the Identification and Analysis of Kiln Remains, in *Prospezioni Archeaologiche, Quaderni* I (L. Cavagnaro and M. Cucarzi Eds.), pp. 63-7.

——— 1993. The Archaeological Context of Stoneware Firing at Mohenjo-daro, *East and West* 43 (1-4): 23-68.

Rao, S.R. 1979. *Lothal: a Harappan Port Town (1955-62).* New Delhi: Archaeological Survey of India, Memoirs of the Archaeological Survey of India 78 (1).

——— 1984. *Lothal: a Harappan Port Town (1955-52).* New Delhi: Archaeological Survey of India, Memoirs of the Archaeological Survey of India 78 (2).

Reeves, R. 1962. *Cirè Perdue Casting in India.* New Delhi: Craft Museum.

Rice, P.M. Evolution of Specialized Pottery Production: a Trial Model, *Current Anthropology* 22 (3): 219-40.

Rissman, P. 1989. The Organization of Seal Production in the Harappan Civilization, in *Old Problems and New Perspective in the Archaeology of South Asia* (J.M. Kenoyer Ed.), pp. 159-70. Madison: Wisconsin Archaeological Reports 2.

Ritchie, C.A.I. 1973. Firing Soapstone, in *Soft Stone Carving*, pp. 48-51. London: A Scopas Handbook.

Rodgers, W.B. 1966. Development and Specialization: a Case from the Bahamas, *Ethnology* V: 409-14.

Roux, V. and J. Pelegrin 1990. Knapping Technique and Craft Specialization: an Ethnoarchaeological Investigation in Gujarat, *Puratattva* 19: 50-9.

Rye, O.S. and C. Evans 1976. *Traditional Pottery Techniques of Pakistan.* Washington: Smithsonian Contribution to Anthropology, No. 21. Smithsonian Institution Press.

Santoni, M. 1989. Potters and Pottery at Mehrgarh During the Third Millennium BC (Periods VI and VII), in *South Asian Archaeology 1985* (K. Frifelt and P. Sörensen Eds.), pp. 176-85. London: Curzon Press.

Sax, M. 1991. The Composition of the Material of First Millennium BC Cylinder Seals from Western Asia, in *Archaeological Science 1989* (P. Budd, B. Chapma, C. Jackson, R. Janaway and B. Ottaway Eds.), pp. 104-14. Exeter: Oxbow Monograph 9.

Schneider, G. 1984. Chemical Analysis of Stoneware Bangles and Related Materials from Mohenjo-daro, in *Interim Report*, Vol. 2 (M. Jansen and G. Urban Eds.), pp. 73-8. Rome-Aachen: IsMEO-RWTH.

——— 1989. A Technological Study of North Mesopotamian Stoneware, *World Archaeology* 21 (1): 30-50.

Shaffer, J.G. 1991. The Indus Valley, Baluchistan and Helmand Traditions: Neolithic Through Bronze Age, in *Chronologies in Old World Archaeology,* Vol. 1 (3rd Edition) (R. Ehrich Ed.), pp. 441-64. Chicago: Chicago University Press.

Shar, G.M. and M. Vidale 1985. Surface Evidence of Craft Activities at Chanhu-daro, March 1984, *Analli dell' Istituto Universitario Orientale* 45: 585-98.

Sinopoli, C.M. 1991a. Seeking the Past Through the Present: Recent Ethnoarchaeological Research in South Asia, *Asian Perspective* 30 (2): 177-92.

——— 1991b. *Approaches to Archaeological Ceramics*. New York: Plenum.

Sonawane, V.H. 1992. Fresh Light on the Specialized Crafts of the Harappans in Gujarat, *The Eastern Anthropologist* 45 (1-2): 155-72.

Sonawane, V.H., V.S. Parekh, P. Ajithprasad, K.K. Bhan, K. Krishnan, Ajita Patel and P.C. Chaudhari 1996. Excavations at Bagasra 1996: A Preliminary Report. A Paper presented in the XXIV Annual Conference of ISPQUS (unpublished), New Delhi.

Stech, T. and V. Pigott 1986. The Metals Trade in Southwest Asia in the Third Millennium B.C., *Iraq* 48: 39-64.

Thomas, K. 1986. The Bangles, in *Lewan and the Bannu Basin* (F.R. Allchin, B. Allchin, F.A. Durrani, M.F. Khan Eds.), pp. 145-56. Oxford: BAR International Series 310.

Tite, M.S. and M. Bimson 1989. Glazed Steatite: an Investigation of the Methods of Glazing Used in Ancient Egypt, *World Archaeology* 21 (1): 30-50.

Tosi, M. 1984. The Notion of Craft Specialization and Its Representation in the Archaeological Record of Early States in Turanian Basin, in *Marxist Perspectives in Archaeology* (M. Spriggs Ed.), pp. 22-52. Cambridge: Cambridge University Press.

Ullah, K.B.M.S. 1931. Copper and Bronze Utensils and Other Objects, in *Mohenjo-daro and the Indus Civilization,* Vol. II (J. Marshall), pp. 481-8. London: A. Probsthain.

Vats, M.S. 1940. *Excavations at Harappa*. New Delhi: Government of India.

Vidale, M. 1984. Surface Evaluation of Craft Activity Areas at Mohenjo-daro 1982-85, *East and West* 34(4): 516-28.

——— *Surface Evaluation of Craft Activity Areas at Mohenjo-daro 1982-1985*. Rome: IsMEO.

——— 1986. Steatite Cutting on Glazing: Relational Aspects of Two Technological Environment in Harappan Urban Context, *East and West* 36 (4): 520-25.

——— 1987a. The Paste Plaques and Cylinders of Chanhu-daro: a Descriptive Report, *Annali dell' Istituto Universitario Orientale* 47 (1): 57-66.

——— 1987b. More Information on a Protohistoric Ceramic Puzzle, in *Interim Report,* Vol. 2 (M. Jansen and G. Urban Eds.), pp. 105-11. Rome-Aachen: IsMEO-RWTH.

——— 1987c. Some Observations and Conjectures on Group of Steatite-Debitage Concentrations on the Surface of Mohenjo-daro, *Annali dell' Istituto universitario Orientale* 47 (2): 113-29.

——— 1987d. Some Aspects of Lapidary Craft at Mohenjo-daro in the Light of Surface Record at the Moneer South East Area, in *Interim Report*, Vol. 2 (M. Jansen and G. Urban Eds.), pp. 113-50. Rome-Aachen: IsMEO-RWTH.

——— 1989a. Early Harappan Steatite, Faience and Paste Bead in a Necklace from Nausharo (Pakistan), *East and West* 39 (1-4): 300.

——— 1989b. A Steatite-Cutting Atelier on the Surface of Mohenjo-daro, *Annali dell' Istituto Universitario Orientale* 49 (1): 29-51.

——— 1989c. Specialized Producers and Urban Elites: on the Role of Craft Industries in Mature Harappan Contexts, in *Old Problems and New Perspective in the Archaeology of South Asia* (J.M. Kenoyer Ed.), pp. 171-82. Madison: Wisconsin Archaeological Report.

——— 1990a. On the Structure and the Relative Chronology of an Harappan Industrial Site, *in South Asian Archaeology 1987,* Part 1 (M. Taddei and P. Callieri Eds.), pp. 203-44. Rome: IsMEO.

——— 1990b. Stoneware Industries of the Indus Civilization, in *Ceramic and Civilization* (D. Kingery Ed.), pp. 231-56. Westerville, Ohio: American Ceramic Society.

——— 1990c. Study of the Moneer South East Area, a Complex Industrial Site of Mohenjo-daro, *East and West* 40 (14): 301-14.

——— 1993a (in press). Early Beadmakers of the Indus Tradition: Reconstructing the Manufacturing Technology of Talc Disk Beads at Mehrgrah in Vth Millennium B.C., *East and West*.

——— 1993b. Produzione Artigianale Prorostorica, *ethnoarcheologia e Archeologia dal Laboratorio del Piovego* 4.

Vidale, M. and C. Balista 1988. Towards a Geo-Archaeology of Craft at Mohenjo-daro, in *Interim Reports* Vol. 3 (M. Jansen and M. Tosi Eds.), pp. 93-108. Rome-Aachen: IsMEO-RWTH.

Vidale, M. and G.M. Shar 1990. Zahr-Muhra: Soapstone Cutting in Contemporary Baluchistan and Sind, *Annali dell' Isttiuto Universitario orientale* 50 (1): 61-78.

Vidale, M.J.M. Kenoyer and Kuldeep K. Bhan 1992. A Discussion of the Concept of 'Chaine Opératorie' in the Study of Stratified Societies: Evidence from Ethnoarchaeology and Archaeology, in *Ethnoarchaèologie: Justification, Problèms, Limites* (A. Gallyy Ed), pp. 181-94. Juan-Le-Pins, France: Centre de Recherches Archeologiques.

Wenke, R.J. 1980. *Patterns in Prehistory*. New York: Oxford University Press.

Wheeler, Sir R.E.M. 1947. Harappa 1946: the Defense and Cemetery R-37, *Ancient India* 3: 59-130.

——— 1968. *The Indus Civilization*. Cambridge: Cambridge University Press.

Wilson, J.G. 1989. The Addition of Talc and Asbestos to Pot Clay by Past and Present Inhabitants of Karamoja District in Uganda and Adjoining Districts of Kenya, *Man* 8 (2): 300-2.

Wraight, E.A. 1940: Report on the Metallography of the Ancient Bronze Specimen Found at Harappa in *Excavation at Harappa*, Vol. I Text, Vol. II Plates (M.S Vats), pp. 382-3. New Delhi: Government of India.

Wright, R.P. 1989. The Indus Valley and Mesopotamian Civilizations: a Comparative View of Ceramic Technology, in *Old Problems and New Perspectives in the Archaeology of South Asia* (J.M. Kenoyer Ed.), pp. 145-6. Madison: Wisconsin Archaeological Reports.

——— 1991. Patterns of Technology and the Organization of Production at Harappa, in *Harappa Excavations 1986-1990: a Multidisciplinary Approach to third Millennium Urbanism* (R.H. Meadow Ed.), pp. 71-88. Madison: Prehistory Press.

Yerkes, R.W. 1983. Microwear, Microdrills, and Mississippian Craft Specialization, *American Antiquity* 48 (3): 499-518.

Yule, P. 1985a. *Figuren, Schmuckformen und Täfelchen der Harappa-Kultur* (I). München: C.H. Beck'sche Verlagsbuchhandlung.

——— 1985b. *Haarappazeitliche Metallefäbe in Pakistan und Nordewetindien* (II). München: C.H. Beck'sche Verlagsbuchhandlung.

Re-thinking 'Thinking': Ceramic Studies in Gujarat

ARCHANA CHOKSI

INTRODUCTION

Pottery is one of the landmarks of the 'Neolithic Revolution', along with agriculture and sedentary village settlements. The ubiquity of pottery in archaeological sites can make it one of the most useful kinds of data on chronology, site-to-site relationships, ritual practices, dietary practices, economic relationships of production and exchange, and many other aspects of cultural behaviour. In Harappan studies, archaeologists have relied heavily on pottery, using it to construct a chronology and site-to-site relationships across the abundant Harappan sites spread over a vast geographical area. Despite the acknowledged importance of ceramics to archaeology, however, Harappan studies have not yet fully exploited the interpretive potential of the ceramic assemblage. We do not understand adequately the variations occurring in the ceramic assemblage in terms of texture, colour, decoration or form; or regional variations in the ceramic assemblage. A reasonably detailed picture of pottery styles, designs and technologies is not yet available. Most striking is the absence of detailed work on the social significance of pottery, and its relationship with culture: we understand little of the relationship between ceramics and society.

An understanding of the relationship between material culture and society provides a framework through which the ancient record can be interpreted. Within Harappan studies, the use of ceramics has been limited to cataloguing sherds into typologies which are used to illuminate chronologies and site-to-site relationships. Much of this is highly interesting, but it neglects the social significance of pottery as an aspect of material culture. Archaeological projects are about connections, past, present and future. Shanks and Hodder (1995: 14) argue that the 'meaning of things can only be approached if contexts of use are considered', so 'placing things in context is fundamental to understanding the past'. If archaeologists want to move away from cataloguing sherds to interpreting their social significance, they will remember that pottery vessels reflect the culture of the people who made and used them.

It is the contention of this paper that typologies are of limited relevance to that archaeological aim. I will argue that Harappan studies would benefit from closer archaeological attention to what sherds can tell us about the socio-cultural and technological importance of ceramic wares. I begin by outlining the major findings in Harappan studies after the partition, and how ceramics have been used by archaeologists. I then draw on a model developed by Van der Leeuw (1984) which outlines phases of archaeological inquiry, to explain the limitations of the typological approach that has been favoured, and the significance of recent tentative movements towards understanding the people behind the artefacts. Ethnographic perspectives are a powerful—and in Harappan studies much under-used—tool to illuminate how socially complex pottery manufacture and usage is, and I draw on one example to illustrate this. This complexity is not recognized in the oversimplified treatment of potsherds by archaeologists, and this prevents the ceramic assemblage from fulfilling its potential in archaeological attempts to understand Harappan Culture.

HARAPPAN SITES IN GUJARAT AFTER PARTITION

The discovery of the ancient cities of Harappa and Mohenjo Daro rejuvenated Indian archaeology. At a stroke, the antiquity of civilization on the subcontinent was thrown back by at least two millennia. The two excavations, initially by Daya Ram Sahni in 1921 at Harappa, in the then Montgomery district of Punjab, and by R.D. Banerji in 1922 at Mohenjo Daro, in the then Larkhana district of Sindh, yielded rich findings. The formative stage of Indian civilization was established; and the view that Indian civilization had only begun after the invasion of Alexander in 326 BC was summarily dismissed.

The political bifurcation of the Indian subcontinent in 1947 provided the impetus for the Archaeological Survey of India to launch a programme of exploration of the regions south and east of the Indus river 'for tracing Harappan sites, if any, within the present-day borders of India' (Rao 1985: 1-2). For, when the subcontinent was divided, only two sites—Kotla Nihang and Rangpur—were known within India. By that time the controversial site of Rangpur—situated on the river Sukhabhadar in Surendranagar district of Gujarat—had been excavated three times. Initially suspected to be a Harappan outpost (Rao 1985), its identification with the Harappan Culture was established in 1935 (Vats 1937) and confirmed in 1937 (Ghurye 1939). The findings of a third excavation in 1947, which showed that it represented only a post-Harappan phase (Dikshit 1950), were challenged by Rao in the excavation he led between 1953-6, hoping to confirm the Harappan affiliation within the present political boundaries of India. He established that Rangpur represented a late phase of Mature Harappan Culture, though the absence of Indus seals and the occurrence of new ceramic wares at the site called for an explanation (Rao 1985). As a result, Rao turned his attention to trying to trace the route followed by the Harappans from Sindh into Saurashtra (Rao 1985). In further explorations of the Sabarmati River Valley, Lothal—a Mature Harappan site—was discovered.

Since then, Gujarat has become one of the best explored areas of the Harappan Culture. Major excavations in Gujarat have been conducted at Lothal (Rao 1963, 1979, 1985); Rangpur (Rao 1963); Surkotada (Joshi 1972); Nagwada (Hegde et al. 1988); Rojdi (Possehl and Raval 1989); and Dholavira (Bisht 1991). Smaller excavations have been conducted at Desalpur (Soundara Rajan 1984); Nageshwar (Hedge et al. 1984) and Padri (Shinde and Kar 1992).

On the basis of excavations at Rangpur (1962-3) and Lothal (1973), Rao divided the

LOTHAL				RANGPUR
			1300 BC	Period III Lustrous Red Ware culture (Late Harappan)
		1600 BC	1600 BC	
				Period II C Transition
Period B Late Harappan				1700 BC
				Period II B
Phase V A-B				Late Harappan (initial phase)
		1900 BC	1900 BC	
				Period II A
Period A				
	Phase IV A-B		2000 BC	
		2000 BC		
	Phase III A-B			
		2200 BC		?
Mature Harappan	Phase II A-C	2350 BC		Hiatus
		Phase I		
		2450 BC		Period I

Fig. 1. Rao's chronology of Harappan Gujarat.

entire period of Harappan occupation in Gujarat into three major sub-periods: Mature Harappan, Late Harappan and Post Harappan. Figure 1 summarises Rao's sequence:

CERAMIC ASSEMBLAGE IN RAO'S CHRONOLOGICAL SEQUENCE

The ceramic assemblage was central to the construction of Rao's chronological sequence in Gujarat. Early Harappan pottery was

> wheel-made, red to pink wares, with slips in red and darker tones. Painting, also in dark colours, with some white infilling is present, along with comb incised wares. 'Reserved slip' ware is also reported. There are deep dishes and jars but little more has been reported on ceramic forms (Bisht 1991: 79)

Mature Harappan pottery consisted of well fired red wares painted with black designs of vegetal and geometric patterns. The major shapes include dish-on-stand, 'S' shaped jars, straight-sided beakers, pointed goblets, perforated jars, etc. (Joshi 1972). Red Ware was occasionally chocolate slipped, but was often painted in crimson, black and rarely in white (Rao 1985). Buff Slipped Ware and Buff Ware, painted in black or chocolate are also typical of this period. In Gujarat, Micaceous Red Ware, Prabhas Ware, Black-and-Red Ware, Coarse Grey Ware, Cream-Slipped Bichrome Ware, Red-Slipped Polychrome Ware, Reserve Slip Ware, etc., have also been found in association with the Mature Harappan phase.

In the Late Harappan, 'transition' phase, pottery shows indifferent treatment of the surface of the vessel and the coarseness of fabric (Rao 1963). It is characterized by Lustrous Red Ware complex, painted Black-and-Red Wares, and Coarse Wares.

THE RANGPUR CULTURAL SEQUENCE

Rangpur revealed a cultural sequence from Mature Harappan period IIA to the end of Harappan tradition of Gujarat, Period III. Based on findings at Lothal and Rangpur, it was thought that, after the initial penetration of the Harappans into Gujarat, the Harappan tradition in Gujarat reflected a high degree of continuity from Mature to the Late Harappan phase. On the basis of the material recovered from Lothal, Rao (1985) reported the increase in the frequency of Coarse Red Ware, indicating that the Harappan ceramic tradition had 'started to deteriorate' during the late phase of Mature Harappan, represented by Lothal A, Phase IV. After the transition phase at Rangpur IIA, Lothal A IV, Nagwada, Surkotda IC and perhaps Desalpur IB, the Harappans of Gujarat were thought to have entered the initial phase of Late Harappan, represented by Period II B-C at Rangpur. The final phase of the Harappan tradition in Gujarat, defined by a further increase in the frequency of Lustrous Red Ware and Coarse Wares, is represented by Rangpur Period III.

Because Rangpur had been the only site to show continuous Harappan occupation in Gujarat, the ceramic variability it displayed was taken as the reference point of the definition of site periodization in Harappan Gujarat. Due to the absence of suitable materials, it was not possible to confirm the sequence through radiocarbon dating at this site.

The characteristic cultural items of Mature Harappan like square steatite seals inscribed in the Indus script, terracotta toy carts, Indus type human figurine and a truly characteristic range of painted design on pottery were missing at Rangpur. But there are elements present at Rangpur which are not found elsewhere in Harappan settlements, except those in Gujarat, the Micaceous Red Ware and Black-and-Red Ware. Two vessel forms common to Gujarat; like the stud handled bowl and storage jar with club rims, seem not to be found elsewhere.

Radiocarbon determination from Lothal and Surkotda suggested that the Mature (Urban) phase Harappans settled in Gujarat, including Kachchh in *c*. 2400-2300 BC. They apparently came to Gujarat in an effort to gain access to the raw material wealth of this region, and to western India in general (Possehl 1976). Earlier it was thought that Mature Harappan sites were most frequent in Kachchh, while in other regions of Gujarat settlements were few and far between. There was much speculation on the reason behind this expansion. Nageshwar and Lothal were thought to be outlying resource areas for Indus urban centres. The settlements of Kachchh had been interpreted as settlements located to facilitate administration (Joshi 1979: 64; Soundara Rajan 1984: 219; Chitalwala 1982: 198).

Sequencing before the Rojdi Dates

In 1974 and 1980 Possehl and in 1986 Bhan presented maps showing the distribution of sites from the three phases of the Harappan settlements (Possehl 1980: 57-9; Bhan and Shah 1990: 221-7). These maps showed an 'Urban Phase' penetration of Gujarat through Kachchh (Joshi 1972) proceeding to Rangpur, Koth and Lothal. These latter sites were then thought to be on the south-eastern borders of the 'Urban Phase' Indus states (Possehl 1976). In the succeeding Rangpur II B-C phase there appeared to have been a significant increase in the number of sites, especially in Saurashtra. The surveys carried out by Possehl (1980) in eastern Saurashtra, Bhan (1983) in western Saurashtra and Momin (1979) in north Gujarat also revealed an increase in the number of settlements in the 'Late Harappan' phase. The significant shift in the settlement pattern was thought to have been related to the introduction of bajra, jowar and ragi.

The final phase of the Harappan tradition of Gujarat, represented by Rangpur Period III, is defined by a further increase in the frequency of Lustrous Red Ware and Coarse Wares. This phase was marked by a decrease in settlements in Saurashtra. Surveys carried out near the western section of north Gujarat bordering the Little Rann of Kachchh revealed 30 settlements (Hegde and Sonawane 1986). This cluster of sites was hypothesized as pastoral camp sites (Bhan 1989: 232). This was attributed to the reemphasis of herding over farming by part of the settled population, which led to the development of pastoral sites in north Gujarat (Bhan 1989) and Saurashtra at Oriyo Timbo (Rissman 1985).

Until 1980 there was no radiocarbon determination available for the Rangpur sequence. For almost three decades, Rangpur had been the reference point of the definition of site periodization in the Harappan Gujarat. The role of ceramics was prime in this sequencing: sequences were defined by ceramic changes, grouped into four phases (Rao 1963).

Post-Rojdi Chronology

The whole chronology of the Harappans in Gujarat changed in 1989, when a series of twelve radiocarbon dates became available from the Rojdi excavation (Possehl and Raval 1989). Ceramics from Rojdi (Herman 1989) and Vagad (Sonawane and Mehta 1989) show typological similarities with Rangpur II A, II B and perhaps II C. This period of occupation must thus be placed within the time bracket of 'Mature Harappan'. All the sites of Rangpur II B-C category, which had previously been thought to represent the 'Late Harappan' (Rao 1963) or 'Post Urban' (Possehl 1980) or 'Initial phase of Late Harappan' (Rissman 1985; Bhan 1989: 227-31) phase fell into the time bracket of 'Mature Harappan'. Emerging from the research at Rojdi is a sense that there are at least two kinds cf 'Harappans' in Gujarat during the third millennium. The concepts of 'Sorath Harappan' and 'Sindhi Harappan' were proposed as explanatory models (Possehl 1989).

The first of these, 'Sorath Harappan', is represented by Rojdi A and B, and probably by the early Rangpur sequence. It is interpreted as small rural villages and dry seasonal pastoral camps (Possehl 1980, 1989; Momin 1981; Mehta et al. 1980; Mehta 1984; Sonawane and Mehta 1985; see Reddy 1990 for alternative explanation). The pottery from Rojdi is clearly of Harappan tradition, but it lacks the key Urban Phase Harappan ceramic markers. Rojdi has not yielded a single sherd with the Indus black on red painting style (Herman 1989). The second, 'Sindhi Harappan', has been unearthed at places like Desalpur, Surkotda, Dholavira, Nageshwar, Nagwada and Lothal. 'Sindhi Harappan' shares material inventory of Harappan sites of Sindh alongwith local 'Non-Harappan' and Early/Pre-Harappan ceramic types (Possehl 1989:15).

Sonawane and Ajithprasad (1994: 135) challenged the 'Sorath' definition on the basis of north Gujarat findings. They proposed an alternative, named the 'Anarta' after the traditional name of north Gujarat, where more than 80 Harappan sites with different degrees of affiliation to the Harappan Culture were discovered. The ceramic assemblage is dominated by a series of Non-Harappan pottery types: Gritty Red Ware (dominant type), Fine Red Ware, Burnished Red Ware and Burnished Grey/Black Ware—peculiar to the region. The vessels are painted with different shades of black and red on a white or cream background thereby producing a bichrome effect. All pottery types except Black-and-Red Ware have common vessel shapes and patterns suggesting that they belong to a single pottery tradition. The north Gujarat pottery tradition is distinct from the Harappan and Sorath Harappan (ibid. 1994: 135).

THE TYPOLOGICAL APPROACH

As the above overview has shown, Harappan Gujarat offers numerous varieties of ceramics, in terms of texture, colour, decoration and form. Yet most reports of excavations of Harappan sites do not attempt to interpret the ceramic assemblage. Instead, they tend to adopt a 'typologising' approach to sherds, classifying them to produce a catalogue of sherds found. Where ceramics themselves are given greater attention, there is a tendency to view them solely in typological terms - texture, colour, decoration and form, wheel/handmade, etc. The variations which are thus catalogued have been used to establish typologies which put the site in its chronological and/or site-to-site context. For example, Joshi (1972), in his discussion of Harappan ceramic types, writes in the Surkotda report:

> The distinguishing feature of this phase (period IIC) ... is the introduction of a palpably hand-made very coarse and red ware of granulated texture, which account for 40-70% of the ceramic yield. The types represented in this fabric includes big storage jars with ridged shoulder, jars with short vertical or slightly outturned rims, vases with long concave necks and carinated profile, basins with perforated vertical lugs, dishes, bowls, etc. ... Associated with it is ... a meagre amount (only up to 4.5%) of a white painted black and red ware represented by large and small bowls with or without carination. ... The interior surfaces on these vessels are painted in fugitive white with designs comprising groups of multiple straight or wavy lines and spirals. ... (Joshi 1972: 133)

This report discusses painting, shape and style but omits any consideration of the sociological context—it offers a one-sided rather than holistic interpretation of excavated pottery. The author, in defining finds in this way, implicitly poses questions about regionality, evolution of shape, painting, etc., but is not concerned to raise them explicitly, nor to attempt an answer.

In this process, the social significance of ceramics is neglected. Sherds seem to become more important than the people who created and used them. The ceramic assemblage is simplified, without understanding its complex relationship with society. Despite considerable and sustained interest over the years, Indian archaeologists have in general adopted an approach which does not permit study of the social context in which these artefacts were made and used. Typological descriptions of pottery sherds, narrowly focused on chronology and site-to-site relationship, tend to neglect issues concerning other aspects of cultural variation (Ajithprasad 1993). There appears therefore to be an identifiable archaeological 'mind-set' which underpins interpretations of the material record, especially in case of pottery.

Van der Leeuw's Model

This 'mind-set' is consistent with the first phase identified by Van der Leeuw (1984) in his model of the summary of shifts in archaeologists' thinking. This model is a useful tool in explaining the interpretive dimension of Harappan studies in Gujarat—past, present, and perhaps future. Van der Leeuw discusses the three phases of development of archaeologists' thinking which he summarizes as:

(i) the typological approach
(ii) the people behind the artefacts
(iii) the cultural element.

The aim of the first, 'typological' approach has been to distinguish types by measuring artefacts and assigning them to categories by such means which eliminate the subjective bias of the observer. No attempt was made to identify the sherds themselves with the people in the past. As Van der Leeuw points out (1984: 710):

> Differences between groups of sherds were also assumed to point to different groups of people or cultures, which resulted in the 'migration' approach as a means of explaining the distribution of a set of artefacts.

That this approach is dominant in investigations of Harappan Culture can well be illustrated. For instance:

> Another possible explanation for the presence of Padri ware in the Harappan levels is that there was cultural contact with the first farmers of the Decaan (Savalda Culture). ... (But) In the absence of evidence for migration into Gujarat, cultural contact with the Harappans cannot be ascertained. (Shinde and Kar 1992: 110)

A further characteristic of the typological approach is a tendency to attribute differences in pottery found between two stratigraphic layers to cultural deterioration, migration, invasion, a transition phase, etc. For instance:

> It is also certain that Prabhas Ware is an intrusion in Late Harappan settlements in Kathiawar. It does not occur either in Rangpur IIA or Lothal A. The presence of pot sherds painted in brown, violet or black on a white or creamy slip in Prabhas IA may, as suggested by one of the excavators, indicate contact with Ahar. (Rao 1963: 182-3)

In sum, the typological approach is polarized: it exhibits a complete distinction between the archaeologist and the sherds; and a complete absence of distinction between the sherds and the people associated with them in the past.

This tension can be resolved through a shift in thinking, which recognizes that it is not possible to create objective typologies, and that there is a 'relationship between the typology, and the aims and approach of the person making it' (Van der Leeuw 1984: 711). This second phase distinguishes three levels of analysis: the lower (micro) level, operating between artefact and artefact pattern; the middle level, operating between the artefact pattern and the human activities involved; and the upper (macro) level, operating between humans involved, and the structure of which they are assumed to be a part.

The micro level distinguishes 'the nature of individual remains of past activity (the data), the nature of the patterning, and ... the nature of the reasoning that brings them together' (Van der Leeuw 1984: 712). The objective approach was projected onto human behaviour itself, which was held to be bound by laws of nature and thus 'deemed knowable with as much certainty as any other natural phenomenon' (ibid). But technological studies have made it apparent that potters adopt alternatives which are not necessarily subjected to the laws of nature; some degree of subjectivity is therefore apparently inherent.

The middle level evolved as it became apparent that types themselves are subjective patternings created by archaeologists. The options which potters exercise point also to the fact that not everyone in any society conforms exactly to norms, which gave rise to the notion of 'polythetic types'. At this stage ethnographic work played its part in influencing archaeologists to consider the multi-faceted nature of real life in the archaeological record too: the 'people behind the artefacts' were discovered.

To bridge the gap between artefact patterns and human behaviour, the 'middle range' theory evolved (Binford 1977). This was most successful in areas where it was possible to be relatively objective and rely on the laws of nature. Where these laws do not operate, archaeologists met with much less success and the most obvious lacuna is in the study of entirely cultural phenomena. Van der Leeuw contends that this lack of success is inevitable since it is very difficult not to identify with other human beings and because 'we cannot really study human behaviour on the basis of artefact patterns without a conception of how humans learn and think. Without the latter we have no "grip" on humans in the past' (Van der Leeuw 1984: 714).

The macro level is concerned with the relationship between the activity of individuals and groups, and the context in which they operate, that is the relationship between potters and their environment.

The major contribution of this way of thinking has been 'an increased facility in distinguishing the various dimensions of variability which are responsible for the nature of archaeological artefacts as we encounter them' (Van der Leeuw 1984: 715). For example, to explain variations in ceramics in detail, one needs to make distinctions 'between the perspectives of the maker, the trader and the user; or the distinction between the technological and the social, political, economic and communications components of variation' (Van der Leeuw 1984: 718).

The subjectivity/objectivity dilemma remained, however, and the model's third phase—study of the cultural element—is characterized by more detailed analyses and the modelling of cultural aspects of ceramics. This phase retains the three levels of analysis but recognizes that the individual, system and context are not independent, and can only be understood in relation to each other:

> The fundamental assumption is that no matter how many constraints are placed on human behaviour by natural variables, there is always room for alternative choices. Which alternatives are chosen within these confines, are dependent upon the perception of the people who make the choices. (Van der Leeuw 1984: 716)

Although an increasing fragmentation of ceramic studies may result, Van der Leeuw (1984: 717) sees this phase as a

> response to the long overdue need to search for the organising principles underlying human behaviour; thus it moves away from the stress on non-human phenomena, and the role played by these in the past.

He sounds a cautionary note, however, that as long as it is assumed that

> the perceptive framework of each group of humans is specific, this approach will be very difficult to apply within archaeology, because of the limitations of the archaeological data set which makes the testing of hypotheses so difficult. (ibid.)

The 'mental map', or perceptive framework, determines the patternings (Van der Leeuw's 'organising principles') underlying the potter's material output:

> If the potter is truly crucial in creating his/her products, then the potter's knowledge and approach decide how this is done. Thus, an anlysis of pottery-making should ... focus on the choices a potter makes, about the use of environment and the raw materials it contains, as well as about the use made of tools and of technical capabilities. The choices are deemed as crucial in determining the nature and shape of the product, its effectiveness and its life-expectancy as the materials and tools. (Van der Leeuw and Papousek 1992: 137)

In this respect, it is worth emphasizing that these patternings 'are anchored in a much wider conceptual world' (Van der Leeuw et al. 1991: 145) and arguing, with Van der Leeuw et al. (1991), that

> The true locus of both change and stability is at the interface between these two aspects, the purely technical and the conceptual. (Van der Leeuw et al. 1991: 145)

The salient details of Van de Leeuw's model, with its movement from the objective towards the subjective, can be summarized (Fig. 2):

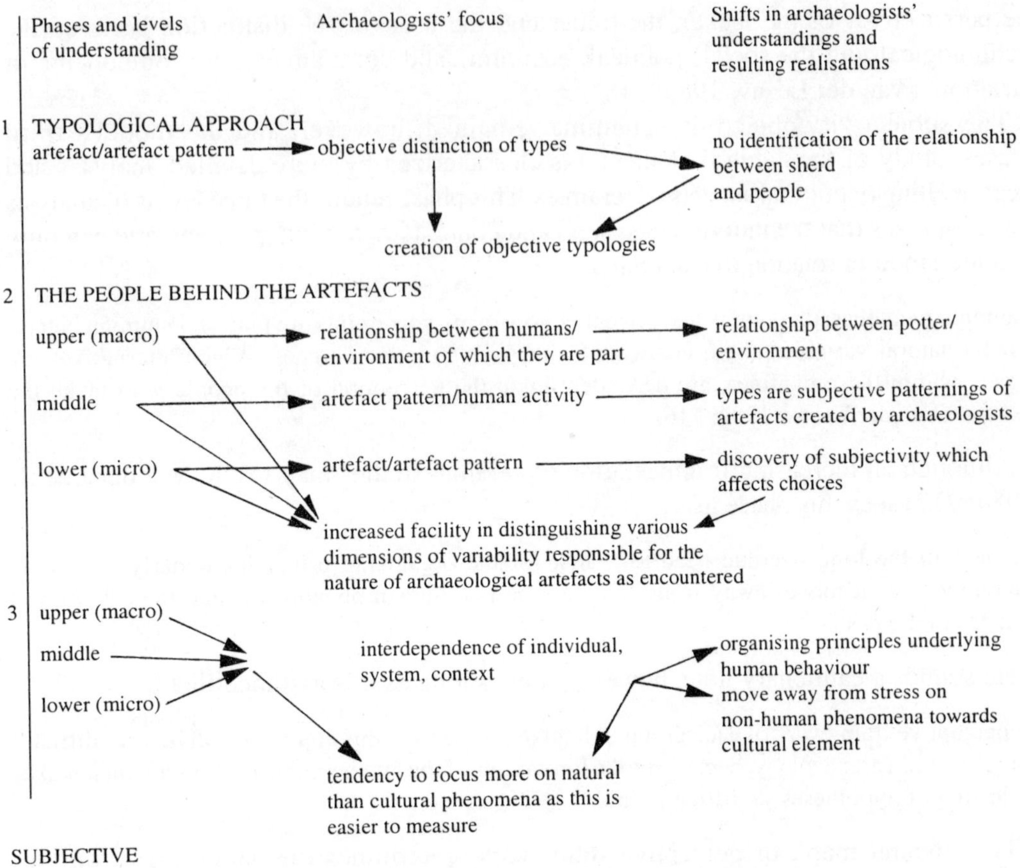

Fig. 2. Harappan Studies in Van der Leeuw's model of archaeologist's thinking.

HARAPPAN STUDIES IN VAN DER LEEUW'S MODEL

Investigations of Harappan Culture have tended to remain at the typological level of conceptualization in this model. This is useful in cataloguing and reporting archaeological data but 'has proved relatively inadequate for understanding cultures holistically' (Possehl 1980: 2).

It is not difficult to trace the origin, and perhaps the reasons for the perpetuation, of this approach. Faced with the total absence of any important Harappan site in post-partition India, Rao was under pressure to establish the Harappan connection in India. This he was able to do, but in so doing he excavated material which did not fit into the homogeneous—or classic—ceramic assemblage of Mohenjo Daro and Harappa. In further explorations in Gujarat, what he was not able to find at Rangpur, he was able to find at Lothal—a classic Harappan site. In discussing the chronology of the Harappan Civilization (and to account for post-partition India's ancient history) Rao attempted to show continuity from Mature Harappan to Post Harappan Culture in Gujarat. This was done on the basis of stratigraphic analysis of pottery at the two sites of Lothal and Rangpur. Continuity could only be posited by attributing pottery found in Rangpur Period II C to a 'transition' phase.

In subsequent excavations, ceramic assemblages have been classified and used to strengthen or contest the chronology proposed by Rao. Their reports illustrate clearly that the focus has tended to be on classifying sherds into types which can provide the site in question with a chronological designation. It seems, as Ucko (1989: xii) points out, that 'archaeologists themselves have been influenced in their interpretation by the received wisdom of their times'. Because chronology and site-to-site relationships have been the centre of interest, there has been no incentive to use ceramics in any other context: 'the usual, and often the only question asked of the data is whether it constitutes an example of Early, Mature or Late Harappan cultural development' (Schaffer 1982: 42).

For example, adhering to the tradition established by Rao, Bhan and Sonawane (1988: 123), report on Nagwada:

> A majority of the vessels are made of a coarse red ware with a gritty core. These vessels were made on a slow wheel and hand finished or modelled. ... This ware is represented by bowls with panelled designs near the rim, dishes and basins showing a similarity to coarse red ware and Micaceous red ware of Lothal A, Phase IV, Surkotda IB and IC. (Bhan and Sonawane 1988: 123)

Reports of Mohenjo Daro and Harappa seem to have created 'the impression of an over-standardized pottery assemblage' (Ajithprasad and Sonawane 1993: 2). Yet, along with the examples of the classic Harappan assemblage, many sites also revealed Non-Harappan pottery in varying proportions. Regional variation and/or diffusion and deterioration was posited as an example for this phenomenon, but although this possibility has been recognized, the tendency has been to subsume these variations under the blanket term Harappan, or at best to designate such incongruous material as a regional variant of the Harappan Culture (Sonawane and Ajithprasad 1994: 130).

PEOPLE BEHIND THE ARTEFACTS

During the last two decades, studies of Harappan Culture in Gujarat have become more problem-orientated and region-specific (ibid.). Recent excavations have brought to light several interesting aspects of the Harappan Culture and its cultural dynamism. An important point that emerges is the recognition of Non-Harappan Chalcolithic traditions contemporary with, if not earlier than, the Harappan Culture in Gujarat (ibid.). This concern to understand regionality has seen the distribution of sites.and the relationship between site and variability in artefact/artefact patterns emerge as a research concern. Indian archaeology is beginning to embrace the second phase of van der Leeuw's model as excavations begin to attempt to understand Harappan Culture more holistically than before—in both economic and ecological terms. An attempt has been made to deal with various aspects of Harappan subsistence in Gujarat, by differentiating between the various economies: urban pastoralism, and the rural village economy. The place of pastoralists, dry cropping, irrigation and so on have been considered within this framework.

The new concern with ecology and economy is marked in Possehl's (1980) study. New focal points include the transition from Urban to Post Urban Harappan; the definition of a cultural tradition; the demonstration that the Post Urban phase of Indus Civilization should not be treated as a period of total decline; and attempts to understand the position of Lothal within the broad structure of Harappan organization (Possehl 1980: 10-11). He concluded 'the adaptation to dry farming and the introduction of bajra appears to have been a significant part of Late Harappan subsistence in Gujarat' (ibid.: 83). Lothal was thought to be a focal point of trading activities between hunter-gatherers of north Gujarat and the Harappan hinterland (ibid.: 76). Similarly, Hegde and Sonawane's (1986) study of the 21 Rupen sites of north Gujarat show a rural way of life mainly based on agrarian economy.

The argument that changes took place in the economy still relegates ceramics to a place within the framework of the Rangpur sequence and site-to-site relationships. Pottery is again used to indicate site-to-site relationships and migration. Hegde and Sonawane (1986: 29) conclude, for example,

> Rupen sites show greater affinities in ceramic types and forms and also other material assemblages to Saurashtra, and are analogus to Rangpur period IIB, IIC and III ... since our sites show much greater affinities with Saurashtra than with those of Kachchh it is possible to infer that the Harappan immigrants came to Rupen valley from Saurashtra.

At this stage, archaeologists were still struggling with the absence of radiocarbon dates for site-to-site relationship and chronology. The Rojdi excavation provided some resolution to this problem as new radiocarbon dates emerged. It revealed the existence of pottery which could clearly not be identified as classic Mature Harappan in Sindh, although the time bracket is the same. This appears to confirm the notion of regionality: 'It appears that Rojdi, and many other sites in Saurashtra and possibly north Gujarat as well represent a newly-discovered regional expression of the Harappan Urban phase' (Possehl and Raval 1989: 13). Ajithprasad and Sonawane's (1993) challenge, and proposal of 'Anarta' rests on their assertion that the Sorath Harappan concept does not adequately account for the pottery found in north Gujarat 'which is very different from the Mature Harappan and the Sorath Harappan pottery'.

THE ELUSIVE CULTURAL ELEMENT

Yet, effectively, the proposal of all these—Sorath, Sindhi and Anarta—categories serve to create further typologies. Still we find a reluctance to engage with the issues of how the lives of these different peoples and economies in the region are reflected in the ceramic assemblage. Regional variations abound, with almost all important excavated sites yielding cultural relics predominated by pottery that is different from the Harappan (Rao 1963, 1979, 1985; Hegde et al. 1988; Joshi 1972; Possehl and Raval 1989). The very existence of regional variability implies that cultural mechanisms must have existed to ensure a certain degree of continuity in local pottery styles, while limiting their diffusion and the intermingling of styles between regions. Typological categorizations are limited in their ability to advance what is surely the underlying goal of archaeology—to understand past societies. For, if it is 'an accepted fact that a given type of pottery shows certain amount of variation within the site and between the sites' (Ajithprasad and Sonawane 1993: 5), archaeologists surely need to shift their focus to understanding why there should be not only inter-site variations, but also intra-site variations in pottery. Why is it that a pottery type is found at three sites but not at a fourth one nearby? Why should it be that at one site there is a very high proportion of one particular category of vessel that hardly appears at a similar site in the same region assigned to the same time bracket? It seems, as Rice (1984: 233) says, that 'we are looking where it is easier to look, not where the object actually is'.

These apparent anomalies can be understood only if the whole notion of culture is placed at the centre of archaeological problematization:

> (One) must start with the concept of culture, since the artefacts are cultural objects. One must go beyond the appearance of the pottery to examine the standards, customs and beliefs to which the artisans conformed in making it. It is these standards, customs and beliefs which constitute the culture of the community, and only by knowing them will one be able to determine whether a given potsherd belongs to the local culture, is a personal aberration or has been brought in from another culture as the result of trade. (Rouse 1965: 94-5)

The culture of the community in turn cannot be understood unless the cognitive processes which constitute culture are explored; the particular cultural system of which the potter is a constituent part. If the relationship between the larger system (culture) and the sub-system (potter) can be established, the complexity of the artefacts in society can be understood. The extent of this complexity is, as yet, rather poorly understood for the archaeological record. Indeed, Harappan studies seem to be a case substantiating Ucko's (1989) concern that 'archaeological classification may often serve to camouflage the more subtle messages of style and technique which probably symbolize complex patterns of behaviour, as well as individual aspirations within any society'.

ROLE OF ETHNOARCHAEOLOGY

Ucko (1989) argues that throughout the history of archaeology, objects of material culture have been taken to reflect the activities of special groups or 'societies', whose physical movements have often been postulated on the basis of the distribution patterns of such objects. The physical or ethnic identities of such groups have often been assumed to correlate with such artefactual grouping. The distinctive material culture complex may represent activities of a vast variety of social grouping and subgroups.

One way of improving our understandings of cultural complexities is to make use of ethnography, which allows 'direct observation of an on-going society'. This in turn 'permits one to correlate activities and even patterns of thought or social organization, with material by-products that may be preserved in the archaeological record' (Yellen 1977: 11). There can be no doubt that 'real life is multi-faceted, and therefore there are a large number of dimensions of variability in the "real world"... which are worth exploring in archaeology' (Pritchard and Van der Leeuw 1984: 10). An ethnoarchaeologist may be very well placed 'to think in terms of the variables which affected daily life (and pottery making) in the past' (Pritchard and Van der Leeuw 1984: 5) and 'to refine the interpretation of ... excavated material' (Rye and Evans 1976: 4):

> Without a broad set of comparative data concerning how, where, or by whom pottery is produced, distributed, and used, archaeological reconstructions of these patterns are on shaky ground. (Rice 1987: 168)

Ethnography is of real value if the evidence it produces is carefully analysed and that analysis is used to establish 'rules' governing cultural processes, of which artefacts, and those who create and use them, form an integral part.

Ethnoarchaeology in Harappan Studies

Some ethnoarchaeological attempts have been made to study the Harappan ceramic heritage. Dales (1965) describes the pottery manufacture at Balreji, near Mohenjo Daro in Pakistan. Other, more general, ethnographic studies have been carried out by Sharma (1965), who studied the potters of Uttar Pradesh; Rye and Evans (1976), on potters in Pakistan; and Roux (1989) on craft specialization and technical competence. Saraswati and Behura (1966) included in their wide-ranging study two potters from Kachchh but based their work on short visits to each site of production. Such brief studies have little 'time-depth' and characteristically 'focus on one or two workshops, where production is described in detail with only a brief mention of other aspects' which are then 'related to features of production in other workshops' which have not been studied in detail (Pritchard and Van der Leeuw 1984: 12). Most studies have focused on technological issues, as they can be approached more or less 'objectively' through the use of experimentation and methodologies drawn from the hard science (Pritchard and Leeuw 1984: 14).

Two attempts to categorize and explain variability with reference to the social context have been made, by Miller (1985), who carried out a study of ceramic variability in central India, and Choksi (1994) who carried out an ethnoarchaeological study of the social context of pottery manufacture and usage. I will draw here on my earlier study (Choksi 1994) to illustrate that at each stage of its life, a ceramic vessel tells a story which has social significance. The scope of this study was limited but it serves as a demonstration of culturally located patterns of behaviour among manufacturers and consumers which determine the choices made at various stages during the life of the pot—for instance in form, design, function, usage (Choksi 1995, 1997, 1998). The analytical frameworks furnished by such an ethnographic study of these patterns of behaviour can be applied to interpretations of the ceramic assemblage, allowing sherds themselves to tell those stories. Perhaps this sort of approach may assist Harappan studies in the move towards the third phase of understanding the cultural element.

The Stories Colours Tell: an Ethnographic Interpretation

I will take one example, that of colour, to show how ethnographic study can shed new light on the significance of colour and dramatically broaden possible interpretations in the archaeological record.

Colour has provided a basic criterion for categorizing vessel sherds. Depending on the colour of the sherd, it may be classified as a sample of Red Ware, or Buff Ware, or Black-and-Red Ware, etc. Some reports go further, and note which slip is applied to which ware:

> A red-ochre slip is found to have been applied over the Red Ware and the Micaceous Red Ware, but rarely on the coarse red wares. ... The Micaceous Red Ware vessels are treated with an orange slip. ... Patches of red, buff and pinkish slips noticed on some pots and various shades of yellow, red and orange occurring on others may be due to the presence of iron compounds in the clay or due to differential firing. ... A chocolate slip is noticeable on some vessels of the Red Ware as well as the Buff Ware groups. (Rao 1985: 336)

This observation attributes the different coloured patches and shades of vessels to the composition of the clay, and/or differences in firing. This is to some extent corroborated by the ethnographic evidence which indicates that colour variations do arise from both—many colour variations can occur in a single kiln, according to the type of slip applied, and the firing process itself. However, Rao's report does not acknowledge that the potter/painter might have intentionally produced a colour variation in the ceramic assemblage. In one of the case study villages, potters/painters applied a very light slip to a water pot in order to obtain the particular light orange tint preferred by their pastoralist clientele. Similarly, a pink tint is produced for ritual vessels through the application of very thin white slip on a red vessel. The potters/painters deliberately manipulate their materials in order to produce the type of wares that are in demand from the community whose demands they seek to fulfil.

The existence of different colours applied to a 'homogenous body of material' is acknowledged in the Rojdi report, again with reference to the differences in colour being produced either by firing techniques or different clays:

> The Fine Red, Fine Buff and Fine Grey Wares of Rojdi are all clearly a part of the general Harappan ceramic tradition. These three wares, distinct from one another only in their fabric colour, may be seen as an homogenous body of materials in terms of ceramic production. The quality of the fabric, slips, vessels forms, styles and motifs are fundamentally the same. It is common for red slips to have been applied to Fine Red fabrics and for brown slips to cover Fine Buff Ware. At this moment it is not known if the difference in fabric colour of the Rojdi Fine Wares is only due to the manipulation of firing techniques or whether it was achieved by using different clays. (Possehl and Raval 1989: 57)

Although this report makes it clear that the potter may have deliberately manipulated his materials or technique, one could argue that even if the technological reasons resulting in the difference in fabric colour were known, no advance would be made in understanding either the social role of the Fine Wares, or the social reasons for the differences in their colours. In my 1994 study, the ethnographic evidence indicated very clearly that variations in colour occur for a reason; the nature of the economy or preferences of the particular community which purchases a particular pot for a particular reason.

Understanding sherds in this way can lead an archaeologist to approach their classification in a different way. For instance, one could try to use the proportions of particular coloured wares at a site as an indicator of community demand: if there is a set of sherds which occur in a very low percentage, this might be because the vessels had ritual significance; or they could be the remains of a less-used vessel of a very small community. Colour variation in the same vessel is again often an indicator of community preference, and could for instance explain the Rojdi finding cited above. Ethnographically, it was seen that in a single village, potters simultaneously manufacture water vessels which are identical in every respect except colour, to fulfil the demands of different communities. One community prefers white slipped water pots, while another prefers red slipped water pots.

Direct comparisons between contemporary and ancient systems are of little value, since what exists today may have no ancient counterpart. However, this example of colour illustrates that, from careful probing of the underlying patterns of contemporary society, and of the sub-system of pottery production, the ethnographer can abstract rules and frameworks which provide the archaeologist with a different way of seeing. Ethnographic evidence shows the sheer complexity of the pottery system, and that a potter works in a symbiotic relationship with society, and the complexities of this relationship condition his material output. This understanding of the social role of pottery can add many more dimensions to the possibilities of interpreting the ancient record.

THE WAY FORWARD

As Van (1984: 132) comments, 'there are as many uses of potsherds in archaeology as ideas one might wish to gain or test concerning past societies: functional, chronological, technological, spatial, cultural, etc. Each requires its own kind of ceramic analysis.' I have argued that at present, the archaeological focus has tended to neglect the cultural dimension, and that because of this, the static objects (in this case ceramic) of material culture are not being equated with dynamic human culture (Ucko 1989: xiii). In this, it seems that we are overlooking the flexibility and variety of past human endeavour, and interpreting material culture only in relation to concerns with chronology and site-to-site relationships.

Bhattacharya (1989: 21) very usefully reminds us that 'dynamic processes of culture and strategies of adaptation chosen by a community alone can help in interpretation of symbolic objects. A more stylistic or morphological description will serve no purpose in our understanding of the prehistoric mind, and hence the society'. In our attempts to understand material culture, we must think beyond it, penetrating surface appearance to reach underlying realities:

> We need to think in terms of relationships between things, rather than simply in terms of the things themselves and to remember that 'each individual act of material culture production and use has to be regarded as a contextualized social act. (Tilley 1989: 188)

If archaeologists want to understand culture, they must try to understand why things are made as they are. What prompted a potter to produce a particular type of ceramic ware in an assemblage? It is more than just observing what is present—but also what is absent, and above all, asking why? Why is this sherd found in this context, rather than, any other? Such questioning could usefully lead to the construction of new interpretative categories, which begin to move Harappan studies towards the third phase of archaeological thinking, a concern with the cultural element. For instance, by attempting to establish the types of vessels and the percentage of each in a particular location, an archaeologist would be able to interpret the socio-economic and cultural characteristics of the community residing in the area where the vessel or vessel sherds were found.

Social contexts provide the clues as to why a vessel is as it is, but these clues are excluded by the dominant typological approach. If archaeologists are to come closer to understanding past societies, they must steer a different course. The ethnographic evidence suggests that it is quite possible to find conceptual frameworks by which to begin to explain issues such as variation in texture, colour, decoration and form in the ceramic assemblage (Choksi 1994). But this can only be done if archaeologists try to use pottery sherds to focus on the people who created and used ceramic artefacts, rather than treating the artefacts themselves as people.

REFERENCES

Ajithprasad, P. 1993. Harappan Culture and North Gujarat. Unpublished Paper, Deptartment of Archaeology the M.S. University of Baroda.

Ajithprasad, P. and V.H. Sonawane 1993. Harappa Culture in North Gujarat: a Regional Paradigm. Paper Presented at the conference on 'the Harappans in Gujarat: Problems and Prospects' at Deccan College Pune.

Bhan, K.K. 1983. Archaeology of Jamnagar District Gujarat. Ph.D. Dissertation. Vadodara: the M.S. University of Baroda.

——— 1989. Late Harappan Settlements of Western India: with Specific Reference to Gujarat, in *Old Problems and New Perspectives in the Archaeology of South Asia* (J.M. Kenoyer Ed.), pp. 219-42. Madison: Prehistory Press. Wisconsin Archaeological Reports 2.

Bhan, K.K. and D.R. Shah 1990. Pastoral Adaptation in the Late Harappan Tradition of Western India: with Specific Reference to Gujarat. Paper Presented at International Seminar on Rising Trends in Paleoanthropology: Environmental Change and Human Response. Pune.

Bhattacharya, D.K. 1989. Terracotta Worship in Fringe Bengal, in *The Meaning of Things: Material Culture and Symbolic Expression* (Ian Hodder Ed.), pp. 12-22. London: Unwin Hyman.

Binford, L.R. 1977. *Theory-Building in Archaeology*. New York: Academic Press.

Bisht, R.S. 1991. Dholavira: a New Horizon of Indus Civilisation, *Puratattva* 20: 71-82.

Chitalwala, Y.M. 1982. Harappan Settlements in the Kutch-Saurashtra Region: Patterns of Distribution and Routes of Communication, in *Harappan Civilization* (G.L. Possehl Ed.), pp. 197-202. Delhi: Oxford-IBH and the American Institute of Indian Studies.

Choksi, A. 1994. An Ethnoarchaeological Study of Pottery Manufacture in Kutch. Ph.D. Dissertation. Vadodara: the M.S. University of Baroda.

——— 1995. Ceramic Vessels: Their Role in Illuminating Past and Present Social and Economic Relationship, *Man and Environment* XX (1): 87-108.

——— 1997. Painted Pots: an Expression of Aesthetics or of Social Identity? *South Asian Studies* 13: 227-40.

——— 1998. Pottery Manufacturing Techniques: the Role of Technical Constraints and Personal Choices, *Man and Environment* XXIII (2): 107-118.

Dales, G.F. and J.M. Kenoyer 1986. *Excavation of Mohenjo daro, Pakistan: the Pottery.* Philadelphia: University Museum.

Dixit, M.S. 1950. Excavation at Rangpur 1947, *Bulletin of the Deccan College Research Institute* 7: 3-55.

Ghurye, G.S. 1939. Two Old Sites in Kathiawar, *Journal of the University of Bombay* VIII: 3-12.

Hegde, K.T.M., K.K. Bhan and V.H. Sonawane 1985. Excavation at Nageshwar 1984: a Preliminary Report, *Journal of the M.S. University of Baroda* 33-4: 3-20.

Hegde, K.T.M. and V.H. Sonawane 1986. Landscape and Settlement Pattern of Harappan Culture Villages in Rupen Estuary, *Man and Environment* X: 23-31.

Hegde, K.T.M., V.H. Sonawane, D.R. Shah, K.K. Bhan, P. Ajitprasad, K. Krishnan and S. Pratapachandra 1988. Excavation at Nagwada 1986-87: a Preliminary Report, *Man and Environment* XII: 55-65.

Herman, C.F. 1989. The Sorath Harappan Ceramics, in *Harappan Civilization and Rojdi* (G. Possehl and M H Raval Eds.), pp. 53-159. New Delhi: Oxford-IBH and the American Institute of Indian Studies.

Joshi, J.P. 1972. Exploration in Kutch and Excavation at Surkotada and New Light on Harappan Migration, *Journal of the Oriental Institute* XXII: 22: 98-144.

——— 1979. The Nature of Settlement at Surkotda, in *Essays in Indian Protohistory* (D.P. Agrawal and D.K. Chakrabarti Eds.), pp. 59-64. Delhi: B.R. Publishing Corporation.

Mehta, R.N. 1984. Vallabhi: a Station of Harappan Cattle Breeders, in *Frontiers of the Indus Civilization* (B.B. Lal and S.P. Gupta Eds.), pp. 227-30. New Delhi: Books & Books.

Mehta, R.N., K.N. Momin and D.R. Shah 1980. *Excavation at Kanewal.* Vadodara: the M.S. University of Baroda.

Miller, Daniel 1985. *Artefacts as Categories: a Study of Ceramic Variability in Central India.* Cambridge: Cambridge University Press.

Momin, K.N. 1979. Archaeology of Kheda District (Gujarat) up to 1500 AD Ph.D. Dissertation. Baroda: the M.S. University of Baroda.

——— 1981. Excavation at Zekhada, *Puratattva* 12: 120-5.

Pritchard, A.C. and Sander E. Van der Leeuw 1984. Introduction: the Many Dimension of Pottery, in *Ceramics in Archaeology and Anthropology* (S. Van der Leeuw and A. Pritchard Eds.), pp. 1-24. Amsterdam: Amsterdam University Press.

Possehl, Gregory 1976. Lothal: a Gateway Settlement of the Harappan Civilization, in *Ecological Background of South Asian Prehistory* (K.A.R. Kennedy and G.L. Possehl Eds.), pp. 118-31. Ithaca: Cornell University South Asia Program.

——— 1980. *Indus Civilisation in Saurashtra.* New Delhi: B.R. Publishing Corporation.

Possehl, G. and M.H. Raval 1989. *Harappan Civilisation and Rojdi.* New Delhi: Oxford-IBH and the American Institute of Indian Studies.

Rao, S.R. 1963. Excavation at Rangpur and Other Exploration in Gujarat, *Ancient India* 18-19: 5-201.

——— 1979. *Lothal: a Harappan Port Town (1955-62).* New Delhi: Memoirs of the Archaeological Survey of India 78 (1).

——— 1985. *Lothal: a Harappan Port Town (1955-62).* New Delhi: Memoirs of the Archaeological Survey of India 78 (2).

Raval, R.L. 1976. A Transition Profile of Kutch, 1809-1860, *Bhuj Museum Bulletin* XXVI: 35-58.

Reddy, S.N. 1990. Food or Fodder: Complementary Approaches to Late Harappan Subsistence Studies, Project Proposal (MSS). Department of Anthropology, University of Wisconsin.

Rice, Prudence. M. 1984. Change and Conservatism in Pottery-Producing Systems, in *Ceramics in Archaeology and Anthropology* (S.Van der Leeuw and A. Pritchard. Eds.), pp. 231-87. Amsterdam: Amsterdam University Press.

——— 1987. *Pottery Analysis: a Source Book*. Chicago: The University of Chicago Press.

Rissman, Paul. C. 1985. Migratory Pastoralism in Western India in the Second Millennium BC: the Evidence from Orio Timbo (Chirod). Ph.D. Dissertation. Philadelphia: University of Pennsylvania.

Rouse, Irving 1965. Caribbean Ceramics: a Study in Method and Theory, in *Ceramics and Man* (F.R. Matson Ed.), pp. 88-103. Chicago: Aldine Publishing Company.

Roux, Valentine 1989. *The Potter's Wheel: Craft Specialisation and Technical Competence*. New Delhi: Oxford-IBH.

Rye, O.S. and C. Evans 1976. *Traditional Pottery Techniques of Pakistan: Field and Laboratory Studies*. Washington, D.C.: Smithsonian Institute Press. Smithsonian Contributions to Anthropology 21.

Saraswati, B. and N.K. Behura 1966. *Potters Techniques of Peasant India*. Calcutta: Anthropological Survey of India Memoir 13.

Shaffer, Jim G. 1982. Harappan Culture: a Reconsideration, in *Harappan Civilization: a Contemporary Perspective* (G.L. Possehl Ed.), pp. 41-50. New Delhi: Oxford-IBH.

Shanks Michael and Ian Hodder 1995. Processual, Post Processual and Interpretive Archaeologies, in *Interpreting Archaeology: Finding Meaning in the Past* (Ian Hodder, Michael Shanks, Alexandra Alexandri, Victor Buchli, John Carman, Jonathan Last and Gavin Lucas Eds.), pp. 3- 29. London-New York: Routeledge.

Sharma, R.C. 1965. Pottery Industry in U.P., in *Census of India 1961, 15: Uttar Pradesh Part 7A*. New Delhi: Handicraft Survey Monograph 3.

Shinde, Vasant and Kar, Sonya Bhagat 1992. Padri Ware: a New Painted Ceramic Found in the Harappan Levels at Padri in Gujarat, *Man and Environment* XVII (2): 105-10.

Sonawane, V.H. and R.N. Mehta 1985. Vagad: a Rural Harappan Settlement Gujarat, *Man and Environment* IX: 38-44.

Sonawane, V.H. and P. Ajithprasad 1994. Harappan Culture and Gujarat, *Man and Environment* XIX (1-2): 129-39.

Soundara Rajan, K.V. 1984. Kutch Harappan: a Corridor of the Indus Phase, in *Frontier of Indus Civilisation* (B.B. Lal and S.P. Gupta Eds.), pp. 217-26. New Delhi: Books & Books.

Tilley, Christopher 1989. Interpreting Material Culture in *The Meaning of Things: Material Culture and Symbolic Expression* (Ian Hodder Ed.), pp. 185-94 London: Unwin Hyman.

Ucko, P.J. 1989. Forward, in *The Meaning of Things: Material Culture and Symbolic Expression* (Ian Hodder Ed.), pp. ix-xvii. London: Unwin Hyman.

Van As, Abraham 1984. Reconstructing the Potter's Craft, in *Ceramics in Archaeology and Anthropology* (S. Van der Leeuw and A. Pritchard Eds.), pp. 129-60. Amsterdam: Amsterdam University Press.

Van der Leeuw, S. 1984. Dust to Dust: a Transformational View of the Ceramic Cycle, in *Ceramics in Archaeology and Anthropology* (S. Van der Leeuw and A. Pritchard), pp. 707-74. Amsterdam: Amsterdam University Press.

Van der Leeuw, S. and A.C. Pritchard (Eds.) 1984. *The Many Dimensions of Pottery: Ceramics in Archaeology and Anthropology*. Amsterdam: Amsterdam University Press.

Van der Leeuw, S. and D. Papousek 1992. Tradition and Innovation in Ethnoarchaeologie: Justification, Problemes, pp. 135-58. Juan-les-Pins: Limites Editions APDCA.

Van der Leeuw, S., D. Papousek and Anick Coudart, 1991. Technical Traditions and Unquestioned Assumptions: the Case of Pottery in Michoacan, *Techniques et Culture* 17-18: 145-73.

Vats, M.S. 1937. *Annual Report of the Archaeological Survey of India 1934-37.* New Delhi: Archaeological Survey of India.

Yellen, J. 1977. Archaeological Theory and Ethnographic Fact, in *Archaeological Approaches to the Present: Models for Reconstructing the Past* (J. Yellen), pp. 1-12. New York: Academic Press.

Biological Anthropology of Human Skeletons from Harappa

KENNETH A.R. KENNEDY

INTRODUCTION

The resumption of archaeological excavation at Cemetery R-37, Harappa, in 1986 and the successful recovery of human skeletal remains from this locality in 1987 and 1988 revives questions about the phenotypic pattern and biological affinities of the ancient Harappans. Over the past 60 years answers to the question 'Who were the Harappans'? have been offered by historians, archaeologists, linguists, and indologues of various persuasions without the emergence of any single hypothesis overshadowing competing explanations. This state of affairs is due, in large part, to a failure to allow the skeletal record to 'speak for itself', i.e. to reveal its nature and degrees of genetic distance from ancient and contemporary populations unhindered by the preconceptions of how the Harappans might fit into traditional scenarios of South Asian prehistory based upon quasihistorical and religious tradition or upon racial typologies created by anthropologists. The four biological anthropologists affiliated with the University of California Archaeological Expedition to Pakistan during the 1987 and 1988 field seasons have approached the question of Harappan identity by focusing upon the skeletal material itself on the assumption that answers to a biological inquiry must be sought primarily in biological source material. This is a complex research strategy involving specialized study of the dentition, nonmetric variables, markers of pathological and occupational stress, indicators of growth and development pattern, and a basic morphometric analysis of individuals' bones and skeletal regions. From these data it is possible to apply robust multivariate statistical procedures that transcend the inadequate methods of racial typology and carry the results of laboratory analysis and a clearer light where real biological relationships of ancient and contemporary populations are demonstrated. This paper examines earlier morphometric and statistical analysis of the Harappan skeletons and demonstrates the value of a recent application of Principal Componenets Analysis (PCA) to new interpretations of their place within the broader arena of other prehistoric populations for which skeletal remains are available.

HARAPPAN MORTUARY SERIES

The existence of an advanced civilization in the Indus Valley region during the second and third millennia BC was unknown before 1921 when exacavtions were initiated by Daya Ram Sahni at Harappa in the Punjab and by Sir John Marshall (1931) at Mohenjo

Daro in Sindh. Site surveys and exacavations by their asssociates and successors led to the discovery of several hundred sites of the Harappan Culture, of which some are large urban centres. The sphere of Harappan cultural influence extended from north Afghanistan and the Makran coast of Baluchistan eastwards to the Indo-Ganga plain and beyond the outskirts of modern Delhi, while 700 miles separate the sub-Himalayan site of Rupar (Ropar, Rupnagar) on the Sutlej river in the Indian Punjab from Bhagatrav, and outpost on the banks of Narmada river in central India. The larger urban sites have yielded human skeletal remains which, in addition to skeletal series from several non-urban localities, constitute a total sample of over 500 individuals. This figure includes the more than 100 skeletal specimens excavated from Cemetery R-37 at Harappa in 1987 and 1988, 25 of which are relatively complete specimens from primary burial contexts.

This entire skeletal sample is a very broad representation of the 'Harappan population' coming as it does from different temporal contexts and across an immense geographical portion of the north-western sector of the Indian subcontinent. Treatment of this Harappan skeletal assemblage as a single Mendelian panmictic population is untenable. An example of such misinterpretation of data concerns the skeletons recovered from deposits at Mohenjo Daro which are unassociated with formal burial practices. Nevertheless, these specimens have been treated as though they were representative of a single population of contemporary individuals of the late Mature period despite the archaeological and biological evidence that these so-called 'massacre victims' were unceremoniously interred at different periods of time in different parts of the ancient city and do not exhibit markers of traumatic stress on their bones (Dales 1964, 1965; Kennedy 1984b).

Radiocarbon dates for the urban phase of the Mature Harappan Civilization are *c*. 2550-2000 BC (Possehl 1989, 1992), the period of deposition of the human remains from Mohenjo Daro, Chanhu Daro, and Cemetery R-37 at Harappa. Most of the skeletons from this latter necropolis were excavated between 1937 and 1941, and other specimens were collected during 1946 and 1966 field seasons. In addition to the discovery of these R-37 primary burials, comingled and secondary burials of human remains were found at Mound AB and Mound G between 1921 and 1934. Area G at Harappa is dated to a late Mature Period and Cemetery H, which lies adjacent to Cemetery R-37, is Post-Harappan with dates closer to 1850-1700 BC. Cemetery H contains two stratigraphic levels and distinctive ceramic wares, as revealed in excavations carried out between 1929 to 1930 and 1933 to 1934. All of the skeletons from Harappa and Mohenjo Daro were transported to Banaras in 1943, arriving at their present repository at the Anthropological Survey of India, Calcutta, in 1948.

The Lothal skeletons from Gujarat are Late Harappan and date to around 1900-1850 BC. Lothal is a trade outpost on the periphery of the Harappan realm. Skeletons from the large urban centre of Kalibangan in Rajasthan are dated to the Mature Harappan period, but comparative analyses of these specimens await publication (Sharma 1969-70, 1972, 1982). Rupar does not provide radiocarbon dates for the settlement prior to the cultural horizon associated with Northern Black Polished Ware (NBP) of the fourth and fifth centuries BC, although analysis of the skeletons associated with the Mature Harappan period has been published (Dutta et al. 1987). Fragmentary human remains from Damb Buthi in Sindh were excavated from Mature Harappan levels, but these were never fully described (Guha 1934). Additional skeletons associated with the cultural and geographical sphere of Harappan influence have been recovered in Baluchistan from Nal (Sohr Damb) (Sewell and Guha 1929) and Shahi Tump (Sewell and Guha 1931a), from Allahadino near Karachi (Khan 1968; Shaffer 1947; Hoffman and Shaffer 1976), and from Rojdi in central Gujarat (Possehl and Raval 1989). These specimens were not included in the present study for the reasons that some of the bones are remains of immature individuals while many adult bones are too fragmentary or lack good archaeological context to merit morphometric analysis.

In addition to the problem of establishing chronological and cultural contemporaneity of this Harappan mortuary sample is the trend of earlier investigators to omit incomplete or damaged specimens from laboratory examination. Much more concern has been directed to the selection of skeletal specimens which are in a good state of preservation. Postcranial bones have been overlooked in studies where descriptions of cranial specimens predominate. Thus in one study of the 265 individuals represented in the mortuary series from Harappa, only 72 specimens were included in the laboratory analysis (Chatterjee and Kumar 1962, 1963a). Another study of 42 crania from Mohenjo Daro was based upon a selection of only 12 specimens (Cappieri 1970). In certain cases excavated human skeletal remains have never been described by skeletal biologists. A relatively complete adult male skeleton removed in 1966 from Cemetery R-37 and placed in the Harappa Museum was not examined until 1988 when it was removed from its glass case for cleaning, restoration, and morphometric analysis (Mughal 1968). Some 11 human skeleton specimens from the 1966 excavation await laboratory analysis in the collections of the Archaeological Survey of Pakistan in Karachi.

UNIVARIATE ANALYSIS STUDIES

The first anthropometric description of Harappan skeletons appeared in 1931 following Marhsall's excavations of 1922-7 at Mohenjo Daro (Sewell and Guha 1931b). This was supplemented seven years later by the description of additional skeletons collected at the same site in 1927-31 by Mackay (Guha and Basu 1938). The methodology followed in both reports was that of anthropometric description based upon procedures for taking straightline measurements and angles, determining indices, and noting certain nonmetric morphological variables, as prescribed in the 1928 English language edition of Martin's *Lehrbuch der Anthropologie* (Martin 1928). Statistical analysis was limited to recording ranges of variation and calculating means, with considerable emphasis placed upon the significance of the cranial length-breadth index. Conclusions arising from these procedures reflected theories of racial typology and taxonomy favoured by B.S. Guha, Director of the Anthropological Survey of India. In his important contribution to the Census of India for 1931, Guha classified the living ethnic groups of India into seven racial categories, and he assigned his Mohenjo Daro cranial material to four of these (Guha 1935). He concluded that the dominant racial type at Mohenjo Daro found its biological affinites with past and present populations of western Asia and the Mediterranean Basin rather than with the peoples of peninsular India, Sri Lanka, or South-East Asia. His work was influenced to a considerable degree by the Vedic and Brahmanical traditions concerning a dichotomy of Aryan and non-Aryan populations of the subcontinent and by the approach to the study of human diversity taken by Roland B. Dixon, his mentor at Harvard University during the 1920s.

Guha's claim to have identified four separate racial types in the ancient population of Mohenjo Daro—types he labelled as Proto-Australoid, Mediterranean, Mongolian branch of Alpine, and Alpine—as well as the anthropometric and univariate statistical methods he employed were perpetuated by subsequent officers of the Anthropological Survey of India whose report of the skeletal series from the Harappa site appeared in 1962 (Gupta et al. 1962). The skeletons they described had been excavated from 1927 to 1944 under the directorships of Vats and Sastri and in 1946 when Wheeler conducted a major excavation. The writers of the 1962 report refer to several ethnic elements of which A-1 is dolichocranic and gracile with a receding frontal region while B-1 is mesobrachycranic, orthocranic, and mesorrhinic with temporal fullness and moderately developed brow ridges. There is a third group called A which is encountered in Cemetery R-37 and is characterized by dolichocrany, chamaecrany, orthocrany, and moderately formed muscular ridges. Gupta (et al. 1962) have proposed that this latter racial element represents the earliest population substratum at Harappa. The A-1 people, however, are members of the indigeneous population—the 'true Harappans'—but were overwhelmed demographically by the B-1 people of uncertain origins but physically quite different. Finally, a small-headed form of A-1 cranial type is a fourth racial element called A-2, its chief feature being its possession of mesocrany. The distribution of each of these so-called racial types in the various mortuary sites of the Harappan cities is discussed in detail by the inventors of these racial taxa, but it is not difficult to see that they can be matched quite easily with the elements of Guha's scheme: A = Proto-Australoid; A-1 and A-2 = Mediterranean; B-1 = Alpine + Alpine form of Mongoloid. Guha's approach is seen as well in later reports of skeletons from Chanhu Daro, which were excavated 1935-6 (Krogman and Sassman 1943), from Lothal excavated after 1954 (Rao 1973), and in the publications of others who re-examined the Harappa and Mohenjo Daro series (Chaterjee and Kumar 1963b; Sarkar 1964).

The single important departure from Guha's scheme was taken by Sarkar (1964). In 1964 this biological anthropologist of Calcutta University was writing about the '71 index people', i.e. the Harappan skeletons with cranial length-breadth indices clustering around this figure which Sarkar considered to be the hallmark of the architects of the high culture in the Indus Valley. He concluded from study of trait distribution curves that the dominant racial element was closely related to, if not derived from, waves of the Tepe Hissar populations whose final migrations from western Asia via the Ukraine and central Russia brought the mesocranic 'Scythian element' presented by broader-headed racial specimens from Area G and Stratum I of Cemetery H at Harappa.

Sarkar's racial typology was strongly influenced by the work of Kappers (1934), especially the latter's 1934 study of Western Asiatic populations and the skeletal series of Tepe Hissar. According to Sarkar, the Harappans had their origins with the group, Kappers called Indo-Aryan, although Sarkar preferred the term Indo-Caspian in the light of his thesis that these people of Western Asia reached the Indus plain via the Ukraine and neighbouring regions of Russia and Central Asia. Sarkar substituted Guha's Proto-Australoid type for Australoid, regarding this as a submerged autochthonous element already present in the subcontinent before the arrival of the ancestors of the architects of the Harappan civilization. Thus the argument for the heterogeneity of the Harappans was maintained within the methodological framework of univariate analysis.

The single female skull found at Chanhu Daro is assigned to 'a Proto-Mediterranean type in which ancestral Negroid traits have manifested themselves', according to its describers Krogman and Sassman (1943). Their study served to reinforce the thesis that Harappan biological affinities were to be found among the builders of high culture in the Mediterranean basin and western Asia, although appearance of non-Mediterranean phenotypic variables required explanation too. The answers were sought in the idea of 'submerged racial substrata' of Australoid, Veddoid, Negroid, Negritoid, and other 'foreign' or 'autochthonous' primitive survivals.

Chatterjee and Kumar (1963b) assigned the Lothal skeletal material they examined to three racial types—Proto-Nordic, Proto-Mediterranean, and Alpine—based upon the criteria of a limited number of nonmetric variables and the cranial length-breadth index. This classification was reduced to two types by Sarkar (1964), who used the cranial length-breadth index as the single criterion. Sarkar went on to claim to have established an affinity of the Lothal series to the dolichocranic and brachycranic peoples of ancient Sialk.

The past several years of Harappan skeletal series witnessed a reversal of opinion concerning the thesis of biological heterogeneity of these ancient people. Scholars who have contributed most significantly to the view that the Harappans were a fundamentally homogeneous population are Cappieri (1971) and Dutta (1972, 1974, 1975). While their conclusions are similar, their analytical methods are strikingly different.

Cappieri followed a traditional model of human racial typology concurring with Guha that the basic pheonotypic pattern of the Harappans finds its closest biological affinities with both earlier and contemporary populations of Western Asia and the Mediterranean basin. But Cappieri rejected those particular racial classifications which his Indian colleague applied to the Harappans, especially in the case of the skeletal specimens accorded distinct racial status on the basis of possessing the shape variable of brachycrany. The Italian investigtor assigned all Harappans to the eastern branch of his sevenfold division of what he calls Asian Proto-Mediterranean, as defined by configurations of physical similarities which, he says, were preserved through regional persistence of strict endogamous practices and absence of disruptive invasions of foreign groups and absence of movements of groups within the various kinds of uniform settlement patterns prevailing over long periods of time. In other words, homogeneity of Cappieri's Indian type is the consequence of both social and geographical isolation. He sought to demonstrate this phenomenon by quantification of morphological traits combined with characters derived from anthropometric mensural data for which he established means, standard deviations, determination of differences of means, analysis of variance, and levels of intersex variability for specimens of different skeletal series. He dismissed brachycranialization as a criterion for any separate racial enclave wherever the trait appears. Rather, he hypothesized, broad-headedness is an evolutionary process involving the morphoarchitecture of the cranium and face which has been manifested in varying degrees among widely dispersed and biologically distant human populations. Because he regarded all native inhabitants of north-western sector of the Indian subcontinent as a homogenous biocultural population which has remained relatively unchanged over the course of many millennia, it followed in his argument that components of his eastern branch of Asian Proto-Mediterraneans, such as the Harappans, were homogeneous also. Cappieri has noted that populations represented by cranial series from Lothal and Langhnaj (a Mesolithic population) in Gujarat reveal some regional variations when compared with the Indus Valley folk, but such differences are not significant within the range of phenotypic characters defined by his macro-populational division of mankind.

In his study published in 1972, Dutta sought to identify the particular population responsible for the Harappan Civilization and to determine if the skeletal series from the three Harappa site localities of Cemetery R-37, Area G, and Cemetery H were representative of a homogeneous Harappa type population or were representative of two or three unique racial lines. In short, Dutta was asking if it was possible to discern a racial strain that might be characteristic of all or some Harappan series. His sample contained 72 adult male and female crania, and he compared 15 anthropomorphic variables recognizable in his sample with the same variables described for an ancient Egyptian series called the Egyptian E skeletons from a single cemetery in the vicinity of the Gizah pyramids. This African sample was selected on the basis of its presumed phenotypic homogeneity, as asserted by Pearson and Davin (1924). Following the trend of previous investigators, Dutta chose his comparative data from skeletal series to the west of the Indian landmass. He tested for homogeneity of his Harappa crania by employing the univariate method of Chi-squre analysis, concluding from the results that 'The Harappan C series (R-37+G may thus be regarded as a sufficiently homogeneous population and responsible for the mature Harappan culture' (Dutta 1972). He observed that coefficients for variation of the Harappa males from Cemetery R-37 and Area G are greater than those same characters coefficients for females of Cemetery R-37 and area G are greater than those of Egyptian E females for 9 characters and smaller for 4. But when Dutta compared the Harappan specimens of his series B (R-37+H), he obtained results indicating heterogeneity, a conclusion apparently supported by his results when all three Harappa series were pooled into a single sample called series A (R-37+G+H).

The same conclusions reappear in Dutta's paper of 1974 in which he applied Chi-square method to 12 nonmetrical quantifiable variants observed in the same Harappa sample examined in 1972. But in this second study he states that 'the entire material belongs to a single homogeneous population group representing the Bronze Age Harappans', and 'that neither there exist differences between the sexes nor (could there) be found differences between populations of Cemetery R-37 and Cemetery H in regard to the indices for most of the discontinuous morphological characters' (Dutta 1974: 103, 113).

The contradiction between Dutta's observation of heterogeneity in the Harappa series stated in 1972 and his claim two years later that homogeneity characterizes the entire skeletal sample from the site is hardly explicable on the grounds of differences in research results derived from biometrical *versus* discrete trait anthropometric data. I submit that the resolution of this confusion is to be found in a third publication which Dutta authored in 1975. In this Dutta seeks to free himself from a narrow commitment to the typological racial concepts characterizing all earlier descriptions of the population, including his own contribution to the Harappa report of 1962. Dutta recognized some of the difficulties inherent in this static approach to the phenomenon of human biological diversity, and he turned to what he terms the currently more accepted 'population concept'. By this he meant the substitution of traditional multifactorial measurements and nonmetrical observations for observation of variables understood to be under genetic control and, therefore, less modifiable by environmental stresses. But his conversion to population genetics was not a radical one, and he attempted to bring about 'a synthesis of the older classical morphological anthropology with the new population genetics' (Dutta 1975: 35).

If I am correctly interpreting the views of this investigator, I should say that he labours under a powerful desire to define the architects of the Harappan Cultural achievements as a unique and homogeneous population, according them an ethnic integrity presumed to be inherent in the older typological concept of human races as natural biological entities (Kennedy 1987). Indeed, Dutta refers to his series as belonging to a single biological subspecies, a conclusion he restates in his book published in 1983—*The Bronze Age Harappans*. In the text of this major statement of his life's work, Dutta states, 'The ethnic identity of the entire cranial series may, therefore, be established as the Bronze Age Harrapan (race)' (Dutta 1983: 63). Furthermore, Dutta's analysis of variability of cranial specimens from Harappa for 19 measurements along with calculations of standard deviation and X^2 approximation for homogeneity of variance lead him to conclude that, 'It becomes pragmatical now to conceive a new concept of race ... the term "race" in palaeontological sense, may be defined as a "a natural biological unit" the membership of which is dependent solely upon the morphological homogeneity of the individual skeletal specimens obtained from a single locality' (Dutta 1983: 63).

To support this thesis, Dutta minimizes the significance of the anthropometric and morphological differences he had observed earlier in series from Cemetery H, concluding that 'there is no evidence to suggest that the tree samples—Cemetery R-37, Area G and Cemetery H—could have arisen from different population' (Dutta 1975: 45), and elsewhere, 'The entire material which can be considered a unit sample, deserves to be viewed as possessing a continuous spectrum of variation.' This view is repeated by Dutta (1984) in a later publication.

To summarize what has been discussed thus far, we can discern four assumptions supported by studies utilizing univariate/bivariate statistical techniques.

1. The ancient Harappans find their closest biological affinities with past and present populations inhabiting Western Asia and the Mediterranean Basin. Earlier and contemporary populations of peninsular India, Sri Lanka, South-East Asia, and the Far East have been omitted from comparative studies of biological distance.
2. Harappans are biologically homogeneous population.
3. Harappans are a biologically hetergeneous population. Where this assumption is made, it is associated with the claim that micropopulations within the Harappan gene pool are easily definable by observation of specific morphometric variables and that the individuals exhibiting these traits are all within the 'normal' range of pheotypic variability of a single Mendelian population.
4. Harappans are not the Aryans of Indian traditional accounts. One difficulty in arguing that invading Aryans brought about the decline of Harappan Culture is that the traditional date of their invasion, 1500 BC, is too late to coincide with the close of the Late Harappan period in about 1700 BC. The absence of 'Aryan skeletons' (whatever these might be and however they might be recognized!) precludes the possibility of a comparative morphometric analysis and any statistical measures of biological affinity. Among a minority of investigators of Harappan skeletal series who consider that there is an affinity of these materails with the Aryans is Rao (1973) who would assign the Harappans to an early infiltration of Aryan-speakers rather than to the Vedic Aryans of Indian religious accounts.

MULTIVARIATE ANALYSIS STUDIES

Until recently, multivariate analysis has not played a significant role in these inquiries, notable exceptions being Bartel's (1979) and Dutta's (1983) investigations of Harappan skeletal remains and Bernhard's (1967, 1968, 1969) analysis of materials from Timargarha and Sarai Khola. Bartel's study of 1979 is a significant application of the multivariate procedure of stepwise discriminant analysis undertaken with South Asian skeletal series. Bartel derived his methods of analysis from procedures described by Howells (1972, 1973a, 1973b) and othes (Janz 1973; Marriott 1974) writing in the early 1970s. He noted that the aim of discriminant analysis is to transform a set of P values into K linear functions in order to discern maximum degrees of dispersion between individual cranial specimens consituting the population being studied. Estimations of distance from group centroids may permit classification of individuals within a given cluster, and a canonical analysis can then be carried out towards a correlation of characters with a set of orthogonal axis developed to maximize the degree of dispersion between the groups. The problem posed by Bartel was to determine if groupings could be associated with measurements. He chose discriminant analysis in order to investigate the relationships between a known or presumed grouping of the data and the variables recorded. This multivariate approach could reveal a joint distribution of several varieties, a feature unattainable by univariate analysis.

Bartel included in his analysis 13 straightline cranial measurements derived from published sources. He did not collect these data from direct observation of the research specimens. His comparative samples from outside South Asia were selected in the same way from published records of prehistoric and historic crania from the Caucasus (Abdushelishvili 1960). Given the incomplete nature of this published record, certain criteria and adjustments had to be established before his data were run through the Biomedical Series stepwise discriminant computer program BMD 07M, which was used in all analyses (Dixon 1973).

Bartel's interpretations of his results were as follows: There is a significant discrimination of 95 per cent between crania from Cemetery R-37 and Area G, both males and females being included in this analysis.

Dutta's original observations that heterogeneity characterizes the interrelationships between specimens from Cemetery H and all other Harappa specimens, i.e. from Cemetery R-37 and Area G, are confirmed. The Cemetery H people appear to be distinct from the Mature Harappan people.

When comparing results to determine the degree of genetic distance between Cemetery R-37 males and males from Mohenjo Daro, Bartel observed the two series to be significantly discriminated.

Males from rural sites contemporary with the Harappan Civilization, either within or outside the sphere of its direct cultural influence, also tend to be discriminated from Harappa Cemetery R-37 males. It is interesting to note that there are some obvious sexual differentiations here, many of the rural males falling directly within the classification of urban Harappa females.

When Indian cranial data from these previous computer runs were compared with series from the Caucasus, as well as with a skeletal series from the prehistoric Timargarha cemetery of the Gandhara region of north-western Pakistan (Bernhard 1967), the Caucasus materials is observed to be significantly discriminated from the Indian series, and Timargarha males and females overlap with crania of both sexes from Harappa Cemetery R-37.

Earlier univariate approaches to racial classification of South Asian skeletal series could not be confirmed from discriminant analysis without risk of compounding a great number of artificial groupings or types and misclassifying some specimens into unrealistic categories. In short, the efforts to establish racial-types by statistical methods used by Guha and others appear to be quite irrelevant to interpretation of Bartel's scatter plot diagrams.

Finally, the population of prehistoric South Asia may be considered relatively homogeneous when compared with other populations from outside the subcontinent.

PRINCIPAL COMPONENTS ANALYSIS

The present writer and his associates (Kennedy et al. 1984) have produced a bivariate summary of the relationships of 15 prehistoric South Asian populations by a multivariate analysis of craniometric data in order to demonstrate the utility of Principal Components Analysis (PCA) as an investigative tool in palaeoanthropology. This multivariate ordination technique was used in the analysis of 12 cranial measurements from a total Harappa Area AB and Cemetery R-37, and Lothal. With these series from mature food-producing and pastoral populations were included series from hunting-gathering populations (Bellanbandi Palassa, Langhnaj, Mahadaha, Sarai Nahar Rai), early farming populations (Burzahom, Tekkalakota), non-Harappan mature agriculturalist-pastoralist populations (Nevasa), and iron-using populations with successful food-production (Adittanalur, Brahmagiri, Timargarha, Yeleswaram (Fig. 1). Pleistocene hunter-gatherers from Upper Palaeolithic sites of France, Italy, Belgium, and Czechoslovakia constituted the remainder of the sample. The senior author had examined at first hand the bulk of this cranial collection, but some data were derived from published and unpublished sources (Kennedy 1980; Kennnedy and Caldwell 1984). Procedures for anthropometric measurements were based upon standards established by Martin and Sallar (1957).

The hypothesis-generating features of PCA are becoming familiar to anthropologists and prehistorians through a number of articles published by the statistical community (Gauch 1977, 1982a, 1982b; Gauch et al. 1977; Barnett 1981; Diaconic and Efron 1983). In standard descriptive and inferential statistics, mathematical procedures are used to summarize large quantities of data and to test hypotheses. While multivariate analysis is often used in these modes, it can be developed to an exploratory mode wherein the researcher interacts with the data matrix through a generalized set of computer programs and searches for significant structures in the matrix. When the researcher is satisfied that structures seen under a particular analysis are stable, then localities of unknown relationships can be added to the matrix and their placement within the established framework can be scrutinized. Clusters of localities are relatable to clusters of variables in a single low-dimensional ordination space, hence it is a straightforward matter to determine which variables are most important in the definition of locality subsets.

In the present study, a preliminary survey of the entire data matrix (117 crania by 12 measurements = 1404 information bits), using the SAS program package PRINCOMP procedure (Ray 1982), did not produce unambiguous clusters either by sex, site, or stratigraphic horizon. Therefore, it was decided that this original data set contained too many missing values. A second analysis, using the ORDIFLEX program package PCA procedure, was performed on the much condensed matrix of 14 sites (Lothal excluded in the original analysis) by 12 measurements (Gauch 1977). Grand means for measurements were available. Because the data set consisted of measurements with a small range in any variable and a high similarity between samples, PCA was used (Gauch, et al. 1977). Results of centred, centred and standardized, and reciprocal averaging analyses were distinctly different. The three distinct PCA ordinations produced by the ORDIFLEX package showed that the first and third arranged sites into a crescent with respect to first and second principal components, thereby spreading out the sites along a single gradient while the centred and standardized method produced a rough two-dimensional scatter of sites. Inspection of these three ordinations revealed a rough north-south axis perpendicular to a temporal axis. It should be emphasized that this particular ordination was chosen not for *a priori* mathematical reasons, but based on information about geography and chronology known to the researcher but not to the computer (Fig. 2).

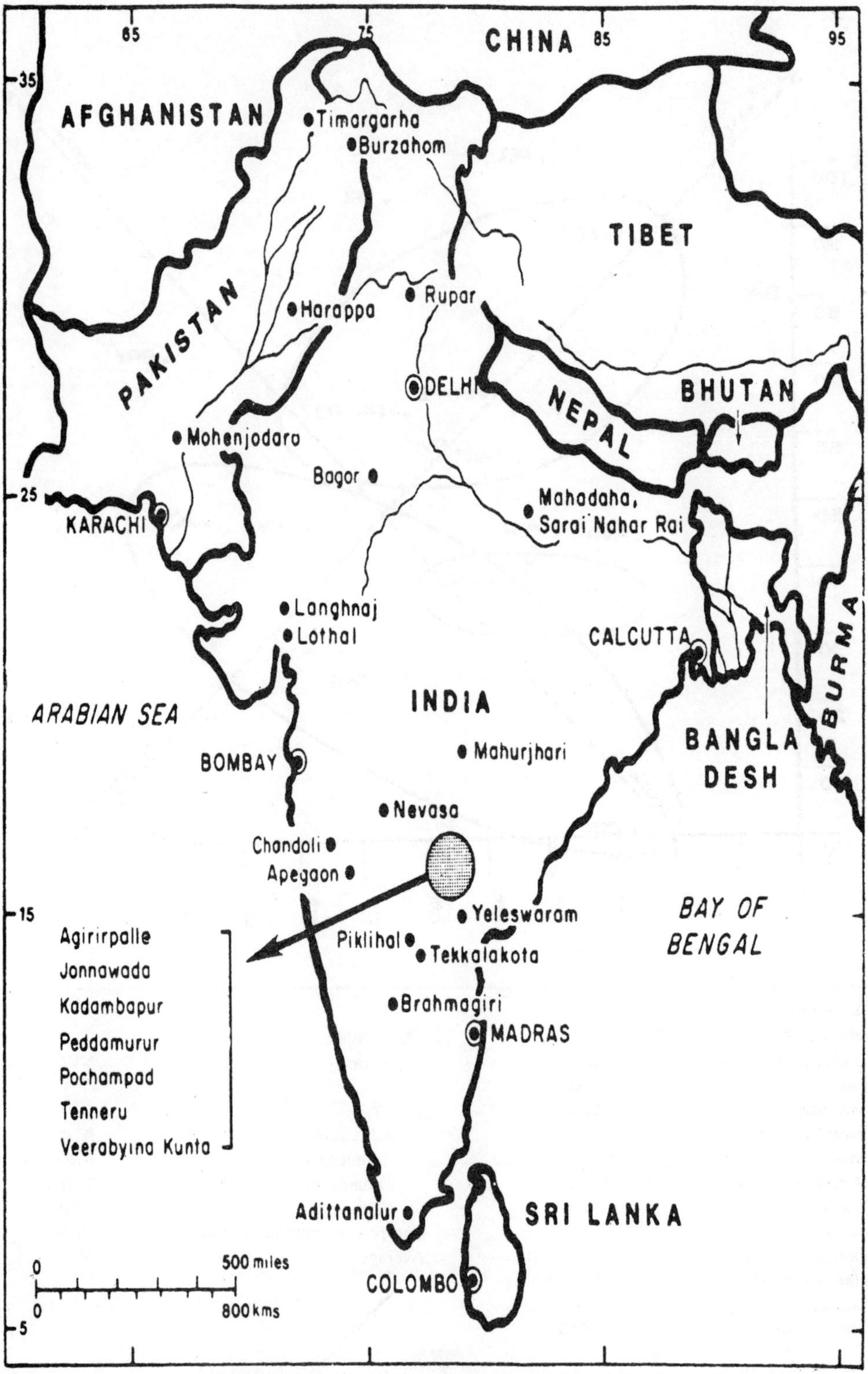

Fig. 1. Map of Archaeological sites mentioned in the text.

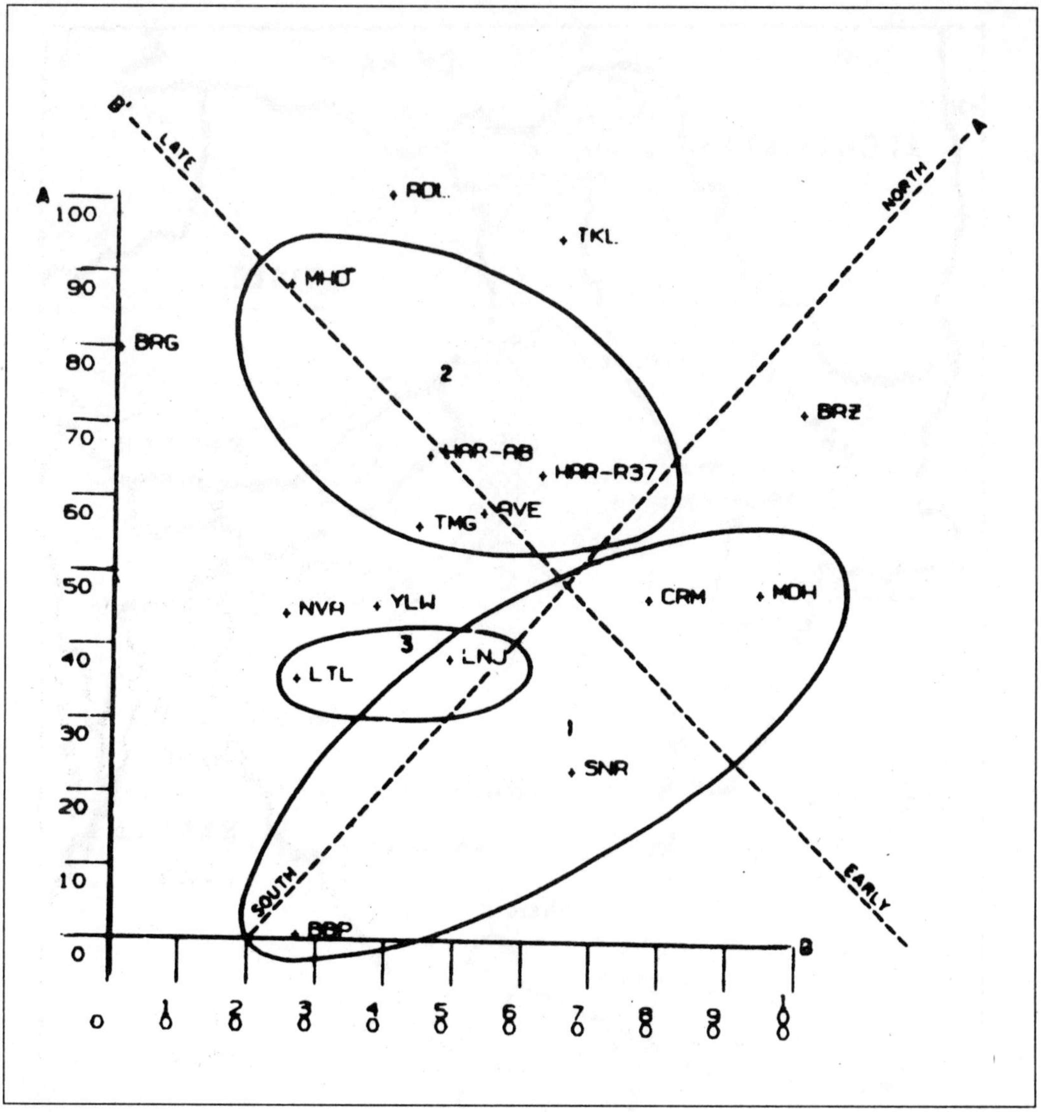

Key to abbreviations:

Mesolitihic		Chalcolithic	
Bellanbandi Palassa	BBP	Nevasa	NVA
Langhnaj	LNJ		
Mahadaha	MDH	Iron Age	
Sarai Nahar Rai	SNR	Adittanalur	ADL
Neolithic		Brahmagiri	BRG
Burzahom	BRZ	Timargarha	TMG
Tekkalakota	TKL	Yeleswaram	YLW
Harappan		European Upper Palaeolithic	CRM
Harappa, Area AB	HAR-AB	Average	AVE
Harappa, R-37	HAR-R37		
Lothal	LTL		
Mohenjodaro	MHD		

Fig. 2. Distribution and cluster of prehistoric skeletal series included in the principal component analysis.

The results of the PCA studies are the following: (1) A north-south distribution of prehistoric sites along the axis A'; (2) A temporal distribution of sites along the axis B'; (3) One cluster of sites of hunting-gathering populations from South Asia and the European Upper Palaeolithic and a second cluster of sites including food-producing communities. A third cluster includes the late hunting-gathering population of Langhnaj and the site which is a distant outlying trade centre of the Harappan Civilization at Lothal. Sites falling outside these clusters find their place with respect to geographical and temporal axis.

In determining which biological variables affected the clustering of hunter-gatherers from food-producers, it was found that features of facial architecture (internal and external palatal breadths, bizygomatic breadth, intraorbital breadth, bifrontal breadth, Nasion-Prosthion height) were the most significant characters for the former group. The food-producers were marked by somewhat different cranial variables (bigonial breadth, maximum cranial breadth, bicondylar breadth, nasal breadth) which exerted the greatest 'pull' away from the average. For example, the dolichocranic skulls of the hunter-gatherers cluster contrast markedly with the high incidence of mesocrany and appearance of brachycrany in the food-producing populations from Brahmagiri and, to a lesser degree, Mohenjo Daro and Lothal. Noses are broadest among the hunter-gatherers of Sri Lanka and narrowest among the Harappans. The position of the European Upper Palaeolithic crania within the cluster of Indian and Sri Lankan prehistoric hunter-gatherers does not imply genetic affinity but, rather, parallel development of certain facial morphologies and proportions in the hunting-gathering populations.

DISCUSSION

Bartel's observations that series from Cemetery R-37, Area G, and Cemetery H are discriminant makes good sense in the light of the archaeological contexts of these mortuary localities. These deposits are by no means contemporary in time, the skeletons from Cemetery R-37 belonging to the Mature phase of occupation whereas Cemetery H skeletons are Post-Harappan and mark a settlement which dates to a time just before the total abondonment of the city. Some investigators have identified the Harappa Cemetery H people with a culture called Jhukar, and debate continues as to whether this represents a final gasp of the Harappan Culture or should be attributed to non-Harappan people arriving from lands to the west of the Khyber or from elsewhere (Wheeler 1947; Casal 1964). Archaeologically the Cemetery H mortuary and artefactual records bear the stamp of impermanency. Area G burials are now assigned to a late phase of the Mature Harappan. Thus the dating of these three mortuary series ranges over a span of several centuries. It is hardly surprising that heterogeneity is an obvious feature of Harappan skeletal material when it is assembled for comparative analysis.

The argument for biological heterogeneity finds some support from the examination of the several modes of disposal of the dead practised at Harappa over the long period of the city's occupation. At Cemetery R-37 the usual burial pattern is dorsal extension of the body which is laid in a north-south orientation and accompanied by food and grave goods. In area G fractional burials predominate with the bones packed together in a limited amount of space and with fewer funerary goods associated with them. Flexed burials are most common at Cemetery H, Stratum II, and the skeletons are accompanied by grave goods; but urn burials of infants and fractional burials of adults characterize Stratum I. To be sure, several different burial customs may prevail in a society at the same time as in some present-day Western cultures. However, given the temporal distribution of the Harappa cemeteries, it is more probable that differences in burial practice indicate distinct cultural traditions of more than one ethnic group. These groups would include enclaves of immigrants from outside or members of different established social classes. The differences in burial customs and the difference in physical features of the skeletons are exactly what is to be expected in the kind of cosmopolitan life characteristic of other large urban settlements with extensive trade connections and exploratory commercial and military activities in the ancient world. It is not remarkable that results of Bartel's multivariate analysis suggest that the Harappan citizenry was composed of more than a single homogeneous ethnic element.

Further support for the argument in favour of Harappan heterogeneity is found in the results of Principal Components Analysis. The degrees of biological affinity identified by Bartel, whereby Harappa series from Mound AB and Cemetery R-37 are more proximate than both are to the series from Mohenjo Daro, are confirmed by our results (Fig.2). Lothal specimens are distant from all three Indus Valley series and are more proximate to series from Langhnaj and other series from Gujarat and the Deccan plateau. Racial classifications advanced by Guha (1935) and Sarkar (1972) on the basis of their univariate analyses of most of the same metrical variables employed in Bartel's and our studies are not confirmed by this multivariate analysis, nor do other racial classificatory schemes for prehistoric South Asians find a place in our analysis of results. For these reasons, we must look to factors beyond genetic affinity to explain the distributions of the series included in the PCA study.

It is proposed that the positions of hunter-gatherer series from South Asia and Europe reflect real differences of craniofacial anatomy which set apart Terminal Pleistocene and early post-Pleistocene populations from more recent food-producing groups. This documents a trend from pronounced skeletal robusticity and large body size towards skeletal gracility and reductions of body size over the past 1,00,000 years of sapiens evolution. It is most dramatically demonstrated by comparisons between anatomically archaic and anatomically modern *Homo sapien's* skeletons (Wolpoff 1980). This trend accelerated for those populations making the transition from hunting and gathering to food-producing life-ways in the last period of the Quaternary. It is most obvious in populations with a long history of sedentary agriculture or pastoralism within rural and urban contexts. The evolutionary process which accounts for this change is natural selection, for smaller body size becomes adaptive for village and urban lifeways with their higher percentages of carbohydrate nutritional resources and lower percentages of available protein (Stini 1975). Selection towards larger and more robust bodies may be relaxed as the physical strength of the hunter is no longer of such high selective value in the food-producing ecological and cultural setting. More advanced technologies serve as a more effective buffer between the food-producer and his nutritional resources than is the case between the hunter and his prey. A recent study of stature variability in prehistoric and modern South Asian populations indicates that standing height was greater in pre-agricultural skeletal series than in both ancient and modern food-producing populations of the Indian subcontinent, the trend towards decreased stature being attributed to responses to chronic protein deficiency as well as to relaxed natural selection where large body size no longer plays a significant role in survival (Baernstein and Kennedy 1990).

Tooth size reduction parallels these trends towards reduced muscular-skeletal development and stature, as has been effectively documented for South Asia by Lukacs (1982, 1983, 1985) and others (Brace and Mahler 1971; Brace and Montagu 1977). They have observed that today in South Asia smallest teeth appear among populations in the northern and north-western sectors of the subcontinent, becoming larger in the western and central Deccan and largest in southern India and Sri Lanka. Their surveys are correlated with the archaeological record which reveals that higher technologies, including those relating to food procurement and preparation, are of greater antiquity in northern India and Pakistan than in the peninsula, as attested by the emergence of the Harappan Civilization some 5000 years ago. Indeed, there appears to be a parallel trend towards tooth size reduction in other parts of the world where more advanced technologies have evolved. Thus the greater the period of time a population has practised advanced technologies and food production, the smaller are its teeth, with parallel reduction of other physical components. It is hypothesized that this is due to relaxation of selective pressures upon skeletal robusticity, body height, and dental size (Brace 1978).

If these hypotheses to explain the fact of skeletal-muscular-dental size reduction are correct, then the clustering of Harappan and other food-producing populations apart from hunter-gatherer populations, as indicated by PCA, may be due less to ties of genetic affinity than to parallels that are manifested in regional populations with long histories of food-production. The data from this analysis suggest that the significant variables which form the clusters for these two groups are related to features of facial architecture. Dental size is a function of facial size and robusticity, and which dental data are not included in our PCA study, the osteological data accord well with what is known from other studies about comparative facial and dental size in South Asia (Lukacs 1985).

The close proximity of the Langhnaj and Lothal series may offer a better case for identification of genetic distance within the sample, for both populations were coexisting in Gujarat at the same time. Archaeological evidence from Langhnaj reveals trade contacts of its hunting-gathering population with the Harappan Civilization, presumably through local emporia (such as Lothal; Possehl 1976). This study confirms conclusions reached by an earlier univariate analysis of skeletal series from Langhnaj and Lothal that the Lothalians were not derived directly from Indus Valley populations but were members of local population enclaves in Gujarat (Ehrhardt and Kennedy 1965). This is supported by observations that there is a high degree of phenotypic heterogeneity in the skeletal biology of the Lothal series when it is compared with the mortuary series from

Harappa and Mohenjo Daro. Furthermore, the Lothalians are not so similar in phenotypic pattern to their contemporaries in the Indus Valley as to suppport a hypothesis that the inhabitants of the settlements were reproductively isolated from the macropopulation of the region. Indeed, there is evidence of a biological continuum of ancient and present-day populations in this part of the subcontinent of which the Lothalians are a single geographical varient. Furthermore, there is every reason to hypothesize from the results of multivariate analysis that there was a regular pattern of gene flow between Lothal and hunting-gathering populations in Gujarat during late Harappan times, and this is strongly upheld by the archaeological evidence (Possehl and Kennedy 1979) and recent studies in dental anthropology (Lukacs 1990).

A very significant aspect of the dynamics between tribal populations and village agriculturalists is that the rural setting is the scene of the initial step in the urbanization of tribal enclaves which move from regions of relative isolation into centres of high culture based upon food-production. Such demographic transitions are registered in the gene pool of urban populations, and there is every reason to hypothesize that new genetic material was added to centres of Harappan activity through this process. It is one which continues to the present-day in South Asia (Kennedy 1984a). This demographic process may be documented by the presence of skeletal specimens that Guha classified as Proto-Australoid in his racial classification of Mohenjo Daro skeletons. Another specimen with similar cranial features was found in the 1988 excavations at Cemetery R-37 at Harappa, the striking differences in cranial architecture and metrical values for these 'exotic' specimens placing them well outside the range of variation of other crania in these Harappan urban centres.

The apparently significant distance between the skeletal series from Mohenjo Daro and Harappa which is indicated by the Principal Components Analysis may be interpreted as a measure of differences in demographic histories, composition of ethnic enclaves, social groupings with separate burial practices, as well as of differences in health status, occupational stresses, and other physical variables which are of nongenetic origin. The contrasts in the ecologies of Sindh and the western Punjab 4,500 years ago and today indicate that human biological reponses have been different in the two regions. This discrepancy in statistical measures is unsettling only if those who assume that all of the participants in the achievements of the Indus Valley Civilization constituted a homogeneous racial element. One argument against that assumption is that the modern inhabitants of Sindh are not biologically identical with the modern habitants of the western Punjab, a predictable phenomenon which may have a long biological history covering many millennia in this part of southern Asia.

A related issue is the matter of a prehistoric pan-South Asian ethnic identity and the discovery by various methods of statistical analysis of closely related populations from beyond the banks of the Indus. As noted already, there exists a strong bias on the part of many investigators to establish the ethnic origins of the Harappans with ancient populations of western Asian and the Mediterranean region, some scholars suggesting a migratory route via Central Asia. All earlier theories of demographic movements have been based upon results of univariate analysis which employed a limited number of mensural and morphological features of which the cranial length-breadth index asserted an overwhelming role in establishing racial identities.

The important question of Harappan ethnic identity is raised consistently in the anthropological literature over the past 70 years. There are three reasons for this failure to achieve a 'final solution':

(1) the published studies give little, if any attention to multivariate analysis of morphometric data of ancient skeletal specimens from peninsular India, save for studies of prehistoric skeletal remains from Iron Age sites (Kennedy and Levisky 1985) and the PCA analysis by the author and his associates (Kennedy et al. 1984);
(2) almost all comparative data bearing upon this problem have been focused upon anthropometric study of living populations in which the variables observed are distinct from those encountered in skeletal analysis, viz., pigmentation variables of skin, hair, and eyes or hair form or other features of soft part anatomy;
(3) all studies of the biological affinities of historic populations have been unduly influenced by theories based upon traditional or literary sources. (Bowles 1977)

Almost all treatment of the skeletal series discussed above is haunted by the shades of the typological race concept and the search for the identification of an Aryan racial element. Western scholars have been as devoted to this preoccupation as have their South Asian colleagues (Childe 1926; Poliakov 1974; Erdosy 1989), but with one significant difference. The fall of the race or subspecific concept in Western taxonomic biology by 1940 is variably interpreted in Asian cultures where established social groups and castes form integral parts of contemporary life. In a cultural context where race is not easily distinguished from social classifications, those populations occupying the lower rungs of the social hierarchy by reason of caste status are considered to be farthest removed from prestigious Aryan origins. While we must recognize the Aryan presence as an irrefutable linguistic phenomenon, its biological significance remains unestablished. We do not encounter 'Aryan skeletons'. Attempt by archaeologists to relate certain Post-Harappan prehistoric cultures with Aryans have not met with general acceptance (Shaffer 1984).

Certainly we do discern unifying physical features among the present-day peoples of South Asia, especially when study samples are compared with ethnic groups from outside the geographical landmass of the subcontinent. Even univariate analysis studies go far to suggest the existence of biological continua of prehistoric and contemporary populations within sectors of this part of the world (Kennedy 1965; Kennedy and Malhotra 1966; Kennedy et al. 1987). But we are not able to comprehend the scope and distribution patterns of the biological variability characterizing this immense area of investigation with its many aboriginal tribes, castes, long-settled agricultural village communities, urban dwellers, and migratory groups of pastoralists, military and commerical socieites, and immigrants from lands bordering the Himalayas or from regions across the waters of the Indian Ocean.

Finally, we should note that multivariate analysis has an important contribution to make in the area of palaeodemography. We have observed already the question of discerning apparent sexual dimorphism in the Harappan skeletal record, i.e. rural Harappan females. Apart from problems of sampling error or mixing of skeletons in the laboratory, a more likely resolution to this problem is that these similarities are statistically significant and may reflect a combination of environmental and genetic factors having to do with a population's overall realization of ontogenetic growth potential during early years of life, metabolic responses to nutritional resources and their quantities, adaptations to a broad spectrum of social and natural stressors, and the consequences of endemic diseases and other health-related variables. Still other palaeodemographic phenomena which can be better understood through multivariate studies include measures of habitat preference (urban *versus* rural settlements; rock-shelters and caves *versus* open air camps), demographic movements (nomadic herding practices or the pioneering of new ecological settings by resettled communities exploiting natural resources), and health profiles (adaptations to areas of endemic malaria; adaptations to iron deficiency; consequences of high population density, especially in regions of high incidence of disease vectors and their parasites dependent upon a large host population) (Kennedy 1981; Lovell and Kennedy 1989). Multivariate studies of palaeodemographic data will require the close collaboration of archaeologists, ecologists, and biological anthropologists, an ideal that was realized at the Harappa excavations by the University of California, Berkeley, and the Government of Pakistan since 1986.

It is anticipated that with the morphometric and statistical analysis of the recently recovered human remains from Cemetery R-37 at Harappa during the 1987 and 1988 field seasons the biological identities and affinities of the ancient Harappans may be understood more clearly. Not only is the size of the skeletal record increased substantially (> 100 specimens of which 25 are relatively complete skeletons from primary burial deposits), but modern methods of skeletal conservation guarantee the preservation of material for future generations of biological anthropologists. The intense analysis of these newly acquired specimens from Cemetery R-37 has involved radiographic and photographic records, microscopic and chemical analysis of osseous and dental tissues, and careful study of each bone and tooth by the four biological anthropologists trained in the specialities of morphometrics, palaeopathology, discrete trait analysis, and dental anthropology. Reports of this intensive research project are in manuscripts in process of publication (Dales and Kenoyer 1987, 1988, 1989).

CONLCUSION

This paper reviews the history of research involving univariate, bivariate, and multivariate analysis studies of prehistoric skeletal series from South Asia with particular attention to the mortuary series recovered from sites of the Harappan Civilization. The questions of genetic homogeneity-heterogeneity of prehistoric populations and estimates of the degrees of biological affinity between them are evaluated in the context of a recent application of Principal Components Analysis. Results of this study are incorporated in the following conclusions:

If we are to find better solutions to problems of biological constitution and affinities of prehistoric populations in South Asia within the context of cultural succession, then the modern methods of multivariate analysis may prove helpful.

Principal Components Analysis is a useful procedure in hypothesis formation. When applied to a number of cranial series from widely scattered prehistoric sites and cultural periods in South Asia, results show a distribution of traits that form clusters based upon anatomical variables responsive to stresses of the socio-economic and technology environments of human culture and not to criteria of racial identification derived from earlier unvariate and bivariate statistical studies.

An examination of the distribution of populations from Harappa, Mohenjo Daro, and Lothal, as formed by PCA (Fig. 2), reveals that no single phenotypic pattern defines them as a single Mendelian population. While the proximity of the mortuary populations of Harappa's Mound AB and Cemetery R-37 is apparent, the individuals from these series are not so anatomically similar as interpretaions of univariate studies suggest. Regional populations of Harappans at Mohenjo Daro and Lothal reinforce the conclusion that heterogeneity rather than homogeneity characterized the ethnic profile of the ancient Harappans. This is exactly the genetic picture we should predict from the archaeological record of diverse burial customs and regionally unique features of the widely scattered urban centres of large size. As with other ancient cities, Harappan cities witnessed demographic shifts of ethnic enclaves in commerce as well as the continuing urbanization of sectors of the population derived from rural towns and villages and from areas of relative isolation occupied by tribal groups. Many of these hunter-gatherer peoples formed symbiotic ties with sedentary, food-producing populations in the course of their eventual socialization to more complex urban life. These are the features of cultural succession most contributory to changes in the gene pools of cities. It is this biological diversity we encounter in Harappan mortuary sites.

The multivariate studies discussed here do not support schemes of racial typology proposed by earlier investigators using univariate and bivariate analyses of South Asia's mortuary populations. Nor does the concept of an 'Harappan race' have any significance once the principles of population genetics and multivariate analysis are properly understood.

REFERENCES

Abdulshelishvili, M.G. 1960. Craniology of the Caucasus, in *Contribution to the Physical Anthropology of the Soviet Union, Peabody Museum of Archaeology and Ethnology* (V.V. Bunak, G.F. Debets and M. Levin Eds.), pp. 24-65. Cambridge: Harvard University.

Baernstein, A. and K.A.R. Kennedy 1990. Stature Variability in Prehistoric and Modern South Asian Populations: a Biocultural Approach, *Journal of Human Ecology* 1 (2): 81-108.

Barnett, V. (Ed.) 1981. *Interpreting Multivariate Data*. New York: John Wiley and Sons.

Bertal, B. 1979. A Discriminant Analysis of Harappa Civilization Human Populations, *Journal of Archaeological Science* 6: 49-61.

Bernhard, Wolfram 1967. Human Skeletal Remains from the Cemetery of Timargarha (A.H. Dani Ed.). Timargarha and Gandhara Grave Culture, *Ancient Pakistan* 3: 291-407.

——— 1968. Human Skeletal Remains from the Bronze and Early Iron Age Cemetery of Timargarha (Dir State, West Pakistan), Tokyo, *Proceedings of the 8th International Congress of Anthropological and Ethnological Sciences* 2: 144-54.

——— 1969. Preliminary Report on the Human Skeletal Remains from the Prehistoric Cemetery of Sarai Khola, *Pakistan Archaeology* 6: 100-16.

Bowles, Gordon T. 1977. *The People of Asia*. New York: Charles Scribner's Sons.

Brace, C. Loring 1978. Tooth Reduction in the Orient, *Asian Perspectives* 19: 203-52.

Brace, C. Loring and Ashley Montagu 1977. *Human Evolution: an Introduction to Biological Anthropology*. New York: Macmillan and Sons.

Brace, C. Loring and P.E. Mahler 1971. Post-Pleistocene Changes in Human Dentition, *American Journal of Physical Anthropology* 34: 191-203.

Cappieri, Mario 1970. The Population of the Indus Civilization. *Coconut Grove: Field Research Projects, Occasional Papers* 11: 1-46.

——— 1971. The Population of the Indus Civilization, in *The Roots of Ancient India* (Walter A. Fairservis, Jr.), pp. 425-43. New York: Macmillan.

Casal, Jean-Marie 1964. *Fouilles D'Amri,* 2 Vols. Paris: Publication de la Commission des Fouilles Archaeologiques, Fouilles du Pakistan. Librairie C. Klinchsieck.

Chatterjee, B.K. and G.D. Kumar 1962. Etude comparee at Analyse Racial des Restes Humains de Harappa, Pakistan Occidental, *L'Anthropologie* 66: 335-7.

——— 1963a. *Comparative Study and Racial Analysis of the Human Remains of Indus Valley Civilization with Particular Reference to Harappa*. Calcutta: W. Newman and Co.

——— 1963b. Racial Elements in Post-Harappan Skeletal Remains at Lothal, in *Anthropology on the March* (R. Ratnum Ed.), pp. 104-10. Madras: Social Sciences Association.

Childe, V. Gordon 1926. *The Aryans: a Study of Indo-European Origins*. London: Kegan Paul, Trench and Trubner.

Dales, George F. 1964. The Mythical Massacre at Mohenjo Daro, *Expedition* 6 (3): 36-43.

——— 1965. New Investigations at Mohenjo Daro, *Archaeology* 18 (2): 145-50.

Dales, George F. and Jonathan Mark Kenoyer 1987. Preliminary Report on the University of California at Berkeley's Second Season at Harappa, Pakistan, January-April 1987, Manuscript (Photocopy): 19.

——— 1988. Preliminary Report on the Third Season (January-March 1988) of Research at Harappa, Pakistan, Manuscript (Photocopy): 62.

——— 1989. Preliminary Report on the Fourth Season (January 15-March 31, 1989) of Research at Harappa, Pakistan, Manuscript (Photocopy): 33.

Diaconic, P. and B. Efron 1983. Computer Intensive Methods in Statistics, *Scientific American* 248 (5): 116-30.

Dixon, W. 1973. *Biomedical Computer Programs*. Los Angeles: University of California.

Dutta, P.C. 1972. The Bronze Age Harappans: a Re-examination of the Skulls in the Context of the Population Concept, *American Journal of Physical Anthropology* 36: 391-6.

——— 1974. Non-Metrical Variation in the Cranial Material from Harappa, in *Indian Anthropology Today* (D. Sen Ed.), pp. 103-13. Calcutta: University of Calcutta.

——— 1975. Race Concept and Palaeoanthropology: a Research Model for Interpreting Ancient Human Remains, *Anthropologie* 13: 35-46.

——— 1983. *The Bronze Age Harappans: a Bio-Anthropological Study of the Skeletons Discovered at Harappa.* Calcutta: Anthropological Survey of India.

——— 1984. Biological Anthropology of the Bronze Age Harappans: New Perspectives, in *People of South Asia: The Biological Anthropology of India, Pakistan and Nepal* (John R. Lukacs Ed.), pp. 59-75. New York: Plenum Press.

Dutta, P.C., A. Pal, P. Gupta and B.C. Dutta 1987. *Ancient Human Remains from Rupar.* Calcutta: Anthropological Survey of India.

Ehrhardt, Sophie and Kenneth A.R. Kennedy 1965. *Excavations at Langhnaj*: 1944-63. *The Human Remains.* Poona: Deccan College.

Erdosy, George 1989. Ethnicity in the Rigveda and Its Bearing on the Question of Indo-European Origins, *South Asian Studies* 5: 35-47.

Gauch, H.G. Jr. 1977. *Ordiflex—A Flexible Computer Program for Four Ordination Techniques, Weighted Averages, Polar Ordination, Principal Components Analysis and Reciprocal Averaging. Release* B. Ithaca: Cornell University.

——— 1982a. *Multivariate Analysis in Community Ecology.* Cambridge: Cambridge University Press.

——— 1982b. Noise Reduction by Eigenvactor Ordinations, *Ecology* 63 (6): 1643-9.

Gauch, H.G., Jr., R.H. Whittaker and T.R. Wentworth 1977. A Comparative Study of Reciprocal Averaging and Other Ordination Techniques, *Journal of Ecology* 65: 157-74.

Guha, B.S. 1934. Human Remains, in *Explorations in Sind* (N.G. Majumdar), pp. 157-8. New Delhi: Memoirs of the Archaeological Survey of India, No. 48.

——— 1935. Racial Affinities of the Peoples of India, in *Census of India 1931, 13a (India), Part III* (Ethnographical). Simla: Government of India.

Guha, B.S. and P.C. Basu 1938. Report on the Human Remains Excavated at Mohenjo Daro in 1928-29, in *Further Excavations at Mohenjo Daro* (Ernest J.H. Mackay), pp. 613-38. Delhi: Government of India.

Gupta, P., P.C. Dutta and A. Basu 1962. Human Skeletal Remains from Harappa, in *Memoirs of the Anthropological Survey of India* 9: 13-188.

Hoffman, Michael A. and Jim G. Shaffer 1976. The Harappan Settlement of Allahdino, Analyzing the Sociology of an Archaeological Site, in *Ecological Backgrounds of South Asian Prehistory* (Kenneth A.R. Kennedy and Gregory L. Possehl Eds.), pp. 4: 94-117. Ithaca: Cornell University South Asia Programs, Occasional Papers and Theses, No. 4.

Howells, W.W. 1972. Analysis of Patterns of Variation in Crania of Recent Man, in *The Functional and Evolutionary Biology of Primates* (Russell Tuttle Ed.), pp. 123-46. Chicago: Aldine.

——— 1973a. Measures of Population Distances, in *Methods and Theories of Anthropological Genetics* (M.H. Crawford and P.L. Workman Eds.), pp. 159-76. Albuquerque: University of New Mexico.

——— 1973b. Cranial Variation in Man, in *Papers of the Peabody Museum of Archaeology and Ethnology*, Cambridge: Harvard University.

Janz, R.L. 1973. Microevolutionary Change in Arikara Crania: a Multivariate Analysis, *American Journal of Physical Anthropology*, 38: 15-26.

Kappers, C.U.A. 1934. *An Introduction to the Anthropology of the Near East in Ancient and Recent Times.* Amsterdam: N.Y. Noord-Hollandsche Uitgeversmaatschappis.

Kennedy, Kenneth A.R. 1965. Human Skeletal Material from Ceylon with an Analysis of the Island's Prehistoric and Contemporary Populations, *Bulletin of the British Museum of Natural History* (Geological [Palaeontological] Series) 11: 135-213.

——— 1980. Prehistoric Skeletal Record of Man in South Asia, *Annual Review of Anthropology*, 9: 391-432.

——— 1981. Skeletal Biology: When Bones Tell Tales, *Archaeology*, 34 (1): 17-24.

——— 1984a. Reassessment of the Theories of Racial Origins of the People of the Indus Valley Civilization from Recent Anthropological Data, in *Studies in the Archaeology and Palaeoanthropology of South Asia* (Kenneth A.R. Kennedy and Gregory L. Possehl Eds.), pp. 99-107. New Delhi: Oxford-IBH.

——— 1984b. Trauma and Disease in the Ancient Harappans: Recent Reassessment of the Skeletal Record, in *Frontiers of the Indus Civilization* (B.B. Lal and S.P. Gupta Eds.), pp. 425-36. New Delhi: Books & Books.

——— 1987. Review of *The Bronze Age Harappans* by P.C. Dutta, *Human Biology* 59 (3): 569-71.

Kennedy, Kenneth A.R. and K.C. Malhotra 1966. *Human Skeletal Remains from Chalcolithic and Indo-Roman Levels from Nevasa: Anthopometric and Comparative Analysis*. Poona: Deccan College.

Kennedy, Kenneth A.R. and Peggy C. Caldwell 1984. South Asian Prehistoric Human Skeletal Remains and Burial Practices, in *The People of South Asia* (John R. Lukacs Ed.), pp. 159-97. New York: Plenum Press.

Kennedy, Kenneth A.R., John Chiment, Todd Disotell and David Meyers 1985. Principal Components Analysis of Prehistoric South Asian Crania, *American Journal of Physical Anthropology* 64 (2): 105-18.

Kennedy, Kenneth A.R. and J. Levisky 1985. The Element of Racial Biology in Indian Megalithism: a Multivariate Analysis Approach, in *Recent Advances in Indo-Pacific Prehistory* (V.N. Misra and Peter Bellwood Eds.), pp. 455-64 Delhi: Oxford-IBH.

Kennedy, Kenneth A.R., Siran U. Deraniyagala, William J. Roertgen, John Chiment and Todd Disotell 1987. Upper Pleistocene Fossil Hominids from Sri Lanka, *American Journal of Physical Anthropology* 72: 441-61.

Khan, A.R. 1968. Ancient Settlements in the Karachi Region, *Dawn: Sunday Magazine Section,* 21 and 28 July.

Krogman, Wilton M. and William H. Saasman 1943. Skull found at Chanhu Daro, in *Excavations at Chanhu Daro 1935-36* (Ernest, J.H. Maccay), pp. 252-63. New Haven: American Oriental Society, American Oriental Series 20.

Lovell, Nancy C. and Kenneth A.R. Kennedy 1989. Society and Disease in Prehistoric South Asia, in *Old Problems and New Perspectives in the Archaeology of South Asia* (Jonathan Mark Kenoyer Ed.), pp. 89-92. Madson: Wisconsin Archaeological Reports 2.

Lukacs, John R. 1982. Cultural Variation and the Evolution of dental Reduction: an Interpretation of the Evidence from South Asia. Calcutta: Paper Presented at the Golden Jubilee Conference on Human Genetics and Adaptation, Indian Statistical Institute, 1-5 February 1982.

——— 1983. Human Dental Remains from Early Neolithic Levels at Mehrgarh, Baluchistan, *Current Anthropology* 24 (3): 390-3.

——— 1985. Tooth Size Variation in Prehistoric India, *American Anthropologist* 87 (4): 811-25.

——— 1990. On Hunter-gatherers and their Neighbours in Prehistoric India: Contact and Pathology, *Current Anthropology* 31 (2): 183-6.

Marriott, F.H.C. 1974. *The Interpretation of Multiple Observations*. London: Academic Press.

Marshall, Sir John 1931. *Mohenjo Daro and the Indus Civilization.* London: Arthur Probsthain.

Martin, R. 1928. *Lehrbuch der Antropologie*. Stuttgart: Fischer Verlag.

Martin, R. and K. Saller 1957. *Lehrbuch der Anthropologie*. Stuttgart: Fishcer Verlag.

Mughal, M. Rafique 1968. Excavations: Harappa 1966 (Cemetery R-37), *Pakistan Archaeology* 5: 63-8.

Pearson, K. and A.G. Davin 1924. On the Biometric Constants of the Human Skull, *Biometrika* 16: 328-68.

Poliakov, L. 1974. *The Aryan Myth*. New York: Basic Books.

Possehl, Gregory L. 1976. Lothal: a Gateway Settlement of the Harappan Civilization, in *Ecological Backgrounds of South Asian Prehistory* (Kenneth A.R. Kennedy and Gregory L. Possehl Eds.), pp. 118-31. Ithaca: Cornell University South Asia Programs, Occasional Papers and Theses, No. 4.

——— 1989. *Radiocarbon Dates for South Asian Archaeology*. Philadelphia: The University Museum, an Occassional Publication of the Asian Section.

——— 1992. The Harappa Cultural Mosaic, in *South Asian Archaeology 1989* (Catherine Jarrige and Richard Meadow Eds.), pp. 237-44. Madison: Prehistory Press. Monographs in World Archaeology 14.

Possehl, Gregory L. and Kenneth A.R. Kennedy 1979. Hunter-gatherer/Agriculturalist Exchange in Prehistory: an Indian Example, *Current Anthropology* 20 (3): 592-3.

Possehl, Gregory L. and M.H. Raval 1989. *Harappan Civilization and Rojdi*. New Delhi: Oxford-IBH and the American Institute of Indian Studies.

Rao, S.R. 1973. *Lothal and the Indus Civilization*. Bombay: Asia Publishing House.

Ray, A.A. (Ed.) 1982. *Sas User's Guide*. Cary, North Carolina: Statistics Sas Institute, Inc.

Sarkar, S.S. 1964. *Ancient Races of Baluchistan, Punjab and Sind.* New Delhi: Munshiram Manoharlal.

——— 1972. *Ancient Races of the Deccan*. New Delhi: Munshiram Manoharlal.

Sewell, R.B.S. and B.S. Guha 1929. Report on the Bones Excavated at Nal, in *Memoirs of the Archaeological Survey of India* 35: 56-86.

——— 1931a. Report on a Collection of Bones Made by Sir Aurel Stein in Makran, *Memoirs of the Archaeological Survey of India* 43: 191-200.

——— 1931b. Human Remains, in *Mohenjo Daro and the Indus Civilization* (Sir John Marshall Ed.), pp. 599-648. London: Arthur Probsthain.

Shaffer, Jim G. 1974. *Allahadino and the Mature Harappan: a Preliminary Report on the Cultural Stratigraphy*. Cleveland: Department of Anthropology, Case Western Reserve University.

——— 1984. The Indo-Aryan Invasions: Cultural Myth and Archaeological Reality, in *The People of South Asia* (John R. Lukacs Ed.), pp. 77-90. New York: Plenum Press.

Sharma, A.K. 1969-70. Kalibangan Human Skeletal Remains: an Osteological Approach, *Journal of the Oriental Institute* 19: 109-13.

——— 1972. Harappan Cemetery at Kalibangan: a Demographic Survey, in *Archaeological Congress and Seminar Papers* (S.B. Deo Ed.), pp. 113-16. Nagpur: Nagpur University.

——— 1982. The Harappan Cemetery at Kalibangan: a Study in *Harappan Civilization* (Gregory L. Possehl Ed.), pp. 297-9. New Delhi: Oxford-IBH and the American Institute of Indian Studies.

Stini, William A. 1975. Adaptive Strategies of Human Population Under Nutritional Stress, in *Biosocial Interrelations in Population Adaptation* (E.S. Watts, F.E. Johnston and G.W. Lasker Eds.), pp. 19-41. The Hague: Mouton.

Wheeler, R.E.M. 1947. Harappa 1946: The Defences and Cemetery R-37, *Ancient India* 3: 58-130.

Wolfpoff, M. 1980. *Palaeoanthropology.* New York: Alfred A. Knopf.

Issues in Harappan Archaeobotany: Retrospect and Prospect

DORIAN Q. FULLER and MARCO MADELLA

INTRODUCTION: THE HISTORICAL DEVELOPMENT OF HARAPPAN ARCHAEOBOTANY

Human use of plants is universal and therefore the study of people-plant relationships in the past is a crucial aspect of any holistic understanding of past societies. Integral to the development of complex societies and states is an agricultural surplus and some level of redistribution, and it is archaeobotany that provides the most direct evidence for the nature of agricultural production. Plant remains from archaeological sites provide insights into cultural ecology, agriculture and food habits and their study is therefore crucial to a number of issues in the study of the Harappan Civilization, its rise and demise. In particular archaeobotany is called upon to support, modify or contradict theories about the organization and intensity of cultivation, its seasonality, irrigation technology, and the impact of hypothesized environmental changes on urban society. In addition, the potential significance of newly introduced species in transforming agricultural ecology and the potential role of the Harappans in disseminating crops to other regions have also emerged as areas of interest. Most of this paper consist of a review of these issues after a short historical outline of the archaeobotany of the Indus Valley and adjacent areas, and detailed consideration of the hard evidence for various crops and food plants.

In general terms, the history of archaeobotany in South Asia can be divided into three broad stages in terms of the way in which research was carried out and the sophistication of understanding the nature of the evidence (see Fuller, in Vol. III of this series, for a more detailed history of the subject in South Asia). The first stage can be called the 'consultant-palaeobotanist' period, to distinguish it from subsequent periods in which individuals came to specialize in the study of archaeological plant remains. Archaeobotanical evidence at least on a small scale, has been a component of Indus Valley archaeology since the first excavations at Mohenjo Daro, Chanu Daro and Harappa in the 1930s and 1940s (Stapf 1931; Luthra 1936, 1941; Burts 1941; Shaw 1943). For the first several decades of research into this civilization, however, archaeobotanical evidence remained haphazard, collected by hand when chance led to the finding of charcoal rich pockets in the archaeological record. Such finds were then sent to botanists, who generally had little knowledge of the archaeology, and who provided species lists, with little interpretation. Early discussions of Harappan agriculture were based upon these few botanical assemblages and guesswork based on artistic depictions (e.g. Marshall 1931: 27; MacKay 1931: 324-5, 1938: 220-1). For example, Wheeler (1968: 84-6) in his discussion of farming simply catalogued the recovered seeds and those assumed to be present based on the interpretation of artefact form or pottery designs. Three field crop species (wheat, barley and peas) and three other food species (melons, sesame and dates) were then recorded from archaeological finds. Cotton cloth was taken to imply cotton cultivation. On the basis of artefact form, coconuts and possibly pomegranates were suggested to have been known, while bananas were inferred on the basis of ceramic decoration (Wheeler ibid.; MacKay 1938: 220). Fairservis (1961, 1967, 1982) and subsequently numerous other scholars reconstructed agricultural practices from settlement patterns and the position of sites in relation to local features of topography and soil types (e.g. Allchin and Allchin 1968: 236-7, 258-61; Flam 1976, 1986; Hoffman and Shaffer 1976; Suraj Bhan and Shaffer 1978; Possehl 1980; Jarrige and Tosi 1981; Mughal 1982; Lal 1984; Dales 1986). An early attempt to synthesise the available archaeological evidence within a broader South Asian context was prepared by Allchin (1969). The botanist Hutchinson (1976) considered the then known archaeobotanical evidence in relation to cropping season and modern crop geography, to argue that the basic agricultural systems of the various parts of South Asia were already established in prehistory.

The above approaches, and more general economic interests in archaeology, led to the second phase of archaeobotany when full-time archaeobotanical specialists emerged. Growing interest in early agriculture encouraged the increasing collection of archaeobotanical evidence, eventually through the use of systematic methods, such as flotation of macro remains (i.e. seeds and charcoal). With increases in the amount of evidence collected, a small number of more or less full-time archaeobotanists emerged in the 1970s, which can be considered the professionalization phase of archaeobotany (see for example, Kajale 1974; Vishnu-Mittre 1977; Vishnu-Mittre and Savithri 1982; Chowdhury et al. 1977). Subsequent to this, we can now be seen to be in a third phase of maturation as increasing thought is given to issues of taphonomy and quantification. Archaeobotanists are now coming to grips with the uniquely archaeological nature of their data and its potential for elucidating the past. In addition, other kinds of plant remains have been studied, including pollen from archaeological deposits (Singh et al. 1974; McKean 1983) and, more recently, phytoliths (Madella 1995, 1997, 1998).

The archaeobotanical evidence from Harappan sites and those in contemporaneous, adjacent regions has grown considerably since the first finds at Mohenjo Daro (see Table 1). It is only in the last two decades that there has been sufficient evidence from a number of sites to allow generalization and theorization about Harappan agriculture. Although the available evidence is still very sparse for such a large area, especially for sites in core areas like the river floodplains of Sindh, and much of it comes from unsystematically collected samples, it is at least possible to place our understanding of Harappan agriculture into an interregional context and to begin to assess its potential impact on broader historical patterns in South Asia. In the lengthy section that follows, the archaeobotanical record for north-western South Asia is criticall reviewed, with consideration given to the likely geographical sources of particular crops and the periods and directions of their dispersal. After this review of the evidence for crops, we turn to discussion of the issues surrounding the introduction of African crops to South Asia, and the analysis of non-crop (weed) taxa in archaeobotanical samples. Then we turn to

TABLE 1. INDUS VALLEY TRADITION SITES AND SITES FROM ADJACENT REGIONS WITH REPORTED ARCHAEOBOTANICAL EVIDENCE

Site Period	Map	Seeds, charred	Impressions	Charcoal	Other wood finds	Pollen	Phytoliths	Inferences from artefacts	References
Baluchistan									
Mehrgarh, I-VII, *c*. 6000 BC *c*. 2500 BC	17	+	+	x					Costantini 1983; Costantini and Biasini 1985; charcoal: Theibault 1988, 1989, 1992, 1995
Nousharo 2600-1900 BC	18	+	+	+					Costantini 1986; 1990a; charcoal: Theibault 1988, 1989,1992,1995
Pirak I-II	19	+	+	+					Costantini 1979; Costantini and Biasini 1985; charcoal: Theibault 1988, 1989, 1992, 1995
Sindh									
Mohenjo Daro, 2600-2000 BC	2	+						+	Stapf 1931; Luthra 1936; Vishnu-Mittre and Savithri 1982
Chanu Daro,	3	+						+	Shaw 1943; Vishnu-Mittre and Savithri 1982
Kot Diji, 3000-2000 BC				+			+		Castelletti et al. 1994; Madella 1995, 1997
Allahdino 2600-2000	20	$+^F$							Fairservis 1982
Balakot 2600-2000	21	$+^F$				+			McKean 1983; see Dales 1986
Northern/Eastern Harappan									
Harappa, 2600-2000 BC (earlier phases not reported	1	$+^F$			+		+	+	Burts 1941; Luthra 1941; Vishnu-Mittre and Savithri 1982; phytoliths: Madella 1998 and unpublished
Kalibangan, 3000-2000 BC	4	+	+			+			Vishnu-Mittre and Savithri 1975, 1982; pollen: Singh et al. 1974
Rohira 2300-1900 BC	5	$+^F$		$+^F$					Vishnu-Mittre et al. 1985; Saraswat 1986; Saraswat et al. 1990; Saraswat and Chanchala 1994
Sanghol	6	+		+					Saraswat et al. 1992; Saraswat and Chanchala 1997
Rupar 2500-1700 BC	7	+							Vishnu-Mittre and Savithri 1979a
Daulatpur 2000-1700 BC	8	+							Vishnu-Mittre and Savithri 1982; Vishnu-Mittre et al. 1985

(contd.)

Site Period	Map	Seeds, charred	Impressions	Charcoal	Other wood finds	Pollen	Phytoliths	Inferences from artefacts	References
Banawali *c*. 3000- *c*. 1600 BC	15	+							Lone et al. 1987
Mahorana 2300-1900 BC	9	+		+					Vishnu-Mittre et al. 1986b; Saraswat and Chanchala 1994, 1996
Burthana Tigrana 2500-2000 BC	10	+[F]							Willcox 1992
Laduwala 2800-2300 BC	11	+[F]							Willcox 1992
Mitathal 2000-1400 BC	12	+[F]							Willcox 1992
Ganga-Yamuna Late Harappan/Ochre-Coloured Pottery									
Hulas 1800-1200 BC	13	+[F]							Saraswat et al. 1992; Saraswat 1993
Lal Quila 1800-1200 BC	14	+							Kajale and Deotare 1993; Kajale 1995
Atranjikhera 1800-1200 BC	16	+		+					Chowdhury et al. 1977, 1983
Northern Periphery									
Rehman Dheri 3200-2000 BC	36	+							Durrani 1988: 28, 30
Tarakai Qila, 3000-2000 BC	35	+[F]							K. Thomas 1983a, 1983b, 1989
Ghaleghay I-III 3000-2000 BC	32	+							Costantini 1987
Bir-Kot- Ghwandai 1700-1400 BC	33	+							Costantini 1987
Loebanhr 3 1700-1400 BC	34	+							Costantini 1987
Burzahom, I-II 2350-1000 BC	30	+[F]		+					Lone et al. 1993
Semthan, I 1500-600 BC	31	+[F]		+					Lone et al. 1993
Areas within trade contact to West and North									
Shortugai (Harappan enclave?)	46	+[F]							Willcox 1991
Mundigak 3000-2000 BC	47	+							Porteres 1961; Costantini and Biasini 1985
Sharh-I-Sokhta 3200-2100 BC	48	+		+					Costantini and Biasini 1985

(contd.)

Site Period	Map	Seeds, charred	Impressions	Charcoal	Other wood finds	Pollen	Phytoliths	Inferences from artefacts	References
Tepe Yahya, VII-IV 4500-2200 BC	49	+							Costantini and Biasini 1985
Hili, Oman 3000-2000 BC	50	+	+						Cleuziou and Costantini 1980, 1982; Cleuziou 1989
Harappan Gujarat									
Lothal 2500-1900 BC	24	+	+	+					Ramesh Rao and Lal 1985
Rangpur IIA-III 2500-1400 BC	25	+	+	+					Ghosh and Lal 1963
Rojdi, A-C 2600-1700 BC	27	$+^F$							Weber 1991
Oriyo Timbo 1700-1400 BC	29	$+^F$							Reddy 1994, 1997
Babor Kot, I-III 2200-1700 BC	28	$+^F$							Reddy 1994, 1997
Kuntasi 2600-2000 BC	23	$+^F$							see Dhavalikar 1995
Surkotada, IC 2000-1800 BC	26	+							Vishnu-Mittre and Savithri 1982
Shikarpur 2500-2000 BC	22	+		+					Saraswat et al. 1995
Eastern Periphery									
Ahar 2500-1500 BC	37		+						Vishnu-Mittre 1969
Balathal 2500-2000 BC	38	$+^F$							Kajale 1996
Southern Periphery of Late Harappan (Chalcolithic Maharashtra)									
Kayatha 2400-1400 BC	40								Vishnu-Mittre et al. 1985
Kaothe *c*. 2000 BC	41	+							Kajale 1990
Daimabad 2000-1100	42	$+^F$		$+^F$					Kajale 1977; Vishnu-Mittre et al. 1986a
Inamgaon 1700-900 BC	43	$+^F$							Kajale 1988
Apegaon 1700-1200 BC	44	$+^F$							Kajale 1979
Navdatoli 2000-1700 BC	45	+							Vishnu-Mittre 1961

NOTE: ^{F}= indicates that at least some samples were collected through flotation.

discussing more general agricultural issues, including irrigation and seasonality. Finally, some of the key issues and datasets of South Asian palaeoecology of the later Holocene are reviewed. An understanding of the issues and hypotheses relating to climatic change in South Asia is important for putting the agricultural evidence into its environmental context.

THE HARD EVIDENCE FOR CROPS

In reviewing the archaeobotanical evidence for the presence of various crops, an attempt will be made to assess the significance of their apparent presence or absence from different regions within the Harappan Civilization and between the Mature/Urban and Late/Post-Urban phases (i.e. Integration and Localization Eras in the terminology of Kenoyer 1991). In Weber's (1991, 1992) review of South Asian archaeobotanical variability, it is clear that some categories of crops are more often recovered than others. These differences are likely the results of factors of preservation and sampling. Thus cereals, especially the large seeded ones (wheat, barley, rice), have been much more widely reported than any other category of plant. Smaller cereals (millets) have also been quite widely reported. Pulses have not been reported from as many sites, but are widely enough reported that presence or absence in particular regions and periods can be reconstructed with a fair degree of certainty. Other types of crop plants, including oilseeds, fibre crops and fruit or nuts, have only been recovered occasionally. These differences doubtless reflect biases in the archaeobotanical record and recovery methods, thus limiting the conclusiveness of histories of crops other than the cereals and pulses. For these reasons the distribution maps in Figures 1 and 2 are limited to cereals and pulses, although other categories of food plant are included in the present tables (Tables 2-3).

As it is of interest to see which crops diffused as a package and which individually, the crops reviewed below will also be grouped according to those which share general geographical regions of origin, as this should facilitate an understanding of diffusion processes. Evidence for the geographical origins of plants comes largely from their living relatives, especially the distribution of wild relatives, and this evidence will not be reviewed in any detail in this paper (see Fuller, in Vol. III of this series for discussion of this evidence). However, not all crops have been equally researched in terms of genetic and geographical origins. Crops which have been most extensively studied are those which originated in South-West Asia and form the basis of traditional agriculture in the Mediterranean and Europe, and a synthesis of the evidence can be found in Zohary and Hopf (1993). Crops of tropical origin are very often documented on the basis of very little real evidence. There has, however, been an accumulation of new studies during the past two decades and a picture of the geographical origins of several African crops has emerged (see Fig. 3, and Fuller, in Vol. III of this series). Some discussion will be given of millets and pulses that are of particular importance to the agriculture of the Indian subcontinent. Crops of South and South-East Asian origin are often poorly documented as to the likely regions of their origin, although an assessment of current evidence can be informative (Fuller ibid.; Fuller et al. n.d.).

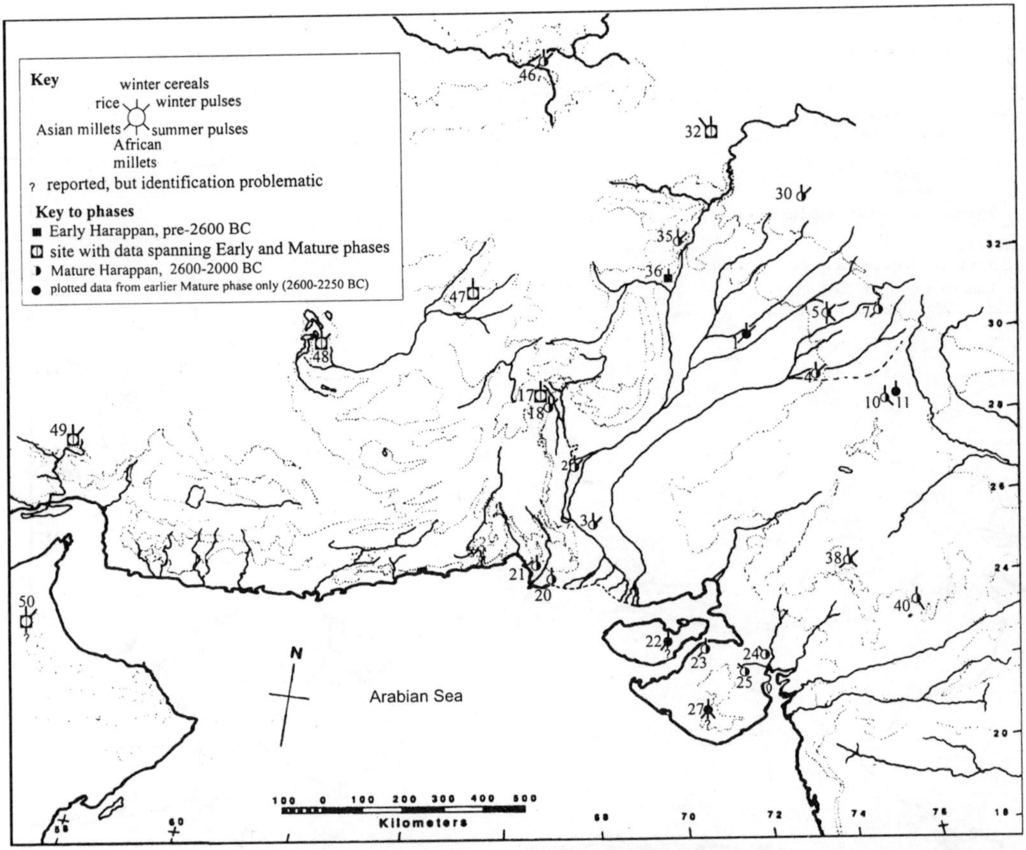

Fig. 1. Map showing distribution of archaeobotanical finds within the Harappan orbit and adjacent regions during the Mature Harappan phase and preceeding early period. Finds are summarized in terms of major crop groups defined on the basis of seasonality, and geographical origin. Site numbers, details of species reported and references can be found in Tables 1-3. Base map shows reconstructed drainage system of greater Indus Valley, including ancient Ghaggar-Hakkra river (after Kenoyer 1998).

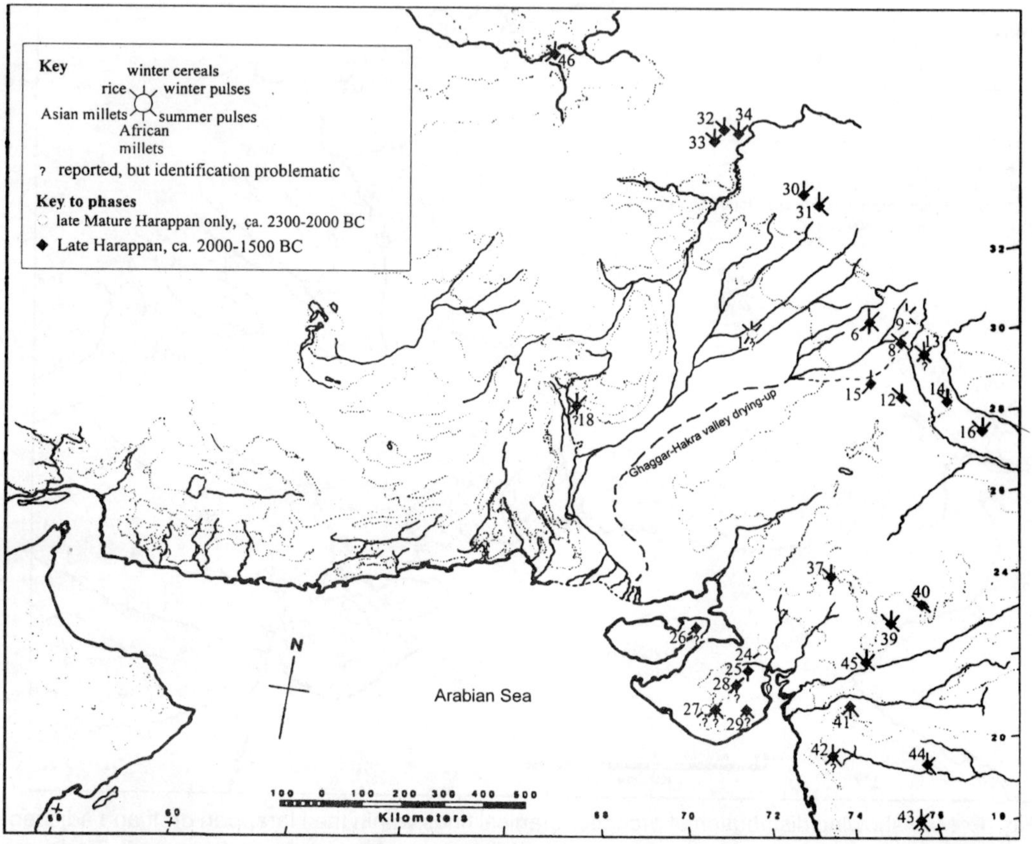

Fig. 2. Map showing distribution of archaeobotanical finds within the Harappan orbit and adjacent regions during the late Mature and late (post-Urban) phases. Finds are summarized in terms of major crop groups defined on the basis of seasonality, and geographical origin. Site numbers, details of species reported and references can be found in Tables 1-3.

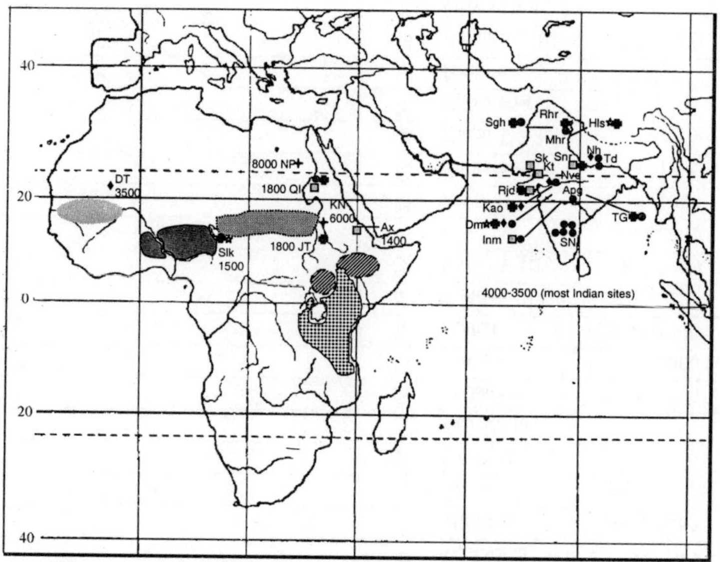

Modern wild progenitor populations of *Pennisetum glaucum* (L.)R. Br.

Early archaeological finds of domesticated *P. glaucum* (pearl millet/ bajra)

Modern wild progenitor populations of *Sorghum bicolor* (L.) Moench.

Early archaeological finds of wild type *S. bicolor*

Early archaeological finds of domesticated type *S. bicolor* (sorghum/ jowar)

Modern wild progenitor populations of *Eleusine coracana* (L.) Gaertn.

Early archaeological finds of *E. coracana* (finger millet/ ragi)

Region in which wild *Lablab purpureus* (L.) Sweet ssp. *Uncinatus* Verdc. occurs

Early archaeological finds of *Lablab* (hyacinth bean/ sem)

Modern wild progenitor populations of *Vigna unguiculata* (L.) Walp.

Early archaeological finds of *V. unguiculata* (cow pea/ chowli)

8000 NP Approximate archaeological age, years BP, and site/culture initials.

African sites: DT= Dhar Tichitt, Slk= Salak,and nearby sites in Cameroun, NP= Nabta Playa, QI= Qasr Ibrim, KN= Khartoum Neolithic, JT= Jebel Tomat, Ax= Axum.

Indian sites: Hls= Hulas, Sgh= Sanghol, Rhr= Rohira, Mhr= Mahorana, Snr= Senuwar, Sk= Shikarpur, Nh= Narhan, Td= Taradih, Kt= Kuntasi, Rjd= Rojdi, Nvd= Navdatoli, Kao= Kaothe, Dm= Daimabad,Apg= Apegaon, Inm= Inamgaon, SN= Southern Neolithic (Ashmound culture), TG= Tuljapur Garhi.

Fig. 3. Map showing the probable regions of demonstration for African millets and pulses present in protohistoric India, and early archaeobotanical finds of these species in Africa and India. World progenitor distributions based on the following sources: Tostain 1994, 1998 (*Pennisetum*), Rawal 1975; Vailencourt and Weeden; Panella et al. 1993 (*V. unguiculata*), Harlan 1992, 1995 (*Sorghum*), Verdcourt 1971 (Lablab), Harlan 1992, 1995 (Eleusine). Sources for African archaeobotanical evidence: Amblard and Pernes 1989; Wasylikowa et al. 1993; Clark and Stemler 1975; Stemler 1990; Rowley-Conwy 1991; Otto and Delneuf 1998; Sheila Boardman: personal communication 1998 (Axum); Alan Clapham, personal communication 1999 (Qasr Ibrim). Archaeobotanical evidence for all South Asian sites shown can be found in Fuller, Vol. III, in this series.

TABLE 2. CHECKLIST OF MAJOR CULTIVATED TAXA REPORTED FROM SITES OF THE HARAPPAN CIVILIZATION (INCLUDING LATE PHASES)

	Region	Baluchistan					Sind				Northern and Eastern provinces									Late period			Upper Ganga			Gujarat						Late period							
	Culture Period						Mature period				Mature period									Late period			OCP			Mature period													
	period B.C.	4500-4000	3200-3000	2600-2000	1950-1550	2600-2000					2600-2300	2250-2000	2500-2000	2000-1500	2500-1700		3000-1600	2500-2000	2800-2300	2000-1700	?2300-1900?	2000-1400	1800-1200			2500-2000	2500-2000	2000-1700	2600-2200	2000-1700	2600-2200	2200-2000	2000-1700				1700-1400		
	Site/phase	Mehrgarh II	Mehrgarh V	Mehrgarh VII-VIII	Pirak I	Nausharo	Allahdino	Balakot	Chanu Daro	Mohenjo Daro	Harappa	Harappa	Kalibagan II	Sanghol	Rupar	Rohira	Banawali	Burthana Tigrana	Laduwala	Daulatpur	Mahorana	Mitathal	Hulas	Lal Quila	Atranjikhera	Shikarpur	Kuntasi	Lothal	Rangpur IIA	Rangpur III	Rojdi A	Rojdi B	Surkotada III	Babar Kot I	Babar Kot II	Rojdi C	Babar Kot III	Oriyo Timbo I	Oriyo Timbo II
Pulses	Map no. seasonality	17	17	17	18	19	20	21	3	2	1	1	4	6	7	5	15	10	11	8	9	12	13	14	16	22	23	24	25	25	27	27	26	28	28	27	28	29	
Cajanus cajan	*kharif*																																						
Dolichos biflorus	*kharif*												x		x		x				x	x													x				
Dolichios lablab	*kharif*													x							x																		
Vigna sp. *(radiata/mungo)*	*kharif*																	x				x																	
Vigna radiata	*kharif*																						x													x			
Vigna mungo	*kharif*																			x											x					x		x	x
Vigna unguiculata	*kharif*																						x																
Cicer arientinum	*rabi*				x						x	x	x										x		x														
Lathyrus sativus	*rabi*										x	x		x									x		x										x	x			
Lens esculenta	*rabi*											x	x		x		x					x	x	x											x	x	x	x	
Pisum sativum	*rabi*					x			x	x	x	x	x	x									x													x			
Trigonella foenum-graecum																																							
Cereals																																							
Hordeum vulgare	*rabi*	x	x	x	x	x	x	x	x	x	x	x	x	x		x	x	x	x		x	x	x	x	x		x				x								
Triticum sp.	*rabi*	x	x	x	x	x	x	x	x	x	x	x	x	x	x	x		x			x	x	x	x	x	x	x												
Avena sativa	*rabi*		?	?	?																																		
Oryza sativa	*kharif*				x							x								x		x	x	x	x			|	|	|									
Sorghum bicolor	*kharif*				[i]									x		x							x									x				x			

Eleusine coracana	*kharif*											[ ]											[ ]			[ ]	[ ]				[ ]	[ ]	[ ]			[ ]		[ ]	[ ].
Pennisetum typhoides	*kharif*																													x							x?		
Panicum sp.	*kharif*				x																												x						
Panicum milaceum	*kharif*																																						
Panicum sumatrense	*kharif*																														x	x		x	x	x	x	x	x
Setaria sp.	*kharif*												x			x						?			x	x				x	x	x		x	x	x	x	x	
Paspalum scrobiculatum	*kharif*														x																								
Oilseeds/Fibres																																							
Sesamum indicum	*kharif*										x			x																									
Gossypium sp.	*kharif/peren*	x?					x															x																	
Linum usitatissimum	*rabi*			x	x								x																				x	x	x				
Cannabis sativa	*rabi/kharif*																																						
Carthamus tinctorius	*rabi*																																						
Rincinus communis	*kharif*																						x																
Papaver sp.	*rabi*													x																									
Phoenix dactylifera	September	x				x				x	x				x																								
Vitis vinifera	summer		x	x	x	x									x						x																		
Prunus sp.	May-Oct.	x	x			x																																	
Prunus dulcis (*Amygdalus communis*)	Feb.-June																						x																
Juglans regia	Mar.-June																						x																
Citrus limon	year round													x																									
Ziziphus sp.	Arp.-Oct.	x	x	x	x	x					x	x						x	x			x				x				x	x								

NOTES: Botanical authorities have been omitted from this table for reasons of space. They can be found throughout the text. For references, see Table 1.

x = presence reported (seed remains); i = present as impression only; x? = reservations expressed by original author(s);

[ ] = identification considered problematic by the present authors; ? = probably present, based on reconsideration of literature by this study.

TABLE 3. CHECKLIST OF MAJOR CULTIVATED TAXA REPORTED FROM SITES IN REGION ADJACENT TO, OR IN CONTACT WITH, THE HARAPPAN CIVILIZATION

	Region	Kashmir			Swat Valley					Bannu		Maharashtra												regions in contact to the North and West					
	Culture Period	Neolithic			Chalcolithic					Basin		Banas			Pre-Malwa			Malwa			Jorwe								
	Period BC	2375-1700	1700-1000	1500-600	3000-2500	2500-2000	1900-1700	1700-1400	1700-1400	late 3rd Mill.	3000?-2500	2600-1500		2000-1500	2450-1400	*c.* 2000	2000-1700	1700-1500	1700-1500		1500-1200	1500-1100		2500-2000		3000-2000	3200-2100	4500-2200	*c.* 2900
	Site/Phase	Burzahom I	Burzahom II	Semthan I	Ghaleghay I	Ghaleghay II	Ghaleghay III	Bir-Kot-Ghwandai	Loebanhr 3	Tarakai Qila	Rehman Dheri	Ahar	Balathal	Dangwada	Kayatha	Kaothe	Daimabad II	Daimabad III	Inamgaon	Apegaon	Inamgaon	Daimabad IV	Navdatoli	Shortugai 1.1	Shortugai 1.2	Mundigak	Sharh-I-Sokhta	Tepe Yahya VII-IV	Hili 8
Pulses	Map no. seasonality	30	30	31	32	32	32	33	34	35	36	37	38	39	40	41	42	42	43	44	43	42	45	46		47	48	49	50
Cajanus cajan	*kharif*																												
Macrotyloma uniflorum	*kharif*														x	x		x	x	x	x	x	x						
Lablab purpureus	*kharif*																	x	x	x	x		x						
Vigna sp. (*radiata/mungo*)	*kharif*												x	x															
Vigna radiata	*kharif*			x																x	x		x						
Vigna mungo	*kharif*														x		x		x		x	x							
Vigna unguiculata	*kharif*																	x				x							
Cicer arientinum	*rabi*																												
Lathyrus sativus	*rabi*																x	x	x	x	x	x	x					x	
Lens esculenta	*rabi*	x	x	x				x	x	x				x			x	x	x	x	x	x	x	x	x		x	x	
Pisum sativum	*rabi*	x							x				x					x	x	x	x	x	x	x				x	
Trigonella foenum-graecum																													
Cereals																													
Hordeum vulgare	*rabi*	x	x	x			x	x	x	x	x	x	x				x	x	x	x	x	x	x	x	x	x	x	x	x
Triticum sp.	*rabi*	x	x	x		x		x	x	x	x	x	x	x	x		x	x	x	x	x	x	x	x	x	x	x	x	x
Avena sativa	*rabi*			x				x																			x	?	

Oryza sativa	*kharif*			x	i	i	i	x	x			x		x					x			x	x							
Sorghum bicolor	*kharif*										[ ]											x							[ ]	
Eleusine coracana	*kharif*																	[ ]	[ ]		[ ]	[ ]								
Pennisetum typhoides	*kharif*															x		x												
Panicum sp.	*kharif*													x								x								
Panicum milaceum	*kharif*												x												x			x		
Panicum sumatrense	*kharif*																													
Setaria sp.	*kharif*																		?				x							
Paspalum scrobiculatum	*kharif*																					x								
Oilseeds/Fibres																														
Sesamum indicum	*kharif*															x					x?									
Gossypium sp.	*kharif/peren.*																													
Linum usitatissimum	*rabi*								x				x?									x	x		x		x			
Cannabis sativa	*rabi/kharif*																													
Carthamus tinctorius	*rabi*																					x								
Rincinus communis	*kharif*																													
Papaver sp.	*rabi*																													
Fruits/Vegetables	season of fruiting																													
Phoenix dactylifera	September																											x	x	
Vitis vinifera	summer		x						x															x			x	x		
Prunus sp.	May-Oct. (?)	x		x																								x		
Amygdalus communis	Feb.-June		x																											
Juglans regia	Mar.-June	x	x	x																										
Citrus limon	year round																													
Ziziphus sp.	Apr.-Oct												x	x			x	x	x	x	x	x	x	x			x			x

NOTES: Botanical authorities have been omitted from this table for reasons of space. They can be found throughout the text. For references, see Table 1.
x = presence reported (seed remains); i = present as impression only; x? = reservations expressed by original author(s);
[ ]= identification considered problematic by the present authors; ?= probably present, based on reconsideration of literature by this study.

South-West Asian Cereals

Wheat and barley, seem to have formed one of the major bases of Harappan agriculture, at least within the Greater Indus Valley. Wheat and barley based agriculture spread from the Near East and reaching Baluchistan, as represented by Mehrgarh, by 6000 BC (Costantini 1983; Meadow 1996), with more recent dates possible pushing this evidence back considerably further to the eighth millennium BC (Meadow 1998). As noted in several previous syntheses (Fairservis 1971; Vishnu-Mittre and Savithri 1982; Costantini and Biasini 1985; Meadow 1989, 1996, 1998; Saraswat 1992; Franke-Vogt 1995), wheat and barley are the two most often recovered cereals on Harappan sites.

Barley/*jau* (*Hordeum vulgare L.*[1]) was once claimed to have been largely absent from prehistoric/protohistoric sites in South Asia (e.g. Vishnu-Mittre 1968c, 1970a), although it is now clear that this conclusion was a product of haphazard sampling prior to the professionalisation of archaeobotany and employment of sieving/flotation (cf. Kajale 1991; Saraswat 1992). Wheat/*gehu* (*Triticum* sp.) has been a widespread find on Harappan sites since the first excavations of Mohenjo Daro (Vishnu-Mittre and Savithri 1982; Kajale 1991; Willcox 1992; Saraswat 1992).

It is notable that wheat and barley are poorly represented on sites from Gujarat either from Harappan or Late/Post-Urban levels, the probable significance of which will be taken up below in 'Seasonality and Intensity of Agriculture' (Vishnu-Mittre and Savithri 1982; Weber 1991, 1992; Reddy 1994, 1997; Meadow 1989, 1996). For example, at Rojdi, despite intensive sampling, only 13 grains of barley were identified by comparison to thousands of millet grains (Weber 1991); at Oriyo Timbo, Babar Kot and Surkotada, wheat and barley were absent (Reddy 1994, 1997; Vishnu-Mittre and Savithri 1982). On the other hand wheat and barley are widely reported, often in considerable quantity from sites in 'inner' India from the second millennium BC, i.e. from Chalcolithic Maharashtra, Rajasthan, and the Ganga Valley (see Kajale 1988, 1991, 1996; Saraswat 1986, 1992; Vishnu-Mittre 1989). Thus the diffusion of these two crops eastwards into tropical India, which occurred during and after the Mature Harappan phase, was a selective process in which certain regions may not have participated, presumably for a combination of ecological and cultural reasons. Indeed, it can be argued that a major reason for the rapid and wide dispersal of these cereals, perhaps barley in particular, was due to cultural associations (such as prestigious or ritual value) associated with the Harappans (Fuller, in press).

Both wheat and barley include a number of different cultivated species or varieties, and it is of interest to trace these archaeologically. Barley can be sub-divided by two variables, the number of fertile (grain-producing) florets per spikelet and whether or not the grains are naked (free-threshing) or hulled (Renfrew 1973; Vishnu-Mittre and Savithri 1982; Jacomet 1987; Zohary and Hopf 1993). Two-rowed inflorescences and hulled grains are the primitive, wild characteristics of barley (Zohary 1969; Zohary and Hopf 1993). Amongst the impressions from Mehrgarh the derived naked six-row form is thought to dominate, while two-row and hulled six-row appear to be minor components (Costantini

1983). Unfortunately, it is not clear how seriously the quantification based on plant impressions should be taken, since the number of impressions depends on the size of the sherd and the number of breaks. At least the presence of these three varieties is clear. Six-rowed, naked barley is also reported from Mohenjo Daro (Luthra 1936) and Harappa (Vishnu-Mittre and Savithri 1982), while hulled barley dominates a large assemblage from Kalibangan in which naked grains were approximately 5 per cent and grains with a twisted appearance indicate the presence (preponderance?) of six-row (Vishnu-Mittre and Savithri 1982). Six-row hulled has also been identified at Banawali (Lone et al. 1987) and Hulas, a Late Harappan site of the Ganga-Yamuna Doab (Saraswat 1993). The small amount of barley from Rojdi also appears to be six-row hulled (Weber 1991). From the available evidence, it is six-row, hulled (*H. vulgare* L. subsp. *vulgare*) which appears to be most widespread in the Harappan Civilization, and it is this variety which diffused eastwards into subsequent cultures of the Ganga Valley, as indicated for example at Atranjikhera, Radhan and Narhan in the Painted Grey Ware phase, latter half of second millennium BC (Buth and Chowdhury 1971; Kajale and Lal 1989; Saraswat et al. 1994), and peninsular Indian village cultures of the second millennium BC (e.g. Kajale 1979, 1984, 1988).

The existence of a distinct, local variety of spheroid barley in Pre-Harappan Baluchistan must be assessed critically. Costantini (1983: 31) has referred to much of the barley at Mehrgarh as '*Hordeum sphaerococcum*', implying that it is a distinct morphological type similar to that recovered from early periods in Armenia, the Caucasus and southern Turkmenia (Janushevich 1978). It was later suggested that 'by the end of the Neolithic (sixth millennium BC) . . . the grain and barley underwent the peculiar local adaptations leading to a morphological convergence of the kernels of the two cereals nowadays classified as *Triticum sphaerococcum* and *Hordeum sphaerococcum*' (Costantini and Biasini 1985: 26). Neither this trend, nor the distinctiveness of '*H. sphaerococcum*' has been established by published morphometric data. Furthermore, such an approach to cereal grains is highly problematic, as noted below for archaeological '*Triticum sphaerococcum*', since charring distorts the size of grains and tends to make them more spheroid.

Unfortunately, despite reported species level identifications of wheats in the Greater Indus Valley, most of these identifications cannot be accepted. It is now well-established that the characteristics of wheat grains as unreliable for specific identification and difficulties are exacerbated in the case of charred material (van Zeist 1976; Kislev 1984; Miller 1992; Zohary and Hopf 1993; Hillman et al. 1996, Maier 1996; for further details see Fuller, in Vol. III of this series). the archaeological and agricultural literature on South Asia makes frequent reference to the presence of hexaploid wheats, especially *Triticum sphaerococcum* Perc., the Indian Shot Wheat (e.g. Vishnu-Mittre 1974a; Hutchinson 1976; Vishnu-Mittre and Savithri 1982; Costantini and Biasini 1985; Saraswat 1986, 1992, 1993; Zeven 1978; Randhawa 1980; Kulshrestha 1985; Meadow 1998). The purported former dominance of *T. sphaerococcum* Percival must be disregarded until there is adequate evidence from wheat rachis remains. From Shortugai, Afghanistan, which shows Harappan affinities in its earliest levels, hexaploid wheat (*T. aestivum* sensu lato) occurs. There is little evidence as yet for hulled wheats. A hulled wheat is present amongst the impressions from early Mehrgarh (*c.* 6000-5000 BC), although whether emmer or einkorn is unsure (Costantini 1983; subsequently both reported as present in Costantini and Biasini 1985). A hulled wheat also appears to have been present amongst the impressions from Harappan Kalibangan (cf. Vishnu-Mittre and Savithri 1975), perhaps emmer. Emmer grains have been identified nearby from Late Harappan Rohira, a site on a tributary system of the former Ghaggar-Hakkra river (Saraswat 1986), as has free threshing-wheat ('*T. sphaerococcum*'). It can tentatively be concluded that free-threshing wheats (of uncertain ploidy level) and hulled barley dominated winter cereal cultivation throughout most of the Harappan world, with the notable exception of Gujarat. Distinguishing these various wheat types is of interest for understanding their separate histories, although there may also be ecological and cultural implications in some cases. For example, *T. sphaerococcum* is generally considered highly drought resistent (Percival 1921), and emmer as a hulled wheat may be prone to less loss during storage.

South-West Asian Pulses

The argument can be made that wheat and barley were part of a crop package which included four likely legume (pulse) species: peas/*mattar* (*Pisum sativum* L., incl. *P. arvense* L.), grasspea/*khasari* (*Lathyrus sativus* L.), lentils/*masur* (*Lens culinarius* Med.), and chickpea/gram/*chana* (*Cicer arietinum* L.) (for evidence of their South-West Asian origins see Zohary and Hopf 1993). Although these species have not been reported from the early periods at Mehrgarh (Costantini 1983), this cannot be taken to indicate their actual absence, as the evidence for the cereals comes from impressions, a category of remains which one would not expect to include leguminous crops. Unfortunately because there are still few systematically studied flotation samples from the Harappan phase of the Indus Valley itself, it is nuclear the extent to which each of the South-West Asian pulse species contributed to the agriculture of the various regions. Nevertheless, the available evidence suggests that each of these species was at least present in the north-western subcontinent at this time. In addition, the Post/Late-Harappan evidence from areas to the east and south in India, suggest that all or most of these pulses were cultivated in the same areas as wheat and barley in the second millennium BC (see Fuller, in Vol. III of this series; Fuller et al., n.d.; cf. Kajale 1991; Saraswat 1992). This suggests that these crops diffused out of the Indus Valley as something of a package, although it is unclear if they entered the region as such. Peas have been reported from Nausharo (Costantini 1990); Chanu Daro/Mohenjo Daro, Harappa and Kalibangan (Vishnu-Mittre and Savithri 1982), in addition to Burthana Tigrana and Mitathal in Haryana (Willcox 1992). Lentils and chickpeas are also known from Kalibangan, while lentils and *Lathyrus* are reported from Harappa. Lentils were also found at Daimabad in Maharashtra and in the subsequent period lentils, peas and *Lathyrus* are known from several Chalcolithic Maharashtra sites, while all four pulses are known from second millennium Ganga Valley sites.

Tropical Pulses

Of particular importance in South Asian agriculture are pulses that are adapted to the savannas and are generally cropped in the summer/monsoon season, many of which are indigenous of South Asia. Unfortunately, these species have been subject to much nomenclatural confusion and revision (reviewed in Fuller et al., n.d.; for taxonomy, see Smartt 1990). Horsegram/*kulthi* (*Macrotyloma uniflorum* (Lam.) Verdocurt 1970, based on *D. uniflorus* Lam.)[2] is generally accepted as native to South Asia, its main region of cultivation, although no wild populations are known (Smartt 1985a, 1990). Horsegram has not been reported from Mature/Urban Harappan period sites, but moves into the north-western subcontinent in the early second millennium BC, with finds from Rojdi Period C in Saurashtra (Weber 1991), Rohira and Hulas in Indian Punjab (Saraswat 1986, 1993), and Haryana sites (Willcox 1992). The *Vigna* grams have also suffered from some nomenclatural confusion: green gram/*mung* (*V. radiata* (L.) R. Wilczek, syn. *Phaseolus radiatus* L., *Phaeseolus aureus* Roxb.)[3], and black gram/*urid*, *V. mungo* (L.) Hepper, syn. *Phaseolus mungo* L.)[4] are both indigenous to tropical/sub-tropical South Asia, although they derive from distinct wild progenitors and presumably have disparate geographical origins (Smartt 1985b, 1990); for further references see Fuller et al., n.d.; Fuller, in Vol. III of this series). These two species can be difficult to distinguish if the hilum is not preserved, although statistical differences exist between the ratio of plumule length to cotyledon length. One or both of these species are reported from sites around the periphery of the Harappan Civilization, in Saurashtra (Weber 1991) and Haryana (Willcox 1992), beginning in levels contemporary with the Mature period. These earliest finds may be entirely of black gram (*V. mungo*), as is the case with Rojdi A (Weber 1991) and Banawali (Lone et al. 1987). Green gram/mung (*V. radiata*) may only have become available in these areas in the second millennium BC, e.g. Rojdi C (Weber 1991), Atranjikhera (Chowdhury et al. 1977), and Hulas (Saraswat 1993). Both pulses have been reported from Balathal, Rajasthan from levels that may be late third millennium (Kajale 1996), as well as from Burthana Tigrana(?) in Haryana (Willcox 1992); species level identification uncertain). Another South Asian cultivar in the same section of this genus (section *Ceratropis*) is the golden gram/*moth* (*Vigna aconitifolia* (Jacq.) Marechal). Moth, however, is not evident in the archaeobotanical record until the latter first millennium BC, and does not concern us in an account of Harappan agriculture. Two pulses of African origin, hyacinth bean/sem (*Lablab purpureus*) and cowpea (*Vigna unguiculata* (L.) Walp, Hindi *chowli* or *lobia*), became available in regions peripheral to the Indus Valley during the Late Harappan phase (after *c.* 1900 BC), with cowpea from Hulas (Saraswat 1993) and Daimabad (Vishnu-Mittre et al. 1986a) and *Lablab* from Sanghol (Saraswat and Chanchala 1997) and Mahorana (Saraswat and Chanchala 1994) in addition to numerous peninsular Chalcolithic sites, and the Southern Neolithic (see Fuller et al., n.d., Fuller, Vol. III of this series, for full details of archaeobotany).

Millets

'Millets' during the Harappan Civilization have drawn much attention, especially those from external geographical sources, due to their potential role in a Late Harappan agricultural 'revolution'. Millets are a heterogenous group of small-seeded, edible (usually cultivated) grasses, which include species in some nine different genera (*Brachiaria, Digitaria, Echinochloa, Eleusine, Panicum, Paspalum, Pennisetum, Setaria, Sorghum*). In some cases there is more than one species in a genus that is known ethnographically to be used as a millet. Most millets can, with some degree of certainty, be assigned to their probable geographical regions of origin, which include Africa, East Asia (probably north China) and South Asia. Within these geographical millet groups no single diffused package is discernible, so that the history of each crop must be traced individually. Unfortunately it can be difficult to distinguish native South Asian species in the genera *Setaria* and *Panicum* from sister species originating in East Asia, and discussion of useful criteria needs to be pursued by practising archaeobotanists (for discussion of some of these criteria see Fuller et al. n.d.; Fuller, in Vol. III of this series). Since reliable and generally accepted criteria for the identification of the range of millets potentially encountered in South Asian archaeobotany is not available, published reports must be assessed critically. Especially problematic are reports of finger millet/*ragi* (*Eleusine coracana* (L.) Gaertn.) unaccompanied by illustrations, since a critical review of the illustrated specimens in addition to ongoing comparative study of modern and archaeological millet specimens, indicates that *Eleusine* has been frequently misidentified, and many reports consist of mistaken interpretations of charred caryopses of *Setaria* sp. and perhaps *Echinochloa* (Fuller et al. n.d.; see section 4.2 in Fuller, in Vol. III of this series). Possible misidentifications are indicated in Tables 2-3 and with question marks on Figures 1-2. Reports which cannot be assessed for accuracy due to lack of illustrations and clear criteria are *tentatively* accepted for the sake of discussion.

Attention has often focused on Gujarat as the most likely region for the initial adoption of African millets (Possehl 1980, 1986; Weber 1991, 1998; Meadow 1996; Kenoyer 1998: 163). It was in this region where some of the earliest finds of African millets had been reported. These millets did not appear in this region as a single package but at different times. The reported evidence puts '*Eleusine*' at Rojdi by *c.* 2500 BC, while *Sorghum bicolor* (L.) Moench. and *Pennisetum glaucum* (L.) R. Br. (syn., *P. typhoides* (Burm.) Stapf. & Hubb.) appear as much as 500 years later in the Rangpur phase (Weber 1990, 1991, 1998; Ghosh and Lal 1963; Saraswat et al. 1995). At this time, the early second millennium BC, *Sorghum* and *Pennisetum* probably occur at Kaothe south of the Tapi river (there is some possibility of contamination at this site, Kajale 1990). Other early reports in Maharashtra are not until the Jorwe period, after *c.* 1500 BC, as at Daimabad (Kajale 1977) and possibly Inamgaon (Vishnu-Mittre and Savthri 1976; reservation is warranted, however, as this report was not accompanied by illustration and this presence was not confirmed through the systematic sampling programme reported in Kajale (1988). However, there is now evidence for African crops, including *Sorghum*, the pulse *Lablab*, and possibly *Eleusine* in Indian Punjab in the later Mature Harappan era, 2300-2000 BC, at Mahorana and Rohira (Saraswat and Chanchala 1994; Saraswat 1986). This suggests that earlier evidence for these crops in more coastal regions must await discovery. Reports of *Eleusine* from the Harappan north are more problematic. It has recently been reported from Harappa (Weber 1998), although full publication is still awaited. In the early second millennium BC, *Eleusine* is reported further east at Hulas in the Ganga-Yamuna Doab (Saraswat 1993), although the illustrations are more suggestive of *Setaria* caryopses and fragments of the rugose lemma/*palea* of *Setaria.* An impression of *Sorghum* has been reported from Pirak west of the Indus Valley, after *c.* 1900 BC (Costantini 1979) and, if confirmed, suggests that indeed *Sorghum* (and possibly other millets) spread throughout the Harappan region and were taken up in appropriate localities only after the collapse of Harappan integration (this issue is addressed further, below).

In considering evidence for foxtail millets (*Setaria* spp.) and panic grasses (*Panicum* spp.) it must be recognized that there are species indigenous to China and native to the monsoon grasslands of South Asia. Although both Chinese millets (*Setaria italica* (L.) P. Beauv. and *Panicum miliaceum* L.) have been identified on Late/Post-Harappan sites in Gujarat, it is unclear how these species were definitively distinguished from indigenous congeneric species, such as the edible *S. verticillata* (L.) P. Beauv., *S. intermedia* Roem. & Schult. (syn. *S. tomentosa* (Roxb.) Kunth.) and *S. pumila* (Poir.) Roem. & Schult. (the latter also domesticated) and the little millet (*Panicum sumatrense* Roth. ex Roem. & Schult.). The work by Weber (1991) and Reddy (1994) appears to have relied on differences of size alone, although no statistical studies of modern samples nor the effects of experimental charring are reported to support these metrical criteria. *Panicum miliaceum* L. has been positively identified from Kashmir in the Indo-Greek period, i.e. late first millennium BC (Lone et al. 1993). *Setaria* probably to be identified with *S. italica* (L.) P. Beauv. also comes from roughly the same period and region (ibid.). In addition, *Setaria* sp. caryopsis, and a rugose lemma similar *S. italica* type is illustrated from Hulas (Saraswat 1993; Pl. II, 10-12), although it was misidentified as *Eleusine coracana* (L.) Gaertn. *S. italica* (L.) P. Beauv. is also reported from Banawali (Lone et al. 1987). *Panicum miliaceum* L. is present at Shortugai in Afghanistan but not in the earliest levels that are thought to be associated with a Harappan foundation. This millet remains prominent at the site throughout the second millennium BC, i.e. after those levels with Harappan affinities, while *S. italica* is absent (Willcox 1991). If reported identifications are accepted, then *Setaria italica* is present in the north-western part of the subcontinent by the mid-third millennium BC, with only a few possible grains of *Panicum miliaceum* (Kajale 1996; Reddy 1997; Weber 1998); most *Panicum* having been attributed to the little millet (*Panicum sumatrense* Roth. *ex* Roem. & Schult.), a native of India (De Wet et al. 1983a; Hiremath et al. 1990). While De Wet et al. (1983a) tended towards the possibility of multiple domestications across India, Hiremath et al. (1990) argued that a region of the eastern peninsula was likely to have been a primary centre. The report of *Panicum sumatrense* Roth. *ex* Roem. & Schult. from Harappa back to *c.* 3000 BC (Weber 1998; Meadow 1998) could be indicative of a separate domestication in the north-western subcontinent. *Panicum/Setaria* type articulated phytoliths have been recently noted in samples from Harappa (Madella, unpublished data).

Other millets do not appear to have played a significant role during the Harappan periods in the north-western subcontinent. Two millets native to peninsular grasslands, Kodo millet (*Paspalum scrobiculatum* L.), a relic crop in parts of peninsular India today (De Wet et al. 1983b), and sawa millet (*Echinochloa colona* (L.) Link) was found from Rojdi C, in the Rangpur phase (Weber 1991), although the quantities were fairly small and could indicate that the species was present as a weed, or was insignificant in the overall subsistence. Another peninsular millet, browntop millet (*Brachiaria ramosa* (L.) Stapf, still lacks an archaeobotanical record.

The available evidence raises important questions about the eras of domestication and the routes of dispersal of these species. The presence of *Lablab*, *Sorghum* and perhaps *Eleusine* during the later urban period (Late Mature Harappan) on sites not too distant from Harappa, indicates that these crops must have become available through the trade networks of the Harappan Civilization and adjacent regions. The resource maps of Kenoyer (1995, 1998: 91-4) indicate that the most likely routes are via the Indus/Ghaggar-Hakkra Valley or perhaps up the Luni river and across the Thar desert. That these species were not adopted in more of the Harappan regions cannot be attributed to their unavailability but must be sought in cultural factors such as agricultural organization. While *Panicum sumatrense* Roth. *ex* Roem. & Schult. and the native *Setaria* spp. could have been native components of the Kathiawad grasslands, utilization of which was taken up independently by local communities, it is also possible that the practice of their utilization spread from the Deccan. Hiremath et al. (1990) suggested, although on admittedly slim evidence, that *P. sumatrense* may have origin in northern Andhra. If more detailed genetic studies on wild and cultivated populations bear this out, then a diffusion of this crop westwards prior *c.* 2500 BC would have to be envisioned. *P. sumatrense* Roth. *ex* Roem. & Schult., *Setaria verticillata* (L.) P. Beauv. and possibly *S. pumila* (Poir.) Roem. & Schult., and/or *S. intermedia* Roem. & Schult., were all cultivated by the Southern Neolithic peoples (northern Karnataka) from sometime in the third millennium BC (not yet well-dated) and these crops could have dispersed from there, although the lack of village sites back to 2500 BC in Maharashtra does not favour this view. On current evidence, therefore it seems plausible that the inhabitants of Gujarat (or elsewhere in the north-western subcontinent) began to utilize and domesticate *Panicum* and *Setaria* species that were available as wild components in the native flora.

Rice

The presence or absence of rice (*Oryza sativa* L.) from Harappan agriculture has long been an issue of controversy. While there is growing evidence for the cultivation of rice during this period in various regions of the subcontinent, there is no reason as yet to believe that it was an important crop for the Harappan Civilization, although it appears to have been locally important in some areas. Reported rice impressions from Kalibangan were mis-identified (Vishnu-Mittre and Savithri 1975). Impressions are also known from contemporary sites in Gujarat (Ghosh and Lal 1963; Ramesh Rao and Lal 1985) and

Rajasthan (Vishnu-Mittre 1969), while actual grain evidence for rice comes from Haryana (Willcox 1992) and Balathal in Rajasthan (Kajale 1996). In addition, rice phytoliths have been reported from Harappa (Fujiwara et al. 1992), and ongoing phytolith studies from the site confirm this presence (Madella, unpublished data). The macrobotanical remains also indicate rice at Harappa but only in the later urban period, after *c.* 2200 BC (Weber 1997). Impression of rice are also known from Ghaleghay II, 2500-2900 BC (Costantini 1987). This evidence suggests that rice was *available* as a crop for the Integration Era cities and towns of the Harappan region but not adopted. That rice does not feature in the agriculture, as it is presently understood, of the core regions of the Indus (including the Ravi river, e.g. Harappa during the early Mature phase, 2600-2300 BC) and Ghaggar-Hakkra systems, indicates that there must have existed aspects of the agricultural traditions and organization of Harappan Civilization which prevented the adoption of rice. Systems of irrigation, tillage and seasonal labour scheduling could all have operated against the spread of rice. Or less tangible cultural food values may have been involved. As previously discussed by Allchin (1984) regions along the northern Indus Basin, such as the Gomal and Swat Valleys, appear not to have participated in the urbanization and interaction systems that characterized the Mature Harappan Civilization despite the presence of Early Harappan sites in these areas. One of the contributing factors of this could have been that the rest of the Indus system, where the Harappan Civilization was established, shared in separate developments of agricultural production (Allchin 1984).

Fibres/Oilseeds

After the cereals and pulses, the most significant category of agricultural plants was likely to have been those that yielded fibres and/or edible oils. The most significant crop in this broad category for the Harappans may have been cotton which produces both textile fibres and oil from its seeds. Although disagreements persist, there are plausible arguments for the origin of one of the old world cottons, tree cotton (*Gossypium arboreum* L.) somewhere in South Asia, although the wild progenitor populations may now be extinct (Zohary and Hopf 1992; Wendel 1995). Early evidence of cotton seeds has been reported from Merhgarh, *c.* 5000 BC (Costantini 1983). Although some concern may be warranted given the uncharred preservation of this find (cf. reservations in Costantini and Biasini 1985: 24), the date is approximately as should be expected given that cotton had reached the Arabian peninsula by *c.* 4400 BC (Betts et al. 1994), although cotton cultivation in Mesopotamia is not documented until much later in the first millennium BC. Cotton cloth was found at Mohenjo Daro (Gulati and Turner 1929; Janaway and Coningham 1995), while better evidence for cultivation, seeds, have only been reported from Hulas in the Late Harappan, 1800-1300 BC (Saraswat 1993), and Loebanr 3 in Swat (Costantini 1987). Possible cotton pollen was reported from Balakot (McKean 1983; see Dales 1986).

Somewhat better documented archaeobotanically is flax/linseed (*Linum usitatissimum* L.), which is of South-West Asian origin and was incorporated from an early date into the

Neolithic package of the fertile crescent (Zohary and Hopf 1993). Although the cereals and most of the pulses of this package are known from Urban period Harappan sites, flax has only been reported from Nausharo (Costantini 1986, 1990) and at Chalcolithic Balathal, a site outside the Harappan orbit but contemporary (Kajale 1996). There are numerous finds, however, from the Late/Post-Urban phase, i.e. early second millennium BC, such as at Rojdi, phase C (Weber 1991) and Pirak (Costantini 1979b).

Possible seeds of jute (*Corchorus capsularis* L. or *C. olitorius* L.) were recovered from Rojdi (Weber 1991: 69). Although most of the *Corchorus* seeds recovered represented modern contamination, 19 charred examples came from secure archaeological contexts. Although two of the species in this genus are cultivated today for fibre, it is generally assumed that they were domesticated as fibre crops relatively recently as 'a deliberate attempt to search for new fibres to replace hemp in cordage and sacking' (Singh 1995: 476). Nevertheless, these and related species could have been utilized for fibre from a wild state, and some species also have edible parts. As these species are herbaceous annuals, their archaeological occurrence could also be due to their presence as arable weeds in the past. Another possible fibre crop which entered South Asia during the Harappan era may have been hemp (*Cannabis sativa* L.). Hemp has been reported in the form of charcoal from Neolithic Senuwar in Bihar, 1800-1200 BC (Saraswat et al. 1995). This species is thought to originate in temperate Central Asia, Afghanisatan or parts of the Himalayas (Small and Cronquist 1976; Zohary and Hopf 1993: 126). It is thought to have been present in China by the early third millennium BC (Li 1974). Preliminary study of phytolith samples from Harappa include morphotypes that have been provisionally identified as hemp (Madella, unpublished data). As is well-known, this species provides a psychotomimetic drug as well as fibres.

Oilseed finds have also been rare. Sesame (*Sesamum indicum* L.), which may have originated in South Asia (Bedigian and Harlan 1986; Zohary and Hopf 1993) has been reported from Harappa (Vats 1941: 467; Allchin 1969) and a Mature Harappan phase site in Makran (Tengberg 1998). That sesame had been domesticated by this time is given further confirmation by its presence in the third millennium in Mesopotamia (Charles 1989), thus making the identification of sesame with 'oil-plant' in Sumerian literature plausible (cf. Postgate 1985; Zohary and Hopf 1993: 133).

There are number of other oil crops, of various origins, that have been sparsely reported. The source of castor oil (*Ricinus communis* L.), thought to have originated in Africa is reported from Hulas, 1800-1300 BC (Saraswat 1993), and must therefore be added to the list of early crops to arrive in South Asia from Africa. Some sort of mustard (*Brassica* sp., probably *B. campestris* L., brown sarson) was also probabaly cultivated for its oily seeds, with occassional finds of *Brassica* from Rojdi (Weber 1991: 66), Babar Kot and Oriyo Timbo (Reddy 1994: 253, 284), and Mohenjo Daro (Vishnu-Mittre and Savithri 1982). A single record of poppy seeds (*Papaver* sp.) comes from the Bara phase at Sanghol in Punjab (Saraswat and Chanchala 1997); these seeds are to differ from the domesticated *P. somniferum* L. As this species probably arose from the wild *P. somniferum* subsp. *setigerum* (DC) Arc. of the western Mediterranean (Zohary and Hopf 1993: 128-30), we would expect it to be fully recognizable by the time it reached India and the Hulas find should perhaps be attributed to another species in the genus. The safflower, *Carthamus tinctorius* L., probably from South-West Asia (Zohary and Hopf 1993), has been recovered only from sites of inner India in Post-Harappan periods, including Jorwe phase Daimabad (Kajale 1977) and second millennium BC Senuwar in Bihar (Saraswat et al. 1995).

Melons, Cucumbers, Squashes

Seeds of the cucurbitaceae have been reported from a number of sites. Melon (*Cucumis melo* L.) seeds were recovered in the early excavations at Harappa (Vats 1941). *C. melo* L. was probably domesticated in South-West Asia from wild types indigenous to that area. while modern Indian and East Asian forms are thought to derive from a separate domestication from tropical varieties (Zohary and Hopf 1993: 182). Which type was present in the Harappan region is unclear. *C. melo* L. was also probably present on the Peninsula from at least the Malwa period, 1700-1500 BC (Kajale 1988). At Hulas, 1800-1300 BC, seeds of the Ivy gourd/*kundru* (*Coccinia grandis* (L.) Voigt., syn. *C. cordifolia* (L.) Cogn.) were found (Saraswat 1993); this species is wild and sometimes cultivated in India. *Cucumis* spp. have also been identified from Rojdi C, 2000-1700 BC, which include the native, wild *C. prophetarum* L., and two other undetermined species (Weber 1991). *Cucumis* sp. (which could be a wild species, *C. melo* L. or *C. sativus* L., the cucumber, probably native to the Himalayan belt) is reported from Chalcolithic Balathal (Kajale 1996) and Loebanr 3, 1700-1300 BC (Costantini 1987: 158). Pollen of a cucurbit was present in the archaeological strata at Balakot (McKean 1983; Dales 1986).

Arboriculture

Fruit trees (and perennial vines) are a category of food plant that almost certainly had a separate history from the cereals and pulses and developed through a different process of arboricultural domestication (Zohary and Spiegel-Roy 1975; Zohary and Hopf 1993: 134-7). Cultivated dates (*Phoenix dactylifera* L.) are probably of South-West Asian origin and the earliest archaeological finds come from Ubaid period Mesopotamia, fifth millennium BC (Zohary and Hopf 1993). The reported stones from Mehrgarh appear to be broadly contemporary with this (Costantini 1983). Dates have presumably had a presence in the Indus Valley ever since, with reported finds coming from Harappa, Mohenjo Daro (Marshall 1931: 27; Sahni 1931: 215; MacKay 1938: 220, Vats 1940) and Nausharo (Costantini 1990a). The domesticated date, important in the north-western subcontinent must not be confused with the Indian wild species, *Phoenix silvestris* (L.) Roxb. which has been reported from a few sites in inner India (e.g. Kajale 1988). Palm phytoliths, although not identifiable to species, are a regular component of samples from Kot Diji Harappa (Madella 1995, 1997, 1998, unpublished), and are most likely to have derived from groves of date palms. Also palms (perhaps dates) were a common motif on Harappan painted pottery (MacKay 1931: 324, 1938: 220; Vats 1940: 290).

Other fruits that came to the Indus Valley from the west were grapes (*Vitis vinifera* L.) and hackberries (*Celtis caucasica* Willd., syn. *C. australis* auct. pl. non L.). Grape pips have been reported from Nausharo, Baluchistan (Costantini 1990a), Rohira, Punjab (Saraswat 1986), Mahorana (early Bara Culture/Late Harappan), *c.* 2300-2000 BC (Vishnu-Mittre et al. 1986b), as well as Post-Harappan contexts in the Swat Valley, such as Loebanr 3, *c.* 1700-1400 BC (Costantini 1987) and Burzahom in Kashmir after *c.* 1700 BC (Lone et al. 1993). In addition, the cultivation of grapes is suggested by wood charcoal from Baluchistan, Punjab, and Post-Harappan Kashmir (Thiebault 1988a, 1988b, 1989, 1992, 1995; Saraswat et al. 1990; Lone et al. 1993: 180). Hackberries/*kharak* (*Celtis caucasica* Willd.) may have come to South Asia in the Late Harappan period where they have been recovered from sites in the northern periphery, such as Swat (Costantini 1987) and Kashmir (Lone et al. 1993). This species is thought to originate in the eastern Mediterranean (Zohary and Hopf 1993).

Arriving in South Asia also originally from the West were two nuts. One is the almond (*Amygdalus communis* L., syn. *P. amygdalus* Batsch., *Prunus dulcis* (Miller) D. Webb) an early nut of South-West Asia (Zohary and Hopf 1993; Browicz and Zohary 1996) reported from Late Harappan Hulas, after *c.*1800 BC (Saraswat 1993) and Kashmir after *c.* 1700 BC (Lone et al. 1993). Almonds are reported wild over a wide area from the Levant and Turkey to Central Asia. While some authorities have considered Central Asia as the likely home of the Almond (e.g. Kester et al. 1991), more recently Browicz and Zohary (1996) have questioned this since wild species of the same subgenus are absent form this region. Thus South-West Asia is most likely to have been the region where almonds were originally wild (Zohary and Hopf 1993: 173-7). The two early finds from India are both from the only regions where almonds have been grown in recent times, namely Kashmir and Punjab (Watt 1908). Also common walnuts (*Juglans regia* L.) arrived by this time. They have been reported from Neolithic Kashmir (Lone et al. 1993) and Late Harappan Hulas (Saraswat 1993). This species could have come into Kashmir from the north as it is known wild in pockets today from the north-eastern Turkey, north Iran through the Caucasus to Central Asia and the Tien Shah province of western China (Zohary and Hopf 1993: 177-8).

Several fruits native to South Asia may have already been present in the Indus Valley or else derive from further east. *Zizyphus mauritania* Lam. (syn. *Z. jujuba* (L.) Gaertn., nom. illeg.), a frequent archaeobotanical find was available locally, as the widespread occurrence of *Zizyphus* wood charcoal attests (Thiébault 1988a, 1988b, 1989, 1992, 1995; Castelletti et al. 1994). At some undetermined period, this species was brought into cultivation and diffused westwards to South-West Asia, Egypt and sub-Saharan Africa (Zohary and Hopf 1993). In addition the sour caper (*Capparis decidua* (Forsk.) Edgew.), present in wood charcoal assemblages (Castelloeti et al. 1984), was probably utilized from the local flora although hard evidence is still lacking. Fruits from more tropical regions to the east that may have been utilized in mango (*Mangifera indica* L.), *jamun* (*Syzygium cumini* (L.) Skeels) and *amla* (*Phyllanthus emblica* L, syn. *Emblica officinalis* Gaertn.) but hard evidence has not yet been recovered archaeobotanically. Evidence for the latter two crops comes from the Chacolithic Deccan (Vishnu-Mittre 1961; Kajale 1988), while the only evidence for mangoes comes from Iron Age wood charcoal in the middle Ganga plain at Narhan (Saraswat et al. 1994). Seeds of some sort of fig (*Ficus* sp.) were present through the cultural sequence at Rojdi and probably indicate the collection and use of wild(?) fruits (Weber 1991). A single find of a *Ficus* sp. seed from Babar Kot, although classified by Reddy (1994: 269, 285) as a weed of crop processing, could also indicate a one-off inclusion of seed from fruit consumption. The leaves of the *pipal* tree (*Ficus religiosa* L.) are amongst the most common plant motifs on Harappan painted pottery (MacKay 1938: 220; Vats 1940: 290).

The only early archaeobotanical evidence for *Citrus* fruits comes from the Late Harappan (Bara phase) site of Sanghol in Punjab where seeds of lemon (*C. limon* (L.) Burm. f.) have been reported (Saraswat and Chanchala 1997). This is of great interest as these fruits are thought to have been domesticated somewhere in the area spanning from north-eastern India to south China and South-East Asia, although there remains no firm evidence for precisely where or when (Roose et al. 1995). This evidence suggests that lemons diffused westwards, presumably along the Ganga Valley in the early second millennium BC. Further west, in South-West Asia, the citron (*C. medica* L.) occurs as early as *c.* 1200 BC, while the lemon arrives later in the first millennium AD (Zohary and Hopf 1993).

Additional fruits which entered the subcontinent during this general period were two species of *Prunus*, which being better suited to more temperate climates, appear to have been adopted only in Neolithic Kashmir (Lone et al. 1993), including peach (*P. persica* (L.) Batsch), and apricot (*P. armeniaca* L.). Both of these species are thought to be native to mountainous areas in Tibet, western China and the Tien Shah mountains of Central Asia (Zohary and Hopf 1993: 172; Watkins 1995). These species, like the lemon, only reached South-West Asia and Europe much later, at the end of the first millennium BC. An additional *Prunus* sp., but presumably not almond, has been reported from Baluchistan from as early as Mehrgarh II, 4500-4000 BC (Costantini and Biasini 1985; Costantini 1986, 1990). It may be that this represents locally wild, collected fruits. Otherwise they would indicate quite early arboriculture. More specific identification details are needed.

The above evidence suggests that these fruits species diffused from further west. Their arrival should not be seen as part of the initial Neolithic founder package, as there is no evidence that they were cultivated yet in South-West Asia at the period contemporary with early levels at Mehrgarh. In general, grapes and arboriculture may not have become important agricultural practices until *c.* 4000 BC (Zohary and Hopf 1993). Thus the adoption of fruit vine and tree crops in the Greater Indus Valley should be seen as part of a process of agricultural expansion during the Regionalization Era in which more complex forms of social organization and redistribution emerged in the Pre-Harappan cultures and long-distance trade with the west made exotic perennial corps available. The above evidence suggest that there was little diffusion of fruit crops from South Asia to the west until the period that is definitely Post-Urban/Late Harappan. This is in contrast with the adoption of fruits from the West into South Asian cultivation prior to or during the Harappan era, continuing during the Post-Urban/Late phase, and the spread of selected South Asian field crops like sesame and cotton further west also during this earlier period.

Bananas (*Musa paradisiaca* L.), have been identified on the basis of a common ceramic motif, noted first as Mohenjo Daro (Wheeler 1968: 85; MacKay 1938: 220, Pls. LXIX 15, LXX 5, 18; Marshall 1931: Pl. XCII 5, although this latter images were first suggested to be a 'millet' by MacKay 1931: 324). As domesticated bananas are seedless, they cannot be recovered through conventional archaeobotanical sampling, although it is clear that they produce distinctive phytolith forms (Tomlinson 1969; Wilson 1985). Ongoing study of phytolith samples from Kot Diji by one of us (Madella), indicates the presence of possible *Musa* phytoliths, and the necessary comparative study is underway. If confirmed this is of great interest, as domesticated bananas are thought to have originated from southern South-East Asia, in present-day Indonesia, from mutations in wild *M. acuminata* Colla. Within India, these cultivars were hybridized with *M. balbisiana* Colla, presumably native to the southern and eastern India and Sri Lanka, which provided adaptation to drier and monsoonal climate (Simmonds 1995). Evidence of wild banana seeds from an Early Holocene site in Sri Lanka (Kajale 1989) probably attest to traditions of utilization of *M. balbisiana* by cultures in southern India, within which hybridization with domesticates could have occurred at a later date. *M. balbisiana* Colla, does not have a sweet flavour and is seldom eaten as a fruit today. Sweet hybrid varieties of bananas were apparently not present in Sindh at the beginning of the twentieth century AD. Cultivation of *M. paradisiaca* L. hybrids on an intensive scale began only after partition (Rahman 1993: 186-7). The Harappan period evidence could indicate either a discontinuity in the cultivation of sweet bananas in some Post-Harappan era or else the utilization of non-sweet, starchy varieties.

THE HARAPPAN ROLE IN THE DIFFUSION OF AFRICAN CROPS: A RECONSIDERATION

A popular theme in discussions of Harappan archaeobotany is the presumed role of Harappan long-distance trading networks in introducing and disseminating crops, especially millets of African origin. Possehl (1980: 8-9, 54) suggested that millets from Africa played an important role in the subsistence of Gujarat in the Harappan and Post-Harappan periods. These millets included *bajra*/pearl millet (*Pennisetum glaucum* (L.) R. Br.), *jowar*/sorghum (*Sorghum bicolor* (L.) Moench., and ragi/finger millet (*Eleusine coracana* (L.) Gaertn.). In addition, there has been much interest in reports of *Sorghum* in the early second millennium BC of North-Western South Asia (e.g. Costantini 1979; Costantini and Biasini 1985; Jarrige 1985; Tosi 1986; Ratnagar 1994: 123; Haaland 1995; Possehl 1997, 1998). The presence of these crops on sites in this peripheral region contrasted with the dominance of winter crops in the Harappan 'core' (the Greater Indus Valley). The distinctiveness of cropping in Gujarat has been taken up by other authors and supported by a growing archaeobotanical database in which wheat and barley are under-represented while millets play an important role (e.g. Meadow 1989, 1996; Dhavalikar 1995; Weber 1991; Reddy 1994, 1997). This evidence has been compared with that from Pirak in Baluchistan from the Late/Post-Harappan period (early second millennium BC), where *Sorghum* sp. and *Panicum* sp. were reported (Costantini 1979), in order to argue that on the periphery of the Harappan Civilization a transformation in agriculture took place in the Late Harappan period in which exotic summer crops were adopted (Costantini and Biasini 1985; Jarrige 1985, 1997; Cleuziou and Tosi 1989; Meadows 1989, 1996, 1998; Franke-Vogt 1995: 32-4; Singh 1996). Possehl (1986) also put forward the hypothesis that millets of African origin (finger millet/*ragi*, pearl millet/*bajra*, and sorghum/*jowar*), which became available through Harappan long-distance trade by the end of the third millennium BC, played a critical role in the establishment of agriculture in peninsular India and allowed agricultural lifeways to develop in the savanna environments of inner India (cf. Hutchinson 1976). However, despite the continuing attraction of this narrative, it remains a 'just-so' story.

A critical re-examination of the available evidence for crops of African origin (not just the millets) in prehistoric South Asia undermines the likelihood both of the primary importance of African crops and the role of Harappan long-distance trade (see Fig. 3; for details of the evidence beyond that discussed earlier, see Fuller, in Vol. III of this series; Fuller et al. n.d.; cf. Kajale 1991). First of all, a number of the earlier reports of *Sorghum*, especially from pottery impressions, have been called into doubt (Willcox 1992; Rowley-Conwy et al. 1997; Deakin et al. 1998; Fuller et al. n.d.; Fuller, in Vol. III of this series). Nevertheless, there remain valid reports of prehistoric *Sorghum* from India which argue against Rowley-Conwy et al. (1997) hypothesis of a late domestication. In addition, finger millet has been widely identified, although critical re-examination of the published record suggests that many of these are mistaken identifications of other small millets, especially *Setaria* spp. and possibly *Echinochloa* spp. (see above and Fuller et al., n.d., Fuller, in Vol. III of this series). When the doubtful reports are removed, the distribution of most of the finds falls outside the Harappan area. Although less widely reported, pearl millet also is both external to and post-dates the Harappan Civilization. Also of critical importance but largely undiscussed in the past are two pulses of African origin, *Lablab purpureus* (L.) Verdc. and *Vigna unguiculata* (L.) Walp. (which is *not* the *V. unguiculata* reported by Weber from Rojdi, see note 1). These finds make it hard to accept a dispersal through Harappan trade. *Ricinus communis* L., the castor plant, also probably came from Africa and was present at Hulas in the early second millennium BC. The evidence as it stands does not suggest that any of the African millets were crucial to the settlement of the Indian peninsula as Possehl (1986) had suggested, but rather that they were incorporated at an early stage into pre-existing agricultural systems. Indeed finds of winter cereals (wheat, barley), as well as winter and summer pulses are as early or earlier than African millets at all well-reported sites. More importantly, as Weber (1998) suggests, the African millets appear to be adopted into a region where there is evidence for indigenous millets already present (also, Meadow 1998), and indeed emerging evidence from the southern Deccan suggests that the first cultivation in that region may have depended entirely on indigenous pulses and millets, and could have provided a pre-existing monsoonal cropping system (Fuller et al. n.d.).

The available evidence is suggestive of a gradual and piecemeal adoption of African crops in South Asia. This need not surprise us, since our current understanding of the botanical evidence for wild progenitors of African crops indicates that they were domesticated in widely separated regions of Africa (Fig. 3). None of the sites from which one species has been reported have evidence for the rest of the crops of African origin, although African crops do often co-occur in pairs. Hyacinth bean (*Lablab purpureus* (L.) Verdc.) co-occurs with one or the other of the reported millets from peninsular sites of the early second millennium BC (see Fig. 3). However, hyacinth bean also appears to have spread more widely, and has been found recently in relatively large quantities for the latter period of Southern Neolithic sites for which there is no evidence for African millets (finger millet reports appear to be largely mistaken from this region; see Fuller et al., n.d.; Fuller, in Vol. III of this series). The co-occurrence of *Sorghum* with other African crops, such as cowpea and castor at Hulas. (Saraswat 1993), and both *Lablab* and cowpea at Daimabad (Kajale 1977; Vishnu-Mittre et al. 1986a), strengthen the case for the presence of *Sorghum*. These finds therefore contradict the claims for a late first millennium BC domestication of this crop, argued from Nubian evidence by Rowley-Conwy (1991; Rowley-Conwy et al. 1997; Deakin et al. 1998).

Despite enthusiastic arguments on the part of a number of archaeologists, there remains no good archaeological evidence for trade or direct contact between prehistoric South Asia and Africa. S.R. Rao (1973) argued for contact with East Africa and Egypt on the basis of supposed baboon and mummy figurines, although these have not been accepted as Egyptian types (Chakrabarti 1990: 40). Similarly, some authors have pointed to ceramic headrests from south Indian sites as evidence for contact with Africa, where this tradition is known, spanning back to ancient Egypt (Allchin 1966; Nagaraja Rao 1970). However these latter arguments ignore the existence of a similar tradition in South-East Asia and the Pacific; and do not take into account the equally likely possibility of a local development (and subsequent abandonment) of such a tradition. Dhavalikar (1995) presents an argument that the presence of finger millet on sites in Saurashtra indicates contact with East Africa and Egypt, since *Eleusine* comes from Ethiopia—ancient Axum and/or *Punt*(?)—and Ethiopia was part of the Egyptian Empire. The latter claim is certainly not accepted by most Egyptologists, and finger millet is not known from Pharaonic Egypt (for a recent review of the relationship between Egypt and ancient Ethiopia, see Phillips 1997; Kitchen 1993; for Egyptian archaeobotany, including artistic evidence, see Germer 1985). Despite the wealth of evidence for Harappan involvement in trade with Mesopotamia and the Persian Gulf (Powell 1983; Cleuziou 1984; Mitchell 1986; Tosi 1986; Chakrabarti 1990; Potts 1993; Ratnagar 1994; Possehl 1997, 1998), there is nothing to indicate contact with Africa, or even with the Yemen side of Arabia. The archaeobotanical presence of crops of African origin, despite a number of likely misidentifications, is suggestive of at least indirect contact, but this evidence is stronger for peninsular India than sites within the Harappan orbit, although the earliest evidence to date does appear to occur in Harappan Punjab (see above). As a number of Harappan and Post-Harappan sites have now been explored in Gujarat without any clear evidence of contact, there is need for a contemporaneous site to be found and explored on the Konkan-Kerala coast where the first evidence of African-Yemeni contact should perhaps be sought.

NON-CROP SEEDS

Archaeobotanical samples often contain seeds of herbaceous species that are not those of well-established crop plants, both in India and elsewhere. Large assemblages of non-crops species were quite rare prior to the use of flotation in sampling, although one large, anomalously diverse assemblage including 25 species was recorded from Late Harappan Surkotada (Vishnu-Mittre and Savithri 1978; Vishnu-Mittre 1990). A few other samples with quantities of non-corps come from Sanghol (Saraswat and Chanchala 1997), Shikarpur (Saraswat et al. 1995), Loebanr 3 (Costantini 1987). On the other hand, most sites sampled using flotation have yielded relatively large numbers of non-crop species, e.g. Rojdi (Weber 1991), Babar Kot and Oriyo Timbo (Redy 1994), Balathal (Kajale 1996) and Burzahom (Lone et al. 1993). The traditional approach to these taxa has been to assume that these were utilized and therefore to seek ethnographically documented uses, as famine foods, condiments, medicines or the like (e.g. Weber 1991). However, ethnoarchaeological studies and a large number of archaeobotanical analyses in Europe and the Near East argue strongly that most, if not all, of the non-crop seeds recovered archaeologically because they were weeds that infested cultivated fields and were therefore harvested inadvertantly with the crop and removed during crop processing leading to their presence in significant quantities in habitation areas (e.g. Hillman 1981, 1984; Jones 1984, 1987; Reddy 1994, 1997). Subsequently, charring leads to their preservation. Thus the taxa present may not provide the type of information suggested by Weber, can on the other hand offer potentially more important insights into the ancient ecology of cultivated fields, while changes in the assemblage composition can be used to infer changes in agricultural practices (or the practices of crop-processing). Another potential source argued for South-West Asian and some South Asian weed assemblages is through dung used as fuel (Bottema 1984; Miller 1984; Reddy 1994; Charles 1998).

Some taxa may occur as either weeds or crops and their status must be assessed for each individual case. Kodo millet (*Paspalum scrobiculatum* L.), for example, is today a well known weed of cultivation, especially of rice, as are *Echinochloa colona* (L.) Link and *Coix lachryma-jobi* L. (Job's tears) (Hohn et al. 1977). Indeed all of the native millets are potential weeds. But experience has shown that most charred assemblages are dominated by likely crop plants (especially cereals), so that large quantities of potential millets in an assemblage can be assumed to represent a crop [good examples are furnished by the quantities of *Setaria*, *Panicum* and '*Eleusine*' at Rojdi, Babar Kot and Oriyo Timbo (Weber 1991; Reddy 1994, 1997)]. Large quantities of species other than cereals or pulses, are more difficult to interpret.

A controversial example is that of *Chenopodium album* L. at Rojdi, which Weber (1991) argues was harvested as a crop. *C. album* L. is widespread in Eurasia as a weed (Hanf 1983; Langer and Hill 1991: 207), and in modern times at least has been widespread in South Asia as a weed of cultivation and disturbed ground. It is nuclear whether or not *C. album* occurred wild in India in the past, although a perusal of floras does not suggest populations unassociated with human impact. Thus we can expect it to turn up on archaeological sites as a weed. Within South Asia, however, there is ample ethnographic evidence for this species being harvested and indeed cultivated in widely separated regions both as fodder and for human consumption, including both leaves and seeds (Watt 1908: 293; Weber 1991: 67-8, 121-2; Reddy 1994: 201). Weber's attribution of crop status to *C. album* at Rojdi during phase B rests on the ubiquity (32 per cent of secure provenances) and large quantities (57 per cent of seed from secure provenances) recovered from Phase B, in particular stratum 9: 'In light of the large volume of *C. album* seeds and their density, it is difficult to imagine how their presence could be due to anything other than intentional collection' (Weber 1991: 121). However, most of this quantity is accounted for by a single sample that contained 476 *C. album* seeds (Trench 46L, stratum 9). Reservation is warranted as *C. album* is a prolific seed producer, with individual plants averaging 3,000 seeds and having as many as 20,000 seeds (Hanf 1983: 202). In many other samples *C. album* occurs as one or a few seeds, not significantly different than the *Chenopodium* sp. quantities reported by Reddy (1994) from Babar Kot and Oriyo Timbo. Weber further argued that because the seeds of this species could be harvested and processed much like the small millets (see also Reddy 1994: 201), which were also present at Rojdi, this species may have been categorized together with the millets (Weber 1991: 122, 144). While *C. album* does occur in higher densities and ubiquities than most non-millet taxa, it remains less frequent than the millets overall, and notably so when the one sample with 476 seeds is removed from consideration. The overall ubiquity of *C. album* is not significantly different from *Trianthema*, a well-documented weed of millets (cf. Reddy 1994, 1997). It is certainly possible the *C. album* was used, and it is likely that it was utilized on at least a small scale, but it is difficult to accept the argument that it was utilized as a crop when this interpretation relies on its large quantity in a single sample. At present, therefore, the evidence for whether or not *Chenopodium album* was cultivated at Rojdi during any period remains inconclusive. If Weber's argument is considered plausible, then it raises the question as to why at the particular site of Rojdi during this particular period, late Mature Harappan (2200-2000 BC), *Chenopodium album* L. became important Weber (1991: 122) suggests that decreasing production of millet surpluses may have promoted use of *C. album*. That this may have been connected to decreasing security in intersite trade in foodstuff is worth considering, and it is notable that while barley was recovered in Rojdi, phase A, in small quantities, probably imported, it and other winter crops are absent from Rojdi B. Weber's (ibid.) contention that it would have been harvested in spring, rather than autumn, seems problematic, given that floristic reports indicate the normal flowering time as November after the monsoons (Cooke 1908), similar to that of millets.

If we accept that most of the taxa present in the Rojdi samples were crop weeds, entering the archaeological record through repetitive crop-processing activities, it become possible to examine changes in the composition of the Rojdi assemblages through time in terms of changes in either arable ecology or the organization of crop-processing activities. The evidence from Rojdi points to a substantial change in assemblage composition between phases B and C, i.e. *c.* 2000 BC (Weber 1991: 135-8). Rojdi C showed a greater diversity of taxa, especially a greater range of recovered food plants, such as pulses, additional millet taxa (*Sorghum*, possibly-cultivated *Echinochloa* and *Paspalum*), and possible oilseeds (*Linum* and *Brassica*). In addition, several new 'weed' taxa occurred while others were present in much larger quantities than previous levels. Most notably *Carex* was found in large quantities while it has previously been absent. *Cyperus articulatus* L./*rotundus* L. and *Fimbristylis* cf. *tenera* Roem. & Schult., although present previously, were recovered in larger quantities. As all of these taxa are sedges (cyperaceae), a family generally associated with wetlands, it suggests that a new or previously lightly-exploited type of micro-environment was being used for cultivation, areas with higher water tables, such as river or pond edges. Several of the other taxa present only in phase C. could also have come from such environments, including *Echinochloa colona* (L.) Link, *Paspalum scrobiculatum* L., and *Neptunia* sp., which could be the aquatic *N. prostrata* (Lam.) Baillon, although this genus also includes non-aquatic shrubs.

Another possible change in Rojdi C may have been in the organization of crop processing. Weeds in general were more common and more diverse than in previous periods (Weber 1991: 152). Their presence could be due to cultivation in a greater range of micro-environments or alternatively be a simple reflection of processing techniques that allowed more efficient separation of weeds from crops. In addition, as Weber (1991: 154) notes, there is a decrease in the density of wood charcoal which could suggest that other fuel sources, in particular dung, were increasingly used, and may have introduced more non-crop seeds to the site and/or to the record, since they would get charred. The relative proportions of the different millets also underwent change, with *Setaria*, including *S.* cf. *italica* (L.) P. Beauv. and *S.* cf. *pumila* (Poir.) Roem. & Schult. (reported as *Setaria glauca* nom. illeg.) becoming more common. *Setaria* was also found in a less-processed state in this level, often retaining its glumes (Weber 1991: 131). While Weber sees this increase in *Setaria* as indicating an increase in the use of this species, the fact that it is found in a different state than previously, i.e. less-processed, suggests that the change might be due to differences in handling the crop in period C. This suggests that *Setaria* was less fully processed at the time of harvest which might mean that harvesting and storage had become less centralized, at least for this particular crop, since the large labour investment needed to process an entire harvest at one time would imply some sort of community centralization. This lack of community-based labour investment could reflect actual social change or reflect a decrease in importance for this particular crop that relegated it to family-level processing, due to increasing emphasis placed on other, more productive crops, such as the newly adopted *Sorghum*.

Thinking of archaeobotanical assemblages in terms of crop-processing, it becomes possible to examine issues of the social organization of agricultural production. Hillman (1981, 1984) first suggested that producer sites, those that harvest and process grain from their own fields, and consumer sites, i.e. those that import their grain, ought to be distinguishable on the basis of the chaff components and weed types present (see also M. Jones 1985; Van der Veen 1992; Thompson 1996; Fuller, in Vol. III of this series, section 3.1). This model was adapted by Reddy (1994, 1997) for millet-based agriculture and applied in her interpretation of the archaeobotany of Oriyo Timbo and Babar Kot. Reddy observed that the weed taxa and chaff that are normally by-products from the early stages in crop processing were absent from Oriyo Timbo but present at Babar Kot, and therefore concluded that Oriyo Timbo had been consuming millets cultivated elsewhere. This assumes, however, that all stages of crop-processing will be preserved archaeologically in all cases; there are obvious problems with any assumption of 'total' preservation. It is more parsimonious to assume that those processing stages represented by archaeological assemblages are the activities carried out most frequently (repetitively) on site, in the vicinity of fires, during the life of the site: this latter approach argues from what is preserved rather than what is not. While the contrast between Oriyo and Babar Kot is significant, it may well be attributable to a different form of organization of the harvest and storage, in which at Oriyo Timbo move of the processing was done in bulk prior to storage, with only the final phases of cleaning done immediately before food preparation. While there are other reasons to believe that cultivation was not carried out at Oriyo, in particular evidence that it was inhabited seasonally in the dry season, March-June (Rissman 1986), the archaeobotany does not reflect 'consumption' so much as a greater degree (and organization?) of crop-processing done ahead of time, before the millets are taken up for day-to-day preparation on site. This could indicate a greater degree of community organization in the processing, storage and redistribution of millets during this later phase, 1700-1400 BC, at least in some areas of Gujarat where cultivation and transhumant pastoralism were well integrated.

Despite the remaining uncertainties, the evidence from the systematically reported samples from Rojdi, Babar Kot and Oriyo Timbo clearly illustrate the potential of archaeobotanical evidence for more than merely assessing crop presence. Instead, assemblages can be related to practices of cultivation and crop-handling. These practices in turn may relate to larger issues of social organization and complexity.

ISSUES OF IRRIGATION

The question of the presence of an irrigated agriculture in the Greater Indus Valley has often been an issue of controversy (see, e.g. Chakrabarti 1995: 43-6, 49-51, 87-8; Misra 1984). The Indus flows in a typical alluvial plain as a result of two main features: the insufficiency of the main channel for carrying the maximum flood discharge and the immense quantity of silt suspended in river's water (Lambrick 1986). During periods of maximum flooding, the river tops its banks and the bed is incapable of containing the muddy waters which pour out over the plains. This process leads to the formation of gentle slopes on either side of the river bed, leaving the river 'suspended' with respect to the rest of the landscape. Nevertheless, part of the flood concentrates into well-defined flood channels, which in turn often overspill their banks. The whole alluvial plain then is constructed by the ridges (*kacchas*) along the river beds and the secondary channels and valleys in between. The ridges and parts of the valleys must have been covered in the past with forest growth of varying extent and density. It is still possible to observe tracts of this forest in Sindh today. In Punjab, where the high gradient of the river is still sufficient to cause erosion during any season, the river beds are carved into the plain. These floodplain beds, known as *khadir*, may be several miles wide and the river is free to meander within them. The raised land between two *khadirs* is known as *bhangar* or *bar*.

Prehistoric agriculture in the Greater Indus plain would probably have been carried out in areas with different hydrological characteristics, and it might be envisaged that lands were arranged along a gradient of water availability. *Rabi* (winter) crops could have been grown following the *sailabi* (inundation) technique along the spillage areas (in the valleys) and the *kacchas* (river ridges). During the nineteenth century, and the first half of this century the sailabi technique was still used in Sindh (Chakrabarti 1995: 49-50; Lambrick 1986). The land is submerged by the spill of the flood and is sown in autumn (October-November) when the inundation passes, often without ploughing or manuring the fields, especially in the *kacchas*. The *rabi* crops (barley, wheat and associated pulses) can be reaped in March or April. Further watering is not necessary, but additional water might come from winter rains in early January. The whole procedure involves minimal labour, energy and use of implements. Raised land like the *bhangar* might have seen the use of the *shadoof* technique, where water is raised from a well and distributed in the field by means of small (ephemeral) earth-works. A linear representation of a man operating a *shadoof* is reported by Lambrick (1986; provenance unclear) to suggest that the Harappans were acquainted with this technique.

In the Harappan agricultural economy there is also evidence for some *kharif* (summer) crop production. Once more there is no need to infer the presence of complex architectural structures devoted to irrigation, as *kharif* cultivation was still practised, until very recently, without the need of canal irrigation systems (Misra 1984; Chakrabarti 1988: 96, 1995: 50; Lambrick 1986). The chosen piece of land, normally near the Indus or one of the old inundation canals, was surrounded with an earth embankment with an opening to admit the flood water as soon as the first spill occurred. Then the opening is blocked, trapping the water in the field, and the land is ploughed and sown. While the inundation continues, potentially damaging water is kept outside by the earth bunds and let in only when needed. The best areas for *kharif* cultivation are the ones in the vicinity of regular flood channels where the farmers can exercise greater control over the water. It should, however, be noted how risky this cultivation method might be, since there is always the possibility of water overtopping the bund an destroying the fields.

Fairservis (1967) argues, on the basis of the modern hydrology of the central Indus Valley and the distribution of Harappan sites in northern and western Sindh, that the central-western portion of the ancient Indus system (until the Mature Harappan period) is generally comparable with the modern one (for geography, see Fig. 4). Spills of the flood along the western banks of the Indus north of Sukkur are documented in Moghul times (Raverty 1979). The flood water would have moved westwards, passing south of Jacobabad and north of Larkana and might have been the main water supply for Judeirjo Daro and Jhukar (Fairservis 1967). Moving south, the water from the Indus would have been channelled again along the edge of the Khirtar Range in east Baluchistan where

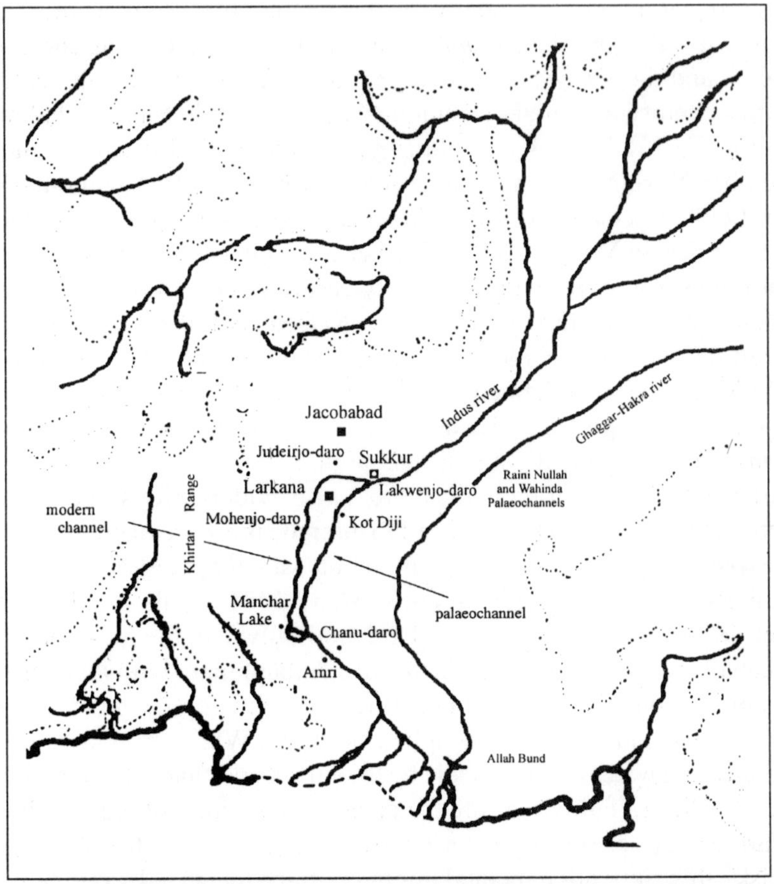

Fig. 4. Map showing modern and geographical feature mentioned in the text and selected sites of the Indus Valley tradition in central Sindh falling in the active area of the Indus river system.

water discharge from seasonal streams originating in the range could have increased the flow. The river course would eventually have opened into the shallow body of water of Manchar lake were two Harappan village sites are to be found (Fairservis 1967). Finally, the water would have rejoined the main stream of the Indus river via the Aral Channel. Mohenjo Daro, Lohumjo Daro, Kot Diji, Naru Waro Daro, Lakwenjo Daro and Amri all fall in the active area of this river system of the Indus Valley. For all these Harappan sites (and many others not mentioned here), their location suggests easy access to the flood waters of the Indus river and its related drainage system for agricultural purposes. There is no evident pattern of site distribution in respect to a possible artificial system of canal irrigation, but rather the location of the sites seems to be related to maximizing access to the Indus flood plain (see also 1967: 24-9, Fairservis 1971; Flam 1986).

This small-scale approach may have contrasted with that which has been envisioned for parts of the eastern Harappan province in the upper regions of the Ghaggar-Hakkra system. In this region, artificial canal systems have been reported through reconnaissance and test-pitting (Bisht 1982; Francfort 1992: 88-100; Chakrabarti 1995: 50-1, 87-8). However, as noted by Francfort (ibid.) much of the water for irrigation may have been provided by the natural network of meandering channels, thus obviating the need for large-scale irrigation works of the sort necessary for agricultural production in Mesopotamia.

A brief remark is needed on the peculiar structures known as *gabarbands*, which have attracted the attention of several archaeologists. *Gabarbands*, dam-like structures observed in Baluchistan and south-western Sindh (see Dales 1962: 30-9; Fairservis 1967: 10; Raikes and Dyson 1961: 265-81) and assumed by Stein (1937) to be built to store water from seasonal streams, can effectively trap water runoff, slowing water speed and allowing the silt in suspension to be deposited. These dam-like structures are often built in sequence, along the direction of drainage (Fairservis 1967, Fig. 5). This process in turn creates small patches of cultivable, rich and moist soil in an otherwise barren landscape. It can also support the formation of small bodies of standing water and marshes. Similar structures have been noted by Lambrick (1986) in southern Kohistan where *barani* (rain-fed) cultivation is practised. *Gabarbands* can sometimes be very complex structures, such as the ones observed in the valley of the Has river (Sindh Kohistan) by H. Buller (*Jhalawan Gazetteer*: 227). The valley, about 7 miles in width in its southern portion, provides a great expanse of cultivable land with rich soils reaching as deep as 30 feet. Rainfall in Sindh is highly variable and there might be years of less than average rainfall, during which time the structures are often abandoned. However, there are also years when rainfall is more abundant and it is worthwhile to cultivate on these fields, as they can yield good crops with sufficient water.

As this short description demonstrates, the Greater Indus Valley environment accounted for several different realities in terms of landform and water availability. This in turn might have required from the Harappans a certain flexibility in the exploitation of the land. However, it is worth remembering that cultivation in Sindh at the beginning of this century (and also in the Thar desert), under a dry climatic regime, was undertaken on rain

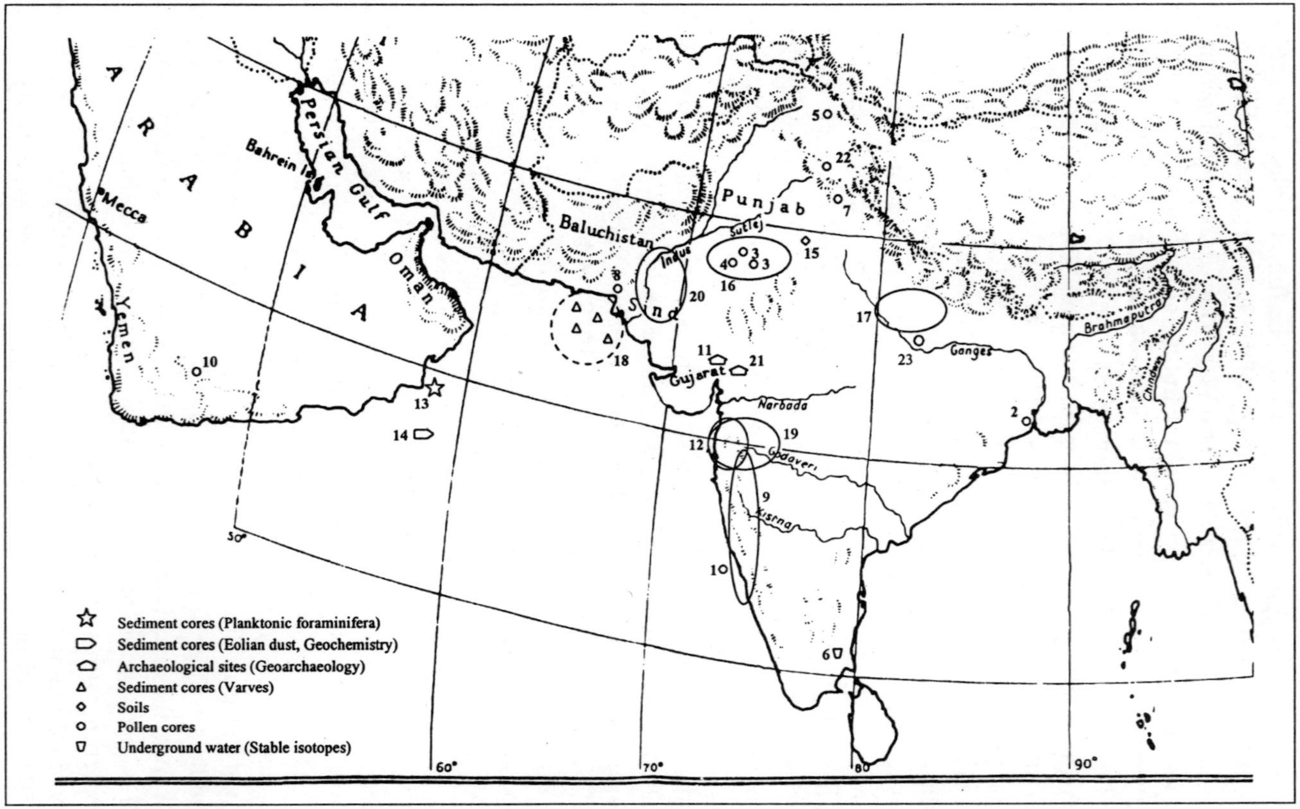

Fig. 5. Map showing the distribution of sites and regions of palaeoenvironmental studies. Site/region numbers and references are given in Table 4.

alone (Lambrick 1986). Under these circumstances and given the complete absence of archaeological evidence, it does not seem necessary to invoke, during the Harappan period, complex canal systems and centralized management for the irrigation of the land. This argues strongly against the application of Wittfogel's (1957) 'Oriental Despotism' model of the state to the ancient Indus Valley (Morrison 1994). More possibly there was a small scale association, possibly at the extended family level, to organize and manage the fields and the inundation water. As noted by Meadow (1989, 1996) and Kenoyer (1998), more important to the maintenance of Harappan urbanism than a highly organized or technologically complex irrigation system was the 'safety net' which provided inter-regional trade in foodstuffs in order to buffer local failures.

SEASONALITY AND INTENSITY OF AGRICULTURE

Beyond tracing the individual histories of particular crop plants, of particular importance for understanding an ancient civilization like the Harappan are reconstructions of the economic organization of agriculture. Although the number of intensively sampled Harappan sites are few, some important insights have come from the discussion of agricultural systems. The first systematic consideration of Harappan agricultural practices was carried out by Fairservis (1961, 1967, 1971: 304) who worked from archaeological settlement distribution patterns in the hilly and piedmont areas west of the Indus to infer factors of water, soils and topography. Fairservis hypothesized a winter (*rabi*), rainfed cultivation that utilized systems of bunds to conserve and channel water. Working from this model, Fairservis explored both the evolving subsistence system which allowed settlement on the Indus alluvium with subsequent urbanization and possible agricultural changes associated with the demise of the Harappan urbanism. In discussing the end of urbanism, Fairservis (1967, 1971: 311) attributed a role to the development of rice agriculture in regions east and south of the core Harappan region, which encouraged the dispersal of population and decentralization. While this hypothesis lacks the support of much hard evidence, as Fairservis himself admitted, it takes a form similar to explanations that have been offered by several authors more recently, usually involving millets rather than rice.

The accumulation of further data has continued to demonstrate the importance of the winter (*rabi*) crops in the Indus Valley, with summer (*kharif*) crops being represented largely by oilseed and fibre crops, such as sesame and cotton. While it can be argued by modern analogy that two cropping seasons must have been undertaken in Harappan times (e.g. Chakrabarti 1988: 96, 1995: 50), the archaeobotanical evidence suggests that Harappan subsistence agriculture was focused most intensively on one season of crops, namely the winter (*rabi*) crops. The food staples were probably the winter-sown, spring-harvested cereals and pulses of South-West Asian origin. Some summer crops (*kharif*) were present, in the form of fibres such as cotton and flax, as well as sesame (see Meadow 1989), but there is no evidence as yet for cereals or pulses of summer seasonality in the core Harappan regions (Indus or Ghaggar-Hakkra valleys). It must be remembered, however, that systematically-collected archaeobotanical samples are still lacking from this region, so that current conclusions are somewhat precarious. While *rabi* crops could have been fairly easily irrigated by winter rains, combined with harnessing run-off and river-flooding through fairly simple means (see discussion of irrigation, above), crops that flower and fruit in the late summer-autumn would have required greater efforts at water management. As their growing season coincides with the flood season of the Indus system, their cultivation in flood plain areas would have risked destruction by inundation if water was not diverted by barriers. On the other hand, soils at higher levels would have been particularly dry at this period. Such higher and drier sites would have required labour-intensive irrigation, probably from wells by *shadoof.* It is conceivable that the combination of readily available stores of winter staples and the labour needed for summer crops would have promoted concentration on smaller areas of cultivation for 'important' crops, not otherwise available, such as the fibre crops of sesame, and perhaps some fruits. Cotton and fruits were all probably grown as perennials and would have required some irrigation and attention throughout the dry season.

Kharif crops were of importance in a number of regions outside the 'core' Harappan region, especially in the later part of the Mature Harappan period ('Integration Era', after *c.* 2300 BC) and during the Post-Urban period. Gujarat, throughout the era of the Mature Harappan, focused on *kharif* cropping of small millets, and the little wheat and barley which were present may have been imports. On the other hand, in the region east of Harappan near the head waters of the ancient Ghaggar-Hakkra system and present-day Yamuna, several Harappan sites show that winter cereals and pulses were cultivated in addition to some summer crops, such as at Hulas, Rohira and Sanghol (see Table 2, and 'Hard Evidence,' above). This indicates that double-cropping was present during the Mature Harappan phase, even if this was not adopted in some of the core regions of the Indus and Ghaggar-Hakkra valleys. It is notable that this eastern region falls definitely within the area watered by monsoon rains which would have made such *kharif* cropping readily possible. The presence of two cropping seasons could have offered an extensive approach to agriculture as an alternative to the more intensive agriculture that might be postulated for the core Harappan regions. Double cropping allowed productivity to be spread across time, and in order to maintain soil fertility it may also have been spread across space, or else cereals could have been alternated with nitrogen-fixing pulses.

Another summer crop, present in the eastern province and at Harappa after 2200 BC was rice. Details about the nature of rice cultivation are still lacking, however. Rice can be cultivated as an irrigated crop, a labour intensive form of cultivation, or as a 'dry' crop, in which it is watered only be the monsoon, as in usually the case with millets (Grigg 1974). For wet-rice cultivation, fields need to be flooded, either by bunding or channeling water, and the seed planted in soils of a muddy condition, usually ploughed. Understanding which approach to rice cultivation was utilized is of interest both for tracing the history of this farming technique and for assessing the agricultural complexity of the eastern Harappan regions. The systematic collection and analysis of weed assemblages and phytolith samples should be able to indicate whether the rice crop was significantly associated with wetland species or showed a range of weeds similar to those of millets, as would be expected in the case of dry-cropping. If rice was dry-cropped, then this provides one possible explanation of why rice cultivation may have been slow to spread westward, since the summer rains are likely to have been inadequate in most of Pakistan for growing summer crops. The adoption of rice in the west may have had to wait until more labour-intensive, irrigated system of cultivation was developed. The presence of rice at Pirak in the second millennium BC, together with evidence for *Panicum* millet and possibly *Sorghum* (Costantini 1979; Jarrige 1985), should probably be seen not merely as the adoption of new crops and a new cropping season, but also new systems of cultivation. In this regard, it is interesting that rice turns up so early in Swat (Costantini 1987): could irrigated, wet-field systems have already been in operation there in the third millennium BC?

In general, while there has been a great awareness of the seasonality of different crops, there has been less discussion of issues of intensity. These are clearly issues of importance for understanding the organization of Harappan agricultural production and the stability of the agricultural base of the civilization. Intensive agriculture, although normally more productive, might also have been more prone to catastrophic failure in bad years. On the other hand, extensive systems which included double-cropping are likely to have had more inherent buffering from the vagaries of climatic variability. It is perhaps in regions with the latter kinds of agriculture systems, such as the Eastern Harappan province and probably Gujarat, where greater long-term stability might be expected, and indeed it is these areas where much of Late Harappan continuity has been identified (Allchin and Allchin 1982, 1997; Chakrabarti 1995; Kenoyer 1991, 1995, 1998; Possehl 1997). The issue of agricultural stability, raises the question of climatic stability and climatic change, to which we turn next.

THE CHANGING ENVIRONMENT AND CHANGING SOCIETY

The area spanned by the Harappan Civilization was vast and encompassed several ecological areas, with rainfalls varying from less than 50 to *c*. 600 mm per year. However, on the whole, the entire area can be considered as arid or semi-arid, with a few semi-humid sectors (e.g. the gallery forest along some of the rivers) (Agrawal and Sood 1982; Allchin and Allchin 1997: 21-5; B. Allchin 1998). This geographical region is nowadays dominated by two main climatic systems, the winter cyclone from the west and the summer monsoon from the east. There has been considerable debate about the degree and extent of climatic changes that occurred in this large area before and during the Harappan Civilization, and also the degree of influence of such hypothetical climate changes in driving the transformation of Harappan society during the second millennium BC.

Early theories about climatic change were based on the evidence of settlement distribution. Stein (1937) inferred wetter conditions on the basis of the presence of settlements and *gabarbands* in Baluchistan (see 'Issues of Irrigation' above). But there is no need to postulate a higher precipitation rate to justify the construction of *gabarbands*, as the production of silt deposits would be worthwhile even for sporadic cultivation at long intervals because of the very poor, thin soils present in the area. Also, the process of building these structures does not always involve high energy expenditure (Madella, personal observation during a survey in the wadis of the Rohri Hills—Thar desert, Sindh). Piggott (1950) and Wheeler (1959) postulated a more luxuriant environment on the basis of the fauna depicted on the Harappan seals and pottery, considered to be typical of a jungle environment (rhinoceros, elephants, tigers, etc.). The Indus and many other important rivers are nowadays still flanked for good tracts of their banks by dense gallery forest which creates a more humid microclimate. The survival of this type of forest is not influenced by the general climate but only by the conditions set by the presence of a river, and such forests represent an ideal environment for all the species depicted in the Harappan pictography. The gallery forest and associated riverside swamps could probably have supported these animals with little or no change in climate; the absence of these species today is probably to be attributed to human impact, including agricultural development and hunting. The Moorish traveller Ibn Batuta described an encounter with two rhinoceros, in an environment similar to the modern one, during his travel in Sindh in 1333 AD (Dafremery and Sanguinetti 1855: 100). It is also important to stress, as already noted by Fairservis (1967), that most of the 'Harappan' animals represent species adapted to survive in a range of environments and they are today to be found also in open forest and grasslands. Furthermore, Harappan pictography on artefacts such as seals might represent 'special' animals rather than those that were part of the everyday repertoire (one might note Ashoka's wide use of the lion in regions where such animals were unlikely to have lived; or even the use of the lion as a royal symbol in Britain!).

A further argument for change was based on the archaeological observation of the enormous quantities of baked bricks in Harappan cities (Marshall 1931; Piggott 1950). It was suggested that the production of burned bricks would have required quantities of wood that could only be accommodated in an environment of more forest cover. However, Raikes and Dyson (1961) calculated that only 400 acres of gallery forest would be needed for each rebuilding of Mohenjo Daro. Modern production of bricks in Sindh is still largely based on the same technology utilized by the Harappans (Madella, forthcoming) and the wood is supplied by the three main trees today growing in areas of water availability within this arid zone: *Acacia arabica* Willd. (babul), *Tamarix* sp. (lai) and *Prosopis cineraria* (L.) Druce (kandi, khejri). Other wood is also available in well-watered sectors (e.g. along the river banks) in the form of *Populus euphratica* Olivier (bahan), *Dalbergia sisso* Roxb. (tali, sheesham), *Salvadora persica* L., *S. oleoides* Decaisne, *Ficus* sp, and *Tamarix* sp. In general, these seem to be the same species of tree/shrub that dominate charcoal assemblages thus far analysed from the Greater Indus Valley (Saraswat et al. 1990; Castelletti et al. 1994; Saraswat 1994; Thiebault 1988b, 1989, 1992, 1995; Saraswat and Chanchala Srivastava 1997). Alongside wood, dung and the crop processing by-products from wheat, barley, rice and cotton are sometimes used in brick production. There is then no need to postulate a higher wood availability to produce the quantity of bricks involved in the construction of the Harappan settlements.

From the 1960s, scientific palaeoenvironmental and geological studies in Sindh suggesting possible climatic or environmental changes appeared to support the archaeological evidence. In this perspective, the Indus river emerged as one of the dynamic factors that intervened in processes of cultural change during the Late Harappan period. In 1965 Raikes published his famous article, 'The Mohenjo-daro floods', in which he suggested that an uplift or a series of uplifts of the Indus Valley in the areas of Sehwan were responsible for the creation of a permeable natural dam which retained the solid fraction transported by the water. These sediments slowly engulfed several settlements of the area in mud (see also Raikes 1964, 1967a, 1967b, 1968, 1979). This hypothesis was sustained also by Dales (1965a, 1965b, 1966a, 1966b; also Dales and Raikes 1968; Raikes and Dales 1977, 1986). The evidence adduced to support this theory is quite inadequate and prompted several critiques (Lambrick 1967; Possehl 1967; Agrawal 1971, 1982; Wasson 1984, 1987). It is argued that if the barrier was permeable it would have been unlikely to endure the force of the hundred thousand cubic feet per second of the Indus floods for more than a few years (Lambrick 1967; Wasson 1984, 1987). A similar geomorphological occurrence, known as the Allah Bund, took place in northern Kachchh in 1819 (Fig. 4). A structure of soil was created by an earthquake and obstructed the Nara (one of the eastern canals from the Sukkur barrage and possibly the southern portion of the bed of the former Ghaggar-Hakkra river). This bund was destroyed only after 7 years by what was probably the first flood of spill water (Lambrick 1967). Lambrick suggests instead a major change in the course of the Indus river upstream from Mohenjo Daro. This might have shifted the bed of the river about 30 miles eastward, depriving the town of nearby inundation and thus encouraging the dispersal of population from the city.

Tectonic uplift and changes in the course of river beds also had a major impact on another area of the Harappan Civilization. Archaeological research in Cholistan, along the dry channels of the Ghaggar-Hakkra river (often identified with the lost Sarasvati and Drishadvati rivers) has led to the discovery of a large number of sites (Stein 1942, 1943; Gosh 1952, 1953; Field 1959; Suraj Bhan 1971-2, 1972, 1973, 1975; Bisht 1976, 1977; Lal 1954-5; U.V. Singh 1977; Joshi 1978a, 1978b; Dikshit 1979, 1981; Flam 1976, 1981, 1986; Dalal 1980; Mughal 1982, 1997; Misra 1984). Both in Cholistan and along the Ghaggar-Hakkra there is a relatively high frequency of settlements during the Mature Harappan which suggests a well-watered river and inland delta (in a area around Derawar). In comparison, there are fewer sites during the Early Harappan, which might reflect a decreased amount of water in the drainage system during this earlier period (see also Mughal 1997 and Possehl 1997b for an extensive review). By the time of the Painted Grey Ware (PGW) the river must have been dry, because several sites of this period are found in the fixed river beds. Lack of water in the Gagghar-Hakkra fluvial system seems to be related to possible tectonic and geomorphological processes (Agrawal and Sood 1982; Agrawal 1992: 237-42) rather than climatic changes. Although most authors have seen the drying up as a rather sudden, Late Harappan event, micromorphological work by Courty and colleagues (Courty 1986; Courty and Federof 1985; Courty et al. 1989: 269-83) calls this view into question. The study of sediments from the paleochannels suggests instead a much longer, more drawn out process of drying-up, although it is clear that during the Mature Harappan period these channels were subject to regular flooding, presumably during the monsoon/Indus flood season. The presence of river with variable water flow can be seen as according with the name given to the Gagghar-Hakkra in the *Rigveda*, '*Saraswati*' which means 'Chain of Pools' (Possehl 1999). The description of the Sarasvati in the *Rigveda* as a mighty and powerful river can be seen in the light of the seasonal floods which might have transformed an intermittent flow of water (indeed, a chain of pools) into a full flowing river. Contrary of what Possehl (1999) argues and in the light of the works of Courty and colleagues, the description of the river in the *Rigveda* and the literal meaning of the name can be reconciled and seen as two (seasonal) expressions of the same river. By the time of the Painted Grey Ware, these channels were being infilled by windblown sand. Movements of sand in the Cholistan and Thar deserts could be, indeed, responsible for the absence of physical evidence of the river between the Derawar Fort inland delta and the two palaeochannels east of Sukkur, the Raini Nala and the Wahinda (cf. Possehl 1999).

The relation between the drying up the Ghaggar-Hakkra course and the consequential depopulation of the area, and the general decline of the Harappan Civilization is not clear. Misra (1984) and Chakrabarti (1995: 274) suggest that the disappearance of the Ghaggar-Hakkra introduced a weakness that affected the entire Harappan distribution area and resulted in de-urbanization. However, the causative link between the river system and the Harappan settlements remains unexplored (Fuller and Boivin, in Vol. of IV this series). A possible explanation is that the valley of the Ghaggar-Hakkra represented the grain basket of the Harappan Civilization, with the surplus production of wheat and barley redistributed in the settlements of Sindh and Punjab. This would explain why changes in the Ghaggar-Hakkra system would have had such a destabilizing effect on Harappan society.

Nevertheless data representative of possible changes in the climate have been documented in north-western India over the past 11,000 years (Table 4; Fig. 5). Widely influential and controversial was the analysis of pollen and sediments from four lakes in Rajasthan (G. Singh 1971; G. Singh et al. 1974; Vishnu-Mittre 1976, 1978; Meher-Homji 1980, 1994a, 1994b; Bryson and Swain 1981; Swain et al. 1983; Wasson 1995). Additional relevant evidence comes from the study of oxygen isotope ratios and pollen assemblages from the Arabian Sea (Van Campo 1986; Caratini et al. 1994), the assessment of Quaternary geomorphology in Rajasthan (Allchin et al. 1978) and Maharashtra (Kajale et al. 1976; Kale and Rajaguru 1987), and the climatic modelling of monsoon intensity and area of influence in the past (Kutzbach 1987; Prell and Kutzbach 1987; Wasson 1995; Meher-Homji 1994a, 1996a; Naidu 1996; Sirocko 1996). Certain disagreement remains between different authors, but in general terms it is possible to highlight that the period between 11,000 BP and 10,000 BP represented a peak in seasonality with stronger monsoons from the west and considerably higher rainfall. This situation persisted, although slowly decreasing, until *c.* 3500 BP.[5] The summer monsoon today does not reach the highlands of Baluchistan, but it has been suggested that it may have been of some importance in the

TABLE 4. SOURCE OF PALAEOECOLOGICAL EVIDENCE FOR THE LATER HOLOCENE OF INDIA AND ADJACENT REGIONS, GROUPED INTO BROAD REGIONS, INDICATING THE TYPE OF EVIDENCE THE NATURE OF THE INFERRED CHANGE, AND GIVING REFERENCES (Numbered sites are plotted in Fig. 4).

Site or Region (numbers refer to Fig. 4)	Map no.	Discipline	Climatic Evidence for Change around 2nd millennium BC	Reference
North-western Subcontinent				
North-west India/Pakistan		Climatology	Monsoon	Ramaswamy 1968
Western Rajasthan (India): salt lakes Didwana and Lukranasar	3	Pollen analysis; also micro-charcoal count	Changes in pollen assemblage and grass/tree ration (also micro-charcoals) Vegetation changes linked to winter and summer rainfall quantities	Singh 1971; Singh et al. 1974; Bryson and Swain 1981; Swain et al. 1983; Wasson 1995 critiques: Vishnu-Mittre 1976; Meher-Homji 1980
Rajasthan and Sindh (India-Pakistan)	16	Geoarchaeology		Allchin et al. 1972
Indus Valley (Pakistan)	20	Geology	Tectonic	Snelgrove 1979
Western Rajasthan (India)	16	Geology	Calcrete/Dunes (not adequately dated)	Agrawal 1992
Indus Valley (India)	20	Geology	Tectonic	Raikes 1984a, 1984b
Haryana-Rajasthan (Ghaggar River Valley, India)	15	Pedology/Soil micromorphology	change in sedimentation, decreasing alluviation, increasing wind-blown sand, indicates drying-up of Ghaggar-Hakkra	Courty 1986; Courty and Federoff 1985; Courty et al. 1989: 269-283
Balakot (Pakistan)	8	Pollen analysis	No change	McKean 1993; synopsis in Dales 1986
Western Rajasthan (India): salt lakes	4	Pollen analysis and Sedimentology		Deotare and Kajale 1996; Kajale and Deotare 1997; Deotare et al. 1998
Thar Desert (India)	16	Stable isotopes		Andrews et al. 1998
Western India				
Langhnaj (Gujarat, India)	21	Archaeology/ Geomorphology	Re-activated sand dunes	Sankalia 1965
Maharashtra (India)	19	Geoarchaeology	Alluvial fills	Kajale et al. 1976
North-west Deccan (India)	12	Geomorphology	Landforms	Kale and Rajaguru 1987

(contd.)

Site or Region (numbers refer to Fig. 4)	Map no.	Discipline	Climatic Evidence for Change around 2nd millennium BC	Reference
Kanewal (Gujarat, India)	11	Archaeology/ Geomorphology	Re-activated sand dunes	Rajaguru and Mishra 1997
Himalayas				
Kashmir Himalaya (India)	5	Pollen analysis	Changes in pollen assemblage	Gupta 1975
Siwalik (India)	22	Pollen analysis		Awashi 1992
Western Himalaya (India)	7	Pollen analysis	Changes in pollen assemblage	Sharma 1992
Kashmir		synthesis of various data sets		Agrawal 1992; 1995
Ganga plain				
Meander lake, Sarai-Nahar-Rai Uttar Pradesh	23	Pollen analysis	Changes in pollen assemblage	Gupta 1976
Bengal Basin (India)	2	Pollen analysis		Gupta 1981
Calcutta peat (India)	2	Pollen analysis	Changes in pollen assemblage	Barui and Chanda 1992
West Bengal (India)	2	Pollen analysis		Arghya et al. 1996
North-central India	17	Pedology		Srivastava and Parkash 1998
Southern India				
Karwar (West South India)	1	Pollen analysis	Changes in pollen assemblage and grass/tree ration	Caratini et al. 1991; 1994 critique: Meher-Homji 1994b, 1996a, 1996b
Western Ghats (India)	9	Ecology, synthesis	Vegetation history	Subash Chandran 1997
South India: Tamil Nadu	6	Ground water isotopes		Sukhija et al. 1998
Arabian Sea and Arabia				
Arabian Sea	14	Climatology	Eolian dust and geochemistry	Sirocko 1996
Arabian Sea	13	Climatology	Monsoon upwelling	Naidu 1996
Southern Arabia (Yemen)	10	Pollen analysis and Palaeohydrology		Lezine et al. 1998
North-eastern Arabian Sea	18	Sedimentology	Precipitation and river runoff	Von Rad et al. 1999

TABLE 5. ARGUMENTS IN FAVOUR OF CLIMATIC CHANGES AND COUNTER ARGUMENTS TO SUPPORT ANTHROPIC INTERFERENCE IN THE LANDSCAPE OF SOUTHERN WEST INDIA (Western Ghats, Karnataka) (modified after Meher-Homji 1994b)

	Interpretation of the pollen assemblages in favour of climatic change around 3500 bp (uncalibrated). (Caratini et al. 1991 and 1994)	Interpretation of the pollen assemblages in favour of anthropic interference on the environment (Meher-Homji 1994a, 1994b and other authors)
Point 1	Decline of pollen from evergreen and deciduous forest taxa and parallel increase of savanna suggesting a more dry climate with less overall rainfall.	Savanna vegetation at low and moderate altitude in the Western Ghats could be the result of repeated fires (Pascal 1984). If change in vegetation cover should be related to a drier climate, then the species of the thorn forest not the savanna would replace the evergreen and deciduous forests (Meher-Homji 1994b).
Point 2	Reduction of mangrove pollen in the pollen rains suggesting the contraction of humid areas.	Mangrove can grow in semi-arid to humid conditions and are not good climatic indicators (Meher-Homji 1994b). According to Gadgil and Subash Chandran (1988) shrinkage of mangrove vegetation may be due to the introduction of paddy cultivation in the estuaries.
Point 3	Flow of water of terrestrial origin from rivers diminishes as indicated by to an increase of ^{13}C stable isotope in the sedimentary organic matter.	Bruijnzeel (1986) argues that deforestation and burning of grasses would result in increased water discharge. Large scale deforestation may affect the local, convectional rainfall without causing any change in the monsoon pattern (Meher-Homji 1991).
Point 4	Notably lower rate of sedimentation (7cm/100 years) in recent period as compared with rate prior 3500 bp (18cm/100 years) could indicate a decrease in rainfall.	Soil erosion on slopes should be higher under savanna vegetation cover than under forests (Meher-Homji 1994b).

past (Snead 1968). The interpretation of seasonal laminated sediments (varves) deposited in the oxygen minimum zone (OMZ) off the Makran and Karachi coasts indicates a decrease in sedimentation which von Rad et al. (1999) suggest could indicate a decrease in precipitation in southern Pakistan after 4000-3500 year BP (*c.* 2000-1750 cal BC). They attempt to correlate this with hypothetical aridification in the Near East. The chronometrical control on sedimentation rate does not appear to be sound, however, with only four radiocarbon dates available for the entire sedimentary sequence (Von Rad et al. 1999, Fig. 6), and thus the chronology of the crucial changes is based on assumptions of sedimentation rates. Furthermore, Von Rad et al. (1999) do not take into account the potential impact on sedimentation rate of the capture of the Ghaggar-Hakkra water by the Ganga system, postulated for about this time (e.g. Agrawal and Sood 1982; Misra 1984; Courty and Federof 1985; see above). Thus the absolute chronology of the changes in this varve sequence is not clear, and their linkage to climatic changes rather than tectonic processes is insecure.

The monsoon is the very pulse of the Indian subcontinent, and affects the Indus Valley even if to a lesser degree than the eastern and peninsular areas. The south-west monsoon of the summer months is the origin of most of the rain for the semiarid and arid regions of the Thar desert. Naidu (1996), on the basis of distinctive planktonic foraminiferas from Arabian Sea core especially the indicator species *Globigerina bulloides*, calculated the upwelling due to the south-western monsoon in the Arabian Sea over the past 19,000 years. Upwelling indices reveal the lowest values during the Holocene occurred between *c*. 3500 BP (*c*. 1500 BC) and 1200 BP (*c*. 800 AD) suggesting a decrease in the monsoon activity over the Indian subcontinent during this period, followed by some increase. Ramaswamy (1968), however, had argued for an opposite situation on the basis of the data supplied by Lamb et al. (1966) and an accurate study of modern daily charts for the northern hemisphere, that between 2000 BC and 500 BC the south-west monsoon must have extended into Pakistan far more frequently than today because low pressure troughs would have been present in the west. This would have induced monsoon activity and also caused any monsoon from the Bay of Bengal to move further and to curve to the north, north-east. Ramaswamy might be disregarded, however, on the ground of poor dating evidence. Indeed, the pollen data of G. Singh et al. (1974) from Lunkaransar lake (Bryson and Swan 1981; Swain et al. 1983) were interpreted as representative of higher monsoon activity and winter rains during Early and Mature Harappan period. This was followed by the much debated hypothetical climatic change towards dryness, postulated by G. Singh et al. (1974) and Bryson and Swan (1981) around 3700 BP (2129, 2982, 2043 cal. BC intercepts), leading to the mobilization of sand dunes. Although it is clear that sand dunes have formed and moved in the past across parts of Rajasthan where they are today stabilized by vegetation (Allchin et al. 1971, 1978; Allchin and Allchin 1982: 19-22), the dating of these dune-movement episodes (and the implied aridity) is still unfixed—a parallel case exists for the sand dunes of the central Sudan (Warren 1970). Modern chronometric techniques need to be applied to the problem.

The most detailed studies on pollen from the Greater Indus Valley are those of G. Singh and his colleagues already referred to above (G. Singh 1971; G. Singh et al. 1972, 1974; discussed by Bryson and Swain 1981; Swain et al. 1983). Recently, Kajale and Deotare (1997) have undertaken new work in this region. The sediments of three salt lakes or playas (Lunkaransar, Didwana and Sambar) in north-western Rajasthan were analysed by G. Singh et al. (1974). However, several saline playas are found west of the Aravalli range. The origin of these depressions is heterogeneous, some being the result of old channels of a disorganized drainage system (i.e. Pachpadra and Thob) while others are due to structural depressions (i.e. Didwana and Kuchman) (Kajale and Deotare 1997). The basal deposits of the studied lakes consisted mainly of aeolian sand overlaid by lake sediments with variable preservation of pollen grains. Pollen assemblages are interpreted by Singh (1971) as showing a dryer phase around 18,000 BP, followed from around 16,000 BP by a more seasonal climate and higher summer precipitation. The assemblage is rich in the pollen of grasses, sedges, *Chenopodiaceae/Amaranthaceae* and *Artemisia*, and it is interpreted as reflecting the development of a grass-steppe vegetation following a period of extreme aridity. Between 5000 BP (3900-3700 cal BC) and 3800 BP (2400-2100 cal. BC), the pollen of trees and shrubs became more frequent, reflecting a possible moist phase. Starting sometime before 3500 BP (1900-1700 cal BC), wetter phase was interrupted by a drier period. Pollen of trees and shrubs disappear from the sediments and the lakes became gradually drier until *c.* 1500 BP (400-640 AD) when the lakes had dried up completely and conditions similar to the present day set in. This interpretation of the pollen data, which emphasises climatically-driven desertification processes in the north-west of the Indian subcontinent was contested by Vishnu-Mittre (1974b, 1976, 1979, 1982), whose criticism was based upon the use of certain pollen types as climatic indicators. Vishnu-Mittre (1974b, 1976, 1979, 1982) and the bio-climatologist Meher-Homji (1980, 1994a, 1994b, 1996a, 1996b) are inclined to see the onset of local aridity as the result of anthropic action rather than climatic factors.

Further work on three more playas of western Rajasthan has been carried out by Deotare and Kajale (1996; Kajale and Deotare 1997; Deotare et al. 1998). The litho-stratigraphic column at Bap-Malar playa (Jodhpur district) suggests that the final activity of the now stabilised dunes around the lake is *c.* 7000 BP and the lakes appear to have dried up by around 6000 BP (Deotare et al. 1998). This would imply relative stability of the level of precipitation since well before the Early Harappan period. The pollen analysis at Pachpadra and Thob playas (Barmer district) (Deotare and Kajale 1996; Kajale and Deotare 1997) shows fluctuating plant assemblages which might be a response to changes in *local* hydrological conditions. An episode of relatively dry (local?) conditions is suggested for the end of the Pleistocene on the basis of the presence of *Ephedra* pollen. However, for Deotare and Kajale (1997) it does not seem necessary to invoke climate to explain most intra- and inter-lake variations. Changes in vegetation and hydrology, if present at a given lake, should not be generalized into climatic changes for the whole of Rajasthan, let alone the entire Harappan region. Indeed, many other processes, like geomorphological, topographical and tectonic changes, could be responsible for local changes in hydrology and vegetation. Other pollen sequences near the core Harappan region come from the archaeological site of Balakot, north-west of Karachi near the Arabian Sea coast (McKean 1983; synopsis in Dales 1986), where sediments dated between 5500 and 3500 BP were analysed. The interpretation of pollen from anthropic sediments in terms of climatic characteristics is never totally safe. Several variables, related to human occupation, might influence the pollen rain and make the data set less sound as a source for reconstructing natural vegetation (and therefore climate). In addition, there are serious taphonomic and preservation concerns, as archaeological pollen is prone to mixing and contamination by intrusive pollen from insect-pollinated plants (Bottema 1975). Nevertheless it is worth noting the conclusion of McKean (1983) that: 'there is nothing in the Balakot pollen data, which might suggest that the climate during the protohistoric period in Las Bela was decidedly wetter than at present'.

Human interference could also have significantly influenced the structure of the vegetation at different scales. The decline of evergreen, deciduous and mangrove pollen in favour of grassland species in the off-shore Karwar core (Caratini et al. 1991; 1994) was interpreted as marking the onset of a weaker phase of the monsoon, indicating a less humid phase around 3700-3500 BP (*c.* 1430 cal BC). However, deforestation for intensified agriculture and exploitation of the land cannot be ruled out. Anthropogenic interference related to slash and burn practices and possible heavy deforestation has probably had an important role in shaping the vegetation, as already pointed out by Meher-Homji (1994a, 1994b, 1996a, 1996b) and Subash Chandran (1997). The Chalcolithic and Neolithic archaeological and archaeobotanical evidence in peninsular India for the second millennium BC suggests intensification in the form of a proliferation of villages and the adoption of double-cropping (Fuller, in Vol. III of this series; Fuller et al. n.d.). Unfortunately, most of the available palynological data for the subcontinent during the Holocene appear to have some ambiguity and observed changes could be related to both climatic variables or anthropic action (see Table 5). In the case of the middle Ganga region, the palynological evidence has been taken to suggest that the early cultivation (early second millennium BC) did not significantly affect the forest cover (Gupta 1976; Erdosy 1998).

A final remark about temporal correlation of the various sedimentological sequences from north-west South Asia and the Arabian Sea is due. Unfortunately there is weak evidence for sound correlation on the basis of calibrated radiocarbon dates, which further adds to problems arising from inter-laboratory variations (Edwards 1979). When calibration is performed and dates transformed into calendar years, climatic events recorded in the sediments and considered to be contemporaneous with socio-political and agricultural changes in the Indus Valley may effectively be separated by a time lapse of about 500 years (e.g. the 'dry' event in the Rajasthan pollen sequence of G. Singh et al. 1974 and the offshore pollen sequence of Caratini et al. 1991, 1994).

Some information about ancient climate might be gathered, with caution, from carbonized wood recovered from archaeological sites (anthracology). In the interpretation of this evidence it is especially important to consider the presence of human choice and the fact that the wood represented may not all be available in the vicinity of the site or may represent several ecological zones around the site. Preliminary studies from the sites of Mehrgarh and Nausharo (Thièbault 1988a, 1988b, 1989, 1992, 1995) show that *Tamarix* sp. (lai), *Acacia* sp. (babul?) and *Prosopis* sp. (kandi?) dominate the charcoal assemblages from the eighth till the mid-fifth millennium BP. The same taxa are dominant in the present vegetation. By the third millennium BP, a more diverse assemblage of wood seems to be exploited, with *Juniperus* sp. (juniper), *Zizyphus* sp. (jujuba), *Vitis vinifera* L. (grape) and *Populus* cf. *euphratica* (poplar, bahan) found alongside the previous taxa. In Mehrgarh there seems to be an increase in the use of tamarisk wood in the late third millennium, but this might be related to the particular context analysed, a kiln (Thièbault 1995). As observed by one of the authors (Madella) during several survey journeys in Sindh, tamarisk wood is still very much in use today as kiln fuel and sometime forms the only wood used for firing. This is possible connected to the widespread availability of the plants, along rivers and canals, and in the wastelands and saline areas. Charcoal analysis from Kot Diji (Castelletti et al. 1994), in the middle Indus Valley (Sindh), has shown that both Pre-Harappan and Harappan populations exploited a wide array of wood from several ecological areas, spanning from arid and semi-arid zones (*Calotropis* sp., *Capparis decidua* [Forsk.] Edgew, *Zizyphus nummularia* [Burm.] Arn., *Prosopis cineraria* [L.] Druce, *Acacia* sp.) to salty lands (*Tamarix* sp.) and the riverine hygrophylus forest (*Populus euphratica* Olivier). Poplar is predominant in all but one of the samples, the Pre-Harappan layer 5A, where *Capparis decidua* Forsk. (Edgew). (caper) is more abundant. However, the wood assemblage tends to be quite homogeneous over time and does not show any appreciable variability between the Pre-Harappan and Harappan cultural levels. The plants exploited in Mehrgarh, Nausharo and Kot Diji do not indicate wetter conditions in Baluchistan and the central Indus Valley during the Pre-Harappan, and the Early and Mature Harappan. Instead, they indicate the presence of xerophytic forests and pockets of mesophytic and hygrophylus vegetations. Indeed the exploitation of several ecological niches available in the territory of the settlements is likely. There may even have been substantial trade of exotic wood from the Himalayan foothills towards Punjab and Sindh. For example, a wooden coffin excavated in Harappa (Cemetery H) was made with *Ulmus* sp. (elm) and *Cedrus deodara* (Roxb. ex Lamb.) G. Don f. (deodar) wood (Chowdhury and Ghosh 1951). Charcoals from the Late Harappan site of Sanghol (Punjab) yielded a more diverse assemblage where along with *Acacia* sp. *Ziziphus* sp., and *Tamarix* cf. *articulata* were also identified *Ficus glomerata* Roxb., *Albizzia lebbeck* Benth., *Ephedra* sp. and *Jasminum* sp. (jasmine) (Saraswat and Chanchala 1997). At the Pre-Harappan and Mature Harappan site of Rohira, in Punjab, *Tectona grandis* L. (teak), *Cedrela toona* Roxb. (toon), *Manilkara hexandra* (Roxb.) Dubard (khirani), *Cedrus deodara* (Roxb. ex Lamb.) G. Don f. (deodar), *Lawsonia inermis* L. (henna) and *Nyctanthes arbor-tristis* L. (parijat) charcoals were also identified. These charcoal assemblages suggest the exploitation of the sub-Himalayan and Himalayan valleys which lay to the north and north-west of the sites.

There is also additional 'climatic' evidence in terms of Mesolithic sites observed near Thari village during a survey carried out by the Rohri Hills Archaeological Project in the westernmost part of the Thar desert (Sindh, Pakistan) (Biagi and Kazi 1995 and Madella: personal observations). All those sites are to be found on stabilized sand dunes highlighting that, at least for the western portion of the desert, climatic characteristics were more or less stable since the deposition of these artefacts (i.e. early Mid-Holocene). Site LSI produced both Mesolithic artefacts and a few Harappan potsherds (Biagi and Kazi 1995). The potsherds were heavily weathered, red or brown in colour. It is useful to recall here that Mesolithic hunter-gatherers might have coexisted for a long period with the urban Harappan Culture communities (Possehl and Kennedy 1979; Allchin 1982; Possehl and Rissman 1992; cf. Guha 1994). Additional evidence for the co-existence of Mesolithic (hunter-gatherer) communities alongside the Harappan urbanized society come from hinterland regions such as Langhnaj in north Gujarat (Sankalia 1965) and Budha Pushkar in Rajasthan (Allchin et al. 1978). Mesolithic continuity up to and possibly through the

Harappan period provides general but non-conclusive support for relative stability of the environment.

The Greater Indus Valley and the Harappan Civilization have often been discussed by archaeologists as a single geographical entity to be understood in terms of unitary changes. However, this area comprises several ecological zones, from the coast of Sindh and Gujarat to the sub-Himalayan hills via the 'valleys' of the Indus and several other rivers in Sindh and Punjab, including the former Ghaggar-Hakkra. The scanty palaeoclimatic data available are often extended to the whole area. Thus, even assuming that there may have been a more arid phase in the general climate starting in the early second millennium BC, the reaction of the various ecosystems to it might have been quite different (cf. Vishnu-Mittre 1982). Indeed such local and regional variations in response to climatic variation may be shown through a comparison of the pollen assemblages from different lakes in Rajasthan, such as Lunkaransar lake in comparison with that from Didwana lake, separated by only 150 km (see Bryson and Swain 1981). Thus while the Indian subcontinent must have been affected by global or large scale climate changes like those in the Indian Ocean monsoon system (reflected also in the palaeoclimatic record in north Africa, see Grove 1993; Sirocko 1996) and in East Asia or north Australia (see Wasson 1995), it is unclear what the rapidity or intensity of these changes were within South Asia, and how these might have affected local regions, their fauna, vegetation and human societies (see also F.R. Allchin 1982). There is a growing discomfort with simplistic environmentally determined understandings of change (Paddayya 1994). When environmental data are confronted with the archaeological evidence for change, which begins in some areas *c.* 2200 BC and continues through the second millennium BC, it is no longer possible to attribute a single collapse of the Harappan Civilization to a single episode of climatic change. The picture seems to be less unitary and interpretations should allow for more locally articulated explanations of the changes in relation to regional variables during the late third and second millennia BC.

DISCUSSION: AGRICULTURAL CONSERVATISM AND CHANGE

The agricultural basis that allowed the rise of urbanism in the Indus Valley is a familiar one, shared with the early civilizations of Mesopotamia and Egypt. As noted in numerous pervious reviews, a crop complex based on winter-sown, spring-harvested crops all watered by winter rains or run-off, with their origins much further west in the fertile crescent, became established in the valleys and piedmonts west of the Indus before the sixth millennium BC (Costantini 1983; Meadow 1989, 1996, 1998; Kenoyer 1991, 1998: 37-9; Bar-Yosef and Meadow 1995; Franke-Vogt. 1995). Subsequently, these winter crops were taken out onto the vast Indus and Ghaggar-Hakkra flood plains, where the ability to produce large surpluses presumably fueled social differentiation and craft specialization. The rise of cities was dependent upon an integrated trade network that allowed surplus in one region to furnish the towns and cities in another during times of local shortage: 'The geographic and climatic diversity of the Indus Valley was a kind of safety net, because if the crops failed in the hinterland around one city, surplus production in other regions could have been brought in to feed the general population' (Kenoyer 1998: 162). Although there is no direct evidence for the trade in foodstuffs, the abundant evidence for trade in minerals and seashells attests to the development of the kinds of trade networks necessary for agricultural integration. It is the same kind of developments, based incidentally on the same group of crops, that allowed the development of early civilizations in the Nile Valley and Mesopotamia.

There is no evidence for any major agricultural changes correlating with the rise of the Harappan Civilization, but rather a continuation of diverse local cultivation practices tied to local hydrological conditions and cultural traditions. There is, however, one possible agricultural development that could have been important. It may have been the case that the adoption of animal-drawn ploughs allowed more efficient cultivation in the river flood plains (Allchin and Allchin 1997: 169). The earliest clear evidence for ploughing in South Asia comes from preserved tillage marks sealed beneath Early Harappan levels at Kalibangan on the erstwhile Sarasvati river in northern Rajasthan (Lal 1971). These show that ploughing was established prior to urbanization in the major river basins. In addition, there is a possible schematic depiction of ploughmarks painted on a piece of pottery from Mohenjo Daro (MacKay 1938: 221, Pl. LXVIII, 25). However, it is possible that ploughing was not a widespread, common practice and that the inundated soils were not subjected to this practice. With the collection of systematic archaeobotanical samples it may become possible to corroborate this through the analysis of weed assemblages which would also allow some assessment of the importance of tillage in other regions.

At present there are important limitations to what we can irrefutably claim about Harappan agriculture. There is still a real dearth of published archaeobotanical assemblages that have been collected through systematic means such as flotation or sieving. This is especially the case for most of the core Harappan areas, including the middle-lower Ghaggar-Hakkra and Indus valleys. Although systematic archaeobotanical samples are lacking from most of the Indus Valley, evidence from Baluchistan (Mehrgarh, Nausharo and Pirak) has been taken to represent the situation in the Indus Valley (Costantini 1979, 1990; Jarrige 1985, 1997; Meadow 1989, 1996; Franke-Vogt 1995). As already stated earlier, the Greater Indus Valley is not a homogeneous area and several microclimates and ecotones are present. It might be possible that the archaeobotanical assemblages taken as general examples are, in fact, geographical variants of a more complex agricultural package, flexible and adaptable to regional climatic, geological and geographical characteristics of the territory. The flotation of samples from Harappan town and village sites in floodplain areas should be a priority for future research.

When Harappan agriculture is discussed, the great regional differences must be acknowledge (Vishnu-Mittre 1982). Several authors have recognized different regional traditions within the Harappan Civilization, and amongst the differences between these regions, aspects of cultural ecology are likely to have been significant (Possehl 1989, 1997b). Despite the still slim database, differences between some of the regions in terms of the crops they utilized is clear. While winter crops were probably the norm in core areas, in regions east of the main Indus and Ghaggar-Hakkra valleys, other crops were already being utilized, especially *kharif* crops that are well-suited to cultivation in monsoonal environments. During the Mature Harappan period summer crops, including millets and at least one of the South Asian *Vigna* pulses were present in Gujarat. Also *Macrotyloma uniflorum* (Lam.) Verdc. and *Vigna* spp. were being cultivated in Haryana (Willcox 1992). Irrigation practices also are likely to have varied between sites in different parts of the river valleys, as well as between flood basin sites and sites in the uplands. In regions where summer crops were the norm, i.e. Gujarat, irrigation may have been largely absent, with dependence on rainfall instead. As noted earlier, in the discussion of the Rojdi weed flora, the strong presence of sedges in the final period at that sites, dating to the early second millennium BC, suggests cultivation in areas with high water tables, such as wetlands or perhaps along the edges of ponds. That such ponds could have been artificial, a kind of simple tank irrigation, is worth exploring.

There is an apparent half millennium lagtime between when *kharif* cropping of annual field crops was practised in peripheral areas like Gujarat and Haryana and when it may have become important in core Harappan areas, i.e. west of Gujarat or the Ganga-Yamuna Doab region. It must be noted, however, that the only real evidence for this comes from the archaeobotanical sequence from Mehrgarh-Nausharo-Pirak (Costantini 1979, 1986, 1990; Costantini and Biasini 1985). Meadow (1989, 1996, 1998) argued for an agricultural transformation on the southern and eastern fringes of the Harappan Civilization, facilitated primarily by the African millets, with the arrival of 'Asian' millets, possible from the west, *Panicum miliaceum* L. and *Setaria italica* (L.) P. Beauv., also summer crops. This supposed *kharif* crop revolution opened up new zones to extensive agriculture as opposed to the intensive, presumably irrigated, Harappan system (Possehl 1980: 33). The first adoptions of these crops, alongwith rice, in the Harappan core area may date of after 2000 BC (Franke-Vogt 1995: 32-4). Meadow (1989, 1996, 1998) has suggested that these hypothetical Late Harappan cropping transformations are part of a broader economic revolution. This would have included new livestock species that facilitated transport and communication, namely horses, donkeys and camels. This transport revolution may have facilitated the migration of Harappan agriculturalists into areas where the new crops could be exploited, such as peninsular India. Reliable evidence for domestic horse (*Equus caballus*) in South Asia dates to *c.* 2000 BC at Pirak in Baluchistan (Meadow 1986, 1987: 907-10), although earlier evidence for domesticated horses has been reported from Surkotada (Sharma 1993). Meadow and Patel (1997) question this evidence, while other experts maintain it. Resolution of this issue must await the discovery of new osteological remains. Setting aside the problems of new animals, however, the role of African crops appears to be overstated, and the presence of the Chinese millets is not entirely clear. That there may have been a certain agricultural conservatism inherent in the bureaucratic urban system of the Harappan Civilization which resisted the adoption of new crops in core areas is worth considering. However, this concept of an agricultural 'revolution' correlating roughly with the end of Harappan urbanism needs to be carefully assessed as new data become available. As Weber's (1997) preliminary discussion of data from

Harappa indicates, the major agricultural changes there appear to occur by *c.* 2200 BC, well before the period of devolution, and he has elsewhere attempted to address the apparent disjunction between agricultural and other kinds of change (Weber 1996). Furthermore, the choice not to utilize millets in the major river valleys may have had more to do with emphasis on other kinds of crops in the summer, such as fruits and fibres, which had important non-subsistence economic roles.

Environment has evidently played an important role in shaping and, up to a certain point, promoting changes in the Harappan economic and sociocultural systems. The shift of the Ghaggar-Hakkra drainage system from west to east must have had tremendous repercussions on the agricultural productivity of one of the cardinal areas for the production of wheat and barley, and one of the most heavily populated Harappan regions. The vagaries of the bed of the Indus river could have played some role in diminishing the importance of towns left too far away from the main course (Mohenjo Daro?) or heavily inundated during the floods. Global and regional scale climatic changes would also have had some effect on the environments of the Greater Indus Valley. These effects might be reflected in some of the *adjustments* produced by the Late Harappan societies during the second millennium BC. However, the comparison of environmental data—even if scanty—and the Post-Urban archaeological assemblages found in the Greater Indus Valley give evidence that an explanation based only upon environmental determinants is simplistic and unrealistic.

The transformation that occurred during the second millennium in North-Western South Asia is one of decline in the core area but also of regional developments in the periphery, i.e. a localization era (Kenoyer 1991; Shaffer and Lichtenstein 1992). New political powers seem to develop from the Pre-Harappan cultural traits thus destroying the apparent consolidation achieved by the Harappan Culture during the integration era. New political foci appear in the north, in Afghanisatan and Central Asia, and in the east, in the Ganga-Yamuna Doab, while more localized chiefdoms emerged in the northern Deccan and possibly Gujarat. Some of the shifts might be explained by core-periphery models (Kenoyer 1991, 1995, 1998; Lamberg-Karlovsky 1989; 241-50) which were helped along by the concomitance of environmental changes, regardless of whether they were induced by global changes or human impacts. In the core area of the Harappan Civilization, power may have been too consolidated to allow for new social, political and possibly religious ideas, whereas the periphery may have offered the ideal setting for the emergence of new indigenous polities and a new urban process (Kenoyer 1998). The process of de-urbanization in the Indus Valley was certainly facilitated by hydrographic and climatic changes (even of local scale), but it is hard to see these as driving and determining the course of change. Possible important factors were the captures of several river courses, especially the Sutlej, and tributaries of the Ghaggar-Hakkra which left totally deserted of water the area that is now the Cholistan desert, as well as vagaries of the Indus in the lower valley, south of the Sukkur gorges. The new environmental conditions of the southern portion of the Indus Valley might have also forced some movement of population towards the south-east and the north-east (Misra 1984). Within this context of decentralization and population relocation, additional crops, such as millets and pulses from peninsular India or those from Africa, become more widely available, although their separate adoptions should be seen as local choices rather than some nebulous 'revolution' over a vast area. In some areas, such as in Gujarat and eastern Punjab, these monsoon watered crops may have allowed for more local subsistence independence, and such adaptation may have both decreased the need for and the maintenance of the interregional 'safety-net' presumed to have been so important for the establishment of Harappan urbanism (if such a system indeed existed).

Although the cultural legacy of the Harappan Civilization in later South Asian cultural traditions is clear (Allchin 1982; Allchin and Allchin 1997), its agricultural legacy is not. Evidence for the adoption of wheat, barley and several winter legumes (i.e. the Harappan staples) during the second millennium BC may link these crops with the first fully settled agriculturalists of the northern Deccan (Maharashtra). Peas, lentils and *Lathyrus* became important counterparts to the summer-sown grams, i.e. *Vigna* spp, *Macrotyloma uniflorum* (Lam.) Verdc. While there is some evidence for possible *Eleusine* and *Sorghum* at this time (i.e. 2000-1500 BC), the *rabi* cereals may have been more important for the establishment of sustained agriculture in the Deccan (contra Possehl 1986). This evidence supports, to an extent, the contention of Chakrabarti (1995: 164-7) that the development of agriculture in peninsular India came about through a process of interaction between 'Harappan plough-agriculturalists' (presumably immigrant) and local Mesolithic populations. However, there is a small body of evidence to indicate that agriculture had spread east of the Indus system into areas such as Rajasthan and parts of Gujarat during the pre-Urban/Early Harappan phase. The evidence from Balathal, now dating to the beginning of the third millennium, indicates reliance on the *rabi* crop complex, including wheat, barley and lentils (Shinde 1999). It is perhaps more likely that these extra-Harappan societies provided many of the crops for the development of village in Maharashtra rather than that came from the Harappans as Chakrabarti implies. Also, there is as yet no firm evidence for plough agriculture in Chalcolithic Maharashtra, with the data suggesting instead the use of hand-held implements such as digging sticks and hoes (Shinde 1987). In addition, these introductions must be considered against a background of cattle pastoralism and indigenous pulse-millet agriculture which was established in the southern Deccan (Karnataka-Andhra Pradesh), perhaps between 3000 and 2500 BC (Allchin and Allchin 1982: 122-5; Possehl and Rissman 1992; Devaraj et al. 1995; Korisettar et al., in Vol. I of this series; Fuller et al., n.d.). This southern agricultural complex appears to have provided *kharif* crops to the evolving villages further north, and it is unclear if some of the millets cultivated in Gujarat during the Mature Harappan phase might be derived from contemporary societies of the Indian Peninsula or could have been locally domesticated in Gujarat.

Although many practices from the Harappan period, such as irrigation techniques, have continued into modern times, the most significant agricultural developments for later South Asian history may have been those which took place in the Late Harappan period in areas peripheral to the urban core. The integration of summer and winter crops in Chalcolithic Maharashtra, and perhaps even more significant, the double-cropping which included rice that became the norm in the Ganga Valley, became the most widespread agricultural systems on the subcontinent in more recent times. The surpluses that could be produced, especially through a combination of rice agriculture and irrigated winter cereals, was a prerequisite for South Asia's second urbanization. It is perhaps not surprising then, that the regions identified as 'nuclear regions' for post-Harappan cultural developments in South Asia (Allchin and Allchin 1982: 249-50), correspond roughly to the regions in which these agricultural syntheses occurred. It is also these regions of agricultural synthesis, in particular the upper Ganga Valley-Yamuna region, where the agricultural system was probably more stable, and better buffered against the social and tectonic upheavals of Harappan decentralization.

Since the first excavation report of an Indus Valley site (Marshall 1931), archaeobotanical evidence and discussions of possible environmental changes have been a part of Harappan studies. The collection of evidence to address these issues in a systematic way, however, has only just begun. The gaps in the available evidence, due to unsystematic methods of collection in the past must be bept firmly in mind. Nevertheless, it is clear that the Harappan Civilization arose out of and devolved within a diverse set of environments in north-western South Asia which both constrained and enabled this civilization. These environments were not static but dynamic on several time scales, from the variations in annual floods and rainfall, to longer term trends of change due in part to larger processes of climatic change but also to the impact of human agro-pastoral activities. The understanding of these environmental processes must rely upon a judicious use of palaeoecological data that takes into account difficulties of correlation and the confounding effects of climatic and anthropogenic forces. In order to better understand these relationships, far more environmental archaeology is needed, and continual dialogue must be maintained between those scientists involved in palaeoecological work and those involved with interpreting the archaeology. In the review here, we have hoped to lay some groundwork for such a dialogue, by laying out the available sources of data and by highlighting important issues of debate.

ACKNOWLEDGEMENTS

The authors would like to thank the several colleagues who read earlier drafts of this paper and provided useful comments and suggestions, especially Bridget Allchin, Raymond Allchin, Dilip Chakrabarti, Martin Jones, Victor Paz, Chris Stevens and Nicole Boivin. We would also like to acknowledge our respective sources of funding for laboratory and fieldwork, especially St. John's college for its support of Dorian's research, and the Rohri Hills Archaeological Project and Harappa Archaeological Research Project for supporting Marco's work in Pakistan.

NOTES

1. Throughout this text botanical species names are followed by the standard abbreviation for the authority upon which the species definition is based. Although these letters may appear cumbersome to the archaeologist, we feel these are necessary in this context as several of crop taxa have been subject to taxonomic confusion in the archaeobotanical literature. The abbreviation in parentheses, if present, refers to the first author(s) to describe the species and establish the specific epithet, while the abbreviation without prentheses refers to the authors who first established the full genus-species binomial.
2. Horsegram (Hindi *kulthi*) is usually referred to in Indian floristics and agronomic literature as *Dolichos biflorus* L. However, this species of Linnaeus actually describes catjang type cowpea (Hindi *chowli, lobia*), now grouped in the polytypic species *Vigna unguiculata* (L.) Walp. Thus *D. biflrous* L. is a synonym for *V. unguiculata* (L.) Walp. This equation has, however, been wrongly used by Weber (1991: 98), Reddy (1994), and Kroll (1996, 1997, 1998), since the archaeological finds traditionally described as *D. biflrous* are *not* cowpeas! *D. biflorus* is an invalid name for the horsegram/*kulthi*, which was first properly described by Lamarck as *Dolichos uniflorum*. It has now been transferred to the genus *Macrotyloma* (Verdcourt 1970, 1971; Smartt 1985a, 1990). The recent suggestion that '*Dolichos uniflorus*' is the wild form of '*Dolichos biflorus*' and localized in the southern and eastern peninsula (Mehra 1997), requires botanical clarification.
3. *Phaseolus aureus* and *P. radiatus* are *not* domesticated and wild forms, respectively, as suggested by Lone et al. (1993), but synonyms for the domesticated crop, the wild form of which is *Phaseolus sublobatus* Roxb. As they have all been transferred to *Vigna* and the wild progenitor has been demoted to subspecies following the nomenclatural system of Harlan and De Wet (1971), the wild progenitor is now known as *Vigna radiata* subsp. *sublobata* (Smartt 1985b, 1990).
4. The equation of *Phaseolus mungo* L. with *Vigna angularis* (Weber 1991; Reddy 1994) is an incorrect synonomy, as *V. angularis* (Willd.) Ohwi & Ohashi, the adzuki bean, is a distinct domesticated species cultivated in China, Korea and Japan where its wild progenitor also occurs (Smartt 1985b, 1990; Lawn 1995).
5. Dates are hereafter calibrated to a calendar timescale with CALIB 4.0 (Stuiver and Reimer 1993; Stuiver et al. 1998), which includes the most recent corrections for marine carbon reservoir effects. Uncalibrated dates are given as small capital case BC or BP. It should be noted that when marine reservoir effects and calibrations are taken into account the various *c.* 3700-3500 BP events cited by several authors *do not* correlate, and are separated by as much as 500 years.

REFERENCES

Agrawal, D.P. 1971. *The Copper Bronze Age in India*. New Delhi: Munshiram Manoharlal.

——— 1982. *The Archaeology of India*. Copenhagen: Scandinavian Institute of Asian Studies, Monograph Series 46.

——— 1992. *Man and Environment in India Through Ages*. New Delhi: Books & Books.

Agrawal, D.P. and R.K. Sood 1982. Ecological Factors and the Harappan Civilisation, in *Harappan Civilization: a Contemporary Perspective* (G.L. Possehl Ed.), pp. 223-31. Warminster: Aris & Phillips.

Allchin, B. 1998. Early Man and Environment in South Asia 10,000 BC-AD 500, in *Nature and the Orient: the Environmental History of South and Southeast Asia* (R. Grove, V. Damodaran and S. Sangwan Eds.), pp. 29-50. Delhi: Oxford University Press.

Allchin, F.R. 1966. Pottery Headrest from Narsipur Sangam, in *Studies in Prehistory (Bruce Foote Memorial Volume)* (D. Sen and A. Gosh Eds.), pp. 58-63. Calcutta: Firma K.L. Mukhopadhyay.

——— 1969. Early Cultivated Plants in India and Pakistan, in *The Domestication and Exploitation of Plants and Animals* (P.J. Ucko and G.W. Dimbleby Eds.), pp. 323-30. London: Duckworth.

——— 1982. The Legacy of the Indus Civilization, in *Harappan Civilization* (G.L. Possehl Ed.), pp. 325-33. Warminster: Aris & Phillips.

——— 1984. The Northern Limits of the Harappan Culture Zone, in *Frontiers of the Indus Civilization* (B.B. Lal and S.P. Gupta Eds.), pp. 51-4. New Delhi: Books & Books.

Allchin, Bridget and Raymond Allchin 1982. *The Rise of Civilization in India and Pakistan.* Cambridge: Cambridge University Press.

——— 1997. *Origins of a Civilization: the Prehistory and Early Archaeology of South Asia.* New Delhi: Viking Penguin Books India.

Allchin, Bridget and A. Goudie 1971. Dunes, Aridity and Early Man in Gujarat, Western India, *Man* 6 (2): 248-65.

Allchin, B., A. Goudie and K. Hegde 1978. *The Prehistory and Palaeogeography of the Great Indian Desert.* London: Academic Press.

Amblard, S. and J. Pernes 1989. The Identification of Cultivated Pearl Millet (*Pennisetum*) Amongst Plant Impressions on Pottery from Oued Chebbi (Dhar Oualata, Mauritania), *The African Archaeological Review* 7: 117-26.

Andrews, J.E., A.K. Singhvi, A.J. Kailath, R. Kuhn, P.F. Dennis, S.K. Tandon and R.P. Dhir 1998. Do Stable Isotope Data from Calcrete Record Late Pleistocene Monsoonal Climate Variation in the Thar Desert of India? *Quaternary Research* 50: 240-51.

Arghyia, K.H., H.K. Das, S. Ghosh, A.K. Ray and S. Chanda 1996. Environmental Variations in Late Quaternary Sequence of Kolaghat, West Bengal, India, *Current Science* 70 (12): 1089-93.

Awasthi, N. 1992. Changing Patterns of Vegetation Through Siwalik Succession, *The Palaeobotanist* 40: 312-27.

Bar-Yosef, O. and R. Meadow 1995. The Origins of Agriculture in the Near East, in *Last Hunters-First Farmers: New Perspectives on the Prehistoric Transition to Agriculture* (T.D. Price and A.B. Gebauer Eds.), pp. 39-94. Santa Fe, New Mexico: School of American Research Advanced Seminar Series.

Barui, N.C. and Chanda S. 1992. Late-Quaternary Pollen Analysis in Relation to Palaeoecology, Biostratigraphy and Dating of Calcutta Peat, *Proceedings of the Indian National Science Academy* B 58 (4): 191-200.

Bedigian, D. and J.R. Harlan 1986. Evidence for Cultivation of Sesame in the Ancient World, *Economic Botany* 40: 137-54.

Betts, A., K. van der Borg, A. de Jong, C. McClintok and M. van Strydonck 1994. Early Cotton in North Arabia, *Journal of Archaeological Science* 21: 489-99

Biagi and Kazi 1995. A Mesolithic Site Near Thari in the Thar Desert (Sindh, Pakistan), *Ancient Sindh* 2: 7-12.

Bisht, R.S. 1976. Transformation of the Harappa Culture in Punjab with Special Reference to the Excavations at Sanghol and Chandigarh, in *Archaeological Congress and Seminar* (U.V. Singh Ed.), pp. 16-22. Kurukshetra: Kurukshetra University Press.

——— 1977. *Banawali: a Look Back into the Pre-Indus and Indus Civilization.* Chandigarh: Government of Haryana.

Bottema, S. 1975. The Interpretation of Pollen Spectra from Prehistoric Settlements (with Special Attention to Liguliflorae), *Palaeohistoria* 17: 17-36.

——— 1984. The Composition of Modern Charred Seed Assemblages, in *Plants and Ancient Man* (W. van Zeist and W.A. Casparie Eds.), pp. 207-12. Rotterdam: Balkena.

Bruijnzeel, P.S. 1986. Environmental Impacts of Deforestation in the Humid Tropics—a Water Shed Perspective, *Wallaceana* 46: 3-13.

Bryson, R.A. and A.M. Swain 1981. Holocene Variations of the Monsoon Rainfall in Rajasthan, *Quaternary Research* 16: 135-45.

Burts, B.C. 1941. Comments on Cereals and Fruits, in *Excavations at Mohenjo-Daro* (M.S. Vats), p. 466. New Delhi: Archaeological Survey of India.

Buth, G.M. and K.A. Chowdhury. 1971. Plant Remains from Atranjikhera Phase III, *Palaeobotanist* 20: 280-7.

Caratini, C., M. Fontugne, J.P. Pascal, C. Tissot and I. Bentaleb 1991. A Major Change at *c.* 3500 Years bp in the Vegetation of the Western Ghats in North Kanara, Karnataka, *Current Science* 61: 669-72.

Caratini, C., I. Bentaleb, M. Fontugne, M.T. Morzadec-Kerfourn, J.P. Pascal and C. Tissot 1994. A Less Humid Climate Since *c.* 3500 yr B.P. from Marine Cores Off Karwar, Western India, *Palaeogeography, Palaeoclimatology, Palaeoecology* 109: 371-84.

Castelletti, L., M. Madella and A. Qayom Mahar 1994. Charcoal Analysis at Kot Diji: a Preliminary Report, *Ancient Sindh* 1: 37-41.

Chakrabarti, D.K. 1988. *Theoretical Issues in Indian Archaeology.* New Delhi: Munshiram Manoharlal.

——— 1990. *The External Trade of the Indus Civilization.* New Delhi: Munshiram Manoharlal.

——— 1995. *The Archaeology of Ancient Indian Cities.* Delhi: Oxford University Press.

Charles, M.P. 1989. Crop Husbandry in Lowland Mesopotamia in the Late Uruk-Early Dynastic Periods. Ph.D. dissertation. London: University College London.

——— 1998. Fodder from Dung: the Recognition and Interpretation of Dung-Derived Plant Material from Archaeological Sites, *Environmental Archaeology: The Journal of Human Palaeoecology* 1: 111-22.

Chowdhury, K.A. and S.S. Ghosh 1951. Plant Remains from Harappa Excavations in 1946, *Ancient India* 7: 3-19.

Chowdhury, K.A., K.S. Saraswat and G.M. Buth 1977. *Ancient Agriculture and Forestry in North India.* New Delhi: Asia Publishing House.

——— 1983. Appendix A. Plant Remains, in *Excavations at Atranjikhera. Early Civilization of the Upper Ganga Basin* (R.C. Gaur Ed.), pp. 457-9. Delhi: Motilal Banarsidass.

Clark, J.D. and A.B. Stemler 1975. Early Domesticated Sorghum from Central Sudan, *Nature* 254: 588-91.

Cleuziou, S. 1984. Oman Peninsula and its Relations Eastward During the Third Millennium, in *Frontiers of the Harappan Civilization* (B.B. Lal and S.P. Gupta Eds.), pp. 371-94. New Delhi: Books & Books.

——— 1989. Excavations at Hili 8: a Preliminary Report on the 4th to 7th Campaigns, *Archaeology of the United Arab Emirates* 5: 61-87.

Cleuziou. S. and L. Costantini 1980. Premiers Éléments Sur L'Agriculture Protohistorique de l'Arabie Orientale, *Paléorient* 6: 245-51.

——— 1982. A L'Origine des Oasis, *La Recherche* 13(137): 1180-2.

Cleuziou, S. and M. Tosi 1989. The Southeastern Frontier of the Ancient Near East, in *South*

Asian Archaeology 1985 (K. Frifelt and P. Sörensen Eds.), pp. 15-47. London: Curzon Press.

Cooke, T. 1908. *The Flora of the Presidency of Bombay,* Vol. II. London: Taylor and Francis.

Costantini, L. 1979. Plant Remains at Pirak, in *Fouilles de Pirak,* Vol. 1 (J.-F. Jarrige and M. Santoni Eds.), pp. 326-33. Paris: Diffusion de Boccard.

——— 1983. The Beginning of Agriculture in the Kachi Plain: the Evidence of Mehrgarh, in *South Asian Archaeology 1981* (B. Allchin Ed.), pp. 29-33. Cambridge: Cambridge University Press.

——— 1986. Laboratory of Bioarchaeology, *East and West* 36(4): 354-65.

——— 1987 Appendix B. Vegetal Remains, in *Prehistorc and Protohistoric Swat, Pakistan* (G. Stacul Ed.), pp. 155-65. Rome: Istituto Italiano per il Medio ed Estremo Oriente.

——— 1990a Harrapan Agriculture in Pakistan: the Evidence of Nausharo, in *South Asian Archaeology 1987* (M. Taddei Ed.), pp. 321-32. Rome: Istituto Italiano per il Medio ed Estremo Oriente.

Costantini, L. and L. Costantini Baisini 1985. Agriculture in Baluchistan between the 7th and 3rd Millennium BC, *Newsletter of Baluchistan Studies* 2: 16-37.

Courty, M.A. 1986. Geoarchaeological Approach of Holocene Paleoenvironments in the Ghaggar Plain, *Man and Environment* X: 111-15.

Courty, M.A. and N. Federoff 1982. Micromorphology of Recent and Buried Soils in a Part of North-West India, *Geoderma* 35: 285-332.

Courty, M.A., P. Goldberg and R. MacPhail 1989. *Soils and Micromorphology in Archaeology.* Cambridge: Cambridge University Press.

Dafremery, C. and B.R. Sanguinetti (Translators) 1855. *Voyages d'Ibn Batuta.* Paris.

Dalal, K.F. 1980. A Short History of Archaeological Explorations in Bikaner and Bahawalpur Along the 'lost' Saraswati River, *Indica* 17 (1): 1-40.

——— 1981. RD-89: A New Hakkra Ware Site, *Man and Environment* V: 77-86.

Dales, G.F. 1962. *The Role of Natural Forces in the Ancient Indus Valley and Baluchistan, Anthropological Papers* 62. Utah: University of Utah.

——— 1965a. New Investigations at Mohenjo-daro, *Archaeology* 18 (2): 145-50.

——— 1965b. Re-opening the Mohenjo-daro Excavations, *Illustrated London News* 29 (May): 25-7.

——— 1966a. The Decline of the Harappans, *Scientific American* 241 (5): 92-100.

——— 1966b. Relation of Indus Valley Floods to Decline of Harappan Civilization, *American Philosophical Society Year Book 1965*. Philadelphia.

——— 1986. Some Fresh Approaches to Old Problems in Harappan Archaeology, in *Studies in the Archaeology of India and Pakistan* (J. Jacobson Ed), pp. 117-36. Delhi: Oxford-IBH.

Dales, G.F. and R.L. Raikes 1968. The Mohenjo-daro Floods: a Rejoinder, *American Anthropologist* 70 (5): 957-61.

De Wet, J.M.J., K.E. Prasada Rao and D.E. Brink 1983a. Systematics and Domestication of *Panicum sumatrense* (Graminae), *Journal d'Agriculture Traditionelle et de Botanique Appliquée* 30 (2): 159-68.

De Wet, J.N.J., K.E. Prasada Rao, M.H. Mengesha and D.E. Brink 1983b. Diversity in Kodo Millet, *Paspalum scrobiculatum, Economic Botany* 37 (2): 159-63.

Deakin, W.J., P. Rowley-Conwy and C.H. Shaw 1998. Amplification and Sequencing of DNA from Preserved Sorghum of up to 2800 Years Antiquity Found at Qasr Ibrim, *Ancient Biomolecules* 2 (1): 27-41.

Deotare, B.C. and M.D. Kajale 1996. Quaternary Pollen Analysis and Palaeoenvironemntal Studies on the Salt Basins at Pachpadra and Thob, Western Rajasthan, India: Preliminary Observations, *Man and Environment* XXI (1): 24-31.

Deotare, B.C., M.D. Kajale, A.A. Kshirsagar and S.N. Rajaguru 1998. Geoarchaeological and Palaeoenvironemntal Studies Around Bap-Malar Playa, District Jodhpur, Rajasthan, *Current Science* 75 (3): 316-20.

Devaraj, D.V., Shaffer, J.G., C.S. Patil and Balasubramanya 1995. The Watgal Excavations: an Interim Report, *Man and Environment* XX (2): 57-74.

Dhavalikar, M.K. 1995. *Cultural Imperialism: Indus Civilization in Western India.* New Delhi: Books & Books.

Dikshit, K.N. 1979. The Ochre Coloured Ware Settlement in the Ganga-Yamuna Doab, in *Essays in Indian Protohistory* (D.P. Agrawal and D.K. Chakrabarti Eds.), pp. 285-99. Delhi: B.R. Publishing Corporation.

——— 1981. The Excavation at Hulas and Further Exploration of the Upper Ganga-Yamuna Doab, *Man and Environment* V: 70-6.

Erdosy, G. 1998. Deforestation in Pre- and Protohistoric South Asia, in *Nature and the Orient. The Environmental History of South and Southeast Asia* (R. Gorve, V. Damodaran and S. Sangwan Eds.), pp. 51-69. Delhi: Oxford University Press.

Fairservis, W.A., Jr. 1961. *The Harappan Civilization—New Evidence and More Theory.* New York: American Museum of Natural History, American Museum Novitates 2055.

——— 1967. *The Origin, Character and Decline of an Early Civilization.* New York: American Museum of Natural History, American Museum Novitates 2055

——— 1971. *The Roots of Ancient India—the Archaeology of Early Indian Civilization.* London: George Allen and Unwin.

——— 1982. Allahdino: an Excavation of a Small Harappan Site, in *Harappan Civilization: a Contemporary Perspective* (G. L. Possehl Ed.), pp. 107-13. New Delhi: Oxford-IBH.

Field, H. 1959. An Anthropological Reconnaissance in West Pakistan, Papers of the Peabody Museum of Archaeology and Ethnology, Vol. 3, Cambridge (Mass.): Harvard University.

Flam, L. 1976. Settlement, Subsistence and Population: a Dynamic Approach to the Development of the Indus Valley Civilization, in *Ecological Backgrounds of South Asian Prehistory* (K.A.R. Kennedy and G.L. Possehl Eds.), pp. 76-93. South Asia Occasional Papers and Theses. Ithaca: South Asia Program, Cornell University.

——— 1981. Towards an Ecological Analysis of Prehistoric Settlement Pattern in Sind, Pakistan, *Man and Environment* V: 52-8.

Flam, Louis. 1986. Recent Explorations in Sind: Paleogeography, Regional Ecology and Prehistoric Settlement Patterns (*c.* 4000-2000 BC), in *Studies in the Archaeology of India and Pakistan* (J. Jacobson Ed.), pp. 65-89. Warminster: Aris and Phillips Ltd.

Franke-Vogt, U. 1995. Cultural Ecology of the Greater Indus Valley and Beyond, *The Archaeological Review* (Karachi) 4: 13-64.

Fujiwara, H., M.R. Mughal, A. Sasaki, T. Matano 1992. Rice and Ragi at Harappa: Preliminary Results by Plant Opal Analysis, *Pakistan Archaeology* 27: 129-42.

Fuller, D.Q. (in press). Fifty Years of Archaeobotanical Studies in India: Laying a Solid Foundation, in *Indian Archaeology in Retrospect, Vol. III. Archaeology and Interactive Disciplines*

(S. Settar and R. Korisettar Eds.). New Delhi: Indian Council of Historical Research and Manohar.

——— (in press). Cultural Constraints and Compatibilities in Agricultural Changes: Towards a Culinary Bio-archaeology in South Asia, *Archaeological Review from Cambridge* 17 (1).

Fuller, D.Q., R. Korisettar, P.C. Venkatasubbaiah and M.K. Jones (n.d.). Early Plant Domestications in Southern India: Some Preliminary Archaeobotanical Results, *Vegetation History and Archaeobotany* (submitted).

Gadgil, M. and M.D. Subash Chandran 1988. On the History of Uttara Kannada Forests, Dargavel, in Changing Tropical Forests (J.K. Dixon and N. Semple Eds.), pp. 47-58. Canberra: Australian National University.

Germer, R. 1985. *Flora desw Pharaonischen Agypten.* Mainz: Verlag Philipp von Zabern.

Ghosh, S.S. and K. Lal 1963. Plant Remains from Rangpur and Other Explorations in Gujarat, *Ancient India* 18-19: 161-75.

Gosh, A. 1952. The Rajputana Desert: its Archaeological Aspects, *The Bulletin of the National Institute of Science* 1: 37-42.

——— 1953. Exploration in Bikaner, *East and West* 4 (1): 31-4.

Grigg, D.B. 1974. *The Agricultural Systems of the World: an Evolutionary Approach.* Cambridge: Cambridge University Press.

Grove, A.T. 1993. Africa's Climate in the Holocene, in *The Archaeology of Africa. Food, Metals, and Towns* (T. Shaw, P. Sinclair, B. Andah and A. Okpoko Eds.), pp. 32-42. London: Routledge.

Guha, S. 1994. Recognizing 'Harappan': a Critical Review of the Position of Hunter-Gatherers Within Harappan Society, *South Asian Studies* 10: 91-7.

Gulati, A.N. and A.J. Turner 1929. A Note on the Early History of Cotton, *Journal of the Textile Institute* XX: 1-9.

Gupta, H.P. 1975. Pollen Analytical Reconnaissance of Post Glacial Deposits from Subtropical Zone in Naini Tal District, Kumaon Himilaya, *The Palaeobotanist* 24: 215-44.

——— 1976. Holocene Palaynology from Meander Lake in the Ganga Valley, District Pratapgarh, U.P., *The Palaeobotanist* 25: 109-19.

——— 1981. Palaeoenvironments during Holocene Time in Bengal Basin, India, as Reflected by Palynostratigraphy, *The Palaeobotanist* 27 (2): 138-60.

Haaland, Randi 1995. Sedentism, Cultivation, and Plant Domestication in the Holocene Middle Nile Region, *Journal of Field Archaeology* 22: 157-74.

Hanf, M. 1983. *The Arable Weeds of Europe.* Ludwigshafen: BASF Aktiengesellschaft.

Harlan, J.R. 1992 *Crops and Ancient Man*, second edition New York: American Society for Agronomy.

——— 1995a. *The Living Fields*. Cambridge: Cambridge University Press.

Harlan, J.R. and J.M.J. De Wet 1971. Towards a Rational Classification of Cultivated Plants, *Taxon* 20: 509-17.

Hillman, G.C. 1981. Reconstructing Crop Husbandry Practices from Charred Remains of Crops, in *Farming Practice in British Prehistory* (R. Mercer Ed.), pp. 123-61. Edinburgh: University Press.

——— 1984. Interpretation of Archaeological Plant Remains: the Application of Ethnographic Models from Turkey, in *Plants and Ancient Man—Studies in Paleoethnobotany* (W. van

Zist and W.A. Casparie Eds.), pp. 1-41. Rotterdam: A.A. Balkema.

Hillman, G., S. Mason, D. de Moulins and M. Nesbitt 1996. Identification of Archaeological Remains of Wheat: the 1992 London Workshop, *Circaea* 12 (2): 195-209.

Hiremath, S.C., G. N. V. Patil and S.S. Salimath 1990. Genome Homology and Origin of *Panicum sumatrense* (Graminae), *Cytologia* 55: 315-19.

Hoffman, M.A. and J.G. Shaffer 1976. The Harappan Settlement at Allahdino: Analyzing the Sociology of an Archaeological Site, in *Ecological Backgrounds of South Asian Prehistory* (K.A.R. Kennedy and G.L. Possehl Eds:), pp. 94-117. South Asian Occasional Papers and Theses, No. 4. Ithaca: Cornell University.

Hohn, L.G.D., D.L. Plucknett, J.V. Pancho and J.P. Herberger 1977. *The World's Worst Weeds. Distribution and Biology.* Honolulu: University Press of Hawaii.

Hutchinson, J. 1976. India: Local and Introduced Crops, *Philosophical Transactions of the Royal Society London*, B 275: 129-41.

Jacomet, S. 1987. *Prahistorische Getreidefunde: Eine Anleitung zur Bestimung Prahistorischer Gertsen- und Weizen-Funde.* Basel: Botanisches Institut der Universitat, Abeitlung Pflanzensystematik und Geobotanik.

Janaway, R.C. and R.A.E. Coningham 1995. A Review of Archaeological Textile Evidence from South Asia, *South Asian Studies* 11: 157-74.

Janushevich, Z.V. 1978. Prehistoric Food Plants in the South-West of the Soviet Union, *Berichte der Deutschen Botanischen Gesellschaft*, 91: 59-66.

Jarrige, J.F. 1985. Continuity and Change in the North Kachi Plain (Baluchistan, Pakistan) at the Beginning of the Second Millennium BC, in *South Asian Archaeology 1983* (J. Schotmans and M. Taddei Eds.), pp. 35-68. Naples: Istituto Universitario Orientale, Dipartimento di Studi Asiatici.

——— 1997. From Nausharo to Pirak: Continuity and Change in the Kachi/Bolan Region from the 3rd to the 2nd Millennium BC, in *South Asian Archaeology 1995* (R. Allchin and B. Allchin Eds.), pp. 11-32. New Delhi: Oxfrod-IBH.

Jarrige, J.F. and M. Tosi 1981. The Natural Resources of Mundigak, in *South Asian Archaeology 1979* (H. Hartel Ed.), pp. 115-42. Berlin: Dietrich Reimer.

Jones, G.E.M. 1984. Interpretation of Archaeological Plant Remains: Ethnographic Models from Greece, in *Plants and Ancient Man—Studies in Paleoethnobotany* (W. van Ziest and W. A. Casparie Eds.), 42-61. Rotterdam: A.A. Balkema.

——— 1987. A Statistical Approach to the Archaeological Identification of Crop Processing, *Journal of Archaeological Science* 14: 311-23.

Jones, Martin K. 1985. Archaeobotany Beyond Subsistence Reconstruction, in *Beyond Domestication in Prehistoric Europe* (G.W. Barker and C. Gamble Eds.), pp. 107-28. New York and London: Academic Press.

Joshi, J.P. 1978a. Overlap of the Late Harappan Culture and Painted Grey Ware Culture in the Light of Recent Excavations in Haryana, Punjab and Jammu, in *Indus Civilization: Problems and Issues.* Shimla: IIAS.

——— 1978b. Interlocking of Late Harappan Culture and Painted Grey Ware Culture in the Light of Recent Excavations, *Man and Environment* II: 98-101.

Kajale, M.D. 1974. Ancient Grains from India, *Bulletin of the Deccan College Research Institute* 34 (1): 55-74.

——— 1977. On the Botanical Findings from Excavations at Daimabad, a Chalcholithic Site in Western Maharashtra, India, *Current Science* 46: 818-19.

——— 1979. On the Occurrence of Ancient Agricultural Patterns During the Chalcolithic Periods (*c.* 1600-1000 BC) at Apegaon, District Aurangabad in Central Godavari Valley, Maharashtra, in *Apegaon Excavations* (S.B. Deo, M.K. Dhavalikar and Z.D. Ansari Eds.), pp. 50-6. Pune: Deccan College.

——— 1984. New Light on Agricultural Plant Economy During 1st Millennium BC: Palaeobotanical Study of Plant Remains from Excavations at Veerapuram, District Kurnool, Andhra Pradesh, in *Veerapuram: a Type Site for Cultural Study in the Krishna valley* (T. V. G. Sastri, M. Kasturibai and J. Vara Prasada Rao Eds.), Appendix B (15pp). Hyderabad: Birla Archaeological and Cultural Research Institute.

——— 1988. Plant Economy, in *Excavations at Inamgaon*, Vol. 1, Part ii (M.K. Dhavalikar, H.D. Sankalia and Z.D. Ansari Eds.), pp. 727-821. Pune: Deccan College.

——— 1989. Mesolithic Exploitation of Wild Plants in Sri Lanka: Archaeobotanical Study at the Cave Site of Beli-Lena, in *Foraging and Farming: the Evolution of Plant Exploitation* (D.R. and G.C. Hillman Eds.), pp. 269-81. London: Routledge.

——— 1990. Observations on the Plant Remains from Excavation at Chalcolithic Kaothe, District Dhule, Mahrashtra with Cautionary Remarks on Their Interpretations, in *Excavations at Kaothe* (M.K. Dhavalikar, V.S. Shinde and S.M. Atre Eds.), pp. 265-80. Pune: Deccan College.

——— 1991. Current Status of Indian Palaeoethnobotany: Introduced and Indigenous Food Plants with a Discussion of the Historical and Evolutionary Development of Indian Agriculture and Agricultural Systems in General, in *New Light on Early Farming—Recent Developments in Palaeoethnobotany* (Jane Renfew Ed.), pp. 155-89. Edinburgh: Edinburgh University Press.

——— 1995. Plant Remains from Lal Quila, in *Excavations at Lal Quila* (R.C. Gaur Ed.), pp. 189-93. Jaipur: India Publication Scheme.

——— 1996. Palaeobotanical Investigations at Balathal: Preliminary Results, *Man and Environment* XXI (1): 98-102.

Kajale, M.D. and B.C. Deotare 1993. Palaeobotanical and Pollen Analytical Investigations 2-5, 9-10, *Indian Archaeology 1986-1987– A Review*: 129-31.

——— 1997. Late Quaternary Environmental Studies on Salt Lakes in Western Rajasthan, India: a Summarised View, *Journal of Quaternary Science* 12 (5): 405-12.

Kajale, M.D. and M. Lal 1989. On the Botanical Findings from a Multicultural Site at Radhan, District Kanpur, Uttar Pradesh, *Bulletin of the Deccan College Post-Graduate and Research Institute* 47-48: 109-11.

Kajale, M.D., G.L. Badam, S.N. Rajaguru 1976. Late Quaternary History of the Ghod Valley, Maharashtra, *Geophytology* 6 (1): 122-32.

Kale, V.S. and S.N. Rajaguru 1987. Late Quaternary Alluvial History of the Northwestern Deccan Upland Region, *Nature* 325: 612-14.

Kenoyer, J.M. 1991. The Indus Valley Tradition of Pakistan and Western India, *Journal of World Prehistory* 5 (4): 331-85.

——— 1995. Interaction Systems, Specialized Crafts and Culture Change: the Indus Valley Tradition and the Indo-Gangetic Tradition in South Asia, in *The Indo-Aryans of Ancient South Asia: Language, Material Culture and Ethnicity* (G. Erdosy Ed.), pp. 213-57. Berlin: de Gruyter.

——— 1998. *Ancient Cities of the Indus Valley Civilization.* Karachi: Oxford University Press.

Kislev, M.E. 1984. Botanical Evidence for Naked Wheats in the Near East, in *Plants and*

Ancient Man (W. van Zeist and W.A. Casparie Eds.), pp. 141-52. Rotterdam: A.A. Balkema.

Kitchen, K.A. 1993. Punt and How to Get There, in *The Archaeology of Africa: Food, Metals and Towns* (T. Shaw, P. Sinclair, B. Andah and A. Okpoko Eds.), pp. 567-608. London: Routledge.

Kroll, H. 1996. Literature on Archaeological Remains of Cultivated Plants (1994/95), *Vegetation History and Archaeobotany* 5: 169-200.

——— 1997. Literature on Archaeological Remains of Cultivated Plants (1995/96), *Vegetation History and Archaeobotany* 6: 25-67.

——— 1998. Literature on Archaeological Remains of Cultivated Plants (1996/97), *Vegetation History and Archaeobotany* 7: 23-56.

Kulshrestha, V.P. 1985. History and Ethnobotany of Wheat in India, *Journal d'Agriculture Traditionelle et de Botanique Appliquée* 32: 61-71.

Kutzbach, J.E. 1987. The Changing Pulse of the Monsoon, in *Monsoons* (J.S. Fein and P.L. Stephens Eds.), pp. 247-68. New York: John Wiley and Sons.

Lal, B.B. 1954-5 Excavation at Hastinapura and Other Explorations in the Upper Ganga and Sutlej Basins, *Ancient India* 10-11: 5-151.

——— 1971. Perhaps the Earliest Ploughed Field so far Excavated Anywhere in the World, *Puratattva* 4: 1-3

Lal, Makkhan 1984. *Settlement History and the Rise of Civilization in the Ganga-Yamuna Doab from 1500 BC-300 AD.* Delhi: B.R. Publishing Corporation.

Lamb, H.H., R.P.W. Lewis, A. Woodroffe 1966. Atmospheric Circulation and the Main Climatic Variables Between 8000 and 0 BC: Metereological Evidence, *Quaternary Journal, Royal Metereological Society*, Special Issue: Conference on World Climates 8000-0 BC, London.

Lamberg-Karlovsky, C.C. 1989. Mesopotamia, Central Asia and the Indus Valley: So the Kings were Killed, in Archaeological Thought in America (C.C. Lamberg-Karlovsky Ed.), pp. 241-67. Cambridge: Cambridge University Press.

Lambrick, H.T. 1967. The Indus Flood Plain and the 'Indus' Civilization, *The Geographical Journal* 133 (4): 483.

——— 1986. Sindh, General Introduction, Vol. 1, Hyderabad: Sindh Publishing House.

Langer, R.H.M. and G.D. Hill 1991. *Agricultural Plants,* Second Edition. Cambridge: Cambridge University Press.

Lawn, R.J. 1995. The Asiatic *Vigna* Species, in *Evolution of Crop Plants* (J. Smartt and N.W. Simmonds Eds.), pp. 321-6. Essex: Longman Scientific and Technical.

Lézine, A.M., J.F. Saliège, C. Robert, F. Wertz and M.L. Inizian 1998. Holocene Lakes from Ramlat as-Sab'atayn (Yemen) Illustrate the Impact of Monsoon Activity in Southern Arabia, *Quaternary Research* 50: 290-9.

Li, H.L. 1974. An Archaeological and Historical Account of *Cannabis* in China, *Economic Botany* 28 (4): 437-8.

Lone, Farooq A., Maqsooda Khan and G.M. Buth 1993. *Palaeoethnobotany - Plants and Ancient Man in Kashmir.* Rotterdam: A.A. Balkema.

Luthra, J.C. 1936. Ancient Wheat and Its Variability, *Current Science* 4 (7): 489

——— 1941. Letter Quoted in *Excavations at Mohenjo-Daro* (M.S. Vats), p. 467. Delhi: Manager of Publications.

MacKay, E. 1931. Plain and Painted Pottery with Tabulation, in *Mohenjo-daro and the Indus*

Civilization (J.H. Marshall Ed.), pp. 287-337. London: Arthur Probsthain.

——— 1938. *Further Excavations at Mohenjodaro.* Delhi: Government of India Press.

McKean, M.B. 1983. The Palynology of Balakot, a Pre-Harappan and Harappan Age Site in Las Bela, Pakistan. Ph.D. Dissertation. Dallas: Southern Methodist University. Ann Arbor: University Microfilms.

Madella, M. 1995. A Preliminary Study of Phytolith Analysis, Agriculture and Use of Plants at Kot Diji (Sindh–Pakistan), *Ancient Sindh* 2: 93-108.

——— 1997. Phytolith Analysis from the Indus Valley Site of Kot Diji, Sind, Pakistan, in *Archaeological Sciences 1995,* Oxbow Monograph 64 (A. Sinclair, E. Slater and J. Gowlett Eds.), pp. 294-302. Oxford: Oxbow Books.

——— 1998. *Morphological Analysis of Phytoliths: a Botanical Tool for the Interpretation of Archaeological and Geological Sediments from Eurasia.* Ph.D. Dissertation. Cambridge: Cambridge University.

Maier, U. 1996. Morphological Studies of Free-Threshing Wheat Ears from a Neolithic Site in Southwest Germany, and the History of Naked Wheats, *Vegetation History and Archaeobotany* 5: 39-55.

Marshall, J. 1931. *Mohenjo-daro and the Indus Civilization.* London: Arthur Probsthain.

Meadow, R. 1987. Faunal Exploitation Patterns in Eastern Iran and Baluchistan: a Review of Recent Investigations, in *Orientalia Iosephi Tucci Memoriae Dicata* (G. Gnoli and L. Lanciotti Eds.), pp. 881-916, Serie Orientale Roma LVI, 2. Rome: Istituto Italiano per il Medio ed Estermo Oriente.

——— 1989. Continuity and Change in the Agriculture of the Greater Indus Valley: the Palaeoethnobotanical and Zooarchaeological Evidence, in *Old Problems and New Perspectives in the Archaeology of South Asia* (J.M. Kenoyer Ed.), pp. 61-74. Wisconsin Archaeological Reports. Madison: University of Wisconsin.

——— 1996. The Origins and Spread of Agriculture and Pastoralism in Northwestern South Asia, in *The Origins and Spread of Agriculture and Pastoralism in Eurasia* (D. Harris Ed.), pp. 390-412. London: UCL Press.

——— 1998. Pre- and Proto-Historic Agricultural and Pastoral Transformations in North-Western South Asia, in *The Transition to Agriculture in the Old World* (O. Bar-Yosef Ed.), *The Review of Archaeology* (Special Issue) 19 (2): 12-21.

Meadow, R. and Patel A. 1997. A Comment on 'Horse Remains from Surkotada' by Sandor Bakonyi, *South Asian Studies* 13: 308-15.

Meher-Homji, V.M. 1980. The Thar Desert: its Climatic History, *Man and Environment* IV: 1-7.

——— 1991. Probable Impact of Deforestation on Hydrological Processes, *Climatic Change* 19: 163-72.

——— 1994a. Climate Changes Over Space and Time: Their Repercussion on the Flora and Vegetation, *Palaeobotanist* 42 (2): 225-40.

——— 1994b. Palynology: a Tool to Interpret Past Environments, Climate Change or Human Activity, *The Indian Geographical Journal* 69 (1): 36-8.

——— 1996a. Monsoon: a Bioclimatologist's Point of View, *Current Science* 71 (5): 352-7.

——— 1996b. Past Environments Through Palynology: a Short Appraisal with Reference to the Western Ghats, *Environment and History* 2: 249-52.

Mehra, K.L. 1997. Biodiversity and Subsistence Changes in India: the Neolithic and Chalcolithic Age, *Asian Agri-history* 1 (2): 105-26.

Miller, N.F. 1984. The Use of Dung as Fuel: an Ethnographic Example and an Archàeological Application, *Paleorient* 10 (2): 71-9.

Miller, T.E. 1992. A Cautionary Note on the Use of Morphological Characters for Recognising Taxa in Wheat (Genus *Triticum*), in *Prehistoire de l'Agriculture: Nouvelles Appreoaches Experimentales et Ethnographiques* (P.C. Anderson Ed.), pp. 249-53. Monographie du Centre de Recherches Archeologiques 6. Paris: Editions CNRS.

Misra, V.N. 1984. Climate, a factor in the Rise and Fall of the Indus Civilization, in *Frontiers of the Indus Civilization* (B.B. Lal and S.P Gupta Eds.), pp. 461-89. New Delhi: Books & Books.

Mitchell, T.C. 1986. Indus and Gulf Type Seals from Ur, in in *Bahrain Through the Ages* (S.H.A. Al Khalifa and M. Rice Eds.), pp. 278-85. New York: KPI Ltd.

Morrison, K.D. 1994. States of Theory and States of Asia: Regional Perspectives on States in Asia, *Asian Perspectives* 33 (2): 183-96.

Mughal, R. 1982. Recent Archaeological Research in the Cholistan Desert, in *Harappan Civilization: a Perspective* (G. Possehl Ed.), pp. 85-96. Warminster, U.K.: Aris and Phillips Ltd.

Mughal, M.R. 1997. *Ancient Cholistan: Archaeology and Architecture.* Lahore: Ferozsons.

Nagaraja Rao, M.S. 1970. Significance of Pottery Head-rests from Neolithic Sites of Karnataka, *Indian Antiquary 4: Professor H.D. Sankalia Felicitation Volume* (S.B. Deo and M.K. Dhavalikar Eds.), pp. 141-8. Bombay: Popular Prakashan.

Naidu, P.D. 1996. Onset of an Arid Climate at 3.5 ka in the Tropics: Evidence from Monsoon Upwelling Record, *Current Science* 71 (9): 715-18.

Otto, T. and M. Delneuf 1998. Evolution des Ressources Alimentaires et des Paysages au Nord du Cameroun: Appoert de L'archéologie, *in Plantes et Paysages d'Afrique. Une Histoire à Explorer* (M. Chastanet Ed.), pp. 491-514. Paris: Karthala-CRA.

Paddayya, K. 1994. Investigation of Man-Environment Relationships in Indian Archaeology: Some Theoretical Considerations, *Man and Environment* XIX (1-2): 1-28.

Panella, L., J. Kami and P. Gepts 1993. Vignin Diversity in Wild and Cultivated Taxa of *Vigna unguiculata* (L.) Walp. (Fabaceae), *Economic Botany* 47: 371-86

Pascal, J.P. 1984. Les Forets Denses Humides Sempervirentes des Ghats Occidentaux, *Institute Français de Pondicherry, Travaux Section Scientifique et Technique* 20: 1-365.

Phillips, J. 1997. Punt and Aksum: Egypt and the Horn of Africa, *Journal of African History* 38: 423-57.

Piggott, S. *1950. Prehistoric India to 1000 BC* Harmondsworth: Penguin.

Porteres, R. 1961. Appendix XIII, in *Fouilles de Mundigak* (J.-M. Casal Ed.), pp. 259-60. Memoire de la Délégation Archéologique Fraçaise en Afghanistan, Tome 17. Paris

Possehl, G.L. 1967. The Mohenjodaro-Floods: a Reply, *American Anthropologist* 69 (1): 32-40.

——— 1980. *Indus Civilization in Saurashtra.* Delhi: B.R. Publishing Corporation.

——— 1986. African Millets in South Asian Prehistory, in *Studies in the Archaeology of India and Pakistan* (J. Jacobson Ed.), pp. 237-56. New Delhi: Oxford-IBH.

——— 1989 The Harappan Cultural Mosaic: Ecology Revisited, in *South Asian Archaeology 1989* (C. Jarrige Ed.), pp. 237-43. Madison: Prehistory Press.

——— 1997a. The Seafaring Merchants of Meluhha, in *South Asian Archaeology 1995* (R. Allchin and B. Allchin Eds.), pp. 87-100. New Delhi: Oxford-IBH.

——— 1997b. The Transformation of the Indus Civilization, *Journal of World Prehistory* 11 (4): 425-72.

——— 1998. The Introduction of African Millets to the Indian Subcontinent, in *Plants for Food and Medicine* (H.D.V. Prendergast, N.L. Etkin, D.R. Harris and P.J. Houghton Eds.), pp. 107-21. Kew: Royal Botanic Gardens.

——— 1999. Did the Sarasvati Ever Flow to the Sea?, in *Arabia and its Neighbours: Essays on Prehistorical and Historical Developments* (C.S. Phillips, D.T. Potta and S. Searigh), pp. 339-54. Brepols: ABIEL II.

Possehl, G.L. and K.A.R. Kennedy 1979. Hunter-gatherer/Agriculturalist Exchange in Prehistory: an Indian Example, *Current Anthropology* 20 (3): 592-93.

Possehl, G. and P. Rissman 1992. The Chronology of Prehistoric India from Earliest Times to the Iron Age, in *Chronologies in Old World Archaeology* (R.W. Ehrich Ed.), Vol. 1, pp. 465-90, Vol. 2, pp. 447-74. Chicago: University of Chicago Press.

Potts, D.T. 1993. The Late Prehistoric, Protohistoric, and Early Historic Periods in Eastern Arabia (*c.* 5000-1200 BC), *Journal of World Prehistory* 7 (2): 163-212.

Powell, M.A. 1983. The Standard of Dilmun, in *Dilmun* (D.L. Potts Ed.), pp. 141-2. Berlin: Dietrich Reimer Verlag.

Prell, W.L. and J.E. Kutzbach 1987. Monsoon Variability Over the Past 1,50,000 Years, *Journal of Geophysical Research* 92 (D7): 8411-25.

Rahaman, M. 1993. *Land and Life in Sindh—Pakistan*. Lahore: Ferozsons.

Raikes, R.L. 1964. The End of the Ancient Cities of the Indus, *American Anthropologist* 66: 284-9.

——— 1965. The Mohenjo-daro Floods, *Antiquity* 39: 106-203.

——— 1967a. The Mohenjo-daro Floods, Further Notes, *Antiquity* 41: 64-6.

——— 1967b. The Mohenjo-daro Floods, Reposte, *Antiquity* 41: 309-10.

——— 1968. Kalibangan: Death from Natural Causes, *Antiquity* 42 (108): 286-91.

——— 1979. The Mohenjo-daro Floods: the Debate Continues, in *South Asian Archaeology. 1977* (M. Taddei Ed.), pp. 561-66. Napoli: Istituto Universitario Orientale, Seminario di Studi Asiatici, Series Minor 6.

——— 1984a. *Water, Weather and Prehistory,* Second Edition. New Jersey: Humanities Press.

——— 1984b. Mohenjo-daro Environment, in *Frontiers of the Indus Civilisation* (B.B. Lal and S.P. Gupta Eds.), pp. 455-60. New Delhi: Books & Books.

Raikes, R.L. and G.F. Dales 1977. The Mohenjodaro Floods Reconsidered, *Journal of the Palaeontological Society of India* 20: 251-60.

——— 1986. Reposte to Wasson's Sedimentological Basis of the Mohenjo-daro Flood Hypothesis, *Man and Environment* X: 33-44.

Raikes, R.L. and R.H. Dyson 1961. The Prehistoric Climate of Baluchistan and the Indus Valley, *American Anthropologist* 63 (2): 265-81.

Rajaguru, S.N. and S. Mishra 1997. Late Quaternary Climatic Changes in India: a Geoarchaeological Approach, *Indo-Pacific Prehistory Association Bulletin* 2 (Chiang Mai Papers, Vol. 3): pp 27-32.

Ramaswamy, C. 1968. Monsoon Over the Indus Valley During the Harappan Period, *Nature* 217 (5129): 628-9.

Ramesh Rao and Lal 1985. Plant Remains, in *Lothal* (S.R. Rao), pp. 667-84. New Delhi: Memoirs of the Archaeological Surevy of India 78 (2).

Randhawa, M.S. 1980. *A History of Agriculture in India, Volume I: Beginning to 12th Century.* New Delhi: Indian Council for Agricultural Research.

Rao, S.R. 1973. *Lothal and the Indus Civilization.* Bombay: Asia Publishing House.

Ratnagar, S. 1994. Harappan Trade in Its 'World' Context, *Man and Environment* XIX (1-2): 115-28.

Raverty, H.G. 1979. *The Mihran of Sind.* Lahore: Sang-E-Meel Publishers.

Rawal, K.M. 1975. Natural Hybridization Among Wild, Weedy and Cultivated *Vigna unguiculata* (L.) Walp., *Euphytica* 24: 699-707.

Reddy, Seetha N. 1994. Plant Usage and Subsistence Modelling: an Ethnoarchaeological Approach to the Late Harappan of Northwest India. Ph.D. Dissertation. University of Wiscosin. Ann Arbor, Michigan: University Microfilms.

——— 1997. If the Threshing Floor could Talk: Integration of Agriculture and Pastoralism During the Late Harappan in Gujarat, India, *Journal of Anthropological Archaeology* 16: 162-87.

Renfrew, Jane. 1973. *Palaeoethnobotany.* London: Methuen and Co. Ltd.

Rissman, P. 1986. Seasonal Aspects of Man/Cattle Interaction in Bronze Age Western India, *Journal of Ethnobiology* 6: 257-77.

Roose, M.L., R.K. Soost, and J.W. Cameron 1995. Citrus, in *Evolution of Crop Plants* (J. Smartt and N.W. Simmonds Eds.), pp. 443-9. Essex: Longman Scientific and Technical.

Rowley-Conwy, P. 1991. The Sorghum from Qasr Ibrim, Egyptian Nubia, *c.* 800 BC–AD 1811: a Preliminary View, in *New Light on Early Farming* (J. Refrew Ed.), pp. 191-212. Edinburgh: Edinburgh University Press.

Rowley-Conwy, P., W. Deakin and C.H. Shaw 1997. Ancient DNA from Archaeological Sorghum (*Sorghum bicolor)* from Qasr Ibrim, Nubia: Implications for Domestication and Evolution and a Review of the Archaeological Evidence, *Sahara* 9: 23-34.

Sahni, R.B.D.R. 1931. VS Area, in *Mohenjo-daro and the Indus Civilization* (J.H. Marshall Ed.), pp. 214-32. London: Arthur Pronbsthain.

Sankalia, H.D. 1965. *Excavations at Langhnaj: 1944-63, Archaeology*. Poona: Deccan College.

Saraswat, K.S. 1986. Ancient Crop-economy of Harappans from Rohira, Punjab (*c.* 2000-1700 BC), *The Palaeobotanist* 35: 32-8.

——— 1992. Archaeobotanical Remains in Ancient Cultural and Socio-Economical Dynamics of the Indian subcontinent, *The Palaeobotanist* 40: 514-45.

——— 1993. Plant Economy of Late Harappan at Hulas, *Puratattva* 23: 1-12.

Saraswat, K.S. and Chanchala Sirivastava 1994. Palaeobotanical and Pollen Analytical Investigations, *Indian Archaeology 1989-90—a Review*: 132-33.

——— 1995. Palaeobotanical and Pollen Analytical Investigations, *Indian Archaeology 1990-91—a Review*: 103-4.

——— 1996. Palaeobotanical and Pollen Analytical Investigations, *Indian Archaeology 1991-92—a Review*: 139-140.

——— 1997. Palaeobotanical and Pollen Analytical Investigations, *Indian Archaeology 1992-93—a Review*: 123-4.

Saraswat, K.S., N.K. Sharma and D.C. Saini 1994. Plant Economy at Ancient Narhan (*c.*1300 BC-300/400 AD), in *Excavations at Narhan (1984-1989)* (Purushottam Singh Ed.), pp. 255-346. Varanasi: Banaras Hindu University.

Saraswat, K.S., D.C. Saini, M.K. Sharma and Chanchala Sirivastava 1990. Palaeobotanical and Pollen Analytical Investigations, *Indian Archaeology 1985-86—a Review*: 122-5.

——— 1992. Palaeobotanical and Pollen Analytical Investigations 1, 6-8, 11, *Indian Archaeology 1986-87—a Review*: 129-32.

——— 1993. Palaeobotanical and Pollen Analytical Investigations, 5-7, *Indian Archaeology 1987-88—a Review*: 151-3.

Shaffer, J.M. and D.A. Lichtentein 1992. Indus Valley, Baluchistan, and the Helmand Drainage (Afghanistan), in *Chronologies in Old World Archaeology* (R.W. Ehrich Ed.), Vol. 1, pp. 441-64, Vol. 2, pp. 425-46. Chicago: University of Chicago Press.

Sharma, A.K. 1993. The Harappan Horse was Buried Under the Dunes of ..., *Puratattva*, 23: 30-4.

Sharma, C. 1992. Palaeoclimatic Oscillations Since Last Deglaciation in Western Himalaya: a Palynological Assay, *The Palaeobotanist* 40: 374-82.

Shaw, F.J.F. 1943. Vegetable Remains, in *Chanhudaro Excavations* (E.J.H. Mackay), pp. 250-1. New Haven, Connecticut: Yale University Press.

Shinde, V. 1987. Farming in the Chalcolithic Deccan, India *c.* 2000-1000 BC, *Tools and Tillage* 5 (4): 215-27.

——— 1999. Chalcolithic Balathal, Paper Presented at the Settlement History of South Asia Conference, McDonald Institute for Archaeological Research, Cambridge, 25-6 March, 1999.

Simmonds, N.W. 1995. Bananas, in *Evolution of Crop Plants*, Second Edition (J. Smartt and N. W. Simmonds Eds.), pp. 370-5. Essex: Longman Scientific and Technical.

Singh, D.P. 1995. Jute. *Corchorus* spp (Tiliaceae), in *Evolution of Crop Plants*, Second Edition (J. Smartt and N.W. Simmonds Eds.), pp. 476-7. Essex: Longman Scientific and Technical.

Singh, G. 1971. The Indus Valley Culture Seen in the Context of Postglacial Climatic and Ecological Studies in North-West India, *Archaeology and Physical Anthropology of Oceania* 6 (2): 177-89.

Singh, G., R.D. Joshi and A.B. Singh 1972. Stratigraphic and Radiocarbon Evidence for the Age and Development of Three Salt Lake Deposits in Rajasthan, India, *Quaternary Research* 2: 496-505.

Singh, G., R.D. Joshi, S. Chopra and A.B. Singh 1974. Late Quaternary History of Vegetation and Climate in the Rajasthan Desert, India, *Philosophical Transactions of the Royal Society London* 267: 467-501.

Singh, P. 1986. The Origin and Dispersal of Millet Cultivation in India, in *Interregional Contacts in the Later Prehistory of Northern Africa* (L. Krzyzaniak Ed.). Poznan: Polish Archaeological Museum.

Singh, U.V. 1997. Late Harappan Culture as Revealed by the Excavations at Mirzapur and Daulatpur, District Kurukshetra (Haryana), in *Indus Civilization: Problems and Issues* Simla: IIAS.

Sirocko, F. 1996. The Evolution of the Monsoon Climate Over the Arabian Sea During the Last 24,000 Years, in *Palaeoecology of Africa*, Vol. 24 (K. Heine Ed.), pp. 53-69. Rotterdam: A.A. Balkema.

Small, E. and A. Cronquist 1976. A Practical and Natural Taxonomy for *Cannabis, Taxon*, 25: 405-35.

Smartt, J. 1985a. Evolution of Grain Legumes. II. Old and New World Pulses of Lesser Economic Importance, *Experimental Agriculture* 21: 1-18.

——— 1985b. Evolution of Grain Legumes. III. Pulses in the Genus *Vigna*, *Experimental Agriculture* 21: 87-100.

——— 1990. *Grain Legumes: Evolution and Genetic Resources.* Cambridge: Cambridge University Press.

Snead, R.E. 1968. Weather Patterns in Southern West Pakistan, *Archiv für Metereologie, Geophysik und Bioklimatologie*, Ser. B (16): 316-46.

Stapf, O. 1931. Comments Quoted in *Mohenjo-daro and the Indus Civilization* (J. Marshall Ed.), p. 586. London: Arthur Probsthain.

Stein, M.A. 1937. *An Archaeological Reconnaissance in Northwestern India and Southeastern Iran*. London: Macmillan.

——— 1942. A Survey of Ancient Sites Along the 'Lost' Saraswati River, *The Geographical Journal* 99 (4): 173-82.

——— 1943. *An Archaeological Tour along the Ghaggar-Hakkra River, 1940-42*. American Documentation Institute, Microfilm No. ADI-4861.

Stemler, Ann B. 1990. A Scanning Electron Microscopic Analysis of Plant Impressions in Pottery from Sites of Kadero, El Zakiab, Um Direiwa and El Kadada, *Archeologie du Nil Moyen* 4: 87-106.

Stuiver, M. and P.J. Reimer 1993, Extended ^{14}C Database and Revised CALIB Radiocarbon Calibration Program, *Radiocarbon* 35: 215-30.

Stuiver, M., P.J. Reimer, E. Bard, J.W. Beck, G.S. Burr, K.A. Hughen, B. Kromer, F.G. McCormac, J. V. D. Plicht and M. Spurk 1998a. INTCAL98 Radiocarbon Age Calibration 24,000-0 Cal. BP., *Radiocarbon* 40: 1041-83.

Subash Chandran, M.D. 1997. On the Ecological History of the Western Ghats, *Current Science* 73 (2): 146-55.

Snelgrove, A.K. 1979. Migrations of the Indus River, Pakistan, in Response to Plate Tectonic Motions, *Journal of the Geological Society of India* 20: 392-403.

Sukhija, B.S., D.V. Reddy and P. Nagabhushanam 1998. Isotopic Fingerprints of Palaeoclimates During the Last 30,000 Years in Deep Confined Groundwaters of Southern India, *Quaternary Research* 50: 252-60.

Suraj Bhan 1971/2. Siswal: a Pre-Harappan Site on the Drishadvati Valley, *Puratattva* 5: 44-6.

——— 1972. Changes in the Course of the Yamuna and Their Bearing on the Protohistoric Cultures of Harayana, in *Archaeological Congress and Seminar Papers* (S.B. Deo Ed.), pp. 125-28. Nagpur: Nagpur University.

——— 1973. The Sequence and Spread of Prehistoric Cultures in the Upper Saraswati Basin, in *Radiocarbon and Indian Archaeology* (D.P. Agrawal and A. Ghosh Eds.), pp. 252-63. Delhi: Concept Publishers.

——— 1975. *Excavation at Mitathal (1968) and Other Explorations in the Sutlej-Yamuna Divide*. Kurukshetra: Kurukshetra University Press.

Suraj Bhan and J.G. Shaffer 1978. New Discoveries in Northern Haryana, *Man and Environment* II: 59-68.

Swain A.M., J.E. Kutzbach and S. Hastenrath 1983. Estimates of Holocene Precipitation for Rajasthan, India, Based on Pollen and Lake-Level Data, *Quaternary Research* 19: 1-17.

Thiébault, S. 1988a. Palaeoenvironment and Ancient Vegetation of Baluchistan Based on Charcoal Analysis of Archaeological Sites, *Proceedings of the Indian National Science Academy* 54A: 501-9.

——— 1988b. L'évolution de La Végétation à Mehrgarh, in *Les Cités Oubliées de l'Indus*, p. 45. Paris: Musée National des Artes Asiatiques Guimet.

——— 1989. A Note on the Ancient Vegetation of Baluchistan Based on Charcoal Analysis of the Latest Periods from Mehrgarh, Pakistan, in *South Asian Archaeology 1985* (K. Frifelt and P. Sörensen Eds.), pp. 186-8. London: Curzon Press.

——— 1992. Complentary Results in Anthracological Analysis from Sites in Baluchistan, in *South Asian Archaeology 1989* (C. Jarrige Ed.), pp. 271-6. Monographs in World Archaeology 14. Madison: Prehistory Press.

——— 1995. First Results of the Study of the Ancient Vegetation of Mehrgarh Through Anthracological Analysis, in *Mehrgarh, Field Reports 1974-1985—from Neolithic Time to the Indus Civilization* (C. Jarrige, J.-F. Jarrige, R.H. Meadow and G. Quivron Eds.), pp. 524. Karachi: Department of Culture and Tourism, Government of Sindh, Pakistan in Collaboration with French Ministry of Foreign Affairs.

Thomas, K.D. 1983a. Tarakai Qila: Site, Economy and Environment, in *Site, Environment and Economy* (B. Proudfoot Ed.), pp. 127-44. Oxford: BAR International Series 173.

——— 1983b. Agricultural and Subsistence Systems of the Third Millennium B.C. in North-West Pakistan: a Speculative Outline, in *Integrating the Subsistence Economy* (M.K. Jones Ed.), pp. 279-314. Oxford: BAR International Series 181.

——— 1989. Hierarchical Approaches to the Evolution of Complex Agricultural Systems, in *The Bieginnings of Agriculture* (A. Milles, D. Williams and N. Gardner Eds.), pp. 55-73. Oxford: BAR International Series 496.

Tomlinson, P.B. 1969. *Anatomy of the Monocotyledons: III. Commelinales-Zingiberales.* Oxford: Oxford University Press.

Thompson, G.B. 1996. Ethnographic Models for Interpreting Rice Remains, in *The Excavation of Khok Phanom Di a Prehistoric Site in Central Thailand, Volume IV: Subsistence and Environment: the Botanical Evidence (The Biological Remains, Part II)* (C. Higham and R. Thosarat Eds.), pp. 119-50. London: The Society of Antiquaries of London.

Tosi, M. 1986. Early Maritime Cultures of the Arabian Gulf and the Indian Ocean, in *Bahrain Through the Ages* (S.H.A. Al Khalifa and M. Rice Eds.), pp. 94-107. New York: KPI Ltd.

Tostain, S. 1994. Isozymic Classification of Pearl Millet (*Pennisetum glaucum, Poaceae*) Landraces from Niger (West Africa), *Plant Systematics and Evolution* 193: 81-93.

——— 1998. Le mil, une Longue Histoire: Hypotheses sur sa Domestication et ses Migrations, in *Plantes et Paysages d'Afrique. Une Histoire a Explorer* (M. Chastanet Ed.), pp. 461-90. Paris: Karthala-CRA.

Vaillancourt, R.E. and N.F. Weeden 1992. Chloroplast DNA Polymorphism Suggests Nigerian Center of Domestication for the Cowpea, *Vigna unguiculata*, Leguminosae, *American Journal of Botany* 79: 1194-9.

Van Campo, E. 1986. Monsoon Fluctuations in Two 20,000-yr B.P. Oxygen-Isotope/Pollen Records Off Southwest India, *Quaternary Research* 26: 376-88.

Van der Veen, M. 1992. *Crop Husbandry Regimes: an Archaeobotanical Study of Farming in Northern England 1000 BC-AD 500.* Sheffield Archaeological Monographs 3. Sheffield: J.R. Collis Publications, University of Sheffield.

Van Zeist, W. 1976. On Macroscopic Traces of Food Plants in Southwestern Asia (with Some Reference to Pollen Data), *Philosophical Transactions of the Royal Society London* B. 275: 27-41.

Vats, M.S. 1940. *Excavations at Harappa. I.* Calcutta: Archaeological Survey of India.

Verdcourt, B. 1970. Studies in the *Leguminosae-Papilionoideae* for the 'Flora of Tropical East Africa': III, *Kew Bulletin* 24 (3): 379-443.

——— 1971. Phaeseoleae, in E. Milne-Redhead and R.M. Polhill (Eds.) *Flora of Tropical East*

Africa, Leguminosae (Part 4), Palpilionidae (2). London: Crown Agents for Overseas Governments and Administrations.

Vishnu-Mittre 1961. Plant Economy in Ancient Navdatoli-Maheshwar, *Technical Report on Archaeological Remains*, pp. 13-52. Pune: Department of Archaeology and Ancient Indian History, Deccan College and University of Poona Publications.

——— 1968. Protohistoric Records of Agriculture in India, *Transactions of the Bose Research Institute* 31 (3): 87-106.

——— 1969. Remains of Rice and Millet, in *Excavations at Ahar (Tambavati)* (H.D. Sankalia, S.B. Deo and Z.D. Ansari), pp. 229-35. Pune: Deccan College.

——— 1970. Status of Barley in Indian Archaeology with Remarks on the Aryan Hypothesis, *Puratattva* 3: 1-2.

——— 1974a. Palaeobotanical Evidence in India, in *Evolutionary Studies in World Crops: Diversity and Change in the Indian Subcontinent* (J. Hutchinson Ed.), pp. 3-30. Cambridge: Cambridge University Press.

——— 1974b. Plant Remains and Climate from the Late Harappan and Other Chalcolithic Cultures of India—a Study in Inter-Relationships, *Geophytology* 4: 46-53.

——— 1976. Palaeoecology of the Rajasthan Desert during the last 10,000 years, *The Palaeobotanist* 25: 549-58.

——— 1977. Changing Economy in Ancient India, in *Origins of Agriculture* (C. Reed Ed.), pp. 569-88. Paris: Mouton.

——— 1979. Palaeobotanical Evidence of the Environment of Early Man in Northwestern and Western India, *Grana* 18: 167-81.

——— 1982. The Harappan Civilization and the Need for a New Approach, in *Harrapan Civilization: a Contemporary Perpsective* (G.L. Possehl Ed.), pp. 31-9. New Delhi: Oxford-IBH.

——— 1989. Forty Years of Archaeobotanical Research in South Asia, *Man and Environment* XIV: 1-16.

——— 1990. Plant Remains, in *Excavations at Surkotada* (J.P. Joshi Ed.), pp. 388-92. New Delhi: Memoirs of the Archaeological Survey of India 87.

Vishnu-Mittre and R. Savithri 1975. Supposed Remains of Rice (*Oryza* sp.) in the Terracotta Cakes and Pai at Kalibangan, Rajasthan, *The Palaeobotanist* 22: 124-6.

——— 1976. Ancient Plant Economy at Inamgaon, *Puratattva* 8: 55-63.

——— 1978. *Setaria* in Ancient Plant Economy of India, *The Palaeobotanist* 25: 559-64.

——— 1979. Palaeobotanical and Pollen Analytical Investigations, *Indian Archaeology 1974-75—a Review:* 78-81.

——— 1982. Food Economy of the Harappans, in *Harrapan Civilization* (G.L. Possehl Ed.), pp. 205-21. New Delhi: Oxford-IBH.

Vishnu-Mittre, K.S. Saraswat, A. Sharma and Chanchala Srivastava 1985. Palaeobotanical and Pollen Analytical Investigations, *Indian Archaeology 1982-83—a Review*: 146-50.

Vishnu-Mittre, A. Sharma and Chanchala Srivastava 1986a. Ancient Plant Economy at Daimabad, in *Daimabad 1976-1979* (S.A. Sali Ed.), pp. 588-626. New Delhi: Archaeological Survey of India.

Vishnu-Mittre, K.S. Saraswat, A. Sharma and Chanchala Srivastava 1986b. Palaeobotanical and Pollen Analytical Investigations, *Indian Archaeology 1983-84—a Review*: 174-8.

Von Rad, U., M. Schaaf, K.H. Michels, H. Schulz, W.H. Berger and F. Sirocko 1999. A 5000-Yr

Record of Climate Change in Varved Sediment from the Oxygen Minimum Zone Off Pakistan, Northeastern Arabian Sea, *Quaternary Research* 52: 39-53.

Warren, A. 1970. Dunes Trends and Their Implications in the Central Sudan, *Zeitschrift für Geomorphologie* 10: 154-80.

Wasson, R.J. 1984. The Sedimentological Basis of the Mohenjo-daro Flood Hypothesis, *Man and Environment* VIII: 88-90.

——— 1987. The Sedimentological Basis of the Mohenjo-daro Flood Hypothesis—a Further Comment, *Man and Environment* XI: 122-3.

——— 1995. The Asian Monsoon During the Late Quaternary: a Test of Orbital Forcing and Palaeoanalogue Forecasting, in *Quaternary Environemnts and Geoarchaeology of India* (S. Wadia, R. Korisettar and V.S. Kale Eds.), pp. 22-35. Bangalore: Geological Society of India.

Wasylikowa, K., J.R. Harlan, J. Evans, F. Wendorf, R. Schild, A.E. Close, H. Krolik and R.A. Housely 1993. Examination of Botanical Remains from Early Neolithic Houses at Nabta Playa, Western Desert, Egypt with Special Reference to Sorghum Grains, in *The Archaeology of Africa. Food, metals, and Towns* (T. Shaw, P. Sinclair, B. Andah and A. Okpoko Eds.), pp. 154-64. London: Routledge.

Watkins, R. 1995. Cherry, Plum, Peach, Apricot and Almond, *Prunus* spp. (Rosaceae), in *Evolution of Crop Plants,* Second Edition (J. Smartt and N.W. Simmonds Eds.), pp. 423-9. Essex: Longman Scientific and Technical.

Watt, G. 1908. *The Commercial Products of India—An Abridgement of 'The Dictionary of the Economic Products of India'*. London: John Murray.

Weber, S.A. 1991. *Plants and Harappan Subsistence—an Example of Stability and Change from Rojdi.* New Delhi: Oxford-IBH.

——— 1992. South Asian Archaeobotanical Variability, in *South Asian Archaeology 1989* (C. Jarrige Ed.), pp. 283-90. Madison, Wisconsin: Prehistory Press.

——— 1996. Distinguishing Change in the Subsistence and the Material Records: the Interplay of Environment and Culture, *Asian Perspectives* 35 (2): 155-63.

——— 1997. Harappa Archaeobotany: a Model for Subsistence, in *South Asian Archaeology 1995* (R. Allchin and B. Allchin Eds.), pp. 115-17. New Delhi: Oxford-IBH.

——— 1998. Out of Africa: The Initial Impact of Millets in South Asia, *Current Anthropology* 39 (2): 267-74.

Wendel, J.F. 1995. Cotton, *Gossypium* (Malvaceae), in *The Evolution of Crop Plants* (J. Smartt and N.W. Simmonds Eds.), pp. 358-66. Essex: Longman Scientific and Technical.

Wheeler, R.E.M. 1959. *Early India and Pakistan.* London: Thames and Hudson.

——— 1968. *The Indus Civilization.* Cambridge: Cambridge University Press.

Willcox, G. 1991. Carbonised Plant Remains from Shortugai, Afghanistan, in *New Light on Early Farming: Recent Developments in Palaeoethnobotany* (J.M. Renfrew Ed.), pp. 139-53. Edinburgh: Edinburgh University Press.

——— 1992. Some Differences Between Crops of Near Eastern Origin and Those from the Tropics, in *South Asian Archaeology 1989* (C. Jarrige Ed.), pp. 291-9. Monographs in World Archaeology 14. Madison: Prehistory Press.

Wilson, S.M. 1985. Phytolith Analysis at Kuk, an Early Agricultural Site in Papua, New Guinea, *Archaeology in Oceania* 20(3): 90-7.

Zeven, A.C. 1978. The Prehistoric Spread of Bread Wheat into Asia, in *Proceedings of the Fifth*

International Wheat Genetics Symposium (S. Ramanujam Ed.), pp. 103-7. New Delhi: Indian Society of Genetics and Plant Breeding.

Zohary, D. 1969. The Progenitors of Wheat and Barley in Relation to Domestication and Agriculture Dispersal in the Old World, in *The Domestication and Exploitation of Plants and Animals* (P.J. Ucko and G.W. Dimbleby Eds.), pp. 47-66. London: Duckworth.

Zohary, Daniel and Maria Hopf 1993. *Domestication of Plants in the Old World*. Cambridge: Cambridge University Press.

Zohary, D. and P. Spiegel-Roy 1975. Beginnings of Fruit Growing in the Old World, *Science* 187: 319-27.

From Mehrgarh to Harappa and Dholavira: Prehistoric Pastoralism in North-Western South Asia through the Harappan Period

RICHARD H. MEADOW and AJITA K. PATEL

INTRODUCTION

Pastoralism involves the breeding, raising, and managing of domesticated ungulates by members of a human society (Meadow 1992; Patel 1997). This can be accomplished under many different conditions and does not presuppose any particular degree of economic specialization or mobility or any particular way of life on the part of the pastoralist. The degree to which individuals or groups depend upon domestic animals and animal products and the ways in which they husband their stock can vary from time to time, place to place, and circumstance to circumstance. We, as researchers studying animal usage over the past 9,000 years, wish to investigate the history of the role of domestic animals in human societies and the ways that they were managed. We do not wish to be obliged to identify ways of life as belonging to one pre-defined type or another. Thus when we talk about pastoralism, we do not mean to suggest anything about 'nomadism' or 'transhumance' or about degree of commitment to raising animals as opposed to growing crops or trading or manufacturing. Those are matters to be determined through analysis and evaluation of a wide array of archaeological, textual, and anthropological data, including but not limited to animal bone remains from archaeological sites.

In the South Asian context, we are only at the dawn of the study of ancient pastoralism. Our data include published reports on animal bone assemblages from only a very few archaeological sites and some iconographic representations and artefacts that help us to know a bit about what the animals looked like and how they were being used. There is almost no direct archaeological evidence for how and where domestic animals were being kept at any given locality nor about any possible seasonal variability in the exploitation of those animals. For ideas about these matters we tend to fall back upon 'ethnographic analogy' with all its inherent weaknesses, particularly in the absence of any satisfactory archaeological confirmation.

In this essay we focus on the zooarchaeological and to a minor degree on iconographic evidence for pastoralism in north-western South Asia from the period of the first known villages (seventh millennium BC) through the end of the Indus Civilization (beginning of the second millennium BC). The area covered comprises what is today Pakistan and part of north-western India. We begin with a brief history of the investigation of ancient animal exploitation in the region and then review the state of our current understanding of ancient pastoralism.

A SHORT HISTORY OF ZOOARCHAEOLOGY IN SOUTH ASIA

Zooarchaeology involves the study and interpretation of non-human animal remains recovered from archaeological sites (Meadow 1999). Other terms used are faunal analysis, archaeozoology, paleoethnozoology, and osteoarchaeology. Faunal analysis is the most general of the terms, designating the study of the vestiges of non-human animals in any depositional context. Thus those who study naturally deposited fossils, i.e. those who consider themselves to be doing palaeontology, also carry out faunal analyses. Archaeozoology, largely synonymous with zooarchaeology, is a term widely employed outside of North America and Britain. Practitioners tend to have backgrounds in palaeontology, zoology, or veterinary medicine rather than in archaeology, as is more usual with those who consider themselves as zooarchaeologists. As a result, archaeozoological studies may emphasize biology-based and evolutionary-based interpretations more than the culturally oriented ones favoured by zooarchaeologists. Palaeoethnozoology refers to the study of how humans interacted with non-human animals in the past. Sources of information may be iconographic, textual, architectural, and artefactual as well as faunal. Archaeozoologists and zooarchaeologists also employ such sources as aids to the interpretation of faunal remains, and most of these investigators would agree that they are concerned with the role that non-human animals played in human societies, although few actually use the term palaeoethnozoology. Finally, osteoarchaeology comprises the study of bones and teeth from archaeological sites. As such it includes parts of the domains of both zooarchaeology and physical anthropology, dealing as it does with all animals with endoskeletons (i.e. vertebrates). In contrast, animals with exoskeletons (i.e. invertebrates) also form part of the domains of zooarchaeology, archaeozoology, faunal analysis, palaoethnozoology and palaeontology.

Zooarchaeology in South Asia traces its beginnings to the late 1920s and early 1930s with the analysis by Colonel Robert Beresford Seymour Sewell (Sewell and Guha 1931) and Baini Prasad (1934, 1936) of animal bone remains from Mohenjo Daro, Harappa, and various prehistoric sites in Sindh. Sewell and Prasad were both Zoologists and (successively) Directors of the Zoological Survey of India. As Sewell (Sewell and Guha 1931: 639) notes for his analysis of the faunal remains from Mohenjo Daro, 'So far as I am aware, this is the first occasion on which a thorough investigation of the animal remains obtained by archaeological excavation in India has been carried out...' [The first person is used throughout the text. That this is Sewell is clear from footnote 1 on page 671, even though the chapter is attributed to both Sewell and Guha. See also Prasad (1936: 1).] He goes on to say that

> ... it is therefore of no small interest to see to what extent such investigation can furnish data regarding the conditions in which the early inhabitants of these sites lived, and whether by means of such a study we can confirm or refute conclusions regarding these early peoples that have been drawn from other lines of evidence.

Judged from the standpoint of modern zooarchaeology, these goals are entirely laudable, although they were largely frustrated by the lack of stratigraphic excavations and by incomplete recovery of archaeofaunal materials. Solutions to these problems would come only later with the introduction of stratigraphic methods by Robert Eric Mortimer Wheeler in 1944 and with the use of sieves to screen excavated sediments, although the latter procedure is still employed only haphazardly across the subcontinent.

Two features of the work of Sewell and Prasad deserve notice. One is that they frequently refer to the pioneering work of the Switzerland-based osteologist Johann Ulrich Duerst (1908) on the faunal remains from the site of Anau in modern Turkmenistan. The Anau project was the brainchild of the remarkable American mining engineer turned avocational archaeologist Raphael Pumpelly who led the first multidisciplinary archaeological team to excavate in the greater Middle East, pre-dating by four decades the fielding of multidisciplinary teams by Robert John Braidwood. The inclusion of specialist reports in archaeological monographs throughout the 1920s and 1930s can partly be attributed to the example set by Pumpelly. The second feature that deserves notice is that neither Sewell nor Prasad cite the work of palaeontologists who had been studying the remains of pre-modern faunas (archaeofaunas) in South Asia for nearly a century, some of these remains being associated with stone tools. These early palaeontological investigations (reviewed by Badam [1979] and Sahu [1988] apparently were deemed irrelevant to the study of Holocene (modern) faunas, with the emphasis instead being on the use of modern comparative collections in the Indian Museum, Calcutta, to help identify the archaeofaunal remains. As the palaeontologist Gyani Lal Badam (1979) points out, however,

> It is indeed ideal to trace the history of one animal from the Pleistocene to the Holocene, studying the morphological changes motivated by genes and also brought about by domestication. This, however, can only be achieved by studying within their cultural context, the animal bones from archaeological sites.

From the zooarchaeological (as opposed to the palaeontological) perspective, it is important to try to trace changes in the human exploitation of animals across the Pleistocene-Holocene boundary and within the Holocene from hunting to the keeping of domestic animals. Unfortunately, these transitions are marked by major lacunae in our understanding of the archaeological record in South Asia.

Following the work of Sewell and Prasad, there were very few, if any, publications of faunal remains from South Asian Holocene sites until the 1950s. In 1953, one page of analysis of animal remains by J.C. George was included in Subbarao's *Baroda Through the Ages*. This report appears to represent the first Holocene faunal report published in post-Independence India. J.C. George was Head of the Department of Zoology, the M.S. University of Baroda. The commissioning of his report and a subsequent one published in 1955 is due to the multidisciplinary orientation of the remarkable Indian archaeologist Bendapudi Subbarao, who had been sent by his professor at Deccan College, Pune, Hasmukhlal Dhirajlal Sankalia to form a Department of Archaeology and Ancient History at Baroda. Both Sankalia and Subbarao had interacted extensively with Frederick Everard Zeuner and were also influenced by the exhortations of R.E.M. Wheeler concerning the importance of multidisciplinary research (Sankalia 1978; Paddayya 1994).

The year 1955 also saw the first publication of the work of Bhola Nath (Vertebrate Zoologist, Department of Anthropology, Government of India, Calcutta, subsequently of the Zoological Survey of India) who published faunal reports until *c.* 1985. Other productive scholars have been Krishnarao Raghavendrarao Alur (a retired veterinary anatomist) who published from *c.* 1969 to 1990 and (Mrs.) Dolly Raman Shah (Lecturer in Zoology, the M.S. University of Baroda) with publications from 1965 to 1992. Also carrying out analyses of faunal remains from archaeological sites in India during the late 1950s into the 1970s were P. Srinivasan (Reader in Anatomy in the College of Veterinary Science at Osmania University: 1960, 1961), J. Eapen (the M.S. University of Baroda: 1960), and Juliet Clutton-Brock (then a student of Zeuner at the Institute of Archaeology, University of London: 1962, 1965). In addition, A.K. Sharma (Archaeological Survey of India, Nagpur) published analyses from Surkotada and Gufkral between 1974 and 1993. Useful reviews of the literature are the works of Bhairabi Prasad Sahu (1988) and P.K. Thomas and P.P. Joglekar (1994), where bibliographic entries for the individuals mentioned in this paragraph can be found.

In 1972, with the creation by H.D. Sankalia of a paleontological and bio-archaeological laboratory at the Deccan College Post-Graduate and Research Institute, Pune, G.L. Badam joined that institution to work on Pleistocene remains associated with cultural materials. At the same time, Pappy Kuzuvelil Thomas was a student at Pune, where he continued on the staff after completing his Ph.D. dissertation in 1977, largely on the faunal remains from Bagor, a Mesolithic (microlithic) site in Rajasthan. Of significance for the course of the development of archaeozoology at Deccan College were the contributions of Antje Trientje Clason from the Netherlands (Rijksuniversiteit Groningen, The Netherlands) who spent the second half of 1972 in Pune (Clason 1974, 1977). With her training in the Central European tradition of archaeozoology, she provided a different perspective on the study of faunal remains from archaeological sites. In particular, there was a move away from mere lists of taxa or identified specimens that had characterised most of earlier work towards a more quantitative approach to data presentation. The recording of bone measurements also became important. Unfortunately, the establishment of an extensive comparative collection of modern specimens was not sufficiently emphasized, and this essential aid to the identification of archaeofaunal materials remained underdeveloped at Pune until the end of the 1980s.

The importance of modern comparative collections in the South Asian context lies in the presence in archaeological sites of skeletal parts that are morphologically quite similar between taxa. The most common difficulties of identification relate to distinguishing the bones of different forms of bovid, for example, differentiating *Ovis* (sheep) from *Capra* (goat) from *Gazella* (chinkara) from *Antilope* (blackbuck) as well as *Bos* (cattle) from *Bubalus* (water buffalo) from *Boselaphus* (nilgai). There also can be problems distinguishing the bones of bovids from those of cervids (deer) and the remains of the various cervids from each other. Only comprehensive modern collections and detailed comparative osteologies based on those collections can begin to overcome these difficulties. An especially problematic analytic practice can be to use bones identified from one archaeological site to help identify those from another. While this approach is acceptable if the material has been identified correctly in the first instance, incorrect identifications will perpetuate gross error into subsequent generations of analyses.

Today in India the importance of comparative material has been recognized by zooarchaeologists (although perhaps not understood by most other archaeologists). There are growing collections of South Asian wild and domestic forms at both Deccan College, Pune, and the M.S. University, Baroda, the two centres of Holocene faunal analysis in India. Given the staffing histories of these two institutions, Pune has been the focus of archaeozoological work in India since the mid-1980s. G.L. Badam, and especially P.K. Thomas joined later by P.P. Joglekar, have carried out most of the Holocene faunal studies in India over the last two decades of the twentieth century (for a summary, see P.K. Thomas and Joglekar 1994). At Baroda, J. Eapen was the first zoologist in India appointed to a position in a Department of Archaeology. He was followed in the mid-1960s by D.R. Shah, who carried out significant research to the time of her retirement in 1988. Her work is noteworthy because it remains a more reliable source of information than that of other researchers of her time. For the next eight years, the post at Baroda remained vacant until the 1996 appointment of Ajita Kantilal Patel to the Lecturer in Zoology position. Currently at Baroda, a comprehensive zooarchaeological research program is underway that involves tracing the exploitative histories particularly of wild and domestic bovids.

In Pakistan, the situation is different than that in India. There is no locally established tradition of the analysis of Holocene faunas from archaeological sites, with the result that almost all analyses are done by Western scholars. The first published faunal report is that contained in Quetta Valley report of Walter Ashlin Fairservis, Jr. (1956); it was compiled by Fairservis on the basis of a number of analyses by different specialists in America. Following this, until the middle 1970s there is only the study of Thérèse Poulain-Josien of the fauna from Amri published in 1964. By 1978, however, five collaborative Pakistani-foreign projects—with the Italians in Swat, the British in the Bannu Basin, the Americans at Balakot and Allahdino near Karachi, and the French at Mehrgarh—had included faunal analysts as members of their teams (Caloi and Compagnoni 1976 and Compagnoni 1979; K.D. Thomas 1981; Meadow 1979a, 1981; Turnbull 1983). Since then, faunal analysts have been associated with the American-Pakistani team at Harappa (Meadow 1991; Belcher 1997, 1998) and with the French-Pakistani team working in the Makran (e.g. Desse 1995) as well as continuing work in the Bannu Basin and at Mehrgarh and nearby sites (see Meadow 1993a for a review).

PREHISTORIC PASTORALISM

The earliest evidence for pastoralism in South Asia comes from only one site—Mehrgarh, located at the foot of the Bolan Pass in eastern Pakistani Baluchistan (Meadow 1981, 1984a, 1984b, 1989a, 1993b). This site, situated on the north Kachi plain at the foot of the mountainous edge of the Indus alluvium, is at an ecotone on the margins of foothill, plain and riverine environments (C. Jarrige et al. 1995). The wild-animal remains that dominate the early levels of Aceramic Neolithic Period I reflect this situation with twelve large ungulates represented: wild sheep (*Ovis orientalis*) and goats (*Capra aegagrus*) from the hills, chinkara (*Gazella bennetti*) from the foothills and plains, wild onagers (*Equus hemionus*) and blackbuck (*Antilope cervicapra*) from the drier plains, and nilgai (*Boselaphus tragocamelus*), large deer (*Cervus* (?)*duvauceli*), smaller deer (*Axis* (?)*axis*), boar (*Sus scrofa*), water buffalo (*Bubalus arnee*), wild cattle (*Bos namadicus*), and possibly elephant (*Elaphas maximus*) from better-watered zones.

The wild sheep, goat, cattle, and buffalo all comprise potential ancestral stock for the domestic forms. To judge from the occurrence of infant goats as offerings in a number of burials, however, goats are likely to have been domesticated even at the beginning of Period I, which may date to sometime in the seventh millennium BC (all dates cited here are based on calibrated radiocarbon determinations and thus approach calendar years). The domestic status of at least some of the goats is confirmed by the presence of the remains of relatively small subadult and adult animals in contemporary trash deposits. A decrease in body size of the grown or nearly grown animal is one characteristic of early domestic bovids (see Uerpmann 1979 for sheep and goat, Grigson 1989 for cattle, Meadow 1989b for overall discussion). Goats are also the single most common animal represented in the early Period I assemblages after chinkara which, in contrast, show no size diminution.

Through the course of the Aceramic Neolithic at Mehrgarh (now divided into three phases: IA, IB, and IC: J.F. Jarrige 1999), the remains of sheep and cattle came to increasingly dominate the faunal assemblages of the successive strata while, at the same time, the animals represented grew smaller in body size. By the end of Period IB cattle bones make up well over 50 per cent of the remains recovered from the archaeological deposits. This coincident pair of trends increasing representation and decreasing body size was found to occur in two widely separated deep soundings and strongly supports an hypothesis of local domestication. In addition, both osteological and figurine evidence indicate that zebu (humped) cattle (*Bos indicus*) were present and likely to have been the dominant form (Meadow 1984b). These findings (first published in Meadow 1981) confirmed proposals by others with regard to the indigenous origin of South Asian zebu (reviewed in Grigson 1985). Over the course of the 1990s, the indigenous domestication of cattle in eastern Iran or South Asia from local wild stock has been corroborated by the work of geneticists from Trinity College, Dublin (e.g. Loftus et al. 1994; Bradley et al. 1998). Through examination of mitochondrial DNA, autosomal microsatellites, and Y chromosome polymorphisms, they have shown that the principal genetic divide between forms of cattle is between *Bos indicus* (zebu forms) and *Bos taurus* (European non-humped forms). Furthermore, the degree of this divergence 'strongly supports biologically separate origins for the two domestic taxa' (Bradley et al. 1998: 85).

The situation with sheep is not so straightforward. Cytogenetic studies suggest that modern domestic forms are all descended from a single ancestor related to the current South-West Asian population of mouflon (*Ovis orientalis*: reviewed in Uerpmann 1987). This would seem to preclude a separate origin in South Asia where the local wild species today is the urial (*Ovis vignei*). However, it is possible that the former range of the mouflon extended from the southern Zagros into Baluchistan. It is also possible that sheep domesticated in western South Asia from the urial were replaced later by imported South-West Asian domestic forms descended from the mouflon (Meadow 1989c). Gradual decrease in the size of sheep at Mehrgarh continued well into Mehrgarh Period III (fifth millennium BC) and then stabilized with relatively small animals being the norm at least into the second millennium in that region (at the sites of Sibri and Nausharo situated near Mehrgarh). At Harappa in (Pakistani) Punjab, however, very large domestic sheep occur in third millennium BC. Harappan phase deposits that are contemporary with those at Nausharo (Meadow 1991).

Unlike wild cattle that probably existed through much of South Asia, wild sheep and goats seem to have been confined to the extreme western part of the subcontinent on the eastern margin of the Iranian plateau. Thus finds of these small bovids on sites farther east and south-east are presumed to reflect introductions of the pastoral economy. But the mechanisms and timing of such a movement remain poorly understood, and until recently the possibility of multiple local domestications of cattle (*Bos*) has not been considered. In part, of course, this is linked to the poorly developed nature of our understanding of the earliest village farming communities in these areas. Also imperfectly understood, however, are the nature and degree of use of domesticates by the inhabitants of so-called 'mesolithic' or 'microlithic' communities, which in the Indian context can date anywhere in the Holocene.

The important microlithic site of Bagor in south-eastern Rajasthan provides a good example of the problem. D.R. Shah (cited in *IAR* 1967-8: 42) initially examined the faunal remains and suggested that only wild animals were exploited, at least in Phase I (somewhere between 5000 and 2800 BC). K.R. Alur (reprinted in Alur 1990: 224-31) subsequently studied part of the collection and identified caprines (sheep and goat) and, to a lesser extent, cattle as the most commonly represented taxa. Finally P.K. Thomas (1975) added water buffalo to the list and continued to claim that domestic caprines were the most frequently occurring forms in all periods (I-III: microlithic to Early Historic). This identification of sheep and goat and cattle at Bagor and other microlithic sites has led to the suggestion that domestic animals were adopted quite early by non-agricultural peoples who thus became hunter-pastoralist gatherers. Our observations of the Bagor material (bones and photographs of bones) lead us to believe that identifications particularly of sheep and goats from this site are in error. The fact that Dolly Shah identified only wild taxa has never been fully considered (Shah 1971).

Mis-identifications of material such as that from the Ganga Valley microlithic sites (noted by P.K. Thomas et al. 1995), Inamgaon (noted in Meadow 1996), and Bagor can be traced to a number of factors. These include not using suitable comparative collections and a lack of effort by investigators to carry out necessary comparative osteological studies. The reports of individuals who were careful, consistent, and conservative in their identifications, for example, Juliet Clutton-Brock (1965) at Langhnaj and D.R. Shah at a number of different sites, are more trust-worthy than those of other contemporary investigators. Our own experience with the Mehrgarh and Loteshwar faunal remains has made us extremely cautious in identifying material to species or even to genus or family unless we can observe diagnostic features on a particular specimen that permit us to securely assign it to a taxon.

The site of Loteshwar in Mahesana district of north Gujarat raises some important issues. These concern identification, dating, and the advent of pastoralism in this region. Loteshwar is located on the margin of a salty waste depression north of river Rupen east of the Rann of Kachchh. Partially excavated by a team from the M.S. University of Baroda in 1991, this site, situated on a stabilized sand dune, has two components: microlithic (Period I) and Chalcolithic (Period II: *IAR* 1991-2: 12-16). Neither of the components has shown any evidence of architecture. The Chalcolithic deposits measure between 20 and 30 cm in depth below the surface, although there are pits that penetrate the Period I deposits to natural sediment. Samples of charcoal found in these pits have given conventional calibrated radiocarbon dates of about 3700 and 2900 BC (Sonawane and Ajithprasad 1994). The microlithic (Period I) deposit measures between 50 and 100 cm in depth. No dates on associated charcoal are available from Period I levels.

Among the faunal remains from Period I deposits, only wild forms were identified (Patel and Meadow 1998b). These include predominantly blackbuck with some chinkara, small and large deer, cattle, water buffalo, nilgai, boar, and khur. In the Period II pits, the proportion of cattle bones increases markedly with blackbuck decreasing proportionally. Otherwise the taxa remain pretty much the same. Given that the Chalcolithic pits were dug into and sometimes through the microlithic levels, many and perhaps most of the bones from wild animals found in the pits could have come from the earlier component. What is characteristically different about the pit material is the presence of many bones of domestic cattle. In contrast, in the Period I levels there are very few cattle bones, and to judge from the size of the bones, they come from wild animals. Because of the possibility of pit deposits being mixed, not only is it necessary to be cautious about drawing conclusions with respect to the relative importance of wild *versus* domestic fauna from Period II, but it is also necessary to be cautious about using charcoal from the pits to date their contents. To circumvent this problem, we have begun a project of dating charred animal bone from Periods I and II at Loteshwar using the AMS technique. One burned humerus of a blackbuck from Period I has provided an AMS date of approximately 5550 BC calibrated (Patel and Meadow 1998a). Additional specimens of wild animals from Period I and domestic cattle from Period II await determinations. When these are in hand, we should be able to say more about the beginnings of pastoralism in this part of Gujarat (Patel 1998). Of particular interest will be the dates for the Chalcolithic material. If they approach those of the previously determined charcoal samples (*c*. 3700-2900 BC), this would confirm the presence in north Gujarat of cattle pastoralists (and agriculturalists?) well before the Harappan period. If they are later, one will need to re-evaluate the significance of all of the cultural remains from these contexts at Loteshwar. Whatever the outcome, the results will underline the importance of directly dating carefully analysed and identified faunal specimens from South Asia.

As far as cattle (*Bos* sp.) are concerned, it is important to note that, historically, there have been (and are) pastoralists in India that keep cattle without themselves directly engaging in agriculture (e.g. Chaudhuri 1990: 291-6). Some years ago, Walter Fairservis (1961, 1967) emphasized that, until the recent millennium, most agriculture in north-western South Asia was carried out using ad hoc systems of floodwater farming. This meant that crop-growing was confined to the fertile and well-watered margins of back-swamps, oxbow lakes, and low-lying areas in active flood plains as well as to alluvial fans, inland basins, and artificially constructed terraces on slopes where run-off could be channelled and trapped. This left immense areas of the region open to other kinds of exploitation including hunting, fishing, fowling, plant gathering, woodcutting, and pastoralism. On many occasions, Fairservis (most emphatically in 1986) emphasized what seemed to him to be the overwhelming importance of cattle pastoralism for Harappan society. We feel that, while his interpretation of the Harappan polity as cattle-based chiefdoms lacks credibility, his insistence on the importance of bovines (cattle: *Bos* sp. and secondarily water buffalo: *Bubalus* sp.) is well placed. Even so, no pastoral system exists, or is likely to have existed for very long, without agricultural products being available through one means or another, whether this be tillage, trade or raid. And it is agricultural villages, towns, and cities and not ephemeral pastoral camps that leave the more obvious archaeological traces. Thus almost all of our evidence for pastoralism in South Asia comes from the remains of settled communities.

If there are difficulties in distinguishing the bones of small bovids, the situation is equally problematic for large bovids including cattle (*Bos* sp.), water buffalo and nilgai. This has hampered our understanding of the domestication of the water buffalo in particular. Occasional remains of the wild form (*Bubalus arnee*) have been identified from Mehrgarh Period IA deposits (Meadow 1981). In Period III at that site (*c.* 4800-3300 BC), a complete horncore was uncovered (Meadow 1989a). It is long and sweeping and has basal dimensions that are intermediate between those of two wild specimens from the site of Santhli in Banaskantha district of north Gujarat (Patel and Meadow 1998a). Like Loteshwar, Santhli contains two components, microlithic (Period I) and Chalcolithic (Period II). These components are likely to be more or less contemporary with those at Loteshwar, although there are no dates from Santhli. Period I at Santhli included clusters of skulls and post-cranial material from at least eight water buffalo together with the bones of other wild animals including blackbuck. If Loteshwar during the microlithic may have been a hunting station primarily for blackbuck, Santhli seems to have been a kill site primarily for water buffalo. The complete or partially complete skeletons from such sites provide metrical and morphological data that enable the zooarchaeologist to better evaluate fragmented material from habitation and trash deposits. In particular, the Santhli water buffalo skeletons provide an important baseline with which to identify and evaluate the degree of size diminution that accompanied domestication.

During the Harappan phase, water buffalo appear to have been both hunted and kept as domestic animals. At Balakot, near the coast north-west of Karachi, a small and tightly curled horncore was found that is likely to be from a domestic buffalo (*Bubalus bubalis*) (Meadow 1979a). At Harappa in the Punjab, only a very few bovine bones can confidently be identified as coming from water buffalo even though this form is well represented in the corpus of terracotta figurines. Water buffalo are also depicted in the iconography of Harappa as hunted animals (Patel and Meadow 1998a: Fig. 2). At Dholavira in Kachchh, careful comparative osteology has permitted Patel (1997; Patel and Meadow 1998a) to identify significant numbers of water buffalo post-cranial remains. Evaluation of measurements suggests that both wild and domestic forms are represented. The large Dholavira specimens are comparable in size to those from Santhli and Mehrgarh (Patel and Meadow 1998a: Fig. 7). Generally, however, the Dholavira water buffalo were much smaller, indicating significant size diminution before the Harappan phase. Water buffalo remains have also been identified from a number of other pre- and protohistoric sites in north-western South Asia (compiled in Sahu 1988; P.K. Thomas and Joglekar 1994), but their wild or domestic status is not always clear.

Water buffalo pastoralism is different from husbanding other domestic bovids. While caprines and zebu cattle can be pastured in semi-arid areas, water buffalo require better forage and reliable sources of water for soaking their hides. They are thus likely to have been kept in areas close to permanent water sources. Therefore, it is not surprising that domestic water buffalo were maintained at Dholavira where a remarkable series of reservoirs would have fulfilled their water requirements. As for why they were being kept, there is so far no direct evidence. However, as with cattle, secondary products traction and especially milk are likely to have been important.

In sum, by the end of the third millennium the herding of domestic water buffalo, goats, sheep, and especially cattle characterized village agricultural and urban sites throughout north-western South Asia. In addition, the presence of temporary pastoral encampments has been proposed by a number of scholars. These include sites with sherd scatters and pits in Cholistan (e.g. Mughal 1997) and north Gujarat (Bhan 1994). Only a few of these have been excavated, however, and the possible keeping of animals by presumed hunter-gatherers remains an open question, as does the relationship such communities may have maintained with their settled neighbours, particularly in places like Rajasthan and north Gujarat. What also remains to be studied in a comprehensive fashion is what products besides meat were supplied by domestic stock. The evidence of miniature terracotta bullock cart frames (from Harappan sites throughout the region), yokes (from Harappan phase levels at Nausharo: J.F. Jarrige, personal communication), and ploughs (e.g. from Banawali: R.S. Bisht, personal communication) suggests that bovines were harnessed for draft. Whether they were also used for milk is not yet confirmed, nor is the use of sheep for wool. An inter-site comparative study of the remains of sheep and cattle from Harappa, Dholavira and Nausharo, however, does suggest the presence of animals of different sizes and proportions in different environmental zones during the Harappan phase (Meadow 1991; Patel 1997). This may reflect the development of separate breeds in the region by this time.

By the middle of the second millennium, two and possibly three new species had been introduced into the animal economies of South Asia (Meadow 1989d). These are the camel (probably *Camelus bactrianus*), the domestic donkey (*Equus asinus*) and the domestic horse (*Equus caballus*). None of these is traditionally used as a food animal, but all are commonly employed for transport and communications. Among the earliest evidence for all three comes from the site of Pirak located in the north Kachi plain some distance from Mehrgarh (Meadow 1979b, 1986, 1987). While faunal remains of donkeys, horses, and camels come primarily from Pirak Period III (first millennium BC), figurines of two-humped camels, horses and riders are present from Period I, probably dating between 1800 and 1500 BC (J.F. Jarrige et al. 1979). In contrast, there are no convincing depictions of either horse or camel in Harappan iconography, and the suggestion of Shaffer (1988) that the camel was an animal important for overland trade in the second half of the third millennium does not stand a close scrutiny of the evidence available to date.

Additional reasonably well-dated evidence from north-western South Asia includes depictions of horses painted on pottery from the Swat Valley (Stacul 1987: Fig. 46). Less sure is a camel skeleton from Mohenjo Daro which may possibly date to the end of the Harappan phase (Meadow 1984c) and bones of both horse and camel from the old excavations at Mohenjo Daro and Harappa (Sewell and Guha 1931; Nath 1962). The archaeological context of none of these is secure, however. The contextual integrity of camel and horse specimens reported from Lothal, Kuntasi and Shikarpur (P.K. Thomas and Joglekar 1994: Table 3) also cannot be judged in the absence of detailed discussion of the archaeology of those finds. And the dating of two camel specimens from a pit at Nagwada (Patel 1989) remains to be determined.

A good example of the problems of archaeological context is provided by a complete camel humerus from Harappa excavated in 1995 from nearly 1.5 m below the surface in association with cultural remains of the last two centuries of the third millennium BC. In spite of this association, there was concern over the integrity of the context and a radiocarbon determination was made on the bone itself. The result was *c.* AD 690 (calibrated), clearly indicating the intrusive nature of the specimen and confirming the high degree of disturbance characteristic of the upper levels at Harappa (Meadow 1998).

A number of claims have been made for the presence of the domestic horse in South Asia before the beginning of the second millennium BC. Many of these are reviewed by Sahu (1988: 59-60, 224), R.S. Sharma (1993) and Singh (1995), but most cannot be substantiated because of the absence of proper osteological, contextual, and temporal documentation. These are essential because of the presence in north-western South Asia of the khur (*Equus hemionus*). Bones of a large khur overlap in size those of a small horse, while bones of a small khur overlap in size those of a donkey. In addition, supposed morphological differences between the different equid taxa are not as clear-cut as previously believed. One collection that has been documented and discussed extensively is that from Surkotada, a late third and early second millennium site in Kachchh, Gujarat, India (A.K. Sharma 1974, 1990, 1993; Meadow 1987; Bökönyi 1997; Meadow and Patel 1997). While we do not find identifications of true horse at Surkotada to be convincing, the prolonged and sometimes highly technical debate on the subject shows that study of this material is not always straightforward. We face with equid identifications the same problems we do with small bovids and bovines.

On the basis of present evidence, it seems that horses, donkeys and camels came into South Asia from the north-west perhaps as early as the end of the Harappan phase and became widespread only by the second millennium BC, complementing the existing complex of domestic bovids and helping to change the economic and social face of the subcontinent. Horses were useful for transport, communication, raiding and warfare although keeping them has always required special skills under conditions of extreme heat and humidity. Historically most horses were kept by the elite, while the donkey was very much a work animal of the village. Camels have traditionally been used for long distance trade and for carrying the households of transhumants, roles that they probably took over from cattle, although cattle are still used by people throughout South Asia as transport animals. The early camels were probably of the two-humped variety (Meadow 1984c), supplemented only later by dromedaries with which they were cross-bred to produce a particularly strong caravan animal.

CONCLUSION

Our understanding of prehistoric pastoralism in north-western South Asia has advanced considerably since 1947. Beginning in the mid-1950s increasing amounts of archaeofaunal material have been recovered from archaeological sites, analysed and published, however incompletely. These data indicate that cattle (*Bos* sp.) have long been the most important pastoral animal in the region followed by sheep. As noted above, however, we lack a great deal of information about how these animals were husbanded and for what purposes they were kept. The history of the development of pastoral systems remains sketchy at best.

An important development in South Asian archaeology is the increasing evidence for the establishment of settled communities throughout much of the north-western region by the end of the fourth millennium BC. While it has long been known that such localities existed in the area of what is now Pakistan, many recent excavations have led to their identification in Saurashtra (e.g. Padri and Prabhas Patan), north Gujarat (e.g. Loteshwar and possibly Nagwada and Santhli [burial pottery]), Kachchh (possibly the early levels of Dholavira), Rajasthan (e.g. Balathal and, possibly Kalibangan), and Haryana (e.g. Kunal and, possibly Banawali) (Shinde 1992 and personal communication; Dhavalikar and Possehl 1992; Sonawane and Ajithprasad 1994; Khatri and Acharya 1995; Misra et al. 1995; Misra 1997; Bisht 1993 and personal communication). We do not believe that it is now necessary to posit the Harappan Civilization as having been the ultimate source of the Chalcolithic culture(s) of peninsular India (e.g. Dhavalikar 1994; Shinde 1994). Instead it was farming and herding practices developed in areas peripheral to the Indus Valley proper that are more likely to have established the foundation for settlements to the east and south. Thus it is essential that we understand the forms of both agriculture and pastoralism that developed in these areas. This is a task that has only just begun, as has our understanding of the same phenomena at the same time in the Indus Valley itself.

As for the earliest evidence of pastoralism, we have only Mehrgarh. But, as indicated above, even that site does not take us back to the very beginnings of pastoralism (or of agriculture) in South Asia. Indeed, there is a remarkable dearth of understanding of Early Holocene animal exploitation anywhere in the subcontinent. This can be traced to an apparent absence of sites identified as belonging to this time period. Either the sites have not been found or they have not been dated. Dealing with this evident gap in knowledge should be a priority for future archaeological research.

What we have currently for South Asia in general and for the north-western portion in particular is a patchy archaeological framework with little depth of understanding for any single region, let alone for the entire area. The study of animal remains continues to be rather haphazard and the results are only now beginning to be integrated into the broader archaeological picture. Questions of archaeological provenance and sample integrity are also just beginning to be addressed. The greatest need now for those who analyse animal remains in the South Asian context is that they understand the implications of their work for the archaeology of the region. This demands that results of analyses be not just offered in an undigested form but be critically evaluated, interpreted and presented in such a way that archaeologists understand their worth and significance.

ACKNOWLEDGEMENTS

We wish to acknowledge the support for our research provided by those with whom we work. In particular, RHM wishes to thank J.F. Jarrige, C. Jarrige and J.M. Kenoyer for years of friendship and collegiality, and AKP wishes to thank R.S. Bisht for his unflagging encouragement, support and care. We also gratefully acknowledge the contributions of many workers—Pakistani and Indian—who have made our study of bones both possible and enjoyable.

REFERENCES

Alur, K.R. 1990. *Studies in Indian Archaeology and Palaeontology*. Dharwad: Shrihari Prakashana.

Badam, G.L. 1979. *Pleistocene Fauna of India*. Pune: Deccan College.

Belcher, W.R. 1997. Marine and Riverine Resource Use During the Indus Valley Tradition: a Preliminary Comparison of Fish Remains from Balakot and Harappa, in *South Asian Archaeology 1995* (R. Allchin and B. Allchin Eds.), pp. 173-85. New Delhi: Oxford-IBH.

——— 1998. Fish Exploitation of the Baluchistan and Indus Valley Traditions: an Ethno-archaeological Approach to the Study of Fish Remains. Ph.D. Dissertation. Madison: Department of Anthropology, University of Wisconsin.

Bhan, K.K. 1994. Cultural Development of the Prehistoric Period in North Gujarat with Reference to Western India, *South Asian Studies* 10: 71-90.

Bisht, R.S. 1993. Excavations at Banawali: 1974-77, in *Harappan Civilization* (G.L. Possehl Ed.), pp. 113-24. New Delhi: Oxford-IBH.

Bökönyi, S. 1997. Horse Remains from the Prehistoric Site of Surkotada, Kutch, 3rd Millennium B.C., *South Asian Studies* 13: 297-306.

Bradley, D.G., R.T. Loftus, P. Cunningham and D. MacHugh 1998. Genetics and Domestic Cattle Origins, *Evolutionary Anthropology* 6 (3): 79-86.

Caloi, L. and Compagnoni, B. 1976. Bone Remains from the Site of Loebanr III (Swat, Pakistan), *East and West* (New Series) 26 (1-2): 31-43.

Chaudhuri, K.N. 1990. *Asia Before Europe*. Cambridge: Cambridge University Press.

Clason, A.T. 1974. Archaeozoological Study in India, in *South Asian Archaeology 1973* (J.E. Van Lohuizen-de Leeuw and J.J.M. Ubaghs Eds.), pp. 78-89. Leiden: E.J. Brill.

——— 1977. Wild and Domestic Animals in Prehistoric and Early Historic India, *East and West* (New Series) 30 (3): 241-89.

Clutton-Brock, J. 1965. *Excavations at Langhnaj: 1944-63. Part II: The Fauna*. Pune: Deccan College, Building Centenary and Silver Jubilee Series 27.

Compagnoni, B. 1979. Preliminary Report on the Faunal Remains from Protohistoric Settlements of Swat, in *South Asian Archaeology 1977* (M. Taddei Ed.), pp. 697-700. Naples: Istituto Universitario Orientale, Seminario di Studi Asiatici.

Dhavalikar, M.K. 1994. Early Farming Communities of Central India, *Man and Environment* XIX (1-2): 159-68.

Dhavalikar, M.K. and G.L. Possehl 1992. The Pre-Harappan Period at Prabhas Patan and the Pre-Harappan Phase in Gujarat, *Man and Environment* XVII (1): 71-8.

Desse, J. 1995. Archéo-Ichthyologie du Golfe Arabique et de l'océan Indien, in *Archaeozoology of the Near East II* (H. Buitenhuis and H.-P. Uerpmann Eds.), pp. 72-8. Leiden: Backhuys.

Duerst, J.U. 1908. Animal Remains from the Excavations at Anau and the Horse in its Relation to the Races of Domestic Horses, in *Explorations in Turkestan, Expedition of 1904, Prehistoric Civilizations of Anau* (R. Pumpelly Ed.), pp. 341-442. Washington, D.C.: Carnegie Institution of Washington 2.

Fairservis, W.A. Jr. 1956. *Excavations in the Quetta Valley, West Pakistan*. Anthropological Papers of the American Museum of Natural History 45 (2): 165-402. New York: American Museum of Natural History.

——— 1961. *The Harappan Civilization: New Evidence and More Theory*. American Museum Novitates 2055: 1-35. New York: American Museum of Natural History.

——— 1967. *The Origin, Character, and Decline of an Early Civilization*. American Museum Novitates 2302: 1-48. New York: American Museum of Natural History.

——— 1986. Cattle and the Harappan Chiefdoms of the Indus Valley, *Expedition* 28 (2): 43-50.

George, J.C. 1953. Animal Remains from Baroda, in *Baroda Through the Ages, Being the Report of an Excavation Conducted in the Baroda Area, 1951-1952* (B. Subbarao Ed.), p. 90. Baroda: the M.S. University of Baroda, Archaeology Series 1.

——— 1955. Identification of Bones, in *Report on the Excavations at Nasik and Jorwe, 1950-51* (H.D. Sankalia and S.B. Deo Eds.), pp. 142-6. Pune: Deccan College.

Grigson, C. 1985. *Bos indicus* and *Bos namadicus* and the Problem of Autochthonous Domestication in India, in *Recent Advances in Indo-Pacific Prehistory* (V.N. Misra and P. Bellwood Eds.), pp. 425-8. New Delhi: Oxford-IBH.

——— 1989. Size and Sex: Evidence for the Domestication of Cattle in the Near East, in *The Beginnings of Agriculture* (A. Milles, D. Williams and N. Gardner Eds.), pp. 77-109. Oxford: BAR International Series 496.

IAR. Indian Archaeology—A Review. New Delhi: Annual Bulletin of the Archaeological Survey of India.

Jarrige, C., J.-F. Jarrige, R.H. Meadow and G. Quivron 1995. *Mehrgarh 1974-1985: from Neolithic Times to the Indus Civilization*. Karachi: Department of Culture and Tourism, Government of Sindh, Pakistan.

Jarrige, J.-F. 1999. Mehrgarh Neolithic: New Excavations, in *South Asian Archaeology 1997* (M. Taddei Ed.). Rome: IsMEO (in press).

Jarrige, J.-F., M. Santoni and J.F. Enault 1979. *Fouilles de Pirak*. Paris: Diffusion de Boccard.

Khatri, J.S. and M. Acharya 1995. Kunal: a New Indus-Saraswati Site, *Puratattva* 25: 84-6.

Loftus, R.T., D.E. MacHugh, D.G. Bradley, P.M. Sharp and P. Cunningham 1994. Evidence for Two Independent Domestications of Cattle, *Proceedings of the National Academy of Sciences USA* 91: 2757-61.

Meadow, R.H. 1979a. Prehistoric Subsistence at Balakot : Initial Consideration of the Faunal Remains, in *South Asian Archaeology 1977* (M. Taddei Ed.), pp. 275-315. Naples: Istituto Universitario Orientale, Seminario di Studi Asiatici.

——— 1979b. A Preliminary Note on the Faunal Remains from Pirak, in *Fouilles de Pirak* (J.F. Jarrige, M. Santoni and J.-F. Enault Compilers), p. 334. Paris: Diffusion de Boccard.

——— 1981. Early Animal Domestication in South Asia: a First Report of the Faunal Remains from Mehrgarh, Pakistan, in *South Asian Archaeology 1979* (H. Härtel Ed.), pp. 143-79. Berlin: Dietrich Reimer Verlag.

——— 1984a. Animal Domestication in the Middle East: a View from the Eastern Margin, in *Animals and Archaeology 3: Early Herders and their Flocks* (J. Clutton-Brock and C. Grigson Ed.), pp. 309-37. Oxford: BAR International Series 202.

——— 1984b. Notes on the Faunal Remains from Mehrgarh, Pakistan, with a Focus on Cattle (*Bos*), in *South Asian Archaeology 1981* (B. Allchin Ed.), pp. 34-40. Cambridge: Cambridge University Press.

——— 1984c. A Camel Skeleton from Wheeler's Excavations at Mohenjo-daro, in *Frontiers of the Indus Civilization* (B.B. Lal and S.P. Gupta Eds.), pp. 137-40. New Delhi: Books & Books.

——— 1986. Faunal exploitation in the Greater Indus Valley: a Review of Recent Work to 1980, in *Studies in the Archaeology of India and Pakistan* (J. Jacobson Ed.), pp. 43-64. New Delhi: Oxford-IBH.

——— 1987. Faunal Exploitation Patterns in Eastern Iran and Baluchistan: a Review of Recent Investigations, in *Orientalia Iosephi Tucci Memoriae Dicata* (G. Gnoli and L. Lanciotti Eds.), pp. 881-916. Rome: Istituto Italiano per il Medio ed Estremo Oriente.

——— 1989a. A Note on the Distribution of Faunal Remains During the Later Periods at Mehrgarh (Baluchistan, Pakistan), in *South Asian Archaeology 1985* (K. Frifelt and P. Sörensen Eds.), pp. 167-75. London: Curzon Press.

——— 1989b. Osteological Evidence for the Process of Animal Domestication, in *The Walking Larder* (J. Clutton-Brock Ed.), pp. 80-90. London: Allen and Unwin.

——— 1989c. Prehistoric Wild Sheep and Sheep Domestication on the Eastern Margin of the Middle East, in *Early Animal Domestication and Its Cultural Context* (P.J. Crabtree, D.V. Campana and K. Ryan Eds.), pp. 24-36. Philadelphia: University Museum, University of Pennsylvania, MASCA.

——— 1989d. Continuity and Change in the Agriculture of the Greater Indus Valley: the Paleoethnobotanical and Zooarchaeological Evidence, in *Old Problems and New Perspectives in the Archaeology of South Asia* (J.M. Kenoyer Ed.), pp. 61-74. Madison: Department of Anthropology, University of Wisconsin.

——— 1991. Faunal Remains and Urbanism at Harappa, in *Harappa Excavations 1986-1990: a Multidisciplinary Approach to Third Millennium Urbanism* (R.H. Meadow Ed.), pp. 89-106. Madison, Wisconsin : Prehistory Press.

——— 1992. In-Conclusive Remarks on Pastoralism, Nomadism and Other Animal Related Matters, in *Pastoralism in the Levant: Archaeological Materials in Anthropological Perspectives* (O. Bar-Yosef and A. Khazanov Eds.), pp. 261-9. Madison, Wisconsin: Prehistory Press.

——— 1993a. The Past, Present, and Future of Bioarchaeological Studies in Pakistan with Specific Reference to Mohenjodaro and the Indus Civilization, *Pakistan Archaeology* 28: 183-215.

——— 1993b. Animal Domestication in the Middle East: a Revised View from the Eastern Margin, in *Harappan Civilization* (G.L. Possehl Ed.), pp. 295-320. New Delhi: Oxford-IBH.

——— 1996. The Origins and Spread of Agriculture and Pastoralism in Northwestern South Asia, in *The Origins and Spread of Agriculture and Pastoralism in Eurasia* (D.R. Harris Ed.), pp. 390-412. London: UCL Press.

——— 1998. Pre- and Proto-historic Agricultural and Pastoral Transformations in Northwestern South Asia, *The Review of Archaeology* 19 (2): 12-21.

——— 1999. Zooarchaeology, in *Archaeological Method and Theory: an Encyclopedia* (L. Ellis Ed.), pp. 675-82. New York: Garfield Publishing.

Meadow, R.H. and A.K. Patel 1997. A Comment on 'Horse Remains from Surkotada' by Sándor Bökönyi, *South Asian Studies* 13: 308-15.

Misra, V.N. 1997. Balathal: a Chalcolithic Settlement in Mewar, Rajasthan, India: Results of First Three Seasons' Excavations, *South Asian Studies* 13: 251-73.

Misra, V.N., V. Shinde, R.K. Mohanty, K. Dalal, A. Mishra, L. Pandey and J. Kharakwal 1995. Excavations at Balathal: Their Contribution to the Chalcolithic and Iron Age Cultures of Mewar, Rajasthan, *Man and Environment* XX (1): 57-80.

Mughal, M.R. 1997. *Ancient Cholistan: Archaeology and Architecture*. Rawalpindi: Ferozsons.

Nath, B. 1962. Remains of Horse and Indian Elephant from Prehistoric Site of Harappa, *Proceedings of 1st All-India Congress of Zoology* 2: 1-14.

Paddayya, K. 1994. Investigation of Man-Environment Relationships in Indian Archaeology: Some Theoretical Considerations, *Man and Environment* XIX (1-2): 1-28.

Patel, A.K. 1989. Vertebrate Archaeofauna from Nagwada: a Preliminary Study. M.A. dissertation. Baroda: Department of Archaeology and Ancient History, Faculty of Arts, the M.S. University of Baroda.

——— 1997. The Pastoral Economy of Dholavira: a First Look at Animals and Urban Life in Third Millennium Kutch, in *South Asian Archaeology 1995* (R. Allchin and B. Allchin Eds.), pp. 101-13. New Delhi: Oxford-IBH.

——— 1998. From Loteshwar to Dholavira: the Development of Pastoralism in North Gujarat and Kutch. Paper Presented at the Twenty-Seventh Annual Conference on South Asia. Madison: University of Wisconsin, 16 October 1998.

Patel, A.K. and R.H. Meadow, 1998a. The Exploitation of Wild and Domestic Water Buffalo in Prehistoric Northwestern South Asia, in *Archaeozoology of the Near East III* (H. Buitenhuis, L. Bartosiewicz and A.M. Choyke Eds.), pp. 180-199. Groningen: Centre for Archaeological Research and Consultancy, Rijksuniversiteit Groningen.

Patel, A.K. and R.H. Meadow 1998b. The Problem of Blackbuck (*Antilope cervicapra*) and Gazelle

(*Gazella bennetti*) in the Identification of Faunal Remains from Northwestern South Asia. Paper Presented at the Fourth International Conference on the Archaeozoology of Southwest Asia (and Adjacent Areas). Paris: Museum National d'Histoire Naturelle, 29 June 1998.

Poulain-Josien, T. 1964. Etude de la Faune, in *Fouilles d'Amri* (by J.-M. Casal), pp. 164-9. Paris: Librairie C. Klincksieck.

Prasad, B. 1934. Animal Remains:Appendix A, in *Explorations in Sind* (N.G. Majumdar), pp. 155-7. New Delhi: Memoirs of the Archaeological Survey of India 48.

——— 1936. *Animal Remains from Harappa*. Delhi: Memoirs of the Archaeological Survey of India 51.

Sahu, B.P. 1988. *From Hunters to Breeders*. Delhi: Anamika Prakashan.

Sankalia, H.D. 1978. *Born for Archaeology: an Autobiography*. Delhi: B.R. Publishing Corporation.

Sewell, R.B.S. and B.S. Guha, 1931. Zoological Remains, in *Mohenjo-daro and the Indus Civilization* (J.H. Marshall Ed.), pp. 649-73. London: A. Probsthain.

Shah, D.R. 1971. A Note on Unmodified Animal Remains from Bagor, *The Eastern Anthropologist* 24 (3): 319-20.

Sharma, A.K. 1974. Evidence of Horse from the Harappan Settlement at Surkotada, *Puratattva* 7: 75-6.

——— 1990. Animal Bone Remains, in *Excavation at Surkotada 1971-72 and Exploration in Kutch* (J.P. Joshi), pp. 372-83. New Delhi: Memoirs of the Archaeological Survey of India 87.

——— 1993. The Harappan Horse was Buried Under the Dunes of ..., *Puratattva* 23: 30-4.

Sharma, R.S. 1993. The Aryan Problem and the Horse, *Social Scientist* 21 (7-8): 3-16.

Shaffer, J.G. 1988. One Hump or Two: the Impact of the Camel on Harappan Society, in *Orientalia Iosephi Tucci Memoriae Dicata* (G. Gnoli and L. Lanciotti Eds.), pp. 333-48. Rome: Istituto Italiano per il Medio ed Estremo Oriente.

Shinde, V. 1992. Excavations at Padri 1990-91: a Preliminary Report, *Man and Environment* XVII (1):79-86.

——— 1994. The Deccan Chalcolithic: a Recent Perspective, *Man and Environment* XIX (1-2): 169-78.

Singh, B. 1995. *The Vedic Harappans*. New Delhi: Aditya Prakashan.

Sonawane, V.H. and P. Ajithprasad 1994. Harappa Culture and Gujarat, *Man and Environment* XIX (1-2): 129-39.

Stacul, G. 1987. *Prehistoric and Protohistoric Swat, Pakistan*. Rome: Istituto Italiano per il Medio ed estremo Oriente.

Subbarao, B. 1953. *Baroda Through the Ages, Being the Report of an Excavation Conducted in the Baroda Area, 1951-1952*. Baroda: Faculty of Arts, the M.S. University of Baroda, Archaeology Series 1.

Thomas, K.D. 1981. Palaeoecological Studies in the Bannu Basin: the Sources of Evidence, in *South Asian Archaeology 1981* (H. Härtel Ed.), pp. 227-32. Berlin: Dietrich Reimer Verlag.

Thomas, P.K. 1975. Role of Animals in the Food Economy of the Mesolithic Culture of Western and Central India, in *Archaeozoological Studies* (A.T. Clason Ed.), pp. 322-8. Amsterdam: North Holland Publishing.

——— 1977. Archaeozoological Aspects of the Prehistoric Cultures of Western India. Ph.D. Dissertation. Pune: University of Poona.

Thomas, P.K. and P.P. Joglekar 1994. Holocene Faunal Studies in India, *Man and Environment* XIX (1-2): 179-203.

Thomas, P.K., P.P. Joglekar, V.D. Misra, J.N. Pandey and J.N. Pal 1995. Preliminary Report of the Faunal Remains from Damdama, *Man and Environment* XX (1): 29-36.

Turnbull, P. 1983. Study of Clams and Snails from Archaeological Sites, in *Animals and Archaeology: 2. Shell Middens, Fishes and Birds* (C. Grigson and J. Clutton-Brock Eds.), pp. 53-65. Oxford: BAR International Series 183.

Uerpmann, H.-P. 1979. *Probleme der Neolithisierung des Mittelmeerraums*. Wiesbaden: Ludwig Reichert Verlag.

——— 1987. *The Ancient Distribution of Ungulate Mammals in the Middle East and Northeast Africa*. Wiesbaden: Ludwig Reichert Verlag.

Investigations into the Archaeofauna of Harappan Sites in Western India

P.K. THOMAS

INTRODUCTION

A number of Harappan sites are reported and excavated from western India, however, our knowledge of the man-animal relationship of this period is confined only to a few of the recently excavated sites from this region. The faunal material collected/selected from some of the earlier excavations have not been deliberated scientifically resulting in the permanent loss of the scientific potential of the biological material. However, the last two decades have witnessed a change in the traditional approach of the archaeologists eventually emerging into multidisciplinary research in the field of archaeology. Therefore, some of the recent excavations in western India especially in Gujarat, have brought out significant account of the faunal assemblage of the Harappan period. In the light of the present methodological approach the faunal remains from some of the formerly excavated sites may have to be restudied to get a comprehensive picture of the period under discussion. When some of the older faunal reports are compared with the recent studies, an ambiguity is unavoidable especially pertaining to the stratigraphy of the site, contextual details, identification of species, quantification of faunal remains, and so on.

The excavations have revealed a wide spectrum of animal species associated with the Harappan Culture. It is also interesting to note that a couple of the earliest archaeofaunal reports from the subcontinent belong to the Harappan sites of Mohenjo Daro (Sewell and Guha 1931) and Harappa (Prashad 1936). Faunal assemblage from some of the recently excavated sites such as Kuntasi, Shikarpur, Orio Timbo, Surkotada, Nageshwar, etc., has brought to light interesting perspective on ancient subsistence based on animals and to a certain extent the environment of the region during the Harappan period. In spite of the limited nature of some of the excavations, an astounding number of animal species are reported from Harappan sites. A majority of these animals consisting of both domestic and wild, have contributed to the food economy and wealth of the Harappans of western India (for details see Thomas et al. 1994, 1995, 1997). Animals from different habitats such as the terrestrial, avian and aquatic were exploited for various purposes. The evidence also suggests the significance of animal by-products as well as animal power in the Harappan economy (Thomas 1989).

DOMESTIC ANIMALS UTILIZED FOR FOOD AND OTHER RESOURCES

About 80 per cent of the faunal assemblage from any of the Harappan sites belongs to domestic animals. A significant amount of the animal protein was obtained from domestic animals such as cattle, buffalo, sheep, goats and pig. Invariably cattle bones have been identified from all the excavated Harappan sites (see Table 1) and often they accounted for more than 60 per cent of the total faunal assemblage.

In addition to the regular supply of meat to the inhabitants, cattle also helped in agricultural operations, and as draught animals. One of the earliest evidence of their use as draught animals is depicted at Mohenjo Daro in the form of a toy cart pulled by bullocks (Mackay 1931). The ageing and sexing of cattle remains at Harappan sites have revealed that for much of the animal protein young and sub-adult males were used. The recent faunal studies at Kuntasi (Thomas and Joglekar 1990; Thomas et al. 1996, 1997) and Shikarpur (Thomas et al. 1995) have revealed two peaks in the culling of these animals; a first peak of young and sub-adult animals in the age group of 1.5 to 3 years and the second peak of adult and senile animals of the age group of 4-8 years. Maintaining these animals for a longer period of time suggests that other than breeding, the by-products of cattle and animal power were also significant in the Harappan economy. The socio-economic importance of this animal can be further deduced from the clay figurines of humped cattle and their depictions on seals/sealings from a vast majority of Harappan and later cultural periods all over India. The very docile nature of the animal and the multifold utility of cattle may have been the reason for their preponderance at many of the protohistoric sites. Therefore, cattle pastoralism was one of the main economic pursuits of the Harappans (Possehl 1979), though there were industrial and trade centres among these sites. Rissman also (1985) identifies Post-Urban small seasonal cattle pastoral camps at sites such as Oriyo and Nesadi (Mehta 1984).

In the subsistence economy the second important animals were the sheep and goats which have been identified from all the Harappan sites (Table 1). From the faunal assemblage it is rather difficult to distinguish between the bones of sheep and goats because of their close morphological similarities (Boessneck 1969). Therefore, the bones of sheep and goat have often been referred to as belonging to sheep/goats. However, at sites like Shikarpur (Thomas et al. 1995) and Kuntasi (Thomas et al. 1997), compared to sheep more goat remains were found. Probably it is befitting to state that sheep is a grazer, and goat a browser, and the latter is more adapted to different environmental conditions. Unlike cattle, sheep and goats were killed at an young age (1-2 years) suggesting that these animals were primarily kept for meat rather than for their by-products like wool and milk. In general the bones of sheep/goats accounted for about 10 per cent in the total faunal assemblage. The collection comprises both meat-bearing and non-meat-bearing parts in an almost equal proportion, which indicate rearing and slaughtering of these animals within the settlement.

Buffalo was one of the other bovids which supported the food economy of the Harappans. Buffalo bones are sparse in the faunal collection, nevertheless, apparently from the size of this animal, it provided enough of animal protein to the Harappans. From the fragmentary faunal remains, it is difficult to distinguish between the bones of cattle and buffalo unless specific skeletal parts are available for identification (Thomas 1977). However, to a certain extent they can be separated out on the basis of metrical analysis (Joglekar 1991). If the evidence from Kuntasi and Shikarpur is any indication the bones of this animal represent 5-10 per cent in the total faunal assemblage. Unlike cattle, the elaborate habitat of buffalo has also to be considered. Therefore, for the ancient population, management of cattle was easier than that of the buffalo. This could be the reason for the scant representation of the buffalo at the Harappan sites. In the Harappan context evidence is lacking to associate this animal with agricultural operations and traction. However, buffalo was part and parcel of the Harappan animal husbandry and it has contributed significantly to the food economy.

Domestic pigs are identified (2-3 per cent) at Harappan sites mostly from the Mature Harappan and Post-Urban periods. At sites such as Kuntasi and Shikarpur there was hardly any representation of pigs in the lower strata of the Harappan deposit. A generalization may not be possible here since stratigraphical details of the other Harappan sites are not known. Both at Kuntasi and Shikarpur, piglets were killed in large numbers. However, the real domestic status of this animal in Harappan stock-raising is yet to be ascertained.

The Harappans also kept pet animals like dog and cat. Dog bones were found in almost all the sites. However, domestic cats are identified only at a few sites (Table 1). Since the bones of these animals do not exhibit any human subsistence activity, they were not part of the diet, rather these bones may have been accumulated among the food refuse because of the scavenging and predatory activities of animals at sites (Thomas and Joglekar 1994). This also reveals to a certain extent the site formation process. Nevertheless, dog is important as a pet, a watch animal and its role in the hunting pursuit of man is unmatched. Being social and territorial in habit, dogs protect domestic herds and settlements. Therefore, directly or indirectly, though pets, these animals have contributed to the socio-economy of the Harappans.

Camel bones are reported from six of the Harappan sites mentioned in Table 1. However, their convincing association with the Mature Harappan Culture is a matter of controversy (Meadow 1984; Sathe and Atre 1989). Also whether it was the Dromedary (*Camelus dromedarius*) or the Bactrian (*Camelus bactrianus*) species is another issue which has been debated (Meadow 1993). A calcaneum of a camel was reported from the slope of the eastern side of the main mound at Kuntasi. At present it is difficult to establish its cultural context, since the sample had no stratigraphical control. The identification of camel at Rojdi is also enigmatic (Kane 1989).

Likewise, the identification of the equid bones from Harappan sites is more complicated, especially the horse (*Equus caballus*) remains. As per record horse bones have been reported from eight of the nineteen Harappan sites mentioned in Table 1.

The identification of true horse bones from the Mature Harappan period is questioned especially, the horse remains from Surkotada (Bökönyi 1997; Meadow and Patel 1997; Anthony 1997). The stratigraphical and contextual details of the finds were often neglected in the faunal report thereby, creating ambiguity in dating these remains (Meadow 1993). In India wild horses are not reported from the Pleistocene or post-Pleistocene deposits. Therefore, it is believed that the domestic horse was introduced into India from the area of its existing wild counterparts, where early domestication of these animals had taken

TABLE 1. MAMMALIAN FAUNA AT HARAPPAN SITES

	MHJ	HPA	KLB	RPR	BAR	AGR	RGR	LTL	KTS	SKD	NGR	OTB	KPR	RJD	MVN	BKT	SKR	PDR	DHV
Domestic																			
Canis familiaris	+	+	+	+	-	+	+	+	+	+	+	-	-	+	+	+	+	+	+?
Felis domesticus	-	+	-	-	-	-	-	-	+	-	-	-	-	+?	-	-	-	-	-
Camelus dromedarius	+	+	+	-	-	-	-	-	+	+	-	-	-	+?	-	-	-	-	-
Equus caballus	+	+	+?	-	-	-	-	+	+	+	-	-	-	-	+	-	+	-	-
Equus asinus	-	+	+	-	-	-	+	-	+	+	-	-	-	-	-	-	-	-	-
Sus domesticus	+	+	+	+	+	+	+	+	+	+	+	+	+	+	-	+	+	+	+?
Bos indicus	+	+	+	+	+	+	+	+	+	+	+	+	+	+	+	+	+	+	+
Bubalus bubalis	+	+	+	+	+	+	+	+	+	-	+	+	+	+	-	+	+	+	+
Ovis aries	+	+	+	+	+	+	+	+	+	+	+	+	+	+	+	+	+	+	+
Capra hircus	-	+	+	+	+	+	+	+	+	+	+	+	+	+	+	+	+	+	+
Wild																			
Presbytis entellus	-	-	-	-	-	-	-	-	+?	-	-	-	-	-	-	-	-	-	-
Cuon alpinus	-	-	-	-	-	-	-	-	-	-	-	-	-	+	-	-	-	-	-
Canis aureus	-	+	-	-	-	-	-	+	-	+	-	-	-	+	-	-	+	-	+?
Canis lupus	-	+	-	-	-	-	-	-	+?	+	-	-	-	-	-	-	-	+	-
Hyaena hyaena	-	-	-	-	-	-	-	-	+	-	-	-	-	-	-	-	-	-	-
Felis chaus	-	-	-	-	-	-	-	-	+	-	-	-	-	-	-	-	-	+	-
Felis libyca	-	-	-	-	-	-	-	-	-	-	-	-	-	+?	-	-	-	-	-
Elephas maximus	+	+	+	+	+	-	-	+	-	+	-	-	-	+?	-	-	-	-	-
Rhinoceros unicornis	-	+	+	-	-	-	-	+	+	+	-	+?	+	-	-	-	+	-	-
Equus hemionus	-	-	-	-	-	-	-	-	+	+	-	-	-	+	-	-	+	-	+
Sus scrofa	-	-	-	-	-	-	-	-	+	-	-	-	+	+	+	+	+	+	+?
Bos sp.	-	-	-	-	-	-	-	-	+	-	-	-	-	-	-	-	+	-	-
Bubalus arnee	-	-	-	-	-	-	-	-	+	-	-	-	-	-	-	-	+	-	-
Muntiacus muntjak	-	-	-	-	-	-	-	-	+	-	-	-	-	-	-	-	+	-	-
Cervus unicolor	+	-	-	-	-	-	+	+	+	-	+	+?	-	+?	-	-	+	-	-
Cervus duvauceli	-	+	+	-	-	+	-	-	+?	-	-	-	-	+?	+	-	-	-	-
Cervus elaphus hanglu	+	-	-	-	-	-	-	-	-	-	-	-	-	-	-	-	-	-	-
Axis axis	+	-	+	-	-	+	-	+	+	+	+	-	-	+	+	+	+	+	-
Axis porcinus	+	-	-	-	-	-	-	-	+	-	-	-	-	+	-	-	+	-	-
Boselaphus tragocamelus	-	-	-	-	-	-	-	+	+	-	+	+	-	+	-	+	+	+	-
Gazella bennetti	-	-	-	-	-	-	-	-	+	-	+	+?	+	+?	-	+	+	-	+
Tetracerus quadricornis	-	-	-	-	-	-	-	-	+	-	-	-	-	+?	-	+	+	+	-
Antilope cervicapra	-	-	-	-	-	-	-	-	+	-	+	+?	-	+?	-	+	+	+	+
Hystrix indica	-	-	-	-	-	-	-	-	+	-	-	-	-	+	-	-	-	-	-
Suncus stoliczkanus	+	-	-	-	-	-	-	-	-	+	-	-	-	-	-	-	-	-	-
Lepus nigricollis	-	-	-	-	-	-	-	+	+	+	+	+	-	+	-	+	+	-	+
Herpestes edwardsi	+	+	-	-	-	-	-	+	+	+	-	-	-	-	-	+	-	+	-
Rattus rattus	+	+	-	+	-	-	-	+	-	+	+	-	-	+	-	+	+	+	-
Cervids (deer)	-	-	-	-	-	-	-	-	-	-	-	-	-	-	-	-	-	-	+

NOTES:

+	=	Presence	KTS	-	Kuntasi (Thomas et al. 1996)
-	=	Absence	SKD	-	Surkotada (Sharma 1990)
?	=	Species doubtful	NGR	-	Nageshwar (Shah and Bhan 1992)
MHJ	-	Mohenjo Daro (Sewel and Guha 1931)	OTB	-	Oriyo Timbo (Rissman 1985)
HPA	-	Harappa (Prashad 1936)	KPR	-	Khanpur (Thomas 1977)
KLB	-	Kalibangan (Sahu 1988)	RJD	-	Rojdi (Kane 1989)
RPR	-	Rupar (Sharma 1989)	MVN	-	Malvan (Alur 1990)
BAR	-	Bara (Nath 1968)	BKT	-	Babarkot (Ryan, in press)
AGR	-	Alamgirpur (Sahu 1988)	SKR	-	Shikarpur (Thomas et al. 1995)
RGR	-	Rangpur (Nath 1963)	PDR	-	Padri (Joglekar 1997)

place. According to some the arrival of the horse in India is linked with the so called 'Aryan invasion' (Parpola 1988). Anthony (1997) is of the opinion that 'The subject has been complicated by the politicized history of the study of the Aryans and their migrations'.

The close osteological similarities existing between the equid species like *Equus caballus* (horse), *Equus asinus* (donkey) and *Equus hemionus* (onager or khur), and the hybrid animals (mule/henny) make the precise species identification rather difficult from fragmentary and scarce remains of these animals from archaeological sites. Therefore, it is prudent to reconsider some of the earlier identifications of equid bones carried out for Harappan sites in light of the present methodological approach. Horse remains identified in the Harappan context are often the lower limb extremities and dentition. Since the animal was not utilized in the regular diet of the Harappans the scarcity of the bones is understandable. However, the absence of other post-cranial bones are also intriguing. From Kuntasi and Shikarpur bones of wild ass (*Equus hemionus*) with cut marks and charring have been found, suggesting hunting of these animals for food. Wild ass bones were also found at sites such as Surkotada, Rojdi and Dholavira.

Also it is interesting to note that in the other protohistoric cultures outside the domain of the Indus Civilization such as the Neolithic, Chalcolithic and Iron Age, the representation of horse bones was identical with that of the Harappan sites. The Megalithic human graves in the Vidarbha region of Maharashtra have conceded evidence for partial burials of horses. The upper and lower jaw dentition with horse bits and the lower extremities of the limb bones were found in a few of the excavated burials. In addition, the Megalithic settlement sites such as Naikund and Bhagimohari (Thomas 1992) and the Chalcolithic site of Inamgaon (Thomas 1988) have yielded meager evidence of post-cranial bones of the horse with cut marks and charring along with other food refuse. Probably here horses were sacrificed and after offering to the dead, the rest of the body may have been consumed at or outside the settlement in a death ceremony. In the Harappan context also this may have to be considered when one is dealing with Harappan horse remains either from the cemetery or from the settlement areas.

WILD ANIMALS

From the list of wild mammals given in Table 1, it appears that a wide spectrum of mammalian species have been exploited in the food economy of the Harappans. A variety of deer, antelopes and the smaller mammals such as hare (*Lepus nigricollis*) and porcupine (*Hystrix indica*) are common at almost all the sites and much of the animal protein from the wild animals may have been obtained from these animals. Among the deer species *Cervus unicolor* (sambar), *Cervus duvauceli* (barasingha), *Axis axis* (chital/spotted deer), *Axis porcinus* (hog deer) and *Muntiacus muntjak* (barking deer) are important. Likewise, antelopes such as *Antilope cervicapra* (blackbuck/Indian antelope), *Gazella bennetti* (chinkara/Indian gazelle), *Tetracerus quadricornis* (four-horned antelope/chowsingha) and *Boselaphus tragocamelus* (nilgai/blue bull) are the commonly represented species in the Harappan sites. Another important wild animal found in the Harappan context is the wild pig (*Sus scrofa*). It is interesting to note that both domestic (*Sus domesticus*) and wild forms of pigs are reported from a few sites. Compared to deer and antelope species, wild pigs are scarcely represented and also from sites like Kuntasi and Shikarpur they are hardly found in the early phase of the Harappan Culture.

The scavenging and predatory activities of carnivores may have led to their inclusion in a few of the sites mentioned in Table 1. These carnivores are usually associated with human settlement for food, and thereby get killed while robbing or preying on domestic stock. Such accidentally killed animals may have been utilized for food. Of the cat family the jungle cat (*Felis chaus*) is identified from Kuntasi and Padri while the desert cat (*Felis libyca*) is found only at Rojdi, where species identification of this animal is not certain. However, the jungle cat is reported from a vast majority of the Chalcolithic sites of the Deccan (Pawankar and Thomas 1997). The selective collection of faunal assemblage may have been responsible for the absence of some of the smaller species of animals from archaeological sites (Thomas 1979, 1984). Among the dog family three species are reported from Harappan sites such as *Cuon alpinus* (Indian wild dog/ dhole), *Canis aureus* (jackal) and *Canis lupus* (wolf). However, the Indian wild dog bones are found only at Rojdi. The wolf and jackal are reported from a few of the Harappan sites (Table 1). *Hyaena hyaena* (striped hyena) has been identified only at Kuntasi. These are not the animals regularly hunted by the inhabitants of the ancient settlements. The bones of these carnivores are meager in the collection. Sometimes a species is represented by a single bone. Therefore, the role of these animals in the Harappan food economy is minimal.

The other set of wild animals represented at the Harappan sites are the large mammals such as the *Elephas maximus* (elephant), *Rhinoceros unicornis* (rhinoceros), *Bos* sp. (cattle like) and *Bubalus arnee* (wild buffalo). As mentioned above in the discussion of carnivores, the bones of these large mammals are also scarce in the collection. Often the elephant is identified at a site from the ivory pieces utilized for making different objects. Also from some sites, rib fragments are reported. Elephant remains are identified from sites such as Mohenjo Daro, Harappa, Kalibangan, Rupar, Bara, Lothal, Surkotada and Rojdi. The rhinoceros is identified from a large number of Harappan and Chalcolithic sites of Gujarat. The lower extremities of limb bones like the carpals, tarsals, metapodia and phalanges are found at Kuntasi and Shikarpur. A shoulder bone of rhinoceros was identified at Langhnaj, a Mesolithic occupation contemporary with the Harappans of Gujarat (Clutton-Brock 1965). This animal inhabited a major part of the Gujarat plains in the protohistoric period and in the medieval period it was restricted to certain ecological niches. The strips of grassland along the banks of the rivers may have supported the habitat of animals like rhino and wild buffalo during the Harappan cultural period (Chitalwala 1977, 1990). Wild buffalo is represented at Kuntasi and Shikarpur by cranial and post-cranial bones bearing cut and butchering marks. Probably this indicate the contribution of wild buffalo in the food economy unlike the other larger mammals like elephant and rhinoceros whose bones are sparse in the collection and probably the bones were brought into the site for other functions such as making bone tools and bone objects. Such bone and ivory objects have been reported from a number of Harappan sites.

Both at Kuntasi and Shikarpur, a few bones of cattle such as humerus, astragalus and metapodials revealed characters which were uncommon in domestic cattle. Apparently some of these bones were also larger in size suggesting the possibility of some affinity with their wild counterparts or these animals were in the early stage of domestication. However, the impact of individual, functional and/ or breed differences cannot be ruled out at this stage. They also formed a part of the diet of the Harappans.

NON-MAMMALIAN SPECIES AT HARAPPAN SITES

The subsistence economy of the Harappans was not only based on the mammalian species but they exploited a variety of animals belonging to the family of birds, reptiles, fish, crustacea and molluscs. Unfortunately species identification of this large group was not attempted at many sites mainly because of the lack of expertise and the non-availability of modern reference skeleton of these animals. The recovery method employed in the collection of artefacts at various sites may have been another culprit. In the Harappan Culture the domestic fowl (*Gallus domesticus*) is reported from quite a few sites. At Khanpur and Babarkot the species identification is not certain. Other species of birds such as jungle fowl (*Gallus gallus*) and pea fowl (*Pavo cristatus*) are common. Reptiles like monitor lizard (*Varanus monitor*), crocodile (*Crocodilus* sp.), gharial (*Gavialis* sp.), turtle/tortoise species such as *Trionyx gangeticus*, *Batagur baska*, *Chitra indica*, *Kachuga* sp. and *Lissemys punctata* are found at almost all the sites.

The Harappan sites have yielded large quantities of fish, crab and molluscs remains. As mentioned above the species of fish and crab remains have not been identified at many of the western Indian Harappan sites. General terms like catfish and carp are mentioned at a few places. However, recent studies on fish remains from Balakot and Harappa in Pakistan have revealed extensive use of both riverine and marine fish in the Harappan economy. And also long distance trade of some species of marine fish has also been suggested (Belcher 1997). The fish species at the coastal Balakot site include shark, sting rays and bony fish. Dominance of grunters (*Pomadays* sp.) and the presence of other species like *Acanthopagrus* sp., *Argyrops* sp., *Protonibea* sp. and a variety of *Arius* sp., has been noticed. Harappa, the inland Urban centre has yielded many species of riverine catfish, carps, snakeheads and spiny eels. In addition the identification of the remains of marine jacks and catfish at Harappa suggests long distance trade of these items (Belcher 1977). However, the exact role of fish in the Harappan subsistence is at present unknown. Therefore, a great deal of emphasis should be given to these finds in future archaeological research in order to get an insight not only into their role in the subsistence economy but also the environmental factors prevailed during the Harappan period.

After the excavations at Mohenjo Daro and Harappa, in recent years many people have tried to appraise the role of molluscs in the economy of the Harappans at sites such as Mohenjo Daro and Harappa (Kenoyer 1983), Nageshwar (Bhan and Kenoyer 1984), Nagwada (Hegde et al. 1988), Surkotada (Joshi 1990), Shikarpur (Thomas et al. 1995) and Kuntasi (Deshpande 1995, 1996; Deshpande-Mukherjee 1998). Both marine and fresh water species of molluscs belonging to three major classes of Phylum Molluscs such as Bivalvia, Gastropoda and Schaphopoda are reported from a large number of

Harappan sites. From the studies carried out it has been inferred that molluscs were collected mainly for shell working and also for food. Compared to marine very few fresh water shells are reported from the Gujarat Harappan sites. At Kuntasi more than 50 species of shells were identified (Deshpande 1995).

Bivalves such as *Anadara* sp., *Paphia gallus*, *Meretrix* sp., *Marcia recens*, *Crassostrea* sp., *Acanthocardia* sp., *Trachicardium enode*, *Lamellidens marginalis*, etc., and Gastropods such as *Agaronia nebulosa*, *Thais* sp., *Telescopium telescopium*, *Terebralia palustris*, *Pila globosa*, etc., were the edible species found at some of the Harappan sites mentioned above. Species like *Turbinella pyrum*, *Pugilina buchephala*, *Chicoreus ramosus*, *Placuna placenta*, *Anadara* sp., *Dentalium* sp., *Polinices didyma*, *Agaronia nebulosa*, *Nerita* sp., etc., were associated with shell industry especially in the manufacture of bangles, ladles, inlays, beads, pendants, gamesmen, chisels, etc. (Deshpande-Mukherjee 1998). The vast amount of complete shells, finished and unfinished shell objects, and waste products of shell manufacture at many of these sites indicate a technologically advanced shell industry during the Harappan period and this tradition continued till historical times in Gujarat.

CONCLUSION

From the foregoing discussion it can be inferred that the Harappans had a very close fellowship with the animal world in and around them. A wide spectrum of animal species has been utilized for various purposes. The absence and presence of certain species of animals from sites which were excavated earlier may be observed with caution. Nevertheless, domestic animals such as cattle, buffalo, sheep, goat, pig and certain deer species and antelopes are common at almost all the sites.

Cattle were the predominant animals in the Harappan Culture. This is true for all excavated protohistoric and Early Historic settlements of the subcontinent. The Harappans were well acquainted with the multiple utility of the cattle, and cattle pastoralism was an indispensable profession in the Harappan economy. Interestingly this animal attained a prestigious position in the Harappan Culture which is evident from the depiction of cattle in various forms at a large number of sites. The other domestic animals such as buffalo, sheep, goat and pigs have also contributed substantially to the diet of the ancient population. In the subsistence system of the Harappans the domestic animals have contributed more than 80 per cent of the animal protein. The remaining 20 per cent is obtained from the wild animals consisting of the terrestrial, avian and aquatic fauna. Wild mammals, birds, reptiles, fish, molluscs and crustaceans were part of the Harappan diet. The role of molluscs in the shell industry and as source of food has been attested at various Harappan settlements.

In addition, the presence of the horse, ass and camel in a few of the sites suggest the utilization of these animals as beasts of burden and may have been associated with industrial and trade centres where these animals can accelerate the mobility of the people. However, in the light of the present controversy over the Harappan horse, the equid remains from some of the Harappan sites need to be reinvestigated.

The identification of large herbivores like rhinoceros, wild buffalo and probably wild cattle at many of the Gujarat Harappan sites suggests that the ecological conditions were more congenial for animal life during the protohistoric period in Gujarat. Wild cattle reportedly missing from the Holocene period of India, may have existed somewhere in this region (Joglekar and Thomas 1992). Rhinoceros reported from a number of Chalcolithic and Harappan sites in Gujarat may have inhabited a major part of the Gujarat plains in the protohistoric period and in the Medieval period it was restricted to certain ecological niches. The strips of grassland along the banks of the rivers may have supported the habitat of animals like rhino and wild buffalo during the Harappan period (Chitalwala 1977, 1990). Elephant bones and ivory from Harappan sites were associated with craftsmanship and probably were trade items acquired through commercial activities.

In general, the representation of wild animals, in the northern group of Harappan sites, shows a slight variation from those sites in the Saurashtra-Kachchh group. The typical semi-arid animals like the blackbuck, gazelle, nilgai, etc., are not identified from the northern group of sites like Harappa, Kalibangan, Rupar, Alamgirpur, etc. Probably this can be attributed to the different ecological settings of these sites. The maximum exploitation of wild fauna was noticed in the Post-Urban period at Rangpur, Surkotada, Nageshwar, Mohenjo Daro, Kuntasi, Shikarpur, etc. Culturally the Post-Urban period marks the decline of the Harappan Culture at these places. Probably in adverse conditions the people had to depend more on animal food for sustenance. From the type of activities identified, it can be presumed that social stratification and division of labour prevailed during the Harappan Culture. The planned economic strategies of the Harappans can be visualized from the animal husbandry practices and the exploitation pattern of both domestic and wild animals.

REFERENCES

Alur, K.R. 1990. *Studies in Indian Archaeology and Palaeontology*. Dharwad: Shrihari Prakashana.

Anthony, D. 1997. Current Thoughts on the Domestication of the Horse in Asia, *South Asian Studies* 13: 315-16.

Belcher, W.R. 1997. Marine and Riverine Resource Use During the Indus Valley Tradition: a Preliminary Comparison of Fish Remains from Balakot and Harappa, in *South Asian Archaeology 1995*, Vol. 1 (R. Allchin and B. Allchin Eds.), pp. 173-86. New Delhi: Oxford-IBH.

Bhan, K.K and J.M. Kenoyer 1984. Nageshwar a Mature Shell Working Site on the Gulf of Kutch (Gujarat), *Journal of the Oriental Institute* 34: 67-75.

Boessneck, J. 1969. Osteölogical Differences between Sheep (*Ovis aries Linne*) and Goats (*Capra hircus Linne*), in *Science in Archaeology* (D.R. Brothwell and E. Higgs Eds.), pp. 331-58. London: Thames and Hudson.

Bökönyi, S. 1997. Horse Remains from the Prehistoric Site of Surkotada, Kutch, Late 3rd Millennium B.C., *South Asian Studies* 13: 297-307.

Chitalwala, Y.M. 1977. Harappan and Post-Harappan Settlement Patterns, in *Ecology and*

Archaeology of Western India (D.P. Agrawal and B.M. Pande Eds.), pp. 93-8. New Delhi: Concept Publishers.

——— 1990. The Disappearance of Rhino From Saurashtra: a Study in Palaeoecology, *Bulletin of the Deccan College Post-Graduate and Research Institute* 49: 79-82. Pune: Deccan College.

Clutton-Brock, J. 1965. *Excavations at Langhnaj, Part II, The Fauna*. Pune: Deccan College.

Deshpande, A. 1995. Application of Molluscan Studies in Archaeology with Reference to Western India. Ph.D. Dissertation. Pune: University of Poona.

——— 1996. Shell Remains, *in Kuntasi, a Harappan Emporium on West Coast* (M.K. Dhavalikar, M.R. Raval and Y.M. Chitalwala Eds.), pp. 331-47. Pune: Deccan College.

Deshpande-Mukherjee, A. 1998. Shellfishing and Shell Crafts During the Harappan Period in Gujarat, *Man and Environment* XXIII (1): 63-80.

Hegde, K.T.M., V.H. Sonawane, D.R. Shah, K.K. Bhan, A. Prasad, K. Krishnan and S.P. Chandran 1988. Excavation at Nagwada, 1986 and 1987: a Preliminary Report, *Man and Environment* XII: 55-65.

Joglekar, P.P. 1991. A Biometric Approach to the Faunal Remains of Walki and Kaothe. Ph.D. dissertation. Pune: University of Poona.

——— 1997. Faunal Remains from Padri: Second Preliminary Report, *Bulletin of the Deccan College Post-Graduate and Research Institute* 56-7: 55-68.

Joglekar, P.P. and P.K. Thomas 1992. Ancestry of *Bos* species: Myth and Reality IV. The Origins of Humped Cattle, *Man and Environment* XVII (1): 51-4.

Joshi, J.P. 1990. *Excavations at Surkotada 1971-72 and Explorations in Kutch*. New Delhi: Memoirs of the Archaeological Survey of India 87.

Kane, V.S. 1989. Animal Remains from Rojdi, in *Harappan Civilization and Rojdi* (G.L. Possehl and M.H. Raval Eds.), pp.182-4. New Delhi: Oxford-IBH.

Kenoyer, J.M. 1983. Shell Working Industries of the Indus Civilization: an Archaeological and Ethnographic Perspective. Ph.D. Dissertation. Department of South and Southeast Asian Studies. Berkeley: University of California.

Mackay, E.J.H. 1931. Games and Toy, in *Mohenjo-daro and the Indus Civilization*, Vol. 2. (Sir John Marshall Ed.), pp. 554-5. London: A. Probsthain.

Mehta, R.N. 1984. Valabhi: a Station of Harappan Cattle Breeders, in *Frontiers of the Indus Civilization* (B. B. Lal and S.P. Gupta Eds.), pp. 227-30. Delhi: Books & Books.

Meadow, R.H. 1984. A Camel Skeleton from Mohenjo Daro, in *Frontiers of the Indus Civilization* (B.B. Lal and S.P. Gupta Eds.), pp. 133-9. New Delhi: Books & Books.

——— 1993. The Past, Present and Future of Bio-Archaeological Studies in Pakistan with Special Reference to Mohenjodaro and the Indus Civilization, *Pakistan Archaeology* 28: 183-215.

Meadow, R.H. and A. Patel 1997. A Comment on 'Horse Remains from Surkotada' by Sandor Bökönyi, *South Asian Studies* 13: 308-15.

Nath, B. 1962-3. Animal Remains from Rangpur, *Ancient India* 18-19: 153-60.

——— 1968. Advances in the Study of Prehistoric and Ancient Animal Remains in India: a Review, *Records of the Zoological Survey of India* 61 (1-2): 1-63.

Parpola, A. 1988. The Coming of the Aryans to Iran and India and the Cultural and Ethnic Identity of the Dasas, *Studia Orientalia* 64: 195-302.

Patel, A. 1997. The Pastoral Economy of Dholavira: a First Look at Animals and Urban Life in the Third Millennium Kutch, in *South Asian Archaeology 1995*, Vol. 1 (R. Allchin and B. Allchin Eds.), pp 101-13. New Delhi: Oxford- IBH.

Pawankar, S.J. and P.K. Thomas 1997. Fauna and Subsistence Pattern in the Chalcolithic Culture of Western India with Special Reference to Inamgaon, *Anthropozoologica* 25-6: 737-46. (Section 5: Post Palaeolithic Europe II, Asia, Africa).

Possehl, G.L. 1979. Pastoral Nomadism in the Indus Civilization: an Hypothesis, in *South Asian Archaeology 1977* (M. Taddei Ed.), pp. 537-51. Naples: IsMEO.

Prashad, B. 1936. *Animal Remains from Harappa*. New Delhi: Memoirs of the Archaeological Survey of India 51.

Rissman, P. 1985. Migratory Pastoralism in Western India in the Second Millennium B.C.: the Evidences from Oriyo Timbo (Chiroda). Ph.D. Dissertation. USA: University of Pennsylvania.

Ryan, K. (in press). Faunal Analysis, in Report on the Excavations at Babarkot: 1990-91 (G.L. Possehl and M.H. Raval Eds.).

Sahu, B.P. 1988. *From Hunters to Breeders*. New Delhi: Anamika Prakashan.

Sathe, V.G. and S. Atre 1989. The Problems of Camel in the Indus Civilization, *Bulletin of the Deccan College Post-Graduate and Research Institute* 47-8: 301-6.

Sewell, R.B.S. and B.S. Guha 1931. Zoological Remains, in *Mohenjodaro and the Indus Civilization* II (John Marshall Ed.), pp. 649-73. London: A. Probsthain.

Shah, D.R. and K.K. Bhan 1992. Faunal Remains, in *Excavation at Nageshwar, Gujarat: a Harappan Shell Working Site on the Gulf of Kutch* (K.T.M. Hegde, K.K. Bhan, V.H. Sonawane, K. Krishnan and D.R. Shah Eds.), pp. 145-7. Vadodara: the M.S. University Archaeology Series 18.

Sharma, A.K. 1990. Animal Bone Remains, in *Excavations at Surkotada 1971-72 and Explorations in Kutch* (J.P. Joshi), pp. 372-83. New Delhi: Memoirs of the Archaeological Survey of India 87.

Sharma, Y.D. 1989. Rupar, in *An Encyclopaedia of Indian Archaeology* 2 (A. Ghosh Ed.), pp. 377-81. Delhi: Munshiram Manoharlal.

Thomas, P.K. 1977. Archaeological Aspects of the Prehistoric Culture of Western India. Ph.D. Dissertation. Pune: University of Poona.

——— 1979. Archaeozoological Aspects of the Prehistoric Culture of Prabhas Patan, in *Archaeozoology,* Vol. I (Marian Kubasiewicz Ed.), pp. 176-86. Szezecin, Poland: Agricultural Academy.

——— 1984. Faunal Background of the Chalcolithic Culture of Western India, in *Animals and Archaeology: 3. Early Herders and their Flocks* (J. Clutton-Brock and C. Grigson Eds.), pp. 355-61. Oxford: BAR International Series 202.

——— 1988. Faunal Assemblage, in *Excavation at Inamgaon* I, Pt. ii (M.K. Dhavalikar, H.D. Sankalia and Z.D. Ansari Eds.), pp. 822-961. Pune: Deccan College.

——— 1989. Utilization of Domestic Animals in Pre- and Protohistoric India, in *The Walking Larder: Patterns of Domestication, Pastoralism and Predation* (Clutton-Brock Ed.), pp. 108- 12. London: Unwin Hyman.

——— 1992. Faunal Background of the Iron Age Culture of Maharashtra, *Man and Environment* XVII (2): 75-9.

Thomas, P.K. and P.P. Joglekar 1990. Faunal Remains, in *Excavations at Kaothe* (M.K. Dhavalikar, V. Shinde and S. Atre Eds.), pp. 233-64. Pune: Deccan College.

——— 1994. Holocene Faunal Studies in India, *Man and Environment* XIX (1-2): 179-204.

Thomas, P.K., P.P. Joglekar, Arati Deshpande-Mukherjee and Seema J. Pawankar 1995. Harappan Subsistence Patterns with Special Reference to Shikarpur, a Harappan Site in Gujarat, *Man and Environment* XX (2): 34-41.

Thomas, P.K., Y. Matsushima and Arati Deshpande 1996. Faunal Remains, in *Kuntasi: a Harappan Emporium on West Coast* (M.K. Dhavalikar, M.R. Raval and Y.M. Chitalwala Eds.), pp. 297-330. Pune: Deccan College.

Thomas P.K., P.P. Joglekar, Y. Matsushima, S.J. Pawankar and A. Deshpande 1997. Subsistence Based on Animals in the Harappan Culture of Gujarat, India, *Anthropozoologica* 25-6: 767-76. (Section 5: Post Palaeolithic Europe II, Asia, Africa).

Archaeology of the Harappan Civilization: An Annotated List of Excavations and Surveys

GREGORY L. POSSEHL

INTRODUCTION

This is an annotated list of the major excavations and survey efforts that have documented the Harappan Civilization. The documentation of the excavations has been made as comprehensive as the records available to the author allow them to be. Documentation of survey efforts has been more selective. The list is organized by work at individual sites and as individual survey efforts. The alternative organization, a straight year by year listing, was evaluated by two or three colleagues. While this approach has the value of being able to follow the unfolding events in chronological order, it was decided that most scholars would want to know when work at an individual site took place. Thus, organizing the list with this as the unifying principle was selected—although it could have been done both ways in one book.

ANNOTATED LIST OF EXCAVATIONS AND SURVEYS

Adatjo Daro 1930. N.G. Majumdar of the Archaeological Survey of India conducted a test excavation at this Mature Harappan site, also known as Badh, first examined by Rao Bahadur K.N. Dikshit in 1925-6. The site is *c.* 16 km north-west of Mohenjo Daro. Fairservis in an examination of collections later suggests that there is a Jhukar occupation as well (Dikshit 1925-6: 99; Majumdar 1934: 47-8).

Afghanistan Survey 1956. An Indian delegation led by T.N. Ramachandran and Y.D Sharma of the Archaeological Survey of India undertook a reconnaissance in Afghanistan. This was very preliminary in nature, but they visited Mundigak, Deh Morasi Ghundai, Shamshirgar and several other protohistoric sites. R.E.M. Wheeler had taken the first delegation to Afghanistan in 1946 (Ramachandran and Sharma 1956).

Ahichchhatra 1862-3. Sir Alexander Cunningham of the Archaeological Survey of India conducted a brief excavation at Ahichchhatra in Bareilly district of Uttar Pradesh. He does not find the Ochre Coloured Pottery but begins a long series of excavation projects at the site (Ghosh 1989, Vol. 2: 7-9).

Ahichchhatra 1891-2. A. Fuhrer of the Archaeological Survey of India conducted a brief excavation at Ahichchhatra in Bareilly district of Uttar Pradesh (Ghosh 1989, Vol. 2: 7-9).

Ahichchhatra 1940-1. Rao Bahadur K.N. Dikshit and A. Ghosh of the Archaeological Survey of India conducted the first of four seasons of excavation at Ahichchhatra in Bareilly district of Uttar Pradesh. They investigate the fortifications and city mound (Ghosh 1989, Vol. 2: 7-9).

Ahichchhatra 1941-2. Rao Bahadur K.N. Dikshit and A. Ghosh conducted the second of four seasons of excavation at Ahichchhatra, continuing the investigation of the fortifications and city mound (Ghosh 1989, Vol. 2: 7-9).

Ahichchhatra 1942-3. Rao Bahadur K.N. Dikshit and A. Ghosh conducted the third of four seasons of excavation at Ahichchhatra (Ghosh 1989, Vol. 2: 7-9).

Ahichchhatra 1943-4. Rao Bahadur K.N. Dikshit and A. Ghosh conducted the fourth and final season of excavation at Ahichchhatra (Ghosh 1989, Vol. 2: 7-9).

Ahichchhatra 1963-4. After a lapse of a century following Sir Alexander Cunningham's first excavations here, N.R. Bannerji of the Archaeological Survey of India conducted the first of two seasons of renewed excavation at Ahichchhatra in Bareilly district of Uttar Pradesh. He investigates the lower levels of the site, seeking the relationship between Painted Grey Ware and Northern Black Polished Ware (*IAR* 1963-4: 43-4).

Ahichchhatra 1964-5. N.R. Bannerji of the Archaeological Survey of India undertook the second of two seasons of renewed excavation at Ahichchhatra in Bareilly District of Uttar Pradesh. He investigates the lower levels of the site and finds Ochre Coloured Pottery (*IAR* 1964-5: 39-42).

Ahmadwala Ther 1942. Sir Aurel Stein of the Archaeological Survey of India undertook a trial excavation at Ahmadwala Ther on the ancient Sarasvati river in what is now Pakistan. This is a Mature Harappan site also surveyed by M.R. Mughal (Stein 1943a: 115-16).

Alamgirpur 1958-9. Y.D. Sharma of the Archaeological Survey of India conducted one season of excavation at Alamgirpur in Uttar Pradesh, district Meerut. He discovered Harappan pottery, published a schematic section and pottery drawings (*IAR* 1958-9: 50-5).

Ali Murad 1930-1. N.G. Majumdar of the Archaeological Survey of India conducted a test excavation at this site near Lake Manchar in Sindh. He found a Mature Harappan site (Majumdar 1934: 89-91).

Aligrama 1974. Giorgio Stacul of IsMEO undertook excavation at Aligrama in the Swat Valley of Pakistan. In Period I he found a settlement of the 'Swat Valley Protohistoric, Period IV'. There are both semi-subterranian houses and those with dry stone masonry at ground level (Stacul 1987: 63).

Allahdino 1972. Walter A. Fairservis, Jr. of the American Museum of Natural History undertook a reconnaissance in the Karachi area that led to the excavation of Allahdino (Nel Bazar) beginning in 1973 (Fairservis 1982).

Allahdino 1973. Walter A. Fairservis, Jr. conducted the first season of excavation at Allahdino on the Malir river just east of Karachi. He found a Mature Harappan site that appears to be an outpost, rather than a farming community. Jim Shaffer defined five phases of occupation (Shaffer 1974; Fairservis 1982).

Allahdino 1974. Walter A. Fairservis, Jr. conducted the second season of excavation at Allahdino (Fairservis 1982).

Allahdino 1976. Walter A. Fairservis, Jr. conducted the third season of excavation at Allahdino (Fairservis 1982).

Allahdino 1978. Walter A. Fairservis, Jr. conducted the fourth season of excavation at Allahdino (Fairservis 1982).

Allahdino 1983. Walter A. Fairservis, Jr. conducted the fifth season of excavation at Allahdino (Fairservis, unpublished).

Ambkheri 1963-4. M.N. Deshpande of the Archaeological Survey of India undertook one season of excavation at this Ochre Coloured Pottery site in Uttar Pradesh, District Saharanpur with a possible 'degenerate Harappan' link to Painted Grey Ware (*IAR* 1963-4: 55-6).

Amra 1955-6. P.P. Pandya of the Gujarat State Department of Archaeology and B. Subbarao of the M.S. University of Baroda conducted a test excavation at this site in Gujarat, district Jamnagar. They found three periods: Period I, Sorath Harappan with Black and Red Ware and some Lustrous Red Ware; Period II, Red Polished Ware; Period III, Medieval. Amra is about 5 km from Lakhabaval (*IAR* 1955-6: 7).

Amri 1831. Alexander Burnes of the Indian Army visited Amri (Amree) in Sindh during his exploration of the Indus river. He recognizes it as an archaeological site (Burnes 1834, Vol. III: 58-9).

Amri 1929. N.G. Majumdar of the Archaeological Survey of India excavated Amri in Sindh. He found a stratified Early and Mature Harappan settlement which firmly establishes the 'Bichrome' Amrian ceramics as coming before the 'Mohenjo Daro Age' (Majumdar 1934: 24-33).

Amri 1959-60. Jean-Marie Casal of the Musee Guimet conducted the first of three seasons of excavation at Amri. He opened trenches on both Mounds A and B and found stratified Mature Harappan and Amri-Nal material (Casal 1964: 3)

Amri 1960-1. Jean-Marie Casal undertook the second of three excavation seasons at Amri with a large excavation on Mound A. His trench is 32 x 4.5 m. He learned that the earliest settlement at Amri was confined to Mound A. Later Amrian inhabitants moved to Mound B as well (Casal 1964: 3).

Amri 1961-2. Jean-Marie Casal conducted the third and final season of excavation at Amri. In the course of his work he discovered a cultural sequence: Amri-Nal, Transitional Early Harappan-Mature Harappan, Mature Harappan then Jhangar (Casal 1964: 3).

Anjira 1957. Beatrice de Cardi of the British Academy conducted one season of excavation at Anjira in Baluchistan, Kalat Division. She found a five phase settlement beginning with Burj Basket-marked Phase nomadic encampment followed by the Togau, Kechi Beg, Amri-Nal and Quetta Phases. Anjira Ware was defined at this site (de Cardi 1965).

Arabjo Thana 1931. N.G. Majumdar of the Archaeological Survey of India conducted a small excavation at this site on the Baran Nai in western Sindh. He found an Amri-Nal site (Majumdar 1934: 136-7).

Atkot 1957-8. P.P. Pandya of the Gujarat State Department of Archaeology undertook an exploratory excavation at this site on the Bhadar river in Gujarat, Rajkot district. He found Harappan (Rojdi A) pottery (*IAR* 1957-8: 20-3).

Atranjikhera 1962-3. R.C. Gaur of Aligarh Muslim University conducted the first of six seasons of excavation at this site in Uttar Pradesh, district Etah. During the first season found nothing relating to the Harappan Civilization; however, he later finds Ochre Coloured Pottery (*IAR* 1962-3: 34-6).

Atranjikhera 1963-4. R.C. Gaur continues the second of six seasons of excavation and finds Ochre Coloured Pottery (*IAR* 1963-4: 45-9).

Atranjikhera 1965-6. R.C. Gaur conducted the third of six seasons of excavation at this site (*IAR* 1965-6: 44-7).

Atranjikhera 1967-8. R.C. Gaur conducted the fourth of six seasons of excavation at this site (*IAR* 1967-8: 45-6).

Atranjikhera 1968-9. R.C. Gaur undertook the fifth of six seasons of excavation at this site (*IAR* 1968-9: 37-8).

Atranjikhera 1979-80. R.C. Gaur undertook the sixth and final season of excavation at this site (*IAR* 1979-80: 75-6).

Babar Kot 1990-1. Gregory L. Possehl of the University of Pennsylvania Museum and M.H. Raval of the Gujarat State Department of Archaeology conducted one season of excavation at Babar Kot in district Bhavnagar, Gujarat. They seek to understand this fortified site on the Bhadar drainage, *c.* 40 km west of Rangpur and to check the chronology of the site against the dates secured from Rojdi, as well as expand the information on Harappan palaeobotany. They found a Rojdi B-C site (Sorath Harappan and Post-Urban Harappan) with a massive fortification wall (Possehl 1994; Reddy 1994).

Bahadrabad 1952. Y.D. Sharma of the Archaeological Survey of India excavated this Copper Hoard site in Saharanpur district, Uttar Pradesh. The copper implements were found by chance while irrigation works were being constructed. Sharma's excavation does not recover any copper implements but he does find Ochre Coloured Pottery (Y.D. Sharma 1989: 37-9).

Baharia 1966-7. V.D. Misra and B.B. Misra of Allahabad University excavated this site in district Shahjahanpur, Uttar Pradesh where they find Ochre Coloured Pottery, Northern Black Polished Ware and other material. Two implements from a copper hoard were also found (*IAR* 1966-7: 43-4).

Bahawalpur Survey 1955. Henry Field of Harvard University and F.A. Khan of the Pakistan Department of Archaeology conducted a brief survey of Bahawalpur. Very few new sites are registered (Field 1959).

Bahawalpur Survey 1974-5. M.R. Mughal of the Pakistan Department of Archaeology conducted a survey in Bahawalpur district. He found 99 Hakkra Wares sites, 40 Early Harappan sites, 174 Mature Harappan sites, 50 Cemetery H sites and 14 Painted Grey Ware (Mughal 1980, 1982: 87).

Bahawalpur Survey 1975-6. M.R. Mughal conducted a second year of survey in Bahawalpur district (Mughal 1980).

Bahawalpur Survey 1976-7. M.R. Mughal conducted a third season of survey in Bahawalpur district (Mughal 1980).

Bahawalpur Survey 1977-8. M.R. Mughal conducted a fourth season of survey in Bahawalpur district (Mughal 1980).

Balakot 1972-3. George F. Dales of the University of California, Berkeley conducted the first of four seasons of excavation at Balakot, between Karachi and Las Bela. He found a stratified Early Harappan, Mature Harappan site near the sea coast (Dales 1979a, 1979b).

Balakot 1973-4. George F. Dales undertook the second of four seasons of excavation at Balakot (Dales 1979a, 1979b).

Balakot 1974-5. George F. Dales conducted the third of four seasons of excavation at Balakot (Dales 1979a, 1979b).

Balakot 1975-6. George F. Dales conducted the fourth and final season of excavation at Balakot (Dales 1979a, 1979b).

Balathal 1992-3. V.N. Misra and Vasant Shinde of Deccan College began excavations at Balathal in Udaipur district of south-eastern Rajasthan. This is a site with Ahar type chalcolithic pottery, including the distinctive white painted, fine Black and Red Ware. Sorath Harappan fine Red Wares are present, as is an Iron Age occupation (unpublished).

Balathal 1993-4. V.N. Misra and Vasant Shinde of Deccan College continue the excavations at Balathal (unpublished).

Balathal 1994-5. V.N. Misra and Vasant Shinde of Deccan College continue the excavations at Balathal (unpublished).

Balathal 1995-6. V.N. Misra and Vasant Shinde of Deccan College continue the excavations at Balathal (unpublished).

Baleli 1885. Major Shepherd, Royal Engineers collects pottery from Baleli mound, north of Quetta City in Baluchistan. It is equivalent to Kili Ghul Mohammad II and III, but he does not recognize its importance (Garwood 1887: 163).

Balu 1978-9. U.V. Singh and Suraj Bhan of Kurukshetra University conducted the first of five seasons of excavation at Balu, district Jind in Haryana. They found Late Siswal ceramics, Mature Harappan ceramics, structures, terracotta objects, copper objects (*IAR* 1978-9: 69).

Balu 1979-80. U.V. Singh and Suraj Bhan conducted the second of five seasons of excavation at Balu (*IAR* 1979-80: 31-2).

Balu 1983-4. U.V. Singh and Suraj Bhan conducted the third of five seasons of excavation at Balu. They discovered a Harappan fortification, Post-Urban Harappan kilns, ovens and other structures (*IAR* 1983-4: 28-9).

Balu 1984-5. U.V. Singh and Suraj Bhan conducted the fourth of five seasons of excavation at Balu, district Jind in Haryana. They undertook the excavation of the Mature Harappan fortification wall (*IAR* 1985-6: 20, 22).

Balu 1985-6. U.V. Singh and Suraj Bhan conducted the fifth and final season of excavation at Balu (*IAR* 1985-6: 29-30).

Baluchistan Survey 1904-5. Sir Aurel Stein of the Archaeological Survey of India conducted his first explorations in Baluchistan at the request of Sir John Marshall. Marshall was especially interested in having a report from Stein on the site of

Nal in Kalat where ancient pottery had recently been found. The pottery was published in the Annual Report of the Survey (Marshall 1904-5: 105-6). Stein visited a number of sites, including Dabar Kot on this exploratory trip (Stein 1905; Mirsky 1977: 215-16).

Baluchistan Survey 1927-8. Sir Aurel Stein undertook a survey of Gedrosia. He excavated at Kulli, Mehi and Sutkagen-dor (Stein 1931).

Baluchistan Survey 1955. Henry Field of Harvard University and F.A. Khan of the Pakistan Department of Archaeology conducted a brief survey of Baluchistan from Quetta to Pasni. Very few new sites are registered (Field 1959).

Baluchistan Survey 1955-6. Robert Raikes, an independent hydrologist, explored southern Jhalawan and Las Bela as a part of his hydrological research for the Government of Pakistan (Raikes 1968).

Baluchistan Survey 1956-7. Robert Raikes continued his exploration of southern Jhalawan and Las Bela (Raikes 1968).

Baluchistan Survey 1960-1. Robert Raikes continued his exploration of southern Jhalawan and Las Bela (Raikes 1968).

Baluchistan Survey 1972. R. Mughal of the Pakistan Department of Archaeology conducted a survey in northern Baluchistan. He found, or revisited a number of protohistoric sites and conducted a small excavation at Damb Sadaat (Mughal 1972a: 137-58).

Banawali 1973-4. R.S. Bisht of the Haryana Department of Archaeology and Museums undertook the first of five seasons of excavation at Banawali, district Hissar in Haryana. Period I is an Early Harappan settlement with two architectural levels. It is claimed that this settlement is fortified and that it is laid out with a grid plan. Period II is a Mature Harappan town, with stratigraphic and cultural continuity from Period I. There is also probably a transitional period from Early to Mature Harappan at the site. Continuation of Period I has ceramics side by side with Mature Harappan. There is a defensive wall with moat and gate complex. Period III is a Post-Urban Harappan settlement with stratigraphic discontinuity with the past. Ceramics are of Bara, Sanghol IB and Mitathal IIB (Bisht 1982; *IAR* 1983-4: 24)

Banawali 1974-5. R.S. Bisht conducted second of five seasons of excavation at Banawali (Bisht 1982; *IAR* 1983-4: 24)

Banawali 1975-6. R.S. Bisht undertook the third of five seasons of excavation at Banawali (Bisht 1982; *IAR* 1983-4: 24)

Banawali 1976-7. R.S. Bisht conducted the fourth of five seasons of excavation at Banawali (Bisht 1982; *IAR* 1983-4: 24)

Banawali 1983-4. R.S. Bisht, now with the Archaeological Survey of India, undertook the last of five seasons of excavation at Banawali in Haryana, district Hissar (*IAR* 1983-4: 24-9).

Bandhri 1930. N.G. Majumdar of the Archaeological Survey of India undertook a brief excavation at this Sindhi Harappan site near Jhangar in the Lake Manchar area of Sindh (Majumdar 1934: 120-2).

Bara 1954-5. Y.D. Sharma of the Archaeological Survey of India excavated at Bara, district Rupnagar in the Punjab. He found Bara pottery at a single occupation site (Y.D. Sharma 1982b; *IAR* 1954-5: 9-11).

Bara 1971. Y.D. Sharma excavated again at Bara in the Punjab, district Rupnagar. He found Bara pottery at a single occupation site (Y.D. Sharma 1982b, 1989).

Bargaon 1963-4. M.N. Deshpande of the Archaeological Survey of India conducted excavation at Bargaon, district Saharanpur in Uttar Pradesh. He found Harappan Ware including the Indus goblet, as well as unslipped Ochre Coloured Pottery (*IAR* 1963-4: 56-7).

Bagasra 1995-6. The M.S. University of Baroda excavates at Bagasra in northern Rajkot district of Gujarat. The site is near Kuntasi, also an excavated site. They find a Sorath Harappan site and a seal impression with a unicorn motif (unpublished)

Bhagatrav 1957-8. S.R. Rao of the Archaeological Survey of India undertook a test excavation at this site on the southern side of the mouth of the Kim river, just south of the Narmada on the Gulf of Cambay. He found a Sorath Harappan type site (Rao 1963: 190).

Bhagwanpura 1975-6. Jagat Pati Joshi of the Archaeological Survey of India conducted excavation at Bhagwanpura in Haryana, district Karnal and found a distinctive Post-Urban Harappan and a 'Late' Harappan with a transition to Painted Grey Ware (*IAR* 1975-6: 16-17; Jagat Pati Joshi 1993).

Bhavnagar District Survey 1980-2. V.K. Jairath of the M.S. University of Baroda undertook an exploration of Bhavnagar district in Gujarat. His work follows that of P.P. Pandya, P.D. Chudasama and Gregory L. Possehl (Jairath 1986).

Bhorgarh 1992-3. B.S.R. Babu of the Department of Archaeology, Government of Delhi undertook the first of two seasons of excavation at Bhorgarh, 30 km north of central Delhi. He found a three period site: Post-Urban Harappan, Painted Grey Ware and Kushana (Babu 1995).

Bhorgarh 1993-4. B.S.R. Babu undertook the second of two seasons of excavation at Bhorgarh (Babu 1995).

Bhudan 1975-6. Suraj Bhan of Kurukshetra University conducted a small scale excavation at Bhudan in Sangrur district of the Punjab. He found an Early Harappan, Mature Harappan and Post-Urban Harappan site (Suraj Bhan and Shaffer 1978: 67, fn 1; Shaffer 1981: 87-8).

Binjor 1970. Katey Feroz Dalal, a graduate student at Deccan College, working with Z.D. Ansari also of Deccan College, conducted a small scale excavation at Binjor on the ancient Sarasvati river in Ganganagar district of Rajasthan. She found a site with a microlithic component and Mature Harappan occupation (Dalal 1980: 37-8).

Birkot Ghwandai 1977. Giorgio Stacul of IsMEO began the first of four seasons of excavation at Birkot Ghwandai in the Swat Valley of Pakistan. In Period I he found a settlement of the Swat Valley Protohistoric Period IV. As at Loebanr III, there are two building levels, the earliest consisting of semi-subterranean houses, the second with dry stone masonry at ground level (Stacul 1978, 1979, 1980, 1981a, 1981b, 1987: 60-3, 1989).

Birkot Ghwandai 1978. Giorgio Stacul conducted the second of four seasons of excavation at Birkot Ghwandai (Stacul 1978, 1980, 1981a, 1981b, 1987: 60-3, 1989).

Birkot Ghwandai 1979. Giorgio Stacul conducted the third of four seasons of excavation at Birkot Ghwandai (Stacul 1978, 1980, 1981a, 1981b, 1987: 60-3, 1989).

Birkot Ghwandai 1985. Giorgio Stacul undertook the final season of excavation at Birkot Ghwandai (Stacul 1978, 1980, 1981a, 1981b, 1987: 60-3, 1989).

Bisauli 1949. B.B. Lal of the Archaeological Survey of India goes to Bisauli in Budan district of Uttar Pradesh for a small excavation at the site of a Copper Hoard. He found Ochre Coloured Pottery, but prior to his definition of it at Hastinapura in 1954-5 (Lal 1951: 27-8).

Burj 1977. Manmohan Kumar of Kurukshetra University carried out a small scale excavation at Burj, a site in Patiala district of the Punjab. The excavation is undertaken as part of his exploration of Ambala and Kurukshetra districts in neighbouring Haryana. He found a Late Harappan site with Bara pottery (Kumar 1978: 77, 87-8).

Burzahom 1935. Hellmut de Terra, in association with T.T. Paterson and P. Teilhard de Chardin, sponsored by the Carnegie Institution of Washington, DC, Yale University, Cambridge University and the American Philosophical Society, conducted archaeological and geological research on the Himalayan glacial sequence and palaeolithic archaeology in the subcontinent. They undertook a trial excavation at Burzahom, later identified as a site of the Northern Neolithic, and Iron Age Megalithic assemblages (de Terra and Paterson 1939: 233-5, Plate XXIV).

Burzahom 1960-1. T.N. Kazanchi of the Archaeological Survey of India undertook the first of nine seasons of excavation at Burzahom, a Northern Neolithic and Megalithic site in the Kashmir Valley near Srinagar. He found Neolithic pit houses and the pottery characteristic of the Northern Neolithic (*IAR* 1960-1: 11)

Burzahom 1961-2. T.N. Kazanchi conducted the second of nine seasons of excavation at Burzahom. He found sixteen pit houses, Northern Neolithic pottery, plus knives and other jadite tools along with a rich bone industry (*IAR* 1961-2: 17-21).

Burzahom 1962-3. T.N. Kazanchi conducted the third of nine seasons of excavation at Burzahom. He found more materials of the Northern Neolithic, including dog burials (*IAR* 1962-3: 9-10).

Burzahom 1964-5. T.N. Kazanchi undertook the fourth of nine seasons of excavation at Burzahom. Excavation efforts are directed to uncovering Northern Neolithic structures. Period II produced two fine Red Ware pots, one a typical Kot Dijian type with the 'Horned Deity' painted on it. This pot contained approximately 950 beads of carnelian and agate. An inscribed stone slab with a hunting scene on it is found in Period Ib contexts (*IAR* 1964-5: 13).

Burzahom 1965-6. T.N. Kazanchi conducted the fifth of nine seasons of excavation at Burzahom. This season of work is terminated prematurely. A second inscribed stone slab is found in Period Ib contexts. It has an abstract 'tectiform' design (*IAR* 1965-6: 19).

Burzahom 1966-7. T.N. Kazanchi conducted the sixth of nine seasons of excavation at Burzahom. More Northern Neolithic structures are excavated. Crucible found (*IAR* 1966-7: 16-17).

Burzahom 1968-9. T.N. Kazanchi undertook the seventh of nine seasons of excavation at Burzahom. Excavation of structures make clear that they were semi-subterranean with interior hearths and a central pillar (*IAR* 1968-9: 10).

Burzahom 1971-2. T.N. Kazanchi undertook the eighth of nine seasons of excavation at Burzahom. Excavation of Northern Neolithic structures. Over 400 carnelian and agate beads and pendants were found. Period III produces 26 beads, probably of gold (*IAR* 1971-2: 24).

Burzahom 1973-4. Sardari Lal of the Archaeological Survey of India conducted the last of nine seasons of excavation at Burzahom. This year's work involved exposing structures of Period I. Two copper rings and a copper needle were found (*IAR* 1973-4: 15).

Butkara One. Giorgio Stacul of IsMEO excavated at Butkara One, a Buddhist stupa and monastery in Swat. This season he found a Neolithic site on a river terrace that can be correlated to the second Neolithic at Ghalegay Cave, also in Swat. It dates to 2000-1750 BC (Faccenna 1981).

Chak 86 1951. A. Ghosh, Director General of the Archaeological Survey of India, conducted a small excavation at this site on the Sarasvati river in northern Rajasthan. The excavation is coordinated with his excavation at Tarkhanawala Dera. Chak 86 has Harappan wares, along with Painted Grey Ware and Rang Mahal ceramics. Sothi (Early Harappan) Wares may also be present (Ghosh 1952: 215; Dalal 1980: 26).

Chandigarh 1970-1. The Archaeological Survey of India and the Punjab State Department of Archaeology investigate a Harappan cemetery unearthed in the course of building a shopping area (Sector 17C) in Chandigarh. Their excavations locate the Mature Harappan cemetery and habitation area 100 m to the east-north-east. The pottery has affinities with Kalibangan I and II as well as Bara (*IAR* 1970-1: 7-8).

Chandigarh 1985-6. The Archaeological Survey of India and the Punjab State Department of Archaeology investigate an area of Chandigarh with Harappan artefacts uncovered while excavating the foundations of a building. Small scale trial excavation reveals two periods of occupation: Period IA, Mature Harappan, Period IB, Bara (*IAR* 1985-6: 15).

Chanhu Daro 1930. N.G. Majumdar of the Archaeological Survey of India conducted a test excavation at Chanhu Daro in Nawabshah district of Sindh. His work confirms the relative chronological ordering of the Mature Harappan and the Jhukar Phase (Post-Urban) (Majumdar 1934: 35-44).

Chanhu Daro 1935-6. Ernest J.H. Mackay, formerly of the Archaeological Survey of

India, but now working for the American School of Indic and Iranian Studies, conducted the first American excavation in the subcontinent at Chanhu Daro in Nawabshah district of Sindh. He found a Mature Harappan settlement with evidence for bead and seal manufacture. Period II is the Jhukar Phase of the Post-Urban Harappan. Some Jhangar material is found as well (Mackay 1943).

Chanhu Daro 1984. G.M. Sher and Massimo Vidale of IsMEO conducted a surface survey at Chanhu Daro in Nawabshah district of Pakistan. They corroborate Mackay's conclusion of intense industrial activity at the site (Sher and Vidale 1985).

Chauro 1930. N.G. Majumdar of the Archaeological Survey of India undertook a small scale excavation at Chauro, south of Lake Manchar in western Sindh. He found an Amri-Nal site (Majumdar 1934: 123-5).

Dabar Kot 1898. Fritz W. Noetling of the Geological Survey of India, visits Dabar Kot in Marri-Bugti hills of Baluchistan. He published Mature Harappan pottery, but does not understand the age of his find (Noetling 1899: 101-2; Pedde 1993a, 1993b).

Dabar Kot 1904. Sir Aurel Stein of the Archaeological Survey of India visits at Dabar Kot near Duki in the Marri-Bugti Hills of Baluchistan. He is there in December as a part of his first Baluchistan survey. Stein was aware of Noetling's visit (Stein 1905: 45-9; Pedde 1993a, 1993b).

Dabar Kot 1927. Sir Aurel Stein excavated at Dabar Kot in the Marri-Bugti Hills of Baluchistan. He had first been there in 1904, on a hurried visit. Stein finds and publishes Mature Harappan pottery and small finds along with later historical find (Stein 1905: 52; 1929: 55-64; Pedde 1993a; 1993b).

Dabar Kot 1950-1. Walter A. Fairservis, Jr. of the American Museum of Natural History visited Dabar Kot in the Marri-Bugti Hills of Baluchistan. He conducted a systematic surface survey, collecting pottery sherds *in situ* from exposed cuts. His work confirms that of Sir Aurel Stein (Fairservis 1959: 308-26; Pedde 1993a; 1993b).

Dadheri 1976-7. Jagat Pati Joshi of the Archaeological Survey of India conducted one season of excavation at Dadheri in the Punjab, district Ludhiana. He found a Post-Urban Harappan ceramic with a transition to Painted Grey Ware (*IAR* 1976-7: 43-4; Jagat Pati Joshi 1993).

Daimabad 1958-9. M.N. Deshpande of the Archaeological Survey of India conducted excavation at Daimabad in Maharashtra, district Ahmednagar and found a Chalcolithic deposit. Later excavation at the site by S.A. Sali will have what he calls a 'Late Harappan' (*IAR* 1958-9: 15-18).

Daimabad 1974-5. S.A. Sali of the Archaeological Survey of India undertook his first of five seasons of excavation at Daimabad in Maharashtra, district Ahmednagar, prompted by the find of four large bronzes. Period I, Savalda Culture; Period II, Late Harappan; Period III, Daimabad Culture; Period IV, Malwa Culture; Period V, Jorwe Culture (*IAR* 1974-5: 29-31; Sali 1986).

Diamabad 1975-6. S.A. Sali conducted his second of five seasons of excavation at Daimabad (*IAR* 1975-6: 31-4; Sali 1986).

Daimabad 1976-7. S.A. Sali conducted his third of five seasons of excavation at Daimabad (*IAR* 1976-7: 34-8; Sali 1986).

Daimabad 1977-8. S.A. Sali undertook his fourth of five seasons of excavation at Daimabad (*IAR* 1977-8: 34-7; Sali 1986).

Daimabad 1978-9. S.A. Sali conducted his fifth of five seasons of excavation at Daimabad (*IAR* 1978-9) 46-52; Sali 1986).

Damb Buthi 1930-1. N.G. Majumdar of the Archaeological Survey of India conducted a small scale excavation at Damb Buthi just south of Lake Manchar in western Sindh. He found a stratified Amri-Nal and Mature Harappan site (Majumdar 1934: 114-17).

Damb Sadaat 1950-1. Walter A. Fairservis, Jr. of the American Museum of Natural History and Harvard University directed a single season of excavation at this site in the Quetta Valley of Baluchistan as a part of the Second Afghan Expedition. The Second Afghan Expedition was in the field for ten months, from August 1950 until May 1951. The work is supervised by Howard Stoudt and Leslie Alcock, the latter had just worked at Mohenjo Daro with Wheeler. They found a three period site beginning with a Kechi Beg Phase occupation and ending with the Quetta Phase (Fairservis 1956).

Damb Sadaat 1972. M.R. Mughal of the Pakistan Department of Archaeology directed a test excavation of the upper levels of this site in the Quetta Valley to check the stratigraphic sequence (Mughal 1972a: 138)

Damkot 1968. The Department of Archaeology at the University of Peshawar conducted excavation at Damkot on the right bank of the Swat river near the village of Chakdara in Dir district of Pakistan. They found a Buddhist settlement that began with of the 'Swat Valley Protohistoric' or Period IV at Ghaligay Cave (Rahman 1968-9).

Daulatpur (Haryana) 1968-9. U.V. Singh and Suraj Bhan of Kurukshetra University excavate Daulatpur in Haryana, district Karnal to investigate the relationship between the Post-Urban Harappan and Painted Grey Ware (*IAR* 1968-9: 8-9).

Daulatpur (Haryana) 1976-7. U.V. Singh resumed excavation of Daulatpur to investigate the relationship between the Late Harappan (Post-Urban Harappan) and Painted Grey Ware. The 'Late' Harappan occupation has ceramics like the Early Harappan of Kalibangan (*IAR* 1976-7: 19).

Daulatpur (Haryana) 1977-8. U.V. Singh resumed excavation of Daulatpur to Painted Grey Ware settlement. Period II, with Painted Grey Ware has iron in the upper levels (*IAR* 1977-8: 23).

Daulatpur (Uttar Pradesh) 1984-5. R.C. Gaur of Aligarh Muslim University undertook excavation at Daulatpur in Uttar Pradesh, district Bulandshahr and found an Ochre Coloured Pottery camp on the Kali Nadi. There are post holes and hearths in rectangular and round huts but no architecture except stratified floors (IAR 1984-5: 86-8).

Deh Morasi Ghundai 1951. Louis Dupree excavated Deh Morasi Ghundai 25 km south-west of Kandahar in southern Afghanistan. He found a settlement with a Damb Sadaat Phase occupation and a final occupation contemporary with the Post-Urban Harappan (Dupree 1963).

Derawar Ther 1935. In about this year H.H. the Nawab '... ordered an excavation in search for hidden treasure' at Derawar Ther (Mughal Bahawalpur Site Number 209) on the ancient Sarasvati river. This is a Mature Harappan site (Stein 1943a: 173-9).

Desalpur 1963-4. K.V. Soundara Rajan of the Archaeological Survey of India undertook excavations at Desalpur in Gujarat, district Kachchh. He found a Mature Harappan settlement including and a Post-Urban Harappan (*IAR* 1963-4: 10-12; Soundara Rajan 1984).

Dhansa 1975-6. Suraj Bhan of Kurukshetra University conducted a small scale excavation at Dhansa in the Union Territory of Delhi. He found a Mature Harappan and Post-Urban Harappan site (Suraj Bhan and Shaffer 1978: 67, fn 1; Shaffer 1981: 87-8).

Dhatva 1967-8. R.N. Mehta of the M.S. University of Baroda conducted excavation at Dhatva in Gujarat, district Surat. He found a Chalcolithic settlement with links to the Harappan of Saurashtra, as well as Red Polished Ware and amphora (*IAR* 1967-8: 19-20).

Dher Majra 1951. Olaf Prufer of Harvard University excavated four trenches in this Harappan site, also known as Bikkun, in the Punjab, former Nalagarh State, during the summer of 1951. He found two periods of occupation: (1) Mature Harappan with evidence for bead manufacture and (2) Post-Urban Harappan, probably related to Cemetery H (Prufer 1952).

Dholavira 1967-8. Jagat Pati Joshi of the Archaeological Survey of India discovers Dholavira on Khadir Island in the Great Rann of Kachchh. He calls the site 'Kotadi' which arouses some debate about the proper name since the 'i' at the end would normally indicate a 'diminutive' fort and this is a large site (*c.* 60 ha) (*IAR* 1967-8: 14-16).

Dholavira 1984-5. R.S. Bisht of the Archaeological Survey of India goes to Dholavira (Kotadi) on Khadir Island in the Great Rann of Kachchh. This is a large site (*c.* 60 ha) and R.S. Bisht engages in mapping and surface exploration in preparation for excavation (*IAR* 1984-5: 14, 17).

Dholavira 1990. Beginning in January, R.S. Bisht of the Archaeological Survey of India undertook the first season of excavation at Dholavira. He found a major Harappan settlement that appears to be a fourth, large, Mature Harappan settlement. There is also an Early Harappan component at Dholavira, which may relate to the Amri-Nal Phase (Bisht 1991: 71-82).

Dholavira 1991. R.S. Bisht continued excavation at Dholavira. He found a large mosaic with the Indus script, gateways and evidence for an Early Harappan occupation (Bisht 1991).

Dholavira 1992. R.S. Bisht continued excavation at Dholavira. He continued an investigation of the city (*IAR* 1991-2).

Dholavira 1993. R.S. Bisht continued excavation at Dholavira. He conducted his fourth season of excavation at the site (*IAR* 1992-3).

Dholavira 1994. R.S. Bisht continued excavation at Dholavira in Kachchh. He completed the fifth season of work (unpublished).

Dholavira 1995. R.S. Bisht continued his excavations at Dholavira (unpublished).

Dwarka 1979-80. S.R. Rao of the Archaeological Survey of India conducted excavation in the forecourt of the Dwarkadhish temple in the town of Dwarka in northwestern Saurashtra. He found Lustrous Red Ware in the lowest levels and an historical sequence above it (*IAR* 1979-80: 25-9).

Ganeshwar 1981-2. Vijay Kumar of the Rajasthan Department of Archaeology excavated the first of two seasons of work at Ganeshwar, a site in Rajasthan, district Sikar. He found Ganeshwar-Jodhpura Pottery and microliths, associated with many copper tools. The Rajasthan State Department of Archaeology earlier had found 58 flat axes and two barbed arrow heads. More copper is found during the excavation this season (*IAR* 1981-2: 61-2; Agrawala and Kumar 1982).

Ganeshwar 1983-4. Vijay Kumar conducted the second of two seasons of excavation at Ganeshwar in Rajasthan, district Sikar. The site has many copper implements associated with microliths. This season reveals an early period with pottery possibly related to the Sothi material of the Sarasvati Valley (Agrawala and Kumar 1982; *IAR* 1983-4: 71-2).

Ghalegay Cave 1967. Giorgio Stacul of IsMEO undertook the first of two seasons of excavation at Ghalegay Cave in the Swat Valley of Pakistan. He found four periods of occupation beginning with a Northern Neolithic which is succeeded by a 'Late Kot Dijian' which is in turn followed by a return of the Northern Neolithic in Period III. Period IV of Ghalegay Cave is the so-called 'Swat Valley Protohistoric' also found at Loebanr III, Birkot Ghundai, Aligrama, Damkot, Barama, Kalakoderay and the Kherai graveyard (Stacul 1987: 29-54).

Ghalegay Cave 1968. Giorgio Stacul undertook the second of two seasons of excavation at Ghalegay Cave in the Swat Valley of Pakistan (Stacul 1987: 29-54).

Ghazi Shah 1930-1. N.G. Majumdar of the Archaeological Survey of India undertook a test excavation at Ghazi Shah near Lake Manchar in Sindh. He found a stratified Amri-Nal and Mature Harappan settlement (Majumdar 1934: 79-86).

Ghazi Shah 1985. Louis Flam undertook the first of three seasons of excavation at Ghazi Shah near Lake Manchar in Sindh. He found a stratified Amri-Nal and Mature Harappan settlement. Working from March to June he began excavation at the summit of the mound (Flam 1993).

Ghazi Shah 1986. Louis Flam conducted the second of three seasons of excavation at Ghazi Shah, near Lake Manchar in Sindh. Working from January to May he continued excavating at the summit of the mound and one of the adjacent slopes. He uncovers a portion of the Harappan occupation (Flam 1993).

Ghazi Shah 1987. Louis Flam conducted the third of three seasons of excavation at Ghazi Shah, near Lake Manchar in Sindh. Working from January to May he uncovers a bead manufacturing workshop, a transitional Amri-Nal to Mature Harappan Transitional Stage and both Amri-Nal and Mature Harappan occupations (Flam 1993).

Ghelo and Kalubhar Valleys Survey 1960-1. P.D. Chudasama of the Gujarat State Department of Archaeology conducted a survey of the Ghelo and Kalubhar Valleys in Bhavnagar district of Saurashtra on behalf of the Gujarat State Department of Archaeology (*IAR* 1960-1: 7-9).

Ghelo and Kalubhar Valleys Survey 1970-1. Gregory L. Possehl, then of the University of Chicago, undertook an intensive survey of the Ghelo and Kalubhar Valleys in Bhavnagar (Possehl 1980).

Ghelo Valley Survey 1980. Gregory L. Possehl of the University of Pennsylvania Museum conducted a survey of the eastern end of the Ghelo Valley (unpublished).

Ghuram 1976-7. Manmohan Kumar of Kurukshetra University, in conjunction with G.B. Sharma of the Punjab Department of Archaeology carried out a small scale excavation at Ghuram, a site in Patiala district of the Punjab. This excavation is undertaken as part of his exploration of Ambala and Kurukshetra districts in neighbouring Haryana. He found a small amount of Late Harappan material, associated with Painted Grey Ware, Early Historical, Medieval and Islamic remains (Kumar 1978: 78-9, 81-7).

Gomal Valley Survey 1970-1. A.H. Dani of Quaid-i-Azam University undertook a survey of the Gomal Valley near Dera Ismail Khan. He excavated at Gumla and Hathala (Dani 1970-1).

Gufkral 1981-2. K.D. Banerji and A.K. Sharma of the Archaeological Survey of India undertake one season of excavation at Gufkral in Pulwama district of Kashmir. They found a Northern Neolithic site, much like Burzahom, but with an Aceramic Neolithic deposit (*IAR* 1981-2: 19-25).

Gumla 1970-1. A.H. Dani of Quaid-i-Azam University conducted one season of excavation at Gumla near Dera Ismail Khan in Pakistan. He found a six period site, including an Early Harappan occupation which sketches the cultural historical outline of the Bronze Age in his region (Dani 1970-1).

Harappa 1826. Charles Masson, a deserter from the Indian Army, is the first visitor to Harappa who publishes an account of his observations. Masson suggests that the site is Sangala, the capital of Porus, defeated by Alexander the Great in his last great battle in 326 BC (Masson 1842, Vol. I: 452).

Harappa 1831. Alexander Burnes of the Indian Army visited Harappa. He is the second European to recognize it as an archaeological site of importance. Burnes visited Amri in Sindh as a part of his exploration of the Greater Indus River Valley (Burnes 1835, Vol. 3: 137).

Harappa 1853. Sir Alexander Cunningham of the Archaeological Survey of India makes his first visit to Harappa. He found the mounds in good condition (Cunningham 1875: 108).

Harappa 1856. Sir Alexander Cunningham made his second visit to Harappa and reports the mounds in good condition (Cunningham 1875: 108).

Harappa 1872-3. The third visit of Sir Alexander Cunningham took place. He noted that the mounds had been subjected to brick robbing and he conducted a small excavation. Cunningham published a plan of the site and a unicorn seal belonging to a Major Clark. Because the bull on the seal has no hump Cunningham suggested that it was non-Indian (Cunningham 1875: 108).

Harappa 1884. J. Harvey, Inspector of Schools, Multan purchased an inscribed bar seal from a farmer at Harappa on November 21, 1884 (Dames 1886). The date that Harvey acquired the seal is given as December 1885 in Fleet (1912: 700).

Harappa 1886. T.A. O'Connor, District Superintendent of Police, dug up a unicorn seal at Harappa in, or shortly before, August 1886. This seal was given to M. Longworth Dames and published by J.F. Fleet along with the Cunningham and Harvey seals (Fleet 1912).

Harappa 1909. Pundit Hira Nanda Sastri of the Archaeological Survey of India went to Harappa in January 1909 on the orders of J.Ph. Vogel, Officiating Director General of the Archaeological Survey of India. Sastri reports that the mounds are not likely to repay excavation (Sahni 1920-1: 9).

Harappa 1914. Sir John Marshall of the Archaeological Survey of India sent Henry Hargreaves to assess the mounds for excavation. Hargreaves was not enthusiastic about excavation but recommended work on Mound F at the northern end of the site near the old bed of the Ravi river (Majumdar 1939: 99).

Harappa 1916-17. Rai Bahadur Daya Ram Sahni of the Archaeological Survey of India visited Harappa in December 1917. He prepared a site plan and began the process of bringing the site under the protection of the government. Sahni noted that brick robbing continued at the site (Sahni 1916-17).

Harappa 1920-1. Rai Bahadur Daya Ram Sahni excavated on Mounds F and A-B, as indicated on Cunningham's 1875 site plan. He located two more seals later said to be Pre-Mauryan (Sahni 1920-1: 8-26).

Harappa 1923-4. Rai Bahadur Daya Ram Sahni continued to excavate Mounds F and A-B. He opened, or expanded the trenches of 1920-1 and used the rain gullies to reach early levels. It is during this season that he discovered the metal ear cleaning implement with parallels at Ur and Kish (Sahni 1923-4: 22, Pl. XIX).

Harappa 1924-5. Rai Bahadur Daya Ram Sahni excavated on Mound F in the 'parallel walls' area now associated with the 'granary'. There was continued digging on the A-B Mound as well. This was Sahni's final season of excavation at Harappa. His findings were incorporated into the Vats report on the site (Vats 1940).

Harappa 1926-7. M.S. Vats of the Archaeological Survey of India moved from Mohenjo Daro to Harappa, taking over from Rai Bahadur Daya Ram Sahni. There were no excavations at Harappa in 1925-6. Vats continued the exploration of Mounds F and A with two objectives: investigate the parallel walls and ascertain the stratigraphy of the site. He exposed 4,690 sq m and found 350 seals and inscribed objects. The area of the 'parallel walls' was declared a storage building by Sir John Marshall (1926-7: 53) based on its similarity to storage rooms associated with Cretan Palaces. Marshall knows the Cretan remains well since he was trained in excavation at Knossos by Sir Arthur Evans (Vats 1926-7).

Harappa 1927-8. M.S. Vats expanded old trenches on Mounds F and A-B and moved about 8,500 cu. m of earth. He began the excavation of Cemetery H burials adjacent to the A-B Mound and continued work in the area of the 'granary' (Vats 1927-8).

Harappa 1928-9. M.S. Vats continued work on the 'granary' on Mound F. He opened new trenches opposite the *thana* mound and near the Museum designated Areas G and H. The red sandstone torso was found on Mound F just to the north of the circular threshing floors and attributed to the Harappan Civilization by Vats, but this was disputed by Marshall. An important hoard of jewelry was also found this season (Vats 1928-9).

Harappa 1929-30. M.S. Vats continued the excavation of Cemetery H and threshing platforms near the 'granary' on Mound F. He conducted a documentation of Cemetery H interments and does a plan of skeletal materials in Site G. There was an unsuccessful search for additional parts of the red sandstone torso found the previous year (Vats 1929-30).

Harappa 1930-1. M.S. Vats continued his excavation of Cemetery H as well as Site J on the A-B Mound. A grant of Rs. 20,000 supports the work (Vats 1930-4a).

Harappa 1931-2. M.S. Vats continued his excavation of Mound F at the 'workmen's quarters' on Mound F. A grant of Rs. 5,000 supports the work (Vats 1930-4b).

Harappa 1932-3. M.S. Vats undertook further excavation of the 'workmen's quarters' and threshing platforms on Mound F (Vats 1930-4c).

Harappa 1933-4. M.S. Vats continued excavation of the threshing floors on Mound F. Grant of Rs. 3,000 supports the work (Vats 1930-4d).

Harappa 1934-5. H. Nazim of the Archaeological Survey of India excavated a trench measuring 27 x 9 m on Mound F. A second trench of 28 x 4.5 m was laid on the A-B Mound. Seals and many other antiquities are published in *Annual Report*, but there was no final report on these materials (Nazim 1934-5: 31-3).

Harappa 1935-6. M.H. Kuraishi of the Archaeological Survey of India excavated an extension of Trench I on Mound D. His report on this work was less than one page and there are no illustration of the binds (Kuraishi 1935-6: 35-6).

Harappa 1936-7. H.L. Srivastava of the Archaeological Survey of India excavated a further extension of Trenches I and II on Mound D. Seals and terracottas were found but there are no illustrations of seals and no final report on this excavation (Srivastava 1936-7: 39-41).

Harappa 1937-8. K.N. Sastri of the Archaeological Survey of India discovered Cemetery R-37 and undertook the first of four seasons of excavation there in collaboration with H.K. Bose (Sastri 1965, Vol. 2: 39-40; Anonymous 1968: 63-8).

Harappa 1938-9. K.N. Sastri undertook the second of his four seasons of excavation at Cemetery R-37 in collaboration with H.K. Bose (Sastri 1965, Vol. 2: 39-40).

Harappa 1939-40. K.N. Sastri conducted the third of his four seasons of excavation at Cemetery R-37 in collaboration with H.K. Bose (Sastri 1965, Vol. 2: 39-40).

Harappa 1940-1. K.N. Sastri conducted the fourth and final season of his excavations in Cemetery R-37 in collaboration with H.K. Bose. They found a total of fifty Mature Harappan burials which have never been published (Sastri 1965, Vol. 2: 39-40).

Harappa 1946. R.E.M. Wheeler, Director General of the Archaeological Survey of India undertook excavation of the defenses on the A-B Mound as well as Cemetery R-37. He excavated a trench connecting Cemetery R- 37 and Cemetery H. Cemetery H habitations were found in the vicinity of the west gates and terraces, demonstrating the stratigraphic relationship between the Mature Harappan and this Cemetery. Deep digging produced Kot Diji type pottery in deposits below the fortifications of the A-B Mound. Wheeler proposed the Aryans as the destroyers of the Harappan Civilization (Wheeler 1947).

Harappa 1966. M.R. Mughal of the Pakistan Department of Archaeology conducted one season of excavation in Cemetery R-37. He lays one trench 30 m long and 4.5 m wide as well as a second excavation unit that was 6 sq m. Burials are found 1 m below the surface in the square trench. Eleven interments were discovered. The cemetery was originally located on sloping ground, outside the bounds of the city (Mughal 1968: 63-8).

Harappa 1986. George F. Dales of the University of California, Berkeley and J. Mark Kenoyer in partnership with the Pakistan Department of Archaeology conducted their first season of resumed excavations at Harappa. They set seven objectives for the first season: (1) they remap surface features, (2) conducted extensive and intensive surface surveys to found activity areas, (3) excavate small test trenches to guide later excavation, (4) begin a conservation program, (5) begin a program of field training for Pakistani students, (6) construct staff quarters and laboratories to be used in later seasons, and (7) initiate a search of old excavation records. Good progress was made on all of these matters (Dales 1986; Dales et al. 1991).

Harappa 1987. George F. Dales, J. Mark Kenoyer and the Pakistan Department of Archaeology conducted their second season of excavation at Harappa. They excavated Cemetery R-37 Harappa as well as the central area of Mound A-B. Forty-nine human specimens were recovered from the cemetery. A trench on A-B Mound produced Cemetery H sherds. Palaeoenvironmental studies were begun and conservation and analytical laboratories were established (Dales and Kenoyer 1987; Dales et al. 1991).

Harappa 1988. George F. Dales, J. Mark Kenoyer and the Pakistan Department of Archaeology conducted their third season of excavation at Harappa. They worked in Cemetery R-37, and Mounds A-B and E. The cemetery excavations yielded 34 individuals. A small excavation on Mound E revealed Early Harappan, Transitional Early to Mature Harappan and Mature Harappan occupations are found in trenches on A-B Mound. Palaeoenvironmental studies are also undertaken (Dales and Kenoyer 1988; Dales et al. 1991).

Harappa 1989. George F. Dales, J. Mark Kenoyer and the Pakistan Department of Archaeology conducted their fourth season of excavation at Harappa. They resumed excavations on Mound E and A-B. Mound E has an Early Harappan occupation with pottery and kilns, including domestic structures and a perimeter wall. There was a Mature Harappan occupation well. Two test trenches were put on the plain between Mounds E and A-B. Late remains (Cemetery H) were found in the A-B Mound trench in disturbed context. Fragments of structures and kilns were found. Palaeoenvironmental studies continued (Dales and Kenoyer 1989; Dales et al. 1991).

Harappa 1990. George F. Dales, J. Mark Kenoyer and the Pakistan Department of Archaeology conducted their fifth season of excavation at Harappa. They undertook excavations on Mound E which confirm the Early Harappan occupation followed by a Transitional Stage between the Mature Harappan and Early Harappan Stages as well as a very prominent Mature Harappan (Dales and Kenoyer 1990; Dales et al. 1991).

Harappa 1991. There was no field season at Harappa in 1991.

Harappa 1992. The Joint US-Pakistani team undertook excavations on Mound E which confirm the Early Harappan occupation followed by a Transitional Stage between the Mature Harappan and Early Harappan Stages as well as a very prominent Mature Harappan (Kenoyer and Meadow 1992).

Harappa 1993. George F. Dales died on April 18, 1992 and passed the leadership of the Harappa Project to Richard Meadow, Director, and J. Mark Kenoyer, Field Director in cooperation with the Pakistan Department of Archaeology. They continued excavation of the site focusing on Mound F, where they investigated the Early, Transitional and Mature Harappan levels (Meadow and Kenoyer 1993).

Harappa 1994. The Pakistan Department of Archaeology undertook exploratory excavation in the area between Mound A-B and Harappa village. They found habitation deposits, demonstrating that this area of the site was occupied in prehistoric times (unpublished).

Harappa 1994. Richard Meadow, J. Mark Kenoyer and their Pakistani collaborators continued excavation of the site focusing on Mound F, where they investigated the Early, Transitional and Mature Harappan levels (Meadow and Kenoyer 1994).

Harappa 1995. Richard Meadow, J. Mark Kenoyer and their Pakistani collaborators continue their excavations at the southern end of Harappa.

Harappa 1996. Richard Meadow, J. Mark Kenoyer and their Pakistani collaborators continue their excavations. They find a well preserved Cemetery H habitation area and more Early Harappan material. The possibility of a Hakkra Wares component is also present.

Haryana Survey 1976-7. Manmohan Kumar of Kurukshetra University undertook a exploration of Ambala and Kurukshetra districts in Haryana (Kumar 1978).

Haryana Survey 1977. Suraj Bhan of Kurukshetra University and Jim G. Shaffer of Case Western-Reserve University undertook a survey in northern Haryana (Suraj Bhan and Shaffer 1978).

Haryana Survey 1979-80. Amar Singh of Kurukshetra University undertook a exploration of Karnal and Jind districts in Haryana (Singh 1981).

Hastinapura 1950-1. B.B. Lal of the Archaeological Survey of India undertook the first of two seasons of excavation at Hastinapura in Meerut district. This site was the capital of the Kauravas of the *Mahabharata*. Lal found a long historical sequence beginning with Ochre Coloured Pottery followed by Painted Grey Ware. Ochre Coloured Pottery was first defined through Lal's work at Hastinapura (Lal 1954-5).

Hastinapura 1951-2. B.B. Lal conducted the second of two seasons of excavation at Hastinapura. He found a long historical sequence beginning with Ochre Coloured Pottery followed by Painted Grey Ware. Ochre Coloured Pottery was first defined through Lal's research (Lal 1954-5).

Hathala 1970-1. A.H. Dani of Quaid-i-Azam University undertook one season of excavation at this site near Dera Ismail Khan in Pakistan. He found that later graves have disturbed the site and he abandons excavation after two weeks. There was, however, an Early Harappan occupation (Dani 1970-1: 24, 54-63).

Hathial West 1980. F.R. Allchin of Cambridge University discovered Hathial West, inside Sirkap Mound at the ancient city of Taxila where he found an Early Harappan (Kot Dijian) settlement (Allchin 1982).

Hathial West 1981. F.R. Allchin cleans a stratigraphic face at Hathial West, inside Sirkap Mound at the ancient city of Taxila where he found an Early Harappan (Kot Dijian) settlement (Allchin 1982).

Hathial West 1989. The Pakistan Department of Archaeology continued clearing this Kot Dijian occupation inside the ancient city of Taxila (A.N. Khan 1988: 76-7).

Hathial West 1990. The Pakistan Department of Archaeology continued clearing this Kot Dijian occupation inside the ancient city of Taxila (A.N. Khan 1988: 76-7).

Hulas 1978-9. K.N. Dikshit of the Archaeological Survey of India conducted the first of five seasons of excavation at Hulas in Uttar Pradesh, district Saharanpur. He found the remains of Harappan settlement followed by historical occupations (*IAR* 1978-9: 60-1).

Hulas 1979-80. K.N. Dikshit conducted the second of five seasons of excavation at Hulas. In Period I he found Harappan occupation followed by Painted Grey Ware, Kushanas and other historical material (*IAR* 1979-80: 82).

Hulas 1980-1. K.N. Dikshit undertook the third of five seasons of excavation at Hulas. In Period I he found Harappan mud platform. Period II was Painted Grey Ware. Later historical material was present as well (see *IAR* 1980-1: 73-6).

Hulas 1981-2. K.N. Dikshit conducted the fourth of five seasons of excavation at Hulas. In Period I he found a Harappan mud platform small furnaces, burnt brick (*IAR* 1981-2: 72-4).

Hulas 1982-3. K.N. Dikshit undertook the fifth and final season of excavation at Hulas. He investigates the three phases of Harappan occupation and found that it covers 2,000 sq m and has 43 structures including rectangular and brick structures, circular structures, furnaces and *chulas*. Found in Harappan context: rice, wheat, barley, horse gram, green gram, black gram, peas, and ragi or finger millet. Non-

Harappan pottery was found in lowest levels. Copper fish hooks, chisels, needles, spiral rings are also found (*IAR* 1982-3: 100-3).

Iran Survey 1932-3. Sir Aurel Stein of the Archaeological Survey of India undertook exploration in south-eastern Iran. He revisits Sutkagen-dor on this visit and publishes the correct spelling of the name (Stein 1937).

Iran Survey 1934-5. Sir Aurel Stein undertook exploration in Iran (Stein 1940).

Iran Survey 1935-6. Sir Aurel Stein undertook exploration in Iran (Stein 1940).

Islam Chowki 1985. The Bannu Archaeological Project, a joint undertaking by the University of Peshawar, the British Museum and the University of London, Institute of Archaeology undertook one season of test excavation at Islam Chowki in Bannu. The site has Early Kot Dijian and Late Kot Dijian occupation (Khan et al. 1991).

Jakhera 1974-5. K.A. Nizami and M.D.N. Sahi of Aligarh Muslim University began the first of three seasons of work at Jakhera in Uttar Pradesh, district Etah. Period I, which was stratified under a Painted Grey Ware settlement, has Black and Red Ware, Black Slipped Ware and Coarse Red Ware. There are no painted ceramics in Period I. Period II has Painted Grey Ware and Period III has Northern Black Polished Ware (*IAR* 1974-5: 43-5).

Jakhera 1975-6. K.A. Nizami and M.D.N. Sahi undertook the second of three seasons of work at Jakhera (*IAR* 1975-6: 50-1).

Jakhera 1985-6. K.A. Nizami and M.D.N. Sahi undertook the third of three seasons of work at Jakhera. The revised sequence for this site indicates that Period I was an Ochre Coloured Pottery settlement (*IAR* 1985-6: 79-81).

Jalilpur 1971. M.R. Mughal of the Pakistan Department of Archaeology conducted excavations at Jalilpur in the west Punjab. He found an Early Harappan settlement with two phases of occupation. The earliest seems to be equivalent to the Hakkra Wares or Amri I, the second was a more conventional Kot Diji Phase, Early Harappan (Mughal 1972b).

Jalilpur 1975. M.R. Mughal conducted a second season of excavations at Jalilpur (Mughal, unpublished).

Jamnagar District Survey 1978-9: Kuldeep Bhan of the M.S. University of Baroda undertook a survey of Jamnagar district in Saurashtra. He found over 100 Protohistoric sites (Bhan 1986: 1-21).

Jamnagar District Survey 1979-80. Kuldeep Bhan continued his survey of Jamnagar district (Bhan 1986: 1-21).

Jamnagar District Survey 1980-1. Kuldeep Bhan continued his survey of Jamnagar district (Bhan 1986: 1-21).

Jamnagar District Survey 1981-2. Kuldeep Bhan continued his survey of Jamnagar district (Bhan 1986: 1-21).

Jekhada 1990-1. A team from the M.S. University of Baroda excavated this site in Banaskantha district of north Gujarat. They found a site very much like Nagwada (Bhan 1994: 80-1).

Jhang 1974. The Pakistan Department of Archaeology excavated Jhang in Campbellpur district. They found a site with both an Early and Late Kot Dijian occupation (unpublished).

Jhang 1981-2: F.R. Allchin and the Cambridge-Peshawar Team collect radiocarbon samples from a foundation trench excavated by a contractor at Jhang; an Early and Late Kot Dijian site (Thomas and Allchin 1986).

Jhangar 1930. N.G. Majumdar of the Archaeological Survey of India undertook a brief excavation at Jhangar, near Lake Manchar in Sindh. He found a small settlement with grey incised pottery that remains undated, but does not seem to be associated with iron (Majumdar 1934: 68-70).

Jhukar 1927-8. N.G. Majumdar excavated the site of Jhukar in Sindh. He found a stratified Mature Harappan and Jhukar settlement (Majumdar 1927-8, 1934: 5-18).

Jhukar 1973. M.R. Mughal of the Pakistan Department of Archaeology conducted the first of two seasons of excavations at Jhukar in Sindh. He found that the Jhukar levels have a considerable amount of Mature Harappan ceramics associated with this distinctive ware (Mughal 1992).

Jhukar 1973-4. M.R. Mughal conducted the second of two seasons of excavations at Jhukar (Mughal 1992).

Jodhpura 1972-3. Vijay Kumar of the Rajasthan Department of Archaeology conducted one season of excavation at Jodhpura in district Jaipur, Rajasthan. He found a site closely to Ganeshwar. Period I was an Ochre Coloured Pottery occupation with copper. Period II has plain Black and Red Ware with similarities to that at Noh. Period III has Painted Grey Ware and Period IV has Northern Black Polished Ware. Period V was a Sunga-Kushana occupation (*IAR* 1972-3: 29-30; Agrawala and Kumar 1982).

Jokha 1966-7. R.N. Mehta of the M.S. University of Baroda conducted excavations at Jokha, district Surat in Gujarat. He found a Chalcolithic site with relationships to the Harappan sites of Saurashtra. There are also Malwa and Jorwe ceramics (*IAR* 1966-77: 10).

Kalako-deray 1989. Giorgio Stacul of IsMEO conducted excavation at Kalako-deray of the Swat Protohistoric (both Periods III and IV). Much material relating to the Northern Neolithic was also recovered (Stacul 1993).

Kalako-deray 1990. Giorgio Stacul undertook the second season of excavation at Kalako-deray of the Swat protohistoric (both Periods III and IV) (Stacul 1993).

Kalat Survey 1948. Beatrice de Cardi of the British Academy conducted a survey of Kalat in Baluchistan (de Cardi 1983).

Kalat Survey 1957. Beatrice de Cardi continued a survey of Kalat in Baluchistan (de Cardi 1983).

Kalayat 1969. S.R. Phogat of Kurukshetra University conducted a small excavation at Kalayat in Jind district of Haryana. He found a Post-Urban Harappan and Painted Grey Ware site (Phogat 1970: 137-40).

Kalepar 1942. Sir Aurel Stein of the Archaeological Survey of India conducted a trial excavation at Kalepar on the ancient Sarasvati river in what is now Pakistan. It was an Early Harappan site, later surveyed by M.R. Mughal. It was also known as 'Bhoot' (Stein 1943a: 118-21).

Kalibangan 1917. Luigi P. Tessitori of the Archaeological Survey of India visited Kalibangan in April 1917 (Tessitori 1917-18; Stein 1943a: 51).

Kalibangan 1918. Luigi P. Tessitori undertook a small excavation. He called the site Kali Vangu in his manuscript (Tessitori n.d.), but Kali Banga in another report (Tessitori 1918-19: 23). Stein noted from Tessitori: '... it appears that according to information he received from Warren, an employee of the Bikaner State Railway, much had been removed from the mounds for ballast in constructing the railway' (Tessitori 1918-19; Stein 1943a: 51).

Kalibangan 1941. Sir Aurel Stein of the Archaeological Survey of India visited the site and discussed Tessitori's work. Stein gives no hint that the site was Harappan (Stein 1943a: 49-52).

Kalibangan 1950. A. Ghosh of the Archaeological Survey of India visited Kalibangan as a part of his survey of the ancient Sarasvati river. He recognized it as an Harappan settlement (Ghosh 1952).

Kalibangan 1960-1. B.B. Lal of the Archaeological Survey of India began the first of nine seasons of excavation at Kalibangan in Rajasthan. This work was based on A. Ghosh's exploration. The site will be the training excavation for students during all nine seasons of work. Lal set two objectives for the first season of work: (1) to look for variation in the Harappan Culture as represented at Kalibangan and (2) determine the pattern of habitation at the site. He found definite evidence of town planning at Kalibangan, just as at Mohenjo Daro and Harappa (*IAR* 1960-1: 31-2).

Kalibangan 1961-2. B.K. Thapar of the Archaeological Survey of India undertook the second of nine seasons of excavation at Kalibangan. He set two goals for work: (1) to assess the non-Harappan elements found in the pottery from the lowest levels during the previous season and (2) determine the presence or absence of a citadel or acropolis (*IAR* 1961-2: 39-44).

Kalibangan 1962-3. B.B. Lal and B.K. Thapar conducted the third of nine seasons of excavation at Kalibangan. They set the following objectives for the third season: (1) elaborate the Pre-Harappan cultural assemblage, (2) to determine whether there was, or was not, a rampart at the smaller of the two mounds and (3) expose a portion of the Harappan township through horizontal digging. They also defined Fabrics A-F for the pre-Harappan pottery (*IAR* 1962-3: 20-31).

Kalibangan 1963-4. B.B. Lal and B.K. Thapar conducted the fourth of nine seasons of excavation at Kalibangan. They set four objectives (in addition to training): (1) complete the plans for the pre-Harappan houses, (2) continue the investigation of the fortification wall around the smaller of the two mounds, (3) expose more of the Harappan architecture on the larger of the two mounds, and (4) locate the cemetery and expose interments (*IAR* 1963-4: 30-9).

Kalibangan 1964-5. B.B. Lal and B.K. Thapar conducted the fifth of nine seasons of excavation at Kalibangan. The following objectives were set for this season:

(1) investigate the fortification wall, (2) obtain plans of Harappan houses in different periods, (3) excavate more Harappan graves to assess burial practices (*IAR* 1964-5: 35-9).

Kalibangan 1965-6. B.B. Lal and B.K. Thapar undertook the sixth of nine seasons of excavation at Kalibangan. They set four objectives: (1) complete the details of the fortification wall for Period II Mature Harappan on the southern half of the Citadel, (2) investigate the occupation on the northern half of the citadel, (3) determine whether or not there was a Period II fortification wall around the Lower Town, and (4) uncover Harappan house plans of successive structural phases in the Lower Town (*IAR* 1965-6: 38-41).

Kalibangan 1966-7. B.B. Lal and B.K. Thapar undertook the seventh of nine seasons of excavation at Kalibangan. They set five objectives for this season: (1) investigate the fortification wall around the northern half of the citadel, especially on the eastern and western sides (2) investigate the structures on the northern half of the Citadel, (3) completely expose one of the mud brick platforms of Period II on the southern half of the Citadel, (4) continue the investigation of the fortification wall around the Lower Town, and (5) further the exposure of the thoroughfares on the Lower Town (*IAR* 1966-7: 31-3).

Kalibangan 1967-8. B.B. Lal and B.K. Thapar undertook the eighth of nine seasons of excavation at Kalibangan. They set the following objectives for this season: (1) to further investigate the fortification wall on the western side of the Lower Town, (2) to create sections in the Lower Town that connect the fortification wall with the north-south streets on both the eastern and western sides of the Lower Town, (3) uncover house plans of successive structural phases in the Lower Town, and (4) determine in as many cases as possible the extent of Harappan platforms on the citadel. The first plan of the site was prepared (*IAR* 1967-8: 42-5).

Kalibangan 1968-9. B.B. Lal, B.K. Thapar and Jagat Pati Joshi set four objectives for the ninth and final season of work: (1) further trace for fortification wall of the Lower Town on the northern, southern and western sides, (2) uncover the lay-out of streets on the northern half of the Lower Town, (3) investigate the structure to the east of the Lower Town known as KLB-3, and (4) expose more burials in the cemetery. There was no suggestion that this would be the last season of work (*IAR* 1968-9: 28-32).

Kanewal 1977. K.N. Momin a graduate student at the M.S. University of Baroda undertook work at Kanewal, District Kheda in Gujarat. He found a stratified Sorath Harappan settlement in a dune associated with a microlithic component. Some suggestion of a Late Sorath Harappan component was also present in the form of Lustrous Red Ware (*IAR* 1977-8: 21; Mehta et al. 1980).

Kantli River Survey 1978. K.N. Dikshit of the Archaeological Survey of India conducted a survey of the Kantli river in northeastern Rajasthan. He surveys from Neemka-Thana to Pilani (*IAR* 1977-8: 47-9).

Kaothe 1984-85. M.K. Dhavalikar of Deccan College conducted one season of excavation at Kaothe in Maharashtra, district Dhulia. The initial reports on the ceramics from Kaothe linked them with 'Late Harappan' related to the Gujarat sites in this period. This was later changed to reflect an affiliation with the Deccan Chalcolithic, although some 'influence' from the Harappans in Gujarat was still recognized (Dhavalikar et al. 1990).

Kapoto Rock-shelter 1955. Henry Field of Harvard University undertook a test excavation at Kapoto Rock-shelter in Kalat. He found Togau and Kechi Beg ceramics (Field 1959: 97-8, 189).

Karez Site 1950-1. Walter A. Fairservis, Jr. of the American Museum of Natural History directed a test excavation at this site in the Quetta Valley of Baluchistan. He found an Amri-Nal Phase settlement (Fairservis 1956).

Kargushki Damb 1927. Sir Aurel Stein of the Archaeological Survey of India conducted a test excavation at this site in Pakistani Makran. He found a large stratified site with Kechi Beg, Amri-Nal and Early Kulli occupations (Stein 1931: 38-41).

Kathpalon 1976-7. Jagat Pati Joshi of the Archaeological Survey of India undertook one season of excavation at Kathpalon in the Punjab, district Jullundur. He found a 'Late Harappan' site with a progressive evolution to the Painted Grey Ware. A Kushana occupation was also present (*IAR* 1976-7: 42).

Kaudani 1927-8. Sir Aurel Stein of the Archaeological Survey of India excavated a trial trench at Kaudani 8 km south-west of Fort Sandeman in Zhob. He found a site with a Zhob and Quetta occupation followed by Buddhist and Partho-Sassanian material (Stein 1929: 41-2).

Kechi Beg 1950-1. Walter A. Fairservis, Jr. of the American Museum of Natural History directed a test excavation at this site in the Quetta Valley of Baluchistan. He found a Kechi Beg Phase settlement (Fairservis 1956).

Khatoli 1978-9. R.P. Sharma of the Archaeological Survey of India undertook a trial excavation at Khatoli in Mahendragarh district of Haryana. He found a small, simple settlement of the Post-Urban Harappan (Sharma 1982: 123-5).

Kheda District Survey 1977-8. K.N. Momin of the M.S. University of Baroda conducted a survey of Kheda district in Gujarat. He located 20 Sorath Harappan sites, many of which seem to have evidence for interaction with microlithic peoples in the vicinity (Momin 1979).

Kherai Graveyard 1966. Giorgio Stacul of IsMEO conducted an excavation at the Kherai Graveyard in the Swat Valley of Pakistan. He found interments of the 'Swat Valley Protohistoric'; 'Period IV' (Stacul 1987: 64-5, 71-3).

Kili Ghul Mohammad 1950-1. Walter A. Fairservis, Jr. of the American Museum of Natural History and Harvard University directed one season of excavation at this site in the Quetta Valley of Baluchistan as a part of the Second Afghan Expedition. The Second Afghan Expedition was in the field for ten months, from August 1950 until May 1951. The excavation was supervised in large part by Rose Lillian Solecki. They found a four period sequence beginning with an aceramic Neolithic (Kili Ghul Mohammed Phase) and ending with a Chalcolithic (Kechi Beg Phase) occupation (Fairservis 1956).

Kohtras Buthi 1931. N.G. Majumdar of the Archaeological Survey of India conducted a small clearance excavation at Kohtras Buthi on the Baran Nai in Sindh Kohistan. He found a fortified Kot Dijian site (Majumdar 1934: 132-4).

Kot Diji 1935. G.S. Ghurye of Bombay University explored parts of Sindh and visited Kot Diji, among other sites (Ghurye 1936).

Kot Diji 1955. F.A. Khan, Director of the Pakistan Department of Archaeology undertook the first of two seasons of excavation at Kot Diji in Khairpur district, just across the Indus river from Mohenjo Daro. He found a stratified Kot Dijian site, with a Mature Harappan occupation above it (F.A. Khan 1965).

Kot Diji 1957. F.A. Khan conducted the second of two seasons of excavation at Kot Diji (F.A. Khan 1965).

Kotla Nihang Khan 1929-30. M.S. Vats of the Archaeological Survey of India puts four trial trenches at this Harappan site (Vats 1929-30: 131-2).

Kotla Nihang Khan 1955. Y.D. Sharma of the Archaeological Survey of India reopens the excavation of Kotla Nihang Khan 2 km south-east of Ropar. The site was first excavated by M.S. Vats in 1929-30. Sharma found evidence for a Mature Harappan site in contrast to other sites in the neighbourhood such as Bara and Rupar (Y.D. Sharma 1982a: 141).

Kranai Hill 1927. Sir Aurel Stein excavated at Kranai Hill north-east of Pishin in Baluchistan. He found evidence for a site occupied during the Damb Sadaat and Quetta Phases (Stein 1929: 85-6).

Kudwala Ther 1942. Sir Aurel Stein conducted a trial excavation at Kudwala Ther on the ancient Sarasvati river in what is now Pakistan. It was a Mature Harappan and Cemetery H site that Stein reports as being over 80 ha in size (Stein 1943a: 113-15).

Kulli 1928. Sir Aurel Stein conducted a test excavation at this site in the Kolwa Valley of Baluchistan. He found a large stratified site with a Kulli occupation (Stein 1931: 118-27).

Kunal 1985-6. The Haryana Department of Archaeology conducted an excavation at Kunal in Hissar district of Haryana. They found an Early Harappan (Kalibangan I) occupation in Period I which was followed in Period II by a Bara occupation and finally a Medieval Period III (*IAR* 1985-6: 23-5).

Kuntasi 1987-8. M.K. Dhavalikar of Deccan College and Y.M. Chitalwala of the Gujarat State Department of Archaeology conducted the first of three seasons of excavation at Kuntasi near the Little Rann of Kachchh in Rajkot district of Gujarat. They found a Sorath Harappan site that may have been a small port (Dhavalikar 1992, 1993).

Kuntasi 1988-9. M.K. Dhavalikar of Deccan College and Y.M. Chitalwala of the Gujarat State Department of Archaeology conducted the second of three seasons of excavation at Kuntasi (Dhavalikar 1992, 1993).

Kuntasi 1989-90. M.K. Dhavalikar of Deccan College and Y.M. Chitalwala of the Gujarat State Department of Archaeology conducted the third of three seasons of excavation at Kuntasi (Dhavalikar 1992, 1993).

Kachchh Survey 1965. In January 1965 Jagat Pati Joshi of the Archaeological Survey of

India undertook a systematic survey of Kachchh. He found many Protohistoric sites including Dholavira and Surkotada (Joshi 1972: 21-35).

Kachchh Survey 1965-6. In December 1965 Jagat Pati Joshi continued a systematic survey of Kachchh (Joshi 1972: 21-35).

Kachchh Survey 1968. In January 1968 Jagat Pati Joshi continued a systematic survey of Kachchh (Joshi 1972: 21-35).

Lak Largai 1985. The Bannu Archaeological Project, a joint undertaking by the University of Peshawar, the British Museum and the University of London, Institute of Archaeology initiates the first season of excavation at Lak Largai in Bannu. It was a Kot Dijian site equivalent to Rehman Dheri I (Khan et al. 1991: 24-31).

Lak Largai 1986. The Bannu Archaeological Project continued with a second season of excavation at Lak Largai (Khan et al. 1991: 24-31).

Lakhabawal 1955-6. P.P. Pandya of the Gujarat State Department of Archaeology and B. Subbarao of M.S. University of Baroda conducted one season of test excavations at Lakhabawal in district Jamnagar of Gujarat. They found Period I, Sorath Harappan with Black and Red Ware (Rojdi A-B?) and some Lustrous Red Ware. Period II, Red Polished Ware. Period III, Medieval (*IAR* 1955-6: 7).

Lakhiyo 1930. N.G. Majumdar of the Archaeological Survey of India excavated at Lakhiyo just to the east of Lake Manchar in western Sindh. He found a Mature Harappan settlement (Majumdar 1934: 67-8).

Lal Qila 1968-9. R.C. Gaur of Aligarh Muslum University conducted the first of three seasons of excavation at Lal Qila, an Ochre Coloured Pottery site in Bulandshahr District of Uttar Pradesh. A Copper Hoard has been found at Kiratapur, 3 km from Lal Qila. Gaur found the first Ochre Coloured Pottery site with sound evidence for architecture which comes in the form of plastered floors (*IAR* 1968-9: 35-7).

Lal Qila 1969-70. R.C. Gaur of Aligarh Muslim University conducted the second of three seasons of excavation at Lal Qila (*IAR* 1969-70: 38-40).

Lal Qila 1971-2. R.C. Gaur of Aligarh Muslim University conducted the fourth of three seasons of excavation at Lal Qila (*IAR* 1971-2: 45-6).

Las Bela and South-western Sindh Survey 1959-60. Walter A. Fairservis, Jr. of the American Museum of Natural History undertook a survey of Las Bela and South-western Sindh. He visited Tharro Hill and many other sites and discovered a large number of Kulli sites (Complex A) and Complex B in Las Bela (Fairservis 1971: 185-208).

Las Bela Survey 1943. Sir Aurel Stein of the Archaeological Survey of India conducted a survey of Las Bela and excavated at Niai Buthi. This was Stein's final exploratory tour prior to his death in Kabul that same year (Stein 1943b).

Lewan 1977-8. The Joint University of Peshawar-Cambridge University team conducted a single season of excavation at Lewan in the Bannu Basin of Pakistan. They uncovered a small, temporary settlement that seems to have been a factory site for the manufacture of a wide range of stone tools during Kot Dijian times. The site parallels Rehman Dheri in time, although it was much smaller and would have only been occupied sporadically during this long period (Allchin et al. 1986).

Loebanr III 1968. Giorgio Stacul of IsMEO conducted the first of three seasons of excavation at Loebanr III in the Swat Valley of Pakistan. He found a settlement of the Swat Valley Protohistoric; Period IV. There are two building levels, the earliest consisting of semi-subterranean houses, the second with dry stone masonry at ground level (Stacul 1987: 55-9).

Loebanr III 1976. Giorgio Stacul undertook the second of three seasons of excavation at Loebanr III (Stacul 1987: 55-9).

Loebanr III 1979. Giorgio Stacul conducted the third of three seasons of excavation at Loebanr III (Stacul 1987: 55-9).

Lohri 1930. N.G. Majumdar of the Archaeological Survey of India excavated at Lohri near Lake Manchar in western Sindh. He found an Amri-Nal and Mature Harappan settlement with the possibility of a transitional phase between them (Majumdar 1934: 66-7).

Lohunjo-daro 1930. N.G. Majumdar excavated at Lohumjo-daro on the western side of the Indus river near the village of Pat in Dadu taluka. He found a Mature Harappan settlement with a Jhukar occupation above it (Majumdar 1934: 48-58).

Loteshwar 1991. A team from the M.S. University of Baroda excavated this site in Banaskantha district of north Gujarat. They found a two period site with a microlithic occupation below one of the Anrata Chalcolithic. The Anrata Chalcolithic at Loteshwar has no Harappan elements in it (Ajithprasad and Sonawane, in press).

Lothal 1954-5. S.R. Rao of the Archaeological Survey of India began the first of eight seasons of excavation at Lothal in Saurashtra. He undertook the work in February 1955 at the highest point of the mound. He immediately found a small seal with a bird and a single sign. A total of six inscribed objects are found. Ceramics and other finds confirm that Lothal, Rangpur, and other sites in Saurashtra are Harappan (*IAR* 1954-5: 12; Rao 1979: 21-2)

Lothal 1955-6. S.R. Rao undertook the second of eight seasons of excavation at Lothal. Rao conducted deep digging and found evidence for floods in the lowest levels. He uncovers solid brick platforms of the 'warehouse'. Two steatite seals, three terracotta seals and 107 sealings are found (*IAR* 1955-6: 6-7).

Lothal 1956-7. S.R. Rao undertook the third of eight seasons of excavation at Lothal. He set two goals for this season of excavation: (1) to determine the extent and function of the platforms later identified as the 'warehouse'; (2) identify the structural phases of the site. Rao defined six structural phases (*IAR* 1956-7: 15-16).

Lothal 1957-8. S.R. Rao undertook the fourth of eight seasons of excavation at Lothal. He resumed excavation of Lothal with the aim of determining the layout of streets, continued his investigation of the 'warehouse', and to understand further the ceramic sequence, especially with respect to Black and Red Ware. He discovered a bead factory and kiln, a terracotta head of a bearded man and a possible copper anthropomorph (*IAR* 1957-8: 11-13).

Lothal 1958-9. S.R. Rao undertook the fifth of eight seasons of excavation at Lothal. He identified the 'dockyard'. The first good plan of the site was produced. The Post-Urban Harappan (Lothal B) settlement was identified. A twin burial was discovered in the cemetery. Rao publishes an aerial photograph of the site (*IAR* 1958-9: 13-15).

Lothal 1959-60. S.R. Rao undertook the sixth of eight seasons of excavation at Lothal. He proposed that this will be the final season of excavation. The town was divided into six major blocks. The limits of the ancient town are determined along with the function of the 'dockyard'. More excavation in the cemetery (*IAR* 1959-60: 16-18).

Lothal 1961-2. S.R. Rao undertook the seventh of eight seasons of excavation at Lothal. Rao excavated again to determine the position of Micaceous Red Ware and to see if there was a gap between Lothal A and B. Micaceous Red Ware are always associated with Harappan ceramics at the site. A 'Persian Gulf Seal' was reported to have been found on the surface (*IAR* 1961-2: 9-10).

Lothal 1962-3. S.R. Rao undertook the eighth and final season of excavation at Lothal. Rao excavated the northern end of the site and identifies a bund to protect the settlement from flood as well as the 'flow- channel' of the Nala used for access to the 'dockyard' (*IAR* 1962-3: 7).

Mahorana 1982. Y.D. Sharma, working with the Punjab Department of Archaeology undertook one season of excavation at Mahorana in Sangrur district of the Punjab. He found a Bara site (Y.D. Sharma 1987).

Makran Survey 1960. George F. Dales of The University Museum undertook a survey of the Makran and found the new Harappan site of Sotka Koh. He also conducted small excavation at Sutkagen-dor (Dales 1962; Dales and Lipo 1992).

Makran Survey 1987. Roland Besenval, a scholar from the Centre National de la Recherche Scientifique, working with an Italian research team and the Pakistan Department of Archaeology undertook a survey in the western Makran. He began by visiting sites such as Sutkagen-dor and Shahi Tump, known from Sir Aurel Stein's surveys, but discovered many more new settlements. The presence of Bampur material in the area documents contact with eastern Iran (Besenval and Sanlaville 1990).

Makran Survey 1988. Roland Besenval undertook the second season of survey in the western Makran. He defined a third millennium, pre-Harappan, Dasht Period; there was a Kulli-Harappan presence in the second half of the third millennium. Shahi Tump material was also present in the area, but was undated. Finally, his Zangian Period was associated with burial carins and Londo Ware, as well as other related pottery (Besenval and Sanlaville 1990).

Makran Survey 1989. Roland Besenval continued his survey of the Makran. He continued exploration of the region, undertook georchaeological studies and collects samples for radiocarbon dating (Besenval and Sanlaville 1990).

Malvan 1969-70. Jagat Pati Joshi of the Archaeological Survey of India and F.R. Allchin of Cambridge University conducted one season of excavation at Malvan in district

Surat, Gujarat. They found a Rojdi B-C site (*IAR* 1969-70: 7-9; Allchin and Joshi 1995).

Manda 1977. Jagat Pati Joshi of the Archaeological Survey of India conducted one season of excavation at Manda in district Jammu, Jammu and Kashmir, in April 1977. He found Early Harappan Red Ware associated with Mature Harappan Red Ware, both Plain and Painted, along with Harappan script, Early Historical and Kushana pottery (*IAR* 1976-7: 19-23).

Mashak 1930. N.G. Majumdar of the Archaeological Survey of India excavated at Mashak near Lake Manchar in western Sindh. He found a Mature Harappan settlement (Majumdar 1934: 63-4).

Mehgam 1957-8. S.R. Rao of the Archaeological Survey of India undertook a test excavation at this site on the northern side of the estuary of the Narmada river on the Gulf of Cambay. He found a Sorath Harappan type site (Rao 1963: 189-90).

Mehi 1928. Sir Aurel Stein of the Archaeological Survey of India undertook a test excavation at this site in Pakistani Baluchistan. He found a large stratified site with a Kulli occupation and some material relating to Dashli 3 in northern Afghanistan (Stein 1931: 153-63).

Mehrgarh 1974-5. Jean-Francois Jarrige of the Centre National de la Recherche Scientifique and the Musee Guimet directed the first season of excavation at Mehrgarh in Kachi. The work began on 17 November 1974. Excavation in that part of the site yields a cultural sequence parallel to that of Damb Sadaat in Quetta. This report contains the first mention of Nausharo as an Harappan site (Jarrige 1979).

Mehrgarh 1975-6. Jean-Francois Jarrige directed the second season of excavation at Mehrgarh. He excavated in areas which yield material comparable to the first season (Jarrige and Lechevallier 1979: 465).

Mehrgarh 1976-7. Jean-Francois Jarrige directed the third season of excavation at Mehrgarh. Exposure of Periods I and II, the ceramic and aceramic Neolithic levels began (Jarrige and Lechevallier 1979: 465-7) and produces the first seven period chronology (Jarrige and Lechevallier 1979).

Mehrgarh 1977-8. Jean-Francois Jarrige directed the fourth season of excavation at Mehrgarh. The focus of the season was on Period I, the aceramic Neolithic, with some probing of Periods II and III (Meadow 1993).

Mehrgarh 1978-9. Jean-Francois Jarrige directed the fifth season of excavation at Mehrgarh. All of the major areas are sites of excavation this season. A new cemetery in MR.1 south was found. This was said to date to the beginning of the second millennium BC. There was a report on palaeobotany by L. Costantini (Jansen et al. 1991; Meadow 1993).

Mehrgarh 1979-80. Jean-Francois Jarrige directed the sixth season of excavation at Mehrgarh. There was excavation in all of the major areas of the site, with clarification of Periods IB and IIB. Marielle Santoni directed the first season at Sibri, or the South Cemetery at Mehrgarh (Meadow 1993).

Mehrgarh 1980-1. Jean-Francois Jarrige directed the seventh season of excavation at Mehrgarh. Excavation focuses on Periods I, II and III as well as in area MR.1, with the later part of the sequence. Marielle Santoni directed the second season at Sibri, or the South Cemetery at Mehrgarh and publishes a major summary in the preliminary report (Jansen et al. 1991; Meadow 1993).

Mehrgarh 1981-2. Jean-Francois Jarrige directed the eighth season of excavation at Mehrgarh. Periods I and II are the focus of the season. The cliff face along the Bolan river was exposed, illustrating the early stratigraphy of the site. There was some excavation in MR.1, with the later portion of the Mehrgarh sequence. Marielle Santoni directed the third season at Sibri, or the South Cemetery at Mehrgarh (Jansen et al. 1991; Meadow 1993).

Mehrgarh 1982-3. Jean-Francois Jarrige directed the ninth season of excavation at Mehrgarh. The aceramic Neolithic of Period I was the focus of work, with additional excavation of areas with Period II, III and the later part of the sequence. The beginnings of the 'Physical Anthropological Project' are outlined in the preliminary report (Jansen et al. 1991; Meadow 1993).

Mehrgarh 1983-4. Jean-Francois Jarrige directed the tenth season of excavation at Mehrgarh. There was excavation of all periods, except Period II. The pottery kiln at Lal Shah was discovered by workmen and then studied by Rita Wright and Stephano Pracchia. A substantial review of the Lal Shah was included in the preliminary report which concludes that it belongs to Period VIIC. See Santoni (1989) for Lal Shah. There was a report on lithic use-ware outlined. The Physical Anthropological Project continued (Jansen et al. 1991; Meadow 1993).

Mehrgarh 1984-5. Jean-Francois Jarrige directed the eleventh season of excavation at Mehrgarh. There was excavation in all areas of the site, including Lal Shah. There are reports on fauna, use wear on stone tools, physical anthropology, dental anthropology and environmental reconstruction through the use of ancient charcoal (Jansen et al. 1991; Meadow 1993).

Mehrgarh 1985-6. Jean-Francois Jarrige directed the twelfth season of research at Mehrgarh. There was no excavation at Mehrgarh, but L. Wengler continued the geomorphological studies of the region in connection with the settlement of Mehrgarh. This was the first season at Nausharo (Jarrige 1986).

Miri Qalat 1990. Roland Besenval, a scholar with the Centre National de la Recherche Scientifique, working with an Italian Research team, and the Government of Pakistan excavated the Miri of Turbat in the Makran. The site is locally known as Miri Qalat. He found a Mature Harappan site to the east of the Islamic fortress and stratified Early Harappan materials to the west. The presence of Shahi Tump Grey Ware was attested in this western sondage (Besenval and Marquis 1993).

Miri Qalat 1991. Roland Besenval excavated Miri Qalat (Besenval 1994).

Miri Qalat 1992. Roland Besenval excavated Miri Qalat in the Makran. He found a four period site with a Mature Harappan occupation on the top. The presence of Shahi Tump Grey Ware was attested in Period II (Besenval 1994).

Miri Qalat 1993. Roland Besenval excavated Miri Qalat (Besenval 1994).

Miri Qalat 1994. Roland Besenval excavated Miri Qalat (unpublished).

Mirzapur 1975-6. U.V. Singh and Suraj Bhan of Kurukshetra University conducted excavations at Mirzapur in Kurukshetra District of Haryana. They found a Mature Harappan site (*IAR* 1975-6: 18).

Mitathal 1968. Suraj Bhan of Kurukshetra University excavated Mitathal in Haryana. He found a Mature Harappan and Post-Urban Harappan settlement. A Copper Hoard was also found at the site, but not as part of systematic excavation (Suraj Bhan 1975).

Moghul Ghundai 1927. Sir Aurel Stein of the Archaeological Survey of India excavated Moghul Ghundai in Zhob district of Baluchistan. He found a Quetta Period site with a Buddhist occupation following it (Stein 1929: 43-9).

Mohenjo Daro 1911-12. D.R. Bhandarkar of the Archaeological Survey of India visited Mohenjo Daro and suggests that it was only 250 years old (Bhandarkar 1911-12).

Mohenjo Daro 1919-20. R.D. Banerji of the Archaeological Survey of India visited Mohenjo Daro (Banerji 1920-1).

Mohenjo Daro 1922-3. R.D. Banerji returns to Mohenjo Daro and excavated 'Sites 1 and 2' on the Mound of the Great Bath and 'Site 3' just to the north. He discovered Harappan seals below the Kushana stupa and monastery (Banerji 1926: 29).

Mohenjo Daro 1923-4. M.S. Vats of the Archaeological Survey of India puts two long trenches in VS Area. He confirms that Harappan remains are directly under the surface and that there was good stratigraphy in the Lower City. Baked brick drains and ten more Harappan seals are discovered (Vats 1923-4).

Mohenjo Daro 1924-5. K.N. Dikshit of the Archaeological Survey of India excavated in the DK Area on the northern part of the Lower City. There are many good antiquities, including a large carnelian bead necklace or girdle. The first contour plan was published (Dikshit 1924-5).

Mohenjo Daro 1925-6. Sir John Marshall of the Archaeological Survey of India excavated the stupa area and uncovers the Great Bath. This was Marshall's only season of excavation at Mohenjo Daro. B.L. Dhama excavated another portion of the Mound of the Great Bath, referred to as DM Area. This was just to the south of the Stupa. Hargreaves began work in HR Area, which today is the eastern portion. Vats extended his area of excavation begun in 1924-5. The 'Priest King' and major limestone statues are discovered (Marshall 1925-6).

Mohenjo Daro 1926-7. Rai Bahadur Daya Ram Sahni and Ernest J.H. Mackay of the Archaeological Survey of India work jointly at Mohenjo Daro. Sahni excavated in HR and VS areas. Mackay works in L Area on the southern end of the Mound of the Great Bath. Mackay uncovers the 'Assembly Hall'. Cotton cloth adhering to a copper vase was discovered. The Bronze Dancing Girl was found in House LV of Block 7 in HR Area (Sahni 1926-7).

Mohenjo Daro 1927-8. Ernest J.H. Mackay of the Archaeological Survey of India was placed in charge of field work. He excavated the area between the Great Bath and stupa on the Mound of the Great Bath and in DK Area where he found what he calls a series of artisan's houses adjacent to Dikshit's 1926 trenches. He exposed 11,236 sq m (Mackay 1927-8: 67).

Mohenjo Daro 1928-9. Ernest J.H. Mackay works in DK Area and found more artisan's houses and investigated the Early Period. The Proto-Siva seal and the seal with the adoration of the plant goddess were discovered. He exposed 3,790 sq m (Mackay 1928-9).

Mohenjo Daro 1929-30. Ernest J.H. Mackay excavation takes DK Area down 4.9 to 5.5 m, the Intermediate Levels. He attempted to go deeper but unusual rains prevent digging. There was a major exposure of main street of the Intermediate Period (Mackay 1929-30).

Mohenjo Daro 1930-1. Ernest J.H. Mackay conducted an excavation on the north side of DK Area. He uncovered *c.* 1,50,000 sq m and works on Central Street. A second Bronze Dancing Girl was found. A second 'Proto-Siva' seal, a ship seal and a soft, grey stone hut pot were found. He digs 30 to 150 m out from the northern end of the Lower City and located remains. Deep digging in last year's area goes down 10 m below datum (Mackay 1930-4).

Mohenjo Daro 1931-2. Ernest J.H. Mackay undertook excavation immediately north of Site 3 on the Mound of the Great Bath, 3 November 1931. Mackay's work at Mohenjo Daro was suspended three days later, on the afternoon of 6 November 1931 (Mackay 1930-4: 70).

Mohenjo Daro 1932-3. Ernest J.H. Mackay asks K.N. Puri to excavate a trial trench to the lowest possible level in the DK Area. Puri's excavation reaches 13.8 m below datum. He found Reserved Slipped Ware in the lowest levels (Mackay 1930-4: 70-1).

Mohenjo Daro 1933-4 . Q.M. Moneer of the Archaeological Survey of India excavated the DK-I Area, also called the 'Moneer Area' to the south of the main DK Area. He investigates the upper levels of the site, but has few financial resources (Moneer 1930-4).

Mohenjo Daro 1936-7. K.N. Puri of the Archaeological Survey of India excavated a trench 45 by 37 m in the DK-I Area, south of Mackay's excavations. He investigates the late levels. Three hundred antiquities are found, including 26 seals. 'The discovery of a good number of beads 16 small weights, a pair of small copper scale pans together with a fulcrum made in a room directly accessible from the lane suggests that this was a lapidary's shop' (Puri 1936-7: 41).

Mohenjo Daro 1938. A small excavation was undertaken in DK-B. It was never published, but the Field Book was signed by A. Rahman. A brown limestone head was found and only recently published (Dales 1985).

Mohenjo Daro 1950. Sir Mortimer Wheeler undertook excavation of the Mound of the Great Bath in vicinity of the 'granary' and the south-eastern walls. Deep digging was also undertaken (Alcock 1952).

Mohenjo Daro 1964. George F. Dales of The University Museum undertook excavation on the eastern edge of HR Area. There are three goals for this undertaking: (1) determine the maximum depth of habitation, (2) obtain a stratified collection of artefacts to understand better the evolution of material culture at the site and (3) examine the existing theories regarding the decline and disappearance of the Indus Civilization. R. Raikes drills three bore holes and found artefacts up to 12 m below the modern ground surface. He discovered a massive platform and investigates the Late 'Squatter' Levels. Dales offers a challenge to the theory that the skeletons in the upper levels were killed as a result of warfare. The most detailed report on Harappan ceramics results from this work (Dales 1965a,1965b; Dales and Kenoyer 1986).

Mohenjo Daro 1979-80. Michael Jansen of the Reinisch Westfalische Technische Hochschule, Aachen undertook the remapping and architectural study of Mohenjo Daro in cooperation with the Pakistan Department of Archaeology. They engage in a restudy of the buildings and town planning in HR Area. The documentation of photographs from Mohenjo Daro with the Archaeological Survey of India in Delhi was undertaken (Jansen and Urban 1984).

Mohenjo Daro 1980-1. Michael Jansen continued the remapping and architectural study of Mohenjo Daro (Jansen and Urban 1984).

Mohenjo Daro 1981-2. Michael Jansen continued the remapping and architectural study of Mohenjo Daro (Jansen and Urban 1984).

Mohenjo Daro 1982-3. Michael Jansen continued the remapping and architectural study of Mohenjo Daro. An IsMEO team headed by Maurizio Tosi studied craft production at the site. The team began using a balloon for photographic documentation (Jansen and Urban 1984).

Mohenjo Daro 1983-4. Michael Jansen and the IsMEO team continued the remapping and architectural study of Mohenjo Daro. They engage in a restudy of the buildings and town planning in DK-G Area. The IsMEO team studies craft production at the site. The team relocates the noted from Wheeler's excavation in 1950 and the survey noted of N.G. Majumdar who surveyed Sindh (Jansen and Urban 1984).

Mohenjo Daro 1984-5. Michael Jansen of Aachen continued the remapping and architectural study of Mohenjo Daro in cooperation with the Pakistan Department of Archaeology and IsMEO in Rome (Jansen and Tosi 1988).

Mohenjo Daro 1985-6. Michael Jansen continued the remapping and architectural study of Mohenjo Daro in cooperation with the Pakistan Department of Archaeology and IsMEO in Rome. They restudy the buildings, town planning and conducted surface surveys looking for craft activity. The team employs a dry core drilling machine to probe the lower levels of the site. They also locate the cards used by E.J.H. Mackay in recording his fiunds. The 'Forma Orbis' project, which investigates the structure of the Mound of the Great Bath was begun (Jansen and Tosi 1988).

Mohenjo Daro 1986-7. Michael Jansen in cooperation with the Pakistan Department of Archaeology and UNESCO undertook a condition report on the city of Mohenjo Daro (Jansen: personal communication).

Mohenjo Daro 1987. The Pakistan Department of Archaeology undertook a salvage excavation in March 1987 at 'Spur Number 3' of the Indus River Training Project. This was *c*. 500 m east of the eastern edge of the Lower Town. They found baked brick buildings, Harappan Red Ware and two unicorn seals (Hussain 1989).

Mohenjo Daro 1988. The Pakistan Department of Archaeology continued its salvage excavation in conjunction with the river training constructions adjacent to the site. From 11 April to 5 May 1988 work was carried out on the Indus river side of the site (A.N. Khan 1988: 75-6).

Motidharai 1957-8. P.P. Pandya of the Gujarat State Department of Archaeology conducted a test excavation at Motidharai in Bhavnagar district of Saurashtra. He found a Sorath Harappan site in Period I and a Lustrous Red Ware occupation in Period II (*IAR* 1957-8: 20-1).

Moti-Pipli 1993. A team from the M.S. University of Baroda excavated this site in Banaskantha district of north Gujarat. They found Amri-Nal type pottery associated with burials at a site of the Anarta Chalcolithic (Ajithprasad and Sonawane, in press).

Multan District Survey 1988. Pakistan Department of Archaeology explored Multan district and surrounding areas. Two Mature Harappan sites are found (A.N. Khan 1988).

Mundigak 1951. Jean-Marie Casal of the Musee Guimet directed the first of eight seasons of excavation at Mundigak on the upper Helmand river of southern Afghanistan. Casal discovered Mundigak in April of 1951 and immediately opened a test trench on Mound A, the principal settlement. In the course of his work Casal defined seven major periods of occupation beginning with a Togau Phase agricultural village and ending with an historical occupation. During Period IV (Quetta Phase) was the major 'urban centre' in its region. Period V at the site was important for understanding Post-Urban Harappan times in the region (Casal 1961).

Mundigak 1952. Jean-Marie Casal directed the second of eight seasons of excavation at Mundigak (Casal 1961).

Mundigak 1953. Jean-Marie Casal directed the third of eight seasons of excavation at Mundigak (Casal 1961).

Mundigak 1954. Jean-Marie Casal directed the fourth of eight seasons of excavation at Mundigak (Casal 1961).

Mundigak 1955. Jean-Marie Casal directed the fifth of eight seasons of excavation at Mundigak (Casal 1961).

Mundigak 1956. Jean-Marie Casal directed the sixth of eight seasons of excavation at Mundigak (Casal 1961).

Mundigak 1957. Jean-Marie Casal directed the seventh of eight seasons of excavation at Mundigak (Casal 1961).

Mundigak 1958. Jean-Marie Casal directed the final, eighth season of excavation at Mundigak (Casal 1961).

Nagal 1961-62. K.V. Soundara Rajan of the Archaeological Survey of India undertook a test excavation at Nagal in Broach district of Gujarat. It was an historical mound with a little known period at the beginning. The excavator believes that this period might fill all, or a portion of, the gap between the end of the Lustrous Red Ware and the beginnings of Northern Black Polished Ware in Gujarat (*IAR* 1961-2: 11-12).

Nagar 1976-7. Jagat Pati Joshi of the Archaeological Survey of India undertook one season of excavation at Nagar in the Punjab, district Jullundur. He found an early Painted Grey Ware site with a 'sprinkling' of Post-Urban Harappan Red Ware indicating the interlocking of these two cultures (*IAR* 1976-7: 42).

Nageshwar 1983-4. K.T.M. Hegde of the M.S. University of Baroda conducted one season of excavation at Nageshwar in district Jamnagar, Gujarat. It was a Mature Harappan site on a lake at the western tip of Saurashtra, with Sindhi Harappan style painted pottery. The inhabitants were involved with the working of *Turbinella pyrum* and *Chicoreus ramosus*. There are two structural phases, IA and IB with historical continuity. An Harappan 'fire alter' was presented (*IAR* 1983-4: 17-18).

Nagwada 1985-6. K.T.M. Hegde conducted the first of five seasons of excavation at Nagwada in the Rupen Valley of northern Gujarat. He found a site of the Anrata Chalcolithic with Harappan pottery, Ahar Black and Red Ware and cenotaphs with Amri-Nal pottery (Hegde et al. 1988: 55-65).

Nagwada 1986-7. K.T.M. Hegde conducted the second of five seasons of excavation at Nagwada (Hegde et al. 1988: 55-65).

Nagwada 1987-8. K.T.M. Hegde conducted the third of five seasons of excavation at Nagwada (Hegde et al. 1988: 55-65, 1990).

Nagwada 1988-9. K.T.M. Hegde conducted the fourth of five seasons of excavation at Nagwada (Hegde et al. 1988: 55-65, 1990).

Nagwada 1989-90. K.T.M. Hegde conducted the fifth of five seasons of excavation at Nagwada (Hegde et al. 1988: 55-65, 1990).

Nal 1903. Merza Sher Mohammad, a government official in Kalat State undertook excavation at Nal in Kalat. He found prehistoric (Nal) burials. Sir John Marshall describes them in the *Annual Report of the Archaeological Survey of India* (Marshall 1904-5: 105-6).

Nal 1908. Colonel (later General Sir) Claud Jacob excavated at Nal in Kalat State using the Hazara Pioneers under his command. He found prehistoric (Nal) burials and recovers *c.* 250 pots, one fifth of which were donated to the McMahon Museum in Quetta (Hargreaves 1929: 17).

Nal 1923 or 1924. Bizarjau Sardar of Kalat, in 1923 or 1924, undertook excavation at Nal in this region. He found prehistoric (Nal) burials. All the found were broken when transported to Quetta following this work (Hargreaves 1929: 18).

Nal 1925. Harold Hargreaves of the Archaeological Survey of India undertook excavation at Nal. He found prehistoric (Nal) burials and evidence for habitation in this first full-scale excavation of a prehistoric site in Baluchistan (Hargreaves 1929).

Naru Waro Dharo 1955. The Pakistan Department of Archaeology undertook one season of excavation at Naru Waro Dharo, a large, low mound 10 km north of Kot Diji.

The site was also known as Kotasur and was explored by M.S. Vats in 1935-6. A Mature Harappan site with a very thin deposit and no architecture was found (Anonymous 1964: 43-4).

Nausharo 1985-6. Jean-Francois Jarrige of the Centre National de la Recherche Scientifique and the Musee Guimet directed the first season of excavation at Nausharo in Kachi district of Baluchistan. He defined three periods: Period I, Early Harappan; Period II, Transitional Early Harappan-Mature Harappan and Period III, Urban Harappan (Jarrige 1987).

Nausharo 1986-7. Jean-Francois Jarrige Guimet directed second season of excavation at Nausharo. He defined Period IA-D. There was a major conflagration in Period ID, just preceding the appearance of the Mature Harappan. He found a Kulli figurine in Period III (Jarrige 1988).

Nausharo 1987-8. Jean-Francois Jarrige Guimet directed the third season of excavation at Nausharo. Excavation on the Transitional and Mature Harappan levels was continued. There was some evidence for a conflagration associated with the Transitional levels (Jarrige 1990a).

Nausharo 1988-9. Jean-Francois Jarrige directed the fourth season of excavation at Nausharo. Excavation on the Early Harappan, Transitional and Mature Harappan levels continued (Jarrige 1990b).

Nausharo 1989-90. Jean-Francois Jarrige directed the fifth season of excavation at Nausharo (Jarrige 1990c).

Nausharo 1990-1. Jean-Francois Jarrige directed the sixth season of excavation at Nausharo. He found a wall around most or all of the settlement and a large Period II platform (Jarrige 1991).

Nausharo 1991-2. Jean-Francois Jarrige directed the seventh season of excavation at Nausharo (Jarrige 1992).

Nausharo 1992-3. Jean-Francois Jarrige directed the eighth season of excavation at Nausharo (Jarrige 1993).

Nausharo 1993-4. Jean-Francois Jarrige directed the ninth season of excavation at Nausharo (Jarrige 1994).

Nausharo 1994-5. Jean-Francois Jarrige directed the ninth season of excavation at Nausharo (Jarrige 1995).

Nausharo 1995-6. Jean-Francois Jarrige directed the tenth and final season of excavation at Nausharo. For the next season he plans to return to Mehrgarh and work on the earliest levels there (J.-F. Jarrige: personal communication).

Niai Buthi 1943. Sir Aurel Stein of the Archaeological Survey of India excavated at Niai Buthi in Las Bela. He found a stratified Amri-Nal, Kulli site (Stein 1943b).

Niai Buthi 1959-60. Walter A. Fairservis, Jr. of the American Museum of Natural History conducted a survey of Las Bela and south-western Sindh. He reinvestigates Niai Buthi. His findings confirm and expand those of Sir Aurel Stein (Fairservis 1961, 1971: 195-216)

Nindowari 1962-3. Jean-Marie Casal of the Musee Guimet conducted the first of three seasons of excavation at this large Kulli site in southern Baluchistan. He found a large town, with monumental architecture and also found Harappan seals (Casal 1966, 1968).

Nindowari 1963-4. Jean-Marie Casal undertook the second of three seasons of excavation at this large Kulli site in southern Baluchistan (Casal 1966, 1968).

Nindowari 1964-5. Jean-Marie Casal conducted the third of three seasons of excavation at this large Kulli site in southern Baluchistan (Casal 1966, 1968).

Noh 1963-4. R.C. Agrawala of the Rajasthan Department of Archaeology undertook the first of seven seasons of excavation at Noh in district Bharatpur, Rajasthan. It is an Ochre Coloured Pottery and Painted Grey Ware site (*IAR* 1963-4: 28-9).

Noh 1964-5. R.C. Agrawala conducted the second of seven seasons of excavation at Noh (*IAR* 1964-5: 34-5).

Noh 1965-6. R.C. Agrawala undertook the third of seven seasons of excavation at Noh (*IAR* 1965-6: 38).

Noh 1966-7. R.C. Agrawala conducted the fourth of seven seasons of excavation at Noh (*IAR* 1966-7: 30-1).

Noh 1968-9. R.C. Agrawala conducted the fifth of seven seasons of excavation at Noh (*IAR* 1968-9: 26).

Noh 1970-1. R.C. Agrawala undertook the sixth of seven seasons of excavation at Noh (*IAR* 1970-1: 31-2).

Noh 1971-2. R.C. Agrawala conducted the seventh and final season of excavation at Noh (*IAR* 1971-2: 41-2).

Nohar 1950-1. A. Ghosh of the Archaeological Survey of India undertook a test excavation at Nohar on the Sarasvati river near the village of the same name. He found a stratified Sothi-Siswal (Early Harappan) and Mature Harappan site (Ghosh 1952).

Nohar 1978. K.N. Dikshit of the Archaeological Survey of India excavated two test trenches, each 2 x 2 m at Nohar near the modern town of the same name on the ancient Drishadvati river. He found a Sothi-Siswal settlement. Nohar was first discovered by A. Ghosh in the course of his explorations of the Sarasvati (Dikshit 1980: 35).

Nundara, Siah Damb 1928. Sir Aurel Stein of the Archaeological Survey of India undertook a test excavation at this site in Pakistani Baluchistan. He found a large stratified settlement with an Amri-Nal occupation (Stein 1931: 138-44).

Oriyo Timbo 1981-2. Gregory L. Possehl of The University Museum and C.M. Atri of the Gujarat State Department of Archaeology conducted a season of excavation at Oriyo Timbo in Bhavnagar district, Gujarat. This was a Lustrous Red Ware site shown to have been the settlement of pastoral nomads during the Late Sorath Harappan. Flotation recovers significant palaeobotanical information (Rissman and Chitalwala 1990).

Oriyo Timbo 1989-90. Gregory L. Possehl of The University Museum and M.H. Raval of the Gujarat State Department of Archaeology undertook another season of excavation at Oriyó Timbo in Bhavnagar district, Gujarat. They found a living surface with a *tandoor* at this Lustrous Red Ware site of the Late Sorath Harappan (Possehl, unpublished).

Othmanjo Buthi 1931. N.G. Majumdar of the Archaeological Survey of India excavated at Othmanjo Buthi on the Baran Nai in western Sindh. He found an Amri-Nal settlement (Majumdar 1934: 139-41).

Pabumath 1977-8. Y.M. Chitalwala of the Gujarat State Department of Archaeology conducted the first of three seasons of excavation at Pabumath in district Kachchh, Gujarat. He found a Mature Harappan settlement on the fringe of the Rann (*IAR* 1977-8: 21).

Pabumath 1978-9. Y.M. Chitalwala undertook the second of three seasons of excavation at Pabumath. Finds include a copper arrowhead and a broken unicorn seal (*IAR* 1978-9: 67-8).

Pabumath 1980-1. Y.M. Chitalwala conducted the third of three seasons of excavation at Pabumath. Finds include an inscribed seal with the unicorn motif (*IAR* 1980-1: 14).

Padri 1990-1. Vasant Shinde of Deccan College undertook the first season of excavation at Padri near the Gulf of Cambay in Bhavnagar district of Gujarat. It was a Sorath Harappan site. During the first season he recovers two large storage jars from villagers with the 'Horned Deity' on them. Shinde proposes that the site was a place where people who made salt were living (Shinde 1991).

Padri 1991-2. Vasant Shinde undertook the second season of excavation at Padri (Shinde 1992).

Padri 1992-3. Vasant Shinde undertook another season of excavation at Padri (Shinde 1992).

Padri 1993-4. Vasant Shinde undertook the fourth season of excavation at Padri (V. Shinde: personal communication).

Paijo-kotrio 1938. N.G. Majumdar of the Archaeological Survey of India undertook trial excavations at Paijo-kotrio, at the mouth of the Gaj Nai in Sindh. This was a very large Amri-Nal site with a Mature Harappan occupation as well. Majumdar was killed by bandits on 11 November, shortly after the excavation was concluded on 4-5 November 1938 (Krishna Deva and McCown 1949: 14-16).

Pandi Wahi 1931. N.G. Majumdar of the Archaeological Survey of India excavated at Pandi Wahi to the north of Lake Manchar in western Sindh. He found an Amri-Nal and Mature Harappan settlement (Majumdar 1934: 91-5).

Pariar 1978-9. B.B. Lal and K.N. Dikshit of the Archaeological Survey of India carry out one season of excavation at this OCP site in Unnao district of Uttar Pradesh. They lay five trenches and found a sequence beginning with OCP followed by a level with Black and Red Ware, Black Slipped and Red Slipped Wares. This was followed by Period III with Painted Grey Ware and Period IV with Northern Black Polished Ware (*IAR* 1978-9: 60-1; Lal and Dikshit 1982).

Periano Ghundai 1897. Fritz W. Noetling of the Geological Survey of India visited Periano Ghundai and recognizes it as an ancient site (Noetling 1898: 460-71; Pedde 1993a, 1993b).

Periano Ghundai 1927. Sir Aurel Stein of the Archaeological Survey of India undertook an excavation at Periano Ghundai in Zhob district of Baluchistan. He recognizes it as a Chalcolithic settlement and relates the pottery to Rana Ghundai and Moghul Ghundai (Stein 1929: 73-7).

Periano Ghundai 1950-1. Walter A. Fairservis, Jr. of the American Museum of Natural History revisits Periano Ghundai in Zhob district of Baluchistan and conducted a systematic survey of the site, removing pottery sherds from exposed sections. Fairservis publishes an analysis of the material and suggests a relative stratigraphy for Periano Ghundai, Rana Ghundai and other sites in the region (Fairservis 1959: 293-300).

Periano Ghundai 1972. M.R. Mughal of the Pakistan Department of Archaeology directed a test excavation at this site in Zhob to check stratigraphy and assist with the collection of additional material (Mughal 1972a: 139).

Pirak 1968. Jean-Marie Casal of the Musee Guimet undertook a test excavation at Pirak, on the Kachi Plain of Pakistan in February. He found distinctive pottery and iron implements of the Early Iron Age in the region. These discoveries lead him to undertake six full seasons of work there (Jarrige and Santoni 1979).

Pirak 1968-9. Jean-Marie Casal undertook the first of six seasons of excavation at Pirak on the Kachi Plain of Pakistan. He found distinctive pottery and iron implements of the Early Iron Age in the region as well as a Late Protohistoric settlement quite different from the Harappan Civilization (Jarrige and Santoni 1979).

Pirak 1969-70. Jean-Marie Casal undertook the second of six seasons of excavation at Pirak (Jarrige and Santoni 1979).

Pirak 1970-1. Jean-Marie Casal undertook the third of six seasons of excavation at Pirak (Jarrige and Santoni 1979).

Pirak 1971-2. Jean-Marie Casal undertook the fourth of six seasons of excavation at Pirak (Jarrige and Santoni 1979).

Pirak 1972-3. Jean-Marie Casal undertook the fifth of six seasons of excavation at Pirak (Jarrige and Santoni 1979).

Pirak 1973-4. Jean-Marie Casal undertook the last of six seasons of excavation at Pirak (Jarrige and Santoni 1979).

Pithadia 1957-8. P.P. Pandya of the Gujarat State Department of Archaeology undertook a test excavation at Pithadia in Rajkot district of Saurashtra. He found a site that was probably Late Sorath Harappan followed by Lustrous Red Ware (*IAR* 1957-8: 20-1).

Pokran 1931. N.G. Majumdar of the Archaeological Survey of India excavated at Pokran on the upper Baran Nai in western Sindh. He found an Amri-Nal and Mature Harappan settlement (Majumdar 1934: 128-9).

Punjab Survey 1931. Sir Aurel Stein of the Archaeological Survey of India explores the north-western Punjab in connection with his research on Alexander the Great's campaign in ancient India. He records no new prehistoric sites (Stein 1937: 1-69).

Punjab Survey 1993-5. Director General M. Rafique Mughal of the Pakistan Department of Archaeology began a comprehensive survey of the west Punjab (Mughal 1995).

Quetta Miri 1886. Major J.F. Garwood, Royal Engineers excavated the Quetta Miri as part of the work of turning this huge mound into an arsenal. He did not recognize the prehistoric pottery there, but did find a large bronze statue of Heracles two feet three inches high, holding the skin of the Nemean lion (Garwood 1887).

Quetta Treasury 1985. Digging undertaken in connection with the construction of a hotel in Quetta uncovers a lavishly equipped grave of the early second millennium BC with important ties to Sibri in Kachi, Central Asia (Saipalli Tepe), Central Iran (Shahdad) and northern Afghanistan (Dashli 3) (Jarrige and Hassan 1989).

Quetta Valley Survey 1950-1. Walter A. Fairservis, Jr. of the American Museum of Natural History and Harvard University undertook a survey of the Quetta Valley (Fairservis 1956).

Raja Karna Ka Qila One and Two 1970-1. U.V. Singh and Suraj Bhan of Kurukshetra University undertook the first of five seasons of excavation at Raja Karna Ka Qila in Haryana, district Karnal. During this season they found no evidence of Harappan occupation, but it appears later (*IAR* 1970-1: 15-16).

Raja Karna Ka Qila One and Two 1971-2. U.V. Singh and Suraj Bhan undertook the second of five seasons of excavation at Raja Karna Ka Qila (*IAR* 1971-2: 23-4).

Raja Karna Ka Qila One and Two 1972-3. U.V. Singh and Suraj Bhan undertook the third of five seasons of excavation at Raja Karna Ka Qila (*IAR* 1972-3: 12-13).

Raja Karna Ka Qila One and Two 1974-5. U.V. Singh and Suraj Bhan undertook the fourth of five seasons of excavation at Raja Karna Ka Qila. During this season they found evidence for a Post-Urban Harappan occupation (*IAR* 1974-5: 16).

Raja Karna Ka Qila One and Two 1975-6. U.V. Singh and Suraj Bhan undertook the fifth and final season of excavation at Raja Karna Ka Qila (*IAR* 1975-6: 18).

Rajasthan Survey 1963-4. V.N. Misra surveys the Berach Basin of south-eastern Rajasthan. This was the region associated with the Ahar Complex (Misra 1967).

Rajasthan Survey 1983-4. Henri-Paul Francfort, head of the French Archaeological Mission to India, in cooperation with the Archaeological Survey of India, conducted a survey in northern Rajasthan along a portion of the Chautaung palaeochannel and in neighbouring areas. He located *c.* 30 Protohistoric sites and undertook research on the ancient environment and irrigation (*IAR* 1983-4: 95-8; Francfort 1985).

Rajasthan Survey 1982-3. Rima Hooja surveys south-eastern Rajasthan as a part of her dissertation research at Cambridge University. She covers the area associated with the Ahar Complex (Hooja 1988).

Rajkot District Survey 1975-8. Y.M. Chitalwala of Deccan College undertook an exploration of Rajkot district in Gujarat. His work follows on that of P.P. Pandya. He located 25 Sorath Harappan sites, some with Lustrous Red Ware (Chitalwala 1979).

Rajpur Parsu 1949. B.B. Lal of the Archaeological Survey of India went to Rajpur Parsu in Binjor district of Uttar Pradesh to conduct a small excavation at this site where a Copper Hoard had been found. He found Ochre Coloured Pottery, which was prior to his definition of it in 1954-5 (Lal 1951: 37).

Rana Ghundai 1898. Fritz W. Noetling of the Geological Survey of India visited Rana Ghundai in Loralai district of Baluchistan and published it as an ancient site (Noetling 1899: 101-2; Pedde 1993a, 1993b).

Rana Ghundai 1927. Sir Aurel Stein of the Archaeological Survey of India visited this site in Loralai district of Baluchistan and noted its great size and the damage done to it. He identifies Rana Ghundai (Queen's Mound) as a prehistoric site (Stein 1929: 52-3).

Rana Ghundai 1935-40. Brigadier E.J. Ross of the Indian Army undertook extensive sampling at Rana Ghundai in Loralai district of Baluchistan. He found a stratified site ranging from the beginnings of villages through a settlement contemporaneous with the Harappan Civilization (Ross 1946).

Rana Ghundai 1950-1. Walter A. Fairservis, Jr. of the American Museum of Natural History visited this site in Loralai district of Baluchistan. He undertook a systematic collection of pottery sherds from stratigraphic positions and publishe a revision of the Ross chronology (Fairservis 1959: 300-8).

Rana Ghundai 1972. M.R. Mughal of the Pakistan Department of Archaeology visited Rana Ghundai in Loralai district of Baluchistan. He made a surface collection and took material for two radiocarbon dates (Mughal 1972d: 142-3).

Rangpur 1934-5. M.S. Vats of the Archaeological Survey of India conducted one season of excavation at Rangpur, district Surendranagar in Gujarat, at the invitation of the Thakore Sahib of Limbdi State. He put in three trenches and found much pottery but little architecture. He determined that some of the pottery was definitely in the category of Indus Black and Red Ware with strikingly similar shapes and decorations. The presence of triangular terracotta cakes and perforated vessels reinforced his conclusion. But, he also noted that other ceramics seem to be more evolved than those found in the Early and Intermediate periods of Mohenjo Daro or Harappa. He suggested that provisionally it may be taken to correspond with the Late Period of the Indus Valley sites or perhaps intercalated between that and the date of the Cemetery H at Harappa (Vats 1934-5).

Rangpur 1936. G.S. Ghurye of Bombay University excavated Rangpur in Gujarat and found Chalcolithic pottery. Ghurye also excavated the Early Historic city of Vallabhipur (Ghurye 1939).

Rangpur 1947. M.G. Dikshit of Deccan College conducted one season of excavation at Rangpur in Gujarat, district Surendranagar. He feels that the site was not Harappan, based on an examination of the pottery. In Dikshit's opinion the major occupation represents a Post-Harappan Period (Dikshit 1950).

Rangpur 1953-4. S.R. Rao of the Archaeological Survey of India conducted the first of three seasons of excavation at Rangpur to settle the cultural affiliation of the ancient inhabitants of the site. Rao discovered a microlithic level, under a Chalcolithic occupation and a late Chalcolithic occupation. He indicates that the Chalcolithic occupation was Harappan (*IAR* 1953-4: 7; S.R. Rao 1963).

Rangpur 1954-5. S.R. Rao undertook the second of three seasons of excavation at Rangpur. The work firmly established that Rangpur was a part of the Harappan Civilization. He also noted that there was a gradual evolution of the ceramics at Rangpur from the Mature Harappan to the Post-Urban Harappan (Lustrous Red Ware) without a break. This was different from the cultural sequence in Sindh. Rao also began work at Lothal this season (*IAR* 1954-5: 11-12).

Rangpur 1956. S.R. Rao put in two small trenches at Rangpur during April 1956. This was the third and final season of his research at the site. This work was not noted in *Indian Archaeology—A Review* (Rao 1963: 8).

Ratanpura 1984-5. K.T.M. Hegde of the M.S. University of Baroda undertook one season of excavation at Ratanpura in the Rupen Valley of northern Gujarat. He found a Lustrous Red Ware site with a fair amount of Ahar Black and Red Ware (*IAR* 1984-5: 17-18).

Rehman Dheri 1976. Farzand A. Durrani of Peshawar University undertook the first of five seasons of excavation at Rehman Dheri near Dera Ismail Khan in Pakistan. The site was discovered in 1971 by A.H. Dani. This excavation had four goals: (1) to determine the cultural stratigraphy, (2) to form a chronology for the region, including radiocarbon determinations, (3) to conduct an horizontal excavation to gain insights into town planning, (4) to collect botanical and faunal remains for insights into the economy and environment (Durrani 1988: 19). Durrani found a stratified settlement with three periods: two of the Early Harappan and Late Kot Dijian (Durrani 1988).

Rehman Dheri 1977. Farzand A. Durrani undertook the second of five seasons of excavation at Rehman Dheri (Durrani 1988).

Rehman Dheri 1978. Farzand A. Durrani undertook the third of five seasons of excavation at Rehman Dheri (Durrani 1988).

Rehman Dheri 1979. Farzand A. Durrani undertook the fourth of five seasons of excavation at Rehman Dheri (Durrani 1988).

Rehman Dheri 1980. Farzand A. Durrani conducted the fifth and final season of excavation at Rehman Dheri (Durrani 1988).

Rehman Dheri 1991. Farzand A. Durrani reopens excavations at Rehman Dheri near Dera Ismail Khan. He found significant quantities of lapis lazuli, a massive platform in Period III and evidence for a wall surrounding the settlement (Durrani et al. 1991).

Rohenjo Kund 1938. N.G. Majumdar of the Archaeological Survey of India conducted two days of excavation at Rohenjo Kund on the Gaj Nai in Sindh. He found an Amri-Nal settlement (Krishna Deva and McCown 1949: 16-25).

Rohira 1982-3. The Punjab Department of Archaeology conducted excavation at Rohira in district Sangrur; a multiperiod site. Period IA was an Early Harappan. Period IB has Mature Harappan and the older Early Harappan pottery together with (Siswal B). Period IC was a Bara establishment (*IAR* 1982-3: 65-6).

Rojdi 1957-8. P.P. Pandya of the Gujarat State Department of Archaeology directed excavation at Rojdi in Gujarat, district Rajkot. He found a Sorath and Late Sorath Harappan site with a wall of large boulders around the site, as well as a Red Ware sherd with four Harappan characters inscribed on it (*IAR* 1957-8: 18-23).

Rojdi 1958-9. P.P. Pandya conducted a second season of excavation at Rojdi. He found rammed earth platforms and Prabhas Ware at this Sorath and Late Sorath Harappan site (*IAR* 1958-9: 19-21).

Rojdi 1962-3. M.A. Dhaky renews excavation at Rojdi. He found two occupations of a Sorath and Late Sorath Harappan site. Phase A structures built on a platform and seven plasterings; the first three burned. Phase B has Sorath Harappan pottery and ties to Prabhas Ware. Period II, Red Polished Ware (*IAR* 1962-3: 8).

Rojdi 1964-5. M.A. Dhaky continues excavation at Rojdi. He found two occupations: Sorath and Late Sorath Harappan (*IAR* 1964-5: 12).

Rojdi 1982-3. Gregory L. Possehl of the University of Pennsylvania Museum and M.H. Raval of the Gujarat State Department of Archaeology conducted the first of four seasons of renewed excavation at Rojdi. They work at the Gateway of the circumvallation, the Large Square building and begin a sondage on the Main Mound of this Sorath and Late Sorath Harappan site. They also conducted intensive flotation for the recovery of palaeobotanical information at the site (*IAR* 1982-3: 28).

Rojdi 1983-4. Gregory L. Possehl and M.H. Raval conducted the second of four seasons of renewed excavation at Rojdi. They work on the South Extension and Large Square Building of this Sorath and Late Sorath Harappan site. Significant architecture associated with Rojdi C, the Late Sorath Harappan, was found on the South Extension (*IAR* 1983-4: 19-20).

Rojdi 1984-5. Gregory L. Possehl and M.H. Raval conducted the third of four seasons of renewed excavation at Rojdi. They work on the South Extension, Main Mound and North Slope of this Sorath and Late Sorath Harappan site (*IAR* 1984-5: 18).

Rojdi 1985-6. Gregory L. Possehl and M.H. Raval conducted the final season of renewed excavation at Rojdi. They work on the South Extension and Main Mound of this Sorath and Late Sorath Harappan site (*IAR* 1985-6: 19).

Rojdi 1992-3. Gregory L. Possehl of the University of Pennsylvania Museum and D.P. Mehta of the Gujarat State Department of Archaeology conducted the first season of further excavation at Rojdi. This follows the project undertook there in the 1980s. They work on the Main Mound and found a well preserved Rojdi C village (Possehl and Mehta 1994).

Rojdi 1993-4. Gregory L. Possehl and Y.M. Chitalwala of the Gujarat State Department of Archaeology conducted the second season of further excavation at Rojdi. They continue work on the Main Mound, further exposing the Rojdi C village (unpublished).

Rojdi 1994-5. Gregory L. Possehl and Y.M. Chitalwala conducted third season of further excavation at Rojdi. They continue work on the Main Mound, further exposing the Rojdi C village (Chitalwala and Possehl, in press).

Ropar 1953-4. Y.D. Sharma of the Excavations Branch of the Archaeological Survey of India undertook the first of two seasons of excavation at Ropar, district Ambala in the Punjab. He wanted clarification of the eclipse of the Indus Civilization and its relationship with the Painted Grey Culture. He uncovers the Harappan and Painted Grey Ware levels (*IAR* 1953-4: 6-7).

Ropar 1954-5. Y.D. Sharma undertook the second of two seasons of excavation at Ropar (*IAR* 1954-5: 9).

Rupen Valley Survey 1979. K.T.M. Hegde of the M.S. University of Baroda conducted a survey of the Rupen Valley of northern Gujarat. He found 21 new protohistoric sites (Hegde and Sonawane 1986: 23-31).

Sahiwal District Survey 1971. M.R. Mughal of the Pakistan Department of Archaeology conducted a survey in Sahiwal district (formerly Montgomery district) of the Punjab. He found no protohistoric sites (Mughal 1972c).

Said Qala 1950-1. Walter A. Fairservis Jr. of the American Museum of Natural History conducted a test excavation at Said Qala Tepe near Kandahar in southern Afghanistan. He found ties to the Quetta Valley and Mundigak and the Quetta Valley. Fairservis' work was later expanded by Jim Shaffer (Fairservis 1952).

Said Qala 1971: Jim G. Shaffer conducted an excavation at Said Qala Tepe near Kandahar in southern Afghanistan. He found a site occupied at the time of Mundigak III to IV, now called the Damb Sadaat Phase (Shaffer 1978).

Saipai 1970-1. The Archaeological Survey of India undertook the first of two seasons of excavation at Saipai in Uttar Pradesh, district Etawah. This work followed a report of a Copper Hoard being found. The excavation produces Ochre Coloured Pottery in association with a copper harpoon of Hoard type (*IAR* 1970-1: 38).

Saipai 1971-2. The Archaeological Survey of India conducted the second of two seasons of excavation at Saipai (*IAR* 1971-2: 46-7).

Salaura 1954-5. Y.D. Sharma of the Archaeological Survey of India excavated at Salaura, next to Bara in the Punjab, district Rupnagar. He found Painted Grey Ware, a Kushana occupation and later historical materials (*IAR* 1954-5: 9-11).

Sandanwala Ther 1941. Sir Aurel Stein of the Archaeological Survey of India conducted an excavation at Sandanwala Ther on the ancient Sarasvati river in Pakistan near the border with India. He found an Early and Mature Harappan settlement (Stein 1943a: 145-56).

Sanghol 1968-9. The Punjab Department of Archaeology conducted the first of nine seasons of excavation at Sanghol in the Punjab, district Ludhiana. In Period I they found a Post-Urban Harappan settlement, followed by Painted Grey Ware and later historical materials (*IAR* 1968-9: 25-6).

Sanghol 1969-70. The Punjab Department of Archaeology undertook the second of nine seasons of excavation at Sanghol. In Period I they found a Post-Urban Harappan settlement with some ceramics that look like those of Cemetery H (*IAR* 1969-70: 31-2).

Sanghol 1970-1. The Punjab Department of Archaeology conducted the third of nine seasons of excavation at Sanghol (*IAR* 1970-1: 30-1).

Sanghol 1971-2. The Punjab Department of Archaeology undertook the fourth of nine seasons of excavation at Sanghol (*IAR* 1971-2: 39, 41).

Sanghol 1972-3. The Punjab Department of Archaeology conducted the fifth of nine seasons of excavation at Sanghol (*IAR* 1972-3: 28).

Sanghol 1977-8. The Punjab Department of Archaeology undertook the sixth of nine seasons of excavation at Sanghol (*IAR* 1977-8: 43-4).

Sanghol 1980-1. The Punjab Department of Archaeology conducted the seventh of nine seasons of excavation at Sanghol. In Period I they found a Post-Urban Harappan occupation with Bara ceramics (*IAR* 1980-1: 46).

Sanghol 1984-5. The Punjab Department of Archaeology undertook the eighth of nine seasons of excavation at Sanghol. Work this year concentrates on the Buddhist stupa, not the Period I Post-Urban Harappan settlement (*IAR* 1984-5: 62, 64).

Sanghol 1985-6. The Punjab Department of Archaeology conducted the ninth and final season of excavation at Sanghol (*IAR* 1985-6: 67-9).

Santhli 1993-4. A team from the M.S. University of Baroda excavated two localities (Santhli-no Thumdo and Ghachiya Wado) in Santhli village of Banaskantha district of north Gujarat. They found Amri-Nal type pottery associated with burials (Ajithprasad and Sonawane, in press).

Sarai Khola 1968. M.A. Halim of the Pakistan Department of Archaeology undertook the first of five seasons of excavation at Sarai Khola in district Rawalpindi, west Punjab. The site, which was near Taxila, was discovered in December 1967 by Muhammad Sharif. The excavation had three goals: (1) determine the potentials of the site, including the culture historical sequence, (2) determine the relationship between the neolithic of Sarai Khola and the Kot Diji (Early Harappan) occupation, and (3) investigate the nature of the graves and their relation to the Gandharan Grave Complex. Period I at Sarai Khola was a Neolithic related to Burzahom in Kashmir. Period II was a Kot Diji Phase occupation. Period III was a cemetery, the later graves of which contain Iron Age implements. Period IV was another Iron Age Cemetery (Halim 1972a,1972b).

Sarai Khola 1969. M.A. Halim undertook the second of five seasons of excavation at Sarai Khola. Work continued on the three goals set for the first season (Halim 1972a, 1972b).

Sarai Khola 1970. M.A. Halim undertook the third of five seasons of excavation at Sarai Khola (Halim 1972a, 1972b).

Sarai Khola 1971. M. A. Halim undertook the fourth of five seasons of excavation at Sarai Khola (Halim 1972a, 1972b).

Sarai Khola 1972. The Pakistan Department of Archaeology and the University of Islamabad conducted the fifth and final season of excavation at Sarai Khola. This work was undertaken to check the stratigraphic position of various artefacts. The new excavation confirms the earlier sequence as published in *Pakistan Archaeology* (Mughal 1972).

Sarai Khola 1981-2. F.R. Allchin and the Cambridge-Peshawar Team collect radiocarbon samples from Sarai Khola (Thomas and Allchin 1986).

Sarangpur 1966. Suraj Bhan of Kurukshetra University excavated at Sarangpur near Chandigarh. He found a Mature Harappan (Siswal B) site with OCP (Suraj Bhan 1967, 1975: 113).

Sarasvati Survey 1917. Luigi P. Tessitori of the Archaeological Survey of India conducted research in the Sarasvati Valley, and undertook a test excavation at Kalibangan (Tessitori 1917-18; Stein 1943a: 51).

Sarasvati Valley Survey 1918. Luigi P. Tessitori conducted research in the Sarasvati Valley, and visited Kalibangan (Tessitori 1918-19; Stein 1943a: 51).

Sarasvati Valley Survey 1940-1. Sir Aurel Stein of the Archaeological Survey of India conducted a survey of the Sarasvati river. He excavated at Sandhanawala. In 1942 he returned to excavate at Ahmadwala Ther, Kalepar (Bhoot) and Kudwala Ther as part of this survey (Stein 1943a).

Sarasvati Valley Survey 1950-1. A. Ghosh, Director General of the Archaeological Survey of India conducted the first season of systematic survey in the Sarasvati and Drishadvati valleys. His work led to the discovery of Sothi, the type site for the 'Early Harappan' in this region as well as to the long-term excavation of Kalibangan (Ghosh 1952, 1953, 1959).

Sarasvati Valley Survey 1951-2. A. Ghosh undertook the second season of systematic survey in the Sarasvati and Drishadvadi valleys (Ghosh 1952, 1953, 1959).

Sarasvati Valley Survey 1952-3. A. Ghosh conducted the third season of systematic survey in the Sarasvati and Drishadvadi valleys (Ghosh 1952, 1953, 1959).

Sarasvati Valley Survey 1970. Katey Feroz Dalal (nee Frenchman) of Deccan College undertook a small scale survey of the Sarasvati Valley as a part of her Ph.D. Dissertation Research (Frenchman 1972; Dalal 1980).

Shahi Tump 1928. Sir Aurel Stein conducted a test excavation at this site in Pakistani Makran. He found a large settlement; a Kulli occupation stratified under a burial complex of unknown affinity (Stein 1931: 88-104).

Shahjo Kotrio 1931. N.G. Majumdar of the Archaeological Survey of India undertook a small excavation at Shahjo Kotrio. It was a Kulli-Harappan site in the Sindh Kohistan (Majumdar 1934: 137-39).

Sheri Khan Tarakai 1986. The Bannu Archaeological Project, a joint undertaking by the University of Peshawar, the British Museum and the University of London, Institute of Archaeology undertook the first of five seasons of excavation at Sheri Khan Tarakai, a Pre-Kot Dijian site in Bannu (Khan et al. 1991).

Sheri Khan Tarakai 1987. The Bannu Archaeological Project undertook the second of five seasons of excavation at Sheri Khan Tarakai (Khan et al. 1991).

Sheri Khan Tarakai 1988. The Bannu Archaeological Project undertook the third of five seasons of excavation at Sheri Khan Tarakai (Khan et al. 1991).

Sheri Khan Tarakai 1989. The Bannu Archaeological Project undertook the fourth of five seasons of excavation at Sheri Khan Tarakai (Khan et al. 1991).

Sheri Khan Tarakai 1990. The Bannu Archaeological Project undertook the fifth and final season of excavation at Sheri Khan Tarakai (Khan et al. 1991).

Shikarpur 1989-90. The Gujarat State Department of Archaeology excavated Shikarpur in Kachchh, near the head of the Gulf of Kachchh. They found a Mature Harappan site (Raval, unpublished).

Shortughai 1976. Henri-Paul Francfort of the Centre National de la Recherche Scientifique directed the first of four seasons of excavation at Shortughai in northern Afghanistan on the Amu Darya. Shortughai was discovered by the French Archaeological team in 1975. It was a Mature Harappan and Post-Urban Harappan outpost (Francfort 1989).

Shortughai 1977. Henri-Paul Francfort directed the second of four seasons of excavation at Shortughai. This was the first large season of work at the site (Francfort 1989).

Shortughai 1978. Henri-Paul Francfort directed the third of four seasons of excavation at Shortughai (Francfort 1989).

Shortughai 1979. Henri-Paul Francfort directed the fourth and final season of excavation at Shortughai (Francfort 1989).

Siah Damb, Surab 1957. Beatrice de Cardi of the British Academy carried out one season of excavation at Siah Damb, Surab in Baluchistan, Kalat Division. She found a three phase site beginning with the Togau Phases and moving through the Kechi Beg and Amri-Nal Phases of Baluchistan (de Cardi 1965).

Sibri 1979-80. Marielle Santoni and Jean-Francois Jarrige of the Centre National de la Recherche Scientifique conducted the first season of excavation at Sibri, just south of Mehrgarh in Kachi. It was an early second millennium funerary site with important ties to Central Asia (Saipalli Tepe), Central Iran (Shahdad) and northern Afghanistan (Dashli 3) (Santoni 1984).

Sibri 1980-1. Marielle Santoni and Jean-Francois Jarrige conducted the second season of excavation at Sibri (Jarrige and Hassan 1989: 150; Santoni 1984).

Sibri 1981-2. Marielle Santoni and Jean-Francois Jarrige conducted the third season of excavation at Sibri (Santoni 1984).

Sindh Survey 1927-8. N.G. Majumdar of the Archaeological Survey of India undertook his explorations in Sindh with an excavation at Jhukar where he discovered a Buddhist site, with a Mature Harappan and a Post-Urban Harappan occupation (Majumdar 1934: 5-18).

Sindh Survey 1929-30. N.G. Majumdar undertook a survey in Sindh. He excavated at Amri and discovered the stratigraphic relationship between the Early and Mature Harappan (Majumdar 1934).

Sindh Survey 1930-1. N.G. Majumdar concluded the first phase of his survey in Sindh (Majumdar 1934).

Sindh Survey 1938-9. N.G. Majumdar resumed his explorations in Sindh with work at the Gaj Nai. He was shot and killed on 11 November while camped there. A short report on this work was later published (Krishna Deva and McCown 1949).

Sindh Survey 1971. Mohammad Sharif of the Pakistan Department of Archaeology conducted a survey in Thar Parkar in south-eastern Sindh. He found, or revisited a number of Protohistoric sites (Mughal 1972a: 131-7).

Sindh Survey 1975-6. Louis Flam of the University of Pennsylvania conducted a survey in the Sindh Kohistan area, between the Laki Hills and Kachi. He visited many of the sites found by N.G. Majumdar and found new prehistoric settlements (Flam 1981).

Sindh Survey 1976-7. Louis Flam continued his survey in the Sindh Kohistan area (Flam 1981).

Sindh Survey 1983 to Present. Louis Flam continues his explorations in the Sindh Kohistan, Kirthar Mountain piedmont, north of Kachi (unpublished).

Sindh Survey 1983. Hans J. Nissen undertook one season of exploration in north-western Sindh between Sukkur and Lake Manchar. During his short project he found two new protohistoric sites (Nissen 1983, 1994).

Sindh Survey 1992-3. Q.H. Mallah, a graduate student at the Shah Abdul Latif University, conducts a survey of Sukkur district in north-eastern Sindh. He records 20 now sites of the Indus Age, mostly of the Mature Harappan (Mallah 1994).

Sindh Survey 1993-5. Director General M.R. Mughal of the Pakistan Department of Archaeology initiated survey in northern Sindh: Jacabobad, Shikarpur, Sukkur and Khairpur districts. His efforts are coordinated with other explorations undertaken by the Shah Abdul Latif University (Mughal 1995).

Siswal 1970. Suraj Bhan of Kurukshetra University excavated one test trench at Siswal in Hissar district of Haryana. He found a site with an Early Harappan (Siswal A or Kalibangan I) occupation followed by a Mature Harappan settlement with Siswal A ceramics in association with Mature Harappan ceramics which he calls Siswal B (Suraj Bhan 1975: 103-9).

Somnath 1955-6. Gujarat State Department of Archaeology and the M.S. University of Baroda undertook the first of three seasons of excavation at Prabhas Patan, or Somnath in Gujarat, district Junagadh. They found a Lustrous Red Ware settlement under a deep historical occupation (*IAR* 1955-6: 7-8).

Somnath 1956-7. Gujarat State Department of Archaeology and the M.S. University of Baroda undertook the second of two seasons of excavation at Prabhas Patan, or Somnath (*IAR* 1956-7: 16-17).

Somnath 1965. Gujarat State Department of Archaeology and the M.S. University of Baroda undertook the third season of excavation at Prabhas Patan, or Somnath. The work was supervised by M.A. Dhaky (Nanavati et al. 1971).

Somnath 1971-2. Gujarat State Department of Archaeology and Deccan College undertook the first of three seasons of renewed excavation at Prabhas Patan, or Somnath (*IAR* 1971-2: 12-13).

Somnath 1975-6. Gujarat State Department of Archaeology and Deccan College undertook the second of three seasons of renewed excavation at Prabhas Patan, or Somnath (*IAR* 1975-6: 13).

Somnath 1976-7. Gujarat State Department of Archaeology and Deccan College undertook the third and final season of renewed excavation at Prabhas Patan, or Somnath. They found a Pre-Prabhas settlement and a Prabhas Period public building (*IAR* 1976-7: 17-18).

Sothi 1950-1. A. Ghosh of the the Archaeological Survey of India lays six trenches at Sothi, 8 km east of Nohar on the ancient Drishadvati. He found pottery like that later identified at Kalibangan Period I. Sothi was the type site for the Early

Harappan Sothi-Siswal Phase in northern Rajasthan and adjacent regions (Ghosh 1952; Dikshit 1984).

Sothi 1978. K. N. Dikshit of the Archaeological Survey of India put one trial trench in the mound of Sothi, 8 km east of Nohar on the ancient Drishadvati (Dikshit 1980: 34-5, 1984).

Spina Ghundai 1881. Captain Lock, the Political Agent for Pishin, Baluchistan, acting under the orders of Colonel, Sir Oliver St. John, excavated Spina Ghundai, near Kila Abdulla, in northern Quetta-Pishin. While most of this mound was historic in date, there was prehistoric pottery there, but Captain Lock does not recognize its antiquity. Sir Aurel Stein revisited the site (1929: 87) as did Walter Fairservis (1956: 200, 351; Garwood 1887).

Sunet 1983-4. The Punjab Department of Archaeology carried out excavation at Sunet in district Ludhiana. It was a multi-period site beginning with an occupation in the Post-Urban Harappan (*IAR* 1983-4: 67-9).

Sur Jangal 1927. Sir Aurel Stein undertook an excavation at Sur Jangal in Loralai district of Baluchistan. He recognized it as a Chalcolithic settlement and relates the pottery to Rana Ghundai and Moghul Ghundai (Stein 1929: 73-7).

Sur Jangal 1950-1. Walter A. Fairservis, Jr. of the American Museum of Natural History revisited Sur Jangal in Loralai district and undertook a systematic survey of the site, removing pottery sherds from exposed sections. Fairservis published an analysis of the material and suggested a relative stratigraphy for Sur Jangal, Rana Ghundai and other sites in the region (Fairservis 1959: 293-300).

Surain Damb 1955. Henry Field of Harvard University undertook a small excavation at Surain Damb in Pakistani Makran. He found a site with Amri-Nal, Kulli and Shahi Tump Grey Ware (Field 1959: 84, 88-9, 105).

Surkotada 1964-5. Jagat Pati Joshi of the Archaeological Survey of India discovered Surkotada in Kachchh district of Gujarat. He returned there for excavation in 1970-1 and 1971-2 (*IAR* 1964-5: 12).

Surkotada 1970-1. Jagat Pati Joshi undertook the first of two seasons of excavation at Surkotada in Gujarat, district Kachchh. He found a fortified Sindhi Harappan settlement in three phases of occupation. There was abundant Ahar Black and Red Ware in Period IC (*IAR* 1970-1: 13-15; Joshi 1990).

Surkotada 1971-2. Jagat Pati Joshi undertook the second of two seasons of excavation at Surkotada (*IAR* 1971-2: 13-21; Joshi 1990).

Sutkagen-dor 1875. Major E. Mockler visited this western-most of the Mature Harappan settlements in Makran on the Iran-Pakistan border (Mockler 1877: 122).

Sutkagen-dor 1876. Major E. Mockler undertook a small excavation at this site. He does not recognize the antiquity of the place (Mockler 1877: 123).

Sutkagen-dor 1928. Sir Aurel Stein undertook a small excavation at this site of the Mature Harappan at the mouth of the Dasht river in the Makran on the Iran-Pakistan Border (Stein 1931: 60-71).

Sutkagen-dor 1932. Sir Aurel Stein revisits Sutkagen-dor (Stein 1937: 70).

Sutkagen-dor 1960. George F. Dales of The University Museum conducted a small excavation at this site and published a preliminary report (Dales 1962; Dales and Lipo 1992).

Taraghda 1978-9. The Gujarat State Department of Archaeology conducted one season of excavation at Taraghada in Gujarat, district Rajkot. They found a Sorath Harappan site with Prabhas Ware, a copper ring, carnelian beads and Harappan weight (*IAR* 1978-9: 68).

Tarakai Qila 1978-9. The Joint University of Peshawar-Cambridge University team undertook one season of excavation at Tarakai Qila in the Bannu Basin of Pakistan. They found a small Kot Dijian site stratified below deposits of the historical period (Allchin and Knox 1981).

Tarkhanewala Dera 1951. A. Ghosh of the Archaeological Survey of India excavated a cremation area at Tarkhanewala Dera in the course of his survey of the ancient Sarasvati river. It was a Mature Harappan settlement (Ghosh 1962: 3).

Tharro Hill 1929. N.G. Majumdar excavated at Tharro Hill near Gujo in southern Sindh, near the northern edge of the ancient Indus delta. He found a site with microliths and an Amri-Nal occupation. This was a poorly understood site that may have evidence for early food production in Sindh (Majumdar 1934: 20-2).

Toji Damb 1927. Sir Aurel Stein undertook a small test excavation at Toji Damb in the Kharan area of Baluchistan. He first visited this site on his 1904-5 tour in this region. Stein found a stratified site with an occupation that probably begins in the Kechi Beg Phase, followed by Amri-Nal and Kulli occupations. There was also historical material at this site (Stein 1931: 22-5).

Trihni 1930. N.G. Majumdar excavated at Trihni (Lal Chhatto) just to the west of Lake Manchar in western Sindh. He found a site with painted black on red pottery and perforated vessels. This site was still not well understood. It may be a Sindhi variant of the late Jhukar in the Post-Urban Harappan (Majumdar 1934: 60-3).

Vagad 1981-2. V.H. Sonawane and R.N. Mehta of M.S. University of Baroda undertook one season of excavation at this large (13.5 ha) Sorath Harappan site just across the Bhadar river from Rangpur (Sonawane and Mehta 1985).

Vallabhi 1979-80. R.N. Mehta conducted one season of excavation at Vallabhi in Gujarat, district Bhavnagar near the well known Early Historical site of Vallabhipur. He found a pastoralists camp with prepared, circular house floors and post holes associated with the Late Sorath Harappan, Lustrous Red Ware ceramic assemblage (Post-Urban Phase) (*IAR* 1979-80: 24; Mehta 1982).

Warthan 1961-2. K.V. Soundara Rajan of the Archaeological Survey of India undertook one season of excavation at Warthan in Gujarat, district Surat. He found a Black-painted Red Ware similar to Nagal, possibly representing the final stage of Chalcolithic occupation in the region. There was Harappan script, 'winged pot sign', as graffiti on pottery. There was also a Red Polished Ware occupation (*IAR* 1961-2: 1)

Waziristan Survey 1927. Sir Aurel Stein conducted a survey of Waziristan. He excavated at Periano Ghundai, Sur Jangal and Dabar Kot (Stein 1929).

Zekhada 1977-8. R.N. Mehta of the M.S. University of Baroda undertook one season of excavation at Zekhada in Gujarat, district Banaskantha. He found a Late Sorath Harappan pastoralist's camp with prepared circular house floors and post holes (*IAR* 1977-8: 20-1; Mehta 1982).

REFERENCES

Agrawala, R.C. and Vijay Kumar 1982. Ganeshwar-Jodhpura Culture: New Traits in Indian Archaeology, in *Harappan Civilization: a Contemporary Perspective* (Gregory L. Possehl Ed.), pp. 125-34. Delhi: Oxford-IBH and the American Institute of Indian Studies.

Ajithprasad, P. and V.H. Sonawane (in press). The Harappa Culture in North Gujarat: a Regional Perspective, in *Harappans and Others in Gujarat* (Gregory L. Possehl and Vasant Shinde Eds.). Delhi: Oxford-IBH.

Alcock, Leslie 1952. Exploring Pakistan's Past: the First Year's Work, *Pakistan Quarterly* 2: 12-16.

Allchin, F.R. 1982. The Legacy of the Indus Civilization, in *Harappan Civilization: a Contemporary Perspective* (Gregory L. Possehl Ed.), pp. 325-33. Delhi: Oxford-IBH and the American Institute of Indian Studies.

Allchin, F.R., B. Allchin, F.A. Durrani and M. Farid Khan 1986. *Lewan and the Bannu Basin: Excavation and Survey of Sites and Environments in North West Pakistan*. Oxford: BAR International Series 310.

Allchin, F.R. and Jagat Pati Joshi 1995. *Excavations at Malvan*. New Delhi: Memoirs of the Archaeological Survey of India 92.

Allchin, F.R. and R. Knox 1981. Preliminary Report on the Excavations at Tarakai Qila, 1978-79, in *South Asian Archaeology 1979* (H. Hartel Ed.), pp. 245-50. Berlin: Dietrich Reimer Verlag.

Anonymous 1964. Departmental Excavations: Mohenjo-daro, Kot Diji, Naru Waro Dharo, Mainamati, Charsada, Banbhore, Lahore Fort, *Pakistan Archaeology* 1: 37-56.

Anonymous 1968. Excavations: Harappa (Cemetery R-37), *Pakistan Archaeology* 5: 63-8.

Babu, B.S.R. 1995. Excavations at Bhorgarh, *Puratattva* 25: 88-90.

Banerji, R.D. 1920-1. Mohen-jo-daro. *Progress Report of the Archaeological Survey of India, Western Circle, for the Year Ending 1 March 1920*: 79-80.

——— 1926 (1984). *Mohenjo-Daro: a Long Forgotten Report*. Varanasi: Prithvi Prakashan.

Besenval, M. Roland 1994. The 1992-3 Field Seasons at Miri Qalat: New Contributions to the Chronology of Protohistoric Settlement in Pakistani Makran, in *South Asian Archaeology 1993* (Asko Parpola and P. Koskikallio Eds.), pp. 81-91. Helsinki: Annales Academiae Scientiarum Fennicae, Series B, Vol. 271.

Besenval, M. Roland and P. Marquis 1993. Excavations in Miri Qalat (Pakistani Makran): Results of the First Field Season (1990), in *South Asian Archaeology 1991* (Adalbert J. Gail and Gerd J.R. Mevissen Eds.), pp. 31-48. Stuttgart: Franz Steiner Verlag.

Besenval, M. Roland and P. Sanlaville 1990. Cartography of Ancient Settlements in Central Southern Pakistani Makran: New Data, *Mesopotamia*: 79-146.

Bhan, Kuldeep K. 1986. Recent Explorations in the Jamnagar District of Saurashtra, *Man and Environment* X: 1-21.

——— 1994. Cultural Development of the Prehistoric Period in North Gujarat with Reference to Western India, *South Asian Studies* 10: 71-90.

Bhandarkar, D.R. 1911-12. Excavation, *Progress Report of the Archaeological Survey of India: Western Circle, for theYear Ending 31 March 1912*: 4-5.

Bisht, Ravi Singh 1982. Excavations at Banawali: 1974-77, in *Harappan Civilization: a Contemporary Perspective*, (Gregory L. Possehl Ed.), pp. 113-24. Delhi: Oxford-IBH and the American Institute of Indian Studies.

——— 1991. Dholavira: a New Horizon of the Indus Civilization, *Puratattva* 20: 71-82.

Burnes, Sir Alexander 1834. *A Voyage on the Indus*. London: John Murray.

——— 1835. *Travels into Bokhara: Containing the Narrative of 'A Voyage on the Indus'*, 3 Vols. London: John Murray.

Cardi, Beatrice de 1965. Excavation and Reconnaissance in Kalat, West Pakistan: the Prehistoric Sequence in the Surab Region, *Pakistan Archaeology* 2: 86-182.

——— 1983. *Archaeological Surveys in Baluchistan, 1948 and 1957*. London: Institute of Archaeology, Occasional Publication 8.

Casal, Jean-Marie 1961. *Fouilles de Mundigak*, 2 Vols. Paris: Memoires de la Delegation Archaeologique Francais en Afghanistan, Tome 17.

——— 1964. *Fouilles d'Amri*. 2 Vols. Paris: Publications de la Commission des Fouilles Archaeologiques, Fouilles du Pakistan.

——— 1966. Nindowari: a Chalcolithic Site in South Baluchistan, *Pakistan Archaeology* 3: 10-21.

——— 1968. Nindo Damb, *Pakistan Archaeology* 5:51-5.

Chitalwala, Y.M. 1979. Harappan and Post-Harappan Settlement Patterns in Rajkot District of Saurashtra, in *Essays in Indian Protohistory* (D.P. Agrawal and Dilip K. Chakrabarti Eds.), pp. 113-21. Delhi: B.R. Publishing Corporation.

Chitalwala, Y. M. and Gregory L. Possehl (in press). Excavations at Rojdi, 1994-1995, *Man and Environment*.

Cunningham, Sir Alexander 1875. Harappa, *Annual Report of the Archaeological Survey of India* 5: 105-8.

Dalal, Katy Feroze 1980. A Short History of Archaeological Exploration in Bikaner and Bahawalpur Along the 'Lost' Sarasvati River, *Indica* 17:3-40.

Dales, George F. 1962. Harappan Outposts on the Makran Coast, *Antiquity* 36: 86-92.

——— 1965a. Re-opening the Mohenjo-daro Excavations, *Illustrated London News, May* 29: 25-7.

——— 1965b. New Investigations at Mohenjo-daro, *Archaeology* 18: 145-50.

——— 1979a. The Balakot Project: Summary of Four Years of Excavations in Pakistan, *Man and Environment* III:45-53.

——— 1979b. The Balakot Project: Summary of Four Years Excavations in Pakistan, in *South Asian Archaeology 1977* (M. Taddei Ed.), pp. 241-74. Naples: Instituto Universitario Orientale. Seminario di Studi Asiatici, Series Minor 6.

——— 1985. Stone Sculpture from the Protohistoric Helmand Civilization, Afghanistan, in *Orientalia Iosephi Tucci Memoriae Dicta* (G. Gnoli and L. Lanciotti Eds.), pp. 219-24. Rome: Instituto Italiano Per Il Medio ed Estremo Oriente, Series Minor 56 (1).

——— 1986. Preliminary Report on the First Season at Harappa, 1986. Typescript Manuscript.

Dales, George F. and J. Mark Kenoyer 1986. *Excavations at Mohenjo Daro, Pakistan: the Pottery*. Philadelphia: The University Museum, University of Pennsylvania.

——— 1987. Preliminary Report on the University of California at Berkeley's Second Season at Harappa, Pakistan: January-April 1987. Typescript Manuscript.

——— 1988. Preliminary Report on the Third Season (January-March 1988) of Research at Harappa, Pakistan. Typescript Manuscript.

——— 1989. Preliminary Report on the Fourth Season (January 15-March 31, 1989) of Research at Harappa, *Pakistan*. Typescript Manuscript.

——— 1990. Excavation at Harappa—1988, *Pakistan Archaeology* 24: 68-176.

Dales, George F., J. Mark Kenoyer, and Staff 1991. Summaries of Five Seasons of Research at Harappa (District Sahiwal, Punjab, Pakistan, 1986-1990), in *Harappa Excavations 1986-1990: a Multidisciplinary Approach to Third Millennium Urbanism* (Richard H. Meadow Ed.), pp. 185-262. Madison: Prehistory Press. Monographs in World Archaeology 3.

Dales, George F. and Carl P. Lipo 1992. *Explorations on the Makran Coast, Pakistan: a Search for Paradise*. Berkeley: Contributions of the Archaeological Research Faculty, University of California, Berkeley 50.

Dames, M. Longworth 1886. Old Seals Found at Harappa, *The Indian Antiquary* 15: 1.

Dani, Ahmad Hasan 1970-1. Excavations in the Gomal Valley, *Ancient Pakistan* 5: 1-177.

De Terra, H. and T.T. Paterson 1939. *Studies on the Ice Age of India*. Washington, D.C.: Carnegie Institute Publication 493.

Dhavalikar, M.K. 1992. Kuntasi: an Harappan Port in Western India, in *South Asian Archaeology 1989* (Catherine Jarrige Ed.), pp. 73-82. Madison: Prehistory Press. Monographs in World Archaeology 14.

——— 1993. Harappans in Saurashtra: the Mercantile Model as Seen from Recent Excavations at Kuntasi, in *Harappan Civilization: a Recent Perspective* (Gregory L. Possehl Ed.), pp. 555-68. 2nd Edition. Delhi: Oxford-IBH and the American Institute of Indian Studies.

Dhavalikar, M.K., V. Shinde and S. Atre 1990. *Excavations at Kaothe*. Pune: Deccan College.

Dikshit, Rai Bahadur K.N. 1924-5. Explorations, Western Circle, Sind, Mohenjo-daro, *Annual Report of the Archaeological Survey of India 1924-25*: 63-73.

——— 1925-6. Exploration, Western Circle, Upper Sind Frontier District, Badah, *Annual Report of the Archaeological Survey of India 1925-26*: 99.

Dikshit, K.N. 1980. A Critical Review of the Pre-Harappan Cultures, *Man and Environment* IV: 32-43.

——— 1984. The Sothi Complex: Old Fecords and Fresh Observations, in *Frontiers of the Indus Civilization* (B.B. Lal and S.P. Gupta Eds.), pp. 531-7. Delhi: Books & Books.

Dikshit, M.G. 1950. Excavations at Rangpur - 1947, *Bulletin of the Deccan College Research Institute* 11: 3-55.

Dupree, Louis 1963. *Deh Morasi Ghundai: a Chalcolithic Site in South-Central Afghanistan*. New York: Anthropological Papers of the American Museum of Natural History 50 (2).

Durrani, Farzand A. 1988. Excavations in the Gomal Valley: Rehman Dheri Excavation Report, No. 1, *Ancient Pakistan* 6: 1-204.

Durrani, Farzand A., Ihsan Ali, and G. Erdosy 1991. Further Excavations at Rehman Dheri, *Ancient Pakistan* 7: 61-151.

Faccenna, Domenico 1981. The Protohistoric Occupation Level, in *Butkara I (Swat, Pakistan) 1956-62* Part 4 (Domenico Faccenna Ed.), pp. 757-65. Rome: IsMEO.

Fairservis, Walter A. Jr. 1952. New Discoveries in Baluchistan, *Archaeology* 5: 100-3.

——— 1956. *Excavations in the Quetta Valley, West Pakistan*. New York: Anthropological Papers of the American Museum of Natural History 45 (2).

——— 1959. *Archaeological Surveys in the Zhob and Loralại Districts, West Pakistan*. New York: Anthropological Papers of the American Museum of Natural History 47 (2).

——— 1961. *Archaeological Studies in the Seistan Basin of Southwestern Afghanistan and Eastern Iran*. New York: Anthropological Papers of the American Museum of Natural History 48(1).

——— 1971. *The Roots of Ancient India*. New York: Macmillan.

——— 1982. Allahdino: an Excavation of a Small Harappan Site, in *Harappan Civilization: a Contemporary Perspective* (Gregory L. Possehl Ed.), pp. 107-12. New Delhi: Oxford-IBH and the American Institute of Indian Studies.

Field, Henry 1959. *An Anthropological Reconnaissance in West Pakistan, 1955*. Cambridge (Mass.): Harvard University. Papers of the Peabody Museum of Archaeology and Ethnology 52.

Flam, Louis 1981. The Palaeogeography and Prehistoric Settlement Patterns in Sind, Pakistan (4000-2000 B.C.). Ph.D. Dissertation. Philadelphia: University of Pennsylvania.

——— 1993. Excavations at Ghazi Shah, Sindh, Pakistan, in *Harappan Civilization: a Recent Perspective* (Gregory L. Possehl Ed.), pp. 457-67. Delhi: Oxford-IBH and the American Institute of Indian Studies.

Fleet, J.F. 1912. Seals from Harappa, *Journal of the Royal Asiatic Society of Great Britain and Ireland*: 698-701.

Francfort, Henri-Paul 1985. *Prospections Archaeologiques au Nord-Ouest de L'inde: Rapport Preliminare 1983-84*. Paris: Editions Recherche sur les Civilizations, Memoire No. 62, Travaux de la Mission Archaeologique Franciase en Inde 1.

——— 1989. *Fouilles de Shortughai: Recherches sur l'Asie Centrale Protohistorique*, 2 vols. Paris: Diffusion de Boccard.

Frenchman, Katy Nariman 1972. Prehistoric Pottery Industries Along the 'Lost' Sarasvati River of the Great Indian Desert. Ph.D. Dissertation. Poona: University of Poona.

Garwood, Major J.F. 1887. Notes on the Ancient Mounds in the Quetta District, *Journal of the Asiatic Society of Bengal* 56:161-3.

Ghosh, A. 1952. The Rajputana Desert: Its Archaeological Aspect, *Bulletin of the National Institute of Sciences in India* 1: 37-42.

——— 1953. Exploration in Bikanir, *East and West* 4: 31-4.

——— 1959. Explorations in Bikanir, in *An Anthropological Reconnaissance in West Pakistan, 1955* (Henry Field Ed.), pp. 212-16. Cambridge (Mass): Harvard University. Papers of the Peabody Museum of Archaeology and Ethnology 52.

——— 1962. The Archaeological Background, in *Human Skeletal Remains from Harappa* (P. Gupta, P.C. Dutta and A. Basu Eds.), pp. 1-5. Calcutta: Memoirs of the Anthropological Survey of India 9.

——— 1989. *An Encyclopaedia of Indian Archaeology*. 2 vols. Delhi: Munshiram Manoharlal.

Ghurye, G.S. 1936. An Account of an Exploratory Tour in Certain Parts of Sind in Search of Prehistoric Culture, *Journal of the University of Bombay* (Arts and Law) 8: 1-18.

——— 1939. Two Sites in Kathiawar, *Journal of the University of Bombay* 8: 3-12.

Halim, M. Abdul 1972a. Excavation at Sarai Khola (Part I), *Pakistan Archaeology* 7: 23-89.

——— 1972b. Excavations at Sarai Khola (Part II), *Pakistan Archaeology* 8: 1-112.

Hargreaves, Harold 1929. Excavations in Baluchistan 1925, Sampur Mound, Mastung and Sohr

Damb, Nal. Delhi: Memoirs of the Archaeological Survey of India 35.

Hegde, K.T.M. and V.H. Sonawane 1986. Landscape and Settlement Pattern of Harappa Culture Villages in the Rupen Estuary, *Man and Environment* X: 23-32.

Hegde, K.T.M., V.H. Sonawane, D.R. Shah, K.K. Bhan, K. Krishnan, Ajithprasad and A. Pratapa Chandran 1988. Excavation at Nagwada—1986 and 1987: a Preliminary Report, *Man and Environment* XII: 55-65.

Hegde, K.T.M., V.H. Sonawane, K.K. Bhan K. Krishnan and Ajithprasad 1990. Excavation at Nagwada—1987-88: a Preliminary Report, in *Adaptation and Other Essays: Proceedings of the Archaeology Conference, 1988* (N.C. Ghosh and S. Chakrabarti Eds.), pp. 191-5. Santiniketan: Visva-Bharati Research Publications.

Hooja, Rima 1988. *The Ahar Culture and Beyond: Settlements and Frontiers of 'Mesolithic' and Early Agricultural Sites in South-Eastern Rajasthan, c. 3rd-2nd Millennia B.C.* Oxford: BAR International Series 412.

Hussain, Majid 1989. Salvage Excavation at Moenjodaro, *Journal of the Pakistan Historical Society* 37: 89-98.

IAR. Indian Archaeology—A Review. Annual Report of the Archaeological Survey of India. New Delhi: Archaeological Survey of India.

Jairath, Virjendra Kumar 1986. Archaeology of the Northern Part of Bhavnagar District, Gujarat State, up to the 15th Century A.D. 2 vols. Ph.D. Dissertation. Vadodara: Maharaja Sayajirao University of Baroda.

Jansen, Michael, Marie Mulloy and Gunter Urban 1991. *Forgotten Cities on the Indus: Early Civilization in Pakistan from the 8th to the 2nd Millennium B.C.* Mainz: Verlag Philipp von Zabern.

Jansen, Michael and Maurizio Tosi (Eds.) 1988. *Reports on Field Work Carried Out at Mohenjo-daro, Pakistan 1983-86 by the IsMEO-Aachen University Mission.* Aachen-Rome: RWTH-IsMEO.

Jansen, Michael and Gunter Urban (Eds.) 1984. *Reports on Field Work Carried Out at Mohenjo-Daro, Pakistan 1982-83 by the IsMEO-Aachen Univeristy Mission.* Aachen-Rome: RWTH-IsMEO.

Jarrige, Jean-Francois 1979. Excavations at Mehrgarh—Pakistan, in *South Asian Archaeology 1975* (J.E. van Lohuizen-de Leeuw Ed.), pp. 76-87. Leiden: E.J. Brill.

——— 1986. *Excavations at Mehrgarh-Naushero: the Twelfth Season: 1985-86: a Preliminary Report.* Paris: Musee Guimet, French Archaeological Mission to Pakistan.

——— 1987. *Excavations at Mehrgarh-Naushero: the Thirteenth Season: 1986-87: a Preliminary Report.* Paris: Musee Guimèt, French Archaeological Mission to Pakistan.

——— 1988. *Excavations at Mehrgarh-Naushero: the Fourteenth Season: 1987-88: a Preliminary Report.* Paris: Musee Guimet, French Archaeological Mission to Pakistan.

——— 1990a. Excavations at Nausharo: 1988-89, *Pakistan Archaeology* 25: 193-240.

——— 1990b. Sedentarite et Semi-Nomadisme dans la Plaine de Kachi du 7e au 2e Millennaire Avant notre Ere, in *Nomades et Sedentaires en Asie Centrale: Apports de l'archeologie et de l'ethnologie* (Henri-Paul Francfort Ed.), pp. 157-68. Paris: CNRS.

——— 1990c. *Excavations at Mehrgarh-Naushero: the Sixteenth Season, 1989-90: a Preliminary Report.* Paris: Musee Guimet, French Archaeological Mission to Pakistan.

——— 1991. *Excavations at Mehrgarh-Naushero: the Seventeenth Season, 1990-91: a Preliminary Report.* Paris: Musee Guimet, French Archaeological Mission to Pakistan.

——— 1992. *Excavations at Mehrgarh-Naushero: the Eighteenth Season, 1991-92: a Preliminary*

Report. Paris: Musee Guimet, French Archaeological Mission to Pakistan.

——— 1993. *Excavations at Mehrgarh-Naushero: the Nineteenth Season, 1992-93: a Preliminary Report*. Parsi: Musee Guimet, French Archaeological Mission to Pakistan.

——— 1994. *Excavations at Mehrgarh-Naushero: the Twentieth Season, 1993-94: a Preliminary Report*. Paris: Musee Guimet, French Archaeological Mission to Pakistan.

——— 1995. *Excavations at Mehrgarh-Naushero: the Twenty-First Season, 1994-95: a Preliminary Report*. Paris: Musee Guimet, French Archaeological Mission to Pakistan.

Jarrige, Jean-Francois and M.U. Hassan 1989. Funerary Complexes in Baluchistan at the End of the Third Millennium in the Light of Recent Discoveries at Mehrgarh and Quetta, in *South Asian Archaeology 1985* (K. Frifelt and P. Sörensen Eds.), pp. 150-66. Scandinavian Institute of Asian Studies, Occasional Papers 4.

Jarrige, Jean-Francois and Monique Lechevallier 1979. Excavations at Mehrgarh, Baluchistan: Their Significance in the Prehistorical Context of the Indo-Pakistan Borderlands, in *South Asian Archaeology 1977* (M. Taddei Ed.), pp. 463-535. Naples: Instituto Universitario Orientale.

Jarrige, Jean-Francois and Marielle Santoni 1979. *Fouilles de Pirak*, 2 Vols. Paris: Publications de la Commission des Fouilles Archaeologique, Fouilles du Pakistan, Vol. 1, No. 2.

Joshi, Jagat Pati 1972. Fresh Light on the Archaeology of Kutch, in *Archaeological Congress and Seminar Papers* (S.B. Deo Ed.), pp. 21-35. Nagpur: Nagpur University.

——— 1990. *Excavation at Surkotada 1971-72 and Exploration in Kutch*. New Delhi: Memoirs of the Archaeological Survey of India 87.

——— 1993. *Excavation at Bhagwanpura 1975-76 and Other Explorations and Excavations 1975-81 in Haryana, Jammu & Kashmir and Punjab*. Delhi: Memoirs of the Archaeological Survey of India 89.

Kenoyer, J. Mark and Richard H. Meadow 1992. *Harappa Archaeological Project 1992: End of Season Report (January 12-April 3, 1992)*. Berkeley, Cambridge, Madison: the Harappa Archaeological Project (photocopy).

Khan, Ahmad Nabi 1988. *Proceedings of Third South Asian Archaeological Congress, Islamabad, 1988*. Karachi: Department of Archaeology and Museums.

Khan, F.A. 1965. Excavations at Kot Diji, *Pakistan Archaeology* 2: 11-85.

Khan, Farid, J.R. Knox and K.D. Thomas 1991. *Explorations and Excavations in Bannu District, North-west Frontier Province, Pakistan, 1985-88*. London: British Museum, Department of Oriental Antiquities, Occasional Paper 50.

Krishna Deva and Donald E. McCown 1949. Further Exploration in Sind, 1938, *Ancient India* 5: 12-30.

Kumar, Manmohan 1978. Archaeology of Ambala and Kurukshetra Districts (Haryana). Ph.D. Dissertation. Kurukshetra: Kurukshetra University.

Kuraishi, M.H. 1935-6. Excavations at Harappa, *Annual Report of the Archaeological Survey of India 1935-36*: 35-6.

Lal, B.B. 1951. Further Copper Hoards from the Gangetic Basin and a Review of the Problem, *Ancient India* 7: 20-39.

——— 1954-5. Excavations at Hastinapura and Other Explorations in the Upper Ganga and Sutlej Basins 1950-52, *Ancient India* 10-11: 5-151.

Lal, B.B. and K.N. Dikshit 1982. Pariar—an Eastern Outpost of the Painted Grey Ware, *Puratattva* 11: 26-31.

Mackay, Ernest J.H. 1927-8. Excavations at Mohenjo-daro, *Annual Report of the Archaeological Survey of India 1927-28*: 67-76.

——— 1928-9. Excavations at Mohenjo-daro, *Annual Report of the Archaeological Survey of India 1928-29*: 67-75.

——— 1929-30. Excavations at Mohenjo-daro, *Annual Report of the Archaeological Survey of India 1929-30*: 98-109.

——— 1930-4. Excavations at Mohenjo-daro, *Annual Reports of the Archaeological Survey of India for the Years 1930-31, 1931-32, 1932-33 and 1933-34* (Part One): 51-71.

——— 1943. *Chanhu-daro Excavations 1935-36.* New Haven: American Oriental Society, American Oriental Series 20.

Majumdar, N.G. 1927-8. Excavations at Jhukar, *Annual Report of the Archaeological Survey of India 1927-28*: 76-83.

——— 1934. *Explorations in Sind.* Delhi: Memoirs of the Archaeological Survey of India 48.

——— 1939. Prehistoric and Protohistoric Civilization, in *Revealing India's Past* (Sir John Cumming Ed.), pp. 91-117. London: The India Society.

Mallah, Qasid Hussain 1994. The Survey/Exploration of Historic Monuments, Archaeological Sites and Ancient Settlement Pattern in Sukkur District. M.Phil. Dissertation. Khairpur: Shah Abdul Latif University.

Marshall, Sir John 1904-5. A New Type of Pottery from Baluchistan, *Annual Report of the Archaeological Survey of India 1904-05*: 105-6.

——— 1925-6. Exploration, Western Circle, Mohenjo-daro, *Annual Report of the Archaeological Survey of India 1925-26*: 72-98.

——— 1926-7. The Indus Culture, *Annual Report of the Archaeological Survey of India 1926-27*: 51-60.

Masson, Charles 1842. *Narrative of Various Journeys in Baluchistan, Afghanistan and the Punjab: Including a Rresidence in Those Countries from 1826 to 1838.* London: Richard Bently.

Meadow, Richard H. 1993. Animal Domestication in the Middle East: a Revised View from the Eastern Margin, in *Harappan Civilization: a Recent Perspective* (Gregory L. Possehl Ed.), pp. 295-320. Delhi: Oxford-IBH and the American Institute of Indian Studies.

Meadow, Richard H. and J. Mark Kenoyer 1993. *Harappa Archaeological Research Project: 1993 Excavations*. Cambridge: Peabody Museum (photocopy).

——— 1994 . Harappa Excavations 1993: the City Wall and Inscribed Materials, in *South Asian Archaeology 1993* (Asko Parpola and Petteri Koskikallio Eds.), pp. 451-70. Helsinki: Annales Academiae Scientiarum Fennicae, Series B, Vol. 271.

Mehta, R.N. 1982. Some Rural Harappan Settlements in Gujarat, in *Harappan Civilization: a Contemporary Perspective* (Gregory L. Possehl Ed.), pp. 167-74. Delhi: Oxford-IBH and the American Institute of Indian Studies.

Mehta, R.N., K.N. Momin and D.R. Shah 1980. *Excavation at Kanewal*. Vadodara: the Maharaja Sayajirao University of Baroda, Archaeology Series 17.

Mirsky, Jeannette 1977. *Sir Aurel Stein: Archaeological Explorer*. Chicago: University of Chicago Press.

Misra, V.N. 1967. *Pre- and Proto-History of the Berach Basin, South Rajasthan*. Poona: Deccan College.

Mockler, E., Major 1877. On Ruins in Makran, *Journal of the Royal Asiatic Society of Great Britain and Ireland* 9: 121-34.

Momin, K.N. 1979. Archaeology of Kheda District (Gujarat) up to 1500 A.D. Ph.D. Dissertation. Vadodara: Maharaja Sayajirao University of Baroda.

Moneer, Q.M. 1930-4. Mr. Moneer's Work During 1933-34, *Annual Reports of the Archaeo-*

logical Survey of India for the Years 1930-31, 1931-32, 1932-33 and 1933-34 (Part One): 72.

Mughal, M. Rafique 1968. Excavations: Harappa, 1966 (Cemetery R-37), *Pakistan Archaeology* 5: 63-8.

——— 1972a. A Summary of Excavations and Explorations in Pakistan, *Pakistan Archaeology* 8: 113-58.

——— 1972b. Excavation at Jalilpur, *Pakistan Archaeology* 8: 117-24.

——— 1972c. Exploration in Central Punjab: Sahiwal District, *Pakistan Archaeology* 8: 127-31.

——— 1972d. Explorations in Northern Baluchistan, *Pakistan Archaeology* 8: 137-50.

——— 1980. New Archaeological Evidence from Bahawalpur, *Man and Environment* IV: 93-8.

——— 1982. Recent Archaeological Research in the Cholistan Desert, in *Harappan Civilization: a Contemporary Perspective* (Gregory L. Possehl Ed.), pp. 85-95. Delhi: Oxford-IBH and the American Institute of Indian Studies.

——— 1992. Jhukar and the Late Harappan cultural mosaic of the Greater Indus Valley, in *South Asian Archaeology 1989* (Catherine Jarrige Ed.), pp. 213-22. Madison: Prehistory Press, Monographs in World Archaeology 14.

——— 1995. A Preliminary Review of Archaeological Surveys in Punjab and Sindh: 1993-95, *South Asian Studies* 13: 241-9.

Nanavati, J.M., R.N. Mehta and S.N. Chowdhary 1971. *Somnath—1956*. Ahmedabad-Vadodara: Department of Archaeology, Gujarat State and Department of Archaeology and Ancient History, the Maharaja Sayajirao University of Baroda, Monograph 1.

Nazim, M. 1934-5. Exploration in the Northern Circle: Harappa, *Annual Report of the Archaeological Survey of India 1934-35*: 31-3.

Nissen, Hans J. 1983. *Report on the Preliminary Archaeological Reconnaissance of the Area of North Western Sind (Between Lake Manchar and Sukkur)*. Berlin: Free University of Berlin.

——— 1994. An Archaeological Surface Survey in Northwestern Sindh, Pakistan, in *From Sumer to Meluhha: Contributions to the Archaeology of South and West Asia in Memory of George F. Dales, Jr.* (J.M. Kenoyer Ed.), pp. 51-8. Madison: Wisconsin Archaeological Reports 3.

Noetling, Fritz W. 1899. *Uber eine Prahistorische Neiderlassungen in Baluchistan*. Berliner Gesellschaft fur Anthropologie Ethnologie und Urgeschichte, 31, Zeitschrift Fur Ethnologie.

Pedde, Friedhelm 1993a. Keramik Aus Nor-Baluchistan: Sie Sammlungen Noetling und Henckmann im Museen fur Indische Kunst, Staatliche Museen zu Berlin, Preussischer Kulturbesitz. *Deutsches Archaologisches Institut Abteilung Tehran, Materialien zur Iranischen Archaologie, Band* 1: Berlin: Verlag von Dietrich Reimer.

——— 1993b. Pottery from Northern Baluchistan—the Noetling Collection in the Museum of Indian Art, Berlin, in *South Asian Archaeology 1991* (Adalbert J. Gail and Gerd J.R. Mevissen Eds.), pp. 215-30. Stuttgart: Franz Steiner Verlag.

Phogat, Silak Ram 1970. Archaeological Remains at Kalayat. *Kurukshetra University Research Journal* (Arts and Humanities) 4: 137-40.

Possehl, Gregory L. 1980. *Indus Civilization in Saurashtra*. Delhi: B.R. Publishing Corporation.

——— 1994. The Indus Civilisation, *Man and Environment* XIX (1-2): 103-13.

Possehl, Gregory L. and Dinker P. Mehta 1994 . Excavations at Rojdi 1992-93, in *South Asian Archaeology 1993*, 2 Vols. (Asko Parpola and Petteri Koskikallio Eds.), pp. 603-14. Helsinki: Annales Academiae Scientiarum Fennicae, Series B, Vol. 271.

Prufer, Olaf H. 1952. *Report on the Trial Excavation Carried Out at Khilokhiri.* Calcutta: Jamia Millia Islamia Historical Research Foundation.

Puri, Kidar Nath 1936-7. Excavations at Mohenjo-daro, *Annual Report of the Archaeological Survey of India 1936-37*: 41.

Rahman, Abdur 1968-9. Excavation at Damkot, in Chakra Fort and Gandhara Art (Ahmad Hasan Dani Ed.), *Ancient Pakistan*, 4: 103-250.

Raikes, Robert L. 1968. Archaeological Explorations in Southern Jhalawan and Las Bela, *Origini* 2: 103-71.

Ramachandran, T.N. and Y.D. Sharma 1956. *Archaeological Reconnaissance in Afghanistan: Preliminary Report of the Indian Archaeological Delegation, 1956.* New Delhi: Archaeological Survey of India.

Rao, S.R. 1963. Excavations at Rangpur and Other Explorations in Gujarat, *Ancient India* 18-19: 5-207.

——— 1979. *Lothal: a Harappan Port Town, 1955-62.* New Delhi: Memoirs of the Archaeological Survey of India 78(1).

Rissman, Paul C. and Y.M. Chitalwala 1990. *Harappan Civilization and Oriyo Timbo.* Delhi: Oxford-IBH and the American Institute of Indian Studies.

Ross, E.J. 1946. A Chalcolithic Site in Northern Baluchistan: Rana Ghundai, *Journal of Near Eastern Studies* 5: 291-315.

Sahni, Rai Bahadur Daya Ram 1916-17. Harappa, District Montgomery, in *Annual Progress Report of the Superintendent, Hindu and Buddhist Monuments, Northern Circle, for the Year Ending 31st March 1917.* Lahore (Punjab): Government Printing.

——— 1920-1. Exploration, Hindu and Buddhist Monuments, Punjab, Harappa, *Annual Report of the Archaeological Survey of India 1920-21*: 15-17.

——— 1923-4. Exploration and Research, Northern Circle, Punjab, Harappa, *Annual Report of the Archaeological Survey of India 1923-24*: 52-54.

——— 1926-7. Mohenjo-daro, *Annual Report of the Archaeological Survey of India 1926-27*: 60-88.

Sali, S.A. 1986. *Daimabad, 1976-79.* New Delhi: Memoirs of the Archaeological Survey of India 83.

Santoni, Marielle 1984. Sibri and the South Cemetery of Mehrgarh: 3rd Millennium Connections Between the Northern Kachi Plain (Pakistan) and Central Asia, in *South Asian Archaeology 1981* (B. Allchin Ed.), pp. 52-60. Cambridge: Cambridge University Press.

——— 1989. Potters and Pottery During the Third Millennium B.C. (Periods VI and VII), in *South Asian Archaeology 1985* (Karen Frifelt and Per Sorensen Eds.), pp. 176-85. London: Curzon Press. Scandinavian Institute of Asian Studies, Occasional Papers 4.

Sastri, K.N. 1965. *New Light on the Indus Civilization.* Vol. 2. Delhi: Atma Ram & Sons.

Shaffer, Jim G. 1974. *Allahdino and the Mature Harappan: a Preliminary Report on the Cultural Stratigraphy.* Cleveland: Department of Anthropology, Case Western Reserve University.

——— 1978. *Prehistoric Baluchistan: with Excavation Report on Said Qala Tepe.* Delhi: B.R. Publishing Corporation.

——— 1981. The Protohistoric Period in the Eastern Punjab: a Preliminary Assessment, in *Indus*

Civilization: New Perspectives (Ahmad Hasan Dani Ed.), pp. 65-102. Islamabad: Quaid-i-Azam University.

Sharma, R.P. 1982 . Khatoli—a Protohistoric Site in Haryana, *Puratattva* 11: 123-5.

Sharma, Y.D. 1982a. Harappan Complex on the Sutlej (India), in *Harappan Civilization: a Contemporary Perspective* (L. Possehl Ed.), pp. 141-65. Delhi: Oxford-IBH and the American Institute of Indian Studies.

——— 1982b. The Pre-Harappans in Punjab, *Puratattva* 11: 34-8.

——— 1987. Fresh Light on the Bara Culture from Mahorana, in *Archaeology and History: Essays in Memory of Shri A. Ghosh*, 2 Vols. (B.M. Pande and B.D. Chattopadhyaya Eds.), pp. 157-76. Delhi: Agam Kala.

——— 1989. Bahadrabad, in *An Encyclopaedia of Indian Archaeology* (A. Ghosh Ed.), Vol. 2 pp. 37-8. Delhi: Munshiram Manoharlal.

Sher, G.M. and M. Vidale 1985. Surface Evidence of Craft Activity at Chanhu-daro, March 1984, *Annali dell'Instituto Universitario Orientale* 45: 585-98.

Shinde, Vasant 1991. The Late Harappan Culture in Maharashtra, India: a Study of Settlement and Subsistence Patterns, *South Asian Studies* 7: 91-6.

——— 1992. Excavations at Padri—1990-91: a Preliminary Report, *Man and Environment* XVII (1): 79-86.

Singh, Amar 1981. Archaeology of Karnal and Jind Districts (Haryana). Ph.D. Dissertation. Kurukshetra: Kurukshetra University.

Sonawane, V.H. and R.N. Mehta 1985. Vagad—a Rural Harappan Settlement in Gujarat, *Man and Environment* IX: 38-44.

Soundara Rajan, K.V. 1984. Kutch Harappan—a Corridor of the Indus Phase, in *Frontiers of the Indus Civilization* (B.B. Lal and S.P. Gupta Eds.), pp. 217-26. Delhi: Books & Books.

Srivastava, H.L. 1936-7. Excavations at Harappa, *Annual Report of the Archaeological Survey of India 1936-37*: 39-41.

Stacul, Giorgio 1978. Excavation at Bir-kot-Ghundai (Swat, Pakistan), *East and West* 28: 137-50.

——— 1979. The Black-Burnished Ware Period in the Swat Valley (*c.* 1700-1500 B.C.), in *South Asian Archaeology 1977* (M. Taddei Ed.), pp. 661-73. Naples: Instituto Universitario Orientale, Seminario di Studi Asiatici, Series Minor 6.

——— 1980. Bir-kot-ghundai (Swat, Pakistan): 1978 Excavation Report, *East and West* 30: 55-65.

——— 1981a. On periods and Cultures in the Swat Valley and Beyond, *Puratattva* 10: 89-91.

——— 1981b. Painted Pottery from the Swat Valley, Pakistan (*c.* 1700-1400 B.C.), in *South Asian Archaeology 1979* (H. Hartel Ed.), pp. 305-11. Berlin: Dietrich Reimer Verlag.

——— 1987. *Prehistoric and Protohistoric Swat, Pakistan (c. 3000-1400 B.C.)*. Rome: Instituto Italiano per il Medio ed Estremo Orientale.

——— 1989. Continuity of forms and traditions at Bir-kot-ghundai, Swat, in *South Asian Archaeology 1985* (Karen Frifelt and Per Sorensen Eds.), pp. 321-6. London: Curzon Press, Scandinavian Institute of Asian Studies, Occasional Papers 4.

——— 1993. Kalako-deray, Swat: an archaeological complex from the early/mid-2nd millennium B.C. in *South Asian Archaeology 1991* (Adalbert J. Gail and Gerd J.R. Mevissen Eds.), pp. 265-72. Stuttgart: Franz Steiner Verlag.

Stein, Sir Aurel 1905. *Report on Archaeological Survey Work in the North-West Frontier Prov-*

ince and Baluchistan for the Period from January 2nd, 1904 to March 31st, 1905. Peshawar: North-West Frontier Province Government Press for the Archaeological Survey of India.

——— 1929. *An Archaeological Tour in Waziristan and Northern Baluchistan.* Delhi: Memoirs of the Archaeological Survey of India 37.

——— 1931. *An Archaeological Tour in Gedrosia.* Delhi: Memoirs of the Archaeological Survey of India 43.

——— 1937. *Archaeological Reconnaissances in North-Western India and South-Eastern Iran.* London: Macmillan and Company.

——— 1940. *Old Routes of Western Iran.* London: Macmillan and Company.

——— 1943a. An archaeological tour along the Ghaggar-Hakra River, 1940-2, *American Documentation Institute Microfilm No.* ADI-4861.

——— 1943b. On Alexander's Route into Gedrosia: an Archaeological Tour in Las Bela, *The Geographical Journal* 102: 193-227.

Suraj Bhan 1967. New light on the Ochre Coloured Ware problem. *Research Bulletin, Arts, Punjab University* 52: 1-9.

——— 1975 . *Excavation at Mitathal (1968) and Other Explorations in the Sutlej-Yamuna Divide.* Kurukshetra: Kurukshetra University.

Suraj Bhan and Jim G. Shaffer 1978. New Discoveries in Northern Haryana, *Man and Environment* II : 59-68.

Tessitori, Luigi P. 1917-18. Exploration, Bikaner, *Annual Report of the Archaeological Survey of India 1917-18*: 21-3.

——— 1918-19. Exploration, Bikaner, *Annual Report of the Archaeological Survey of India 1918-19*: 22-3.

Thomas, Kenneth D. and F.R. Allchin 1986. Radiocarbon Dating of Some Early Sites in N.W. Pakistan, *South Asian Studies* 2: 37-44.

Vats, M.S. 1923-4. Exploration and Research, Sind, Mohenjo-daro, *Annual Report of the Archaeological Survey of India 1923-24*: 97-108.

——— 1926-7. Harappa, *Annual Report of the Archaeological Survey of India 1926-27*: 97-108.

——— 1927-8. Harappa, *Annual Report of the Archaeological Survey of India 1927-28*: 83-90.

——— 1928-9. Excavations at Harappa, *Annual Report of the Archaeological Survey of India 1928-29*: 76-85.

——— 1929-30. Kotla Nihang, *Annual Report of the Archaeological Survey of India 1929-30*: 131-2.

——— 1930-4a. Excavations at Harappa: Excavations During 1933-34, Brick Platform in the Southern Slope of Mound F, *Annual Reports of the Archaeological Survey of India for the Years 1930-31, 1931-32, 1932-33 and 1933-34* (Part One): 89-90.

——— 1930-4b. Excavations at Harappa, *Annual Reports of the Archaeological Survey of India for the Years 1930-31, 1931-32, 1932-33 and 1933-34* (Part One): 72-90.

——— 1930-4c. Excavations at Harappa: Excavations During 1930-31, *Annual Reports of the Archaeological Survey of India for the Years 1930-31, 1931-32, 1932-33 and 1933-34* (Part One): 73-85.

——— 1930-4d. Excavations at Harappa: Excavations During 1931-32, *Annual Reports of the*

Archaeological Survey of India for the Years 1930-31, 1931-32, 1932-33 and 1933-34 (Part One): 85-8.

——— 1934-5. Trial excavations at Rangpur, Limbdi State, Kathiawar, *Annual Report of the Archaeological Survey of India 1934-35*: 34-8.

——— 1940. *Excavations at Harappa*, 2 Vols. Delhi: Government of India.

Wheeler, R.E.M. 1947. Harappa 1946: the Defenses and Cemetery R-37, *Ancient India* 3: 58-130.

Contributors

P. Ajithprasad: Department of Archaeology and Ancient History, Faculty of Arts, the M.S. University of Baroda, Vadodara 390002.

S. Atre: Department of Archaeology, Deccan College, Yeravada, Pune 411006; email: <deccan.college@gems.vsnl.net.in>

Kuldeep Bhan: Department of Archaeology and Ancient History, Faculty of Arts, M.S. University of Baroda, Vadodara 390002; email: bhankuldeep@satyam.net.in

Archana Choksi: School of Education, University of Manchester, Manchester M13 9PL, UK; 123 Longford Road, Chorlton, Manchester M21 9WW UK (Phone: +44-1618819864); email: <archana_choksi@hotmail.com>; 2 Everest SBI Colony, Subhanpura, Vadodara 390007 (Phone: 0265-382451) (Fax: 0265-330430)

R.A.E. Coningham: The Ancient India and Iran Trust, Brooklands House, 23 Brooklands Avenue, Cambridge CB2 2BG, England; Department of Archaeological Sciences, University of Bradford, Bradford BD7 1DP, West Yorkshire, England; email: <r.a.e.coningham@bradford.ac.uk>/<iit2@ula.cam.ac.uk>

M.K. Dhavalikar: Srivatsa, 33 Navketan Society, Kothrud, Pune 411011

D.Q. Fuller: Pit-Rivers Laboratory for Bio-archaeology, Department of Archaeology, University of Cambridge, Downing Street, Cambridge CB2 3DZ; email: <df203@hermes.cam.ac.uk>, <d.fuller@ucl.ac.uk>

Alexandra Ardeleanu Jansen: Department of History of Architecture, Architectural Preservation, AWTH Aachen, Germany; email: <jansen@stadtbaug.rwth-aachen.de>

M. Jansen: Department of History of Architecture, Architectural Preservation, AWTH Aachen, Germany; email: <jansen@stadtbaug.rwth-aachen.de>

K.A.R. Kennedy: Division of Biological Sciences, Section of Ecology and Systematics, Corson Hall, Ithaca, New York 14853-2701; email: <kak10@cornell.edu>

J.M. Kenoyer: Department of Anthropology, University of Wisconsin, Madison, USA

Marco Madella: The Cambridge Phytolith Project, Department of Archaeology and MacDonald Research Institute of Archaeology, University of Cambridge, Cambridge CB2 3DZ, UK

RICHARD H. MEADOW: Director, Zooarchaeology Laboratory, Peadoby Museum, Harvard University, 11 Divinity Avenue, Cambridge MA 02138 USA; email: <meadow@fas.harvard.edu>

AJITA K. PATEL: Department of Archaeology and Ancient History, Faculty of Arts, the M.S. University of Baroda, Vadodara.

GREGORY L. POSSEHL: The University Museum, University of Pennsylvania, Philadelphia, PA 19104-6324, USA; email:<gpossehl@sas.upenn.edu>

JOSEPH SCHULDENREIN: Geoarchaeology Associates, 5912 Spencer Avenue, Riverdale, NY 10471; email:<geoarch@aol.com>

V.H. SONAWANE: Department of Archaeology and Ancient History, Faculty of Arts, the M.S. University of Baroda, Vadodara 390002

P.K. THOMAS: Department of Archaeology, Deccan College, Yeravada, Pune 411006 (Phone: 0212-667037), email: <deccan.college@gems.vsnl.net.in>

MASSIMO VIDALE: Instituto Italiano per il Medio ed Estremo Oriente, Rome.

Index